SECOND INTERNATIONAL HANDBOOK OF
MATHEMATICS EDUCATION

Kluwer International Handbooks of Education

VOLUME 10

A list of titles in this series can be found at the end of this volume.

Second International Handbook of Mathematics Education

Part Two

Edited by:

Alan J. Bishop
Monash University, Australia

M.A. Clements
Universiti Brunei Darussalam

Christine Keitel
Free University of Berlin, Germany

Jeremy Kilpatrick
University of Georgia, Athens, USA

and

Frederick K.S. Leung
The University of Hong Kong, Hong Kong

KLUWER ACADEMIC PUBLISHERS
DORDRECHT / BOSTON / LONDON

Library of Congress Cataloging-in-Publication Data is available.

ISBN 1-4020-1008-7

Published by Kluwer Academic Publishers
PO Box 17, 3300 AA Dordrecht, The Netherlands

Sold and distributed in North, Central and South America
by Kluwer Academic Publishers,
101 Philip Drive, Norwell, MA 02061, U.S.A.

In all other countries, sold and distributed
by Kluwer Academic Publishers, Distribution Centre,
PO Box 322, 3300 AH Dordrecht, The Netherlands

Printed on acid-free paper

Printed and bound in Great Britain by MPG Books Limited, Bodmin, Cornwall.

Table of Contents

Introduction
Alan J. Bishop   ix

PART ONE

SECTION 1: POLICY DIMENSIONS OF MATHEMATICS EDUCATION

Introduction
Christine Keitel   3

1   Mathematics, mathematics education and economic conditions
     Derek Woodrow   9

2   *Is* mathematics for all?
     Peter Gates and Catherine Vistro-Yu   31

3   Mathematical literacy
     Eva Jablonka   75

4   Lifelong mathematics education
     Gail FitzSimons, Diana Coben and John O'Donoghue   103

5   International comparative research in mathematics education
     David Clarke   143

6   Mathematics education in international and global contexts
     Bill Atweh, Phil Clarkson and Benvenido Nebres   185

SECTION 2: RESPONSES IN MATHEMATICS EDUCATION TO
TECHNOLOGICAL DEVELOPMENTS

Introduction
Frederick Leung   233

7   Technology and mathematics education: a multidimensional
     overview of recent research and innovation.
     *Jean-Baptiste Lagrange, Michele Artigue, Colette Laborde
     and Luc Trouche*   237

8   Influence of technology on the mathematics curriculum
     Ngai-Ying Wong   271

9   What can digital technologies take from and bring to research in
     mathematics education
     Celia Hoyles and Richard Noss   323

10   Technology as a tool for teaching undergraduate mathematics
     Mike Thomas and Derek Holton   351

11   Mathematics teacher education and technology
     Judith Mousley, Diana Lambdin and Yusuf Koc   395

                              PART TWO

SECTION 3: ISSUES IN RESEARCH IN MATHEMATICS EDUCATION

Introduction
     Jeremy Kilpatrick   435

12   Getting the description right and making it count
     Jill Adler and Steve Lerman   441

13   The impact of educational research on mathematics education
     Dylan Wiliam   471

14   Preparing mathematics education researchers for disciplined
     inquiry
     Jo Boaler, Deborah Ball and Ruhama Even   491

15   Mathematics teachers as researchers
     Chris Breen   523

16   Researching mathematics education in situations of social and
     political conflict
     Renuka Vithal and Paola Valero   545

17   Obstacles to the dissemination of mathematics education research
     Andy Begg   593

SECTION 4: PROFESSIONAL PRACTICE IN MATHEMATICS
EDUCATION

Introduction
     Ken Clements   637

18   Challenging and changing mathematics teaching classroom
     practices
     Dina Tirosh and Anna Graeber   643

19   Towards a didactic model for assessment design in mathematics
     education
     Marja van den Heuvel-Panhuizen and Jerry Becker   689

20   Values in mathematics teaching – The hidden persuaders?
     Alan Bishop, Wee Tiong Seah and Chien Chin   717

21   Regulating the entry of teachers of mathematics into the
     profession: Challenges, new models, and glimpses into the future
     Max Stephens   767

22   Examining the mathematics in mathematics teacher education
     Thomas Cooney and Heide Wiegel   795

23   Educating new mathematics teachers: Integrating theory and
     practice, and the roles of practising teachers
     Barbara Jaworski and Uwe Gellert   823

24   Professional development in mathematics education:
     Trends and tasks
     Orit Zaslavsky, Olive Chapman and Roza Leikin   877

List of Principal Authors   919

Index of Names   921

Index of Subjects   943

Section 3:

Issues in Research in Mathematics Education

Introduction

JEREMY KILPATRICK
University of Georgia

Research in mathematics education is a young enterprise. For only about a century has mathematics education been recognized as a domain in which serious scholarly work can be done, and some might argue that its status today remains precarious. The earliest international research effort in mathematics education was the set of studies produced for the International Commission on the Teaching of Mathematics (ICTM) from 1908 to 1914 (see Schubring, 1988). These studies reported on such matters as national curricula and teacher-training activities in mathematics, but they did not in general rely on comprehensive evidence systematically gathered. Instead, they often reflected little more than one or two professors' opinions. As international studies waned with the onset of the First World War, researchers in mathematics education began to engage in what were primarily psychological inquiries, asking how children learn mathematics and how one might improve that learning (for a fuller account, see Kilpatrick, 1992). Over the years, communities of researchers in mathematics education developed in many countries, and when the ICTM was reconstituted as the International Commission on Mathematical Instruction in 1964, these communities began to come together and to see that they shared similar interests and problems. Mathematics education research was broadening its focus from children's learning to encompass matters of teaching, curriculum, assessment, teacher education, professional development, and policy. The methods that mathematics education researchers used were also proliferating as they adopted and modified techniques used in sociology, developmental and social psychology, and anthropology, among other fields. Given this expansion, the post-Second World War generation of researchers recognized the value of exchanging ideas about research with their counterparts elsewhere, and the various communities gradually realized that they were at times taking different approaches to similar problems.

Today, there is a healthy exchange of research ideas in mathematics education across national boundaries through conferences, journals, books, and the Internet. Although at times researchers from different countries may use the same words without necessarily meaning the same thing (e.g., *curriculum, problem, geometry, lesson study, constructivist, didactic*), one can point to many instances of cooperative international efforts.

Just as binocular vision requires light of contrasting wavelengths, meaningful research relies on contrast, whether one is comparing methods of teaching a mathematical topic or conducting a case study of a single child's learning (in

Second International Handbook of Mathematics Education, 435–439
A.J. Bishop, M.A. Clements, C. Keitel, J. Kilpatrick and F.K.S. Leung (eds.)
© *2003 Dordrecht: Kluwer Academic Publishers. Printed in Great Britain.*

which case there is an implicit contrast with one's expectations). The International Study of Achievement in Mathematics (Husén, 1967) was conducted not to study mathematics achievement per se but rather to use it as a dependent variable in order to study phenomena such as age of school entry, organization of schools, and graduation rates – phenomena that varied much more across countries than within them. In other words, it was an attempt to examine contrast (variation, in this case) by looking at national systems of education. By the time of the Third International Mathematics and Science Study (TIMSS; see http://timss.bc.edu/timss1995.html) in 1995, researchers in mathematics education, in contrast to researchers in educational policy, had begun to have more influence on such comparative studies, and issues of interest to them were being addressed. (As an aside, TIMSS is discussed in all but the last chapter in this section.) TIMSS is undoubtedly the most prominent, though far from the only, illustration of a study that raises questions about not just how research is to be conducted but also how it should be used. When politicians use a study's results as a basis for legislation and teachers use its results to change curricula and instruction, researchers need to look beyond their own work to the landscape in which they are working.

The present section addresses a variety of issues that have emerged as researchers in mathematics education have adopted a broader perspective, asking questions of what and how: What is ethical practice in our research, and how is that research to be done amid situations of social and political conflict? What impact does educational research have on mathematics education? How is our research to overcome various obstacles to dissemination? What is the role of mathematics teachers as researchers? How is the next generation of researchers in mathematics education to be prepared? These questions would probably not have been posed by most researchers a half-century ago, if only because few then were interrogating their own practice as researchers.

In Chapter 12, Jill Adler and Stephen Lerman offer a framework for ethical practice in mathematics education research that attends to the various goals, responsibilities, and ownership claims of the various participants. Using a fable about a researcher from a developing country who is trained in a developed country and returns to a situation in which studying what the developed world sees as a problem in mathematics education would subordinate systemic concerns to mathematical concerns, they argue for a more inclusive characterization of mathematics education research: any research that informs the knowledge base in mathematics education. They elucidate the issues of validity and power that colour debates about what makes a piece of research legitimate and effective mathematics education research, arguing that 'educational research is always advocacy research' and that the international community should be more open to studies in which mathematics takes a back seat to social and political issues.

Dylan Wiliam, in Chapter 13, examines the notorious failure of educational research to have much effect on the teaching and learning of mathematics, identifying the field's emphasis on analytic rationality as the cause of its impotence. He argues that attention to nature of expertise in teaching would suggest that in framing and conducting research, practical wisdom holds greater promise than any form of analytic rationality. Teachers who incorporate research results into their practice should be seen as creators of knowledge and not simply users, and rather than attempting to find neat resolutions of isolated problems, research in mathematics education ought to be opening up avenues for other voices to be heard. To demonstrate the advantages of expertise over mere competence, Wiliam cites a study in which instructors of life-saving techniques were less able than experienced paramedics to identify the experienced paramedic in a set of video clips of people performing cardiopulmonary resuscitation. The instructors were presumably looking for rule following, whereas the paramedics relied on their expert intuition. Both researchers and teachers need to cultivate the sort of wisdom of practice shown by the paramedics.

The development of research expertise through attention to practice is the dominant theme of Chapter 14, by Jo Boaler, Deborah Ball, and Ruhama Even. Like Adler and Lerman, they begin with the story of a hypothetical Ph.D. student, this one trying to formulate a research proposal with the help of her advisor, to illustrate what might be required to undertake disciplined inquiry in mathematics education. Rather than asking what it is that new researchers should know, Boaler and her colleagues begin by asking what it is that accomplished researchers do – What are their practices? They look at several practices of research: reading, formulating a research question, being rigorous with data, moving from particular observations to general insights, considering the mathematics being investigated, and communicating, whether through writing or other media. The chapter ends with some suggestions as to the ways new researchers might be prepared in the future through opportunities to learn in, from, and for practice.

Recent years have seen greater numbers of practicing teachers engaged in research, and in Chapter 14, Chris Breen explores this phenomenon by asking why research done by teachers appears to have been marginalized in the international community of research in mathematics education. He considers the work by teacher-researchers in mathematics education against the backdrop of the larger teachers-as-researchers movement that crosses both subject matter and national boundaries. Problems he identifies concern the legitimacy of teacher research, its acceptability, how it is to be disseminated, and whether academic researchers have hijacked or otherwise dominated it. Breen offers an example of a promising master's course for teachers that attempts to move beyond these problems, yet he sounds a gloomy note, observing that the current climate of management and accountability in many countries is not auspicious for teacher research. He ends by pointing out that teacher research began with the impulse to improve education by creating discomfort and ought to remain true to its roots.

In Chapter 15, Renuka Vithal and Paola Valero take up the topic of conducting research in mathematics education in situations of social and political conflict. They begin with the view that inasmuch as conflicts are part of our world and mathematics education plays a special role in that world, researchers in mathematics education need to understand how and why mathematics education is involved in those conflicts. They note that very little of the literature in the field deals with social or political conflict, and that such research needs a much fuller development. To illustrate the challenges that conflict situations pose, each author tells her own story of conducting research in a project in which matters of conflict and context were at issue. They use these illustrations to examine ways in which research questions and agendas, theories and methodologies, and criteria for evaluating research quality might be challenged, opened up, and made more useful not simply to those doing research in conflict situations but to others as well. They argue for more dialogue between communities with different research traditions to keep "global fashion trends in mathematics education research" from stifling other views and approaches.

To end the section, Andy Begg, Brent Davis, and Rod Bramald, in Chapter 16, analyse the obstacles to disseminating mathematics education research. First, they parse the major terms in their inquiry – *obstacle, dissemination, mathematics, education,* and *research* – questioning received meanings of these terms, posing alternatives, and attempting to widen the discussion. Then they examine how educational research, development, policy, and practice have been understood and their relationships conceived, offering a succession of models that integrate the components of development and bring practice closer to theory, policy, and research. After examining influences on change in mathematics education, they discuss some obstacles to that change: research and researchers, teachers and schools, and educational systems. As strategies to offset these obstacles, Begg and his colleagues call for researchers to work in classrooms with teachers to improve communication and recognize the complexity of change, for more democratic and inclusive models for developing policy, and for a broader "concept of what is accepted and valued as research".

The chapters in this section have not attempted, singly or collectively, to survey the enormous and diverse terrain of research in mathematics education. Instead, each has taken a set of issues and offered an analysis from one point of view, with other points of view implicitly or explicitly present. Common themes are calls for greater dialogue among the disparate communities of research practice, greater appreciation of contributions from those whose voices have not been heard much internationally, greater tolerance of alternative approaches to research, and greater attention to the ways in which research is being formulated, conducted, and used.

Research in mathematics education has sometimes been portrayed as adolescent and confused (King & McLeod, 1999; Steen, 1999). It certainly has suffered from a lot of abuse and is often greatly burdened with self-doubt. The essays in this section should give researchers not only much on which to reflect but much of which to be proud. We have begun to take ourselves seriously enough to question what we are doing, and that is a kind of maturity that is in short supply everywhere.

The authors and editor of Section 3 are grateful to the following colleagues for either reviewing chapters or supplying additional information: Bill Barton, Andy Begg, Alan Bishop, Jo Boaler, Margaret Brown, Beatriz D'Ambrosio, Rubby Dhunpath, Paula Ensor, Frank K. Lester Jr., Pedro Gómez, Christine Keitel, Gerhard König, Michael Samuel, Ole Skovsmose, and Judith Sowder. In addition, Brian R. Lawler and George Stanic provided valuable editorial assistance.

REFERENCES

Husén, T. (1967). *International Study of Achievement in Mathematics: A comparison of twelve countries* (Vols. 1 & 2). New York: Wiley.

Kilpatrick, J. (1992). A history of research in mathematics education. In D. A. Grouws (Ed.), *Handbook of research in mathematics teaching and learning* (pp. 3–38). New York: Macmillan Publishing Company.

King, K. D., & McLeod, D. B. (1999). Coming of age in academe. *Journal for Research in Mathematics Education, 30,* 227–234.

Schubring, G. (1988). *The cross-cultural 'transmission' of concepts: The first international mathematics curricular reform around 1900, with an appendix on the biography of F. Klein* (Occasional Paper No. 92, corrected ed.). Bielefeld, Germany: Universität Bielefeld, Institut für Didakdik der Mathematik.

Steen, L. A. (1999) Theories that gyre and gimble in the wabe. *Journal for Research in Mathematics Education, 30,* 235–241.

12
Getting the Description Right and Making It Count: Ethical Practice in Mathematics Education Research

JILL ADLER
University of the Witwatersrand

STEPHEN LERMAN
South Bank University

ABSTRACT

Building on the work on ethics in educational research in recent publications, we present a framework for ethical practice in mathematics education research. In particular, we discuss what are the implications of claiming or denying a particular piece of research as acceptable within the community. We argue that researchers must be aware for whom they advocate, thus making it count. We present a map with which researchers should engage the ethics of their practice, and we suggest that they must consider whether they are getting the description right.

INTRODUCTION

All over the world there is a tendency towards reform in mathematics teaching and learning that takes for granted the four following features:

- Rich mathematical tasks
- Relating mathematics to real life experiences and practices
- Learner-centred practice (valuing and working with learners' mathematical meanings)
- Inquiry-based classrooms.

These reform initiatives are being researched and developed, and while emerging from practices in 'developed countries', they are nevertheless objects of desire in the 'developing countries',[1] despite substantive contextual differences. The underlying assumptions in the reform, and in much of its related research, is that these four features of mathematical classroom practice will lead to appropriate, meaningful, and more successful mathematical learning.

Imagine a situation where the dominant forms of schooling are over-determined by mechanisms of selection. In poor countries there are enormous constraints on wide provision of public services (like health care) and public goods (like education). As Mwakapenda (2000) so vividly describes of Malawi, when

Second International Handbook of Mathematics Education, 441–470
A.J. Bishop, M.A. Clements, C. Keitel, J. Kilpatrick and F.K.S. Leung (eds.)
© *2003 Dordrecht: Kluwer Academic Publishers. Printed in Great Britain.*

only 10% of primary school leavers gain access to public secondary schooling, teaching and learning practices are inevitably driven by the forces of selection. Processes of democratisation and development – increasing equitable access to improved social and economic goods – in such a context are significantly different from those in developed countries. It goes without saying that mathematics education reforms will be shaped by such divergent conditions.

Imagine a mathematics education researcher from a developing country as described above, at the level of, say, Ph.D. As is often the case, this person gains entry into Ph.D. study in an institution in a developed country and is sponsored by the ministry of education in his country. He enters a world where what count as problems in mathematics education are framed by the reform movement described above. He decides, after considerable exploration of the field, to study the implementation of inquiry-based mathematics teaching. He believes, as a result of his reading, discussion, and reflection on the educational situation at home, that inquiry-based approaches offer potential for improving mathematics teaching and learning in his country. He communicates with relevant parties at home, and teachers are reported to be interested. He develops a programme and set of materials that he believes are appropriate to his home context, and he returns to set up the project including, at this stage, a series of workshops with a selection of Grade 7 mathematics teachers (the final year of primary school). During this time, he obtains their agreement and support for the project. Indeed, the teachers appear to enjoy the workshops where inquiry-based mathematics learning is modelled and issues discussed. The teachers share with him how they have been challenged mathematically and pedagogically. They express positive views of the potential for such practice in their own classrooms and a willingness to implement these ideas. He then spends a short period of time with one of the teachers in her class, and together they try out activities in her classroom. On the basis of this piloting, he modifies and then leaves a set of materials for all the teachers to try out and develop and reflect on in their respective Grade 7 classes and returns to his academic institution.

Armed now with what has been agreed by his institution as sufficient ground-work and piloting, he proceeds with designing the next and critical phase of the research, the collection of data related to teachers' implementation – and so interpretation – of inquiry-based mathematics learning. Three months later, as planned, he returns home, this time with a range of research tools (instruments) and a carefully formulated participant-observation design process for data collection and analysis. To his dismay and frustration, he finds, across all the teachers, that the materials have barely been touched – only an occasional activity has been tried. Moreover, term dates have been unexpectedly changed. Instead of a process being underway where he could now work with teachers to interrogate their interpretations of inquiry-based mathematics teaching, the teachers are focused on preparing their learners for the kinds of assessments they will face at the end of their primary schooling. Teaching is restricted to providing practice with algorithms for the operations on common and decimal fractions. And the extended time he had thought would be available for participant observation has been curtailed by changed examination times. He now faces considerable practical, methodological, and ethical challenges.

He could continue with a modified exploration of inquiry-based mathematics. He could, for example, organise additional time with learners and teachers from one or two schools after school hours, where he himself teaches mathematics in an inquiry-based way. Through this research strategy, he might be able to identify and describe the kinds of activities the learners engaged with, how, and with what effects. His overall description and explanation is, nevertheless, likely to proceed from a starting point of 'failure' in relation to mathematics education reform by the educational system in his country and include a description of how and why the teachers were unable to implement inquiry-based mathematical learning.

By contrast, he could abandon his orientation to inquiry-based mathematical learning and reorient the study so as to understand why and how assessment has come to overdetermine considerations of epistemology and pedagogy, and how and why the timetable changed, so causing "disruptions in the data" (Valero & Vithal, 1999, p. 7). This decision would be a difficult one to take. Given time constraints for the study, he would need to proceed with a rolling plan for interviews and observations, where time for developing and piloting instruments was curtailed. If he travels that road, he is likely to elicit data related to the selective function of mathematical performance and to a range of socio-cultural and political conditions that shape the forms of school mathematics practice in Grade 7 in his country. His description and explanation of what happened through his research activity is more likely to focus on wider educational issues than strictly mathematical ones. He is also likely to be able to explain resistances in the system (as opposed to in the individual teachers) to the intended 'reforms'. In other words, to explore and understand what happened would require redesigning the study, and most critically, zooming out (Lerman, 1998) of inquiry-based mathematics and into the wider educational practices in which the teachers are positioned.

How should he proceed? Which route should he follow? Depending on where he shares his quandary, he is likely to experience quite diverse and unsettling responses, particularly if he presents a preference for the latter approach. In the wider educational arena, he could be challenged as to his competence to take this more sociological and systemic approach to the research. He is likely to share this concern. At the same time, in the community of mathematics education research, he is likely to experience reactions like: "Well, this is no longer mathematics education research".

From an ethical point of view, as he confronts the multiplicity of goals, responsibilities, and issues of ownership that infuse this research endeavour, some of the questions he must confront are as follows:

How does he continue with confidence and competence?
How does he not do harm to the teachers?
How does he establish respect, reciprocity, and mutual benefit?

What does it mean for him to be 'culturally and contextually sensitive'?
Where does his responsibility lie? With the teachers? With the school system?
   The academy? With himself as a developing researcher?
How does he advance knowledge in and for mathematics education?

As a 'newcomer' to mathematics education research, he could feel pressured to maintain a 'mathematical' focus to the study, that is, continue with the first option described above. This focus is more likely to gain acceptance in the community of mathematics education research. As intimated above, however, in either case he is likely to produce a description of failure as located somewhere between himself as researcher and the teachers and learners. In short, this kind of description would keep intact a decontextualised sense of the potential benefits of inquiry-based mathematics teaching and would lead to recommendations for how school mathematics needs to change in his country and what is needed to support that change.

Is this description 'right'? For some, the pivotal question is whether the design, instrumentation, data collection, interpretations, and claims made are systematic, rigorous, and valid. The above approach might well satisfy these methodological requirements and lead to a successful Ph.D. thesis; that is, it would count in the wider mathematics education research community. But our view is that, however unintentionally, it is likely to do damage to the teachers and so too the context in which they work. It is likely to emphasise the absence of inquiry-based methods and to silence what it is the teachers actually do to meet the mathematical demands of the contexts in which they work.[2] The point we are raising here is that getting the description right and making it count across diverse interests are ethical issues that need to inform the practices of the mathematics education research community.

Let us assume that because of this ethical standpoint and within his financial and time constraints, the researcher proceeds along the more challenging path. He makes this choice despite being aware that, in zooming out to focus on the system, mathematics recedes into the background, and his choice might well undermine goals for his own development and entry into the community of mathematics education research. He works hard to acquire the requisite research skills. He sets out to explore and explain teachers' practices in their mathematics classrooms with tools from the interpretative turn (Hitchcock & Hughes, 1995), and so to chart a less clear methodological path. As intimated above, he finds that his description of teaching practices is framed by an analysis of the educational system in his country, its fiscal constraint, and its overall examination and selection processes. The knowledge produced becomes more about how the teachers interpret and explain their mathematical practice within such systemic affordances and constraints than about their understandings of, and approaches to, inquiry-based mathematics. He goes on to problematise the hegemony of the notion of inquiry-based mathematics and to speculate that a description of its forms and functions is likely to be substantively different from that which permeates dominant mathematics education discussion. It is interesting to note here that even in the context where inquiry-based mathematics is hegemonic, critiques of mathematics education reform come either from mathematicians concerned for the disappearance of what they value in mathematics, from right-wing politicians who fear loss of control, or from sociologists of education asking questions about who succeeds and who fails. They rarely come from within the community of mathematics education research, except where researchers have shifted the focus from students' mathematical activity to the mediation of that mathematics by the teacher (e.g., Adler, 1997; Bartolini Bussi, 1995; Brodie, 1995). This observation suggests that it appears to be difficult for mathematics education researchers to problematise current images of good mathematical practice when the focus of the zoom lens is tightly on mathematical activity. That is not to say that research that focuses in on mathematical activity is inevitably unethical but merely to indicate the questions that it cannot ask or answer.

From our concerns with ethics in this chapter, the emergent description of school mathematical practices in a different context, where systemic concerns overshadow mathematical concerns, is 'right'. But our experience is that this description does not easily count in the dominant field of mathematics education research. From an ethical point of view, we can unpack our position by asking three questions. First, is the research route the researcher took important? Second, is this good research? All mathematics education researchers and readers of such research, implicitly or explicitly, engage these two questions, and based on criteria available through existing research methods, would probably agree that the research route taken is both important and potentially 'good'. But lurking in our midst as mathematics educators is always the additional question: Is this research *mathematics* education research? From a research perspective, this question can be re-interpreted as follows: Can and will it add to the knowledge base in mathematics education?

For some, the answer here would be, "No!" In their view, the research ultimately tells us little about *mathematics* education and more about educational systems and broader constraints in developing countries. From this perspective, the insights from this approach to the study offer no advances to understanding more effective mathematics teaching and learning, despite suggestions from the study as to what these might mean in this different context. In short, that kind of study might be worthwhile in general, but it backgrounds what has come to be valued in school mathematical practice and in so doing offers little of value to the wider and dominant community of mathematics education.

Although the actual story here is fictitious, as Ph.D. supervisors and external examiners, we have constructed it as a generalised case of similar struggles by Ph.D. students and other researchers in mathematics education. Moreover, one of us was witness to precisely this negative reaction when a similar situation was raised for discussion at an international mathematics education research forum. The researcher, on the basis of her experience, suggested that research designs need to be flexible, culturally sensitive, and cautious about importation of ideas from elsewhere. The first response drawn was: "This situation (of disruption of the data) suggests you cannot do research". Other responses were less narrow. They did not bracket out research but instead posited that this was no longer *mathematics* education research, that is, they bracketed out mathematics.

Some, including ourselves, would answer, "Yes! Despite limitations that are inevitable given time and financial constraints, this research could and should inform the knowledge base in mathematics education". The position here is that insights into the challenges of reforming the teaching and learning of mathematics in school lie precisely in an understanding of how mathematics takes shape in teaching and learning situations across school contexts. Such insights entail more than a grasp of the mathematics of the reforms intended and their interpretation. Critically, getting the description 'right' and making it count for its participants entails coming to grips with curriculum as contextualised social process (Cornbleth, 1990). Curriculum change involves changes in how knowledge is classified and framed – and so too in relations of power and social control (Bernstein, 1996). Curriculum change will inevitably be contested terrain. It thus requires an in-depth understanding of school mathematics, and schooling itself, across diverse contexts.

The story above and the questions it provokes are about the worth of the research reported, its quality, its boundaries and its methods, its financial constraints, and ultimately about ethics and values. We have told it in some detail, as we are of the view that there is insufficient debate in the mathematics education research community of the kinds of *ethical* issues we are highlighting. There is insufficient critical reflection on what it means to get the description right and make it count for participants (i.e., locally) as well as for the mathematics education research community (i.e., globally).

In their earlier work and their related chapter in this handbook, Valero and Vithal have problematised some of the elements of the story above as a North-South issue. Their position has provoked interesting, critical methodological debate in a context of wider power relations (Ruthven, 1999; Valero & Vithal, 1999). Our goal is to interrogate the story from the perspective of the ethics of educational research. We are aware, nevertheless, that 'getting the description right' and 'making it count' slide over into questions about validity and relations of power (i.e., the methodological and the political). There is always ideology in what is 'right'.

In our interrogation of mathematics education research activity from the perspective of ethics, we are pointing to what we believe are omissions in recent publications of ethics and research in mathematics education. We need to state up front that we are not trained in moral philosophy, that field typically concerned with questions of ethics. Nor do we intend in this chapter to delve deeply into moral philosophy. We have been motivated by our own experiences of the important ethical questions that we open up in this chapter. Our purpose is to engage such questions as *mathematics education research practitioners, that is, as members of the community of mathematics education researchers.*

We believe, furthermore, that the current context of globalisation raises new ethical questions. A changing world economic order is producing increasing differentiation (inequality) as well as increasing demands for accountability in public spending within and across socio-economic contexts. The story we have told is, in its own way, also about the effects of globalisation. It is about the tension between global trends and pressures for development so as to remain or become 'competitive' in a global world, on the one hand, and democracy and the more equitable distribution of social and economic goods, on the other. How do developing countries embark on educational innovation and development? Do they attempt to keep abreast of developments elsewhere? Perhaps an exploration of inquiry-based mathematics would have been possible in the story above if the study could have been restricted to a careful selection of adequately resourced and developed schools. What then of concerns for deepening democracy in the country? Embedded in that kind of choice would be a commitment to trickle-down notions of development. But does development trickle down? It is beyond the scope of this paper to delve into development theory. It is, however, important to understand that development might well be more effective (in the sense of increasing access and democracy) if research and development activity were grounded in (i.e., took as its starting point) contextual realities. As has been described elsewhere, in a country like South Africa, development and democracy are in constant tension in general and so too in mathematics education (Adler, 1997). This tension produces new ethical challenges for research.

In the next section, we develop an analysis of what we consider to be an ethical framework for mathematics education, building on some of the literature in the field. Following this analysis, we return to the scenario we have presented and then present aspects of three research areas: qualitative studies in teacher education, comparative international studies and studies of teaching and learning mathematics with new technologies. Together these illustrate our position in terms of reading and doing research ethically (Brown & Dowling, 1998). Each area, in recent years, has generated numerous projects, texts, and 'truths' about the teaching and learning of mathematics. Although these by no means exhaust the field, they enable us to prod and probe research practice in terms of whether the description provided is right and for whom it has come to count. In so doing, we come up against challenging ethical questions in both the conducting of research (its processes) and the place such processes and findings come to hold in the mathematics education research community (its products and their dissemination). We conclude the chapter by offering a theoretical framework that locates, and illuminates further, the position of the ethical in our complex research practice.

ETHICS AND EDUCATIONAL RESEARCH

Our rehearsal of key issues in the ethics of educational research draws on two chapters in recent collections: Sowder's 'Ethics in Mathematics Education Research' from 1998 and Howe and Moses's 'Ethics in Educational Research' from 1999. The authors have surveyed the literature thoroughly and written well-constructed chapters that provide clear overviews and insights into the field. We feel privileged by their work, both in their quality and in that they enable us to focus on aspects of ethics that are not covered in those chapters. Nevertheless, no chapter on this area would be complete without summarising the issues they raise, and we therefore proceed to that task. This rehearsal will be a synthesis, and as it would be tedious to the reader to refer to the specific author on every point, we hope it will be acceptable to acknowledge the authors in general and invite readers to consult the individual chapters for further details.

We began this chapter with a scenario to frame the arguments we will be making. We were drawn to start this way through reading the Sowder chapter, in which she introduced her review with three scenarios. The first scenario concerns the issue of confidentiality promised to interviewees when a funding agency asks the researcher to share the interviews at a meeting. The second raises the problem of the public and private, of wanting to report critical things about teachers who, through the research, had become friends of the researcher when it is clear that the teachers would not be happy with the report. The third scenario concerns anonymity, when problematic aspects of the mathematics teaching in a group of schools are to be reported, but the schools are such a special group that they will be recognised. Sowder then goes on to review the history and development of ethics literature in the field of educational research, as does the chapter by Howe and Moses.

Serious considerations of the ethical issues in research owe their origins to the Nuremberg Code, following World War II. This and subsequent guides drew, in the main, on the needs of ethical considerations in bio-medical research. A number of well-known studies, such as the Milgram and the Tearoom Trade studies (in Howe & Moses, 1999, p. 23), resulted in the recognition that specific criteria were required in social science research. Education was often seen as unproblematic because its orientation was to the improvement of the educational experience for school students. Nevertheless, educational research needed its own considerations, leading to the American Educational Research Association ethical standards of 1992 (Howe & Moses, 1999, p. 54), and today probably all universities have codes of ethics and ethical procedures for research in the social sciences. The shift towards interpretative research, drawing more on qualitative approaches than quantitative, has led to substantial developments in ideas and a wider range of potential problems.

The traditional or pre-interpretative approach made a distinction between moral-political issues in research and its scientific-methodological merits – the former concerned with the treatment of participants and the latter with miscon-duct in research practices not directly affecting participants. Moral theories contrast *teleological*, utilitarian principles and *deontological*, Kantian principles. Teleological principles are goal or outcome-orientated, where weighing up the value of a piece of research is, in the main, governed by the significance of the outcomes. This process can be a case-by-case procedure, a kind of cost-benefit analysis, usually called *act-utilitarianism*, or the analysis can be guided by a set of principles, *rule-utilitarianism*. The Kantian, or deontological, approach emphasises the duties of the researcher, and guiding principles insist that the research subjects be seen as ends, not means. Problems with this universal theory (May, 1980) include the following: There is no room for exceptions; it is too individualistic; and it offers a focus on general obligations only. Rawls (1971) outlined a form of the Kantian, deontological position that focused on the rights of the subjects of research, their dignity, liberty, equality, and autonomy, as criteria for action. Regarding research misconduct, issues of concern include intentional deceit, falsification of research, plagiarism, misrepresentation or misinterpretation of results, inappropriate collaboration, inappropriate faculty-student relations, denying knowledge of dishonest research practices, and conflicts of interests with funding agencies.

The traditional or pre-interpretative approach is not uniquely identified with quantitative methods, but such methods are typical of this approach. In relation to current uses of quantitative methods and arising from a study of current texts on statistical techniques in educational research, Jones (2000) points out that ethical issues in quantitative research (e.g., in relation to sampling, data interpretation) tend to be treated as technical in nature. Yet "quantitative-based research in education has had, and continues to have, considerable impact on both policy and practice" (p. 154). As such, ethical questions extend beyond the technical and into the moral-political, and their omission in quantitative educational research is not an oversight, but rather a "significant omission" (p. 161). Jones develops his position through discussion of a range of quantitative studies in education, including international comparative assessments like the Third International Mathematics and Science Study (TIMSS). We develop Jones's concerns for what it means to get a description right and make it count in relation to TIMSS below.

There is both a methodological and epistemological shift with the move to the interpretivist approach; indeed, the distinction between teleological and deontological principles is brought into question. According to this approach, educational research does not have a neutral scientific language on which to draw, social life is dialogical (Howe & Moses, 1999, p. 32), and so the methodology of social science must also be dialogical. As a consequence, a range of other positions on moral and ethical considerations become available to educational researchers: communitarianism or cultural relativism; relational ethics; ecological ethics; critical theory; postmodernism; and contemporary liberal theory. These theories raise a variety of problems for researchers.

Communitarianism or cultural relativism: What is perceived as ethical varies across communities and can only be understood from the inside of those communities. This position would call for the engagement of participants in the planning, conduct, analysis, and dissemination of the research.

Relational ethics: The researcher must actively care about and care for the researched, over and above a concern with the rights of the researched. This position is at the basis of feminist research and differs from communitarianism in that these values transcend the specificity of cultures. The research questions chosen should have the potential to contribute to the future well-being of the subjects, and in our case to teaching and learning and the school community.

Ecological ethics: Research must recognise the interdependence of researcher and researched and the whole environment of the classroom. Focusing on avoiding harm to the individual must therefore be set within the avoidance of harm to the whole system.

Critical theory: Research must be historical; that is, aware of the emergence of the situation to be researched. It must be emancipatory in that its focus is not just on the improvement of the teaching and learning environment for the participants, but also on enabling them to gain a perspective on their own lives and oppression and to change their own lives for the better. The separation of means from ends is not possible, since means are always relative to ends, means are themselves subject to constraints according to values, and a dialogical, democratic approach requires that ends are continually available for renegotiation. Educational research from a critical perspective is always advocacy research.

Postmodernism: People always act in discursive practices that carry their own regimes of truth, normalising individual selves. Researchers are therefore "accomplices in social domination" (Howe & Moses, 1999, p. 35). This position calls, at least, for recognition of the asymmetric relationships in research and the potential for oppression, leading to the notion that participants must take active roles in the research. Researchers should be aware that the notion *progressive* is always local, not universal, and a statement of a particular position. The findings of any research must be self-conscious of how they deal with relations of power.

Contemporary liberal theory: Whilst liberal theory has been under threat for some years, particularly from the five positions preceding this one, contemporary liberal theorists have modified the perspective to insist that participants must be treated as equals in the research and should not be defined in terms outside of their choice, a common failing with earlier utilitarian or Rawlsian liberalism. Justice is to be sought in the distribution of predetermined goods but also in the status and voice of research participants (Howe & Moses, 1999, p. 37).

In terms of operationalising these ethical values in educational research, one has to recognise that interpretative research is ethically more problematic than positivist research precisely because it is always ethically uncharted. It calls, therefore, for: care and reflexivity; refined notions of consent, including participation of research subjects and continual reaffirmation of consent; and a refined notion of autonomy and privacy, including the principle that oppression, especially of children, must be seen as a greater wrong than that done by deceiving oppressors.

Finally, Howe and Moses (1999) and Sowder (1998) have some comments about the honesty of reporting, including the recognition that there is a tension to be continually negotiated between thick description and privacy, between whose version emerges, or who owns the data interpretation, and between responsibilities to outside agencies and to research sites.

In summary, together with these authors, we wish to recognise that educational research is always advocacy research inasmuch as it unavoidably advances some moral-political (and so ideological) perspective, that educational researchers must be able to defend what their research is for (respect for truth), that the research must have points of contact with insiders' perspectives (voice, respect for persons), and that it militates against race, gender, class and other biases (respect for democracy) (Bassey, 1999, p. 37). The duty of the researcher, in taking all these perspectives into account, is to engage continually in the struggle to get descriptions right and make them count.

THE ETHICS OF MATHEMATICS EDUCATION RESEARCH

We consider it uncontroversial to claim that studying aspects of the teaching and learning of mathematics is to be doing social science. As such, we cannot divorce the mathematics from the learners/teachers/texts/classroom/school/society, depending on the chosen focus of the zoom lens – the object of research as created by the researcher. The field inevitably overlaps with other research fields and, like those fields, draws on a number of intellectual resources.

> Educational research is located in a knowledge-producing community. ...
> Of course, communities will display a great deal of variation in their cohe-
> siveness, the strength of their 'disciplinary matrix', and the flexibility of the
> procedures by which they validate knowledge claims. Education as a field
> of research and theorizing is not firmly rooted in any single disciplinary
> matrix and therefore probably lies at the weak end of the spectrum, although
> I think this need not in itself be seen as a weakness.
>
> (Usher, 1996, p. 34)

Recognising and accepting the fuzzy boundaries, we define mathematics education research as the researcher's gaze on the teaching and learning of mathematics, however oblique that gaze might be and down whichever paths such a gaze leads the researcher. But because 'educational research is located in a knowledge-producing community', such a definition must be tempered by where the researcher locates her or his own field and her or his own community. Mathematics education research is not defined by the intellectual resource – sociology or psychology, for example – but by the community to which the research is addressed. The mathematics education research community is quite cohesive and active, as evidenced, for instance, by the fact that the mathematics education group is now the largest special-interest group in the American Educational Research Association. The procedures for validating knowledge claims that have emerged in recent decades, including peer review of journal articles, conference papers, research grant applications, and doctoral thesis examinations, are becoming more flexible and the criteria more varied. The numbers of journals and conferences are increasing, and one can expect that the development of on-line journals, and perhaps video-conferencing too, will accelerate the increasing flexibility. All judgements of what is acceptable at any time as mathematics education research by the various gatekeepers are value judgements. What matters ethically is that those values are made explicit and are constantly under challenge and review by the community. This demand places great responsibility on journal editors, presidents of organisations such as the International Group for the Psychology of Mathematics Education, and the like, but also on all of us as reviewers, Ph.D. examiners, and so on.

Having located mathematics education research within the community, we see eight key questions arising from our overview that frame an ethical approach and must be answered if the description is to be right:

1. On whose behalf is the research advocating? Is it against racism, sexism, classism, and so on?
2. What is the research for? Can the researcher defend the research? On what grounds?
3. Does the research incorporate the insider's perspective?
4. Is the research reflexive?
5. Does the research take care of those being researched, especially avoiding their oppression?
6. Does the research draw on a refined notion of consent?
7. Does the research draw on a refined notion of autonomy?
8. Does the research draw on a refined notion of privacy?

How these questions are answered in research practice will inevitably vary, produce conflicts and contradictions, and involve self-conscious decision making. Sowder's discussion of ethics in mathematics education research deals illustratively and theoretically with respect for democracy and truth and for persons and the tensions between them. What we are foregrounding is that all educational research is also advocacy research. A set of values, and hence a moral and ideological position of some kind, informs all research. Typically, in a great deal of mathematics education research – what we would call the dominant literature – these positions are rarely discussed or made explicit. Perhaps one of the reasons is that university ethics committees typically deal with Questions 6, 7, and 8 above. It is our responsibility to ensure that we render for greater public scrutiny our deliberations over Questions 1 to 5.[3]

Turning back to our opening story, we would argue that the research path chosen by the researcher attempts to address Questions 1, 2, 4 and 5. He could also speak to the remaining questions should he choose to do so and depending on the time and resources he has available. His choice is to advocate against naïve importation of ideas and on behalf of the mathematics teaching and learning community in his country, located as it is within its wider educational system. The research path actively seeks to understand what others might interpret as a deficiency or failure, and so its intention is (ethically) reflexive and against oppression (of developing by developed countries). There are personal and political issues in this, each with its potentialities and costs. The researcher is likely to struggle with the development-democracy tension. As he makes his choice to shift away from prominent values in the mathematics education research community, he will still need to confront development issues – how these are to be identified and addressed. More immediate will be the struggle to get the description right by grounding it in its local context and also to make it count in the wider mathematics education research community. We want to emphasise that in choosing the other path, we are suggesting, perhaps controversially, that Questions 1 to 5 in particular are backgrounded as mathematics is foregrounded.

What then of other current research in mathematics education? How does respect for research practice, democracy, truth, and persons play out as descriptions are produced? Are they right? For whom and how do they come to count?

RESEARCHING FORMALISED IN-SERVICE PROGRAMMES

Sowder drew on qualitative teacher education research as an arena in which the ethical issues of confidentiality, privacy, and anonymity loom large. We too start with a discussion of a mathematics teacher education research project in South Africa so as to illuminate further the ethical questions we have raised.

In 1996, the University of the Witwatersrand introduced an in-service teacher development programme: the Further Diploma in Education (FDE) in Mathematics, Science and English Language Teaching. The FDE is a formalised in-service programme for teachers who have a three-year post secondary school teaching diploma (which in South Africa is abbreviated as an M + 3) and who wish to upgrade to an M + 4 qualification in one of three subject areas: mathematics teaching, science teaching, or English-language teaching. Under apartheid rule, most black teachers in South Africa qualified with an M + 3 through studies in segregated colleges of education. Most white teachers, particularly secondary teachers, completed a three-year degree followed by a one-year post-graduate diploma and thus had an M + 4 qualification. Underscored here is the strong redress motivation in the FDE programme and its broader goals of quality and equity. More specifically, the goals of the programme are as follows:

To broaden and deepen teachers' subject knowledge, pedagogic subject knowledge and educational knowledge;
To extend teachers' reflective capabilities;
To facilitate professional growth (increasing participation and membership in professional activities, networking, associations, workshops, curriculum discussions);
To enable access to further education.

The team responsible for the development of the programme was determined from the outset to develop the programme through research. In 1996, a research project was launched with the aim of investigating the FDE programme effects. An underlying assumption in the programme and the research is an understanding of what was called "the contextualised teacher" (Adler, Lelliott, & Reed et al., 1998, p. 9). This term assumed that teachers' changing knowledgeability (their participation in and take-up from the programme) needed to be located in a conception of knowing as tied to becoming a person-in-context (Lave & Wenger, 1991).

The aims of the overall research project were threefold: (1) to investigate teachers' take-up from the FDE programme in mathematics, science, and English-language teaching and to what extent and how this programme shaped the quality of their classroom practices; (2) to contribute to knowledge about formal in-service professional development (INSET); and, (3) to feed back into the FDE programme's curriculum development through research. The research team set out to describe and analyse continuities and changes in classroom practices within and across some participating FDE teachers over time in relation to conditions in which teachers work and their pupils learn. These multiple goals, and related values, reflected multiple responsibilities (to the teachers and schools, the programme and its funders, and the academy) and multiple levels of ownership of the research agenda, in turn producing an ongoing balancing act of competing interests.[4]

Throughout the three years of the study, the research team confronted and made decisions on a range of complex methodological and ethical issues, all of which involved concerns with respect for democracy, truth, and persons within an overall set of values related to inequality in education in South Africa. These concerns are described in Adler and Reed (2000) and resonate with those raised by Sowder (1998).

Briefly, multiple goals, responsibilities, and ownership of the project pulled at it in challenging ways. We were constrained by a limited research grant and hence by research time. We were not able to employ full-time research assistants and so carried the research alongside the development of the programme. We were constantly concerned with the limits on the time we were able to spend in schools. More time was needed to come to understand teaching practices in all their complexity. We also needed more time than we had to generate in-depth insider perspectives on specific teaching practices as well as the research endeavour as a whole. Within these constraints, we nevertheless strove to produce rich accounts of each teacher's complex practice.

There were tensions in producing rich accounts. We were simultaneously pulled by multiple responsibilities – to the teachers themselves and to the project – in our construction of the descriptions of their practice. Descriptions of 'gaps' in what we saw relative to project goals were important for the project but, coldly, produced the teacher as relatively deficient. We were advocating teacher professional development opportunities in the interests of teaching and learning. We had a responsibility to 'tell it like it is' but within the ethical bounds of confidentiality, privacy, and anonymity, and with care for the teachers themselves. Our pragmatic solution was to develop a detailed portrait of each individual teacher, but these portraits were not made public. They were used, however, as the first step in analysis across teachers, and for reaching "fuzzy generalisations" (Bassey, 1999, p. 44) across teachers. We were thus able to provide for anonymity, privacy, and confidentiality, and at the same time, we were able to describe and illustrate both effective and problematic teaching practices as we interpreted them.

We were continually challenged by ownership of the research, both in terms of a large research team where different members participated in different ways (some feeling more ownership than others) and in terms of the teachers themselves. They were not directly involved in setting the agenda. The ethics of our working with them was at the level of informed consent. Vithal's (2000, p. 569) notion of "democratic participatory validity", where teachers themselves are part of the data collection processes, could perhaps have increased ownership and enabled more grounded questions and insights, and perhaps too a more grounded approach to teacher development. That approach would have meant more time with the teachers, and as we were working across two distant provinces, more money.

Added to the challenge of ownership and voice, and thus whose perspectives came to bear on the research, was that of working in the multilingual South African context. We were constantly aware of how language practices both in the classrooms and in the research context were productive of particular accounts. Some of the research team shared a main language with a particular teacher and were able to have conversations in both that language and English. We were aware not only of the difficulties teachers had in reflecting on their purposes and actions in English but also of how this skill improved over time and with increasing levels of trust. We were aware too that since the programme was delivered in English, the educational discourses produced through their participation in the programme tended to be in English. Discussion about the programme needed to be, at least partly, in English.

In addition, like others in teacher education research (Wilson & Berne, 1999), we struggled with our responsibility to the academy, with how to evidence take-up of practices when these were distributed over reams of qualitative data in videotext, interview recordings, and field notes.

In short, all the way through the project, from design to data collection and analysis, as well as to the production of descriptions and their dissemination, the research team worked to meet and resolve competing goals, responsibilities, and levels of ownership, as reflected in Questions 1 to 8 raised above. In certain moments we self-consciously decided to act in ways that detracted from what we felt was optimum ethical practice. The overarching ethical question remains whether or not we were getting our descriptions right and making them count in the struggle for educational change in South Africa, and in the development of teacher education more generally. Were we actually able to describe what came to count for the teachers as they worked on their practice, what that meant for the FDE programme, and what it meant for the wider field of in-service teacher education?

Various aspects of the research have been, and are still being, published in the mathematics education research community and beyond. This dissemination of the research includes articles in mathematics education research journals (e.g.,

Adler, 2000; Setati & Adler, 2001), papers in refereed conference proceedings (e.g., Setati, 1998; Brodie, 1999), book chapters (e.g., Adler, 2001a) and a dedicated book (Adler & Reed, 2002). It extends outwards towards articles in general education research journals (e.g., Adler & Reed, 2000; Brodie, 2000), language and education research journals (e.g., Setati, Adler, Reed, & Bapoo, 2002) and teacher education research journals (Brodie, Lelliott, & Davis, 2002). In addition, a summary report of the research was produced, offered first to the teachers and schools for comment, and then widely disseminated in South Africa. The point of this elaboration on publication is to demonstrate that in terms of the demands of the academy, the project descriptions count.

But new ethical issues emerged as the research entered the academy and the public domain. An overarching observation through the research was that teachers took up the forms of learner centred practice but not its substance (Adler, Bapoo, Brodie, Davis, Dikgomo, Lelliott, Nyabanyaba, Reed, Setati, & Slonimsky, 1999). Learner-centred practice is not a neutral goal in education. We were conscious that even with rich accounts of how teachers interpreted learner centredness and why, our descriptions inevitably pointed to some inadequacy in relation to a teacher's pedagogic mathematical knowledge. In the current South African context where turning around apartheid education is a mammoth task and one not easily reached, the profession has come under considerable political attack. Any description of inadequacy could feed a political agenda of 'blame the teacher'. In much of the teacher education research literature in the USA (as reported in Wilson & Berne, 1999), inadequate learner-centred practice is typically attributed in part to teachers' lack of depth of mathematical knowledge for teaching. The data in the FDE research project, in general, supports such an attribution. Conditions in schools, however, together with the influence of the wider educational transformation agenda in the country, went a long way to explain why teachers attended to form over substance in their interpretations of learner-centred classroom practice.

From a development perspective, we were concerned that dominant interpretations of learner-centred practice might well be oppressive in the different conditions in which we were working. For example, in contexts of limited English-language infrastructure, revoicing of mathematical English is a critical teaching function. It could be, and often is, interpreted as teacher-centred practice and hence undermined (Adler, 2001b; Setati et al., 2002). Contrary, then, to an interpretation of inadequate learner-centred practice, the research team learned of the need to work instead to reinterpret learner-centred practice so that it enables description and interrogation of practices across diverse contexts. Influencing the dominant literature, however, making a new perspective count in an unequal world, is likely to be a considerable challenge.

A second area of interest that emerged through the research was our observation of the importance of relating resource availability to its use. We have produced accounts of how 'more' resources do not necessarily equate with better practice (Adler, 1998a, 1999). These accounts have been challenged in the wider academy for not including sufficient insider perspectives into the issue of resources. In South Africa, critique has been about feeding a discourse of fiscal discipline that lets the government off the hook from more equitable distribution of educational resources. It gives rope, however unintentionally, to an increasing political claim that good teachers can be successful even with limited resources, a claim not made in celebration of the teachers but in defence of poor delivery on policy and, as a result, enduring inequality. Both challenges to our descriptions are ethical and, in our view, right. They reflect the limited insider perspective of which we were always conscious. Each challenge, however, is quite different. The first is an ethical stance that emphasises the significance on insider perspective, where advocacy is for the researched and hence their voice. The second challenge is that the research does not take sufficient care of those being researched. In its description, it cannot avoid their potential oppression. In short, the research report could feed an oppressive agenda.

The point we are making here is that judgements on whether and how to report research findings are inevitably ideological. We understood that our discussion of resources in particular was controversial and potentially damaging for teachers. Our decision to produce the description was in the interests of the research and of a critical academy in a politically charged context of change. The decision can be defended, though some would disagree with it.

The most complex question to answer for the research project as a whole is, On whose behalf is the research advocating? In all its complexity, the research ultimately advocated improved mathematical opportunities for learners through improved teaching. Yet this advocacy for more and equal access to quality mathematical learning opportunities cannot be separated from the strong and particular conception of *mathematics* and *good teaching* that permeated the FDE programme and so too the research. Defending such research thus includes a need to defend a specific approach to mathematics and its learning and teaching, approaches ultimately informed by a particular ideological perspective.

This detailed discussion of a particular teacher education research project illuminates just how complex are the ethical demands on our practices in mathematics teacher education in particular, and in mathematics education more generally. None of the eight questions we posed at the end of the previous section has a clear, straightforward answer. Ethical decision making means working within and across diverse goals, ownership, and responsibilities, across diverse participant interests. Ethical research practice includes, in our view, more explicit accounts of the kinds of decision making that informs any research agenda, and how and why these have come to shape the description produced.

The detailed discussion of the FDE research project also reveals how ethical issues do not remain bounded by research processes and resultant products. These products will not travel in some benign way into the academic and public arenas. There are ethical issues in how descriptions might be read and in who takes responsibility for such readings and their effects – in short, in how they come to count and for whom. Getting a description right and making it count thus include ideological dimensions. It is this moral advocacy that we feel is insufficiently problematised in the mathematics education research community.

TIMSS

In a globalising world, international comparative assessments make sense. They provide benchmarks for both internal and external comparisons. Such arguments have been made both by the key organisational hub for the Third International Mathematics and Science Study (Plomp, 1998) as well as wider afield (Nebres, 1999). As it re-entered the world in 1994, South Africa found participating in TIMSS in 1995 an attractive option. Here was a possibility for setting up a benchmark against which progress by the post-apartheid government could be mapped and judged (Howie, 1998). The results of TIMSS are now well known and need no rehearsal here. The question we pose is the broader ethical one that drives this whole chapter: Did TIMSS get the description right?

Keitel and Kilpatrick (1999) provide an extensive critique of TIMSS. In their discussion of the promises and perils of international comparisons in mathematics education, they open up numerous ethical issues for the research endeavour. First, they highlight how the direction of the study has been overdetermined by psychometric expertise. In handling the data once collected, and treating possible problems, they argue that "problems of methodological validity, reliability and quality have been resolved purely from a formal point of view. Questions of content – in all its aspects – have usually been seen as secondary" (p. 245).

The second issue they raise is that financial support for the study influences the goals and the extent to which they are politically determined or research oriented, not to mention which countries are able to participate. Few developing countries participated. An interesting and disturbing question is why countries were ranked as in a league table. Whose interests are served by this ranking, and what kind of description is it?

This question points to the third issue they raise: control over the framing and dissemination of results. The power of TIMSS publicly is the sense that numbers do not lie and that the results obtained through the careful data collection and analysis processes were somehow objective. We only need to pause and reflect for a moment on Cooper and Dunne's (2000) extensive research on performance on 'realistic' test items in the United Kingdom. They show convincingly how more complex forms of assessment, like contextualised questions or questions requiring extended elaborated responses, can produce false negatives and tend to do so in ways that disadvantage working-class learners. When Cooper and Dunne interviewed learners who presented or selected wrong answers to such items, they found on probing that the answers selected masked learners' mathematical competence. And there were significant differences here between working- and service-class learners. Cooper and Dunne's research raises important questions about test validity and, we would add, about the ethics of using such results for determining the position of individual learners, let alone countries on a ladder of achievement. A number of the TIMSS items were embedded in realistic contexts. From this perspective, TIMSS could not get the description right. Although the data and analysis revealed important information about how learners across countries performed on a particular construction of the mathematics curriculum and how countries performed in relation to each other, they could not go far enough to reveal false negatives – or, for that matter, false positives.

For South African learners, not only was the test in a second or third language for the majority who took it, but the dominant multiple-choice format was unfamiliar (Howie, 1998). Although these issues were recognised, they were treated as methodological problems. They were described together with sampling and data collection difficulties that were experienced in a country where many schools are in remote areas, difficult to communicate with and to access. Yet the 'result' of South Africa being last out of 42 is the enduring one, and a political tool in all kinds of national education debates.

The final and most significant point made by Keitel and Kilpatrick (1999) concerns the implications of an assumption that curricula across widely diverse contexts can be compared through learner performance presented as an average. What does that mean, ultimately? And moreover, what do such 'numbers' mean when they cannot be located in the full complexity of the cultural contexts. The example Keitel and Kilpatrick provide is of the whole system of afternoon lessons in Japan where examination preparation is emphasised. This contextual information is hidden in a methodology that cannot get beyond surveys, textbook analysis, tests, and classroom observations.

These criticisms of TIMSS are known. Why are we repeating them? Our point is that in the light of the above criticisms, TIMSS cannot get all of the description right, and in its omissions lie significant ethical issues.

Returning to the questions in the introduction that frame an ethical approach to mathematics education research, we need to ask: On whose behalf is TIMSS advocating? Governments and policy makers? Mathematicians? The major arguments for TIMSS are the benefits of benchmarking and thus a conception of progress and development that is facilitated by measurement and comparison. Within the TIMSS descriptions there is little that reflects on the possibilities for oppression arising out of the league table produced, not to mention the idealised curriculum against which the benchmarking and ranking took place.

TIMSS researchers have defended their research (Plomp, 1998). The South African TIMSS researchers, in particular, have provided reflexive discussion of the considerable methodological challenges faced, such as issues raised by sampling, the language of the test, and the format of the questions (Howie, 1998). There is an openness about, and hence some responsibility is taken for, methodological issues, such as the need to improve sampling, improve contextual descriptions, and so too comparisons. Despite these issues and their detraction from getting the description right, it has come to count.

At a conference on TIMSS in South Africa in 1998 (Adler, 1998b), the Director of the IEA was asked whether TIMSS held itself responsible for the ways in which TIMSS results were reported across different national contexts. These questions were framed by a concern that in South Africa, the TIMSS results could feed political agendas. For example, they could be used by minority interests to undermine those now in charge of education in the country. The

Director of the IEA defended the freedom of the research endeavour, arguing that researchers were not responsible for how results are taken up politically, by the public, or by the academy.

Jones (2000) argues that in the United Kingdom, unfavourable international comparisons provided legitimation for the "inclusion of mental arithmetic and no-calculator papers in UK National Tests at 11 and 14" (p. 159) in June 1996. Jones refers to Brown's (1998) claim that international comparisons have been seized by governments and others (media) to justify political moves in education.

Many, if not most, of our community of mathematics education researchers would agree that TIMSS researchers are not responsible beyond their reporting of the results. They would not hold the researchers accountable for how the results are used politically, arguing instead for the benefits of knowing where one stands and of how to plan for progress offered by the benchmarking and comparisons provided. We want to ask where academic freedom begins and ends in the research endeavour. Where does responsibility begin and end in mathematics education research? We ask these questions precisely because of the power mathematics has to include and exclude.

Following the sketch we drew above of the ethical responsibilities in general of educational researchers, we want to argue that researchers *must* do their best to predict the uses that will be made of research findings in order to ensure that they take care of those being researched and that the rights of the insiders are maintained as long as possible beyond publication. A similar situation exists in England, where schools' results in national tests are used to rank schools on league tables published in the press – a ranking that takes no account of what extra 'value' schools can provide for their students. Not surprisingly, well-funded schools in middle-class neighbourhoods appear at the top of the lists. We would argue that no good whatsoever has come out of this process of 'public account-ability' for the disadvantaged except to serve as fuel for conservative groups in society.

What this discussion reveals is that quantitative international comparative studies like TIMSS preclude being able to take care of those being researched beyond individual anonymity, consent, and privacy. At the level of the individual, insider perspectives are not possible within the design of the study. However, there is considerable scope for insider perspectives at the level of participating countries. Yet participation levels in a study like TIMSS are determined by finances available, and thus are inevitably exclusionary. Poorer countries have limited influence over the idealised curriculum that permeates the study, a conception that in the end judges, and so can oppress. The notion of development through progressive benchmarking is in tension with its simultaneous possibility for oppression.

An effect of the publication of TIMSS results in South Africa has been to produce a national discourse of failure at both the level of individual learners and the whole population. For example, media reporting of TIMSS-R (the 1999 repetition of the 1994–1995 TIMSS achievement study) described South Africa's

performance as "last again" (*Business Day*, 7-12-2000) and individual performance as "sheer incompetence" (*The Star*, 7-12-2000). Few would argue against
the position that it is necessary in a globalising world to know and understand
your competitive position and so be able to plan for improvement. From this
perspective, there is little critique as to whether the results of TIMSS count. The
assumption is that the numbers can be trusted and that the description is right.
Our analysis challenges this assumption, and our point, therefore, is that there
needs to be greater critical debate in the mathematics education research community on the ethics of wide-ranging research projects, including those run on
enormous budgets. A colleague, in response to calls for more and continuous
assessment, once noted, "You don't fatten a pig by continually weighing it". Is
the money spent on studies like TIMSS worth it? For whom?

RESEARCHING TECHNOLOGY IN MATHEMATICS EDUCATION

Nowhere is the tension between development and democracy more obvious than
in technology in mathematics education. Whereas some schools and classrooms
are wired, and technological tools (computers and hand-held calculators) are
part of the school's infrastructure and integrated into school mathematical
practices, in others there is neither electricity nor telephone to support computers,
educational software, and Internet access. Nor are there finances to invest in
even one set of graphing calculators for shared use across the school. This
dichotomy exists within and across countries. The technological divide is increasing the gap between those who have (access to material and economic goods)
and those who do not. What is the worth of research that focuses on expensive,
cutting-edge technology – technology that could support an epistemological shift
in mathematical learning – when only a small minority of learners across the
world is likely to benefit in the short to medium term from such a development?

The past two decades, in particular, have seen extensive research and development in technology in and for mathematics education. In the *First International
Handbook for Mathematics Education*, Ruthven (1996) and Balacheff and Kaput
(1996) provide reviews of mathematics education research and development in
relation to hand-held calculators and computer-based learning environments,
respectively. We will not rehearse these in any detail here. Our intention in
drawing from their reviews is to engage with the questions as to whether the
various reports of research on technology and mathematics education have got
their descriptions right, and whether they count.

In his focus on hand-held calculators, Ruthven (1996) argues that these are
likely to become personal technologies. In contrast, computers are likely to be
shared resources in the context of schools for some time to come. In opening
his chapter, Ruthven comments that "most recent contributions to the scholarly
literature and international conferences originate in a rather narrow range of
countries: Australia, England and the United States, but notably also Germany,
the Netherlands and Sweden" (p. 436). Hence, knowledge about technology in

mathematics education has been informed only by European and American classroom practice. This is a limitation. There appears to have been little change since his review. Ruthven discusses tensions between new technologies and equitable access to such tools in schools (but does not take this beyond the UK context). He also refers to gendered effects (girls benefiting more than boys) claimed in some research. In concluding his chapter and summarising the research and developments in technology and its impact on mathematics education practice, Ruthven claims that despite their prevalence in some contexts, and despite research and development, hand-held calculators remain "confined to the margins of classroom life. ... [They are used] casually, instrumentally and often uncritically" (p. 464). He argues for "a renewed curiosity". That was in 1996. Yet research continues in much the same way, exploring the epistemological or pedagogical benefits of using technology in the mathematics classroom without attention to whether it remains on the margins of classroom life. Such discussion, for example, is absent in Graham and Thomas's (2000) report on the potential of the graphing calculator for illuminating the concept of a variable.

For Balacheff and Kaput (1996), the source of power in technological tools is epistemological rather than practical. Technological tools reify mathematical objects and relations enabling students to act more directly on those objects and relations. Their argument is that in this reification "a new mathematical realism" is produced (p. 469). Understanding and improving school learning thus requires moving beyond explorations of didactical transposition to include technological transposition. Like Ruthven, they suggest that research in technology and the teaching and learning of mathematics is at its very beginnings – more is needed.

In many ways, though more or less implicitly, both chapters suggest that the potential for technological tools to transform the nature of mathematical learning in school has not been realised. Through his review of research, Ruthven points to the conceptual limitations of quantitative studies. Their descriptions are suspect, and so too are claims for or against the benefits of using technology to support mathematical learning. He is also cautionary about qualitative studies and uncritical generalisations from such research. Yet both chapters end with a call for more research.

We find these calls for research interesting because we are living in an educational climate where accountability for public spending is on the increase. In teacher education research, for example, there are increasing demands for demonstrating the impact of teacher education on student learning (Taylor & Vinjevold, 1999; Wilson & Berne, 1999). Teacher education needs to demonstrate its worth. Is the same true of technology in support of mathematics teaching and learning?

On whose behalf is technological research advocating? Is it against social discrimination? Is the advocacy for mathematics? Or is advocacy locked into the tool itself? To be specific, on whose behalf was the extensive research on Logo advocating?[5] Who has come to benefit from the money spent on its development and dissemination?

Research into technology and the teaching and learning of mathematics, like the wider reform movement of which it is part, has come to count in the dominant mathematics education research community. The question that needs to be asked, from an ethical point of view, is the following: On what grounds do those researching technological tools in mathematics education defend their research? Presumably, the dominant defence will be from a development perspective, and particularly in relation to the epistemological potential of technological tools in mathematics teaching and learning. In fact, Balacheff and Kaput (1999) argue for the democratising potential of some of the software currently in use. Their argument is based on the new mathematical realism provided and thus the potential for greater access to otherwise abstract mathematical ideas and concepts. The problem, of course, is that they do not simultaneously question the costs of providing and sustaining such technological resources across schools. The serious difficulties in defending the research from a perspective of democracy were evident at the Meeting of the International Group for the Psychology of Mathematics Education in Finland in 1997, where the panel discussion was on technology (see Pehkonen, 1997, Vol. 1, for the presentations by the panel). Most contentious was Kaput's claim about the software program Boxer as a democratising tool. We witnessed some members of the audience arguing that it might be democratising in terms of mathematical mediation, but such opening up of mathematics would only be for a privileged minority. The argument that a technology can democratise mathematics, making it more available and transparent for a particular learner, could not be defended from the perspective of mathematics for all.

At the Ninth International Congress of Mathematics Education in Japan in July 2000, when the Technology Working Group (Working Group for Action 11, 2000) reported on their working group deliberations during the conference, they too expressed the view that technology has not yet fulfilled its promise of educational transformation in mathematics. Yet investment continues, both in improving the tools and in researching their educational use. The Internet is now a new source of knowledge and work for the community of researchers in mathematics education.

We are not suggesting that technology-related research should be abandoned. Most people in the mathematics education community recognise the enormous potential of technology to transform the teaching and learning of mathematics. No doubt most of us are excited by the possibilities, especially the epistemological shifts described by Balacheff and Kaput (1999). We agree with them that research on dynamic geometry is certainly a case in point, and that the way that Logo has been developed in floor turtles and various microworlds is another. Many of the software developments are themselves driven by people with the vision of those potential epistemological shifts. As we have indicated, it is of concern to our community that such potential has scarcely been fulfilled, even in technology-rich environments. Many developments, however, are driven not by people in the mathematics education community with vision but by the market: Incorporating the software program Derive into graphical calculators is an example; the many forms of programmed learning are another. We acknowledge the vision of those of our colleagues who work to realise the potential of even these innovations for teaching and learning of mathematics and for greater equity in achievement. But it is here that the ethical terrain becomes difficult. Were funding for research to be available without preference to particular areas in mathematics education, would it be ethically appropriate to put resources into a field that is aimed at the few, across the world as well as across schools, within technology-rich countries, even in the medium to long term? Where more funding goes into technology disproportionately, additional questions need to be asked about who is providing the funding and why. On whose behalf is the research being done? Does it incorporate the insider's perspective from an equity point of view?

This arena in mathematics education research, particularly because of its obvious position in the tension between development and democracy, requires a greater and more self-conscious ethical stance in its work.

REFLECTIVE COMMENT

Our reflection on research in mathematics teacher education, large-scale international comparative assessments, and technology has been offered to provide illustrations and illumination of the ethical questions that need to frame practice in mathematics education research. Ethical challenges are not exclusive to qualitative research and an obviously conflictual area like teacher education; they also reside in quantitative studies in which anonymity of individuals is secure but that of communities or countries is not. We have extended ethical questions beyond the production processes of research to include its dissemination and have argued that research reported can be and has been used to feed a conservative agenda. This phenomenon extends beyond comparative studies like TIMSS to aspects of teacher development research. Cooper and Dunne (2000) express a similar concern in the introduction to their book. They are aware that their extensive illumination of validity issues in more complex forms of assessment could well be turned to fuel a conservative pedagogical agenda currently in play in the UK. Their response to this ethical dilemma is to make it explicit and to state their position quite clearly. They see the research not as pointing to a return to basics but rather as illuminating the work that needs to be done in teaching and learning of mathematics so that new forms of assessment are not discriminatory.

In addition, we have situated our exploration of ethical practice in the mathematics education community in a globalising and increasingly complex world – a world where mutual respect for truth, persons, and democracy in any research endeavour can pull in contradictory ways. We went further to suggest that the ethical question of 'who benefits' includes a consideration of finances, particularly as the gap between haves and have-nots continues to widen.

There has been a distinct Southern African focus in this chapter. We are aware of the danger that some readers might marginalise the ethical issues we have raised because the history of the region – indeed the continent – is full of very dramatic inequalities, exploitation by developed countries, and so on. We insist, though, that whilst inequalities might be more stark in Southern Africa than in many other places, inequalities and injustices are just as pervasive and ubiquitous in every part of the world and within every society, if sometimes less obvious. The cultural capital of success in school mathematics is common across the world; so too is the failure of so many students from working-class and disadvantaged groups in mathematics. It is precisely the high levels of inequality that throw ethical issues into relief, issues that need to be confronted by all mathematics education researchers wherever they are.

A FRAMEWORK FOR AN ETHICAL APPROACH TO RESEARCH IN MATHEMATICS EDUCATION

We turn now to drawing together and extending our analytic and theoretical framework for working in the mathematics education research community. We have suggested that one should consider educational research as located in a knowledge-producing community. In doing so, what comes to the fore is the engagement with others and with history in an enterprise that should meet, as well as perhaps challenge, sets of socially constituted standards and values. Research communities, like all communities, are fragmented, with subgroups, established and new paradigms, tensions, disputes, and boundary conflicts. These are indications of a normal healthy research community: The modernist image of a unified scientific group achieving universally accepted answers to universally agreed research questions is no longer expected. The complexity of the research enterprise is thus captured in the notion that it is a social practice.

Research can then be seen as a map (Figure 1) whose multiplicity must be taken into account. Thus, in the scenario that opened the chapter, our researcher's dilemmas concern the following:

Goals. To modify his study of inquiry-based mathematical learning or to examine why testing overcame other issues. He needs to be aware of the goals of: (a) his participants, the teachers (to be supported in their struggles, not undermined, and not to have their trust broken); (b) the academy (to do what informs *mathematics education* research in ways that uphold if not develop the ethical standards of the community); and (c) the public (who want the best for their children, whatever that may mean, and who want their privacy respected).

Responsibilities. To his participants, the teachers: to advocate for them, not to hold them up for criticism when they joined him in his plans in good faith, as his understanding of their situation changed; and in addition, to work with refined notions of consent, autonomy, and privacy. To himself: in gaining a Ph.D. within the community to which he belongs and at the same time to be true to what matters to him in his research. To the academy:

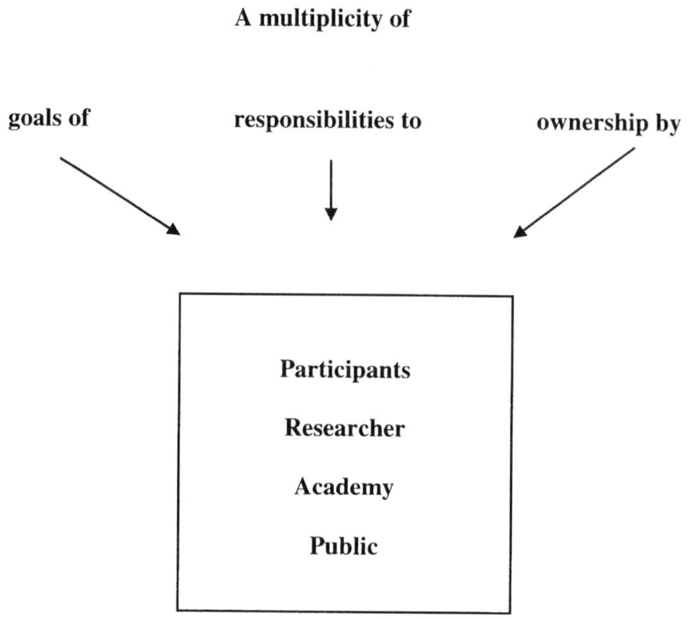

A multiplicity of

goals of   **responsibilities to**   **ownership by**

Figure 1. The map of research.

to advance knowledge of the teaching and learning of mathematics in its widest sense whilst challenging the community to recognise and value the research issue. And to the public: to do research that takes care of teachers and students whilst informing for future policy.

Ownership. By the participants, who see themselves to some degree as framing and conducting the research so as to improve the learning of their students, but who are pulled also by many other, perhaps stronger, constraints. By the researcher, who demands that his community also claim ownership through him. By the academy, that this *matters* to mathematics education research. And by the public, that they should share in researching their schools.

One could carry out a similar analysis for any of the areas of research we have described in our chapter. This map, then, can act as a guide in identifying what and whom research is for and what part all the actors play in the research.
In the introduction, we outlined eight questions to frame an ethical approach aimed at getting the description right. Our proposal here is that answers to those questions lie in engaging with the map, an engagement that must form an integral part of research. But the questions are not answered once, nor are they answered in an uncontested way. Thus they need to be revisited as research proceeds, and the answers and engagement must be addressed in interaction with the community.

CONCLUSION

To conclude, we return to the issue that makes this chapter an extension to the existing work on ethics in educational research; namely, what makes something *mathematics education research*. In conjunction with the need for researchers to address the map and the questions we have set out, there is the need for the community to look into its assumptions regarding what makes a piece of research *mathematics education research*. The community is very successful in locating and engaging with issues and challenges where the mathematics is prominent. A focus on the mathematics, however, requires that researchers are always aware of what is out of focus, the overlapping social practices that constitute the teaching and learning situations. We are convinced that the community also needs to be more open to seeking questions and answers in situations where the mathematics recedes behind a myriad of intersecting social and political issues. Again, this is another focus of the lens in which the researcher creates the object of research through the process of foregrounding and, therefore, backgrounding.

When one is researching social and political forces in education, as in our first scenario, the mathematics is an essential feature in that it constitutes that setting quite differently from any other by virtue of the place that mathematics holds in society in relation to education and to achievement. Let us be clear: Social and political issues are not an irritation that gets in the way of research in mathematics education. We consider it our ethical responsibility to seek out these settings for research. Otherwise, we collude in denying access to power and control over their lives for the majority of students.

NOTES

[1.] In writing this paper we are not yet satisfied with the names given here to mark out difference across countries. The terms we are using, 'developed and developing countries', mask histories. We would have preferred to refer to developed and developing economies, but there are some absurdities in expressions that follow. We could have used 'first and third worlds', 'dominant and dominated countries', but each is problematic for what is produced.

[2.] The second author, on a visit to South Africa soon after the end of the apartheid era, was asked by a Soweto teacher to advise him on how he could reorganise his classroom to facilitate group work. "I have 120 children in my class", he said. The author was made acutely aware of the tensions between his own expertise around group activity in a resource-based context and the teacher's expertise of what it is to teach mathematics in a resource-impoverished context.

[3.] We would go further to argue that this neglect may be bound up with the tendency to focus on methods (techniques of data collection) without methodology (epistemological and ontological assumptions).

[4.] The research methods and outcomes are described in detail in Adler & Reed, 2002; Adler & Reed, 2000; Adler, Lelliott, & Slonimsky et al., 1997; and Adler, Lelliott, & Reed et al., 1998.

[5.] Readers interested in research and development on Logo could refer, for example, to Hoyles and Sutherland (1989).

REFERENCES

Adler, J. (1997). A participatory-inquiry approach and the mediation of mathematical knowledge in a multilingual classroom. *Educational Studies in Mathematics, 33*, 235–258.

Adler, J. (1998a). Resources as a verb: Recontextualising resources in mathematics education. In A. Olivier & K. Newstead (Eds.), *Proceedings of the 22nd Annual Meeting of the International Group for the Psychology of Mathematics Education* (Vol. 1, pp. 1–18). Stellenbosch: University of Stellenbosch, Faculty of Education.

Adler, J. (Ed.). (1998b). *Perspectives on the Third International Mathematics and Science Study.* Proceedings of a National Seminar, Mathematics Education Development Programme. Johannesburg: University of the Witwatersrand.

Adler, J. (1999). Redistribution of resources = equity? In J. Kuiper (Ed.), *Proceedings of the Seventh Annual Meeting of the Southern African Association for Research in Mathematics and Science Education* (pp. 23–32). Harare: University of Harare.

Adler, J. (2000). Conceptualising resources as a theme for mathematics teacher education. *Journal of Mathematics Teacher Education, 3*(3), 205–224.

Adler, J. (2001a). Re-sourcing practice and equity: A dual challenge for mathematics education. In B. Atweh, H. Forgasz & B. Nebres (Eds.), *Sociocultural research on mathematics education: An international perspective* (pp. 185–200). Mahwah, NJ: Erlbaum.

Adler, J. (2001b). *Teaching mathematics in multilingual classrooms.* Dordrecht: Kluwer.

Adler, J., Lelliott, T., & Slonimsky, L., with Reed, Y., Bapoo, P., Brodie, K., Davis, H., De Wet, H., Dikgomo, P., Nyabanyaba, T., & Setati, M. (1997). *A baseline study: Teaching/learning practices of primary and secondary mathematics, science and English language teachers enrolled in the Wits Further Diplomas in Education programme.* Johannesburg: University of the Witwatersrand, Faculty of Education.

Adler, J., Lelliott, A., & Reed, Y., with Bapoo, P., Brodie, K., Davis, H., De Wet, H., Dikgomo, P., Nyabanyaba, T., Setati, M., & Slonimsky, L. (1998). *Mixed-mode FDEs and their effects* (Interim Report June 1998). Johannesburg: University of the Witwatersrand, Faculty of Education.

Adler, J., Bapoo, P., Brodie, K., Davis, H., Dikgomo, P., Lelliott, T., Nyabanyaba, T., Reed, Y., Setati, M., & Slonimsky, L. (1999). *Mixed-mode Further Diplomas in Education and their effects: Summary report on major findings of a three-year research project.* Johannesburg: University of the Witwatersrand, Faculty of Education. (Also published in *Open Learning Through Distance Education (OLTDE), 6*(1), 2000).

Adler, J., & Reed, Y. (2000). Researching teachers' take-up from a formal in-service professional development programme. *Journal of Education, 25,* 192–226.

Adler, J., & Reed, Y. (Eds.). (2002). *Challenges of teacher development: An investigation of take-up in South Africa.* Pretoria: Van Schaik.

Balacheff, N., & Kaput, J. (1996). Computer-based learning environments in mathematics. In A. J. Bishop, K. Clements, C. Keitel, J. Kilpatrick & C. Laborde (Eds.), *International handbook of mathematics education* (pp. 469–501). Dordrecht: Kluwer.

Bartolini Bussi, M. G. (1995). Analysis of classroom interaction discourse from a Vygotskian perspective. In L. Meira & D. Carraher (Eds.), *Proceedings of the Nineteenth Meeting of the International Group for the Psychology of Mathematics Education* (Vol. 1, pp. 77–101). Recife: Universidade Federal de Pernambuco.

Bassey, M. (1999). *Case study research in educational settings.* Buckingham: Open University Press.

Bernstein, B. (1996). *Pedagogy, symbolic control and identity: Theory, research and critique.* London: Taylor & Francis.

Brodie, K. (1995). Peer interaction and the development of mathematical knowledge. In L. Meira & D. Carraher (Eds.), *Proceedings of the Nineteenth Meeting of the International Group for the Psychology of Mathematics Education* (Vol. 1, pp. 216–223). Recife: Universidade Federal de Pernambuco.

Brodie, K. (1999). Working with pupils' meanings: Changing practices among teachers enrolled on an in-service course in South Africa. In O. Zaslavsky, (Ed.), *Proceedings of the Twenty-Third Annual Meeting of the International Group for the Psychology of Mathematics Education* (Vol. 2, pp. 145–152). Haifa: Israel Institute of Technology.

Brodie, K. (2000). Mathematics teacher development in under-resourced contexts: A case study. In J.-F. Matos & M. Santos (Eds.), *Proceedings of the Second International Mathematics Education and Society Conference (MES2)* (pp. 214–223). Lisbon: Faculdade de Ciências da Universidade de Lisboa, Centro de Investigação em Educação.

Brodie, K., Lelliott, A., & Davis, H. (2002). Forms and substance in learner-centred teaching: Teachers' take-up from an in-service programme in South Africa. *Teaching and Teacher Education, 18*(5), 541–559.

Brown, M. (1998). The tyranny of the international horse race. In R. Slee & G. Weiner, with S. Tomlinson (Eds.), *School effectiveness for whom? Challenges to the school effectiveness and school improvement movement* (pp. 38–48). London: Falmer.

Brown, A., & Dowling, P. (1998). *Doing research/reading research: A mode of interrogation for education.* London: Falmer.

Cooper, B., & Dunne, M. (2000). Assessing children's mathematical knowledge: Social class, sex and problem-solving. Buckingham: Open University Press.

Cornbleth, C. (1990). *Curriculum in context.* London: Falmer.

Graham, A. T., & Thomas, M. (2000). Building a versatile understanding of algebraic variables with a graphic calculator. *Educational Studies in Mathematics, 41*(3), 265–282.

Hitchcock, G., & Hughes, D. (1995). *Research and the teacher: A qualitative introduction to school-based research* (2nd ed.). London: Routledge.

Howe, K. R., & Moses, M. S. (1999). Ethics in educational research. In A. Iran-Nejad & P. D. Pearson (Eds.), *Review of Research in Education* (Vol. 24, pp. 21–59). Washington, DC: American Educational Research Association.

Howie, S. (1998). TIMSS in South Africa: The value of international comparative studies for a developing country. In J. Adler (Ed.), *Perspectives on the Third International Mathematics and Science Study* (Proceedings of a National Seminar, Mathematics Education Development Programme, pp. 22–40). Johannesburg: University of the Witwatersrand.

Hoyles, C., & Sutherland, R. (1989). *Logo mathematics in the classroom.* London: Routledge.

Jones, K. (2000). A regrettable oversight or a significant omission? Ethical considerations in quantitative research in education. In H. Simons & R. Usher (Eds.), *Situated ethics in educational research* (pp. 147–161). London: Routledge Falmer.

Keitel, C., & Kilpatrick, J. (1999). The rationality and irrationality of international comparative studies. In G. Kaiser, L. Eduardo, & I. Huntley (Eds.), *International Comparisons in Mathematics Education* (pp. 241–256). London: Falmer.

Lave, J., & Wenger, E. (1991). *Situated learning: Legitimate peripheral participation.* Cambridge: Cambridge University Press.

Lerman, S. (1998). A moment in the zoom of a lens: Towards a discursive psychology of mathematics teaching and learning. In A. Olivier & K. Newstead (Eds.), *Proceedings of the Twenty-second Annual Meeting of the International Group for the Psychology of Mathematics Education* (Vol. 1, pp. 66–81). Stellenbosch: University of Stellenbosch, Faculty of Education.

May, W. F. (1980). Doing ethics: The bearing of ethical theories on fieldwork. *Social Problems, 27*(3), 358–370.

Mwakapenda, W. (2000). *Using everyday experiences in teaching secondary mathematics in Malawi: Possibilities and constraints for change.* Unpublished Ph.D. thesis, Deakin University, Melbourne.

Nebres, B. F. (1999). International benchmarking as a way to improve school mathematics achievement in the era of globalisation. In G. Kaiser, L. Eduardo, & I. Huntley (Eds.). *International comparisons in mathematics education* (pp. 200–212). London: Falmer Press.

Pehkonen, E. (Ed.). (1997). *Proceedings of the 21st Meeting of the International Group for the Psychology of Mathematics Education* (Plenary Panel, Vol. 1, pp. 81–112). Helsinki: University of Helsinki, Department of Teacher Education.

Plomp, T. (1998). Purposes and challenges of international comparative assessments. In J. Adler (Ed.), *Perspectives on the Third International Mathematics and Science Study* (Proceedings of a National Seminar, Mathematics Education Development Programme, pp. 6–21). Johannesburg: University of the Witwatersrand.

Rawls, J. (1971). *A theory of justice.* Cambridge, MA: Harvard University Press.

Ruthven, K. (1996). Calculators in the mathematics curriculum: The scope of personal computational technology. In A. J. Bishop, K. Clements, C. Keitel, J. Kilpatrick & C. Laborde (Eds.), *International handbook of mathematics education* (pp. 435–468). Dordrecht: Kluwer.

Ruthven, K. (1999). The North writes back: North-South dialogue. *Perspectives in Education, 18*(2), 13–18.

Setati, M. (1998). Chanting and chorusing in mathematics classrooms. In A. Olivier & K. Newstead (Eds.), *Proceedings of the Twenty-second Annual Meeting of the International Group for the Psychology of Mathematics Education* (Vol. 4, p. 304). Stellenbosch: University of Stellenbosch.

Setati, M., & Adler, J. (2001). Between languages and discourses: Code-switching practices in primary mathematics classrooms in South Africa. *Educational Studies in Mathematics, 43*(3), 243–269.

Setati, M., Adler, J., Reed, Y., & Bapoo, A. (2002). Incomplete journeys: Code-switching and other language practices in mathematics, science and English language classrooms in South Africa. *Language and Education, 16*(2), 128–149.

Sowder, J. T. (1998). Ethics in mathematics education research. In A. Sierpinska & J. Kilpatrick (Eds.), *Mathematics education as a research domain: A search for identity* (Vol. 2, pp. 427–442). Dordrecht: Kluwer.

Taylor, N., & Vinjevold, P. (1999). *Getting learning right*. Johannesburg: JET/DoE.

Usher, R. (1996). Textuality and reflexivity in educational research. In D. Scott & R. Usher (Eds.), *Understanding educational research* (pp. 33–51). London: Routledge.

Valero, P., & Vithal, R. (1999). Research methods of the 'North' revisited from the 'South'. *Perspectives in Education, 18*(2), 5–12.

Vithal, R. (2000). In the search for criteria of quality and relevance for mathematics education research: The case of validity. In S. Mahlomaholo (Ed.), *Proceedings of the 8th Annual Conference of the Southern African Association for Research in Mathematics and Science Education (SAARMSE)* (pp. 567–573). Port Elisabeth: University of Port Elisabeth.

Working Group for Action 11 (WGA11). (2000). *Mathematics education and technology*. Retrieved October 3, 2002 from http://www.stat.unipg.it/WILMA/sis/199901/msg00080.html.

Wilson, S., & Berne, J. (1999). Teacher learning and the acquisition of professional knowledge: An examination of research on contemporary professional development. In A. Iran-Nejad & P. D. Pearson (Eds.), *Review of Research in Education* (Vol. 24, pp. 173–209). Washington, DC: American Education Research Association.

13
The Impact of Educational Research on Mathematics Education

DYLAN WILIAM

King's College London

ABSTRACT

The failure of educational research to impact teaching and learning has been lamented almost from the beginnings of educational research itself. In this chapter, I explore some of the reasons for this failure and attempt to suggest how educational research might impact the teaching and learning of mathematics more effectively in the future. I begin by arguing that classroom practices in mathematics education are, in fact, relatively stable and have changed little over recent decades. To try to understand why that is, I trace briefly the history of educational research and suggest that the major reason for the failure of research to impact practice is the emphasis on analytic rationality as the method to generate knowledge in education. By focusing on the nature of expertise in teaching, I argue that a focus on Aristotle's intellectual virtue of 'practical wisdom' would be more appropriate and suggest some ways in this change of focus could lead to a more productive relationship between research and practice.

INTRODUCTION

In an interview towards the end of his life, Neville Barnes Wallis (1887–1979), the aircraft designer and creator of the 'bouncing bombs' used in attacks on the Mohne, Eder, and Sorpe dams in the Ruhr valley during the Second World War, was asked about his formative experiences. He described his arrival at a new school (he would probably have been 11 or 13), where his class spent all their mathematics lessons for the first two weeks trying to determine the most accurate value they could for the ratio between the circumference and diameter of a circle. Barnes Wallis spoke about how the teacher had awakened his curiosity to find things out; he felt sure that the quality of the teaching he received was a crucial factor in his later success.

In 1966, a national school leaving examination in mathematics in England gave students four hours to answer one question from five:

1. Discuss the relevance of matrices to networks. Illustrate by suitable examples.

Second International Handbook of Mathematics Education, 471–490
A.J. Bishop, M.A. Clements, C. Keitel, J. Kilpatrick and F.K.S. Leung (eds.)
© *2003 Dordrecht: Kluwer Academic Publishers. Printed in Great Britain.*

2. Discuss 'Relations' with special references to their representations. Illustrate by suitable examples.
3. Discuss the applications of sets to linear programming.
4. [After a definition and an example of a simple continued fraction] Investigate simple continued fractions.
5. Investigate *either*: Quadrilaterals: classification by symmetry, *or*: Triangles and their associated circles.

These two examples raise important questions about the idea of 'progress' in mathematics education. Is mathematics teaching better now than it was when Barnes Wallis was at school? Are the tests and examinations that we set today better than those that were set in 1966?

To some, these questions are hardly worth asking; mathematics teaching must have improved over the last 100 years, and of course our assessments are better than those of 35 years ago. And yet to insist on the possibility of progress is to make a claim about the nature of mathematics teaching and learning. We do not, for example, ask whether musical composition has improved since Mozart, nor whether oil painting has improved since Rembrandt.

Whether or not we believe that mathematics education has improved over the last 100 years, there can be little doubt that is has changed. Describing the nature of those changes, however, and tracing the extent to which they can be attributed to the results of educational research are extremely difficult.

Over the last twenty years, there have been several attempts to review and synthesize research in mathematics education. In 1988 and 1989, the National Council of Teachers of Mathematics (NCTM) published its 'Research Agenda for Mathematics Education' (Charles & Silver, 1989; Grouws, Cooney, & Jones, 1988; Hiebert & Behr, 1988; Sowder, 1989; Wagner & Kieren, 1989) in order to "direct research efforts towards important questions" and "to encourage the development of support mechanisms essential to collaborative chains of enquiry" (Grouws et al., 1988, p. v). Three years later, the NCTM published its *Handbook of Research on Mathematics Teaching and Learning* (Grouws, 1992). Two of the main aims of the handbook echoed those of the research agenda: "to synthesize and reconceptualize past research, [and] suggest areas of research most useful to advancing the field" (p. ix). In addition, a third goal was "where appropriate, provide implications of research for classroom practice". Because of their origins, these resources inevitably focused primarily on research from the Anglophone world, and in particular from the USA. In response to this focus as well as to address the need for synthesis and reconceptualization, the first *International Handbook of Mathematics Education* (Bishop, Clements, Keitel, Kilpatrick, & Laborde, 1997) made explicit efforts to cross national boundaries and to bring in research not published in English. Most recently, the *Handbook of International Research in Mathematics Education* (English, 2002) was initiated "in response to a number of recent global catalysts that have had an impact on mathematics education and mathematics education research" (p. 3) and aimed to "be proactive rather than reactive in examining the emerging and anticipated problems in our field" (p. 4).

These collections have provided an extraordinary level of scholarly synthesis of the research that has been undertaken in mathematics education and have been important in identifying priorities for future research. We have made huge progress in our understanding of "how, where and why people learn or do not learn mathematics" (Begle & Gibb, 1980, p. 8), and yet this knowledge about 'what works' in mathematics education does not appear to have had any great impact on the way that mathematics is taught and learnt around the world.

Of course, the observation that research in education has failed to affect practice is nothing new (see Kilpatrick, 1992), but in this chapter, I want to explore some of the reasons for this failure and to suggest how educational research might influence the practices of learning and teaching mathematics. To do so, I first discuss briefly some of the large-scale changes in mathematics education over the last twenty years or so. My argument here is that mathematics education (at least as it is practiced in classrooms) has changed very little over a considerable period. In order to try to understand why that is so, I then review the history of educational research and suggest that the reason that educational research has impacted so little on practice (in mathematics and in other subjects) has been due to the focus on analytic rationality as the prime method of educational research. In the subsequent section, I suggest that a focus on 'practical wisdom' rather than universal truths is more appropriate for social sciences such as education, and in the concluding section, I suggest how this change in focus might be brought about.

LARGE-SCALE CHANGES IN MATHEMATICS EDUCATION

Attempting to describe changes in mathematics education across any period of time is surely an unwise endeavour. The changes will be different in each nation, and even within each nation, states and provinces often have very different education systems. More importantly, educational provision is rarely homogenous, so that even within a state or province, it will be impossible to describe in any meaningful way what is provided under the broad heading of 'mathematics education'.

A second difficulty is that the changes in mathematics education that take place within any one system are not in any sense a steady progression towards an optimum. For example, consider the 'modern mathematics' movement that began with the Royaumont Seminar in 1959 (Organisation for European Economic Co-operation Office for Scientific and Technical Personnel, 1961). Although not completely without benefit, the assumption that the epistemological hierarchies developed by mathematicians would provide the most suitable didactical hierarchies for students between the ages of 5 and 19 now seems like one of the craziest ideas to take widespread hold in education. There are few today who would argue today that the 'new math' ideas should be tried again (see Moon, 1986, for a history of the controversy). But if we are to learn from history (so that, in the words of George Santayana, we are not condemned to repeat it), we need to understand whether, even with hindsight, the idea of modern mathematics was always wrong, or was it, again with hindsight, right for the 1960s, but not for the 21st century?

Clearly, there is not enough space in this handbook, let alone this chapter, to attempt to cover the whole of research in education and its impact on mathematics education. Therefore, I will instead discuss some of the 'revolutions' that have been claimed in mathematics education. Although inevitably a subjective view, I hope to show that the changes in what actually happens day-to-day in mathematics classrooms (as opposed to what happens across educational systems) over the last twenty or so years have actually been quite modest.

The first revolution I wish to consider is the 'technological revolution', which is perhaps the most visible change in mathematics education, at least in classrooms in Europe and North America. There can be little doubt that the use of information and communications technology (ICT) in mathematics classrooms – specifically of hand-held calculators and computers – is increasing, but the total impact of ICT on the teaching and learning of mathematics is still very limited.

The Third International Mathematics and Science Study (TIMSS) found that in the fourth grade (students typically 9 or 10 years old), there was a huge variation in the use of calculators in mathematics classes (Mullis, Martin, Beaton, Gonzalez, Kelly, & Smith, 1996, p. 178). In several education systems, over 90% of students sampled said that they never used calculators in mathematics classes, while in Scotland, only 5% never used calculators. The median figure across the 26 systems was 79%. In grade 8, calculator usage was much greater, and yet in half the countries studied, the majority of students said that they used calculators "once in a while" or "never" (Beaton, Mullis, Martin, Gonzalez, Kelly, & Smith, 1996, p. 166). Establishing the quality of the use of calculators in schools is much more difficult than establishing its extent, but in concluding a survey chapter on this issue, Ruthven (1997) stated that "calculators are confined to the margins of classroom life: casually used, primarily instrumentally, and often uncritically" (p. 464).

Because of their greater cost, computers are inevitably less widespread than calculators, but many governments have made significant efforts to ensure access to computers in schools. Despite the huge investment in equipment, Balacheff and Kaput (1997) state that, in terms of 'market penetration' in the use of computers "the expectations of thirty years ago have surely not been met" (p. 470). TIMSS found that in the countries on which dependable data were available, the proportion of eighth-grade mathematics teachers saying that computers were never, or almost never, used in their classrooms to solve exercises or problems ranged from 38% to 99%, with a median value of 89% (Beaton et al., 1996, p. 167), and in grade 4, the median value was 93% (Mullis et al., 1996, p. 179). In half the countries studied, at least 85% of 8th-grade students and 80% of 4th-grade students said they never used computers in lessons at all.

Only in 5 of 26 countries did at least 10% of grade 4 students say they used computers in "most lessons", whereas in only 5 out of 44 countries did 10% of grade 8 students say they used computers "pretty often" or "always" in mathematics lessons. In other words, in the vast majority of the mathematics classrooms surveyed in TIMSS, computers were almost never used to solve exercises or problems, and rarely used for anything else.

And, as with calculators, we should also be concerned with the quality of the use of computers, as well as just the extent. Although there is substantial evidence of the utility of computer-based learning environments for teaching mathematics (what Balacheff and Kaput, 1997, call 'epistemological penetration', p. 470), studies of the impact of the use of computers suggest that they are not well integrated into classroom practice (Watson, 1993). As the title of a recent book by Larry Cuban has it, computers in education really have been "oversold and underused" (Cuban, 2002).

The second major 'revolution' in mathematics education that I wish to consider is the 'constructivist revolution'. Before this revolution, the standard psychological models of learning were based on information processing (derived from the idea of the mind as a computer) and before that, in Gestalt psychology, on learning as re-organisation or re-structuring. In terms of teachers' current practice, however, one of the most influential models of thinking appears to be one of the earliest: associationism (Mayer, 1977). In this view, learning consisted of strengthening links between stimulus and response through reinforcement, and failure to learn indicated a failure adequately to form or reinforce the correct links between stimulus and response. From such a perspective errors are random failures in the chain of associations, to be corrected by reinforcement of the correct links. In contrast, constructivist approaches to psychology hold that learning is not the passive acquisition of associations between stimuli and responses, but is rather the result of an active process of sense making on the part of the learner. From such a perspective, the errors that learners make are not random, but, to an extent at least, predictable (Booth, 1984; Hart, 1981, 1984; Kerslake, 1986).

In the mathematics education research community, it seems that 'we are all constructivists now'. And yet, if one observes practice in mathematics classrooms all over the world or looks at textbooks, the predominant activity appears to be the repetition of mathematical techniques through exercises. Even in the education of the youngest students, where 'child-centred' methods have taken greater hold, it seems as if teachers' predominant models of learning, at least for mathematics, are more associationist than constructivist. It is also worth noting that although the writing of Piaget was undoubtedly influential, the adoption of 'child-centred' practices in primary schools during the 1960s and 1970s was due at least as much to changing philosophical views about the nature of the child.

There have, of course, been success stories. The concern with social justice and the search for ways of ensuring that historically disadvantaged groups enjoy greater success in mathematics have resulted in substantial achievements. The gap between female and male achievement in mathematics has been substantially narrowed over the last 50 years (Feingold, 1988; Friedman, 1989; Hyde, Fennema, & Lamon, 1990; Linn, 1992), and in many countries, females now outperform males up to age 18. In this context, however, it is worth noting that socio-economic disadvantage continues to have a profound negative impact on mathematics achievement, and in many countries, the achievement of students from minority ethnic communities is also cause for concern.

Inevitably, the foregoing examples are at best merely suggestive. Nevertheless I hope that even those readers who believe there has been change will agree that such changes have been limited, fragile, and highly vulnerable to changes in government policy.

What are we to make of this lack of significant change? Can lack of change be construed as success? Well, in many cases, yes. In countries that are moving from a system of education for only the elite to a system of mass education, or extending universal education beyond the primary school years, then just maintaining the status quo is an impressive achievement. Similarly, maintaining teacher quality in a changing social order, where the status of teachers and their relative monetary rewards are diminishing, is also an achievement.

Given the tremendous advances in what we know about successful mathematics teaching and learning, however, the huge gulf between what are conceived of as 'good mathematics classrooms' by the research community and the experience of most learners is a severe indictment of the failure of educational research to have an impact on practice in mathematics education. In the next section, I will explore some of the reasons for this failure.

THE (TROUBLING) HISTORY OF EDUCATIONAL RESEARCH

Although the amount of money spent on educational research in most countries has been only a tiny fraction of the total expenditure on education (typically between one-third of a percent and one percent in Europe and North America), the large size of education budgets in most countries has meant that a large amount of money has undoubtedly been spent on educational research. Although there have been some small successes (Tyack & Cuban, 1995), the impact of research on practice is very hard to discern (Travers, 1983). And, notes William Reese (1999), "Nothing like a comprehensive understanding of the overall problem seems likely to appear on the horizon anytime soon" (p. 11).

The failure of educational research to have any real impact on educational practice in general, and on mathematics education in particular, has been lamented for many years (see, e.g., Kilpatrick, 1992). In 1945, J. Cayce Morrison, assistant commissioner for research in the State Education Department in New York, said that there was "too wide a gap between research at its best and much of its practice in education" (Morrison, 1945, p. 243). By the 1970s, there was increasing acceptance that educational research had not had much of an impact either on the practice of teachers in schools (Clifford, 1973) or on policy making (Weiss & Vickers, 1992; Ravitch & Vinovskis, 1995).

Today, there are it seems two broad strands of criticism of educational research. The first is that educational research is unnecessary or irrelevant, perhaps best summed up by Donald Campbell, who suggested that one of the key questions in research is, "If you are wrong about this, who will notice?" Too often, in social science research, he suggests, the answer is, "Nobody" (Campbell, 1986, pp. 128–129). This phenomenon manifests itself either in a belief that expert practitioners already know 'what works' in mathematics classrooms and so novice teachers can learn all they need to know by watching experienced teachers, or that pedagogical practice will always be weak and that the solution lies in prescribing curricula and teaching methods in 'teacher-proof' schemes.

The second strand regards educational research as necessary, but of poor quality. Too often, it is said, educational research produces results that are ambiguous or contradictory (Johnson, 1987). This attitude is perhaps best summed up by Robert F. Kennedy's furious reaction to the ambiguous evaluation of the impact of additional money provided for the education of socioeconomically disadvantaged students: "Do you mean that you spent a billion dollars and you don't know whether they can read or not?" (Lagemann, 2000, p. 202).

More recently, in Great Britain, the government became so frustrated by the 'irrelevance' of educational research that it commissioned a report from a group of social scientists from the Institute of Employment Studies at the University of Sussex. The report concluded:

> Our overall conclusion is that the actions and decisions of policy-makers and practitioners are insufficiently informed by research. Where research does address policy-relevant and practical issues it tends to:
>
> - be small scale and fails to generate findings that are reliable and generalisable;
> - be insufficiently based on existing knowledge and therefore capable of advancing understanding;
> - be presented in a form or medium which is largely inaccessible to a non-academic audience; and
> - lack interpretation for a policy-making or practitioner audience.
>
> This results at least in part from a research effort that is predominantly supply (i.e. researcher) driven. Furthermore, the research agenda tends to be backward rather than forward looking – following policy not prompting it. This is partly due to an emphasis on evaluation within much of the limited volume of government sponsored research, rather than exploration and development. It also reflects a dissonance between the policy making and research production cycles.
>
> (Hillage, Pearson, Anderson, & Tamkin, 1998, pp. xi–xii)

On those few occasions when research does produce unambiguous results, researchers are told that they are telling practitioners and policy makers what they already knew. If educational researchers could only agree how to go about research properly, we are told, educational research could join the elite club of 'hard' sciences producing reliable knowledge (these people have in the past rather unkindly been described as suffering from 'physics envy').

At the beginning of the last century, educational research, to the extent that it existed at all, was either historical or an aspect of philosophy. One of the earliest attempts to use empirical methods in educational research was the 'School Survey' movement in the USA. Beginning around 1910, this movement sought to gather 'objective evidence' about factors influencing the educational progress of school students. However, because of the sheer diversity of the U.S. education system, with over 100,000 school districts each free to determine its own education policy, there was little agreement about the purpose or scope of education, and meaningful comparisons of educational outputs was almost impossible.

In *An Elusive Science* (whose subtitle is the title of this section), Ellen Condliffe Lagemann (2000) shows that the search for ways of producing high-quality research in education has been, in effect, a search for secure disciplinary foundations for the production of reliable knowledge. At first, philosophy and history provided those foundations, but around the turn of the century, these were supplanted by psychology, which dominates to the present day, although since the 1970s sociology and social anthropology have also been influential.

Lagemann argues that the failure of educational research to deliver what has been wanted has arisen from three main causes: the isolation and low status of educational research in the academy; its tendency to focus too narrowly on particular aspects of education rather than looking at education systems; and the weak governance and regulation of educational research. These three causes are of course intimately entwined.

In the USA, teaching had been regarded as 'women's work' since early in the nineteenth century, so that educational research was accorded low status by association. Lagemann also points out that being an applied subject served to marginalise education within the academic mainstream. No doubt partly in an attempt to raise its status, educational research attempted to emulate the hard sciences through the quantification of educational processes, which of course entailed focusing on those aspects of education that could be easily quantified. And whereas most teachers were female, most school supervisors and district administrators were male, so that the emerging field of educational research emphasised educational administration almost from the outset.

This lack of agreement not just about how to undertake educational research but also what should be researched continued to plague attempts to establish 'what works' in education over the next half-century. As Kilpatrick (1992) noted:

> Educational researchers were not satisfying the requests of practitioners that they provide useful information, they were not satisfying the funding agencies and their colleagues in the scientific disciplines that their work was valuable, and they were not satisfying their own expectations for what

research should be. Far from living in a golden age, they seemed to be entering a depression. (p. 31)

However, Lagemann's history closes with an ironic twist. In the final quarter of the last century, educational research finally began to get on the right track with two key realisations. Firstly, the complexity of educational settings requires that insights from all of the 'foundation disciplines' (and not just one) be required to make progress in educational improvement. Secondly, it slowly became clear that centre-periphery models of dissemination are simply ineffective in education. The result was a blossoming of multi-disciplinary research involving teachers in real innovation and improvement. At the same time, however, it seems that the politicians gave up on educational research, and by 1991, federal funding for educational research in the USA stood at approximately one-third the level provided in 1971.

Lagemann's analysis is persuasive, and there are many who believe that the nature of research in the physical sciences can provide a useful model for creating thorough foundations for educational research. For example, in the USA, the Committee on Scientific Principles for Education Research has recently produced a report entitled *Scientific Research in Education* (Shavelson & Towne, 2002) identifying six principles underpinning the conduct of research in all scientific disciplines that, it is argued, are equally appropriate for educational research. Although the invocation of research in the physical sciences as an ideal towards which educational research should aspire may have some merit, I want to suggest here that the goal of educational research as a science, in the same sense as physics is a science, is not just elusive, but impossible.

This claim is in part philosophical, but it is also in part an empirical claim. The phenomena that are studied in educational research (and indeed in all social sciences) are, in the first instance, far more complex than those that are studied by the 'hard' sciences – just imagine trying to set boundary conditions for the initial state of a typical classroom. In addition, however, it is important to realise the autonomy that individual students bring to lessons is not a problem with which physical sciences have to grapple. Bars of iron do not behave differently because someone has been testing them. Or more precisely, although bars of iron may behave differently depending on how they have been treated in the past (e.g., whether they have been annealed or subject to repeated stress and strain), we know what kinds of treatments matter, and we know how to find out in advance how the bar will perform under tests. Even those who believe that there is no such thing as free will and that all human behaviour at time T1 is actually determined by the state of the system at T0 have to concede that it is too difficult to specify the starting conditions precisely enough to determine the outcome. Chaos theory and, at a smaller scale, Heisenberg's uncertainty principle render Laplace's dream of being able to predict all behaviour from initial conditions a nonstarter.

So, if educational research has difficulty in producing (or as I have argued cannot produce) the 'reliable knowledge' (Ziman, 1978) produced by the physical sciences, what is to be done? In the next section, I argue that educational research needs to focus not on the kind of analytic rationality espoused (although not always practised!) in the physical sciences but instead on the pursuit of practical wisdom.

RATIONALITY AND REASON IN EDUCATIONAL RESEARCH

In his Nicomachean Ethics, Aristotle proposes that there are three main types of intellectual virtue: *episteme*, *techne*, and *phronesis*. *Episteme* concerns knowledge of eternal universal truths and equates to the kinds of knowledge that is developed in the physical sciences, often expressed in the form 'know that' and 'know why'. This kind of knowledge is independent of context and persists today in English words like *epistemology* and *epistemic*. *Techne*, in contrast, is the study of how to bring things into a concrete form. It differs from *episteme* in that *episteme* is concerned with things that are the way they are of necessity (otherwise they would not be eternal truths), whereas *techne* deals with things that are contingent and variable. It is thus more about craft knowledge and 'know how' and persists in English words such as *technology* and *technique*. *Phronesis*, often translated as *prudence*, is the ability "to deliberate rightly about what is good and advantageous" (Aristotle, 1976, 1140). This idea, as Aristotle points out, is different from *episteme* since there is no point in debating things that are universally true – *phronesis* requires knowledge of particular circumstances. *Phronesis* is also different from *techne* since it is designed to move people to action rather than production. Aristotle's point here is that *techne* is product-oriented because the aim of the production is not the production itself but the product, whereas action is process-oriented – the end is doing *well*. This distinction inevitably brings in notions of ethics and values. Unlike *episteme*, which aspires to be value free, *phronesis* is based on practical value-rationality. As Flyvbjerg (2001) notes:

> By definition, phronetic researchers focus on values; for example by taking their point of departure in the classic value-rational questions: "Where are we going? Is it desirable? What should be done?" (p. 130)

The choices we make are not right or wrong in an absolute sense, but good or bad according to some set of values and ethical principles. For a fuller discussion of the idea that ethical and value judgements are at the heart of educational research, see Lester and Wiliam (2002).

Since *episteme* deals with universal truths, it is independent of individual experience. Those with different experiences should be able to agree on the extent to which a particular claim is universally true. With *phronesis*, however, individual experience is crucial. Experience can result in an individual reaching universal truths, but that is very rare. More often, the result of experience is not a set of rules but an ability to make good decisions, without necessarily being aware of how these good decisions are arrived at. This ability might be called intuition, but too often, from a standpoint rooted in analytic rationality, intuition is rejected as being 'unscientific'. From the point of view of *phronesis*, intuition is an essential element of practical wisdom – the (albeit implicit) result of a large-scale synthesis of substantial experience.

Although *phronesis* is relevant only when there is no universal truth, that does not mean there are no general principles involved. *Phronesis* involves the practical wisdom to act well by the successful integration of general principles with detailed consideration of context and therefore must be based on substantial experience as well as the use of general principles. In this context, it is worth noting that the word *general* has two meanings in English. To a mathematician, something is generally true only if there are no exceptions (i.e., if it is universally true). In other contexts, however, something is generally true when it is true most of the time but when there are also known to be exceptions. The mathematicians' use of *general* corresponds to *episteme*, whereas the vernacular usage relates more to *phronesis*.

The distinction between *episteme* and *phronesis* is similar to the distinction between analytic and hermeneutic philosophy proposed by Richard Rorty (1979). Analytic philosophy pursues timeless truths, whereas hermeneutic philosophy is intended to help people deal effectively (well?) with issues here and now.

The physical sciences have succeeded because they have focused on *episteme*. But the social sciences have failed for precisely the same reason. For social science in general, and for mathematics education in particular, there cannot be universal truths, because successful action will always require the integration of general principles and specific contextual details. To choose a trivial example, if we want to find the perpendicular bisector of a line, we know that it can always be found by drawing a line between the intersections of circular arcs centred on the endpoints of the line. This statement is true for all lines in Euclidean geometry and is therefore an example of *episteme*. In contrast, how we teach students this technique is contingent, variable, and underdetermined, and therefore requires *phronesis*.

In his most recent book, *Return to Reason*, Stephen Toulmin (2001) makes a similar argument. He suggests that the attempt to emulate the physical sciences by focusing on analytic rationality as the only way for producing knowledge has been crippling to the social sciences. In particular, an emphasis on rationality has focused attention on those aspects of social phenomena that are most amenable to rational analysis. The result has been that the settling of issues that cannot be resolved by the application of universal rules is regarded as 'unscientific'. He suggests that a criterion of 'reasonableness' – research as a guide to action – would be more appropriate.

One of the examples that Toulmin quotes is the work of the U.S. National Commission for the Protection of Human Subjects of Biomedical and Behavioral Research, which was asked to make recommendations about the use of young children in medical and behavioural research. During a six-month period, the Commission discussed the issue intensively and sought the views of others by holding public meetings. At the end of this time, they were able to frame a set of proposals and conditions for acceptable research practices on which they were in almost total agreement.

The Commissioners then went home to write statements about their reasons for approving the recommendations. Toulmin (2001) says,

> At this point Babel set in. Practically speaking, they were in agreement, and agreed what they agreed about. The thing they could not agree about was *why* they had agreed about it – what reasons they had for concurring in the recommendations. Their moral perceptions coincided, but the reasons they gave depended (at least partly) on their backgrounds. In short – and Aristotle would say the same – their shared certitude about their perceptions was greater than the certainty, or uncertainty, that each of them felt about the general systems to which they were professedly committed. (p. 132)

In other words, the Commissioners could agree about what would be 'good and advantageous' but could not agree about any universal rules underlying that agreement.

So not only does the search for universal rules underdetermine action as argued above, it can also prevent agreement about what is best. Had the Commissioners started from their foundational principles, they might never have secured agreement, and the process would certainly have taken longer. Perhaps the resulting consensus might have been even stronger, and longer lasting, but pragmatically the time available for reaching consensus is not unlimited. As I have argued above, I do not believe that universal rules will ever be of value in education, but even if such rules were possible in the future, they are beyond us now. Therefore, educational research ought to place more emphasis on the pursuit of practical wisdom to guide practitioners rather than on the search for absolute truths.

The superiority of intuitive rather than rule-based thinking is demonstrated by an experiment conducted on a group of paramedics (Klein & Klein, 1981) cited by Flyvbjerg (2001). Six short video extracts of a person administering cardiopulmonary resuscitation (CPR) were shown to three groups: experienced paramedics, students being trained as paramedics, and people who taught life-saving techniques. They were then asked which of the six they would choose to resuscitate them if they needed CPR. Five of the six video extracts were of inexperienced trainees just learning CPR, and the sixth was a highly experienced paramedic. Of the experienced paramedics, 90% chose the experienced para-medic, whereas only 50% of the students did so. Only 30% of the instructors, however, chose the experienced paramedic.

Flyvbjerg argues that we can understand this apparently paradoxical result by considering the five levels of expertise in learning proposed by Dreyfus and Dreyfus (1986). At the *novice* level, the individual is guided by rules that are applied irrespective of context. For example, the novice teacher tends to try to apply the same sets of rules to all the classes he or she teaches. The *advanced beginner* begins to take situationally specific factors into account, and personal experience is often relied on more than context-independent rules. As experience accumulates, however, the number of recognisable elements or 'chunks' increases and threatens to overwhelm the individual. For example, the need for the school teacher to attend to the learning needs of her or his students, controlling the behaviour of some while also trying to make sure he or she interacts equally often with female and male students, can lead to a feeling of 'plate spinning' – dashing from one imperative to the next to try to attend to all. The *competent performer* is characterised by performance in which conflicting priorities are resolved through the use of strategies usually derived from conscious problem-solving behaviour. In contrast, the *proficient performer* acts quickly and intuitively, often doing the 'right thing' without conscious awareness. In this context, it is important to realise that 'intuition' is used here not as some irrational prejudice but rather, as outlined above, as the result of the sedimentation and synthesis of vast amounts of experience. Finally, in the *expert*, the ability to act quickly and intuitively in a range of contexts and settings is unified into a 'feeling' of the right thing to do. The use here of an emotive term – 'feeling' – is not coincidental. Experts 'feel' the best course of action, not just with their mind but also in their whole body. Expertise is therefore not the culmination of rationality but rather transcends it. Expertise involves going beyond what can be done through rationality. That is not irrational but meta-rational (i.e., beyond rationality).

Therefore, Flyvbjerg argues, it appears that the paramedic trainers identified the trained paramedics less successfully because they looked for paramedics who followed the rules that they themselves taught. In other words, they were looking for those at the level of competent performers rather than proficient performers or experts. If we accept that the classification proposed by Dreyfus and Dreyfus also applies to teaching, then it seems likely that the failure of educational research to have an impact on educational practice stems from a similar limitation.

If we accept that the prime (although not the only) purpose of educational research is the improvement of educational processes, then it can succeed only if research findings are taken up by teachers and incorporated into their practice. There are, of course, other ways that educational research can influence practice. Ideas about how children learn that were developed in the Concepts in Secondary Mathematics and Science (CSMS) project (Hart, 1981) fed into the construction of the first version of the national curriculum for mathematics in England and Wales (Department of Education and Science & Welsh Office, 1989), and these ideas continue to underpin the national curriculum even though it has been revised three times. Many of those involved in the preservice training of mathematics teachers are themselves actively involved in research, so research can feed into practice in that way. Research can also influence practice through the production of textbooks, although, as Clements (2002) notes, it rarely does so. If educational research is to have any lasting impact on practice, however, it must be taken up and used by practitioners.

The kinds of prescriptions given by educational research to practice have been in the form of generalised principles that may often, even usually, be right but in some circumstances are just plain wrong. Experts can see that a particular recipe is inappropriate in some circumstances, although because their response is intuitive, they may not be able to discern the reason why. What gets learnt by the practitioner is that the findings of educational research are not a valid guide to action.

But more often, research findings also run foul of the opposite problem: that of insufficient specificity. Many teachers complain that the findings from research produce only bland platitudes and are insufficiently contextualised to be used in guiding action in practice. Put simply, research findings underdetermine action. For example, the research on feedback suggests that task-involving feedback is to be preferred to ego-involving feedback (Kluger & DeNisi, 1996), but what the teacher needs to know is, "Can I say, 'Well done' to this student, now?" Moving from the generalised principles produced by educational research to action in the classroom is not a simple process of translation.

In the past, this process has been called dissemination and is now more often called knowledge transfer – both interesting metaphors, suggesting that all that needs to be done is to "share the results" (English, Jones, Lesh, Tirosh, & Bussi, 2002, p. 805) with practitioners about the latest findings and they will be used.

If expertise transcends rationality, as I have argued above, however, then the process of knowledge transfer cannot be one of providing instructions to novices, advanced beginners, or competent performers in the hope that they will get better. Rather what is needed is an acknowledgement that what teachers do in 'taking on' research is not a more or less passive adoption of some good ideas from someone else but an active process of knowledge creation:

> Teachers will not take up attractive sounding ideas, albeit based on extensive research, if these are presented as general principles which leave entirely to them the task of translating them into everyday practice – their classroom lives are too busy and too fragile for this to be possible for all but an outstanding few. What they need is a variety of living examples of implementation, by teachers with whom they can identify and from whom they can both derive conviction and confidence that they can do better, and see concrete examples of what doing better means in practice.
>
> (Black & Wiliam, 1998, p. 15)

CONCLUSION

In this chapter, I have argued that while there may have been large-scale changes in education systems across the world (i.e., the extension of mass schooling), the changes in mathematics classrooms have been relatively modest (and not always for the better). Educational research has failed to affect practice because of an over-attention to analytical rationality, when a greater emphasis on 'practical wisdom' would have served us better as the primary goal of educational research. For too long, we have employed 'centre-periphery' models of dissemination in which researchers suppose that their role is first to work out the best way to teach mathematics and then (optionally) to tell teachers what to do. When teachers fail to 'listen' to researchers, researchers too often adopt habits similar to the Englishman abroad: talk louder, more slowly, and use simpler words. We have treated the 'translation' of research findings into practice as a simple, perhaps even technical, task, when in fact, research on the nature of expertise in teaching suggests quite the contrary (Berliner, Stein, Saberrs, Brown Claridge, Cushing, & Pinnegar, 1989).

Stokes (1997) has rightly pointed out that research should be inspired both by a quest for fundamental understanding and by consideration of its use (what he terms 'Pasteur's quadrant'). I am not suggesting that the quest for fundamental understanding is inappropriate in mathematics education research – we certainly don't yet know everything about 'what works' in mathematics teaching, but I do argue that we know a lot more about 'what works' than we know about how to support teachers in mathematics classrooms to improve their practice. Given the focus on analytic rationality as the criterion against which most educational research has been measured, perhaps that is not surprising. After all, researching the professional development of teachers appears to be much less tractable than researching the best way to learn algebra. But if mathematics education research is to affect practice, then 'considerations of use' need to be given a much higher priority.

If we *are* to take considerations of use more seriously, then we need to understand that teachers who manage to incorporate findings from educational research into their practice are not just 'translating' or 'transforming' knowledge. They are *creating* knowledge, albeit of a distinctive and specialised kind, by integrating the general principles that they can derive from research with the special, detailed knowledge they have of the contexts in which they work.

Fortunately, we have examples that suggest a way forward. Cognitively Guided Instruction (CGI) provided teachers with structures around which they could organise their knowledge of children's thinking, originally in addition and subtraction problems (Carpenter, Fennema, & Franke, 1996; Carpenter, Fennema, Peterson, & Carey, 1988; Carpenter, Fennema, Peterson, Chiang, & Loef, 1989), which resulted in greater self-confidence and enhanced problem-solving ability. In the QUASAR project (Silver & Stein, 1996), 'resource partners' (typically researchers from local universities) assisted schools in improving their practice by helping them formulate their own approaches to curriculum development and professional development. In the Kent-Medway-Oxfordshire Formative Assessment Project (KMOFAP), teachers were supported in developing their own plans in developing their classroom assessment procedures to give them better information about students' learning and to involve students more in their own learning (Black, Harrison, Lee, Marshall, & Wiliam, 2002). What these three projects have in common is that they attend both to the process and the content of teacher development (Reeves, McCall, & MacGilchrist, 2001). They attend to the *process* of professional development through an acknowledgement that teachers need time, and support from colleagues, in order to reflect critically upon and to develop their practice. By themselves, however, these are not enough. Teachers also need ideas about the directions in which they can pro-ductively take their practice, and thus there is a need for work on the professional development of mathematics teachers to pay specific attention to subject-specific dimensions of teacher learning (Wilson & Berne, 1999).

The problem with these three interventions is that they are highly resource intensive and could never, in their current forms, be geared up to provide impact on a national scale. What we therefore need are studies about the extent to which small-scale projects can be scaled up. Within the resources likely to be available, there is no possibility that such studies could establish 'what works' according to the criteria of analytic rationality, but they could just possibly do so if our criterion is one of reasonableness. Similarly, although Geraldine Clifford (1973) notes that proving that research affects teaching is "a near impossibility" (p. 3) within the framework of analytic rationality, if we adopt 'reasonableness' as our criterion, perhaps we can begin to make progress there too.

I am aware that my discussion of *phronesis* has excluded considerations of power, and this is a severe limitation. By founding our basis for action on value-rationality rather than on universal truths, we raise the immediate question of which people's values are to count? Although research cannot tell practitioners what to do, it can problematise all the taken-for-granted assumptions about our practices, such as what we do that serves to restrict opportunities to high-quality mathematics education to some groups of students (Moreno-Armella & Block, 2002; Tate & Rousseau, 2002). As Michel Foucault observed in respect of his work on prisons:

> It's true that certain people, such as those who work in the institutional setting of the prison ... are not likely to find advice on instruction in my books to tell them "what is to be done." But my project is precisely to bring it about that they "no longer know what to do," so that the acts, gestures, discourses that up until then had seemed to go without saying become problematic, difficult, dangerous.
>
> (quoted in Miller, 1993, p. 235)

A focus on *phronesis* can serve to open up debate so that other voices can be heard, thus enabling more conflicting stories to emerge. This process contrasts starkly with *episteme*, which seeks to close down debate by having the last word. In mathematics education research, there can be no objectivity:

> There is *only* a perspective seeing, *only* a perspective 'knowing;' and the *more* affects we allow to speak about one thing, the *more* eyes, different eyes, we can use to observe one thing, the more complete will our 'concept' of this thing, our 'objectivity' be.
>
> (Nietzsche, 1969, p. 119, emphasis in original)

In closing, I can do no better than echo the words of Bellah, Madsen, Sullivan, Swidler and Tipton (1985), by hoping that "the reader will test what we say against his or her own experience, will argue with us when what we say does not fit, and, best of all, will join the public discussion by offering interpretations superior to ours that can then receive further discussion" (p. 307).

NOTE

[1.] The term *systems* is used because in TIMSS the sampling units were sometimes countries (e.g., USA) but sometimes regions (e.g., data for Flemish-speaking Belgium were reported separately from those for French-speaking Belgium).

REFERENCES

Aristotle. (1976). *The Nicomachean ethics.* London, UK: Penguin.

Balacheff, N., & Kaput, J. J. (1997). Computer-based learning environments in mathematics. In A. J. Bishop, K. Clements, C. Keitel, J. Kilpatrick & C. Laborde (Eds.), *International handbook of mathematics education* (pp. 469–501). Dordrecht, Netherlands: Kluwer Academic Publishers.

Beaton, A. E., Mullis, I. V. S., Martin, M. O., Gonzalez, E. J., Kelly, D. L., & Smith, T. A. (1996). *Mathematics achievement in the middle school years: IEA's third international mathematics and science study.* Chestnut Hill, MA: Boston College.

Begle, E. G., & Gibb, E. G. (1980). Why do research? In R. J. Shumway (Ed.), *Research in mathematics education* (pp. 3–19). Washington, DC: National Council of Teachers of Mathematics.

Bellah, R. N., Madsen, R., Sullivan, W. M., Swidler, A., & Tipton, S. M. (1985). *Habits of the heart: Individualism and commitment in American life.* New York: Harper & Row.

Berliner, D. C., Stein, P., Saberrs, D., Brown Claridge, P., Cushing, K., & Pinnegar, S. (1989). Implications of research on pedagogical expertise and experience for mathematics teaching. In D. A. Grouws, T. J. Cooney & D. Jones (Eds.), *Perspectives on research on effective mathematics teaching* (pp. 67–95). Reston, VA: National Council of Teachers of Mathematics.

Bishop, A. J., Clements, K., Keitel, C., Kilpatrick, J., & Laborde, C. (Eds.) (1997). *International handbook of mathematics education.* Dordrecht, Netherlands: Kluwer Academic Publishers.

Black, P., Harrison, C., Lee, C., Marshall, B., & Wiliam, D. (2002). *Working inside the black box: Assessment for learning in the classroom.* London: King's College London, Department of Education and Professional Studies.

Black, P. J., & Wiliam, D. (1998). *Inside the black box: Raising standards through classroom assessment.* London: King's College London School of Education.

Booth, L. R. (1984). *Algebra: Children's strategies and errors.* Windsor, UK: NFER-Nelson.

Campbell, D. T. (1986). Science's social system of validity-enhancing collective belief change and the problems of the social sciences. In D. W. Fiske & R. A. Shweder (Eds.), *Metatheory in social science: Pluralisms and subjectivities* (pp. 108–148). Chicago: University of Chicago Press.

Carpenter, T. P., Fennema, E., & Franke, M. L. (1996). Cognitively guided instruction: A knowledge base for reform in primary mathematics instruction. *Elementary School Journal, 97,* 3–20.

Carpenter, T. P., Fennema, E., Peterson, P. L., & Carey, D. (1988). Teachers' pedagogical content knowledge of students' problem solving in elementary arithmetic. *Journal for Research in Mathematics Education, 19*(5), 385–401.

Carpenter, T. P., Fennema, E., Peterson, P. L., Chiang, C. P., & Loef, M. (1989). Using knowledge of children's mathematics thinking in classroom teaching: An experimental study. *American Educational Research Journal, 26*(4), 499–531.

Charles, R. I., & Silver, E. A. (Eds.). (1989). *The teaching and assessing of mathematical problem solving.* Reston, VA: National Council of Teachers of Mathematics.

Clements, D. H. (2002). Linking research and curriculum development. In L. D. English (Ed.), *Handbook of international research in mathematics education* (pp. 599–630). Mahwah, NJ: Erlbaum.

Clifford, G. J. (1973). A history of the impact of research on teaching. In R. M. W. Travers (Ed.), *Second handbook of research on teaching* (pp. 1–46). Chicago: Rand McNally.

Cuban, L. (2002). *Oversold and underused: Computers in the classroom.* Cambridge, MA: Harvard University Press.

Department of Education and Science & Welsh Office. (1989). *Mathematics in the National Curriculum.* London: Her Majesty's Stationery Office.

Dreyfus, H., & Dreyfus, S. (1986). *Mind over machine: The power of human intuition and expertise in the era of the computer.* New York: Free Press.

English, L. D. (Ed.). (2002). *Handbook of international research in mathematics education.* Mahwah, NJ: Erlbaum.

English, L. D., Jones, G., Lesh, R., Tirosh, D., & Bussi, M. B. (2002). Future issues and directions in international mathematics education research. In L. D. English (Ed.), *Handbook of international research in mathematics education* (pp. 787–812). Mahwah, NJ: Erlbaum.

Feingold, A. (1988). Cognitive gender differences are disappearing. *American Psychologist, 43,* 95–103.

Flyvbjerg, B. (2001). *Making social science matter: Why social inquiry fails and how it can succeed again.* Cambridge: Cambridge University Press.

Friedman, L. (1989). Mathematics and the gender gap: A meta-analysis of recent studies on sex differences in mathematical tasks. *Review of Educational Research, 59*(2), 185–213.

Grouws, D. A. (Ed.). (1992). *Handbook of research on mathematics teaching and learning.* New York: Macmillan.

Grouws, D. A., Cooney, T. J., & Jones, D. (Eds.) (1988). *Perspectives on research on effective mathematics teaching.* Reston, VA: National Council of Teachers of Mathematics.

Hart, K. M. (Ed.). (1981). *Children's understanding of mathematics: 11–16.* London: John Murray.

Hart, K. M. (1984). *Ratio: Children's strategies and errors.* Windsor, UK: NFER-Nelson.

Hiebert, J., & Behr, M. (Eds.). (1988). *Number concepts and operations in the middle grades.* Reston, VA: National Council of Teachers of Mathematics.

Hillage, J., Pearson, R., Anderson, A., & Tamkin, P. (1998). *Excellence in research on schools.* London: Department for Education and Employment.

Hyde, J. S., Fennema, E., & Lamon, S. J. (1990). Gender differences in mathematics performance: A meta-analysis. *Psychological Bulletin, 107,* 139–155.

Johnson, W. R. (1987). Empowering teachers: Holmes, Carnegie and the lessons of history. *History of Education Quarterly, 27,* 221–240.

Kerslake, D. (1986). *Fractions: Children's strategies and errors.* Windsor, UK: NFER-Nelson.

Kilpatrick, J. (1992). A history of research in mathematics education. In D. A. Grouws (Ed.), *Handbook of research on mathematics teaching and learning* (pp. 3–38). New York: Macmillan.

Klein, H. A., & Klein, G. A. (1981). *Perceptive/cognitive analysis of proficient cardio-pulmonary resuscitation (CPR) performance.* Paper presented at the annual meeting of the Midwestern Psychological Association, Chicago.

Kluger, A. N., & DeNisi, A. (1996). The effects of feedback interventions on performance: A historical review, a meta-analysis, and a preliminary feedback intervention theory. *Psychological Bulletin, 119*(2), 254–284.

Lagemann, E. C. (2000). *An elusive science: The troubling history of education research.* Chicago: University of Chicago Press.

Lester Jr., F. K., & Wiliam, D. (2002). On the purpose of mathematics education research: Making productive contributions to policy and practice. In L. D. English (Ed.), *Handbook of international research in mathematics education* (pp. 489–506). Mahwah, NJ: Erlbaum.

Linn, M. C. (1992). Gender differences in educational achievement. In Educational Testing Service (Ed.), *Sex equity in educational opportunity, achievement, and testing: Proceedings of a 1991 ETS Invitational Conference* (pp. 11–50). Princeton, NJ: Educational Testing Service.

Mayer, R. E. (1977). *Thinking and problem-solving.* Glenview, IL: Scott-Foresman.

Miller, J. (1993). *The passion of Michel Foucault.* New York: Simon & Schuster.

Moon, B. (1986). *The 'new maths' curriculum controversy: An international story*. London: Falmer.

Moreno-Armella, L., & Block, D. (2002). Democratic access to powerful mathematics in a developing country. In L. D. English (Ed.), *Handbook of international research in mathematics education* (pp. 301–321). Mahwah, NJ: Erlbaum.

Morrison, J. C. (1945). The role of research in educational reconstruction. In N. B. Henry (Ed.), *American education in the postwar period: Part 2. Structural reorganization* (Forty-fourth Yearbook of the National Society for the Study of Education, pp. 238–265). Chicago: University of Chicago Press.

Mullis, I. V. S., Martin, M. O., Beaton, A. E., Gonzalez, E. J., Kelly, D. L., & Smith, T. A. (1996). *Mathematics achievement in the primary school years: IEA's third international mathematics and science study*. Chestnut Hill, MA: Boston College.

Nietzsche, F. (1969). *On the genealogy of morals*. New York: Vintage Books.

Organisation for European Economic Co-operation, Office for Scientific and Technical Personnel (Ed.). (1961). *New thinking in school mathematics*. Paris: Organisation for European Economic Co-operation.

Ravitch, D., & Vinovskis, M. (Eds.). (1995). *Learning from the past: What history teaches us about school reform*. Baltimore, MD: Johns Hopkins University Press.

Reese, W. J. (1999). What history teaches about the impact of educational research on practice. In A. Iran-Nejad & P. D. Pearson (Eds.), *Review of research in education* (pp. 1–19). Washington, DC: American Educational Research Association.

Reeves, J., McCall, J., & MacGilchrist, B. (2001). Change leadership: Planning, conceptualization and perception. In J. MacBeath & P. Mortimore (Eds.), *Improving school effectiveness* (pp. 122–137). Buckingham, UK: Open University Press.

Rorty, R. (1979). *Philosophy and the mirror of nature*. Princeton, NJ: Princeton University Press.

Ruthven, K. (1997). Calculators in the mathematics curriculum: The scope of personal computational technology. In A. J. Bishop, K. Clements, C. Keitel, J. Kilpatrick & C. Laborde (Eds.), *International handbook of mathematics education* (pp. 435–468). Dordrecht, Netherlands: Kluwer Academic Publishers.

Shavelson, R. J., & Towne, L. (Eds.). (2002). *Scientific research in education*. Washington, DC: National Academy Press.

Silver, E. A., & Stein, M. K. (1996). The QUASAR project: The 'revolution of the possible' in mathematics instructional reform in urban middle schools. *Urban Education, 30*, 476–521.

Sowder, J. T. (Ed.) (1989). *Setting a research agenda*. Reston, VA: National Council of Teachers of Mathematics.

Stokes, D. E. (1997). *Pasteur's quadrant: Basic science and technological innovation*. Washington, DC: Brookings Institution Press.

Tate, W., & Rousseau, C. (2002). Access and opportunity: The political and social context of mathematics education. In L. D. English (Ed.), *Handbook of international research in mathematics education* (pp. 271–299). Mahwah, NJ: Erlbaum.

Toulmin, S. (2001). *Return to reason*. Cambridge, MA: Harvard University Press.

Travers, R. M. W. (1983). *How research has changed American schools: A history from 1840 to the present*. Kalamazoo, MI: Mythos Press.

Tyack, D. B., & Cuban, L. (1995). *Tinkering toward utopia: A century of public school reform*. Cambridge, MA: Harvard University Press.

Wagner, S., & Kieren, C. (Eds.). (1989). *Research issues in the learning and teaching of algebra*. Reston, VA: National Council of Teachers of Mathematics.

Watson, D. M. (Ed.). (1993). *The ImpacT report: An evaluation of the impact of information technology on children's achievements in primary and secondary schools*. London: King's College London, School of Education.

Weiss, C. H., & Vickers, M. (1992). Research impact on educational policy. In M. C. Alkin (Ed.), *Encyclopaedia of educational research* (Vol. 3, pp. 1093–1099). New York: Macmillan.

Wilson, S. M., & Berne, J. (1999). Teacher learning and the acquisition of professional knowledge: An examination of research on contemporary professional development. In A. Iran-Nejad & P. D. Pearson (Eds.), *Review of research in education* (pp. 173–209). Washington, DC: American Educational Research Association.

Ziman, J. (1978). *Reliable knowledge: An exploration of the grounds for belief in science.* Cambridge: Cambridge University Press.

14
Preparing Mathematics Education Researchers for Disciplined Inquiry: Learning from, in, and for Practice

JO BOALER
Stanford University

DEBORAH LOEWENBERG BALL
University of Michigan

RUHAMA EVEN
Weizmann Institute of Science

ABSTRACT

In this chapter we consider what it takes to learn to conduct research in mathematics education. We argue that learning any complex practice requires opportunities to unpack its components in order to see what underlies competence performance. Many of the components of successful research remain implicit and are left to new researchers to glean from finished products. In this chapter we consider: What is it that accomplished scholars do as they conduct research? What are the practices in which they engage? What is it that they have to mobilize, consider, try, and carry out? We unpack the work of research, considering such domains as reading, writing, moving from particular observations to general insights, and communicating through multiple media. We propose that focusing on these practices of research offers a promising avenue for the preparation of beginning scholars.

WHAT IS THE PROBLEM? A DIFFERENT PERSPECTIVE

The earnest Ph.D. student sitting across from the professor had come to seek help with her research proposal: "I am not sure what is wrong, but each time I try to write what it is I want to study, it falls flat, and my committee sends it back, saying that I am not framing my problem in a way that makes it possible to design a study, and I just don't understand. I am getting more and more frustrated." Having read her most recent draft, and having also heard a similar tale of frustration from her advisor, the professor was intrigued. How had this talented doctoral student become stuck at this point? Her draft sketched the problem of teachers' use of curriculum materials, and made a number of claims about how teachers should use such materials. In particular, impressed with Stein, Grover, and Henningsen's (1996) work on the use of mathematical tasks

Second International Handbook of Mathematics Education, 491–521
A.J. Bishop, M.A. Clements, C. Keitel, J. Kilpatrick and F.K.S. Leung (eds.)
© *2003 Dordrecht: Kluwer Academic Publishers. Printed in Great Britain.*

in classrooms, she wanted to focus on improving middle school teachers' interpretation and use of academically challenging mathematical tasks. She seemed to have read widely and well, reaching back into the more general research on teaching literature (e.g., Walter Doyle's work in 1983 and 1988), and she was drawing on her own work as a teacher as well. But her committee was right: More a treatise than a design for research, her proposal identified a problem of practice and discussed ways to solve it. No question was evident. The researcher had chosen and framed an empirical study, yet she seemed to think that she could write the final version now, without collecting any data, doing any analyses, or experimenting with any interventions. What was her conception of research? How had she come so far with such an underdeveloped idea of what it means to conduct 'disciplined inquiry' (Shulman, 1997)? When the professor asked her what she wanted to focus on, she replied unhesitatingly: "When I was teaching seventh grade, I used *Mathematical Pathways* (a new curriculum), and those tasks worked so well with students. I want to study teachers working with this curriculum and show how they are able to use complex tasks with students. We didn't have the sorts of problems that the literature shows. I want to write about how this curriculum works."

Enthusiastic about or committed to one or another approach, method, or idea, novice researchers often set out to describe an approach and show that it works. This researcher already 'knew' that her approach worked. She wanted to write about the ways that it worked. She wanted to show, prove, convince. This problem comes in all shapes and sizes, from the teacher educator who wants to write about his mathematics methods course and show that his course works, to the professional developer whose use of cases produces such good results, to the mathematics curriculum coordinator convinced of the effectiveness of her district's collaborative approach to curriculum planning. Consumed with wanting to find out what works or to prove that some method or another does work, novice researchers often have difficulty framing a problem that can be investigated, designing a way to investigate it strategically, and considering what their study can claim once they do it. They read 'the literature', write 'research questions', develop questionnaires or interview protocols, and too often assume that the sum of these will yield a piece of 'research'.

This scenario illustrates one of the many problems that may be encountered by new researchers – problems that can emerge from any study, whether empirical, theoretical or philosophical. A different example is provided by new researchers who know they need to become familiar with relevant studies in their field but conceive of this task as a goal in its own sake, or even as a ritual, signalling to other members of the community that they are well read. Such researchers often include a summary of related studies without managing to draw connections among the studies or connections between the studies reviewed and the one they are conducting. Although they have acquired lots of knowledge in graduate school, these and other researchers are unprepared for the complex practice of research. In this chapter, we consider the *work* of research, using the notion of *disciplined inquiry* (Cronbach & Suppes, 1969; Shulman, 1997) to call attention to the idea that scholarship is fundamentally about the pursuit of questions and that it is distinguished from everyday curiosity and conclusion by the attentive and rigorous care with which scholars frame problems, design ways to work on them, consider results, and make claims.

The practice of research in mathematics education entails a wide range of knowledge, skills, forms of reasoning, deployment of tools, uses of imagination, and habits of mind. Researchers work to explore and understand the relationship among different factors in educational settings through a process of asking questions, framing and testing hypotheses, reading carefully, gathering evidence, analysing information, revising hypotheses, and making claims. They test their ideas by communicating them to others and improving their claims and arguments on the basis of criticism. In this chapter, we reconsider what it takes to learn to do disciplined inquiry in mathematics education. Rather than treating this question as one of what researchers should know, we turn the question on its head: What is it that accomplished scholars do as they conduct research? What are the practices in which they engage? What is it that they have to mobilize, consider, try, and carry out? We propose that focusing on these *practices of research* offers a promising avenue for the preparation of beginning scholars. If disciplined inquiry rests on such practices, then learning to do such inquiry depends on coming to see and appreciate such practices, understanding their nature and role, and being able to engage appropriately and skilfully in such practices. That is no small order.

WHAT DOES IT MEAN TO CONSIDER RESEARCH FROM THE PERSPECTIVE OF ITS *PRACTICES*?

Pickering (1995) examines the work of mathematicians and scientists and notes that there are "specific, repeatable sequences of activities on which scientists rely in their daily work" (p. 4). He refers to these repeated actions as 'practices' and describes the complex problem solving in which mathematicians and scientists engage as "the mangle of practice" (1995, p. 1). Similarly, mathematics education researchers engage in a repeated set of practices that require knowledge but, more important, that also require the successful enactment of knowledge in different situations. Because research is not merely the validation of common sense but also a set of systematic methods for improving upon everyday knowledge, researchers must develop a peculiar constellation of attitudes that include being sceptical, being open to surprise, trying to prove one's ideas wrong, and considering alternatives. Framing a researchable question is one example of a practice that lies at the heart of the enterprise. Reading widely and making good use of theory and ideas in one's own domain and others are other critical aspects of the research process. Other parts of the work include generalising from particulars – developing concepts and formulating relationships (Shulman, 1997) – revising and improving hypotheses, considering alternative interpretations, using evidence appropriately, and representing ideas in writing. These and other practices comprise the fundamental work of research – of disciplined inquiry and problem solving. Yet many of these core practices of disciplined inquiry are invisible to beginners, and even experienced scholars know and do them tacitly. Consequently, what it takes to do research remains either substantially over-looked or inadequately explicated. We propose that the close examination of core practices offers a way of reconsidering what it might take to prepare beginners to engage in scholarly inquiry.

Because the preparation of mathematics education researchers has rarely been the object of systematic investigation, our field's discussions of learning to do research tend to lack a theoretical frame. Practices are also not often the focus of deliberations about the research preparation curriculum. High-quality research entails a set of practices that depend on the use of a complex combina-tion of knowledge, beliefs, experiences, and habits of mind, yet discussions of the preparation of beginning researchers often focus instead on debates about the necessary base of professional knowledge. This chapter seeks to add to the small but expanding collection of work (Batanero, Godino, Steiner, & Wenzelburger, 1994; Lester & Carpenter, 2001; Lester & Lambdin, in press; Lingefjärd & Dahland, 1998; McIntosh & Crosswhite, 1973; Reys & Kilpatrick, 2000; Schoenfeld, 1999) that examines ways to prepare novices to engage in the work of research in mathematics education. We begin with a brief overview of the range of problems on which researchers in this field focus, for these provide the ground for a discussion of the practices that their investigation entails, and then return to an examination of what might be offered by making the practices of the work more prominent and explicit in the preparation of mathematics education researchers.

THE EXPANSION OF THE FIELD: WHAT IS INVOLVED IN MATHEMATICS EDUCATION RESEARCH?

Researchers of mathematics education seek to gain knowledge that will support the improvement of mathematics teaching and learning, from infancy into the many mathematically demanding parts of adult life, and during the school years in between. For many researchers, that goal has meant focusing on the knowledge and beliefs of learners. Researchers have asked questions about students' mathe-matical trajectories – investigating the ways in which particular mathematical concepts develop over time. In the 1960s and 1970s, researchers compiled repre-sentations of students' cognitive development as it related to particular mathe-matical domains and to curriculum materials. Many of the studies at that time combined statistical analyses of students' responses to questions and assessments, with close analyses of pervasive student conceptions and errors. This work contributed to building an important knowledge base in mathematics education, with an accumulation of studies tracing the development of key mathematical concepts and topics, such as fractions, probability, and geometry. Many of the inquiries at that time drew from psychological theories and frameworks, and in

1976 the International Group for the Psychology of Mathematics Education (PME) was established. This organization brought together researchers from across the world who were investigating students' cognitive development of mathematical ideas. PME continues, to this day, to host the only annual international conference in mathematics education, and although it has expanded its focus beyond the cognitive development of mathematical concepts, psychology continues to be the central discipline employed by researchers who attend the conference, and more generally, by the mathematics education community.

The 1980s witnessed a time of expanded inquiry in mathematics education (for a more comprehensive review of the development of the field of mathematics education research in the U.S., see Lester & Lambdin, in press). Researchers increasingly began to consider teachers and teaching in addition to curriculum and learning, reflecting a greater appreciation of the influence of teachers on students' development. Researchers observed the behaviour of teachers, counting particular teacher actions, analysing the role of their subject knowledge and other teaching variables. In the same decade, researchers increasingly turned their attention to issues of equity as they sought to understand the reasons for differential performance in mathematics, particularly among boys and girls but also among different cultural, linguistic, and ethnic groups in mathematics. Researchers developed questionnaires and assessments and conducted comparative analyses, largely quantitative, of the responses of male and female students, and students of different ethnicities. Inquiries at this time were varied, as the field of mathematics education diversified, continuing its emphasis on curriculum, teaching, and learning, but also embracing issues of assessment, policy, ethnomathematics, philosophy, teacher learning, and professional development.

During this same period, as the areas of inquiry in mathematics education expanded, so too did methods of inquiry. Whereas researchers had tended in the past to conduct their studies in universities or laboratories in an attempt to control all the variables that they observed, they began to study contexts explicitly. Researchers began to situate their inquiries within schools and other educational settings in order to capture, rather than eradicate, "the mobile, complex, ad hoc, messy and fleeting qualities of lived experience" (S.J. Ball, 1995, p. 255). Questionnaires and assessments remained popular as research tools. Researchers were also, however, increasingly turning to classroom observations and interviews to gain information about the dynamics of teaching and learning. By the start of the 1990s, mathematics education inquiries had diversified considerably. Those focusing upon learning started to move beyond students' individual cognitive development to consider socio-cultural and situated aspects of mathematics learning – what Lerman (2000) describes as the "social turn in mathematics education research" (p. 19). Additionally, researchers began to expand their frameworks and analytical perspectives beyond psychology, drawing from a wider range of disciplines including philosophy, anthropology, and sociology (Boaler, 2000; Sierpinska & Kilpatrick, 1998).

The diversification of the field of mathematics education means that beginning researchers face a broad base of perspectives, theories, and frameworks with which they need to become familiar. In addition, new standards are emerging for the dissemination of educational research that are likely to have significant implications for beginning researchers. In the past, educational researchers have aimed to produce new and important knowledge but have not generally concentrated upon the ways such knowledge may be used in practice. Educational research has recently come under significant criticism for its lack of impact in educational settings. Critics assert that researchers focus on questions that are not crucial to those working in practice and produce recommendations that are not workable. In the United States, these criticisms prompted a committee of leading researchers convened by the National Academy of Education (NAE, 1999) to call for research to focus more on what they called "problem-based research and development." The group further recommended that research be judged not only on its intrinsic quality but also on the extent to which it affects practice. In an important report addressing what some perceive as a crisis in the field, the NAE urged those funding research to prioritise studies designed to impact practice – studies that included specific attention to 'travel': the degree to which research is designed to be transportable and useful to practice.

Several specific recommendations frame the National Academy report (NAE, 1999). One is that professional researchers and professional educators collaborate more with practitioners in the framing and conduct of studies, sharing accountability for the goals of the project. A second is that researchers develop materials that explicitly focus upon transporting the aims, concepts, and methods of research to new settings. Third, the report urges researchers to write directly about the results of their efforts to affect practice. These different recommendations for ways of working seem promising, but whether or not these specific ideas are adopted, researchers from across the world will in future need to pay close attention to the question of impact. That high-quality research in mathematics education will be increasingly both rooted in and connected to practice holds important implications for new researchers. This connection to practice will influence the focus of work, the questions and issues being studied, the methods chosen for studying questions, the people involved and, in important ways, the ways in which the products of research are conceived, shared, and used.

This short tour through some of the questions and issues that have occupied researchers of mathematics education over recent decades, and that present pressing issues for new researchers, reveals that our field has considerable breadth. Those preparing to do research in mathematics education in the future need at minimum to understand and respect the nature of different research traditions and paradigms, being sufficiently open to appreciate the value of different perspectives and frameworks. But this breadth of perspective does not only mean that new researchers have a lot to learn, it also means they have an exciting endeavour before them that is full of possibilities. Shulman (1997) notes that researchers may now "investigate an impressive variety of questions from a rich set of alternative social and political perspectives" (p. 18), but their ability to do so will depend, in part, upon being knowledgeable about the philosophical and epistemological foundations of different paradigms and the nature of evidence they provide. The task of research is complex, and as researchers work to "bring out the amazing complexity of what lies in, behind and beyond" (Strauss, 1987, p. 10) data, they will need to deploy considerable knowledge in specific situations, act on the basis of considered professional sensibilities, and exercise both imagination and discipline. We argue that making the development of practices of disciplined inquiry a more specific focus of research preparation could help to prepare beginning scholars with useful resources for the complex work of mathematics education research.

WHAT IS THERE FOR NEW RESEARCHERS TO LEARN? PRACTICES OF MATHEMATICS EDUCATION RESEARCH

Deliberations about the preparation of mathematics education researchers tend to start with questions of knowledge. What and how much mathematics should future researchers know (Dossey & Lappan, 2000)? How may students be introduced to different research methods (Schoenfeld, 1999)? Which theoretical perspectives should they know? In what depth should they know them (Metz, 2001; Page, 2001; Pallas, 2001)? We contend that although such questions are important, future researchers of mathematics education may not be best served by an exclusive focus on conventional knowledge categories. Research, after all, is not *knowledge*. Research, whether empirical, theoretical or philosophical, is an *active process of investigation*, one that relies on strategic use of knowledge, in context. Because it is something people *do*, not just *know*, we turn next to examine a small but illustrative set of core practices of research: reading, formulating a research question, using data carefully to make and ground claims, moving from the particular to the general, considering mathematics, and communicating research findings. Although they are central to disciplined inquiry, these practices are frequently obscured by the products of research. We seek here to make plainer what we mean when we argue that the preparation of new mathematics education researchers may be better informed if more explicit attention is given to the work in which they will engage.

Reading

Reading is a central resource for scholarly work. Scholars read closely in their own fields, keeping up with new developments and deepening their awareness of the historical trajectory and foundations on which contemporary work is based. Mathematics education researchers also read in other fields: sociology, philosophy, psychology, gender studies, anthropology, and mathematics itself, for example. Moreover, because research demands imagination and insight, reading in a wide expanse of public literature is also part of scholarly work. Reading as various as poetry, literary commentary, news analyses, culture and the arts, biography and fiction, all animate and inspire scholars' minds and imagery, contributing to the quality of their thinking.

Reading places many demands on new scholars. First, the sheer volume and complexity of the reading in which they must now engage, although it may be fascinating, is also inundating. Getting through hundreds of pages a week and still making sense, making connections, and keeping track is no small task. Many scholars are transcending disciplinary, cultural, and linguistic boundaries as they engage in this central, but often untutored, practice of research. Equipped with dictionaries and highlighters, they tackle stacks of pages. But rarely is there explicit work on ways to read for different purposes, ways to make records of what one is reading, reasons to read, and ways to pursue questions using reading. For philosophers, reading is their empirical work; even empirical researchers need to come to understand the different roles played by reading.

For example, confronted with a question about the nature of discussion in a mathematics classroom, a researcher might read about mathematical reasoning, or she might survey the work on discourse analysis. Another researcher, his imagination piqued by an essay he reads in a literary magazine, might turn to work on philosophy of language or on how practices of deliberation are structured in law. Reading is both a stimulus of the creative insight and a site for pursuing it.

Reading responsibly means reading to locate one's own work in the ongoing conversation in an area. Novices often fall into one of two chasms in relation to the literature in their field. On the one hand, they may too frequently develop the view that they are the first to discover an idea or consider a relationship, pompously declaring it as 'new', as something about which nothing has been asked and nothing is known. On the other hand, though, new scholars are often tied to the research literature, leaden-footed, unable to speak with their own voice, or think beyond the boxes and categories in which the ideas have been set. What they read functions less as a tool for situating and developing their work than as the subject of their work, and they cite and cite, never bringing their ideas into the mélange. What is involved in reading maturely, giving proper respect to past work, and simultaneously pushing forward and out, contributing to the development of new findings, new ideas, new theory?

A host of auxiliary practices are important to the practice of reading. For example, what can a dictionary offer, and does it matter what sort of dictionary one uses? When, and for what sort of question, might one use a dictionary? For example, many new researchers may not know to investigate the etymology of particular words with which one becomes preoccupied: For which words and which sorts of ideas does this make sense to do? And what does one actually do? Another practice concerns the use of reference lists and footnotes. Seeing the literature as offering gateways to exploration – maps for further journeys – means studying not just what another author has written but also what she has read. Learning a variety of ways to make records of one's reading, for different purposes; storing articles and books for later access; studying a text for what there is to learn about composition, argument, and rhetoric – each of these very different skills plays an important role in the practice we call reading for scholarly work.

Not to be overlooked are ways to read. Graduate students who enter mathematics education from a background in mathematics are likely to read slowly, scrutinizing every word, and contemplating carefully every line. Accustomed to a mathematical precision unequalled in other fields, they may have difficulty interpreting complex texts constructed with a different aesthetic. They may not know how to skim or read for the gist of an argument or a set of results, for 'skimming' is not a practice of reading in mathematics. Similarly, many novice researchers may not know what it means to study text closely. They may read merely for what they think an author is saying and have little experience with interpretation, with examining closely what an author is doing (Schwab, 1958).

Simple and everyday as it may seem, reading is a core practice of disciplined inquiry (Brown & Dowling, 1998). Taking for granted that its skilful development will happen automatically is likely unwise. Preparing new researchers for the work of reading and for learning to use reading as central to their work would mean transcending the often-tacit knowledge of reading possessed by mature scholars to make visible the many elements of the practice.

Forming a Research Question

No practice may be as fundamental to disciplined inquiry than that of framing a productive question or problem for research (Metz, 2001; Schoenfeld, 1999). Without a well-framed question, no amount of method or analysis can lead to quality work. According to Schoenfeld (1999), "The difficulty is to find a problem that is hard enough so that its solution merits publication but not so hard that it cannot be solved. Learning to do this should be part of all doctoral training" (p. 184). Posing a good research question is a practice that may seem mysterious or even misleadingly easy to novice researchers and yet that plays a pivotal role in conducting good research. A number of constituents of this practice become more visible when we consider some different questions that have been asked in a range of studies in mathematics education. Framing a researchable question is the analogue to formulating an interesting and productive problem in mathematics, and just as important to the quality of the resulting inquiry.

Consider an example: the Third International Mathematics and Science Study (TIMSS) video study (Stigler & Hiebert, 1997). In this project, researchers asked a deceptively simple question: "How is mathematics taught in the United States, Germany, and Japan?" Considering that students in the United States score relatively poorly in international achievement tests, the researchers were curious about what U.S. teachers were doing that was similar to or different from teachers in these other countries. The value of a question depends, however, on the way in which answers to it are pursued. Stigler and Hiebert (1997) acknowledged that one approach to this question would have been to give teachers questionnaires asking them to describe their teaching. But recognizing that educators generally lack shared vocabulary when describing teaching, even within single countries, the researchers acknowledged the limits of that approach. To illustrate, they remark, "One teacher will call something 'problem solving' while her colleague next door calls the same thing a 'routine exercise'" (p. 15). They therefore chose to study and analyse a sample of lessons in each country that they captured on videotape. Through a careful process of analysis that is described elsewhere (Stigler & Hicbert, 1997, 1999), the researchers produced a range of important insights about mathematics teaching in the three countries. The success of the TIMSS video study rests upon a range of factors including an unprecedented set of records of practice and innovative analyses of those data. Significant, however, is to note that the ideas grew from a study framed by a single, well-formed core question.

Consider a second study in which K.C. Cheung (1988) asked another simple but important question: How are attitudes towards mathematics related to mathematics achievement? To answer this question, Cheung explored the Second IEA (International Association for the Evaluation of Educational Achievement) Mathematics Study data for students in Hong Kong. This study showed that three specific attitudes did correlate significantly with mathematics achievement: students' perception of their ability to do mathematics, their perception of the importance of mathematics to society, and their perception of the creativity within mathematics. Cheung uses this finding to make recommendations regarding the ways in which teachers may pay attention to the development of positive attitudes amongst students through their teaching.

Another interesting, and very different, question is one posed by Paula Ensor (2001). She surveyed the existing research on mathematics teacher education and found that it left many unanswered questions concerning the impact of teacher education upon teaching. She therefore chose to conduct a two-year longitudinal study in which she tracked seven student teachers in South Africa through a year long methods course and their first year of teaching. Ensor asked: How do students' experiences in teacher education classes affect their subsequent beliefs and actions in teaching secondary mathematics? In the first year of her study, she collected 100 hours of course observations, interviewed student teachers and teacher educators, and collected all assessed work including a teaching practice journal, a reflective journal, a class test, a curriculum project and the scripts of an examination. In the second year, Ensor interviewed the teachers who were teaching in secondary schools, videotaped some of their lessons, and interviewed their heads of department. This collection of data enabled Ensor to consider the questions she posed and to draw some important conclusions. She found that the beginning teachers "drew in two ways from the method course: they reproduced a small number of discrete tasks that had been introduced to them there, and they also deployed a professional argot – a way of talking about teaching and learning mathematics" (p. 296). Ensor also found that student teachers 'recontextualized' what they learned from the course and that the effects of teacher education were not 'washed out' (Zeichner & Tabachnik, 1981), but transformed. Ensor produced some important insights that were clearly related to the framing of her questions and to the appropriateness of the methods chosen to answer them.

What characteristics do these very different questions share that may be helpful in our exploration of the practice of asking a question? One obvious characteristic is that, at their core, they get at a fundamental issue. These researchers framed and asked questions that were central to the puzzles and problems of the field in which they were working. A second characteristic of these questions is the 'fit' between question and method. Although most of the questions could be answered in multiple ways, the methods chosen by these researchers capitalized on the questions they wished to answer. Thus when the TIMSS researchers asked the question of how mathematics is taught in three countries, they were able to answer this question by collecting actual records of teaching in the three countries. Cheung asked about the relationship between attitude and achievement and drew upon a large database including these variables that could be manipulated statistically.

Still another characteristic of these different research problems is the careful attention researchers paid to the size and scope of the questions asked. This is a crucial aspect of research questions that is linked closely to resources. A single student could not, for example, have conducted a cross-national video study. Even with the resources available, the TIMSS researchers needed to make sure that the study was manageable – making decisions to focus only on one grade level, for example, and on lessons addressing particular subject areas. At the same time, the different studies were sufficiently broad to enable the researchers to explore the data and ask different questions of them. Some new researchers pose important questions that are insufficiently focused to be the topic of a research study. Others ask questions that are too small: They can be answered, but they give insufficient space for the researcher to wade around in data, to explore, and to develop important ideas. The size and scope of a study do not have to be completely determined at the outset, as many decisions and adjustments can be made along the way, but they are an important component of any research question.

Yet another aspect shared by these different studies is the importance of the questions asked and their contribution to theory or practice. Some researchers find questions that are of an appropriate grain size and design appropriate methods to answer them, but the new knowledge they produce is not helpful to practitioners and does not contribute to the development of theory. The importance of the question to be asked is a critical dimension to consider, and consideration of its importance is aided both by experience and by careful reading.

The questions in these different studies were also grounded in theory. Ensor (2001) chose to adopt a sociological framework because of gaps she saw in the current knowledge base, and her report gives clear evidence of the ways that the theories she employed were built into the questions she asked, guiding her attention, for example, to the recontexualization (Bernstein, 1996) of pedagogical practices. Research studies are enhanced when questions lie within a coherent theoretical framework. Theory opens new ideas for researchers, helping them to see differently, to go beyond the limits of their experience, and to make sense of findings produced. At the same time, theory adds coherence, helping to bring together the different data and ideas that researchers collect and that may otherwise appear unconnected. Theoretical frameworks help researchers to achieve both the breadth needed for important insights and the focus required by disciplined inquiry. Frameworks may shift as research settings and questions become more familiar (see, e.g., Cobb, 2000). But it is important that questions are theoretically grounded and that the questions draw from a broader, well-chosen framework.

Still another important aspect of these questions is that they connected to an existing knowledge base in meaningful ways (Metz, 2001, p. 13). All of the above researchers identified important gaps in the knowledge base available and used those gaps as targets to pursue. An important part of forming a problem involves considering the place of a new study: Will it add to and build upon prior knowledge? Does it answer the questions that have been raised and not previously been answered? Or questions that have not even been considered? How may prior knowledge be built into the study, so that it provides a productive grounding and springboard for new thoughts? A researcher forming a question needs some knowledge of the research that has been conducted – its character, depth, and breadth – before deciding upon a study.

Forming a coherent question "on which legitimate progress can be made in a reasonable amount of time" (Schoenfeld, 1999, p. 170) is a practice critical for new researchers, but there are few descriptions in the literature of what that actually means, what is involved in doing it well or not well, and what people who do it well actually do. It is important then that beginning researchers receive ample opportunity to reflect upon good questions that have been asked and the ways that productive questions help to frame the problem and methods of gathering evidence. The quality of research depends equally on practices of interpreting and making sense of that evidence. It is to this domain of practice that we now turn.

Being Rigorous with Data

Although questions, theories, and frameworks are crucial, the quality of a study depends just as fundamentally on the rigor and care with which researchers treat their data. Although this domain of practice usually does receive more attention in research training, it is at times reduced to a set of technical decisions regarding methods. Shulman states, "One of the enduring problems in research methodology has been the tendency to treat selection of method as primarily a technical question not associated with the underlying theoretical or substantive rationale of the research to be conducted" (1997, p. 17). Technical decisions are important, and researchers need considerable knowledge of different methods of analysis to support those decisions. But the rigorous and careful analysis of data requires more than just methods. Researchers make many decisions regarding the analysis of data – for example, which of the data that they have gathered should be analysed in depth and which are less crucial to the development of understanding? Which representations of the information might afford analytical insights?

How does one corroborate the reliability of information? What does any particular piece of information mean, and what assumptions are needed to interpret it in that way? These are some of the questions that researchers face and that are dealt with in different and generally unspoken ways.

Debates between qualitative and quantitative researchers and the concomitant dichotomy established by such debates are now a feature of the past, as most contemporary researchers appreciate that the different methodologies give access to different forms of information, all of which are useful and important. Further, they appreciate that it is more productive to consider and clarify the distinctions and similarities between qualitative and quantitative approaches than to argue over their relative worth (Ely, Vinz, Anzul, & Downing, 1997). But the questions of rigor, of what it means to make claims, to produce evidence, and to make warrants for knowledge (Pallas, 2001; Schoenfeld, 1999) persist. In this section, we consider the exploration of data and the production of research claims, including the ways researchers may reflect on the nature of evidence, on which claims are acceptable, and on what particular pieces of information might mean. These two practices – of exploring data and considering the nature of the claims produced – should coexist within studies and be attended to in equal measures by researchers employing qualitative or quantitative methods, but that is often not the case. Indeed, there is a tendency for quantitative researchers to be rigorous in their exploration of data while neglecting exploration of what the data mean. Qualitative researchers, on the other hand, are often reflective about what data mean but do not always employ rigorous methods of data analysis.

Kenneth Ruthven's (1990) exploration of the impact of graphic calculators offers an example of a study in which the researcher explores data and their meaning carefully. Ruthven employed a classic design in this study. He found four schools that each offered two advanced-level mathematics classes, one of which used a graphic calculator, and the other did not. He then gave students a questionnaire – collecting background information – and a 40-minute test of mathematics. Ruthven found that the students using graphic calculators scored significantly higher grades on the test. One approach to this result could be to communicate test scores and link them with characteristics from the questionnaire, but Ruthven engaged in two important practices that went further. First, he spent time addressing the question of what information was collected, giving careful consideration to the questions asked in the test and the reasons for them. Second, he reflected on the limitations of the data, saying, for example, that the students' responses to the tests "cannot be interpreted as accurate records of the reasoning processes of individual students" (p. 439). This exploration of the *meaning of the data* is an important process that is often neglected in reports.

A second example of careful data analysis is evident in a study conducted by James Hiebert and Diane Wearne (1993). In this study, the researchers considered students' learning in six second-grade classrooms that used different instructional approaches. To consider the impact of different teaching approaches, they collected achievement data and analysed them according to the classroom tasks and discourse patterns observed in the different classes. In their analysis of tasks, the researchers considered the problems used in the classes, collecting data on the number of problems posed, the kinds of problems – their contextual and mathematical features – the time spent on each problem, and the physical materials that were available to support problem solving. Classroom discourse was analysed in two ways: The researchers considered who talked and how much they talked, and they considered the kinds of questions teachers asked. For the analysis, they recorded and then coded all of the teachers' questions during class discussion and teacher presentation. After questions were identified, two coders classified them into nine question types that differed in the amount of self-explanation and kinds of cognitive activity they elicited. The researchers then investigated whether the different classroom tasks and questions were associated with differences in learning. The resulting analysis is rich, detailed, and informative. Because of the careful collection and analysis of different forms of data, the researchers were able to provide quantitative comparisons of relationships between tasks, questions, and learning, as well as qualitative descriptions, with examples of particular discourse from the classrooms used to illuminate the general categories found. Capturing the relationship between teaching and learning is extremely difficult work that can be superficial and misleading if it is not performed carefully. Many studies compare classes taught using different curriculum with no evidence of the teaching and learning interactions in classrooms, but Hiebert and Wearne provide insights into these relationships through a careful collection and analysis of data.

A noteworthy aspect of Hiebert and Wearne's (1993) data analysis is the rigor with which it is conducted and explained. One of the most important developments in mathematics education research of recent decades is a move towards in-depth case study research. Strauss (1987) has argued that researchers who employ quantitative methods have an array of standard analytic methods from which to choose, but researchers employing qualitative or mixed methods do not. He also asserts that qualitative researchers have paid considerable attention to the data collection stage but very little to the process of data analysis, with analyses being conducted implicitly by experienced researchers but rarely given explicit attention or taught to new researchers. Learning careful practices of qualitative analysis requires explicit attention to what are often subtle and refined methods of working with narrative data. Some beginning researchers come to regard qualitative methods as an easier option, conducting interviews or observations from which they simply quote in order to support their arguments. This lack of rigor comes about partly when researchers are not taught disciplined procedures for the analysis of qualitative data. One of the greatest contributions of the grounded theory approach has been the development of analytic methods that may constitute the 'microscopic examination' (Strauss, 1987) of qualitative data, including coding – a central analytic method for the analysis of qualitative data that is set out in a number of research manuals (Miles & Huberman, 1994). Data may be examined in many different ways, some of which are superficial. Some researchers read through observation notes or interviews without coding them, merely developing ideas from the notes that they support using extracts from data. But such methods are insufficiently rigorous to reveal the patterns and relationships that lie within data. Hiebert and Wearne's careful study of classroom problems and teacher questioning, including categorical classification and multiple coding, provides an example of the insights that may be achieved when data are explored fully.

An important stage of data analysis, whether researchers employ qualitative or quantitative methods, is that of verification, whereby researchers subject their emerging ideas to careful scrutiny. Different methods exist for verifying, such as searching for counterexamples, conducting respondent validation, and triangulating data. After discovering and naming a phenomenon, researchers are naturally eager to verify its existence, but such fervour may run counter to intellectual integrity and the pursuit of knowledge. It is essential, therefore, to consider the knowledge that researchers may gain of the different methods of verification as well as the beliefs that may encourage the pursuit of such knowledge. At every stage of research, but particularly at the stage of verification, researchers should be encouraged to ask searching questions of their data: Where are these ideas coming from? What evidence do I have for them? What counter-evidence? What would it take to make me think in the *opposite* way from that which I do now? (Lester & Wiliam, 2002). What would be an alternative interpretation? The asking and answering of such questions is an important – but generally hidden – aspect of the research process.

We have considered in this section some ways in which researchers may employ rigor in their work and the different methods and practices that may encourage that. In Schoenfeld's (1999) consideration of the preparation of researchers, he highlights as central the need for "researchers to develop a deep understanding of what it means to make and justify claims," continually asking such questions as "what is the scope of that claim? What kinds of evidence can be taken as a legitimate warrant for that claim?" (p. 180). We contend that this kind of careful inquiry may be supported through more explicit consideration of the work of data analysis. Developing a more careful and nuanced understanding of the ways data may be explored to extract their complexity and of the assumptions behind such work will encourage rigor as well as enable new researchers to move their reports beyond description to *analysis*, an important stage of research to which we now turn.

Moving from the Particular to the General

Perhaps one of the most elusive practices of research is the making of concepts and ideas. Empirical research involves close examination of particulars. How does the analysis of these particulars relate to the questions that researchers seek to investigate? Making sense of the specific details in data, looking for patterns and meaning, and formulating general insights are both important and difficult. Novice researchers often collect a range of data and conduct standard methods of analysis but produce insights that do not extend beyond their particular examples. They offer cases, or tables, and summarize their data.

Description predominates, with little analysis beyond the instances at hand. Leading researchers appear sometimes effortlessly to produce key insights that are generative for other researchers. Such insights rarely come from a standard application of research methods, and they often leave new researchers baffled as to their origin. Where are such insights found? How are they generated? At what stages should they emerge?

Fred Erickson (1977) considers the work of qualitative researchers and concludes that probably 'the most important thing' they do is locate 'key incidents' in their data. Such incidents are elucidated and described so that readers know why the incident is important, how it relates to the broader setting and to other theories, and what about it is general. Although Erickson writes of qualitative research, the process he describes seems important to researchers of all methodologies:

> I think what qualitative research does best and most essentially is to describe key incidents in functionally relevant terms and place them in relations to the wider social context. ... In the research report the generic features of these incidents are highlighted with as much concrete detail as is necessary to make a statement of the relation of the instance to the pattern of the whole. The qualitative researcher's ability to pull out from field notes a key incident, link it to other incidents, phenomena and theoretical constructs, and write it up so that others can see the generic in the particular, the universals in the concrete, the relation between the part and whole may be the most important thing he does. It involves massive leaps of inference over many different kinds of data from different sources – field notes, documents, elicited texts, demographic information, unstructured interviews, and very possibly survey data. This is a decision process analogous to that of the historian or biographer deciding which incidents among many in a person's life to describe. (p. 61)

Erickson describes the way that 'key incidents' may be used to illustrate salient relations in a setting, to elucidate the 'generic in the particular' and even to tie together a whole account. But beginning researchers, often faced with an array of data, frequently find it difficult to appreciate the more critical issues and ideas within data or the ways that these ideas relate to other cases and situations. The more data they collect, the harder the task of making general connections may become. To make this idea more concrete, we turn now to a classic research study in mathematics education conducted by Guy Brousseau.

Brousseau (1984) performed 'clinical observations' of teachers and students to describe a phenomenon that has been generative for many other researchers (Artigue, 1999; Balacheff, 1990; Cobb, Wood, Yackel, & McNeal, 1992; Laborde, 1989). In a short chapter, tucked away in an obscure publication, Brousseau first offered his analysis of the 'didactical contract', (or *contrat didactique*, translated from his native French). As part of his analysis, Brousseau describes a scenario typical in mathematics classrooms: A teacher gives a student a mathematics problem that the student cannot immediately solve. The student asks for help, and the teacher takes the student through a series of questions. The teacher, in making the questions attainable for the student, empties the task of much of its cognitive demand, thereby reducing the opportunities for learning. The 'contract' that Brousseau describes conveys particular roles for teachers and students that reflect deeply held cultural assumptions about the work of teachers and students in classrooms. As part of this didactical contract, the teacher is expected to ask questions that students can answer and that will enable the student to develop new knowledge. The student is expected to answer the questions and learn. But Brousseau points out that this contract may be paradoxical, as the student who accepts it often fails to learn. Brousseau explains:

> The pupil ... is also confronted with a paradoxical injunction; if he accepts that the teacher, according to the contract, teaches him the results, he will not attain them himself and thus will not learn mathematics, i.e., he will not make mathematics his own. *If the pupil accepts the contract, he will refuse it – no learning takes place.* To learn, for him, implies [rejecting] the contract, and to accept being himself engaged in the problem. In fact learning will not be based on the correct functioning of the contract, but rather on breaching it.

(Brousseau, 1984, p. 113, italics in original)

In subsequent years, the idea of the didactical contract, in which teachers and students tacitly collaborate to empty learning situations of their cognitive demand, has been used by numerous researchers to describe and understand interactions in mathematics and other subject classrooms. In the development of the idea of a didactical contract, Brousseau reflected upon one or more incidents he observed and regarded as critical and portrayed them in general terms. Krieger (1991) describes the social science tradition as being one of speaking "specifically in order to speak generally" (p. 4) and "understanding unique and particular phenomena in terms of more general processes" (p. 149). This move from the particular to the general, which is captured by Brousseau's work, is achieved through the identification and naming of a common phenomenon. In his clinical observations, Brousseau presumably witnessed many different interactions between students and teachers, but rather than describe each of them, he generalizes their features into a new and potent concept that can be used to view and understand the interactions of teachers and students in other classrooms. Developing and naming such a concept constitute a process that separates analysis from description. Often researchers describe a case without analysing what it is a case of, what makes it special or interesting, or how it relates to other situations and instances. But it is the extra thought that goes into such analysis that enables the generation of analytical and theoretical insights. Accounts that are purely descriptive cannot by themselves provoke the theoretical understanding of social phenomenon offered by accounts with conceptual density in which researchers look not only for instances in data but also for dimensions and categories that may be explained. Brousseau's didactical contract did not fall out of a standard research method, nor did it emerge from large amounts of data. Instead, it was the product of the practice of "understanding unique and particular phenomena in terms of more general processes" (Krieger, 1991, p. 149).

The practice of identifying and naming general explanatory ideas in research requires a range of capabilities. Naming a phenomenon involves considering what it is, what it is a general case of, and how it relates to other ideas in the literature. The process involves an understanding of the specifics of the context together with the ability to abstract from that context. Developing general ideas from specifics depends also on familiarity with other scholarship – within and outside the field of mathematics education – and of the theories that have been produced in the past that may inform the developing analyses being constructed. Skill with a variety of analytic methods and techniques, such as particular statistical procedures, coding, statistical analysis, textual analysis, and triangulation, can help as researchers can work in multiple ways with different kinds of information. Ideas and insights are also helped, although not produced, by methods of analysis. Statistical procedures, coding, and textual analysis are examples of methods that help researchers notice patterns in data that are invisible to mere inspection. Identifying a central idea requires a substantive perspective – appreciating that not all data are equally important. Indeed, experienced researchers expect and look for unevenness and discrepancies in data. Developing general ideas and concepts also requires particular dispositions and habits of mind. These include the desire to think deeply, to go beyond the surface features of an event to the connections that lie beneath, to wonder, to seek ideas and patterns that might offer a new lens or way of understanding the complexities of the particulars, their dynamics, and their variability. Another disposition is the act of creativity: the generation of ideas and names that open new ways of thinking. The knowledge and dispositions that lie within the practice we have described – of moving from the particular to the general – become more visible as one examines examples of this particular practice. Such close examination is one way that beginning researchers may learn about the practices of research.

Considering the Mathematics

Being a disciplined researcher in mathematics education means knowing when and how to take account of *mathematics* in investigating particular questions. In other words, how does the fact that the learning, the teaching, or the policy being examined is about *mathematics* figure in the ways in which data are collected or analysed? How does it affect the research question itself or the interpretation of the data? Consider the fact that studies of classroom interactions and dynamics can – and often do – proceed independently of the specific content being discussed. How turns are taken, how ideas are validated as correct, whose ideas are used and in what ways, and the role of the teacher – these are all elements of classroom life that researchers seek to understand. But when does it matter that the subject under discussion is mathematics and not literature? And, even more specifically, when does it matter that it is algebra and not probability? Researchers in mathematics education must be sensitive to when the 'subject matters' (Stodolsky, 1988) and when more general issues are more centrally at play. When the mathematics matters, disciplined research requires researchers to know and use mathematics in ways specific to the tasks of systematic inquiry. Knowing mathematics for doing research involves knowledge of specific ideas and practices: the importance of the unit in fractions or what constitutes a mathematical argument, for instance. It also involves sensibilities about what is important mathematically: the role of a particular term, for example, or the need to examine whether and how two representations are equivalent. This sort of mathematical appreciation and understanding is important to being able to make judgments about where to focus on a specific content issue and where to stand back and consider other important elements less focused on the content.

What are some of the specific practices in which mathematics education researchers engage when focusing on mathematics or seeking to uncover the place of the subject matter in their investigations? One such practice is the strategic seeking and use of comparisons and contrasts across disciplines. Stodolsky, in her 1988 book *The Subject Matters*, investigated patterns of instruction in upper elementary classrooms and uncovered sharp differences in those patterns as a function of the subject matter. She continued this work in later collaborations with Pamela Grossman in which the researchers compared teachers' professional interactions and practice in different high school subject matter departments. That life in mathematics departments was different from the professional environment and practice in other subjects was only revealed because of the researchers' explicit and strategic attention to comparisons and contrasts.

In the work on pedagogical content knowledge that began in the mid-1980s at Stanford University, Shulman and his colleagues systematically promoted cross-subject comparisons as a tool for clarifying the issues involved in this new research domain. Some researchers studied the knowledge involved in teaching history and other social studies (e.g., Wilson & Wineburg, 1988), while others investigated the teaching of English (e.g., Grossman, 1990) or science (Carlsen, in press; Hashweh, 1985/1986, 1987). Work on the mathematics knowledge needed for teaching (e.g., Ball, 1988, 1990, 1991; Leinhardt & Smith, 1985; Marks, 1990; Steinberg, Haymore, & Marks, 1985) profited from direct interaction with these related studies in neighbouring subject matters. That one of the dimensions of subject matter knowledge for teaching might be knowledge of the epistemology of the field – how ideas are validated, for instance – was stimulated and advanced by work done on this dimension in history, English, biology, and physics. Across the content areas, many of the researchers drew on ideas developed by Schwab (1958, 1961/1978), and that common theoretical foundation supported productive comparative analyses. When those researchers studying English and history argued that knowledge about different theoretical orientations to the field (Schwab's, 1961/1978, *substantive structures of a discipline*) was a component of a teacher's pedagogical content knowledge, those studying mathematical knowledge came up short, for no clear correspondence existed in mathematics. This finding, too, was helpful in advancing the particular work on mathematical knowledge for teaching, pressing scholars to notice new things specific to mathematics – for example, that the epistemological demands for teaching varied across mathematical domains – from number theory to discrete mathematics, for example. This brief sketch of one domain of mathematics education research – work on teachers' mathematics subject matter knowledge – illustrates the productive use of cross-subject comparisons as a means to develop with precision certain ideas within mathematics education.

A second way in which attention to the specifics of how the subject matters can be realized in mathematics education research is by using mathematical lenses to analyse data on learning, teaching, policy, and implementation. Researchers therefore must know mathematics in ways that enable such uses in their research. Consider, for example, work on equity in mathematics education. A large body of work exists on the differentiated opportunities to learn and outcomes often produced in school. Researchers who study the dynamics of these outcomes sometimes draw exclusively on sociological, economic, anthropological, psychological, and political perspectives in developing their theoretical frames and methods of analysis. But how students and teachers interact in school and the ways in which opportunities to learn are constructed is fundamentally a matter of *what* they are interacting about and the different histories and experiences that they bring to their joint work. That the subject under discussion is mathematics has an impact on students' presentation of self, their teachers' 'reading' of them, and the unfolding of students' consequent opportunities to learn. Probing this phenomenon requires the researcher to know mathematics in ways that enable analyses of curriculum and classroom dynamics that would otherwise fall to the background (e.g., Boaler, 2002a, 2002b; Lubienski, 2000). For example, in investigations of the demands of mathematical discourse in classroom, the precision of the research benefits from an understanding of the role of error analysis in mathematics, of how claims are proved and disproved, and of how tentative ideas are put forth, used, and improved. What does engagement in mathematical argument require of students and their teachers, and how might that differ for different students? Without this understanding, scholars are likely to misinterpret or misdirect their analysis of the course of a particular student interaction in class. Similarly, in applying mathematics to and using it in specific contexts, students may encounter differentially the interface between their knowledge and experience from outside school and what is called for in school. A deep understanding of the role of abstraction and generalization, as well as of localization and application, can help ground studies of students' engagement in school better in the specific entailments of mathematical work. This sort of analysis and perspective implies that researchers need a flexible and unpacked understanding of mathematics, one that can be readily fashioned for use in looking at students' work, listening to their talk, and observing their teachers' moves.

Consider, for example, the development of research tools for probing teachers' or students' learning, or for analysing policy documents or curriculum materials. To design and refine instruments such as student interview protocols, teacher surveys, or document analysis tools, researchers would need a refined understanding of the content, one that permits them to isolate key junctures and elements strategic for observation, measurement, probing, and attention. Information collected in the pursuit of a research question is only as good as the insights that undergird the data-collection design. To develop good insights, researchers need to understand and be able to use the subject in ways not so different from the demands of mathematical knowledge for teaching (Ball & Bass, 2000). This observation suggests an agenda for the development of researchers' skills and capacities that has typically been addressed through the mathematics requirements for the doctoral degree, but these are rarely determined on the basis of an analysis of the mathematical knowledge entailments of research.[1]

Communication of Research

"Research begins in wonder and curiosity but ends in teaching. The process of research is incomplete until the researcher can communicate his or her understandings clearly, persuasively, and effectively" (Shulman, 1997, p. 6). The teaching to which Shulman refers – communicating about research – is the process through which research may become useful, informing the practice and theory of mathematics education. Communication transforms the researchers' amalgam of descriptions, data, and analyses into knowledge, for acts such as writing or drawing diagrams do not just represent ideas that have previously been formed. Communication is a generative act that itself *produces* ideas. Indeed, it could be argued that there is no more critical aspect of the research process. Data, whether they are sets of numbers or reflections from interviews, are the raw constituents of research, but it is the act of representation that transforms data into ideas, and it is in this act of communication that ideas are formed. Communicating ideas, whether through written text or video records, is an act of knowledge generation – of higher order thinking. It is central to the work of disciplined inquiry, and yet many novice researchers have a limited sense of and interest in the act of communication. Although their training may offer some direct guidance about communication, the breadth of what is involved in the act is rarely the subject of explicit analysis and opportunity to learn.

Myriad purposes exist for communicating about research – to different audiences and with different goals. For example, researchers might offer evidence about the viability of an intervention to help those watching it take root improve it and also have the patience to let it develop more fully. Researchers might offer evidence on the effects of maturely developed approaches to provide insight about alternative approaches or regimes. Or researchers might offer conceptual tools for reframing a problem or understanding a question better. Each of these offerings represents a different agenda and requires different skills, methods, modes of presentation, and framing. Being clear about purposes and methods of communication can help make communication more effective, and research therefore also more broadly useful.

Traditionally, mathematics education research has been communicated through written media: in particular, research articles, books, chapters, essays, technical reports, commentaries, and editorials. These are important venues for communication, but as researchers strive more actively to cross the traditional divide between research and practice, they are turning to newer and more varied forms of communication, including the use of cases, classroom video records, and the Internet. Deciding on the nature of the medium through which research knowledge will be communicated is an important aspect of the communication process to which we pay attention in this section. But the practice of communication is varied, with many entailments. Once the medium has been decided on, researchers need to decide which information should be conveyed. They need to consider language that is particularly appropriate for the audience and construct ideas in such a way that they are logically connected, believable, and interesting. Writing is a critical constituent of the communication process, and we turn now to consider this crucial practice and the knowledge, skills, and sensibilities it entails before moving to examine and unpack two other aspects of communication, as well as two particularly interesting examples that exemplify their use.

Writing

Jean-Paul Sartre, at 70, said, "I still think, but because writing has become impossible for me the real activity of thought has in some way been repressed" (cited in Ely, Vinz, Downing, & Anzul, 1997, p. 14). Writing is not merely an act of representing ideas but also of generating them. It is a process of thinking and an act of creation. It can be exhilarating in one minute, frustrating the next. Tom Robbins once described it as "a cross between flying to the moon and taking a shower in a motel", capturing both the magical and the mundane. But for all its mystery and magic, the act of good writing may be taught and learned. It requires a range of knowledge, sensibilities, and skills that may be examined and explicitly encouraged among new researchers. As researchers write, they must consider what their intended audience knows, cares about, believes, and assumes. The writer's job is to capture the essence of her or his work and to convey it with meaning and with accuracy. Writers need to consider how much information they need to portray, providing sufficient details for readers to decide upon its validity. A writer seeks to convey with care the relationship between fact, analysis, truth, and opinion. Shaping the ideas into forms comprehensible to the reader requires the researcher to have a firm grip on the ideas and be able to represent them flexibly. The writer must consider the language that will be accessible to readers as well as the forms of representation that will convey the greatest meaning to particular audiences. Writing entails a fluent use of language at the word, sentence, and text level, as well as the capacity to make a set of ideas accessible using linguistic and rhetorical tools. Shulman (1999) points out that the communication of research cannot mean the retelling of all that was discovered, for "research is about the compressions, transformations and reconstitutions of experience into forms that can be readily stored, displayed, and exchanged" (p. 161). These and other aspects of the writing process may be unpacked and examined so that different opportunities for analysis and learning will be created.

One set of skills is entailed by conventional research writing, when researchers strive to meet the standards of their own disciplinary community and to publish in the journals closest to their own work: mathematics education research journals, for example. Other skills and sensibilities are involved when the purpose is to write for a broad public audience, who share neither the theoretical perspectives nor the language commonly used to express the ideas. The need for communication that crosses into different communities is increasing, for there are new and more demanding calls for researchers to communicate their findings more broadly and to make serious attempts to affect practice. In the next section, we look more closely at broad communicative forms, drawing upon a particular example of two researchers who set out to cross the traditional research-practice divide and were extremely successful in doing so because of the broad forms of communication they employed.

Communicating research in different media

Researchers are often called upon to do more than present research findings to other researchers; they frequently must aim to cross the traditional and enduring divide between educational research and practice, or the one between research and policy. This aim raises new issues about research communication as a domain of skilled practice. Scientific research writing has its own standards and demands, but as researchers write for broader audiences – through newspapers, books, and professional journals – they will need to synthesize and animate their ideas in different ways. They may need to bring more life into their ideas, as they cannot rely upon a shared professional interest in their importance; they may need to convince in different ways, to draw upon different examples, and to arrange the knowledge in more concise forms without losing the integrity or meaning of the research. But this work, whilst unacknowledged in many universities and difficult to achieve, is important, as it frequently serves as the main vehicle by which research ideas are transported into the worlds of educational practitioners.

Two researchers in the United Kingdom – Paul Black and Dylan Wiliam – noted that countries throughout the world were paying significant attention to issues of standards and accountability whilst largely ignoring the most important aspect of learning: the work that takes place in classrooms. They focused upon formative assessment, a process by which teachers use information that they gain from classroom activities as evidence of student learning, which they then use to adapt their teaching. Black and Wiliam asked whether there was evidence that an improvement in formative assessment would raise standards and whether there was evidence about ways to improve formative assessments. Rather than conducting research to answer these questions, they conducted an extensive survey of research literature, including nine years' worth of more than 160 journals. This survey yielded approximately 580 articles to study. The answer to both of the questions was yes, and the evidence that they gained from this review was overwhelming. The evidence suggested that an implementation of formative assessment in classrooms would increase learning to such a degree that a country scoring in the middle of the pack in international comparisons would rise to a place in the top five. Black and Wiliam also found that formative assessment helped low achievers more than high achievers, thus reducing the range of achievement whilst increasing achievement overall. The evidence for these claims was detailed and complex, and the initial communication of the results was in a research article in *Assessment in Education* that, along with six short responses, comprised an entire edition of the journal (Black & Wiliam, 1998a). But the authors believed that the results they had found were important for practitioners to know about and to understand, so they engaged in a number of other forms of communication that extended beyond the traditional writing of journal articles.

One of these forms of communication was an article in the professional journal *Phi Delta Kappan* (Black & Wiliam, 1998b). This journal is published in the United States and read by a large professional audience. The authors needed to communicate their findings convincingly and clearly in a much reduced space and to an audience largely unfamiliar with the jargon of educational research or technical assessment. The authors noted, "Because we are presenting a summary here, our text will appear strong on assertions and weak on the details of their justification. We maintain that these assertions are backed by evidence and that this backing is set out in full detail in the lengthy review on which this article is founded" (p. 140). Black and Wiliam produced a powerful and convincing article, absent of most of the details, illustrating the "compressions, transformations and reconstitutions" that Shulman (1999, p. 161) notes as central to the process of communication.

Black and Wiliam also took a further, highly significant step by arranging for their university to publish a small booklet communicating the main ideas of their study, specifically written for teachers and sold for two British pounds (approximately US$3). The authors also gave a series of presentations on the ideas. In each of these presentations, they combined a summary of research evidence with practical ideas to use in classrooms. News of the importance of the ideas in the booklet and presentation spread throughout the UK, and soon they had sold 20,000 copies, an unprecedented sale of an educational publication (approximately one copy for every school in the country). Black and Wiliam were asked to make hundreds of presentations and in two years addressed over 400 groups of teachers, advisors, and policy makers, making contact with over 20,000 people. Research presentations are a particular form of teaching, and they require substantial design and rehearsal. Whereas there are established norms for written communication, little guidance exists for presentations, sessions, or talks, and learning to do these well is yet another part of the practice of research.

Black and Wiliam also worked closely with government agencies, helping their findings cross the divide between research and policy. They communicated their ideas through the phrase 'assessment for learning', which became a key feature of the Framework for the Inspection of Schools in the UK, an important forum for policy advice given to schools. The varied ways in which Black and Wiliam's results influenced policy and practice would not have been achieved if they had limited their communication to a journal article, and their careful use of forms of media that directly addressed teachers and other educational practitioners, with appropriate writing, use of examples, and summaries of evidence, provides an important illustration of the role of well-crafted communication practices in the transportation of research ideas.

New possibilities for communication

The media of the research enterprise have also been changing. New possibilities exist for representing ideas and engaging people in them, making for better communication and for questions about the ways new technologies may be employed to cross the divide between research and practice. Pea (1999) asserts that new forms of representation, made possible by new communication channels such as the Internet, have the potential to change "fundamentally how education research is conceived, conducted, authored, and critically responded to by its audiences" (p. 336). Such changes are evident in the intense and frequent dialogue about research that is taking place on the World Wide Web and through electronic mail.

One researcher who has grappled with the potential of alternative media for communicating about research is Magdalene Lampert. Lampert, who studies the dynamics of classroom teaching of mathematics and who has contributed exquisitely written articles about the challenges of teaching (Lampert, 1990, 1992), became fascinated with the problem of representing practice. Teaching and learning, which are complex and interactive over time, defy typical forms of representation. Many representations of teaching compress and omit crucial elements of the work for teachers and students: for example, the multiplicity of foci, the ways in which time functions to shape the work, and the kinds of local knowledge and ways of knowing on which teachers' and students' moment-to-moment moves rely. The problem of representation became a direct object of inquiry for Lampert. Drawing on records of her own practice across an entire school year, she explored what might be involved in representing aspects of practice more adequately, paying attention to the numerous considerations teachers take from moment to moment. She strove to represent the complexity of teaching: for example, that teachers work simultaneously with individuals and with groups of students, and that learning occurs over time. She considered varieties of representation and communication that would capture the multiple and layered dimensions of the work. Framing her research problem as that of representing the fundamental unit of practice – the school year – Lampert used multiple media and forms of graphical representation along with text different from classic research writing. Lampert's resulting book (2001) on the problems of teaching illuminates in unprecedented ways what teaching and learning entail, and it also creates a new image of what it might mean to represent – and thus, communicate about – practice. With chapters on different slices of the work – teaching while leading a discussion, teaching students to be people who study in school, teaching with problems, for instance – the book combines diagrams, transcripts, scanned excerpts from the students' notebooks and the teacher's notes, reproductions of the chalkboard across a single class discussion, and a panoply of other images that contribute to representing the threads that weave together dynamically through time and through complex human interactions and relationships to produce the ordinary work we call classroom teaching. What her book achieves is to make vivid the ways in which teaching is far from ordinary work, and it contributes to scholars' and practitioners' grasp of the elements that contribute to the complexity of teaching and that make it possible to do.

But new forms of communication also raise new challenges. Records of practice, for example, may enable new insights into mathematics teaching and learning (Lampert & Ball, 1998, 1999) and can offer material for vivid communication, but researchers must exercise new cautions, for primary records such as videotapes of lessons can be interpreted in multiple ways, and their very potency may also mislead. How, for example, does a researcher responsibly select a representative sample from the data set, and what does it mean to be 'representative'? If the data being shown are not representative, how might researchers provide a useful context for the specific examples being examined? The availability of the potent media of videotapes and other records of practice means that there are new demands on scholars and therefore on beginning researchers.

The practice of making research knowledge accessible, interesting, and useful includes a number of constitutive elements that, like many other aspects of the research process we have considered, are largely invisible to new researchers. We have considered three aspects of the communication process in this section by way of illustration and contend that greater opportunities for learning these practices will serve well the development of mathematics education researchers, as well as the broader education community.

LEARNING IN AND FOR THE PRACTICE OF RESEARCH

Oddly, although research is something researchers *do*, little research preparation seems explicitly designed to develop the complex uses of knowledge, skill, and habits of mind fundamental to the practice of research. In most countries, graduate programs supply the professional training thought to be needed for research (Batanero et al., 1994). The research training that students receive is often made up of two components: (a) an introduction to knowledge of mathematics education and different research methods and approaches; and (b) an introduction to research, at which time in the pursuit of their own research questions, students receive opportunities to use and apply the knowledge to which they have been introduced. Required to conduct a study to earn the degree, beginning researchers seek to demonstrate competence as they complete what is often their first independent research in the form of a dissertation.

Despite the fact that research entails a complex set of practices, most research preparation programs present knowledge of research methods and traditions, separate from the act of conducting research. Thus, beginning researchers in mathematics education generally take courses on research methods as part of a masters or doctoral degree program and then conduct research within a doctoral research study (Batanero et al., 1994). This model of teaching and learning, in which knowledge that is taught is assumed to be available for later application and use, has been questioned in mathematics education and in teacher education, yet it prevails in the corridors of higher education with surprising tenacity.

The absence of opportunities to develop understanding and skill as well as flexibility and reasoning with core practices of research means that new researchers often begin major research studies ill-prepared for the complex demands of the work that they will face. Reading research, doing exercises and assignments in research methods texts, and writing short papers cannot by themselves prepare beginners for the complex practice of disciplined inquiry. A more explicit, purposeful focus on research practices, and the knowledge and habits of mind they require, could provide students with opportunities to learn about research in a deeper and more substantive way in the early stages of their work.

Following this path would entail identifying and unpacking the central domains of the work of disciplined inquiry, a process that we have started by way of illustration in this chapter. But it would also require the design of a curriculum of research preparation replete with opportunities for novice and experienced practitioners to learn to engage in those domains of work. We have not attempted to design such a curriculum as part of this chapter, because to do so would be overly ambitious and necessarily speculative. But such work is being attempted to varying degrees in different institutions across the world.

Our main aim in this chapter has been to raise the possibility that future years may profitably witness ways in which research institutions may offer new researchers experiences, tasks, assignments, and materials that afford opportunities to learn in, from, and for practice. For example, beginning researchers might shadow experienced researchers, observing and querying the current stage of the work, reading rough drafts of papers, and sitting in on group meetings as instruments and analyses are scrutinized and critiqued. Such experiences could function, if designed, as practica in research, and different practices could be in focus at different times. Records of practice could also be created for close scrutiny and opportunities to engage in 'fragments of inquiry' (Schwab, 1978). Possible examples might be drafts of research proposals with critiques, videotapes of conference presentations and discussants' comments, successive diagrams as an idea develops, videotapes of a research team working on an idea or designing a study, researchers' lab notes or analytic memos, and a complete historical record of a particular paper. Beginning researchers might engage in small slices of the work: framing alternative research problems and comparing their merits and problems, writing a précis of an argument, making alternative representations of data, and investigating what each form makes visible.

Many more activities organically connected to the core practices of research could be developed. In future years, a research curriculum could be centred more directly in the critical activities of the work and include opportunities to develop the practices central to that work, including the knowledge and dispositions that undergird skilled design, analysis, interpretation, and communication in disciplined inquiry. Learning any complex practice requires opportunities to unpack its components in order to see what underlies competent performance. In this chapter, we have unpacked some of the practices of mathematics education research in the hope that our writing will inform future dialogue, work, and teaching of the practices of mathematics education research.

NOTE

[1.] We propose a parallel here between current research on the mathematics knowledge required for teaching (Ball & Bass, 2000) and the mathematical preparation of mathematics education researchers.

REFERENCES

Artigue, M. (1999). The teaching and learning of mathematics at the university level: Crucial questions for contemporary research in education. *Notices of the AMS, 46*(11), 1377–1385.

Balacheff, N. (1990). Towards a *problematique* for research on mathematics teaching. *Journal for Research in Mathematics Education, 21*, 258–272.

Ball, D. L. (1988). *Knowledge and reasoning in mathematical pedagogy: Examining what prospective teachers bring to teacher education.* Unpublished doctoral dissertation, Michigan State University, East Lansing.

Ball, D. L. (1990). The mathematical understandings that prospective teachers bring to teacher education. *Elementary School Journal, 90*, 449–466.

Ball, D. L. (1991). Research on teaching mathematics: Making subject matter part of the equation. In J. Brophy (Ed.), *Advances in research on teaching* (Vol. 2, pp. 1–48). Greenwich, CT: JAI Press.

Ball, D. L., & Bass, H. (2000). Interweaving content and pedagogy in teaching and learning to teach: Knowing and using mathematics. In J. Boaler (Ed.), *Multiple perspectives on the teaching and learning of mathematics* (pp. 83–104). Westport, CT: Ablex.

Ball, D. L., & Cohen, D. (1999). Developing practice, developing practitioners. In L. Darling-Hammond & G. Sykes (Eds.), *Teaching as the learning profession: Handbook of policy and practice* (1st ed.). San Francisco, CA: Jossey Bass.

Ball, S. J. (1995). Intellectuals or technicians? The urgent role of theory in educational studies. *British Journal of Educational Studies, 43*(3), 255–271.

Batanero, M. C., Godino, J. D., Steiner, H. G., & Wenzelburger, E. (1994). The training of researchers in mathematics education: Results from an international survey. *Educational Studies in Mathematics, 26*, 95–102.

Bernstein, B. (1966). Sources of consensus and disaffection in education. *Journal of the Association of Assistant Mistresses, 17*(1), 4–11.

Bernstein, B. (1996). *Pedagogy, symbolic control and identity: Theory, research, critique.* London: Taylor & Francis.

Black, P. J., & Wiliam, D. (1998a). Assessment and classroom learning. *Assessment in Education,* *5*(1), 7–74.

Black, P., & Wiliam, D. (1998b, October). Inside the black box: Raising standards through classroom assessment. *Phi Delta Kappan,* 139–148.

Boaler, J. (2000). Intricacies of knowledge, practice, and theory. In J. Boaler (Ed.), *Multiple perspec-* *tives on mathematics teaching and learning* (pp. 1–18). Westport, CT: Ablex.

Boaler, J. (2002a). Learning from teaching: Exploring the relationship between 'reform' curriculum and equity. *Journal for Research in Mathematics Education, 33*(4), 239–258.

Boaler, J. (2002b). *Experiencing school mathematics: Traditional and reform approaches to teaching and* *their impact on student learning.* Mahwah, NJ: Erlbaum.

Brousseau, G. (1984). The crucial role of the didactical contract in the analysis and construction of situations in teaching and learning mathematics. In H. G. Steiner (Ed.), *Theory of mathematics* *education* (pp. 110–119). Bielefeld Germany: Institut für Didaktik der Mathematik der Universität Bielefeld.

Brown, A., & Dowling, P. (1998). *Doing research/reading research: A mode of interrogation for educa-* *tion.* London: Falmer.

Carlsen, W. S. (in press). Domains of teacher knowledge. In J. Gess-Newsome & N. G. Lederman (Eds.), *Examining pedagogical content knowledge: The construct and its implications for science* *education.* Dordrecht: Kluwer.

Cheung, K. C. (1988). Outcomes of schooling: Mathematics achievement and attitudes towards mathematics learning in Hong Kong. *Educational Studies in Mathematics, 19,* 209–219.

Cobb, P., Wood, T., Yackel, E., & McNeal, B. (1992). Characteristics of classroom mathematics traditions: An interactional analysis. *American Educational Research Journal, 29*(3), 573–604.

Cobb, P. (2000). The importance of a situated view of learning to the design of research and instruc-tion. In J. Boaler (Ed.), *Multiple perspectives on mathematics teaching and learning* (pp. 45–82). Westport, CT: Ablex.

Cronbach, L. J., & Suppes, P. (Eds.). (1969). *Research for tomorrow's schools: Disciplined inquiry for* *education.* New York: Macmillan.

Dossey, J., & Lappan, G. (2000). The mathematical education of mathematics educators in doctoral programs in mathematics education. In R. E. Reys & J. Kilpatrick (Eds.), *One field, many paths:* *U.S. doctoral programs in mathematics education* (CBMS Issues in Mathematics Education, Vol. 9, pp. 67–72). Providence, RI: American Mathematical Society.

Doyle, W. (1983). Academic work. *Review of Educational Research, 53*(2), 159–199.

Doyle, W. (1988). Work in mathematics classes: The context of students' thinking during instruction. *Educational Psychologist, 23,* 167–180.

Ely, M., Vinz, R., Anzul, M., & Downing, M. (1997). *On writing qualitative research: Living by words.* London: Falmer.

Ensor, P. (2001). From preservice mathematics teacher education to beginning teaching: A study in recontextualizing. *Journal for Research in Mathematics Education, 32*(3), 296–320.

Erikson, F. (1977). Some approaches to inquiry in school community ethnography. *Anthropology and* *Education, 8*(2), 58–62.

Grossman, P. (1990). *The making of a teacher.* New York: Teachers College Press.

Hashweh, M. Z. (1986). An exploratory study of teacher knowledge and teaching: The effects of science teachers' knowledge of subject matter and their conceptions of learning on their teaching (Doctoral dissertation, Stanford University, 1985). *Dissertation Abstracts International, 46,* 3672A.

Hashweh, M. (1987). Effects of subject matter knowledge in the teaching of biology and physics. *Teaching and Teacher Education, 3*(2), 109–120.

Hiebert, J., & Wearne, D. (1993). Interactional tasks, classroom discourse, and students' learning in second-grade arithmetic. *American Educational Research Journal, 30*(2), 393–425.

Krieger, S. (1991). *Social science and the self: Personal essays on an art form.* New Brunswick, NJ: Rutgers University Press.

Laborde, L. (1989). Audacity and reason: French research in mathematics education. *For the Learning* *of Mathematics, 9*(3), 31–36.

Lampert, M. (1990). When the problem is not the question and the solution is not the answer: Mathematical knowing and teaching. *American Educational Research Journal, 27*, 29–63.

Lampert, M. (1992). Practices and problems in teaching authentic mathematics. In F. Oser, D. Andreas & J. Patry (Eds.), *Effective and responsible teaching: The new synthesis* (pp. 295–314). San Francisco: Jossey Bass.

Lampert, M. (2001). *Teaching problems and the problems of teaching.* Ann Arbor, CT: Yale University Press.

Lampert, M., & Ball, D. (1998). *Teaching, multimedia, and mathematics: Investigations of real practice.* New York: Teachers College Press.

Lampert, M., & Ball, D. (1999). Aligning teacher education with contemporary K-12 reform visions. In L. Darling-Hammond & G. Sykes (Eds.), *Teaching as the learning profession: Handbook of policy and practice* (pp. 33–53). San Francisco: Jossey-Bass.

Leinhardt, G., & Smith, D. (1985). Expertise in mathematics instruction: Subject matter knowledge. *Journal of Educational Psychology, 77*, 247–271.

Lerman, S. (2000). The social turn in mathematics education research. In J. Boaler (Ed.), *Multiple perspectives on mathematics teaching and learning* (pp. 19–44). Westport, CT: Ablex.

Lester, F. K., Jr., & Carpenter, T. (2001). The research preparation of doctoral students in mathematics education. In R. E. Reys & J. Kilpatrick (Eds.), *One field, many paths: U.S. doctoral programs in mathematics education* (CBMS Issues in Mathematics Education, Vol. 9, pp. 63–66). Providence, RI: American Mathematical Society.

Lester, F. K., Jr., & Lambdin, D. V. (in press). From amateur to professional: The emergence and maturation of the U.S. mathematics education research community. In G. M. A. Stanic & J. Kilpatrick (Eds.). *A history of school mathematics.* Reston, VA: National Council of Teachers of Mathematics.

Lester, F. K., Jr., & Wiliam, D. (2002). On the purpose of mathematics education research: Making productive contributions to policy and practice. In L. D. English (Ed.), *Handbook of international research in mathematics education* (pp. 489–506). Mahwah, NJ: Erlbaum.

Lingefjärd, T., & Dahland, G. (Eds.). (1998). *Research in mathematics education: A report from a follow-up conference after PME 1997.* Gothenburg, Sweden: Gothenburg University.

Lubienski, S. (2000). Problem solving as a means towards mathematics for all: An exploratory look through the class lens. *Journal for Research in Mathematics Education, 31*(4), 454–482.

McIntosh, J. A., & Crosswhite, F. J. (1973). *A survey of doctoral programs in mathematics education.* Columbus, OH: ERIC Information Analysis Center for Science, Mathematics and Environmental Education.

Marks, R. (1990). Pedagogical content knowledge: From a mathematical case to a modified conception. *Journal of Teacher Education, 41*(3), 3–11.

Metz, M. (2001). Intellectual border crossing in graduate school. *Educational Researcher, 30*(5), 12–18.

Miles, M., & Huberman, M. (1994). *Qualitative data analysis: An expanded sourcebook.* Thousand Oaks, CA: Sage.

National Academy of Education. (1999). *Recommendations regarding research priorities: An advisory report to the National Educational Research Policy and Priorities Board.* New York: Author.

Page, R. (2001). Reshaping graduate preparation in educational research methods: One school's experience. *Educational Researcher, 30*(5), 19–25.

Pallas, A. (2001). Preparing education doctoral students for epistemological diversity. *Educational Researcher, 30*(5), 6–11.

Pea, R. (1999). New Media Communications Forums for Improving Education Research and Practice. In E. C. Lagemann & L. S. Shulman (Eds.). Issues in Education Research: Problems and Possibilities. Jossey Bass: San Francisco. (pp. 336–370).

Pickering, A. (1995). *The mangle of practice: Time, agency, and science.* Chicago: University of Chicago Press.

Reys, R., & Kilpatrick, J. (Eds.) (2000). *One field, many paths: U.S. doctoral programs in mathematics education* (CBMS Issues in Mathematics Education, Vol. 9). Providence, RI: American Mathematical Society.

Ruthven, K. (1990). The influence of graphic calculator use on translation from graphic to symbolic form. *Educational Studies in Mathematics, 21*, 431–450.

Schoenfeld, A. (1999). The core, the canon, and the development of research skills: Issues in the preparation of education researchers. In E. Lagemann & L. S. Shulman (Eds.), *Issues in education research: Problems and possibilities* (pp. 166–202). San Francisco, CA: Jossey-Bass.

Schwab, J. J. (1958). Inquiry and the reading process. *Journal of General Education, 11*, 72–82.

Schwab, J. J. (1978). Education and the structure of the disciplines. In I. Westbury & N. J. Wilkof (Eds.), *Science, curriculum, and liberal education: Selected essays of Joseph J. Schwab* (pp. 229–272). Chicago: University of Chicago Press. (Original work published 1961)

Shulman, L. S. (1997). Disciplines of inquiry in education: A new overview. In R. M. Jaeger (Ed.), *Complementary methods for research in education* (pp. 3–19). Washington DC: American Education Research Association.

Shulman, L. S. (1999). Professing educational scholarship. In E. C. Lagemann & L. S. Shulman (Eds.), *Issues in education research: problems and possibilities* (pp. 159–165). San Francisco: Jossey-Bass.

Sierpinska, A., & Kilpatrick, J. (Eds.) (1998). *Mathematics education as a research domain: A search for identity. An ICMI Study*. Dordrecht, The Netherlands: Kluwer.

Stein, M. K., Grover, B., & Henningsen, M. (1996). Building student capacity for mathematical thinking and reasoning: An analysis of mathematical tasks used in reform classrooms. *American Educational Research Journal, 33*, 455–488.

Steinberg, R., Haymore, J., & Marks, R. (1985, April). *Teachers' knowledge and content structuring in mathematics*. Paper presented at the annual meeting of the American Educational Research Association, Chicago.

Stigler, J., & Hiebert, J. (1997, September). Understanding and improving mathematics instruction. *Phi Delta Kappan*, 14–21.

Stigler, J., & Hiebert, J. (1999). *The teaching gap: Best ideas from the world's teachers for improving education in the classroom*. New York: Free Press.

Stodolsky, S. S. (1988). *The subject matters: Classroom activity in math and social studies*. Chicago: University of Chicago Press.

Strauss, A. L. (1987). *Qualitative analysis for social scientists*. Cambridge: Cambridge University Press.

Wilson, S. M., & Wineburg, S. S. (1988). Peering at history through different lenses: The role of disciplinary perspectives in teaching history. *Teachers College Record, 89*, 525–539.

Zeichner, K. M., & Tabachnik, B. R. (1981). Are the effects of university teacher education 'washed out' by school experience? *Journal of Teacher Education, 32*(3), 7–11.

15
Mathematics Teachers as Researchers: Living on the Edge?

CHRIS BREEN

University of Cape Town

ABSTRACT

In this chapter, contrasting views on the contributions that teachers as researchers are making to the field of mathematics education are used as a springboard to examine developments over the past decade. On the one hand, there is a growing movement for more teachers to become involved in a critical exploration of their practice through such methods as critical reflection, action research, and lesson studies. The contrasting position makes the claim that these activities have done little to add to the body of knowledge on mathematics education. The chapter starts by scanning the literature in mathematics education and then takes a step back and explores the broad roots and issues of the teacher-researcher movement. A particular example of teachers studying for a higher degree in teaching provides an opportunity to explore the interface between the two contrasting positions. The chapter closes with an appeal to academics in mathematics education to seek ways to listen to and engage with the informed voices of teachers.

INTRODUCTION: A CONFUSED PICTURE?

In a keynote paper to the Fifth Annual Conference of the Department of Science and Mathematics Education in Brunei, Jeremy Kilpatrick (2000) made the case for a return to the scientific base for future educational research and had the following to say about teachers as researchers:

> "Teachers as researchers" has become an important mantra in many programmes of teacher education in mathematics, but it does seem fair to say that, so far, teacher research has not had much impact on the larger community. ... Lately, some questions have begun to be raised about the status of the knowledge produced through teacher research and, in particular, whether that knowledge should be included in the same category as traditional academic research knowledge. (p. 87)

John Malone, who had been present at the talk, used an opportunity that

Second International Handbook of Mathematics Education, 523–544
A.J. Bishop, M.A. Clements, C. Keitel, J. Kilpatrick and F.K.S. Leung (eds.)
© *2003 Dordrecht: Kluwer Academic Publishers. Printed in Great Britain.*

same year to respond to these views in a plenary presentation to the annual conference of the Mathematics Education Research Group of Australasia (MERGA) in Australia:

> It is impossible to gauge how much research teachers have conducted on the teaching of mathematics, and I believe that there is ample evidence to demonstrate that teachers' research is having considerable impact locally, even if it does not have a high profile when viewed from outside the profession ... Reversing the shift in current methodological approaches would certainly highlight the gap between the evidence-based research of the teacher and the form of research they saw us implementing.

> (Malone, 2000, pp. 29–30)

Obviously, something in Kilpatrick's plenary talk served as a stimulus to prompt Malone's defensive response. A closer look at the extract from Kilpatrick's paper suggests that this stimulus could have come from the suggestion of an almost religious fervour around teacher research ('mantra') or from the separation of teachers from 'the larger community' and their research from 'traditional academic research'. However, in his attempt to defend teacher researchers, Malone refers to, without citation, 'ample' evidence of 'local' impact (as opposed to the profile from 'outside the profession') and locates himself as one of 'us' (positioning teachers as 'them'?). In essence, it seems that both accuser and defender share many of the same assumptions and speak as outsiders.

Who are these teacher-researchers that these 'others' are devoting space to in their plenary papers? What is it about their work that prompts these claims and counterclaims? Is this controversy just another form of the well-trodden track of the practice/theory and teacher/researcher divide? How easy is it in mathematics education to access the response of someone responding from within the community of teacher researchers?

This second handbook provides an appropriate opportunity to focus on these and similar questions and to investigate further. As a start, stock is taken of what has been happening in the field of teacher research in mathematics education by scanning some of the recently published literature. This evidence will be offset against a broader perspective of the teacher-research movement, which cuts across the boundaries of subject disciplines. This broad view will hopefully place us in a more informed position to understand some of the issues affecting mathematics education so that some possible fruitful areas for future development can be explored.

TEACHER RESEARCH IN MATHEMATICS EDUCATION

Any scan of the literature of teacher research in any subject area largely depends on the way in which that research is disseminated – a point that is picked up again later. Most of the sources quoted in this section are to be found in the academic literature in the field of mathematics education. The examples given below are also intended to give a flavour of this work rather than be definitive. A conscious attempt has also been made to draw from a diverse geographic spread to ensure a more international perspective.

At one level, there has been a growing use of reflective accounts of teaching and the use of diaries as a means of encouraging teachers to think about their practice. For example, Colyn (1992) presents a series of reflections written by teachers working in partnership with an in-service organisation in Cape Town. Nearly all the teachers who contributed to the book worked in seriously over-crowded and under-resourced classrooms in squatter camps and black townships during the apartheid era. Their contributions to the book represented their first written reflections on their attempts at experimenting with their teaching methods. For example, Nomakhaya Mbeki (1992) writes:

> When I observed them in groups, I noticed two children were making their own triangles. I could see that they were thinking by the way they were touching their foreheads. I noticed that there was a leader in each group (this happened automatically, they didn't select the leader). I noticed in this activity that everybody was willing to do something and be seen by the others and by the teacher. (p. 4)

In the first edition of the *International Handbook of Mathematics Education*, Kathryn Crawford and Jill Adler (1996) pick up on this book and note the astonishing enthusiasm that is present in the way these teachers think about and work on their practice. The authors go on to argue the case for the active participation of teachers in research activities associated with their professional practice as a prerequisite for changes in the processes and quality of mathematics education for school students. They contrast this inquiry into teaching with traditional university-based definitions of research and ask how such teachers can be included in research and inquiry about mathematics education.

In the same chapter, Crawford and Adler (1996) describe a project in which student teachers engage in an action research project focusing on teaching mathematics to pupils as an official part of their university course. They report that these students are generally confronted by tensions and inconsistencies between the learning theories that they have been told about and the models of learning they see in practice in the classroom. The students' involvement in this action research project effectively widens their awareness of the practical implications of educational theory and strengthens their confidence for future classroom decision-making.

A description of a wider range of teacher research projects is provided by the International Group for the Psychology of Mathematics Education (PME), which started a working group called Teachers as Researchers in 1988. This working group was based on the belief that classroom teachers could and should carry out research concerned with the practice of teaching mathematics. The group met annually for nine years before disbanding at the PME conference in

Spain in 1996. This last meeting also coincided with the final stages of the preparation of a publication with the theme of teachers as researchers that was based on contributions from members of the group (Zack, Mousley, & Breen, 1997).

The book contained 18 chapters by authors from different parts of the world (the USA, Canada, South America, England, Australia, Portugal, and South Africa). Of the 18 chapters, 3 were written by teachers (as part of their study for a higher degree), 4 by teams of lecturers and teachers, and the rest by university or college lecturers. The chapters ranged from reports of projects in which the university lecturer facilitated and supported classroom research aimed at empowering or transforming teachers, through accounts of initiatives to include teacher research as a legitimate form of higher degree study, to teacher accounts of moving from being a teacher to being a teacher-researcher. The divergent nature of the papers in the book provides a valuable source for commenting on some of the major issues that arise in teacher research.

In a contribution to a later book on mathematics education research, Hatch and Shiu (1998) include practitioner research in their definition of mathematics education research by placing an emphasis on the process of the research. They argue that teachers are uniquely placed to investigate and record aspects of their teaching, their classroom, and their students that are hidden from others. They describe officially sanctioned practices at their respective universities where teacher research is incorporated into courses at the levels of pre-service, professional development, higher degree, and research degree. At the pre-service level, this incorporation is done through what Hatch and Shiu term *implicit personal research* in which student teachers keep a reflective file. Students are set an explicit action research project in the final year that focuses on a question they identify from their own teaching practice. In the professional development course, students keep diary-type files in which they note classroom observations. The authors' major concern in the chapter is to create ways to ensure that the results from such research activity is properly shared by the community, and they suggest the formation of a network to disseminate the results.

A second Working Group of PME called The Psychology of Inservice Education of Mathematics Teachers met from 1986 in London until 1994 in Lisbon and later published a book with chapters representing the group's work (Jaworski, Wood, & Dawson, 1999). Two of the chapters in that book (Irwin & Britt, 1999; Krainer, 1999) address issues in teacher development that arise when teachers start to undertake research into aspects of their own classroom practice.

Krainer (2000) continued that theme, focusing on what he perceived as a trend in European mathematics teacher education: the attempt to find closer connections between teacher education as a field of practice and as a field of research. He described and analysed six initiatives from different regions (the Netherlands, Portugal, Hungary, Israel, Great Britain, and Austria). The first three examples were taken from pre-service courses in which some form of systematic examination of practice was undertaken by student teachers with the assistance or guidance of one or more teacher educators. The remaining three examples focused on qualified mathematics teachers who became involved in in-service or higher degree study. In these examples, teacher educators observed, or prepared and participated in, specific in-service activities that involved the teachers in an examination and reflection on practice. Krainer concluded that all the projects encouraged reflection based on practical experiences and had at least one differently knowledgeable person present whose main task was to introduce appropriate theory and literature. He recommended building communities of learners so that co-learners can work together to bring about an informed change in practice.

Although most of the reported examples involved an outside agency that drove the writing or the research, a growing practice in teacher research is emerging out of the focus of the Third International Mathematics and Science Study (TIMSS) on an international comparison of mathematics teaching and teacher education (see, e.g., Hiebert & Stigler, 2000). A number of teacher groups in the United States are following the Japanese example of 'lesson study' (see, e.g., Lewis, 2000), a professional development process that allows teachers to systematically examine their practice with the goal of becoming more effective. Teachers work collaboratively on a small number of 'study lessons' whose focus comes from an overarching goal and related research question. Teachers work together in drawing up plans for the lesson, which is then taught by one of the group while the others observe. The group then comes together to discuss their observations and analyse the data recorded, often with a view toward revising the lesson for implementation in another classroom. The teachers produce a final report of what the study lessons have taught them, particularly with respect to their research question (see, e.g., < www.tc.columbia.edu/lessonstudy >). In their original form, these lesson studies were driven by a diverse group of teachers from a school or region with the support and interest of the school management. An outside advisor was often invited to provide further insights for the group's process.

This scan of the dominant literature of teacher education in the field of mathematics education presents a picture of a growing number of teacher education initiatives at both pre-service and in-service levels incorporating teacher research as a means of developing professional practice. Teachers are encouraged to use research methods that allow them to reflect on their practice in both informal and formal settings. In all the examples quoted thus far, this form of teacher research is reported (mainly by academics) in a positive and healthy light. Although there are some tentative hints of issues arising, there is not much sense of the provocative and contrasting positions taken up by the two plenary speakers in the introduction to this chapter.

In an attempt to enable this literature scan to be put under a more careful and informed examination, the next section takes a broader view of the roots of the teacher-research movement. It also probes the objections and issues that have arisen in the field across subject discipline boundaries. This action is likely to allow some of the latent issues hinted at above to stand out in clearer relief.

THE ROOTS OF THE TEACHER-RESEARCH MOVEMENT

Cochran-Smith and Lytle (1999) provide an overview of the roots of the Teacher-Research (TR) movement in the USA and the United Kingdom. They trace these roots as having emerged from a paradigm shift that saw teachers being regarded as knowers and thinkers who did not need more findings from university-based researchers. This group recognised and acted upon a need for more dialogue with other teachers that would ground theory in practice. The involvement of teachers in research was constructed as a form of social change grounded in critical and democratic social theory. This construction was accompanied by an explicit rejection of the authority of professional experts who produced accumulated knowledge in scientific settings for use by others in practical settings. The movement initially consisted of a loosely connected group of school-based and university-based teachers and researchers who were committed to progressive education, the social responsibility of educators, and the construction of alternative ways of observing and understanding students' work. They also wanted to solve educational problems and help teachers uncover and clarify their implicit assumptions about teaching, learning, and schooling.

In addition, a small number of university-based teacher educators and researchers began to juxtapose the purposes and possibilities of teacher research with the assumptions of more traditional research on teaching as part of an effort to challenge the hegemony of an exclusively university-generated knowledge base for teaching. Finally, a common feature of the teacher-researcher movement was that many teachers and teacher groups played major roles in shaping and articulating the agendas of the projects. In many cases, these were not teacher groups initiated by or affiliated with universities or agencies authorised to train or provide professional development for teachers. In this sense, the teacher-research movement had a distinctly grassroots character that informed, and was informed by, a number of provocative intellectual ideas and approaches to educational change.

SO WHAT ARE THE ISSUES?

Is This Research?

Cochran-Smith and Lytle (1999) begin their article by defining *teacher research*. They take it in a broad sense to mean "all forms of practitioner inquiry that involve a systematic, intentional, and self-critical inquiry about one's work in educational settings" (p. 22). Their definition includes inquiries that "others might refer to as action research, practitioner inquiry, teacher or teacher-educator self study, and so on, but it does not necessarily include reflection or other terms that refer to being thoughtful about one's educational work in ways that are not necessarily systematic or intentional" (Cochran-Smith & Lytle, 1999, p. 22).

Sources outside mathematics education indicate an opposing view to this view of teacher research. Their critique is based on the premise that there is a formal, theoretical, and scientific form of knowledge about teaching that is distinguishable from some other kind of knowledge about teaching. Fenstermacher (1994) distinguishes between practical knowledge (bounded by context and particular situations) and formal research (generalisable across contexts). He claims that if teacher research wants to be regarded as formal research, it needs to be governed by the same epistemological traditions as research intended to generate formal knowledge.

Huberman (1996) is certain about his view of teacher-research. He questions whether teacher research in general is research at all and is prepared to accept it, if at all, only under the umbrella of interpretative research. He states that understanding events in which one is a participant is excruciatingly difficult if not impossible. He argues that teacher research must apply the same criteria for assessing truth that are invoked by the deliberate universe of the academy. For him, therefore, if teacher research wishes to be counted as research, it should be bound by the rules of provision of evidence, consistency, and freedom from obvious bias and the perceptions of the people involved.

A closer examination of the writings of the mathematics educators quoted in the survey above shows that this question of whether teacher research is actually research is one that has had to be faced by each author in writing on the topic of teacher research. For example, Mousley (1997) reports that the question "What constitutes research?" was the inevitable starting point each year for the Teachers as Researchers working group as first time attendees at PME wanted to find out where the group was coming from. In her introduction to the Teachers as Researchers book, Mousley tackles the issue as follows:

> I cannot answer this question fully, because Research is an evolving concept, a developing process; a social field constrained somewhat by its own history but continually creating new boundaries. Today I think of research as a field with many criss-crossed pathways along which people move, according to various pressures, essentially personal interest and need. Some of these interlocked pathways are teacher-researcher continua where teachers undertake journeys of inquiry, seeking deeper knowledge about their own work, its effects and how these might be improved. (p. 1)

The difficulty of claiming specific work as research is signalled by the title of the book *Developing Practice: Teachers' Inquiry and Educational Change.* Mousley (1997) explains, "We were keen that the title relate teacher research to practice as well as educational change, but that it use the more inclusive term of inquiry rather than research" (p. 10).

The same tension concerning the acceptability of teacher research is shown by Crawford and Adler (1996). In their acknowledgment that university research does not reach teachers and is certainly not embodied in the teaching and learning practices in schools, they call for teachers to be involved in 'research-like activities' as a means to ensuring professional development. Similarly, Hatch and Shiu (1998) want to include practitioner research in their definition of acceptable research by placing an emphasis on process. They define *mathematics education research* as "*intentionally controlled examination of issues ... through a process of inquiry that leads to the production of (provisional) knowledge both about the objects of inquiry and the means of carrying out that inquiry*" (p. 297, italics in original).

Finally, Krainer (2000) introduces the term *investigation* as a way of getting around the problem of calling the work he reports *research*.

> Whereas in the past, teacher education was mainly seen as a field of practice, it is now increasingly also seen as a field of research. It should be stressed that the term 'investigations' is used here with a broad meaning, ranging from first systematic reflections by teacher students to more elaborate research by experts. (p. 1)

It is clear that these academics are all mindful of the controversy surrounding the legitimacy of teacher research. The introduction of terms such as *investigations, inquiry*, and *research-like activities* instead of *research* indicates an uneasiness that hints at a much larger controversy and contradicts the positive tone of most of these contributions.

It seems that Kilpatrick's (2000) plea for a return to a scientific base for educational research and Malone's (2000) riposte that the research-practice gap has its roots in the concept of technical rationality have their roots in a growing paradigm war for the heart of educational research. This is a fierce debate that has implications far beyond the teacher research movement. 'Constructivist' and 'realistic' research methods are placed at polarities, and uncomplimentary comments are fired across each other's bows.

> But there is a central fallacy at work here that consists in expecting interviewees, for example, necessarily to have access to the grounds for their actions. As Fuchs (199, p. 315) puts it, 'ornithologists don't communicate with one another through chirps and twitters'. Trying to generate 'theory from the ground' is then to mistake 'chirps and twitters' for ornithology.
>
> (Muller, 1999, p. 7)

> Those outside the classroom need to hear what we know and understand. ... We know what others think of us, but we are rarely asked to explain what we really know to others.
>
> (Cochran-Smith & Lytle, 1992, p. 316)

Problems with Dissemination

Cochran-Smith and Lytle (1999) claim that dissemination is one of the major factors that impedes the development of and informed knowledge about teacher research. In the initial stages of teacher research, traditional publications were hesitant to publish teachers' reports of their research as those reports were often conveyed in a less formal manner than was the norm. Teachers often focused on their own localised insights and improvements in practice rather than on more generalisable findings. They often adopted a narrative style of presentation of their findings. One of the main reasons for this focus and style was that teacher research was often prompted by an individual's or group's desire to improve their own practice. Accordingly, there was less investment in publishing their results and findings, especially in journals, which presented obstacles in the form of demands on how these findings should be reported.

In mathematics education, Hatch and Shiu (1998) argued for the importance of setting up a nationwide database of teacher case studies that would give researchers greater access to these data and ensure that teacher research would become more widely accessible. The difficulty of putting this proposal into practice is evidenced by the absence to date of such a resource.

The earlier quote by Mbeki from the book edited by Colyn (1992) provides an interesting example. This book was one of the first collections of teacher writings and was an in-house publication by an organisation that provided the service to teachers. Crawford and Adler (1996) used these accounts of 'astonishing enthusiasm' in making a case for 'research-like' professional development activities. This collection of teacher reflections, however, came to the attention of the academy only because one of the authors had been involved in an evaluation of the service organisation in which the publication was one of the sources of data.

Malone (2000) describes a different type of research community: a community of teachers who are the recipients and consumers of their own research. He typifies their exchange of research findings as taking place in staff rooms and the corridors of school between classes in the form of anecdotes and stories. Such an oral exchange is not ordinarily accessible to a community outside that school, and hence claims of the relative success of teacher research are impossible to judge.

A brief glance at other subject discipline areas such as language education shows a relative reluctance on the part of mathematics education journals to actively promote teacher research.

> In addition to Heinemann/Boynton/Cook, NCTE and other presses that have published teachers' writings for years, many prominent educational journals and yearbooks now include teacher research. For example, *Harvard Education Review, Language Arts, English Journal, Teaching and Change,* and *The National Writing Project Quarterly* regularly publish research by teachers as well as articles about many aspects of teacher research.
>
> (Cochran-Smith & Lytle, 1999, p. 19)

Collaboration or Co-option?

Cochran-Smith and Lytle (1999) report that the teacher research movement had its roots with teachers at the centre, initiating the projects and playing a major role in the decision-making processes. The research reported above from the mathematics education field shows little evidence that the teachers are at the centre of the project. Most of the papers and chapters surveyed were written by university teacher educators and researchers who had initiated the projects with teachers, usually with the aim to empower the teachers and to transform practice.

The reports cited by Krainer (2000) indicate a wide range of university-led endeavours where the use of 'investigative' methods is accepted and promulgated by the university academics involved in the projects. The teacher-researcher endeavour has become accumulated into the normal practice of teacher education in the university with a view to ensuring that student teachers are exposed at an early stage to the process of reflecting on their practice as part of their lifelong learning. Tripp (1987, p. 2) warns that when a research method gains currency and academic legitimacy, it tends to be transformed to serve the interests of the academy.

So what has been lost by this incorporation of the teacher-research movement into ongoing efforts to improve professional development? Perhaps the answer again lies in the roots of the movement, where a strong aim was to influence change in educational settings. Benign forms of teacher research have lost their critical agenda if their democratic edge is blunted (Kincheloe, 1991) and they are separated from the political sphere (Noffke, 1997).

Krainer (2000) makes the plea for the collegiality that exists in many of the projects on which he reports to be extended more widely to include the principals and administrators of schools. In this way, he hopes that the possibilities for change in the system might be more effective. Malone (2000) calls for researchers to double their efforts to understand the practical inquiry undertaken by teachers through collaborative action research ventures. He posits that such a move will result in gains for all involved. Teachers will gain new insights into their practice from academic researchers, who in turn will grow in their understanding of the mathematics teaching-learning context and day-to-day concerns of mathematics teachers.

The problem with both these appeals is that there is a great deal at stake in education, and true collaboration implies a sharing of control and decision-making. In practice, the equation is not equal, and issues of power exist and need to be addressed. It is usually inevitable that someone is going to be co-opted into someone else's agenda, and it is most likely that the university academic will have more access to power and resources than the teacher. Collaboration might well be able to be a win-win situation as Malone suggests, but the things being won are seldom the same. The teacher involved in in-service work might be gaining rewards for himself or herself such as additional resources and trips to conferences rather than increased effectiveness in the classroom. So the optimism for all working together needs to be tempered by the realisation that so many agendas cannot be realised. Either all work on the lowest common denominator, which is likely to be very dull and unimaginative, or else some are working on others' agendas.

In most research projects, for example, it is usually the university researcher who has access to the funds and the resources that are necessary to drive the research process. Boulter (2000) reports on the establishment of a research group with a focus on the ways that individuals construct representations in science and technology. Shortly after the main group was formed, a small group of primary teachers keen on researching their own practice was gathered together and 'collaboratively' chose to explore a topic that fell under the ambit of the topic already decided upon by the main research group! In a recent book arising out of another PME working group, Peter, Begg, Breen, and Santos-Wagner (in press) collected a series of chapters on the topic of collaborative projects in mathematics education. In the book, they examine the pitfalls and difficulties in trying to set up collaborative ventures.

RISKY BUSINESS

It seems clear that teachers who care about what they do in the classroom will always be searching for ways to improve their practice. As they work on their practice, their methods of investigation will inevitably become more and more disciplined and sophisticated. The example of the way in which American teachers have taken on board the example of the Japanese in exploring lesson study investigations at their own initiative shows this inherent drive in teachers. It seems that such efforts are not regarded as being problematic in any way. 'They' are doing a good job as long as 'they' do not get involved with what 'we' do. In this way, the trouble seems to arise when this teacher research impinges on the world of the academy.

Teacher research has been reported as being "risky business" (Lytle, 1993) and as being part of learning to teach "against the grain" (Cochran-Smith, 1991). It has been associated more with uncertainty than with certainty, more with posing problems and dilemmas than with solving them, and with the recognition that inquiry both stems from and generates questions. It seems inevitable that any attempt to remain true to the roots of teacher research yet move beyond the present impasse of the differing perspectives highlighted in this chapter will inevitably step into this murky area of risk. In this section, I try to explore this area of risk and uncertainty by focusing in some detail on an initiative that had as its major aim an attempt to bring teacher research directly into the gaze of the academy.

The year 2000 saw the first intake of students to the newly approved Masters in Education (Teaching) at the University of Cape Town. It is a taught course where students complete four 24-hour modules, each with an assignment, before having the choice (if marks are sufficient) to move on to the dissertation stage. The Masters in Teaching has been designed for teachers who are passionate about their teaching and who wish to remain in teaching but want to take the time to think and read about how they can improve their practice. Twenty students registered for the first intake from a variety of subject disciplines (including mathematics) and a variety of educational sites, with business, adult education, primary, high school, and tertiary institutional backgrounds.

There are two compulsory modules for the course. The first is a course called Teaching and the Modern Condition, in which teachers are asked to think about teaching against a background of society's move from traditionalism to modernism to postmodernism. Students are asked to take a macro-view of their position in society and their beliefs about themselves and their teaching. Assignments consist of letters written to the presenters of the course that combine the personal with the literature that has been offered.

Having completed this course, the students move on to one called Researching Teaching, which is based on some important shifts of attention (see Breen, 2000, 2002). The first step involves a shift from a 'getting an education' paradigm to one of 'becoming more experienced' and is based on the work of Gadamer (1975) and Olson (1997). In the 'getting an education' paradigm, knowledge is an objective truth separate from the knower, and it is the task of the expert to pass this knowledge on to the learner. The learner's task is to co-operate with the expert by apprenticing himself or herself to the expert and endeavouring to understand and adopt the presented facts and discourse. The dominant modes of interaction are telling and discussion to argue the facts. 'Becoming more experienced' presents a different challenge in that knowledge is now seen as embodied and constructed by experience. This view means that the experiences of each participant are welcomed as important and unique and that the task of the teacher is to create the space for participants to engage with the subject matter. The relationship between the teacher and the learner is a collaborative endeavour, and the dominant mode of interaction is conversation in which each experience is presented in the form of a narrative. The crucial importance of this move to any endeavour for teachers to research their own practice is more fully argued in Breen (2002).

A supporting theoretical foundation comes from the adoption of *enactivism* (Maturana & Varela, 1986; Varela, Thompson, & Rosch, 1991) as a model of learning. Based on the work of Merleau-Ponty (1962) as well as on Chaos and Complexity Theory, enactivism seeks a middle way between the mental and physical (inner and outer) by suggesting that the body is that which renders the world and mind inseparable. This premise means that any learning situation is constituted not only by the teacher and the learner but also by the content and the context of the situation, and that each of these factors plays a role in forming the interaction. Mind and body in each participant cannot be separated, and the basis of cognition is to be found in embodied action.

The third important phase involves the introduction of the concepts of 'conversation' and different forms of listening. The aim of a conversation is to allow all participants to deepen their understanding of the issue at hand. Participants allow the subject matter to guide them without allowing issues of self to dominate. Davis (1996) draws on Levin (1989) to identify three forms of listening. *Evaluative listening* is the most common form in society; one listens to judge the value of what the other is saying. It is the type of listening used in the 'getting an education' paradigm in which one's evaluation of the other person's statements would form the basis for the discussion in search of the objective truth.

Interpretive listening allows the listener to focus on the teller and access the subjective nuances of what is being heard with a view to entering the teller's world with compassion. Both of these forms of listening fit into the mind/body divide. In the first, the listener concentrates on the mind to judge the value of the facts, and in the second, the listener focuses on the self (body) of the teller. *Hermeneutic listening* does not accept the divide; it requires the hearer and the heard to become involved in a shared project that respects the views of each as worthy of consideration but uses the opportunity to explore what is heard with a view to coming to a mutually greater understanding of the subject.

Against this theoretical background, students in the first two intakes to this module have explored the possibilities of an experience-based methodology called the Discipline of Noticing, which has been developed by John Mason (2001). In the Discipline of Noticing, the teacher is asked to notice critical classroom incidents and give a brief-but-vivid account-of this instance in a way that avoids as much personal bias and interpretation as possible. This 'account-of' allows others and the teller to enter and re-enter into the incident at a later stage in order to create a range of possible interpretations and possible future actions.

In essence, the orientation of this module provides students with a disciplined method for investigating their practice. They are free to focus on any aspect that emerges from their work in the class and from the moments that they have collected from their day-to-day experience. The assignments submitted by this mixed group of teachers taking the first run of this module have some interesting features. In the first place, few of them chose to focus on aspects that would normally be addressed in traditional research. Rather than focus on content or delivery issues, most of the teachers focused on aspects that related to their own behavioural functions. Topics addressed included impatience, withdrawal, inhibitions, not coping, being silenced, self-doubt, and impulsiveness. These topics are core functions of their persona and are inextricably linked to their teaching practice. In their end-of-course evaluation, they reported that the course had provided them with some important steps in the process of working on their practice. In the first place, the two compulsory modules helped form a community of learners who focused on developing a shared understanding of ways of knowing. The enactivist grounding affirmed the notion of body as instrument, and many drew on visceral triggers as an initial source for the recognition of critical moments. The Discipline of Noticing provided a structure and language for scientifically exploring the teaching analysis that many felt they did naturally. They also described, however, how the identification of patterns of behaviour that they wanted to change was tightly interwoven with their own habitual patterns of behaviour. The task of identifying a habit such as impulsiveness that they wanted to work with was only the first step. Identifying and preparing for alternative ways of acting could only begin to be implemented once they were able to catch themselves *in the moment before* they acted. This task proved to be enormously difficult. Finally, many of the teachers commented on the demanding nature of the assignment, which required them not to understand and repeat the digested words and theories of others but rather to analyse and make sense of their own theories located against a broader literature. Here is what one teacher wrote:

> This has turned out to be one of the most challenging and difficult assignments I have ever had to undertake – and the most time-consuming. I have written and re-written entire paragraphs more times than I can count. I have read and re-read the essay and each time found things that I was not happy with. Indeed this essay has occupied my mind every waking moment for the past 3 weeks.

It is also interesting to note that the whole process of tackling the assignment was filled with unease. The students' immediate response was one of considerable consternation. They felt that the expected time for completion of the project (3 weeks) was far too short a time for them to engage with the topic in the way that they wanted. It would take them a while to understand and capture the full implications of the enactive perspective that worldviews, feelings, and intuitive body beliefs were an essential component of their teaching and could be included in their analysis of teaching at an academic institution. In submitting their assignments, many of them expressed concerns that this format of a linearly presented piece of writing did not do justice to the ways of knowing that had encouraged during the course. Several students responded by following some of the ideas expressed in a handout from a book *Daredevil Research* (Jipson & Paley, 1997) and included photographs, colour-coordinated paper to match themes, parallel commentaries, and other innovations to try to make their point. In many cases, these innovations proved to be exceptionally well chosen.

The above description of the basics of this new course is not intended to advocate any particular aspect of either of the modules. It is rather intended to highlight some of the features of the Masters of Teaching that place it outside the framework of traditional higher degree courses. The advantage of running this activity as a university course is that teacher educators and teachers have been forced to explore each other's worlds. The teachers have been forced to engage with the demands of the university, and at the same time the academy has been forced to address the needs of the teachers. It is indeed a risky business.

The risk is becoming particularly apparent as some of the students move on to the dissertation stage of the course. Masters in Teaching students are encouraged to follow their passion and to research aspects of their teaching that are important to them. Three of the top students from the coursework section of the course, who have also proved themselves as being capable of scoring high marks in more traditionally orientated modules, have chosen to undertake hermeneutically inspired classroom research using the tools that they acquired in the Researching Practice module. Whereas one of these students is working in the field of drama education to understand her own learning process, the other two are working in the field of mathematics education.

The first challenge that has arisen for them has come in the Research Methods module run by different faculty members who employ traditional scientific-based research frameworks. The students have to write a research proposal and have been given an exemplary framework for their submission that is framed by traditional science-based research issues such as 'the research question', validity, and generalisability. The pressure to satisfy these traditional demands has been such that they have all submitted proposals of over double the expected length as they try to counter expected criticisms of their proposal. The results of this possible face-off between teachers and academy are still awaited but provide the opportunity for further engagement and discussion.

EMERGING LEARNING

A number of emerging themes arise from the above description of this new Masters course for teachers that resonate with many of the points raised about teacher research in this chapter yet seem to be missing from the literature in mathematics education. In the first place, the conscious shift of attention and paradigm to one of 'becoming more experienced' and its concomitant emphasis on ways of communicating through conversation has opened the space for the teachers to talk more from their own experience. The extent to which the teachers were able to make their own choices of focus in their assignments also contributed to this open space. The result was that they shared more than usual about themselves and their practice and about those aspects that really mattered to them. They tackled with determination and responsibility the task of exploring and attempting to put into practice changes of habit.

Wood (1999, p. 176) identifies one aspect of teacher development that mathematics educators know very little about as being the processes that are involved as teachers make changes in their teaching. The approach adopted in the course described above seems to provide a starting point for making conjectures about the changes that teachers want to initiate in their own practice. The striking feature is that such a process seems to be one that takes an enormous amount of focus, energy, and time. This feature is already a very different mindset from the current expectation that the main task for change is for 'best practice' to be identified and communicated to teachers who, unless they choose to be resistant to change, will be able to implement the new ideas with little difficulty.

The opening of the discourse to include additional dimensions such as personal uncertainties, beliefs that are not bounded by and restricted to the cognitive, and the acceptance of what one student calls *visceral triggers* also holds enormous potential. One of the challenges for the presenters of the course has been to allow the students the freedom to explore topics about which they care and are hopefully passionate rather than those that are more comfortable to the lecturer. In essence, the challenge is one of setting up a truly collaborative venture rather than one in which the student is co-opted into following the lecturer's agenda. Such an approach will inevitably move the lecturer out of her or his comfort zone, but the possibilities for new insights are enormous.

The extent to which advantage of the possibilities of such an opening is taken by the research community will depend on the degree to which researchers can suspend their own limiting forms of discourse. For example, Ensor (2000) focuses on the importance of trying to access those parts of teachers' and teacher educators' tacit knowledge that she believes cannot be described by language. She gives an extract in which a teacher educator she was interviewing 'had difficulty in expressing why he selected certain tasks for inclusion in his course' (p. 4). She posits two possible reasons for the difficulty. Either the teacher educator was being asked questions for which he was unprepared, or else some of his principles of selection were tacitly held and could not be made completely available in language. An additional reading, arising from the experience of the teachers in the Master's group, could be that the teacher educator was being co-opted into a framework dominated by a preferred theory of discourse and a 'getting an education' mode. Since the aim of the research was to add to a body of knowledge in a manner that privileges the academic insights of the researcher and uses discussion as a means to arrive at the 'truth', an additional reason for the teacher educator's reported difficulty might have stemmed from the mismatch in modes of engagement. The group of teachers doing the Researching Teaching course felt more comfortable and articulate when they were involved in 'becoming more experienced'. In this mode, they were allowed the safety to open up and explore some deeply held personal yet clearly stated aspects of their practice. This way of working through what has been called *sustained conversations* (Hollingsworth, 1997) requires trust and emotional maturity as essential prerequisites to 'break the silence' (McDonald, 1982). Perhaps the inevitably adversarial positioning nature of an academic researcher coming from a limiting perspective causes teachers (and teacher educators?) to become silent about their true craft decisions and aims. One is left to conjecture what new insights will become available to researchers who change their mode of operation with teachers and engage in collaborative conversations.

FUTURE TRENDS?

Cochran-Smith and Lytle (1999) look to the future and report that the standards movement currently dominates the U.S. agenda regarding instruction. They predict that as pressures for school- and classroom-level accountability intensify, research-based, whole-school improvement models will become increasingly widespread. In addition, the concept of 'best practice' will guide discussions about student achievement and teacher education. They believe that the authoritative role of outsiders in school improvement will become the rule rather than the exception. They see that these moves are underpinned by a set of assumptions about school change that de-emphasises differences in local contexts; the construction of local knowledge in and by school communities; and the role of the teacher as decision maker and change agent – ideas that are at the heart of many initiatives in the teacher research movement.

A scan of developments around the world suggests that education at all levels, including teacher education, has become more and more of a service industry based on market principles. The dominant discourse in many countries is for the development of evidence-informed practice, with a growing number of educational initiatives that have a focus on managerial solutions to problems couched in managerial terms.

It seems as though management is likely to be the dominant force in education around the world for the next decade. There seem to be different slants, however, on the best-practice debate. In some countries, evidence-based practice tends to be a tool used to bludgeon academics to conduct their research in classrooms. In others, it is the in-service agencies that are put under the spotlight, with the academic educational researchers being asked to supply evidence of the success or failure of various intervention programmes. In yet other countries, it is the teachers who are on the receiving end of the management gaze. Many calls are likely to be similar to that made by Taole (2000) in South Africa for large-scale longitudinal studies using scientific thinking to find out the facts to get teaching right.

In the United Kingdom, it appears that the government is looking to classroom teachers as opposed to academic researchers to lead the drive towards evidence-based practice through the award of large teacher research grants where successful applications have to have a practicing teacher partnering the higher education institution. A Best Practice research scholarship has also been awarded to teachers wanting to do school-based research. In contrast, Crawford and Adler (1996) agree that in an age of quality management and hierarchical administrative structures, teaching activities are increasingly circumscribed by requirements for planning, documentation and measurable outcomes. In such a strongly regulated environment, teachers will play an educationally powerless and unprofessional role.

This analysis suggests that the future for teacher research as a social inquiry aimed at provoking debate and change in schools is likely to play a dormant role in the next decade as management demands for evidence-based data on best practice solutions to educational problems dominate. Where teacher research does continue to have a role in higher education, it is likely to be in a co-opted role where the form is present but the substance absent as teachers fit in with academically prescribed and advocated forms of research. This analysis suggests that the views reported by Kilpatrick (2000) and noted at the start of this chapter are likely to hold sway in educational research during the next decade.

Cochran-Smith and Lytle (1999) describe ways in which the teacher-research movement has the potential to act as a transformative influence for university cultures as it collides with the long-standing tradition of universities to privilege research while holding teaching and service in relatively low regard. They point to the extent to which such research can become an especially contested terrain when doctoral students and their professors assert the validity of teacher research as dissertation material and when university-based practitioner research is presented by academic staff for promotion or tenure review purposes. The experience of trying to introduce the Masters in Teaching course at the University of Cape Town is a case in point, with early attempts from the academy to block its introduction on the somewhat ironic grounds that it presented a 'monologic' view of education. Even supportive colleagues seemed to collude with the diminishment of teacher research by suggesting that such a course should rather be offered as a reflective practice module for pre-service and in-service teachers rather than being appropriate for higher degree study. Crawford and Adler (1996, p. 1195) claim that academic hegemony runs counter to the goal of teacher ownership of the research agenda and of knowledge generated as they learn through research activity.

CONCLUSION

This chapter has in the main focused on the way in which teacher research is reported in the academic literature of mathematics education. The result of this gaze has been to highlight the fact that academic mathematics educators generally side with the critics of teacher research as a legitimate form of research. Even when the topic is raised in journals, cautious words are chosen to describe the activity, and more generally teachers are co-opted to work with academics.

I have also argued, however, that teachers will always reflect on their work in an attempt to improve their practice. The recent move towards 'lesson study' is a good example of how teachers will refine their methods of researching their practice under their own motivation. The implication of this claim is that teacher research will continue at school level even if it is not recognised by the academy. One challenge to the mathematics education community will be to create ways in which publications adapt to give voice to this form of teacher research. Failure to do so will continue the separation of 'us' from 'them' that will leave the debate on teacher education in the split of factions as evidenced in the excerpts from the plenary speeches quoted in the introduction.

The example of the Masters in Teaching degree in Cape Town was given in an attempt to show the enormous benefits and new knowings and understandings that might become available if university academics and teachers create an opportunity to explore the space that emerges when they can enter into collaborative conversations with each other. I remind the reader that I believe it is up to the academics to make the move to engage the teacher in conversation, not because the academic holds a more enlightened and superior position but because it is the academic who currently holds the power in the discourse and control of the resources. Breen, Lebethe, and Agherdien (in press) describe how essential it is in a collaborative venture for the person with power to acknowledge this power inequity by making herself or himself vulnerable in the initial stages.

Hewitt (1995, p. 15) argues that what is required is a broadening of view as to what constitutes research, how it is done, and what are the 'data' on which generalisations are built. He argues that there is also a need to accept that 'rigour' is problematic within all methodologies. A useful step would apparently be to work at challenging this algorithmic approach to educational research by teachers at the very least at Masters level. Such work would allow students to explore alternative framings of their dissertation topics (such as a critical hermeneutic research, which tends towards a tentative approach and which outlines the area to be investigated rather than the question) as well as alternative methodologies that they develop as appropriate for their search. Such an action could contribute enormously to the development of educational research and researchers and offer new understandings of teacher development. It would also assist in empowering students as independent researchers and indicate that their views and ideas are valued. Teachers are told in their classrooms that they should respect learners as being creative, wise, and responsible who need more space to inquire and explore without being subjected to rote-learnt algorithms. Yet these same teachers are seldom regarded in practice by the academy as being wise, creative, and responsible. Mason (1994) has written that the most important product of any research endeavour is the development of the researcher himself or herself. Similarly, Crawford and Adler (1996) argue on grounds of neo-Vygotskian perspectives that knowledge derived from research is necessarily personal.

Teacher research provides exciting opportunities of tapping into the wisdom of those responsible for classroom practice. It also provides the best opportunity for understanding the dynamics of change in practice and creating a living educational theory (Whitehead, 1989). Many in-service providers are already aware of the enormous enthusiasm and energy generated when teachers take or are given the opportunity to reflect on and improve their practice. The experience of the Masters in Teaching degree in Cape Town has shown the enormous learning opportunities that become accessible to teacher educators when they join in this search for improvement as equal partners. In many ways, it is strange that teacher research is not more widely accepted and encouraged. Visits to Web sites such as <www.actionresearch.net> and <http://www.csci.educ.ubc.ca/publication/insights/> bear witness to the enthusiasm and possibilities that result from collaborative teacher research.

A final irony and warning is to be found in the roots of the teacher-research movement. It would be unfortunate if we were to lose sight of the fact that the essence of the movement came from the dissonance and unease that it caused in its quest to improve the education system. The harsh words of those involved in the mathematics wars and paradigm wars and the extent to which government has decided that it has a crucial role in standing outside the profession to set standards are proof that education is going through troubled times. The teacher-research movement can assist by causing dissonance and trouble. The trouble will come from conviction based on evidence drawn from research by those in the field who know that we haven't got education right and who are prepared to put their energies into getting something changed. The minute teacher research becomes comfortable, someone else needs to take over. We know that distanced research is comfortable compared with teaching or working closely with teachers (Setati, 2000; Vithal, 1998). If your research endeavour is uncomfortable, you know you are close to the edge, and you can be sure that beneficial learning is taking place.

> In our past exploration, the tradition was to discover something and then formulate it into answers and solutions that could be widely transferred. But now we are on a journey of mutual and simultaneous exploration. In my view, all we can expect from one another is new and interesting information. We can not expect answers. Solutions, as quantum reality teaches, are a temporary event, specific to a context, developed through the relationship of persons and circumstances. ... In this new world, you and I make it up as we go along, not because we lack expertise or planning skills, but because that is the nature of reality. ... Every step requires that we stay comfortable with uncertainty, and confident of confusion's role.

(Wheatley, 1992, pp. 151–152)

REFERENCES

Boulter, C. (2000, January). Research by primary school science teachers: Reflections on the relationship of research to professional development at times of curriculum change. In J. Kuiper (Ed.), *Proceedings of the 8th annual conference of the Southern African Association for Research in Mathematics, Science and Technology Education* (pp. 1–12). Port Elizabeth: University of Port Elizabeth Press.

Breen, C. (2000). Re-searching teaching: Changing paradigms to improve practice. In M. A. Clements, H. H. Tairab & W. K. Yoong (Eds.), *Science, mathematics and technical education in the 20th and 21st centuries* (pp. 94–103). Gadong: Universiti Brunei Darussalam, Department of Science and Mathematics Education.

Breen, C. (2002). Researching teaching: Moving from gut feeling to disciplined conversation. *South African Journal of Higher Education, 16*(2), 25–31.

Breen, C., Lebethe, A., & Agherdien, G. (in press). A case for collaborative staff development: A path layered while walking. In A. Peter, A. Begg, C. Breen & V. Santos-Wagner (Eds.), *Collaboration in teacher education: Examples from the context of mathematics education*. Dordrecht: Kluwer.

Cochran-Smith, M. (1991). Learning to teach against the grain. *Harvard Educational Review, 51*(3), 279–310.

Cochran-Smith, M., & Lytle, S. (1992). Communities for teacher research: Fringe or forefront? *American Journal of Education, 100,* 298–324.

Cochran-Smith, M., & Lytle, S. (1999). The teacher research movement: A decade later. *Educational Researcher, 28*(7), 15–25.

Colyn, W. (Ed.). (1992). *Reflections: Mathematics teachers' voices*. Cape Town: University of Cape Town, Mathematics Education Project.

Crawford, K., & Adler, J. (1996). Teachers as researchers in mathematics education. In A. Bishop, K. Clements, C. Keitel, J. Kilpatrick & C. Laborde (Eds.), *International handbook of mathematics education* (pp. 1187–1205). Dordrecht: Kluwer.

Davis, B. (1996). *Teaching mathematics: Toward a sound alternative*. New York: Garland Publishing.

Ensor, P. (2000, July). Recognising and realizing 'best practice' in initial teacher education and classroom teaching. In J. Bana & A. Chapman (Eds.), *Mathematics education beyond 2000: Proceedings of the 23rd Annual Conference of the Mathematics Education Research Group of Australasia* (pp. 235–242). Fremantle, Western Australia: Executive Press.

Fenstermacher, G. D. (1994). The knower and the known: The nature of knowledge in research on teaching. *Review of Research in Education, 20,* 3–56.

Fuchs, S. (1995). The new wars of truth: Conflicts over science studies as differentiated modes of observation. *Social Science Information, 35*(2), 307–326.

Gadamer, H.-G. (1975). *Truth and method* (2nd rev. ed). New York: Crossroad Publishing.

Hatch, G., & Shiu, C. (1998). Practitioner research and the construction of knowledge in mathematics education. In A. Sierpinska & J. Kilpatrick (Eds.), *Mathematics education as a research domain* (Book 2, pp. 297–315). Dordrecht: Kluwer.

Hewitt, D. (1995, May). Response to Paul's comments on the principle of economy in the learning and teaching of maths. *Philosophy of Mathematics Education Newsletter,* 8.

Hiebert, J., & Stigler, J. W. (2000). A proposal for improving classroom teaching: Lessons from the TIMSS video study. *Elementary School Journal, 101,* 3–20.

Hollingsworth, S. (Ed.) (1997). *International action research: A casebook for educational reform.* Washington, DC: Falmer.

Huberman, M. (1996). Moving mainstream: Taking a closer look at teacher research. *Language Arts, 73*(2), 124–140.

Irwin, K., & Britt, M. (1999). Teachers' knowledge of mathematics and reflective professional development. In B. Jaworski, T. Wood & S. Dawson (Eds.), *Mathematics teacher education: Critical international perspectives* (pp. 91–101). London: Falmer.

Jaworski, B., Wood, T., & Dawson, S. (Eds.). (1999). *Mathematics teacher education: Critical international perspectives.* London: Falmer.

Jipson, J., & Paley, N. (Eds.). (1997). *Daredevil research: Re-creating analytic practice.* New York: Peter Lang.

Kilpatrick, J. (2000). Research in mathematics education across two centuries. In M. A. Clements, H. H. Tairab & W. K. Yoong (Eds.), *Science, mathematics and technical education in the 20th and 21st centuries* (pp. 79–93). Gadong: Universiti Brunei Darussalam, Department of Science and Mathematics Education.

Kincheloe, J. (1991). *Teachers as researchers: Qualitative inquiry as a path to empowerment.* London: Falmer.

Krainer, K. (1999). PFL-Mathematics: Improving professional practice in mathematics teaching. In B. Jaworski, T. Wood & S. Dawson (Eds.), *Mathematics teacher education: Critical international perspectives* (pp. 102–112). London: Falmer.

Krainer, K. (2000, August). *Teacher education as research: A trend in European mathematics teacher education.* Paper presented to Working Group for Action 7 at the Ninth International Congress on Mathematical Education, Tokyo.

Levin, D. (1989). *The listening self: Personal growth, social change and the closure of metaphysics.* London: Routledge.

Lewis, C. (2000, April). *Lesson study: The core of Japanese professional development.* Paper presented at the meeting of the American Educational Research Association, New Orleans.

Lytle, S. (1993, Winter). Risky business. *Quarterly of the National Writing Project and the Center for the Study of Writing and Literacy, 15*(1), 20–23.

Malone, J. (2000, July). Bridging the gap: A challenge for the dual community. In J. Bana & A. Chapman (Eds.), *Mathematics education beyond 2000: Proceedings of the 23rd Annual Conference of the Mathematics Education Research Group of Australasia* (pp. 27–36). Fremantle, Western Australia: Executive Press.

Mason, J. (1994, July). Researching from the inside: Locating an I-you relationship. In J. Ponte & J. Matos (Eds.), *Proceedings of the Eighteenth Annual Meeting of the International Group for the Psychology of Mathematics Education* (pp. 176–190). Lisbon: Faculdade Ciencias Universidade de Lisboa.

Mason, J. (2001). *Researching your own practice: The discipline of noticing.* London: Routledge Falmer.

Maturana, H., & Varela, F. (1986). *The tree of knowledge.* New York: Shambhala.

Mbeki, N. (1992). Problems facing our pupils. In W. Colyn (Ed.), *Reflections: Mathematics teachers' voices* (pp. 26–34). Cape Town: University of Cape Town, Mathematics Education Project.

McDonald, J. (1982). *Teaching: Making sense of an uncertain craft.* New York: Teachers College Press.

Merleau-Ponty, M. (1962). *Phenomenology of perception.* London: Routledge.

Mousley, J. (1997). An introduction: Teachers' inquiry. In V. Zack, J. Mousley & C. Breen (Eds.), *Developing practice: Teachers' inquiry and educational change* (pp. 1–10). Geelong: Deakin University Press.

Muller, J. P. (1999). Reason, reality and public trust: The case of educational research for policy. In N. Taylor & P. Vinjevold (Eds.), *Getting learning right* (pp. 37–64). Johannesburg: Joint Education Trust.

Noffke, S. (1997). Professional, personal and political dimensions of action research. *Review of Research in Education, 22,* 305–343.

Olson, M. (1997). Collaboration: An epistemological shift. In H. Christiansen, L. Goulet, C. Krentz & M. Maeers (Eds.), *Recreating relationships: Collaboration and educational reform* (pp. 13–25). Albany: State University of New York Press.

Peter, A., Begg, A., Breen, C., & Santos-Wagner, V. (Eds.). (in press). *Collaboration in teacher education: Examples from the context of mathematics education.* Dordrecht: Kluwer.

Setati, M. (2000, January). Classroom based research: From with or on teachers to with and on teachers. In S. Mahlomaholo (Ed.), *Proceedings of the 8th annual conference of the Southern African Association for Research in Science, Mathematics and Technology Education* (pp. 511–520). Port Elizabeth: University of Port Elizabeth Press.

Taole, K. (2000, January). Calling for a shift in the existing research culture. In S. Mahlomaholo (Ed.), *Proceedings of the 8th annual conference of the Southern African Association for Research in Mathematics, Science and Technology Education* (pp. 37–41). Port Elizabeth: University of Port Elizabeth Press.

Tripp, D. (1987). *Teacher autobiography and classroom practice.* Perth: Murdoch University.

Varela, F. J., Thompson, E., & Rosch, E. (1991). *The embodied mind: Cognitive science and human experience.* Cambridge, MA: MIT Press.

Vithal, R. (1998, January). Disruptions and data: The politics of doing mathematics education research in South Africa. In N. A. Ogude & C. Bohlmann (Eds.), *Proceedings of the 6th annual conference of the Southern African Association for Research in Mathematics and Science Education* (pp. 475–480). Pretoria: University of South Africa.

Wheatley, M. (1992). *Leadership and the new science.* San Francisco: Berrett-Koehler.

Whitehead, J. (1989). Creating a living educational theory from questions of the kind, 'How do I improve my practice?' *Cambridge Journal of Education, 19*(1), 41–52.

Wood, T. (1999). Approaching teacher development: Practice into theory. In B. Jaworski, T. Wood & S. Dawson (Eds.), *Mathematics teacher education: Critical international perspectives* (pp. 163–179). London: Falmer.

Zack, V., Mousley, J., & Breen, C. (Eds.). (1997). *Developing practice: Teachers' inquiry and educational change.* Geelong: Deakin University Press.

16
Researching Mathematics Education in Situations of Social and Political Conflict[1]

RENUKA VITHAL
University of Durban-Westville

PAOLA VALERO
Aalborg University

ABSTRACT

We explore the thesis that given that our societies are fraught with various social and political conflicts, and that mathematics education is concerned with contributing to the life possibilities of students in that world, then mathematics education as a field of practice and research has to be concerned with the implications of recognising those conflicts. In particular, we explore the implications of considering social and political conflict situations for: the kinds of research questions and agendas constructed; the theories and methodologies adopted; and the criteria used for judging the quality of research in mathematics education. In building our argument we draw not only on international literature in the discipline of mathematics education and outside it, but also on our experiences as researchers struggling with the complexity of conflict contexts.

INTRODUCTION

Among all people working in mathematics education, from practitioners, advisors, and policymakers to researchers, there seems to be agreement about the importance of providing students with an adequate mathematical experience in schooling, since that experience, it is hoped, will prepare students to be active members of our societies (Niss, 1996). This kind of statement seems to presuppose that, sooner or later, to a minor or major degree, it is important to establish a connection between what one does in school mathematics education and the broader social world where students act. We argue that the current picture of the world in which students have to live is that of a world filled with all kinds of conflict. Therefore, mathematics education needs to consider conflict in significant ways. Before the attack of 11 September 2001 in the United States of America, conflict and its relevance for mathematics education could have been thought of as an issue of interest mainly to researchers in developing countries,[2]

Second International Handbook of Mathematics Education, 545–591
A.J. Bishop, M.A. Clements, C. Keitel, J. Kilpatrick and F.K.S. Leung (eds.)
© *2003 Dordrecht: Kluwer Academic Publishers. Printed in Great Britain.*

where, in fact, conflict has been evident and in some cases even endemic. The world order that is emerging after the experience of large-scale terrorism in the heart of Western civilisation, however, invites us all to think carefully about the meaning and possibilities that research endeavours in mathematics education acquire if we are interested in facing the challenges of this new order.

If one accepts the thesis that conflicts are part of the societies and world we live in, then it follows that institutions of learning within different societies embed these conflicts and that all of us as learners, teachers and researchers are implicated in the production and reproduction of these conflicts and their inequalities. Furthermore, if one accepts the thesis that mathematics and mathematics education play a very special role in that world, then mathematics education researchers have a very important task to understand how and why mathematics education is implicated in these conflicts. In particular, they need to consider seriously what social and political conflicts mean in the endeavour of mathematics education research in practice, methodologically, and theoretically.

Our argument about the relevance of recognising social and political unrest in mathematics education research is developed by exploring the idea of conflict and distinguishing different categories, meanings, and associations that we then analyse in relation to how mathematics education research has approached them. Facing the lack of consideration of broader social and political conflict as an integral part of mathematics education research problems, we present a critique of mathematics education research and point to emerging and possible directions for recognising the political nature of this activity. As a result, we consider issues connected with the research questions, theories, methodologies, and criteria for research quality in this area. In this way, we hope to engage a broad audience of researchers in mathematics education in a discussion of the field of study we are building, of what it is evidencing, and what it is, at the same time, silencing.

HOW DO SITUATIONS OF SOCIAL AND POLITICAL CONFLICT RELATE TO MATHEMATICS AND MATHEMATICS EDUCATION?

As foundational 'power-knowledge' in the historical construction of the world and its current organisation, mathematics and mathematics education have to acknowledge their participation in the production of social and political conflicts. But how, and in what ways are they implicated? We explore some sources of conflict.

One reason that social and political conflicts in their current shape and manifestations are found in organisations today could be tracked to the foundations of the modern Western world. We not only want to bring to our discussion many criticisms in the Marxist and critical traditions of the inequalities generated by the capitalist economic organisation but also would like to focus on how mathematics has been constructed and used as a tool of power in such a social process. Desrosières (1998) provides a detailed study of the connection between the development of statistics and the construction of the modern state in England, Germany, and France. Statistics, both as a practical knowledge developed to describe the wealth and power of a state and also as a theoretical mathematical knowledge that provided a tool to deal with uncertainty, constituted one of the sources for the adoption and expansion of values like rationality, objectivism, control, normalisation, and abstraction. These values, reinforced by the thrust in science as a kind of legitimate knowledge that allows the 'right' decisions to be made, are at the centre of the modern Western world. We find the dominance of this ideology to be one cause of conflict inside many societies when it silences forms of perceiving the world that differ from the hegemonic, well-established rationality. In this way, in the centre of Western societies, people who think, act, express themselves, or believe differently have been systematically excluded. Exclusion takes place on the basis of, for example, ethnicity, social class, gender, and what is taken to be 'ability'. In mathematics education, exclusion has found expression in, among other forms, the creation of a public image of the fields of mathematics, science, and technology as a cold, abstract, and external world, a male domain that many are scared to join (e.g., Ernest, 1998; Walkerdine, 1988, 1998); the systematic minimal participation of women in the production of mathematics, science, and technology in both developed and developing countries (Beyer, 1995; Gray, 1995; Singh, 1998); and even the exclusion of girls from possibilities for getting engaged in meaningful mathematical learning (Boaler, 1997).

Another source of conflict is to be found in the history and consequences of colonisation. The colonisation of the world by European invaders meant the denial of aboriginal languages, religions, values, and ways of thinking. The establishment of educational systems that followed the rules of the colonial powers was one of the strong means, besides physical extermination, of assuring the imposition of the functional Western values and behaviours in the maintenance of colonial power. Mathematics, as a unique representative of the Western worldview, contributed to that 'occupation of the mind' (Fasheh, 1997; Khuzwayo, 1998, 2000). As D'Ambrosio (1996, pp. 113–114, our translation) reminds us:

Therefore [when talking about Western mathematics] especially in relation to Aboriginal's or Afroamerican's or other non-European people's, to oppressed workers and marginalised classes, this brings the memory of the conqueror, the slaver-owner, in other words, the dominator; it also refers to a form of knowledge that was built by him, the dominator, and that he used and still uses to exercise his dominance.

All these conflicts and tensions are played out in the movements to develop indigenous knowledge systems against and within the dominant value and knowledge frameworks and processes (e.g., Smith, 1999) of the modern or indeed a

postmodern world today, as can be seen in the debates for transforming education through an 'African Renaissance' in a globalising world (Nekhwevha, 2000)
or 'Africanisation' of education (Seepe, 2000). In mathematics education, this
process is directly observed in the challenges of developing a field of study and
practice such as ethnomathematics (e.g., Barton, 1999; Gerdes, 2001; Powell &
Frankenstein, 1997; Vithal & Skovsmose, 1997).

For the former colonies, each with a different post-independence trajectory of
length and patterns of national reconstruction, conflicts have arisen from the
challenge of establishing new social, economic, and political orders, as different
groups in society struggle for fairer and more just distribution of goods, services,
and opportunities for education and work, and for positions of power to control
these. In many of these developing nations, recovering from different forms of
colonisation and struggling to establish democratic regimes, the conflicts are
overt and explicit, often involving their entire nations. Mathematics education
is not innocent in the production of some of these conflicts; especially as a filter
for access to further education (e.g., Volmink, 1994; Zevenbergen, 2000b), it
operates as one of the many barriers that constitute part of the struggle for
access to power resources.

But the former colonisers have also had to contend with migration of people
from their former colonies into their countries. Thus many developed nations
also have a diversity of peoples and associated conflicts because of the ways in
which that diversity in knowledge and value systems is recognised, experienced,
and put into dialogue with dominant ways of knowing and acting in those
countries. The expression of diversity brings conflict when difference is denied,
suppressed, or co-opted, often because of an inadequate understanding of the
nature and quality of the diversity. Given the power of the dominant groups,
social, cultural, and political conflicts are found in all nations. They may be
more masked through the structures and functioning of well-established and
well-resourced democracies in more developed countries. Nevertheless, conflicts
do erupt as the violent riots against and by marginalised groups in many such
countries demonstrate, including riots in schools and classrooms. In mathematics
education this situation is engaged through, among others, multicultural, multilingual classrooms that challenge both the assumptions and the ways of working
of homogeneous groups of students with a teacher in the task of learning
mathematics (Adler, 1996; Licón-Khisty, 1995; Setati, 1999).

Another source of acute conflict may be found in the more recent expansion
of the informational society (Castells, 1999). Here we can refer to at least two
aspects that have relevance for our discussion. The first is the global spread of
neoliberalism as an ideology that supports a new version of a capitalist, free
market economy and that reproduces deeper inequalities (Flecha, 1999;
McLaren, 1999). The global adoption and imposition of this economic approach
has meant the dismantling of social security, an increase in unemployment, and
a rise in the concentration of resources in the hands of fewer individuals and
multinational companies (McLaren, 2000). Second, advances in technology have
also contributed to a change in the traditional sources of value and power,

making technology and technology-based knowledge new key organisers of society and economics. Science and technology have improved life for many, but far more for those few who have the access and control over them, generating a new kind of exclusion and the formation of the 'Fourth World' (Castells, 1999). For mathematics education, these two trends represent a serious challenge. The first is the need to face the risks of a growing exclusion of many local and national communities in the midst of a dominant discourse that praises global inclusion. The second is the need to pay attention to the dangers of the use of mathematics and mathematics education to promote the uncritical reproduction of dominant forms of power-knowledge in an international scene that celebrates the importance of mathematics as a qualification that provides improved life possibilities but that does not seriously address democratic access to such a qualification (Skovsmose & Valero, 2001b). Mathematics is deeply implicated in changing the very structures of society through its applications in almost all facets of modern life, including science, technology, and economics (Keitel, Kotzmann, & Skovsmose, 1993; Skovsmose, 1994). But perhaps of greater concern is the increasing uncertainty of the consequences of the use of mathematics as a foundational resource of power in society (Skovsmose, 2000).

The impact of the new information and global economy is being felt in all societies but most sharply in developing nations, which are especially vulnerable. No doubt conflicts emerge and play out in different ways and to different degrees within different countries and have led to restructuring and transformation of different institutions, perhaps most notably in their educational systems. Two points concerning the depth, breadth, and volume of the changes make conflicts more far reaching and more acutely felt in developing nations with fragile and young democracies than in developed countries. First, in developing countries, changes in the educational system often occur concurrently with widespread, fundamental changes in other institutions such as housing, health, transport, and sanitation. Conflicts in one institution influence conflicts in others, which means that more conflicts may be experienced. Second, conflicts arise within the educational systems in developing nations because of the number and rapidity with which changes are made as new or revised policies are implemented. In South Africa, for example, three waves of curriculum reforms have taken place in less than a decade (Samuel, 1999b). New policies regarding the rationalisation and redeployment of educators, new forms of governance in schools, new appraisal systems, new systems of school funding, and so on have been implemented simultaneously. As different stakeholders – teachers, parents and even students – lobby for better conditions, services, and opportunities in a deeply unequal context, conflicts become sharper, overt, and even violent, and often they enter schools. Teaching and learning in classrooms may be affected, and schools may close. These developments directly influence mathematics education in both positive and negative ways.

A main concern at the heart of this chapter is the question of what it means that the mathematical learning of many students happens in a situation of constant conflict. We have observed a variety of sources of conflict and their possible connections with mathematics and mathematics education. As researchers, we must ask about the characteristics that mathematics education acquires in such situations and about how much we actually know about the meaning of *mathematics education* in environments of ongoing conflicts where teaching and learning nevertheless continue. Is the mathematical experience of, for instance, Northern Irish students the same as that of Danish students? Or was the experience of Lebanese children between 1975 and 1990 – the period of the civil war in the country – similar to that of Colombian students? Abboud (1998) describes the mathematical competencies and understanding of college students in Beirut after the war and comments on their previous school experience:

> We can give a conservative estimate that schools opened for less than two thirds of the required time. When classes were held, material had to be quickly covered, and there was very little time and opportunity for exploration and experimentation to develop higher cognitive skills. Thus, the luxury of exploring, learning concepts and problem solving had to be subordinated to the goal of finishing the curriculum and to prepare the students to sit for the Baccalaureate exams in spite of the war and the continuous interruptions. (p. 52)

There is some recognition of the role that mathematics and mathematics education can play in a particular historical time as a tool in ideological confrontations (Mellin-Olsen, 1987). The evidence found by Mehrtens (1993) about the attempt of the Nazi regime during the Second World War to develop a "German mathematics related to Nazi ideology" (Restivo, 1992, p. 15) raises doubts that mathematics and mathematics education remain neutral in a time of struggle or war. Mathematics education in situations of conflict may get constituted in ways that are particularly significant for the learning experiences of students in that society – and for their ideological upbringing. In South Africa, mathematics was explicitly named and used as a tool to deny access to further opportunities by the apartheid regime (Khuzwayo, 2000). As a consequence, mathematics is still not offered at the senior secondary phase in a significant number of secondary schools. The rise of 'People's Mathematics' (Julie, 1993) as part of the movement of 'People's Education' during the most turbulent times of the uprising against apartheid sought to directly challenge the dominant perspective and offered an alternative, deeply politicised mathematics education.

Another kind of permanent confrontation is that of wealth and poverty found in differing forms and content in both developing and developed countries. Some researchers have begun to analyse what it means to learn and teach mathematics in an under-resourced environment in wealthy countries like the United States (Payne & Biddle, 1999, 2000; Turner, 2000) and in poorer countries like South Africa (Adler, 1998). Mathematics education research related to class conflicts (e.g., Dowling, 1998; Frankenstein, 1995) resonates with, but is also different from that related to poverty, given the vast extent of the inequalities, the numbers of poor learners and poor schools, and the resources needed to address these inequalities in educational systems, particularly in developing countries, in which they are sometimes unavailable and at other times difficult to redistribute. Any equilibration requires political will, legislation, and systemic, structural changes. As inequalities endure, conflicts persist in the competition for scarce resources, opportunities, and service, but mathematics teaching and learning continue where any possibility to do so exists – from the poorest of poor schools to refugee camps to shelters for children who live on the streets to prisons. Within continually war-torn contexts, life resumes its regularity and continues to meet its educational needs. We know little about what happens with mathematics teaching and learning in these environments, except that the mainly large-scale quantitative studies of achievement indicate that these learners do more poorly than those in more favourable environments.

If these are some, among the many possible, sources of conflict in our world – and they are related to mathematics and mathematics education – then we can ask how the field of mathematics education has, in fact, responded to these inequalities and conflicts. What does it mean to develop a strong scholarship in mathematics education – in practice, theory, and research – that brings to the centre what has been underdeveloped, even hidden? We invite mathematics educators and researchers to join us in this search.

HOW IS CONFLICT BEING DEALT WITH IN MATHEMATICS EDUCATION?

To begin to realise a sense of how the notion of conflict features in mathematics education research studies, we examined one of the most comprehensive databases in the field. Searching in the ZDM MATHDI Database for the word *conflict*, we found 100 matching items (see Table 1). Of these, 23 items used the word in a way that was not related to our purposes – for example, in papers about the philosophy of mathematics, general educational essays, or instructional material. Of the remaining 77 items, 47% were related to the idea of *cognitive conflict*. These were papers reporting research exploring student's cognitive conflict in a given mathematical topic, describing the result of experiments using teaching-learning strategies that generated cognitive conflict in students, or reporting on the evolution of students' views about mathematical topics given the emergence of conflict between these views. A second use of the word – in 30% of the entries – was found in papers on *interaction* between teachers and parents or between students and teachers. Many of these papers discussed the effects of classroom interaction or peer interaction on the development of teachers' professional knowledge. A third, less common use of the word – in 12% of the entries – was present in studies dealing with *the cultural dimension of mathematics education* practices and adopting an ethnomathematical point of view, discussing the differences between everyday knowledge and school mathematical knowledge, or concentrating on the whole school mathematical experience of particular people or groups in a foreign environment. The remaining 12% of

Table 1.   Uses of the Word *Conflict* in the Mathematics Education Research Literature

Categories	Frequency	%
Cognitive conflict		
Cognitive conflict	7	
Conflict methodology	14	
Conflicting views	11	
Topics	4	
	36	47
Conflict in the interaction		
Parents-teachers	1	
Classroom	5	
Teachers' professional knowledge	17	
	23	30
Cultural conflict		
Ethnomathematics	2	
School – child's mathematics	3	
Different groups	4	
	9	12
Social and political conflict		
Gender	4	
Politics	5	
	9	12
Total	77	100

Source: MATHDI Database, October 2000.
See *http://euclid.hms.gr/MATH/DI.html*

the entries were papers that considered large *societal conflicts* such as gender issues in connection with future career possibilities and the role of mathematical learning in the power struggles of minority groups or in situations of conflicting social values.

This survey, together with a broader review, leads us to assert that the discussion of conflict cannot be separated from the discussion about *context* in mathematics education research. Conflict is inhered into context. We argue therefore, that a way of approaching confrontations of a social and political nature is through acknowledging them in situations where learning and teaching take place as an integrated part of the study of mathematics education phenomena. The four uses of the word *conflict* in fact coincide with different notions of context.

A first interpretation of *context* present in literature discussing learning processes in mathematics is from a constructivist point of view. 'Cognitive conflict' refers to the mechanism through which a knowledge organisation that is valid in a given developmental stage of thinking comes to be re-accommodated because the individual perceives that her or his cognitive organisation does not allow her or him to approach a given task. The mechanism promotes a re-organisation in actual knowledge structures and therefore can help produce learning. Cognitive conflict is located in the realm of individual cognitive behaviours. A valid interpretation of context is bound to the mathematical task and to what the setting of a mathematical problem might evoke, which triggers the conflict (Wedege, 1999). In a special issue of *Educational Studies in Mathematics* on teaching and learning mathematics in context (see Boero, 1999), 7 of the 12 papers use the word in this sense.

A second interpretation of the words *conflict* and *context* has emerged with the adoption of social constructionism – knowledge has a social nature, and so does mathematical knowledge (e.g., Bloor, 1976; Restivo, 1992) – and of social constructivism – individuals construct knowledge socially (Ernest, 1991; Gergen, 1994). These trends stand on the recognition that "social factors affect the development of mathematical knowledge and, in turn, the conditions for learning mathematics" (Mellin-Olsen, 1992, p. v). One direction in this trend is the empha-sis on social interaction as the sine qua non of learning. In the social interaction between a student and her or his social world represented by the environment of the classroom, the teacher, and other students, more than just cognitive conflicts arise. In this perspective, we could talk about conflict between the teacher's and the students' expectations, beliefs, and so on. This interpretation recognises that interaction in a classroom for the learning and teaching of mathematics is complex and far from being smooth. The reasons for the socio-cognitive conflicts emerge in the characteristics of interpersonal interactions, which constitute their micro-context (De Abreu, 2000).

A third way of connecting conflict and context, which is in fact a further elaboration of the previous interpretation, emanates from the adoption of socio-cultural approaches to cognition in mathematics education (Boaler, 2000; Lave, 1988). In studies using these approaches, the 'situation context' (Wedege, 1999) is related to the evidence that "sociological factors, such as gender, social class, and urban or rural environment [are] associated with children's performances", and that these factors constitute a 'macro-context' (De Abreu, 2000, p. 12). Nevertheless, the influence of these factors is not direct but mediated by some elements of the micro-context of interaction. It makes sense, therefore, to study the way individuals participate in socially organised communities of practice where learning takes place. In this socio-cultural scenario, different conflicts can emerge with relation to mathematical learning: conflicting identities as math-ematics learners or teachers and the conflict between mathematics inside and outside school (Baker, 1996; Nunes, Schliemann, & Carraher, 1993).

From our perspective, the interpretation of *social* in this third kind of study is problematic and underdeveloped. First, it does not transcend the boundaries of the classroom to integrate the full political dimension of the broader social scenario where learning happens. As De Abreu (2000, p. 12) points out, this kind of research does not have enough evidence to argue that sociological differences are directly associated with deep cognitive differences and therefore adopts a mediated view of that possible influence. That is, explanations for mathematics learning, for instance, are not directly connected to macro-structural conflicts that include broad political conflicts – poverty or fear of violence – but are considered indirectly through other data or factors discernible in the classroom environment. Second, even though the adoption of socio-cultural approaches in mathematics education research seems to be related "more to political concerns that inequalities in society were reinforced and reproduced by differential success in school mathematics" (Lerman, 2000, p. 24) than to the realisation in itself of the importance of social theories of learning, this approach does not integrate a political view into the problems of learning and teaching of mathematics. Most research studies taking this approach do not consider context in a broader social and political sense, although there is now an increasing recognition for the need to fully infuse socio-political dimensions into this work.

A fourth connection between conflict and context is evident in the sense that we are conveying. Some developments in mathematics education that have attempted to pay attention to social and political conflicts can be found in areas such as ethnomathematics (e.g., D'Ambrosio, 1985, 1990; Gerdes, 1985, 1988; Knijnik, 1996, 1997, 1998; Powell & Frankenstein, 1997); critical mathematics education (e.g., Frankenstein, 1987, 1995; Mukhopadhyay, 1998; Skovsmose, 1994); gender and mathematics education (e.g., Burton, 1990; Parker, Rennie, & Fraser, 1996; Hanna, 1996; Harris, 1997; Keitel, 1998; Walkerdine, 1998); equity concerns and mathematics education (Rogers & Kaiser, 1995; Secada, Fennema, & Adajian, 1995; Trentacosta & Kenny, 1997); social justice and mathematics education (Cotton, 1998; Gates, 2000; Zevenbergen, 2000b); and anti-racist (e.g., Shan & Bailey, 1991) and multicultural mathematics education (e.g., Gorgorió & Planas, 2000; Nelson, Joseph, & Williams, 1993; Zaslavsky, 1991); and in themes such as mathematics education and democracy (I.M. Christiansen, 1996; D'Ambrosio, 1990; Skovsmose, 1990; Tate, 1996; Valero, 1999a; Vithal, 1999; Volmink, 1994; Woodrow, 1997).

If conflict is being dealt with in some form or other, what then, are our claims? We assert first that the socio-political concerns embedding conflict that have been developed in mathematics education have arguably done so disconnected from, outside of, and parallel to broader mainstream psychological approaches. That is, these concerns have not really been fully integrated into dominant understandings and explanations of teaching and learning mathematics, and hence their recognition in the construction of research questions, methodologies, and theories is seriously limited. Second, much of the development with a concern for social and political conflicts in mathematics education has remained mainly in the domain of theory and prescriptive formulations concerned with advocacy and arguably with much less take-up in practice in broader educational systems. Third, limited development has occurred within research itself; that is, little advance has been made in research processes, criteria, tools of analysis, and forms of representation appropriate to conflict contexts. And fourth, many more areas still need to be problematised and conceived of as situations of social and political conflict. More varied sites for research are needed as well as research into aspects such as mathematics teacher education, policy research, and even mathematics education research communities themselves, nationally and internationally. Our contention is that if we accept that the world nowadays is fraught with conflicts and that mathematics education has in fact something to do with that world, then we need to go much further and deeper in searching the implications of considering the impact of a conflict-laden world not only in mathematics education in general but also in the broad range of mathematics education research. We must also ask the question in reverse: What could mathematics education and its research contribute to living in and making sense of such a world?

WHAT CHALLENGES DO SITUATIONS OF SOCIAL AND POLITICAL CONFLICT POSE FOR MATHEMATICS EDUCATION RESEARCH?

In the remainder of the chapter, we explore the question of the challenges that situations of conflict pose for mathematics education research. We offer as starting points for the discussion two research projects. One of us has been involved in each project over the last few years. We have tried to grapple in these projects with the issues of conflict and context in a broader sense. We do not contend that prescriptions can be advanced for researching in situations of conflict. Rather, we offer ideas and illustrations to illuminate our ways of working and thinking when doing research in such situations.

Paola's Study: 'Reform, Democracy, and Secondary School Mathematics'

My doctoral research builds on three main concerns. First, during the 1990s, there has been an international trend of reform initiatives in the teaching and learning of school mathematics (Clarke, Clarke, & Sullivan, 1996). Despite the efforts of national governments to move these practices into a more desirable direction, not very much has been achieved. Second, ideas of change put forward a discourse that connects mathematics education with democracy. Although there is no concrete meaning for what this connection is about and how it is actually to be achieved, advocates expect that teachers can provide an education that contributes to the consolidation of democracy in those countries. Nevertheless, the changes in policy documents and in discourse remain distant from effective transformations of school mathematics practices. Third, the research literature on change in many countries (e.g., Brodie, 1997; Skott, 2000) has concentrated on exploring isolated factors as the centre of the inefficacy of reform initiatives. There is a critical need to explore change processes in mathematics education inside the structure of the school as a whole (e.g., Perry, Valero, Castro, Gómez, & Agudelo, 1998; Valero, Gómez, & Perry, 1997).

My research work provides further development of the idea that the functioning of the teaching and learning of mathematics inside a school is a system in which at least three types of actors intervene: the school leaders, the group of mathematics teachers in the school, and the teacher as an individual in his or her classroom. The institutional system of mathematics education (ISME) (Perry et al., 1998) gives an account of the interactions among these three in order to constitute the mathematics education in a school. Is this a powerful idea to explore the complexity that actually takes place in a school in relation to change in the teaching and learning of mathematics? Can this theory be developed further from a socio-political perspective to give an account of how that system works in relation to the concerns for a democratic mathematics education in a process of change? With these questions in mind, I approached my research task.

I decided to study these issues in the case of three schools in three very different social, political, and cultural contexts: Nyspor School[3] in a municipality close to Copenhagen, Denmark; Rajas Secondary School,[4] a predominantly 'Indian' school in Durban, South Africa; and Esperanza Secondary School[5] in a working class area of Bogotá, Colombia. My intention was not to compare them but rather to contrast my initial theoretical starting point and see whether it made sense – and how – in each context. I visited each school for around 3 to 4 weeks and collected different kinds of information about the way leaders, teachers as a collectivity, and teachers as individuals worked in the school in building mathematics education practices. A varied set of data emerged from documents, classroom observations, participation in group meetings, interviews with the mathematics teachers and school leaders, and many informal talks about what was going on in the schools in relation to mathematics. I collected the information about each school in a 'scrapbook', an open folder in which I had notes about my observations that the teachers and leaders could look at as a basis for our interviews and discussions. They also contributed to the scrapbook by giving me material that they considered relevant for me to grasp the functioning of school mathematics in their institution.

The process of collecting information was itself a learning process for me inasmuch as I could not only sharpen my observations and questions, but also develop more clarity about the way I wanted to interact with teachers, leaders, and students in the schools. My theoretical critical perspective came to be realised as well in my presence in the schools. What do you do when talking with a teacher who is criticising the bureaucratisation of her time and, in the middle of the conversation, the union leader pops in – constraining the teacher's opinions? How do you face a situation in which you could not get to interview a teacher because he 'was ill again' – and failed to attend school regularly – or simply because he did not have a moment of free time to answer your questions given the alteration of schedule because of a teacher strike? How do you deal with the expectations of teachers, leaders, and students that they will receive feedback about what you as a researcher 'see'? Or what role do you play when you have to stand in for one of the teachers with whom you have been interacting, in a lesson you intended to observe, because the teacher could not come to school that day? Again, there could be very many alternatives for reacting to these situations, each with different consequences for the research process. My reactions in particular situations in these three schools constitute a support for my reflections about how to deal with situations of social and political conflict in mathematics education research.

Renuka's Study: 'A Social, Cultural, Political Approach to a Mathematics Curriculum'

I introduce student teachers to what may be referred to as a social, cultural, and political approach to a mathematics curriculum as part of their mathematics education major (Vithal, 1997). This introduction brings together ideas about ethnomathematics; critical mathematics education; issues of gender, race, and class; and South Africa's own legacy of people's mathematics that could be realised through practices such as project work in a mathematics class. For my doctoral study, I was interested to see what student teachers would do with such ideas and practices, which are mostly imported from other contexts (Vithal, 2000a). I constructed a research design in which the student teachers who accepted the invitation to participate in the study, the teachers in school, and myself as teacher educator/researcher could jointly interpret these theoretical ideas and practices for our classrooms in a two-phase teaching practice programme. The first phase did not take place, because as protest action intensified, the university was shut down. Instead, I held several preparation sessions, but even these were erratically attended because of student mass meetings and other related events. So the student teachers were left on their own to negotiate in schools for an opportunity to try out what they and many principals and teachers considered were to be projects with 'radical ideas'.

Ironically, the university closure gave several student teachers the opportunity to identify and visit the schools in which they were going to do their teaching practice and to meet and talk with teachers. Two weeks into the second phase of teaching practice, just as I began to develop a systematic plan for data collection across the 7 schools in which the student teachers were based, teacher strikes began. Every school in my study was affected with varying degrees of disruption and with different outcomes. Because I did not want to see students' participation disappear from the study and because of the differential impact of the strike on the student teachers' work, I began to consider the notion of 'disruptive' data and the politics of doing mathematics education research in South Africa (Vithal, 1998). What could be learnt in the study from the students' participation in this constant instability and change? How could 'no data' be construed as data? Further, the vast diversity in contexts and conditions made it important for the student teachers and me to think together – to imagine and to anticipate hypothetical situations as the current actual classroom situation was specially arranged for research (Vithal, 2000c; Skovsmose & Borba, 2000).

As a result of the disruption, my inability to be present in each school to work with the student teachers and to produce data from each school brought further modifications to the research process. I had to rely more heavily on the student teachers to assist in data production, which they did to differing degrees and depending also on the availability of resources such as telephones, electricity, and audio-recorders in the school. Besides the disruptions, the material conditions within which and according to which the research proceeded also affected the quantity and quality of the data. My unequal participation across the study also had consequences for my relationship with the student teachers, particularly those students in whose project I was less physically present. Only 6 of the 12 student teachers participated in developing and presenting a joint paper on their projects at a national mathematics education conference (Vithal et al., 1997). This paper was negotiated at the start of the study as an outcome they wanted from participating in the research. My study took up this initial analysis that we collectively developed.

A wide variety of data were collected, including interviews with all the main players, classroom videos, journals, and written documentation. The 'crucial' case description I finally wrote up in my dissertation was that of only one student teacher Sumaiya Desai (Vithal, 2000a). It was constructed from the happenings captured in a grade 6 mathematics classroom over a 6-week period as the project spilled into lunch breaks and other lesson times made possible by Sumaiya's involvement as teacher and co-researcher. Still, my account is privileged as I organised and analysed the case description into five dual-concept themes – authority and democracy, structure and freedom, mathematics and context, differentiation and equity, and actuality and potentiality – each pair of which I theorise are in a relationship best captured by the notion of complementarity (Otte, 1990, 1994). Complementarity as a theoretical analytical tool grasps the complexity of the classroom, allowing us to see both co-operation and contradiction. From these theoretical developments, I put forward a pedagogy of conflict and dialogue also underpinned by complementarity.

Using these two examples and drawing on a broad range of literature inside and outside mathematics education, we examine three broad aspects of research: (a) the kinds of questions asked in mathematics education research that together come to produce a research agenda, (b) the research methodologies and theories employed and developed, and (c) the criteria for evaluating what is deemed quality research. We explore the challenges to existing research trends and traditions that a concern with social and political conflict situations brings. We also look at some developments in research that have attempted to take account of such issues both in mathematics education and outside it.

CHALLENGING AND OPENING RESEARCH QUESTIONS AND AGENDAS

Research begins with questions or concerns. On what kinds of questions is mathematics education currently focussing? No doubt some of the roots of mathematics education research lie in the association between mathematics and psychology, as argued by Kilpatrick (1992). This link has in many ways shaped the questions in which mathematics education as a field or discipline has engaged. A recent handbook on research in mathematics and science education (Kelly &

Lesh, 2000) with a strong North American focus seems to show how deeply rooted and enduring the psychological traditions and perspectives are in mathematics education. In their chapter on research agendas, problems, and theories, Lesh and Lovitts (2000) write:

> We have underlined psychological issues more than other perspectives, because during the past few decades, some of the most productive branches of mathematics and science education research have focussed their investigations on how the ways of thinking of students, teachers, or others who are involved in mathematics and science education develop. Therefore, these are the areas where the development of new design areas has flourished. (p. 49)

We do not disagree. Indeed, this emphasis is reflected in the majority of research designs and procedures discussed in the book. But we argue that this orientation in itself is inadequate to address the kinds of issues raised in the same book when attempting to address, for instance, the challenges of systemic reform concerned with equity and quality, as discussed by Confrey (2000), or when focussing on 'all students' as mathematics and science education reform movements require (Romberg & Collins, 2000) and which invariably involve forms of conflict. In this work and in others such as the volumes edited by Sierpinska and Kilpatrick (1998), the research questions and concerns of situations of conflict, though mentioned, remain underrepresented and underdeveloped.

Analyses of the kinds of articles appearing in international journals and conferences by Gómez (2000) and Skovsmose and Valero (2001b) provide further indication of the dominance of studies focusing on the triad of teacher-mathematics-students in the context of the classroom and mainly from a broad psychological perspective. Although such studies provide valuable insights into particular teaching-learning aspects of specific mathematical notions, they lack a wider location in larger systems of practice and hence limit their explanatory power. For example, one could question the validity of claims made about a student's understanding of particular concepts in mathematics produced out of analysis of data collected through carefully constructed tests and mathematically focused interviews if knowing and doing well in mathematics are not valued in the student's family or community, or if a particular performance could have other negative consequences in other parts of the student's life in the classroom or outside it. If schools and classrooms are part of society, and society is seen as constituting a myriad of different conflicts, then the possibility of 'observing' conflicts or any associated aspect requires the researcher to consider the 'whole life', the 'whole class', and the 'whole school' as units of analysis in the research even if the focus is on exploring a specific aspect of mathematics education.

In Paola's research, the units of analysis were the school organisation and the interactions among the different actors who participate in the practices of mathematics education. This meant that mathematics education was viewed through the complexity of the interactions between different people and in different scenarios – not only in the classroom but also in teachers' meetings, spaces for administrative decision making, and spaces for professional interaction. Opening the focus of explanation for the way in which ideas of reform are brought to practice by the teachers in the classroom and in the school organisation as a whole allows one to explore the complexity of the different social interpretations of theoretical formulations of reform and of the multiple reasons and social enactments of those ideas in multiple levels and spaces. When one explores reform, democracy, and mathematics education in this complex scenario, central ideas emerge: the strong determinant force of the social, political, cultural, and economic context in which a school is immersed; the relevance of school mathematics as seen from the perspective of students' envisioned possibilities for their future life; the dynamics of professional development among the mathematics teachers in a school; and the creation of meaning in the classroom as the result of the meeting between the teachers' 'multiple motives for practice' (Skott, 2000) and the students' perceived relevance of their school mathematical experience (Valero, 2000).

An unintended but nevertheless serious consequence of a research agenda that cumulatively focuses on some specific aspect of, say, conceptual understanding in mathematics also comes to produce a particular view of teachers and learners that places the blame for teachers' or learners' 'poor' or problematic understanding on themselves. After all, much of the research seeks to improve the situation, and mostly for those who fail to learn or know mathematics, it then also selects and inadvertently pathologises particular groups who invariably are the marginalised groups in that context. The more dominant psychological approaches and perspectives need to be brought into dialogue with and developed in relation to others, such as socio-political analyses, to make broader theoretical connections to better understand how particular knowledge, beliefs, attitudes, meanings, and actions come to be produced through particular life trajectories that include diverse reasons and conditions for learning mathematics and its expression in different spaces.

The reasons for opening and broadening questions posed in mathematics education research are particularly important in situations of social and political conflict because of the unstable and disruption prone nature of such environments. In Renuka's study, the research question was posed broadly: "What happens in a mathematics classroom when an attempt is made to realise a social, cultural political approach?" This broadness helps one to anticipate a situation in which it might seem that the research is constantly in danger of collapsing. If flexibility about the research focus and eventual questions is accepted, then several opportunities also seem to be opened. For example, the focus of the study could have moved closer to the student teachers; different aspects of their understanding and interpretation of a social, cultural, and political approach to the curriculum could be explored. The study could have also taken a closer look across schools to examine what happens to mathematics teaching and learning as a result of such disruptions, which are a frequent feature of the educational system in South Africa. How far a researcher might be moved out of her or his initial research focus depends on many different issues, including the severity and length of a particular disruption, the stage of the research in which disruptions happen, the nature and content of the disruption, and the part of the educational system the disruption affects. Broadening or opening the research focus or question does not imply diminishing rigour, clarity, or connectedness in the research design; instead, it allows for flexibility and shifts in a study to improve relevance, responsiveness to context, and possibilities for alternative, even conflicting, analyses that lead to deeper insights.

This point on managing the research focus could be counteracted by arguing that the research site should be carefully chosen in anticipating disruptions. If the main focus is to investigate how student teachers are interpreting a particular approach in practice, choosing schools in areas in which strike action is not likely to take place, such as former 'White' schools in South Africa, would be a safer option. Although this course of action would mean taking a school that does not reflect the broader context, it would have been convenient from a methodological perspective. In this way, we have argued elsewhere (Valero & Vithal, 1998) that researchers in situations of widespread social and political conflict can continue to do 'good' quality research that is methodologically 'correct' but that is marginally relevant to the broader context in which they are working. Researchers can also struggle with doing 'poor' quality research given disruptions that alter the selection of questions and processes but that may result in shedding light on problems that are more relevant to a whole setting or broader regional context.

As a researcher chooses a question for study, she or he has in mind the places in which the study is to be conducted. Open and flexible research foci make it possible to work across very different research settings in ways that are unlikely to set up some as deficient in relation to others. Selecting radically diverse contexts makes powerfully visible the taken-for-granted research assumptions and challenges one's analyses and theories. For instance, three situations are captured in Paola's research.

- In Nyspor School, Gitte, an eighth-grade girl, sits alone at the front of the middle row in Mette's classroom. All the other students sit in pairs. Mette, a young teacher, gives some special tasks to Gitte but most of the time concentrates on helping the other students in the class. The interaction between Gitte and the other students is surprising. They command her to do little things for them: "Gitte, pass me the ruler", "Gitte, pick up the eraser from the floor". When Mette is asked about Gitte, she explains that the girl has learning difficulties. "It's even a family thing", Mette says. "At the beginning, I tried to give her attention but I cannot do it all the time. It's very time consuming". Gitte spends her school life and her mathematical experience as a lonely girl.
- In Rajas Secondary School, many students walk a long distance to school. Most are 'African' students whose parents make an effort to provide them with the necessary means to attend an 'ex-Indian' school. Most of the time, these students are in groups. They are together in class, during breaks, and

when going down the hill to return to their homes in other areas of the city. In mathematics lessons, they do not participate much, and they almost always get a failing mark in the assessment tasks. It appears that allowing 'African' students into this school is an issue of letting outsiders 'creep into' instead of making them legitimate insiders.

* In Esperanza School, Andrés and José, two teenage students, show little interest in their mathematics lessons. Talking about the possibilities that learning mathematics might open in their lives, they show more concern about escaping from an unpromising social situation. School and mathematics have little to offer. José says, "The only class I would like to pay attention to is English because I want to get out of this fucking country and go to the U.S.". Why should Andrés and José study mathematics if there appears to be no future for them?

From the literature on equity and social justice, these three cases could be interpreted as raising problems that have to do with the exclusion of particular individuals in a particular classroom setting on the grounds of their ability, gender, race, or social class. Under that interpretation, one could base explanations of a particular kind of student behaviour on their belonging to a category of people who are disadvantaged by their own intrinsic characteristics like gender, beliefs, or motivations (Brew, Pearn, Leder, & Bishop, 1998; Forgasz, 1998) or by the dominant ways in which mathematics education happens in the school (Boaler, 1997). But one could also offer alternative interpretations of the three episodes from the perspective of the various practices that in the school as a whole result in the creation and perpetuation of these situations for many students. One can look at the general frame of the school in a society that is connected with the situation. In the case of Gitte, the particular democratic conception of Danish schooling that allows all students the right to have a basic education might be the reason for Gitte to be accommodated not in a different learning environment but in her neighbourhood school. The conception results in a paradox in which this attempt at inclusion is manifested in a systematic disadvantage for her. We could broaden the focus to look at the way the teachers are organised in the school and the impact of that organisation on the situation described. In the current structure of teachers' work in Danish primary and lower secondary schools, there are formal spaces of interaction among teachers by grade, class, and interdisciplinary teams, but not by specific school subjects. This structure means that teachers co-operate systematically with teachers from other subjects – it is usual to have mathematics, Danish, and social science teachers working together – but very seldom to collaborate among, say, colleagues teaching mathematics. Mette, as a young, inexperienced teacher, had many questions and doubts about how to deal with her eighth-grade class, among them what to do for Gitte as a person and mathematically. Could it be that the lack of a professional group influences the contribution that Mette can make to Gitte's mathematical and personal development?

In Esperanza School teachers do work together as a professional group, yet what possibility do they have for engaging Andrés and José in mathematics? One could also look at the participation in school mathematics of Gitte, Andrés, José, and the 'African' students in terms of their background in school or in society, but especially in terms of their foreground (Skovsmose, 1994) – understood as their perceptions about their future possibilities that schools and societies make available given their current social condition. In this way, one can offer multiple explanations that draw on more than the students' belonging to a particular disadvantaged group to understand their positioning in the classroom.

Inequities related to gender, ability, class, and race – not to mention language or religion – are part of the complex networks of practice in which school mathematics education is embedded. Possibilities for strongly linking the conflicting context of schooling with mathematics education are particularly visible when mathematics curricula invite teachers to bring outside reality into the classroom to improve relevance. This invitation means that the inequalities and injustices and their associated conflicts are also carried into the classroom, and in diverse classrooms they are embodied in the learners themselves. Friendship groups from outside the classroom and the school, which are often based on associations of gender, race, and class, are carried into group activities that involve mathematics. In Renuka's research, this continuation of associations showed up in the group projects such as 'Money Spent on My Education' and 'Time Spent After School'. These groupings sometimes served to control and dominate the interactions and activities and hence shaped the quality of learning taking place in a group, but they were also challenged at times. The inequalities and conflicts of society, which played out differently in the different groups, were laid bare in the classroom project presentations and discussion.

For example, Devan, whose relative affluence was visible in the discussions and graphs the students each drew to show the money spent on their education, pointed out Harry's graph to the whole class: "Harry lives in Clermont, and every day he comes from Clermont to [school], which costs quite a bit of money. ... And it's quite hard because Harry actually leaves at five o'clock in the morning." Devan, an 'Indian' student had said just a few minutes earlier that his transport cost one hundred rands a year, "Because I live down the road". Whereas Harry, an 'African' student, had indicated one thousand rands on his graph in travelling from one of the 'African' townships to this school in a predominantly middle class 'Indian' area. These inequalities are not taken further, however, and the discussion gets directed into other aspects and, most importantly, into the mathematical 'correctness' of the graph. Unless our research questions open us to broader probing of and explanations for what learners and teachers say and do, we also miss the opportunity to offer the means to make mathematics classrooms into places in which the injustices of society, as revealed by mathematics, can be discussed and debated.

Besides broadening research foci, we also ask what kinds of research questions are not being adequately addressed in places in which social and political conflicts seem to be deeper and broader. In his discussion of the possible contributions of research in mathematics education in developing countries, Gómez (2000) concludes that "mathematics education research ... shows very little production in those themes related to the practices that influence somehow the teaching and learning of mathematics from the institutional or national point of view" (pp. 1–2). To attend to conflicts, one needs to understand and explain the larger forces that shape mathematics education. One can point to, for example, macro concerns such as research in national policy development or policy implementation to ensure equitable outcomes in a host of areas related to mathematics education. These concerns are often dominant in developing countries given the societal restructuring and transformations taking place and the recognition of the pivotal role mathematics – together with science and technology – plays in addressing poverty and underdevelopment. Mathematics educators and researchers from such countries often participate in initiatives at national or regional levels with greater possibilities to affect change than in developed nations with more entrenched systems. Hence their under-representation in bringing these concerns to international attention and into the international literature impoverishes mathematics education as a field of practice and study. As a consequence, the possibility is reduced for mathematics educators to recognise and develop the scholarship needed to understand, research, and work in situations of social and political conflict.

The need for a different research agenda in mathematics education about understanding and contributing to 'systemic reforms' that are currently underway in many countries is being recognised. Confrey (2000), speaking to the U.S. context, argues for research directions to be changed in order to guide, assess, and support reform efforts; she points to the urgency of the situation because these processes are already being carried out widely. In countries where human and material resources are limited, the mathematics education research community is small, and policy decisions require research, there is considerable pressure on mathematics education research to contribute to these large-scale initiatives across diverse classrooms and conditions. Research may demonstrate the power and success of particular 'progressive' processes, tasks, materials, and technologies in smaller and restricted settings of particular mathematics classrooms, but much less is known about their meaning when recontextualised in the diversity of broader and changing systems.

For example, open-ended tasks and investigative approaches that require students to discuss ideas and that are deemed 'good' practices presuppose specially qualified teachers with interest and motivation, particular resources and conditions for teaching and learning, and a particular culture of students' questioning and challenging ideas in the school and classroom. The challenge is that of developing and researching innovative ideas for teaching and learning in, for example, smaller 'teaching experiments' (Kelly & Lesh, 2000), in particular settings, but then opening for critique the outcomes of their theoretical ideas and their practice with further research in more diverse or unstable settings – particularly where the resources provided by the researcher are not available. Indeed, the sustainability of innovations by teachers and schools after the research phase is completed is not well documented. It is also in this respect that researchers have much to gain in having their work developed more rigorously by locating their research in situations of social and political conflict.

Whether researchers in the developed world intend it or not, their research is taken up in less-developed countries in which the capacity to mount studies is limited. The internationalisation and globalisation of the content and practices of mathematics education are not new (Atweh & Clarkson, 2001). Nevertheless, we see that this universalism is now supported by the generalisation of theories and methodologies, as well as the indiscriminate adoption of research findings. National curriculum policies in many countries pressure teachers to engage these ideas even when their validity and suitability may not have been considered or researched in diverse educational settings. Disastrous outcomes may arise when teachers try out such ideas in the uneven contexts so characteristic of places where social and political conflict is present, such as large, diverse, multilingual classes whose teachers are not secure in their knowledge of the mathematics or the educational ideas that they are required to work with. In such contexts, where the severe widespread lack of physical space and learning materials is evident, so-called 'progressive practices' may ironically produce poorer learning outcomes than traditional teaching would.

The absence of a broader policy-related research agenda means that not enough research and discussion seem to be taking place about how policies related to mathematics curricula are being developed at national or local levels, what impact they are having at a system level in the full range of schools and classrooms that constitutes any education system, what forces are driving successive waves of national reforms in mathematics curricula within the broader socio-political transformations, and what kinds of theorising would enhance our understanding of systemic processes in relation to micro-classroom aspects of mathematics education. This gap minimises opportunities for research to significantly affect practice. The gap is crucial also for understanding how macro-level changes shape in various ways what researchers do or can do, as well as how and why teachers and schools may choose to participate in the reforms as well as related research. After carrying out curriculum research in a period of constant structural, curriculum and policy change in the educational system of England and Wales, Paechter (2000) concludes the following:

> Changes at the macro-level can have far-reaching effects even on explicitly micro-focused research. In circumstances in which rapid changes are taking place in national policies, it is essential to set up the research in such a way as to be able to make significant changes in focus without losing the spirit of ones original aims, even if these aims have to be modified in the light of experience in the field. (p. 34)

If mathematics education research is to respond in relevant and meaningful ways to a continually and rapidly changing, conflict ridden, and disruption prone environment in which mathematics and mathematics education play a key role, then the dearth of policy-related research in the field points to the need for new research questions to be posed, for methodologies and quality criteria to be fundamentally rethought, and for a search to be undertaken for different theoretical tools to better explain and act in this changing world.

No doubt a common agenda for national reforms in different countries is needed to improve both equity and quality in mathematics education. Confrey (2000) argues for these two as complementary goals in guiding the selection of priorities in research in the United States. But this analysis needs to be deepened and extended from any within-country research priorities to understanding how mathematics education is recruited and implicated in the challenges and dangers of globalisation and internationalisation (Keitel & Knijnik, 2000; Skovsmose & Valero, 2001b). Recognising the functioning of mathematics education beyond a narrow educational reality of a country, to a broader socio-political reality of the 'global village', the myths and fictions it produces – particularly in relation to 'the promises and perils of the new information technologies' – can allow us to understand and act on, through research, goals seeking social justice. A wider-angle lens on such goals makes more easily visible the sources of inequalities and conflicts in the path of equity and fairness to gaining a mathematics education. These macro global forces play out in ways that make it necessary to come to grips with "the contradictory demands and measures for new qualities of teaching, learning and mathematics education research" (Keitel & Knijnik, 2000) within and across countries. Attending to these issues, revealed in critiques of international studies (Keitel & Kilpatrick, 1998), can open a fuller, richer understanding of the field and a researcher's work and positioning in it.

CHALLENGING AND OPENING RESEARCH METHODOLOGIES AND THEORIES

Research questions are dealt with by researchers adopting a view on the focus of their study and how to approach that focus. That is, research questions go together with theories and methodologies. In a research process these get mutually constituted. If this statement is accepted, then we can ask whether the intention of recognising situations of political and social conflicts in research in mathematics education is a decision that the researcher makes a priori, or whether it is a position that gets developed during the research process.

Paola's study was guided by the following principles in the process of producing data about the practices of mathematics education within the frame of the school organisation. First, the intention and research questions were made available to the people who participated in the research. This principle was part of considering teachers and leaders as dialogic partners (Kögler, 1999) in a process of inquiry rather than as 'objects or subjects of study'. A consequence of this principle was that information collected in the form of notes in a scrapbook was open to the participants, as were the researcher's initial interpretations of the teachers' and leaders' actions. This information and these interpretations were shared in conversations that challenged the researcher's perceptions as much as the participants' points of view and reasons for action. A second, connected principle was the reluctance to 'force' any data collection method that could 'violently' intrude into the lives of people in the school, positioning the researcher as an 'objective outsider' who collects data and interprets it in ways completely unknown to the participants. Hence, Paola shared and negotiated her emerging initial analysis. This approach meant that more than 'objective' observation protocols or recordings of interviews, the data acquired the form of notes from formal and informal conversations, transcriptions of classroom sessions and interviews that built on exchanges about situations of the school life, some photographs, and mainly the systematic reconstruction by the researcher of the episodes that were experienced as significant in relation to the conceptual ideas that were being explored. This principle meant that the collection of data took place in the natural setting in ways that attempted to respect the lives of the participants and their institution. Although it might have been ideal to have interview conversations with all the mathematics teachers in every school, it was not possible to impose the researcher's need for information on the teachers' minimal availability of time amongst their multiple occupations. Reconstruction based on notes taken after informal conversations with the teachers who were not interviewed constituted an alternative source of data. The point is not to deny the presence and participation of the researcher in the very setting being studied but to become aware of her impact and to manage it differently.

Such an approach to data production can be read as a deficient methodological design and, as a consequence, a polluted, incomplete corpus of data that is problematic for the objectivity and substantiation of possible interpretations and claims. One could say that the failure to collect 'complete' data raises questions about the validity of the conclusions, that declaring the researcher's intentions to the participants generates doubts about the objectivity of the information collected and, therefore, of the claims, and that the reliance on subjective reconstruction of episodes and interactions by the researcher raises uncertainty about the credibility of the data set and, therefore, of the whole study and its possible generalisability. The researcher, then, can be judged as failing the basic standards of a 'scientific' endeavour. Such an evaluation depends, however, on the research perspective and approach taken in the study. What the adoption of these methodological principles seeks is a more explicit coherence between a theoretical positioning concerning educational phenomena and its practical manifestations in doing research.

Whether a researcher considers the above as a contamination or corruption of the research reveals the researcher's positioning within particular research paradigms – "belief systems based on ontological, epistemological and methodological assumptions" (Guba & Lincoln, 1998). If research journals and recent handbooks published in mathematics education (Bishop, Clements, Keitel, Kilpatrick, & Laborde, 1996; Grouws, 1992; Kelly & Lesh, 2000; Sierpinska & Kilpatrick, 1998) are taken as indicating the current state of debates and developments in mathematics education research, then it seems reasonable to conclude that the critical paradigm, which most explicitly and directly takes up the concern with conflict, is significantly underrepresented. This situation contrasts with the strong and increasing scholarship in critical perspectives taken up in the social sciences and in general education (e.g., Apple, 1996; Freire, 1999; Giroux, 1997; Macedo, 1999; McLaren & Giarelli, 1995; Popkewitz, 1991, 1998a, 1998b), where research, theories, and methodologies have developed, diversified, and broadened in the critical paradigm. This concern has not been taken up as seriously in mathematics education research, even more when conflict is under consideration, despite the rise in advocacy of such approaches in teaching and learning mathematics and an increasing focus on social, cultural, and political dimensions of mathematics education.

If we turn to mathematics education literature for theoretical and methodological developments, the concern with social and political conflicts may be seen in at least two areas that have received attention recently, namely, critical mathematics education and ethnomathematics, including some works in gender and social class. Much of this work is arguably inspired by and draws on education and social science developments from the broad and extending paradigm described above but has admittedly seen more theoretical advances and ideas for practice than have developments in research methodology. Nonetheless, we refer to and reflect on some emerging theoretical and methodological issues from research in these and related areas that attempts to take account of conflict.

As a field of study and practice, ethnomathematics seeks to give mathematical voice particularly to those deemed disadvantaged. The inequalities in the experiences of such people is present also in any research setting that involves them – in the processes, relationships, and outcomes. The researcher, by virtue of her or his resources in knowledge and skills as a researcher, even if from the group, is positioned differently (Setati, 2000; Smith, 1999). Knijnik (1996, 1997, 1998, 2000) discusses characteristics of research work in the mathematical literacy of landless communities in Brazil. She conceptualises this ethnomathematical research and the mathematical literacy practices as essentially political activities. Research in such an environment has two dimensions. The first dimension deals with the "investigation of the traditions, practices and mathematics concepts of a social group". Of fundamental importance is that Knijnik is aware that her reading of another's culture is not an innocent, objective action but rather her interpretation and re-writing. She states the ethical principle that she is not treating the material collected as 'rocks' that, as a researcher, she could bring home and analyse in a laboratory. Instead, she engages in a continuous process of feedback to the community about her interpretations through a pedagogical process in which the group can interpret and decode its knowledge, acquire the knowledge produced by academic mathematics, and analyse the power relations emerging from the application of each. The second dimension of research tackles one's own actions as the focus of research. One interprets one's practice to break the distinction between who does the research and who is researched. By bridging the gap between this double role, Knijnik can carry out research that is sensitive and committed to the interests of the Landless Movement and its concerns as a human group in a political struggle. An important point is that the researcher has to pay attention to both the broader processes and the consequences of her or his research in any study that attempts to mathematise the practices of people who face and experience conflicts and inequalities.

Theoretical developments that explicitly recognise social and political conflicts may also be observed in the work of Skovsmose (1994), who in building a philosophy of critical mathematics education identifies as a basic assumption "that society is fraught with conflicts and crisis" (p. 12). To this assumption, he connects notions of critique, democracy, emancipation, and empowerment to arrive at a concept of *mathemacy* as a double-edged sword similar to literacy as developed in critical education (drawing on, e.g., Freire, Giroux, and Critical Theory). A main argument is that if people are to have the possibility of acting in a society fraught with conflicts, mathematics education will need to provide more than the ability to know and use formal techniques. "Mathematics as a radical construct, has to be rooted in the spirit of critique and the project of possibility that enables people to participate in the transformation of their society and, therefore, mathemacy becomes a precondition for social and cultural emancipation" (p. 27). Two issues – theoretical and methodological – arise from the work elaborated in this area (see Skovsmose & Nielsen, 1996). First, much of this theoretical work is rather silent on what it means to attempt such a mathematics education when the conflicts are not out there in society but embodied and alive in the classroom or school, and when they refer to the students and teachers themselves. Second, what are the methodological tools and processes for researching these ideas? When the classroom or school itself produces conflicts that explode chaotically and impact in all kinds of unforeseen ways, a fundamental rethinking about research questions, processes, relationships, identities, and ethics becomes necessary – not just as posing practical problems to be dealt with technically or idiosyncratically in a study but also as raising foundational questions about what it means to know anything about teachers and learners. This rethinking means that research is itself seen as socially constructed and politically enacted within shifting relations of power and knowledge and as tied to particular material conditions in which people make choices about their participation and about what to reveal and to conceal in their thoughts and actions, implicitly or explicitly.

No doubt a theoretical orientation that recognises a concern for conflict enhances recognition of different methodological and analytical conflicts in research. The 'theoretical tools' developed in the methodology of Renuka's study attempted to respect student teachers and teachers similarly – not as implementers of a particular curriculum approach but as intellectual beings who bring different thoughts, reasons, and dreams to bear on what they do and say in mathematics classrooms. Thus, the study posited a hypothetical, imagined situation in which researcher and research participants brought their collective thoughts and actions with all their conflicts and hopes into an existing classroom situation to create a different, arranged situation for research (Skovsmose & Borba, 2000; Vithal, 2000c).

The point is not only about how teachers can somehow become co-researchers but also about how teachers can be valued as practitioners within an endeavour of scientific knowledge production. The volatility and unpredictability of situations of conflict 'force' researchers to rethink their roles, relations, and reasons for engaging in a particular research study. These considerations and involvements make research in conflict environments generative, opening possibilities for revealing new dimensions of particular theoretical concepts because multiple vantage points and perspectives are considered essential to the research. Therefore, theory building requires that ideas developed in one setting be continually reinterpreted and recontextualised (Bernstein, 1996) in others, most notably in situations of conflict. However, to be open to this process requires an approach to research premised on different assumptions and concerns. Choice, negotiation, reciprocity, reflexivity, flexibility, change, and instability of context, disruption, and discontinuity have to be embraced and worked into the research (Vithal, 2000c).

These aspects are exemplified in the studies cited above and also in Renuka's study, in which the empirical work eventually comes to yield a pedagogy of conflict and dialogue for mathematics education (Vithal, 2001b). Such a pedagogy renders conflict normal, natural, and, in fact, required in a mathematics classroom or school that seeks to engage the actual and potential reality of students' and teachers' lives. Many and varied conflicts may arise at different distances from their lives. Still, the point is not to resolve them but to find the means to understand their nature and learn how to act towards them. Hence dialogue becomes an essential didactical tool for exploring both agreement and disagreement, containing the dimensions of both reflection and action. Conflict and dialogue are in a complex complementarity; they both co-operate and contradict each other. In a classroom, the nature and outcome of a conflict dialogue cannot be predetermined. Where conflicts arise from structural inequalities, there may be little chance for teachers and students to significantly alter the sources of conflict, which may lead to goals opposite from those envisaged in a culturally, socially, or politically relevant mathematics curriculum (see Duba, 2001).

This theoretical development is underpinned by particular methodological principles that problematise methodology and theory, as well as the relation between them in research. Situations of social and political conflict make visible a much deeper problem inherent in the possible dissonance of an educational theory and the assumptions on which any methodology rests that plans to use that theory in some way. If a theory seeks to advance a particular relationship between teachers and learners, the methodology must also attempt to respect and reflect a relationship of similar quality between researcher and research participants (Vithal, 2000c; Skovsmose & Borba, 2000). If one uses a theory that expounds a view of learners, say, as constructing their own knowledge or as independent and critical agents, then this same view must be maintained within the research methodology and in relationships for the production of data. In Paola's study, mathematics education in a school is conceived of as a network of practices grounded in a broader social, political, cultural, and economic context in which people have reasons to act and position themselves through their interaction with others concerning the teaching and learning of mathematics. Consequently, the role of the researcher as an intruder in that network needs to be understood more as that of a participant in such a network. If the intention of highlighting power in those practices cannot be disconnected, then so too must be the conscious and enacted adoption of a position by the researcher in that network. Still, the choice is to make explicit that positioning – what is considered theoretically, methodologically, and ethically correct from the researcher's perspective.

Several issues arise from this argument that reveal the researcher's positioning in the research. One issue is how she or he understands and manages the theoretical and ideological assumptions in choosing to act in particular ways as a researcher (e.g., in resolving the objectivity-subjectivity dilemma), the quality of research relationships constructed, and what the researcher will construe as data and choose to analyse. Another is how the analysis is conducted and with whom and how claims are presented and acted on in the final product. In situations of social and political conflict, contradictions in the researcher's positioning arise in sharp relief, perhaps because of the multiple roles often required by the researcher in such situations but also because she or he may be forced to rely on research participants in 'unusual' or extended ways in the research enterprise; for example, in collecting data and carrying out initial analyses. The instability and disruptions of conflict often reduce the researcher's control of the research environment, forcing the involvement of the research participants in different ways that can serve ultimately to enhance the quality of the claims and their utility. In this situation, researcher and participants engage in co-learning rather than in data extraction agreements (Wagner, 1997). Notions such as 'practitioner research' or 'teachers as researchers' take on different meanings that may require recognition and management of multiple and possibly conflicting interests in the research project and in its outcomes. Doing research *with* research participants as well as *on* them (Setati, 2000) opens possibilities for seeing changing relations of power and knowledge in the research enterprise.

Broadening the net for data production and analysis in this fashion points to a methodological and theoretical collaboration between researchers and research participants that recognises both co-operation and conflict. In situations of social and political conflict, people often act as collectives rather than as individuals to secure their rights and interests. Learners, parents, and teachers 'organise' themselves to protest particular policies or to lobby for their interests. Hence the notion of *collectivity* (Skovsmose & Valero, 2001a, 2001b; Valero, 1999a) developed in Paola's study to discuss the meaning of democracy in mathematics education also becomes important in the research design. It refers to the way a research process in a situation of conflict will produce particular data as a result of a particular kind of relationship a researcher constructs with participants as a group. Collectivity as a concept in methodology may be important also when approaching research sites that are prone to the violence often associated with conflict. The researcher's presence and participation is negotiated and accepted within the collective, which provides some measure of safety and trust. Here the researcher's group affiliation and identity – in terms of gender, race, ethnicity, culture, class, language, religious affiliation, age, academic background, or geographic identity – may need to be clarified, declared, and accepted, with mutual respect and reciprocity established. Consequently, different vested interests in the research and its intentions and goals will need to be negotiated and accepted. The very notion of a collective goes beyond what is called a focus group in interview research; it expands as working to know, understand, and act together. Collectives will, of course, also embed their own relations of power and knowledge and will generate their own conflicts that in turn will shape the research process. In this way, we observe that methodology and theory offer a source for the development of each other and thus resonate with one another.

If theories are both value laden and context laden, how can they be challenged? One approach may be to provide descriptions of practice from research that are not closely bound to the framework being used in a study. That is, descriptions that "make it possible for an outsider to make a critique of a certain theoretical position in mathematics education" (Vithal & Skovsmose, 1997, p. 150) and that make possible self-critique by the researcher have been developed within research in exploring critical approaches to mathematics education – called 'crucial descriptions of practice'. Crucial descriptions can serve to connect theory to practice, on the one hand, and a theory-practice relation to research, on the other. In Renuka's study (Vithal, 2001a), it is argued that such descriptions provide at least four functions in research. First, they allow for *transparency* – of the practices and theories and of the broader context in which these are being considered. They open up educational and research processes and relations to wider scrutiny so that conflicts and related aspects can be observed and critiqued. Second, crucial descriptions also have a *transformative* function. There is potential for change once particular theoretical ideas and practices in education and research are made visible and enacted within a particular context. The possibility of transforming practice or theoretical ideas implies the possibility of inventing new or different ideas and ways of acting both in education and in research settings – that is, a *generative* function may also be served by a crucial description. *Exemplarity*, the fourth function, allows educators and researcher to understand and reflect on how situations of social and political conflict operate within the general system or society by focussing on a single situation of conflict. The production of a crucial description that provides sufficient depth and detail relies on a methodology that allows for the capture of multiple, broad, and open data and hence is particularly important in the instability and uncertainty of situations of social and political conflict.

In challenging and opening methodologies and theories to recognise a situation of conflict, it is clear that some methods and theoretical frameworks lend themselves better to this task than others. Various forms of ethnography, action research, and narrative, biographical, and life history methodologies, to mention a few, have been appropriated from the human and social sciences into educational and mathematics educational research and have been shown to offer potential for working in situations of conflict (e.g., Cotton 1998, Mellin-Olsen, 1995; Reddy, 2000; Samuel, 1999a; Singh, 2000). Similarly, there are theoretical approaches – other than those discussed earlier – that engage issues of power, inequality, and social justice in mathematics education research and that could serve as well for researching conflict situations. The works of Bernstein, Bourdieu, Foucault, among others, have been taken up and developed in various areas in mathematics education, for example, by Dowling (1998), Zevenbergen (2000a), and Hardy (1998). However, we urge and argue that these efforts need to be reviewed and reworked for research in the conflict contexts of the developing world in order to take account of the more profound inequities, fluidity, discontinuity, and instability of that reality. It might be necessary to introduce the term *Conflict Situations* to refer to the sheer scale, number, prevalence, and explicit manifestation of conflicts in the developing world that often engulf the majority rather than a minority and the term *conflict situations* to refer to the kinds of conflicts that are found in all societies as a feature of human actions and interactions. The periphery, which may be characterised as constituting 'conflict situations' and which is beginning to become a focus of research in mathematics education in the developed world, is often the centre in the developing world.

The difficulties of research in situations of social and political conflict must inform a broad range of questions, frameworks, and approaches. Although critical, feminist, postmodernist, and other approaches have produced excellent research, scholarship, theories, practices, and exemplars of institutional or other change in and related to the many aspects associated with situations of conflict, it is not so clear how such approaches can be broadened to research in macro settings, focussing on systemic change at national levels or on the large-scale studies required in developing world contexts. For example, how can survey research take account of situations of conflict and preserve a concern for research participants both ethically and methodologically? One approach is to consider crossing not only disciplinary boundaries but also paradigm boundaries, for instance, in "feminising a survey" (Singh & Vithal, 1998). This approach means finding a way of doing research in situations of social and political conflict but also providing the potential to enhance and deepen our understanding of the topic under investigation and connecting the processes and outcomes of the research to the lives of the people in the study. This idea of diversifying research questions, methodologies, and analysis that we are arguing as essential for studies located in situations of conflict is being shown to be equally necessary in other areas of research in mathematics education such as in gender research (Boaler, 2000b) and in studies of curriculum innovation (Cline & Mandinach, 2000).

This argument points to the need for creativity and innovation in research to generate new questions, phenomena for study, methods, and outcomes and to bring a diversity of approaches and methods to bear in these studies. This change will undoubtedly produce contradictions and conflicts in epistemologies, ontologies, and methodologies. Situations of conflict invite and open up more complex but also more authentic understandings and explanations of the conflict-laden nature of reality today, which resonates with the lives of researchers and their research participants.

CHALLENGING AND OPENING CRITERIA FOR RESEARCH QUALITY

Mathematics educators have recently shown considerable concern with identifying and discussing appropriate criteria for establishing rigour, quality, and scholarship in mathematics education research. Kilpatrick (1993) and Sierpinska (1993), for instance, refer to criteria such as validity, objectivity, rigour and precision, predictability, reproducibility, and relevance, which they claim need to be considered in mathematics education research. Many of these criteria are revisited in an ICMI study edited by Sierpinska and Kilpatrick (1998) and supported there (e.g., Hart, 1998). But more than presenting criteria, the discussion in the ICMI study also raises questions about their possible sources: Are mathematics education researchers to find criteria in classroom practice, in mathematics, in other foundation disciplines, in the progress of the discipline itself, or in the cultural settings of mathematics education in which research is carried out? Even though quality criteria may not be made explicit, one can infer what counts as quality for the different authors through what they take to count as research. Similarly, in the more recent *Handbook of Research Design in Mathematics and Science Education* (Kelly & Lesh, 2000), the concern for criteria is also taken up by several authors, for example, in action research as a methodology (Feldman & Minstrell, 2000), in interpretive research (Tobin, 2000), and in the naturalistic paradigm (Moschkovich & Brenner, 2000).

It is clear from these works that mathematics education researchers are borrowing from a wide variety of disciplinary fields, though more from some than others. Drawing on broader literature, in this section we show how the discussion of criteria for judging the quality of research in mathematics education is linked to the paradigms, theories and methodologies that researchers adopt. There is no universal set of criteria according to which all research processes can be checked. In this sense, the status of criteria like generalisability, reliability, and validity as "a scientific holy trinity" (Kvale, 1996, p. 229) has been deeply questioned, reformulated, and redefined, even refuted. The history of the rise of qualitative approaches in social science and educational research, for instance, demonstrates an explosion of criteria and discourses for evaluating and judging research (e.g., Denzin & Lincoln, 1998). The variety of criteria does not mean, however, that these are ad hoc. The resonance between the ideological and theoretical orientation of a study and its methodology – as argued in the previous section – now comes to include the criteria by which any study is judged. If such a connection between questions, theory, methods, and criteria is accepted, then the search for quality criteria in research in mathematics education that acknowledges social and political conflict might be found in some of the theoretical and methodological tools developed in the research endeavour. In this way, those criteria are likely to become more relevant to such contexts. Therefore, in this section we share ideas for consideration developed in our research, which attempted to recognise and work with and in conflict situations, and use this opportunity to bring them into dialogue with each other. We explore and organise this section around two main criteria: validity and generalisability, which seem to dominate in discussions in the literature about criteria for quality research.

Validity: Challenged and Changing

Both generalisability and validity originate in the positivistic research paradigm, where they are not only well defined but also intended to be uniformly applied across studies in that paradigm. The rise of interpretative and critical paradigms, feminist, narrative, and a host of other research approaches, however, has prob-lematised validity, giving rise to new questions and challenges as well as new discourses in research. Researchers are reconceptualising validity in a manner and a language that is appropriate for their research within particular paradigms and linked to particular methodologies that preserve a resonance with their theoretical orientations and ideological commitments (see, e.g., Anderson & Herr, 1999, Guba & Lincoln, 1998; Lather, 1994; Scheurich, 1997). These propos-als go beyond a concern with credibility and applicability of the claims of a study to the research process and participants. Furthermore, the concern for validity is no longer left only to the researcher but is shared between the researcher and those who read and use research in various ways, including the research participants.

When, as in Paola's study, research relies on the notion of *collectivity*, simple data-extraction agreements (Wagner, 1997) are unlikely to be accepted or to yield authentic information, and they may even be considered exploitative because information giving or sharing could have serious consequences for research participants and indeed also for researchers. Situations of social and political conflict typically embed some serious inequality around which contesta-tion is occurring that produces the conflict in the first instance. Hence the notions of power and conflict must be constantly kept in view, as well as what interest and whose interest the research processes, relationships, and outcomes will serve. What does it mean to execute a technically 'good' study if its processes or findings serve to further oppress a disadvantaged collective? In this respect, a notion such as *catalytic validity* (Lather, 1991) – "the degree to which research moves those it studies to understand the world and the way it is shaped in order for them to transform it" (Kincheloe & McLaren, 1998, p. 289) – which developed in critical research, may be important as a matter of quality research to help one focus on the consequences of research as part of the research enterprise in contexts of conflict.

The notion of research participants as opposed to subjects signals an important shift and is well established in qualitative research approaches. The question is how the notion of participation – of collectives engaged in deliberative dialogue

– becomes a matter of validity. The task is one of building a concept of *participatory validity* that may be appropriate in situations of conflict where dialogue is important. Such a concept has been developed with reference to critical research in mathematics education (Vithal, 2000b) and to practitioner or action research (Anderson & Herr, 1999). We posit a conception of validity that could be used more generally in research methodology to observe or declare the nature of the relationship between the researcher and the research participants as well as the extent of the involvement of those researched in the research process in its entirety, including the eventual claims made in situations of conflict. Participatory validity could be said to be high when participation is evident or is the basis of the study throughout the research process and when participants can shape the nature and degree of their participation, have a voice in its claims, and can even act on them. It could be said to be low when the participants have no say in any aspect of the research process and are seen only as subjects or respondents. It indicates the nature and quality of 'co-learning agreements' set up between the researcher and participants as opposed to 'data-extraction agreements' (Wagner, 1997).

Participatory validity opens up the notion of partnerships in research. The quality of research relationships is crucial in conflict settings for enhancing the validity of the study and maintaining ethical and nonexploitative terms in the research itself. Participatory validity forces the users of a research methodology to recognise and make transparent the ethnic, gender, and class identities and the socio-political, material, and historical locations of the researcher and the research participants. Within the collectivity, participatory validity lays bare the inescapable and shifting relations of knowledge and power that produce particular meanings in and from the research endeavour through which information is both revealed and concealed. In situations of conflict, relationships are fragile; the potential for all kinds of violence is ever present and must be accounted for. In critical and feminist approaches to research, relationships are characterised by such features as negotiation, choice, and reciprocity while these are also recognised as operating within inevitable and inherent power relations. When such a concern is foregrounded in a study theoretically and methodologically, it is possible to speak of a democratic participatory validity (Vithal 2000b), and crucial descriptions can offer a tool for assessing such validity claims (Vithal, 2001a).

The focus on participation as a validity concern brings into sharper relief the principles of responsibility and responsiveness to the research participants and setting. Responsibility refers to the researcher's capacity to be openly accountable to those involved in the research for the observations, interpretations, and results. Responsiveness is the capacity to reply and react readily to the influence received from the research interaction. In other words, in contrast to the classical situation in which researchers take information out of a social situation and use it outside the research setting for knowledge production purposes, the responsiveness and responsibility principles require a constant and open 'giving back' to the people or situation involved in the research. This giving back contributes to the necessity of establishing a de-objectifying dialogue between researcher and participants so that they can become acquainted with the research purposes and intentions and can also benefit intellectually from it (Valero, 1999a; Valero & Matos, 2000).

Consequently, for any real notion of partnership to survive in research, deliberative dialogue is needed. Such dialogue has been operationalised in some research approaches through the notion of reflexivity. Meaningful and substantial participation in a study is made possible through opportunities for reflection. In situations of conflict and change, a double reflexivity (Apple, 1995) is needed. One reflexivity is directed to the content or topic under study, and the other is directed at the research process and relationships themselves. Reflexivity includes both group reflections by collectives – *coflections* (Valero, 1999a) – and individual reflections, providing a means for managing conflicts, unequal power relations, and hierarchies not only between the researcher and the research participants but also among the research participants themselves – for instance, between teachers, between teacher and pupils, and among pupils, as well as among members of a team of researchers who may also differ according to some dimensions (see Smith, 1999).

An important challenge that notions such as catalytic and participatory validity throw up in situations of conflict is their relevance for other paradigms and approaches, such as, say, survey research in a positivist tradition, that must also find ways to cope with conflicts. Quite clearly these notions could lead to conflicts and contradictions in the epistemological and ontological bases of some research approaches. It may be argued that conflicts and contradictions are the realities of those who inhabit spaces of contestation and hence create an imperative for dealing with them at the heart of the research process. Theoretical and methodological frameworks that prioritise systematisation, logic, and coherence at the expense of the research participants' involvement in a study are unlikely to capture the breadth and depth of the phenomena investigated in conflict situations, yielding processes and claims that may be disputed by the research participants or the broader community represented in the study. This potential weakness is why participation in and outcomes of research need to be problematised and raised as a validity criterion in situations of conflict.

The researcher needs not only to identify, declare, and maintain the values and ideological assumptions embedded in the theoretical and methodological frames chosen or constructed for the study but also to pay equal attention to the particularities of the context, that is, the various conflicts and contestations in it. Questions about unequal relations of power that are greater in situations of conflict need to be addressed and managed across different approaches and paradigms of research rather than to remain as preoccupations only in the critical or feminist domain, which are often at the periphery when one is trying to inform and shape actions and policies at macro or national levels. Processes and outcomes of research such as surveys are often imposed and are used both for and against particular groups, which can acerbate conflicts. We are not arguing for discarding or rejecting research, such as survey research, done in positivist traditions. Such studies are needed in the repertoire of methodologies that address issues in situations of conflict; for example, to establish the extent of poverty or discrimination. Instead, such methodologies need to be reclaimed, and the very concerns that such research approaches currently locate at the margins, as side issues of ethics and politics, need to be brought to their centres. That is, criteria for quality cannot focus only on decontextualised claims and findings but need to include an evaluation of the processes and consequences of research actions and relations. Research practices are not neutral or without impact and must be accounted for in any judgements made about them.

Generalisability Challenged and Connected: Generativity

The issue of validity arises together with concerns about generalisations in research, especially in the positivistic research tradition in which generalisability of findings to other situations is important for verifying knowledge. The rise of new methodologies and paradigms has brought a shift in focus from generalisation to contextualisation. For example, Kvale (1996) discusses several forms of generalisation, such as naturalistic, statistical, and analytic generalisation, and raises questions about "who should conduct the analytic generalisation" and "how much should the researcher formalise and argue generalisations or leave the generalisations to the reader" (p. 233). This observation points to the researcher having to provide sufficient information, for instance, through crucial descriptions, for generalisations to be made by a reader.

In the interpretive and critical paradigms, the concern with generalisation has not been abandoned; instead, it has been reinterpreted and shared with research readers and participants. Gergen's (1992) postmodern conception of generative theory, according to Kvale (1996), refers to research that unseats conventional notions and creates possibilities for alternative thought and action. The transformative agenda of research is integrated into criteria by which research is evaluated. Instead of seeking generalisability of findings, a study could be considered in terms of its capacity for generating ideas in theory, policy, practice, and research (Vithal 2000a). In unstable and rapidly changing situations of conflict, *generativity* is more relevant than generalisability because by the time the generalisation is available, the situation under study may have already changed, or the sheer extent of diversity or inequality may render generalisations inadequate or even inappropriate.

It may be argued that all research is about the generation of knowledge and, in this sense, that generativity is an implicit condition in all research. Our purpose here, however, is to make it an explicit and substantive criterion for scientific quality and relevance in mathematics education research. The question is, What could a study be generative of, and for whom? Adler (1996) argues that a language of description that arises from a study could be generative of new practices and of new knowledge and therefore could refer to the extent to which the research is taken up by teachers and other researchers. Confrey (2000) identifies generativity as a criterion for assessing the impact of "transformative and conjecture-driven teaching experiments" as a "type of research [that] is coupled to a reform agenda" (p. 262). Our assertion is that a study can be judged on the basis of the extent to which it is generative of tools for thinking, acting, and managing the changes and conflicts themselves. In this way, generalisability is reinterpreted; it is confined not to the applicability of findings in a wide variety of contexts but rather to the recontextualisation of the products of research – tasks, methods, conceptual tools, and claims – in practice, policy, theory, other research, and so on.

Researchers and their research never completely escape generalisation. Readers of research and researchers themselves constantly make judgements about the applicability of findings of other research to their own situations. Generativity need not be seen, however, as being in opposition to generalisability. The focus on the capacity of a study to generate new ideas for practice, policy, and theory highlights a different concern that a researcher brings to the study. It may be argued that by studying a particular topic or instance of a phenomenon, one might come to a general understanding of a system or of a totality of which it is a part (a kind of generalisation) and also come to know some new things (generativity). The former refers to the principle of *exemplarity*, which has been theorised in relation to social and political conflicts in critical mathematics education (Skovsmose, 1994). It offers a means for connecting generativity and generalisability in studies of critical mathematics education (Vithal, 2000a) and therefore in research in situations of conflict. The exemplarity principle, particularly as it is applied in the German and Scandinavian educational context, has already acquired some meaning related to research, specifically with respect to project studies (F.V. Christiansen, 1999; Illeris, 1999; Vithal, Christiansen, & Skovsmose, 1995).

In situations of conflict, the principle of exemplarity faces particular difficulties in connecting an educational practice to an educational totality. The research may focus say, on some 'new' educational practice that is not yet very well understood in relation to the educational totality – a totality itself undergoing transformation. Indeed, there may be multiple 'totalities' to which a connection may be created. For instance, in Renuka's research, the totality that the researcher and research participants could come to know might be the complexity of the educational context of which mathematics education is a part, the theory related to the education practice being studied, or the enterprise of research. Whatever the totality, it is dynamic, cannot be completely known, and may contain all sorts of conflicts and crises. In this respect, generativity is an important concept since studying a specific situation can give rise to new ways of understanding the totality or reveal unknown aspects of the totality. Exemplarity allows one to interpret and respond differently to the generalisability problem. Studying the particular can lead to understanding the whole, and knowing the whole implies one can also know about what happens in other parts of that whole. By studying a specific situation, therefore, one can also gain new insight into a totality that may not exist in a stable form. In this way, exemplarity forges a connection between generativity and generalisability that is particularly important for situations of conflict.

The search for relevant criteria in research is part of the attempt to preserve *rigour*, a key feature of any activity deemed research. In research, rigour is typically related to understanding more thoroughly, understanding in greater depth, and arriving at stable findings and frameworks that will endure relatively unchallenged provided the correct steps were taken in the research. In situations of social and political conflict, rigour privileges different features such as interconnectedness, flexibility, breadth in understanding, and fluidity in claims. Diversity and change – so well recognised in society and therefore in the educational system – then also come to reside in the very means for investigating and knowing about that system. Research is not itself a universal, neutral, and value-free 'set of instruments or methods' by which one can interrogate and make claims about the world. A carefully conceived research design in one moment and place can become inappropriate or break down in another. Rigour in such situations must refer to responsiveness and responsibility – how the research responds to a changing environment rather than to how a researcher is adhering to a predetermined research design. The material conditions and historicity of the methodology and participants have to be accounted for by preserving a sense of time and place in the research. Although a single epistemological framework developed in detail is valued in traditional notions of rigour, in conflict situations multiple and even conflicting epistemologies need to be considered and managed (Harding, 1998; Scheurich & Young, 1997). One needs to deal with diverse ways of knowing the world and acting in it, not only in the theory and practice of mathematics education but also in its research. Rigour is about how this complexity is worked with, captured, and finds expression in research.

In this search for criteria of quality and relevance for mathematics education in situations of conflict, one must recognise that there is no neat, coherent, linear progression in the development and use of validity or generalisability. Traditional notions may conflict and yet still coexist with newer criteria "depending on the researchers' ontological, epistemological, and political leanings and assumptions, as well as their situational requirements" (Lenzo, 1995, p. 17) in the untidy world of doing and legitimating research. This observation raises important questions about the ways in which research methodologies in mathematics education are growing, changing, and becoming understood as 'situated' and how notions such as participatory validity, collectivity, coflection, generativity, and alternative forms of rigour and scholarship are taken up and evolve or die in the politics of both knowledge production and its means of production. To make advances in theory and influence policy and practice in mathematics education across all contexts and for *all* learners, fundamental advances are needed in methodologies used to understand and interrogate those policies, theories, and practices. Methodology may need to be theorised differently and different criteria developed for rigour, relevance, and quality. Even then, one still needs constantly to question whether the criteria put forward here are appropriate, what meaning they can and do come to have in the world of doing research, and what other criteria and issues should be considered.

IN CLOSING

Mathematics education as a research domain in search of its identity, as Sierpinska and Kilpatrick (1998) suggest, may not be in an identity crisis (Steen, 1999). Instead, it may be beginning to recognise its multiple and possibly conflicting identities. Viewing the domain in this way allows one to recognise that a rich diversity is emerging in mathematics education as a field of study, just as in the practice of mathematics education that values diversity of learners. Mathematics education is expanding in response to the recognition of a changing world, changing demands for knowledge, skill, and attitude, and the need for inter-, multi- and trans-disciplinarity in education. Different researchers with different theoretical, epistemological, methodological perspectives and approaches as well as different disciplinary expertise are constantly shifting our 'research gaze' within the broadening field we now call mathematics education. They offer multiple lenses and multiple vantage points, not all of which are necessarily coherent and neatly fitting; instead, they may be fraught with conflicts and contradictions. Mathematics education, by its very nature and its status, provides fertile ground for the research paradigm wars to be fought. Although theoretical and practical scholarship in the social and political dimensions of mathematics education has increased significantly – the place where situations of conflict are most likely to be discussed – and mathematics education researchers draw heavily from developments in other disciplines, arguably much less attention has been paid to issues of research processes and relationships and to alternate forms of representing research. That is, the mathematics education literature contains very little dealing explicitly with issues of research, especially at a meta-level, despite these significant borrowings. In fact, this lack of questioning and critiquing of the adoption of approaches from other fields is a particular difficulty in developing countries when researching in situations of social and political conflict. Indeed, the paradigm wars that have disrupted dominant methodological and theoretical trends point to the conflicts in social science and educational research, on the one hand, and in the physical and natural sciences, on the other. They open the possibility of asking similar foundational questions about the context in which they arise. That is, debates about theories and methodologies that have lead to the different research paradigms, perspectives, and approaches must be extended to questions about what those debates could come to mean when recontextualised in settings in the developing world.

There is also a need to recognise that the choice of research question, perspectives, and approaches is shaped in part by the researcher's identity, which is produced through diverse life experiences and struggles from having lived in particular communities. That we, Renuka and Paola, write from and draw attention to a politicised mathematics education is not disconnected from our own life journeys to become educated; the opportunities we have had for mathematics teaching and learning; our identities as women in two continents considered underdeveloped and developing; and our historical, social, economic, cultural trajectories in arriving at a point of doing doctoral studies. We raise questions as to who is represented in the centre of the mathematics education research community not only as a matter of equity – a political or social justice concern – but as a methodological and epistemological issue that impoverishes the discipline itself in generating alternative views, questions, and understandings about what it means to be educated in the discipline of mathematics. Marginalized groups in mathematics education as a field of practice also remain outside mathematics education as a field of study.

This last observation brings us to the thorny and difficult argument about the importation and exportation of research questions, methods, theoretical and conceptual tools, and frameworks and findings in mathematics education between and even within countries. The commerce in knowledge, its means of production, and its products occurs mainly from the developed to the developing world (see Valero & Vithal, 1998), but it is also experienced within countries between what are construed as the centre and the margin. Although the dominant research trends and theoretical approaches in mathematics education research carefully avoid situations of conflict because of the difficulties they pose, many researchers in developing countries affirm and legitimate their work with reference to those who live and work mainly in the developed world and hence also do not pay sufficient attention to the conflicts. This phenomenon, in effect, keeps the work of the margin on the margin and makes a scholarship relevant to situations of social and political conflict difficult to develop. Nevertheless, just as mathematics and mathematics education have been challenged as 'Western' and 'Eurocentric' knowledge forms that sought to historically deny local or indigenous knowledge, a similar charge can be levelled at the means for producing that knowledge. The relatively well-developed arguments for decolonising mathematics and mathematics education now need to be directed to decolonising research methodologies and theories. As an indigenous Maori researcher, Smith (1999) points to particular challenges in "reclaiming indigenous ways of knowing and being" and observes that "research is one of the ways in which the underlying code of imperialism and colonialism is both regulated and realized" (p. 7). Smith recognises, however, the complex differentials of knowledge and power between who does research on or with whom that all researchers must confront whether insiders or outsiders.

To better understand and do research in situations of conflict, an analysis is essential of how and why particular questions, methodologies, and theories are chosen, developed, travel, traded, and appropriated. We note, for instance, the globalisation of mathematics education research that is led in no small measure by large international studies such as the Third International Mathematics and Science Study that are dominated by the concerns of wealthy countries, the migration of research students and researchers across countries, and the dominant voices that get represented in international conferences and journals shaped in the main by funding opportunities. This globalisation has also created global fashion trends in mathematics education research, theory, policy, and practice, and played a part in the spread of those trends to former colonies. We concede and recognise that we too are implicated in this importation because the works we cite in support of our arguments for researching in situations of social and political conflict, particularly for developing world contexts, are largely from the North. However, the different mathematics education research traditions discernible in different countries in Europe and the United States, for example, demonstrate the potential and need to generate homegrown approaches and perspectives relevant to particular contexts.

Finally, as Ruthven (1999) cautions, this focus on researching in difficult situations of social and political conflict could turn into a celebration of the conflicts. In fact, mathematics education research has a long and extensive history of an incessant focus on those who 'fail' to learn or to teach mathematics and in which a pathologising is evident. No doubt, such a focus can also have the opposite effect of celebrating particular individuals, groups, or settings. One must recognise that whatever category or phenomena researchers come to construct, these are then maintained in the questions, theories, analyses and claims; they eventually come to occupy a means through which the world is viewed. In this chapter, we share a view of the world through our eyes and offer an invitation to continue and contribute to a dialogue between North and South, centre and periphery, margin and mainstream, however and wherever each of us comes to be and take a position in this world.

NOTES

1. A longer version of this chapter is published separately as Vithal and Valero (2001). Several parts also appear in Vithal (2000a).
2. Whatever term we choose to refer to the fact of power and resource imbalances among countries in the world is problematic. Therefore, we opt for pairs such as 'developed-developing', 'North-South' and 'First World – Third World' according to the meaning we want to convey in a particular part of our discourse. We want to make clear that the use of any pair does not mean that we think that the world can be portrayed in terms of opposites. However, it is central to acknowledge the structural differences and inequity among communities, countries, and regions in the world.
3. *Nyspor* is a Danish word that translates into 'new tracks'. This fictitious name represents what I see as one of the strongest characteristics of this school: It is a place where different alternative ways and paths are being built to make the 'train' of change in mathematics education run.
4. In the Indian Vedic tradition, *Rajas* represents one of the three basic forces of nature, in charge of change and movement.
5. The word *esperanza* in Spanish means 'hope'. This fictitious name for the school illustrates what I saw in it: teachers who, despite the adversities, have a strong commitment with their work and hope that what they do can contribute to the betterment of their students' life conditions.

REFERENCES

Abboud, M. (1998). Teaching mathematics in Lebanon: A post-war experience. In P. Gates & T. Cotton (Eds.), *Proceedings of the First International Mathematics and Science Education Conference* (pp. 197–206). Nottingham: Nottingham University, Centre for the Study of Mathematics Education.

Adler, J. (1996). *Secondary school teachers' knowledge of the dynamics of teaching and learning mathematics in multilingual classrooms*. Unpublished Ph.D. dissertation, University of the Witwatersrand, Johannesburg.

Adler, J. (1998). Resources as a verb: Recontextualising resources in and for school mathematics. In A. Olivier & K. Newstead (Eds.), *Proceedings of the 22nd Conference of the PME* (Vol. 1, pp. 1–28). Stellenbosch: University of Stellenbosch.

Anderson, G. L., & Herr, K. (1999). The new paradigm wars: Is there room for rigorous practitioner research. *Educational Researcher, 28*(5), 12–21, 40.

Apple, M. (1995). Taking power seriously: New directions in equity in mathematics education and beyond. In W. Secada, E. Fennema & L. Adajian (Eds.), *New directions for equity in mathematics education* (pp. 146–164). Cambridge: Cambridge University Press.

Apple, M. (1996). *Cultural politics and education.* New York: Teachers College Press.

Atweh, B., & Clarkson, P. (2001). Internationalization and globalization of mathematics education: Towards an agenda for research/action. In B. Atweh, H. Forgasz, & B. Nebres (Eds.), *Socio-cultural aspects of mathematics education: An international research perspective* (pp. 77–94). Mahwah, NJ: Lawrence Erlbaum Associates.

Baker, D. (1996). Children's formal and informal school numeracy practices. In D. Baker, J. Clay, & C. Fox. (Eds.), *Challenging ways of knowing: in English, mathematics and science* (pp. 80–89). London: Falmer Press.

Barton, B. (1999). Ethnomathematics: A political plaything. *For the Learning of Mathematics, 19*(1), 32–35.

Bernstein, B. (1996). *Pedagogy, symbolic control and identity: Theory, research, critique.* London: Taylor & Francis.

Beyer, K. (1995). A gender perspective on mathematics and physics education: Similarities and differences. In B. Grevholm & G. Hanna (Eds.), *Gender and mathematics education* (pp. 45–64). Lund, Sweden: Lund University Press.

Bishop, A. (1992). International perspectives in research in mathematics education. In D. A. Grouws (Ed.), *Handbook of research on mathematics teaching and learning* (pp. 710–723). New York: Macmillan.

Bishop, A., Clements, K., Keitel, C., Kilpatrick, J., & Laborde, C. (Eds.). (1996). *International handbook of mathematics education.* Dordrecht: Kluwer.

Bloor, D. (1976). *Knowledge and social imagery.* London: Routledge.

Boaler, J. (1997). *Experiencing school mathematics.* Buckingham: Open University Press.

Boaler, J. (Ed.). (2000a). *Multiple perspectives on mathematics teaching and learning.* Westport, CT: Ablex Publishing.

Boaler, J. (2000b). So girls don't really understand mathematics? Dangerous dichotomies in gender research. *Proceedings of the International Organisation of Women and Mathematics Education IOWME, Sessions in ICME 9* (pp. 29–44). Tokyo: IOWME.

Boero, P. (Ed.). (1999). Teaching and learning in context. *Educational Studies in Mathematics, 39*, 1–3.

Brew, C., Pearn, C., Leder, G., & Bishop, A. (1998). Big fish resizing themselves in the school pond. Why do girls under-rate their ability? In C. Keitel (Ed.), *Social justice and mathematics education: Gender, class, ethnicity and the politics of schooling* (pp. 69–82). Berlin: IOWME – Freie Universität Berlin.

Brodie, K. (1997). A new mathematics curriculum: Reflecting on outcomes in process. In P. Kershall & M. de Villiers (Eds.), *Third National Congress of the Association for Mathematics Education of South Africa. Proceedings 1: General & Primary* (pp. 26–41). Durban: AMESA.

Burton, L. (1990). *Gender and mathematics: An international perspective.* London: Cassell.

Castells, M. (1999). Flows, networks, and identities: A critical theory of the informational society. In M. Castells, R. Flecha, P. Freire, H. Giroux, D. Macedo, & P. Willis (Eds.), *Critical education in the new information age* (pp. 37–64). Lanham, MD: Rowman & Littlefield.

Christiansen, F. V. (1999). Exemplarity and educational planning. In H. S. Olesen & J. H. Jensen (Eds.), *Project studies – A late modern university reform?* (pp. 57–66). Roskilde: Roskilde University Press.

Christiansen, I. M. (1996). *Mathematical modelling in high school: From idea to practice.* Unpublished Ph.D. dissertation, Aalborg University, Aalborg, Denmark.

Clarke, B., Clarke, D., & Sullivan, P. (1996). The mathematics teacher and curriculum development.

In A. Bishop, K. Clements, C. Keitel, J. Kilpatrick, & C. Laborde (Eds.), *International handbook of mathematics education* (pp. 1208–1210). Dordrecht: Kluwer.

Cline, H. F., & Mandinach, E. B. (2000). The corruption of a research design: A case study of a curriculum innovation project. In A. E. Kelly & R. A. Lesh (Eds.), *Handbook of research design in mathematics and science education* (pp. 169–189). Mahwah, NJ: Lawrence Erlbaum Associates.

Confrey, J. (2000). Improving research and systemic reform toward equity and quality. In A. E. Kelly & R. A. Lesh (Eds.), *Handbook of research design in mathematics and science education* (pp. 87–106). Mahwah, NJ: Lawrence Erlbaum Associates.

Cotton, T. (1998). *Towards mathematics education for social justice.* Unpublished Ph.D. dissertation, University of Nottingham, Nottingham, United Kingdom.

D'Ambrosio, U. (1985). Ethnomathematics and its place in the history and pedagogy of mathematics. *For the Learning of Mathematics, 5*(1), 44–48.

D'Ambrosio, U. (1990). The role of mathematics education in building a democratic and just society. *For the Learning of Mathematics, 10*(3), 20–23.

D'Ambrosio, U. (1996). *Educacão matemática: Da teoria à pràtica.* Campinas, Brazil: Papirus.

De Abreu, G. (2000). Relationships between macro and micro socio-cultural contexts: Implications for the study of interactions in the mathematics classroom. *Educational Studies in Mathematics, 41*(1), 1–29.

Denzin, N. K., & Lincoln, Y. S. (1998). *The landscape of qualitative research: Theories and issues.* Thousand Oaks, CA: Sage Publications.

Desrosières, A. (1998). The politics of large numbers. A history of statistical reasoning. Cambridge, MA: Harvard University Press.

Dowling, P. (1998). *The sociology of mathematics education: Mathematical myths/pedagogic texts.* London: Falmer Press.

Duba, N. (2001, July). In response to Vithal. In M. Setati (Ed.), *Proceedings of the Seventh National Congress of the Association for Mathematics Education of South Africa* (pp. 49–52). Johannesburg: University of the Witwatersrand.

Ernest, P. (1991). *The philosophy of mathematics education.* London: Falmer Press.

Ernest, P. (1998). Images of mathematics, values, and gender: A philosophical perspective. In C. Keitel (Ed.), *Social justice and mathematics education: Gender, class, ethnicity and the politics of schooling* (pp. 45–58). Berlin: IOWME – Freie Universität Berlin.

Fasheh, M. (1997). Mathematics, culture and authority. In A. Powell & M. Frankenstein (Eds.), *Ethnomathematics. Challenging Eurocentrism in mathematics education* (pp. 273–290). Albany: State University of New York Press.

Feldman, A., & Minstrell, J. (2000). Action research as a research methodology for the study of the teaching and learning of science. In E. Kelly & R. Lesh (Eds.), *Handbook of research design in mathematics and science education* (pp. 429–455). Mahwah, NJ: Lawrence Erlbaum Associates.

Flecha, R. (1999). New educational inequalities. In M. Castells, R. Flecha, P. Freire, H. Giroux, D. Macedo, & P. Willis, *Critical education in the new information age* (pp. 65–82). Lanham, MD: Rowman & Littlefield.

Forgasz, H. (1998). The 'male domain' of high school and tertiary mathematics learning environments. In C. Keitel (Ed.), *Social justice and mathematics education: Gender, class, ethnicity and the politics of schooling* (pp. 32–44). Berlin: IOWME – Freie Universität Berlin.

Frankenstein, M. (1987). Critical mathematics education: An application of Paulo Freire's epistemology. In I. Shor (Ed.), *Freire for the classroom: A sourcebook for liberatory teaching* (pp. 180–210). Portsmouth, NH: Boyton/Cook Publishers.

Frankenstein, M. (1995). Equity in mathematics education: Class in the world outside the class. In W. Secada, E. Fennema, & L. Adajian (Eds.), *New directions for equity in mathematics education* (pp. 165–190). Cambridge: Cambridge University Press.

Freire, P. (1999). Education and community involvement. In M. Castells, R. Flecha, P. Freire, H. Giroux, D. Macedo, & P. Willis, *Critical education in the new information age* (pp. 83–92). Lanham, MD: Rowman & Littlefield.

Gates, P. (2000). *A study of the structure of the professional orientation of two teachers of mathematics:*

A sociological approach. Unpublished Ph.D. dissertation, University of Nottingham, Nottingham, United Kingdom.

Gerdes, P. (1985). Conditions and strategies for emancipatory mathematics education in undeveloped countries. *For the Learning of Mathematics, 5*(1), 15–20.

Gerdes, P. (1988). On culture, geometrical thinking and mathematics education. *Educational Studies in Mathematics, 19*(2), 137–162.

Gerdes, P. (2001). On the 'African Renaissance' and ethnomathematical research. In I. V. Mutimucuio (Ed.), *Proceedings of the 9th Conference of the Southern African Association of Research in Mathematics, Science and Technology Education* (pp. 1–14). Maputo: Eduardo Mondlane University Press.

Gergen, K. (1992). Toward a postmodern psychology. In S. Kvale (Ed.), *Psychology and postmodernism* (pp. 1–30). London: Sage.

Gergen, K. (1994). *Realities and relationships. Soundings in social construction.* Cambridge, MA: Harvard University Press.

Giroux, H. (1997). *Pedagogy and the politics of hope.* Boulder, CO: Westview.

Gómez, P. (2000). Investigación en educación matemática y enseñanza de las matemáticas en países en desarrollo. *Educación Matemática, 12*(1), 93–106.

Gorgorió, N., & Planas, N. (2000). Researching multicultural classes: A collaborative approach. In J. F. Matos & M. Santos (Eds.), *Proceedings of the Second International Mathematics Education and Society Conference* (pp. 265–274). Lisbon: CIEFC – Universidade de Lisboa.

Gray, M. W. (1995). Recruiting and retaining graduate students in the mathematical sciences and improving their chances for subsequent success. In B. Grevholm & G. Hanna (Eds.), *Gender and mathematics education* (pp. 39–44). Lund, Sweden: Lund University Press.

Grouws, D. A. (Ed.). (1992). *Handbook of research on mathematics teaching and learning.* New York: Macmillan.

Guba, E. G., & Lincoln, Y. S. (1998). Competing paradigms in qualitative research. In N. K. Denzin & Y. S. Lincoln (Eds.), *The landscape of qualitative research: Theories and issues* (pp. 195–220). Thousand Oaks, CA: Sage.

Hanna, G. (1996). *Towards gender equity in mathematics education: An ICMI study.* Dordrecht: Kluwer Academic Publishers.

Harding, S. (1998). Multicultural, postcolonialism, feminism: Do they require new epistemologies? *Australian Educational Researcher, 25*(1), 37–51.

Hardy, T. (1998). Tales of power: Foucault in the mathematics classroom. In P. Gates & T. Cotton (Eds.), *Proceedings of the 1st International Mathematics and Science Education Conference* (pp. 197–206). Nottingham: Nottingham University, Centre for the Study of Mathematics Education.

Harris, M. (1997). *Common threads: Women, mathematics and work.* Staffordshire: Trentham Books.

Hart, K. (1998). Basic criteria for research in mathematics education. In A. Sierpinska & J. Kilpatrick (Eds.), *Mathematics education as a research domain: A search for identity* (pp. 409–414). Dordrecht: Kluwer Academic Publishers.

Illeris, K. (1999). Project work in university studies: Background and current issues. In H. S. Olesen & J. H. Jensen (Eds.), *Project studies – A late modern university reform?* (pp. 25–32). Roskilde: Roskilde University Press.

Julie, C. (1993). People's mathematics and the applications of mathematics. In J. Lange, C. Keitel, I. Huntley, & M. Niss (Eds.), *Innovation in mathematics education by modelling and applications* (pp. 31–40). London: Ellis Horwood.

Keitel, C. (Ed.). (1998). *Social justice and mathematics education: Gender, class, ethnicity and the politics of schooling.* Berlin: IOWME – Freie Universität Berlin.

Keitel, C., & Kilpatrick, J. (1998). The rationality and irrationality of comparative studies. In G. Kaiser, E. Luna, & I. Huntley (Eds.), *International comparisons in mathematics education* (pp. 241–257). London: Falmer Press.

Keitel, C., & Knijnik, G. (2000). *Social and political aspects of mathematics education.* Discussion paper for Working Group in Action 12, ICME 9, Tokyo, Japan.

Keitel, C., Kotzmann, E., & Skovsmose, O. (1993). Beyond the tunnel vision: Analysing the relationship between mathematics, society and technology. In C. Keitel & K. Ruthven (Eds.), *Learning from computers: Mathematics education and technology* (pp. 243–279). Berlin: Springer-Verlag.

Kelly, A. E., & Lesh, R. A. (Eds.). (2000). *Handbook of research design in mathematics and science education.* Mahwah, NJ: Lawrence Erlbaum Associates.

Khuzwayo, H. (1998). Occupation of our minds: A dominant feature in mathematics education in South Africa. In P. Gates & T. Cotton (Eds.), *Proceedings of the First International Mathematics Education and Society Conference* (pp. 219–232). Nottingham: Nottingham University, Centre for the Study of Mathematics Education.

Khuzwayo, H. (2000). *Selected views and critical perspectives: An account of mathematics education in South Africa from 1948–1994.* Unpublished Ph.D. dissertation, Aalborg University Center, Aalborg, Denmark.

Kilpatrick, J. (1992). A history of research on mathematics education. In D. A. Grouws (Ed.), *Handbook of research on mathematics teaching and learning* (pp. 3–38). New York: Macmillan.

Kilpatrick, J. (1993). Beyond face value: Assessing research in mathematics education. In G. Nissen & M. Blomhøj (Eds.), *Criteria for scientific quality and relevance in the didactics of mathematics* (pp. 15–34). Roskilde: Roskilde University.

Kincheloe, J. L., & McLaren, P. L. (1998). Rethinking critical theory and qualitative research. In N. K. Denzin & Y. S. Lincoln (Eds.), *The landscape of qualitative research: Theories and issues* (pp. 260–299). Thousand Oaks, CA: Sage.

Knijnik, G. (1996). *Exclusão e resistencia: Educacão matemática e legitimidade cultural.* Porto Alegre: Artes Médicas.

Knijnik, G. (1997). An ethnomathematical approach in mathematical education: A matter of political power. In A. Powell & M. Frankenstein (Eds.), *Ethnomathematics: Challenging Eurocentrism in mathematics education* (pp. 403–410). Albany: State University of New York Press.

Knijnik, G. (1998). Ethnomathematics and political struggles. *Zentralblatt für Didaktik der Mathematik, 98*(6), 188–194.

Knijnik, G. (2000, July). Challenging the research/practitioner dichotomy: A voice from the South. In K. Safford & M. J. Schmitt (Eds.), *A conversation between researchers and practitioners* (Proceedings of the Seventh Conference of Adults Learning Mathematics). Stevenage, UK: Avanti Books.

Kögler, H. H. (1999). *The power of dialogue: Critical hermeneutics after Gadamer and Foucault.* Cambridge, MA: MIT Press.

Kvale, S. (1996). *Interviews: An introduction to qualitative research interviewing.* Thousand Oaks, CA: Sage.

Lather, P. (1991). *Getting smart: Feminist research and pedagogy with/in the postmodern.* New York: Routledge.

Lather, P. (1994). Fertile obsession: Validity after poststructuralism. In A. Gitlin (Ed.), *Power and method: Political activism and educational research* (pp. 36–60). New York: Routledge.

Lave, J. (1988). *Cognition in practice: Mind, mathematics and culture in everyday life.* Cambridge: Cambridge University Press.

Lenzo, K. (1995, May). Validity and self-reflexivity meet poststructuralism: Scientific ethos and the transgressive self. *Educational Researcher,* pp. 17–23, 45.

Lerman, S. (2000). The social turn in mathematics education research. In J. Boaler (Ed.), *Multiple perspectives on mathematics teaching and learning* (pp. 19–44). Westport, CT: Ablex Publishing.

Lesh, R., & Lovitts B. (2000). Research agendas: Identifying priority problems and developing useful theoretical perspectives. In A. E. Kelly & R. A. Lesh (Eds.), *Handbook of research design in mathematics and science education* (pp. 45–71). Mahwah, NJ: Lawrence Erlbaum Associates.

Licón-Khisty, L. (1995). Making inequality: Issues of language and meanings in mathematics teaching with Hispanic students. In W. Secada, E. Fennema, & L. Adajian (Eds.), *New directions for equity in mathematics education* (pp. 279–297). Cambridge: Cambridge University Press.

Macedo, D. (1999). Our common culture: A poisonous pedagogy. In M. Castells, R. Flecha, P. Freire, H. Giroux, D. Macedo, & P. Willis, *Critical education in the new information age* (pp. 117–138). Lanham, MD: Rowman & Littlefield.

McLaren, P. (1999). Traumatizing capital: Oppositional pedagogies in the age of consent. In

M. Castells, R. Flecha, P. Freire, H. Giroux, D. Macedo, & P. Willis (Eds.), *Critical education in the new information age* (pp. 1–36). Lanham, MD: Rowman & Littlefield.

McLaren, P. (2000). *Che Guevara, Paulo Freire, and the pedagogy of revolution.* New York: Rowman & Littlefield.

McLaren, P., & Giarelli, J. (Eds.). (1995). *Critical theory and educational research.* Albany: State University of New York Press.

Mehrtens, H. (1993). The social system of mathematics and national socialism: A survey. In S. Restivo, J. P. Bendegem, & R. Fisher (Eds.), *Math worlds: Philosophical and social studies of mathematics and mathematics education* (pp. 219–246). Albany: State University of New York Press.

Mellin-Olsen, S. (1987). *The politics of mathematics education.* Dordrecht: D. Reidel.

Mellin-Olsen, S. (1992). Preface. In M. Nickson & S. Lerman (Eds.), *The social context of mathematics education: Theory and practice* (p. v). London: Southbank Press.

Mellin-Olsen, S. (1995). *Mathematics education: Women's talk.* Landas, Norway: Caspar Forlag.

Moschkovich, J. N., & Brenner, M. (2000). Integrating a naturalistic paradigm into research on mathematics and science cognition and learning. In A. E. Kelly & R. A. Lesh (Eds.), *Handbook of research design in mathematics and science education* (pp. 457–486). Mahwah, NJ: Lawrence Erlbaum Associates.

Mukhopadhyay, S. (1998). When Barbie goes to classrooms: Mathematics in creating a social discourse. In C. Keitel (Ed.), *Social justice and mathematics education: Gender, class, ethnicity and the politics of schooling* (pp. 150–161). Berlin: IOWME – Freie Universität Berlin.

Nelson, D., Joseph, G. G., & Williams, J. (1993). *Multicultural mathematics: Teaching mathematics from a global perspective.* Oxford: Oxford University Press.

Nekhwevha, F. (2000). Education transformation and the African renaissance in a globalising world. *Perspectives in Education, 18*(3), 119–131.

Niss, M. (1996). Goals of mathematics teaching. In A. Bishop, K. Clements, C. Keitel, J. Kilpatrick, & C. Laborde (Eds.), *International handbook of mathematics education* (pp. 11–47). Dordrecht: Kluwer Academic Publishers.

Nunes, T., Schliemann, A. D., & Carraher, D. W. (1993). *Street mathematics and school mathematics.* Cambridge: Cambridge University Press.

Otte, M. (1990). Arithmetic and geometry: Some remarks on the concept of complementarity. *Studies in Philosophy and Education, 10,* 37–62.

Otte, M. (1994). *Das Formale, das Soziale und das Subjektive: Eine Einfuhrung in die Philosophe und Didaktik der Mathematik.* Frankfurt am Main: Suhrkamp.

Paechter, C. (2000). Moving with the goalposts: Carrying out curriculum research in a period of constant change. *British Educational Research Journal, 26*(1), 25–37.

Parker, L. H., Rennie, L. J., & Fraser, B. J. (Eds.). (1996). *Gender science and mathematics: Shortening the shadow.* Dordrecht: Kluwer Academic Publishers.

Payne, K. J., & Biddle, B. J. (1999). Poor school funding, child poverty, and mathematics achievement. *Educational Researcher, 28*(6), 4–13.

Payne, K. J., & Biddle, B. J. (2000, October). Funding, poverty, and mathematics achievement: A rejoinder to Sarah E. Turner. *Educational Researcher,* pp. 27–29.

Perry, P., Valero, P., Castro, M., Gómez, P., & Agudelo, C. (1998). *La calidad de las matemáticas en secundaria: Actores y procesos en la institución educativa.* Bogotá: una empresa docente.

Popkewitz, T. (1991). *A political sociology of educational reform: Power/knowledge in teaching, teacher education and research.* New York: Teachers College Press.

Popkewitz, T. (1998a). *Struggling for the soul: The politics of schooling and the construction of the teacher.* London: Teachers College Press.

Popkewitz, T. (1998b). The culture of redemption and the administration of freedom as research. *Review of Educational Research, 68*(1), 1–34.

Powell, A., & Frankenstein, M. (Eds.). (1997). *Ethnomathematics. Challenging Eurocentrism in mathematics education.* Albany: State University of New York Press.

Reddy, V. (2000). *Life histories of black South African scientists: Academic success in an unequal society.* Unpublished D.Ed. dissertation, University of Durban-Westville, Durban.

Restivo, S. (1992). *Mathematics in society and history.* Dordrecht: Kluwer Academic Publishers.

Romberg, T. A., & Collins, A. (2000). The impact of standards-based reform on methods of research in schools. In A. E. Kelly & R. A. Lesh (Eds.), *Handbook of research design in mathematics and science education* (pp. 73–85). Mahwah, NJ: Lawrence Erlbaum Associates.

Rogers, P., & Kaiser, G. (Eds.) (1995). *Equity in mathematics education: Influences of feminism and culture.* London: Falmer Press.

Ruthven, K. (1999). The North writes back: North-South dialogue. *Perspectives in Education, 18*(1), 13–17.

Samuel, M. (1999a). *Words, lives and music: On becoming a teacher of English.* Unpublished D.Ed. dissertation, University of Durban-Westville, Durban.

Samuel, M. (1999b). *Researching in rapidly changing environments.* Paper for Teacher Education in Developing Countries – The Multi-site Teacher Education Research Project (Research Seminar Series). Durban: University of Durban-Westville, Centre for Educational Research, Evaluation and Policy.

Scheurich, J. (1997). The masks of validity: A deconstructive investigation. *Research methods in the postmodern* (pp. 80–93). London: Falmer Press. (Originally published 1996 in *Qualitative Studies in Education, 9*(1), 49–60)

Scheurich, J. J., & Young, M. D. (1997). Colouring epistemologies: Are our research epistemologies racially biased? *Educational Researcher, 27*(3), 4–16.

Secada, W., Fennema, E., & Adajian, L. (Eds.) (1995). *New directions for equity in mathematics education.* Cambridge: Cambridge University Press.

Seepe, S. (2000). Higher education and Africanisation. *Perspectives in Education, 18*(3), 52–71.

Setati, M. (1999). Ways of talking in a multilingual mathematics classroom. In O. Zaslavski (Ed.), *Proceedings of the 23rd Conference of the International Group for the Psychology of Mathematics Education* (Vol. 4, pp. 177–184). Haifa: Israel Institute of Technology.

Setati, M. (2000). Classroom-based research: from *with or on* teachers to *with and on* teachers. In J. F. Matos & M. Santos (Eds.), *Proceedings of the Second International Mathematics Education and Society Conference* (pp. 351–363). Lisbon: CIEFC – Universidade de Lisboa.

Shan, S., & Bailey, P. (1991). *Multiple factors: Classroom mathematics for equality and justice.* Staffordshire: Trentham Books Limited.

Sierpinska, A. (1993). Criteria for scientific quality and relevance in the didactics of mathematics. In G. Nissen & M. Blomhøj (Eds.), *Criteria for scientific quality and relevance in the didactics of mathematics* (pp. 35–74). Roskilde: Roskilde University.

Sierpinska, A., & Kilpatrick, J. (Eds.). (1998). *Mathematics education as a research domain: A search for identity.* Dordrecht: Kluwer Academic Publishers.

Singh, S. (1998). Women's perceptions and experiences of mathematics. In C. Keitel (Ed.), *Social justice and mathematics education: Gender, class, ethnicity and the politics of schooling* (pp. 101–107). Berlin: IOWME – Freie Universität Berlin.

Singh, S. (2000). *'Intruders in the sacred grove of science'? A critical analysis of women academics' participation in research.* Unpublished D.Ed. dissertation, University of Durban-Westville, Durban.

Singh, S., & Vithal, R. (1999, October). *Feminism's courtship with survey: Dangerous liaisons or close encounters of the feminist kind?* Paper presented at the Women-in-Research Conference. Durban: University of Natal, Innovation Centre.

Skott, J. (2000). *The images and practice of mathematics teachers.* Unpublished Ph.D. dissertation, Royal Danish School of Educational Studies, Copenhagen.

Skovsmose, O. (1990). Mathematical education and democracy. *Educational Studies in Mathematics, 21*, 109–128.

Skovsmose, O. (1994). *Towards a philosophy of critical mathematics education.* Dordrecht: Kluwer Academic Publishers.

Skovsmose, O. (2000). Aporism and critical mathematics education. *For the Learning of Mathematics, 20*(1), 2–8.

Skovsmose, O., & Borba, M. (2000). *Research methodology and critical mathematics education* (Pre-print series of the Centre for Research in Learning Mathematics No. 17). Roskilde & Aalborg: CRLM, Danish University of Education, Roskilde University & Aalborg University.

Skovsmose, O., & Nielsen, L. (1996). Critical mathematics education. In A. Bishop, K. Clements,

C. Keitel, J. Kilpatrick, & C. Laborde (Eds.), *International handbook of mathematics education* (pp. 1257–1288). Dordrecht: Kluwer Academic Publishers.

Skovsmose, O., & Valero, P. (2001a). Breaking political neutrality: The critical engagement of mathematics education with democracy. In B. Atweh, H. Forgasz, & B. Nebres (Eds.), *Socio-cultural aspects of mathematics education: An international research perspective* (pp. 37–55). Mahwah, NJ: Lawrence Erlbaum Associates.

Skovsmose, O., & Valero, P. (2001b). Democratic access to powerful mathematical ideas. In L. D. English (Ed.), *Handbook of international research in mathematics education: Directions for the 21st century*. Mahwah, NJ: Lawrence Erlbaum Associates.

Smith, L. T. (1999). *Decolonizing methodologies: Research and indigenous peoples.* Dunedin: University of Otago Press.

Steen, L. A. (1999). Theories that gyre and gimble in the wabe. *Journal for Research in Mathematics Education, 30*(2), 235–241.

Tate, W. F. IV. (1996). Mathematizing and the democracy: The need for an education that is multicultural and social reconstructionist. In C. A. Grant & M. L. Gómez (Eds.), *Making schooling multicultural: Campus and classroom* (pp. 185–201). Upper Saddle River, NJ: Prentice Hall.

Tobin, K. (2000). Interpretive research in science education. In A. E. Kelly & R. A. Lesh (Eds.), *Handbook of research design in mathematics and science education* (pp. 487–512). Mahwah, NJ: Lawrence Erlbaum Associates.

Trentacosta, J., & Kenny, M. J. (Eds.) (1997). *Multicultural and gender equity in the mathematics classroom: The gift of diversity* (1997 Yearbook of the National Council of Teachers of Mathematics). Reston VA: NCTM.

Turner, S. E. (2000, October). A comment on 'Poor school funding, child poverty, and mathematics achievement'. *Educational Researcher*, pp. 15–18.

Valero, P. (1999a). Deliberative mathematics education for social democratization in Latin America. *Zentralblatt für Didaktik der Mathematik, 98*(6), 20–26.

Valero, P. (1999b). Dilemas de la investigación socio-política en educación matemática. In Asociação de Profesores de Matemática de Portugal (Ed.), *Memorias do X Seminario de Investigação em Educação Matemática* (X SIEM, pp. 87–96). Lisboa: APM.

Valero, P. (2000). Reforma, democracia y educación matemática en la escuela secundaria. In J. F. Matos & E. Fernandes (Eds.), *Investigação em educação matemática: Perspectivas e problemas* (pp. 103–111). Funchal, Portugal: Universidade da Madeira, APM.

Valero, P., Gómez, P., & Perry, P. (1997). School mathematics improvement: Administrators and teachers as researchers. In V. Zack, J. Mousley & C. Breen (Eds.), *Developing practice: Teachers' inquiry and educational change* (pp. 113–121). Geelong, Australia: Deakin University, CSMEE.

Valero, P., & Matos, J. F. (2000). Dilemmas of social/political/cultural research in mathematics education. In J. F. Matos & M. Santos (Eds.), *Proceedings of the Second International Mathematics Education and Society Conference* (pp. 394–403). Lisbon: CIEFC – University of Lisbon.

Valero, P., & Vithal, R. (1998). Research methods of the North revisited from the South. In A. Olivier & K. Newstead (Eds.), *Proceedings of the 22nd Conference of the PME* (Vol. 4, pp. 153–160). Stellenbosch: University of Stellenbosch. Reprinted in *Perspectives in Education, 18*(1), 5–12.

Vithal, R. (1997). Exploring student teachers' understanding of a theoretical perspective in mathematics teacher education. In M. Sanders (Ed.), *Proceedings of the Fifth Annual Meeting of the Southern African Association of Mathematics and Science Education* (pp. 331–342). Johannesburg: University of the Witwatersrand.

Vithal, R. (1998). Data and disruptions: The politics of doing mathematics education research in South Africa. In N. A. Ogude & C. Bohlmann (Eds.), *Proceedings of the Sixth Annual Meeting of the Southern African Association for Research in Mathematics and Science Education* (pp. 475–481). Pretoria: University of South Africa.

Vithal, R. (1999). Democracy and authority. A complementarity in mathematics education? *Zentralblatt für Didaktik der Mathematik, 98*(6), 27–36.

Vithal, R. (2000a). *In search of a pedagogy of conflict and dialogue for mathematics education.* Unpublished Ph.D. dissertation, Aalborg University Center, Aalborg, Denmark.

Vithal, R. (2000b). In the search for criteria of quality and relevance for mathematics education research: The case of validity. In S. Mahlomaholo (Ed.), *Proceedings of the 8th Annual Meeting of the Southern African Association for Research in Mathematics and Science Education* (pp. 567–573). Port Elizabeth: University of Port Elizabeth.

Vithal, R. (2000c). Re-searching mathematics education from a critical perspective. In J. F. Matos & M. Santos (Eds.), *Proceedings of the Second International Mathematics Education and Society Conference* (pp. 87–116). Lisboa: Universidade de Lisboa.

Vithal, R. (2001a). Crucial descriptions: Connecting research, theory and practice in mathematics education. In I. V. Mutimucuio (Ed.), *Proceedings of the 9th Conference of the Southern African Association of Research in Mathematics, Science and Technology Education* (pp. 81–90). Maputo: Eduardo Mondlane University Press.

Vithal, R. (2001b, July). A pedagogy of conflict and dialogue for mathematics education from a critical perspective. In M. Setati (Ed.), *Proceedings of the Seventh National Congress of the Association for Mathematics Education of South Africa* (pp. 28–48). Johannesburg: University of the Witwatersrand.

Vithal, R., Christiansen, I., & Skovsmose, 0. (1995). Project work in university mathematics education. *Educational Studies in Mathematics* (Special issue on advanced mathematical thinking), 29(1), 199–223.

Vithal, R., Paras, J., Desai, S., Zuma, Z., Samsukal, A., Ramdass, R., & Gcashbe, J. (1997). Student teachers doing project work in primary mathematics classrooms. In P. Kelsall & M. de Villiers (Eds.), *Proceedings of the Third National Congress of the Association for Mathematics Educators of South Africa* (pp. 261–276). Durban: University of Natal Durban.

Vithal, R., & Skovsmose, O. (1997). The end of innocence: A critique of 'Ethnomathematics'. *Educational Studies in Mathematics, 34*, 131–157.

Vithal, R., & Valero, P. (2001, August). *Researching mathematics education in situations of social and political conflict* (Preprint Series of the Centre for Research in Learning Mathematics). Roskilde & Aalborg, Denmark: Danish University of Education, CRLM.

Volmink, J. (1994). Mathematics by all. In S. Lerman (Ed.), *Cultural perspectives on the mathematics classroom* (pp. 51–68). Dordrecht: Kluwer Academic Publishers.

Wagner, V. (1997). The unavoidable intervention of educational research: A framework for reconsidering research-practitioner cooperation. *Educational Researcher, 26*(7), 13–22.

Walkerdine, V. (1988). *The mastery of reason.* London: Routledge.

Walkerdine, V. (1998). *Counting girls out: Girls and mathematics* (New ed.). London: Falmer Press.

Wedege, T. (1999). To know or not to know – mathematics, that is a question of context. *Educational Studies in Mathematics, 39*(1–3), 229–249.

Woodrow, D. (1997). Democratic education: Does it exist – especially for mathematics education? *For the Learning of Mathematics, 17*(3), 11–16.

Zaslavsky, C. (1991). World cultures in the mathematics class. *For the Learning of Mathematics, 11*(2), 32–36.

Zevenbergen, R. (2000a). 'Cracking the code' of mathematics classrooms: School success as a function of linguistic, social and cultural background. In J. Boaler (Ed.), *Multiple perspectives on mathematics teaching and learning* (pp. 201–224). Westport, CT: Ablex Publishing.

Zevenbergen, R. (2000b). Pathways: Possibilities for reform and social justice. In J. F. Matos & M. Santos (Eds.), *Proceedings of the Second International Mathematics Education and Society Conference* (pp. 45–56). Lisbon: CIEFC – Universidade de Lisboa.

17
Obstacles to the Dissemination of Mathematics Education Research

ANDY BEGG
Open University

BRENT DAVIS
University of Alberta

ROD BRAMALD
University of Newcastle

ABSTRACT

Mathematics education research has often been undertaken with an expectation that the results would have some influence on teachers' practice and on educational policies including curriculum, but numerous obstacles seem to limit that influence. This investigation of the topic begins by exploring the meanings of the words obstacles, dissemination, mathematics, education, and research. In section 2, the development process and the relationship between research, policy, and practice are examined. Next, some variables that influence change are considered. In the fourth section, some of the obstacles are discussed under the headings 'research and researchers', 'teachers and schools', and 'systems'. Finally, three strategies for the future are suggested; these relate to communication and complexity, changing the development model, and extending the boundaries of research.

INTRODUCTION

Talking about the relationship between mathematics and education, Bishop (1992) suggests that mathematics is somewhat unique and therefore that it needs to be seen as a specific subset of education. An alternative view is that mathematics, like every other subject, offers a different but complementary perspective in terms of how learners make sense of their worlds. As such, mathematics education requires no special status inasmuch as the range of perspectives offered by all subjects needs to be acknowledged. This second view is important for elementary school teachers. They teach most subjects and look for commonalities rather than differences, and their approaches to teaching mathematics are often similar to those they use with other subjects. This observation supports the view that in mathematics education and mathematics education research there is a need to be concerned with not only mathematics but also the learning and teaching

Second International Handbook of Mathematics Education, 593–634
A.J. Bishop, M.A. Clements, C. Keitel, J. Kilpatrick and F.K.S. Leung (eds.)
© *2003 Dordrecht: Kluwer Academic Publishers. Printed in Great Britain.*

of all subjects. This rejection of the uniqueness of mathematics is also important because mathematics itself is merely part of a Western partitioning of knowledge. As Bishop (1988) has said, in some cultures there is no grouping of ideas called mathematics, although there are a number of separate activities that involve mathematical thinking.

Four intersecting domains of research influence the curriculum, policies, and practices related to the learning and teaching of mathematics. These are research within mathematics in terms of what mathematicians know and do, research into mathematics pedagogy, research into education in general, and research into the nature of learning. Although the first two of these could be interpreted in terms of the uniqueness that Bishop (1992) spoke of, all four domains influence teaching. For example, within statistics, new topics such as resampling have been developed and may need to be considered in terms of a possible curriculum change to update the subject and with an aim of achieving better understanding of the related concepts. An example of research in mathematics pedagogy is the work on misconceptions that students have or develop with a topic (Assessment Performance Unit, 1985; Cambridge Institute of Education, 1985; Hart, Johnson, Brown, Dickson, & Clarkson, 1989; Hart, Kerslake, Brown, Ruddock, Küchemann, & McCartney, 1981), and it is generally believed that an awareness of such misconceptions helps teachers assist their students to come to acceptable understandings. General educational research involves learning, teaching, curriculum, teacher education, educational policy, assessment, classroom management, and other themes that relate to educational practices in general, and some researchers working in these areas would be using mathematics as the context for their studies. We believe that research that specifically focuses on the nature of learning has emerged as important over the last few decades. Indeed, the most compelling and innovative work in mathematics education research has been linked to new ways of thinking about how people learn and the way that particular teaching practices and schooling structures assume or enact these theories of learning.

Once researchers have been involved in projects and have written up their findings, they would like these to be influential. When that does not occur, they may feel aggrieved and wonder about a system that encourages research but appears to take no notice of the findings. Thus the questions arise, What are the obstacles to dissemination? And what might be done to change the situation? Numerous mathematics educators have commented on these questions, but there is little evidence of research into the questions; thus this chapter is one of scholarship in which comments about the perceived problem have been explored by looking for relationships and reasons. As we develop our argument, our suspicion is that the most significant obstacles to the dissemination of research are *not* the explicit or obvious barriers (although these can be sources of considerable frustration) but rather the habits of perception and interpretation that frame one's immediate actions.

In this chapter, we draw from a number of discourses,[1] among them phenomenology, radical and social constructivisms, enactivism, ecology, and systems and complexity theories – in brief, those domains of inquiry that contribute to what Capra (1996) has described as "a new scientific understanding of living systems". These theories converge around a desire to better understand the tacit ground of human activity – that is, the 'taken for granted', the 'commonsensical', and the 'way things are'. To contextualize these theories within the current mathematics education literature, they might be considered as elaborations of radical and social constructivist epistemologies. They have common views of learning and knowing as complex, emergent processes by which dynamic agents maintain fitness with one another and within dynamic contexts. However, rather than limiting the notion of 'agent' to the body biologic (as radical constructivists do) or to a social corpus (a body of knowledge or a student body, as social constructivists might), these perspectives frame such (knowing) bodies as emerging from and as nested in other complex systems. This move compels attendance to such matters as biologic predisposition as it influences and is influenced by cultural context, which in turn affects and is affected by emergent environmental circumstances.

Two of the key concepts within this shift in thinking are the following:

1. An enlargement of the notion of cognitive (or learning) systems, and
2. The combining together of knowledge, activity, and identity.

On the first concept, a *learning system* is seen as any complex form that can adapt itself to changing circumstances. Examples include a stock market as it adjusts to unexpected economic news, an ecosystem as it establishes a new balance when the climate changes, a child who accommodates to the demands of a new classroom, and a workplace community that adjusts to the expectations within the larger social context. For the most part, such systems are dynamic and robust, able to change and adapt efficiently. Inherent in this notion is the broader definition of cognition as 'coming to know', which includes traditional rational thinking and other forms of learning.

From such a perspective, *learning* refers to transformations, those that expand the learner's potential range of action – and it is here that the second major concept fits into place. The suggestion that learning is a *transformation* is a reference to the physical character of a learning system. Upon learning, a system's patterns of activity and its associations – internal and external, with and in other systems – undergo physical change. Put differently, learning affects the entire web of being, and it follows that what one knows, what one does, and who or what one is cannot be separated.

With the melding of knowing, doing, and being, discussions of learning are broadened to include the unformulated or tacit ground of human activity. Knowledge is seen not in strictly formal or formulated terms, nor as independent of individuals and their environments, nor as something that can be tested and matched against external standards, but rather as embodied action. Such ecological perspectives locate knowing within a complex web of relations, with all decisions and actions being both constrained by and influencing all nodes of the web. In rejecting the separation of self from others, and knowledge from knower, these ecologically minded theories emphasize *being connected*, which is much stronger than the notion of *making connections* (see Dawson, 1999; Kieren, 1995).

1. MEANINGS

The title of this chapter uses five key words – *obstacles, dissemination, mathematics, education*, and *research*. Although these words have generally accepted meanings, each also has some problematic aspects that are worthy of exploration.

1.1. *Obstacles*

An obstacle is usually thought of as "something that obstructs onward movement". This obstruction is usually seen as undesirable. But if the direction or speed of a movement is not the preferred one, then an obstacle may be desirable, although it may then be given a less value-laden label such as a 'retardant'. Although researchers may want their findings used, others may disagree. Thus what is perceived as an obstacle by one person may be seen positively by others, and an obstacle may be temporarily or permanently serving a valuable function. Although some obstacles may be deliberately constructed to retard a change, others emerge from structural circumstances and may not be directly related to specific findings or proposed changes, and yet others emerge accidentally or as the result of unforeseen circumstances. Howson, Keitel, and Kilpatrick (1981) wrote of the "barriers to change as being values, power, practical, and psychological factors", and these are evident in deliberate and structural obstacles.

Prompted by the perspectives on knowing and knowledge from our introduction, we should note that obstacles are not merely things that appear in front of us that compel some sort of change in course. They are also those forms and phenomena that channel our activities in particular ways – the patterns of acting, the habits of interpretation, the momentum of history, and so on that give shape and meaning to our everyday activities. Unfortunately, through familiarity, such forms tend to become invisible to us. As such, they cease to be seen as obstacles; they come to be taken as the natural shoreline, the way things are. The acceptance of such forms and phenomena as the way things are is perhaps the major obstacle to the dissemination of mathematics education research. In fact, the obstacles that appear in the river are insignificant compared with the ones that define the river's course and shoreline. For this reason, we need to consider interrogating the ground of our actions. As we develop the realization that the most significant (and the least noticed) obstacles are those that channel activity (rather than those that are perceived to impede it once channeled), a domain of research questions reopens. They include the following: What is it that we are doing when we claim to be teaching mathematics? How is school mathematics knitted into our collective being? How are cultural beliefs enfolded in mathematics pedagogy?

1.2. *Dissemination*

Dissemination usually implies a process of "sending out and being implemented", but the process often resembles the dictionary meaning of the word: "the process of scattering seeds (often on barren soil)". Under the notion of "sending out and being implemented", dissemination has connotations of expert and learner and of teacher-as-technician rather than teacher-as-professional, and these may prompt negative reactions among teachers. Even without negative reactions, dissemination may still be problematic because the complexity of the research-theory-policy-practice relationship is not perceived in the same way by all participants in the dissemination process (see section 2).

Conversely, the more contingent and accidental definition, "the process of scattering seeds (often on barren soil)", might be used to reframe the project of broadcasting (a notion that is also rooted in the idea of scattering seeds) research developments. In particular, such a shift implies a different role for the academic or researcher, one that might be described in terms of a shift from telling to conversing. This shift recognises that lines of influence are never direct and one-way, as studies of social interaction and other complex events have demonstrated, (see Nørretranders, 1998, for a summary of some of this research). Rather, to be effective, efforts at dissemination must be attentive to the effects of those efforts. On this count, projects of dissemination of research are not unlike the project of teaching mathematics. The stage, the players, and the audiences are different, but the structural dynamics of the project are similar.

For us, there is a range of nested and interacting bodies that must be considered when disseminating findings from mathematics education research. The way findings influence curriculum, policy, and practice can be interpreted at numerous levels varying from the macro to the micro. These include the official, unofficial, school, teacher policy, and teacher practice levels, and some aspects of these are shown in Table 1. These levels are only indicative, and alternative hierarchies

Table 1.   Five Levels of Policy and Practice

Policy and practice level	*Official policy*	*Unofficial policy*	*School policy*	*Teacher policy*	*Teacher practice*
Descriptor	political	professional	community	personal intent	personal enactment
Sphere of influence	regional	various	local	individual	class
Evidence	curricula, regulations	standards, textbooks	programmes, school culture	lesson plans, classroom rules	taught curriculum, classroom practice

are possible; for example, teacher practice could be subsumed by teacher policy, and school policy and school practice could be separated.

Research has implications at all five levels. Traditionally some levels have waited until research findings have impinged at other levels, usually higher ones. For example, teachers' lesson planning influences their practice, their planning in turn is linked to school programme planning, and that is dependent on curriculum and textbooks. Although one may assume such an approach to be the way that policies and practice are influenced, the alternative is to acknowledge that anyone can initiate change. From this perspective, teachers, schools, textbook authors, professional associations, and bureaucrats can all be change agents and can initiate changes at their own levels and subsequently influence other levels. Recognition of that point, with communication between levels, may lead to more effective use of these change agents, which would imply that researchers, policy makers, and practitioners need to communicate to a broad audience, and failure to do so may be an obstacle in the dissemination of educational initiatives.

An alternative view of dissemination arises if one agrees with Mason's (1998) views about the significant products of research in mathematics education. He says, "The most significant products are the transformations in the being of the researchers", whereas "the second most significant products are stimuli to other researchers and teachers to test out conjectures for themselves in their own context" (p. 257). From this perspective, the dissemination that occurs does so without being imposed. It avoids the expert-novice connotation. It is a form of shared collegiality, with teachers encouraged to test things for themselves and become small-scale researchers.

1.3. *Mathematics*

In the context of mathematics education research, mathematics is usually thought of as school mathematics with the aim being preparation for academic mathematics, adult life, and the workplace. Little cognisance seems to be taken of other types of mathematics. These include everyday mathematics that might be learnt outside school, ethnomathematics that depends on ethnic and other cultures, mathematics that may be learnt with home computer use, and other mathematical activities that are embedded in other school subjects, recreation, and outside-school experiences. If a significant amount of mathematics is being learnt in contexts other than school, and if the topics being learned are broader than is implied by the school curriculum, then those topics need to influence what is considered as mathematics.

School mathematics, like mathematics, is a dynamic subject. It is a vibrant and emergent body within a larger and evolving body of knowledge. New areas are continually developing, and new techniques are being developed with the advancement of computing. These changes are based on research that is mainly of the scholarship and creative endeavour form. They slowly influence tertiary education, and some influences are felt in schools. This phenomenon is generally thought of not as an influence of research but as part of a natural evolutionary process. Perhaps following the more tentative definition of *dissemination* offered above, it is appropriate to consider such developments as part of the dissemination process.

To elaborate, school mathematics includes a number of content areas such as number, measurement, geometry, and algebra, and later trigonometry and calculus. These content areas are slowly changing as more countries consider including topics such as statistics and probability in their mathematics curricula. In addition, in the last two decades, influenced by the *Cockcroft Report* (Department of Education and Science and the Welsh Office, 1982) and by the *Standards* (National Council of Teachers of Mathematics, 1989, 2000), the emphasis has moved from mathematical *content* or *what mathematicians know* to include mathematical *processes* or *what mathematicians do*. These processes are problem solving, reasoning, communicating, making connections, and using technology. This emphasis on the processes has altered the way we all think about mathematics.

Such shifts have also opened the door to somewhat more radical attitudes to the nature of mathematics. For example, emerging social constructivist (e.g., Ernest, 1991), critical (e.g., Walkerdine, 1987), and enactivist views break from many traditional perspectives in their emphasis on the co-implication of individual knowing and collective knowledge. Such viewpoints prompt the discussion away from the question of *what mathematics is* and toward *what mathematics does*. Put differently, the emergent perspectives on learning compel us to ask how this subject matter is knitted into our individual and collective beings. How does mathematics infuse worldviews, shape our activities, and define our possibilities? Implicit in this line of questioning is the assertion that knowledge cannot be considered as separable from knowers – a conceptual demand that renders mathematics, as Davis and Hersh (1981) have suggested, a humanity, a study of ourselves-in-the-universe. Taking this viewpoint further, one begins to realize the profound curricular implications of new perspectives on mathematical inquiry.

1.4. *Education*

Among mathematics education researchers, discussions of teaching tend to be framed in terms of the co-implicated matters of "how do students learn" and "what should teachers do to facilitate this learning". In some pre-service teacher education programmes, however, many courses focus on what the teacher does rather than on how students learn. The underlying issue is a critical one: For the most part, in school classrooms and university seminar rooms alike, learning is usually treated as a well-understood phenomenon. Such a tacit assumption may be the greatest barrier to the dissemination of research, as it channels attention away from the complex matter of what learning is to the (technocratically framed) issue of how teachers can make learning (naively understood) happen. In effect, the situation parallels the "conceptual versus procedural understanding" dyad developed by Hiebert (1986), applied in this case to the understanding of human learning rather than the understanding of school mathematics.

This situation may arise in part because schooling is often cast in instrumental or mechanical terms. A more complicated conceptualisation might, for instance, prompt awareness that schooling is complex because teaching is neither a necessary nor sufficient condition for learning. Schooling is influenced not only by how students learn, but also by school and regional curricula, by assessment policies and practice, by the aims of education and of schooling, as well as by other societal, political, and cultural factors. Unfortunately, in mathematics education, research is often stripped of this complexity and considered variable by variable, and often that is done by assuming a simple causality rather than by seeing the educational process as a complex interplay of related influences.

One approach when learning or teaching is being discussed or researched is to consider the theoretical framework that might be used to best make sense of the situation. That often means what learning theory will be assumed. Over the years, such theories have been described by many adjectives, such as associationist, behaviourist, constructivist (with many variations), post-Darwinist, neo-Deweyist, and enactivist. At the same time, progressive, Gestalt, critical, humanist, cognitive science, and numerous other labels indicate other influences. It is often forgotten that different people make different assumptions and may feel uncomfortable with a report based on alternative assumptions. Of even more concern is the notion that a theory or assumption might be considered as if it was true, rather than being acknowledged along with other theories with each providing different insights on a particular situation.

It is not only theoretical frameworks such as the learning theories being assumed that need consideration; other assumptions about learning that infuse present-day efforts in education and schooling need critical examination. One relates to the deep-seated, commonsense assumption that casts the individual student as the 'fundamental particle' of learning. This assumption has had (and continues to have) profound effects on schooling practice with individualised seating, individualised testing, and individualised instruction – sorts of phenomena that are linked to the modern and Western belief in the coherent, stable, fully-knowable self. This is an assumption at which ecological and complex accounts of learning aim their main critiques of conventional educational practice, highlighting the complex, co-emergent natures of events of cognition. They have prompted attention towards the similar and co-implicated dynamics at work in phenomena such as the evolution of a species, the unfolding of a culture, the emergence of a body of knowledge, the learning of an individual, and the transformations of bodily subsystems. They see the individual learner as one of many nested layers of dynamic evolving agents. And it follows that one cannot properly engage in a discussion of a phenomenon at one level, such as the place of formal education, without a willingness to address what it might mean at other levels, such as the viability of the culture or the life of the individual. That, in turn, compels a willingness to interrogate the habits of thinking that have allowed for such taken-for-granted dichotomies as mental/physical, self/other, individual/collective, human/natural, and truth/fiction – and for the ways that these are enfolded into conventional schooling structures.

Another concern is the separation of education and pedagogy or didactics. The first is sometimes considered as a study *about* education, and courses typically focus on historic, philosophical, political, sociological, and psychological aspects of the subject; that is, the 'isms' and 'ologies' of education. The second is thought of as being concerned with *how to* educate. This dichotomy is unreasonable because 'how to' needs to be considered within the broader perspective. Similar undesirable dichotomies arise when mathematics education is separated from general education, from mathematics method courses related to teaching, and from mathematics itself.

1.5. *Research*

Is the aim of research to contribute to knowledge, to inform practice, or to provide an alternative perspective through which to consider things? Or is research simply part of the practice of practitioners? Bishop (1992) said that research is intentional enquiry, it is evidence based, and its goal is theory. An alternative to this claim is that the goal of research is the growth of the researchers. A third alternative is to consider a hermeneutic attitude when thinking about research questions or unfamiliar areas to be explored from which, in time, understandings emerge and questions arise. In considering questions, Gadamer (1990) suggests that most fall into one of three categories: the teacherly, the rhetorical, and the hermeneutic. The teacherly question has an answer that is already known by the questioner. The rhetorical question is not really a question, as the answer is assumed unknowable. Gadamer sees neither teacherly nor rhetorical questions as being oriented toward the development of deeper understandings, and for him the only genuine sort of question is hermeneutic.

Hermeneutics is the study of interpretation. It is concerned with what is believed and how those beliefs were established. Hence, a hermeneutic question is an event of interpretation that is oriented by a desire to expand the sphere of the known. It is a manner of engagement that arrives as a confession of the inadequacy of one's current understandings, a suspicion of the partialities of one's knowings, a realization of the need for constant reinterpretation. Hermeneutics demands of the researcher a willingness to acknowledge the limitations and the fallibilities of his or her current understandings and interpretations. As such, a hermeneutic attitude would exclude research into, for example, optimising instructional sequences. Instead, a hermeneutic researcher would likely ask something along the lines of the following: "What must we believe about teaching and learning for us to think that instruction can or should be optimised?"

In a sense, much of the work in mathematics education research over the past few decades has been hermeneutic, especially those aspects that have drawn on or elaborated radical and social constructivist discourses. That work has genuinely sought to uncover much of what tends to be taken for granted. The extent to which such work has been taken up by policy makers and education managers, however, has been rather underwhelming. What tends to be picked up from the research are often only the aspects that do not compel people to rethink the foundations of their own practices.

From this perspective, it is interesting to ask "Who values research?". The word *research* is a verb and a noun, and both *researching* (the verb) and the *research findings* (the noun) are of value. The 'researching' aspect is often overlooked, it relates to the personal and professional growth of the researcher as implied by Gadamer's (1990) comments on hermeneutic questions. Associated with this growth, and as a result of doing research, researchers in our experience seem to come to value the research of others more than nonresearchers do. A consequence of this phenomenon is that if research is to become more accepted, and if the only people who value research are researchers, then perhaps more people should be encouraged to do research. Such involvement should not be limited to graduate study. If education is to develop a lifelong quest for understanding, then research by learners (including teachers) may be more valuable educationally than mathematics or other subjects that are taught in schools and universities. Young children learn research skills when doing projects, but such activities are often given less emphasis in high school and undergraduate education. Perhaps children need more encouragement to do research throughout their education, and such a focus may need to be sustained as part of learning to seek information and becoming an autonomous learner. In this situation, with more people involved in research, more sympathy to research findings may be evident and the change process enhanced.

A question that arises in the context of 'changing curriculum, policy, and practice' is, What is accepted as research within mathematics education? Traditionally research was acceptable if it was quantitative, either descriptive or experimental. This tradition had an important limitation that concerned many educators. Giorgi (1970), for example, suggested one could almost say "measurement precedes existence" (p. 65). He argued along the lines that priority is given to measurement but that for something to be measured only its tangible aspects can be apprehended. As a result, these aspects of the phenomenon become more important than the phenomenon itself. In the search for a measurable element, the researcher loses sight of the significance of other aspects of the phenomenon. The non-measurable aspects tend to be discarded, and only the measurable element is included in the investigation.

In the 1980s and 1990s, qualitative research became as acceptable as quantitative research in many countries, but both qualitative and quantitative researchers have tended to share similar assumptions. In particular, both have been readily aligned with empiricist sensibilities – in particular, the assumption that the 'real world' is out there and awaiting description. Such an orientation may be appropriate in domains like physics, but in the complex and volatile realms of social engagement, efforts to describe *what's there* can push to the side such concerns as *why should it be there* and *what else should be there*.

For some people, action research is any research that results in an action component, but it is more usually thought of as 'critical' research. Action researchers, often teachers, see themselves empowered to find solutions to problems in their classrooms, and although that view is important, it often undervalues some of the contributions that critical research might make. This undervaluing is due in part to the fact that the discourse of critical research, as picked up by educators, has been skewed toward Marxist preoccupations with 'empowerment' paradigms and can sometimes ignore the full range of critical discourses in education, which include aesthetic, psychoanalytic, and ecological emphases. To include these discourses, one needs to recognise the uniting quality in critical research: a refusal to accept 'the way things are' as 'the way things must be', or phrased differently, a commitment to the questions, 'What are we doing?' and 'Why are we doing it?' This broader view of 'critical research' is evident when one reads how the movement began – with the 'critical hermeneutics' movement that rose to prominence about a century ago (Gallagher, 1992).

To distinguish quantitative and qualitative research from critical hermeneutic research, it is useful to assume that the former tends to begin with a question, whereas the latter tends towards a tentative approach. Such an approach assumes that humans do not always know what the important questions are in advance of an engaged inquiry into the structures that give shape to current preoccupations.

Although quantitative, qualitative, and critical research can all inform policy and practice, other activities might also be regarded as research. These are scholarship, evaluation as part of development, exploratory studies, informal research, reflection on practice, practitioner hunches, and creative work. The meanings of these terms have been summarised in Table 2.

It may be desirable to extend our view of 'research' and acknowledge these activities when making decisions about curriculum, policy, and practice in mathematics education. Such activities usually involve large numbers of practitioners, they tend to occur over a considerable time span, and they involve practitioners' ownership rather than a feeling of imposition.

Table 2.   Other Research Activities

Term	Meaning
Scholarship	study, teachers' professional reading, or theory building
Evaluation	informal processes such as teachers' evaluating lessons or teachers' or authors' evaluating draft resources and textbooks
Exploratory study	small studies by groups of teachers, initiated by them or by another agency to explore new ideas or strategies to inform development
Informal research	minor research activities that are not usually written up
Reflection on practice	cognitive consideration of current and past practice
Practitioner hunches	unformulated, intuitive ideas based on experience
Creative work	original and inventive notions related to possible practice

Lampert (2000) sees teachers as possible initiators and participants in research. She sees them as adding valuable insider knowledge, having the potential to change ideas about who is responsible for producing professional knowledge, and bringing the 'self' into scholarly activity. Others, too, for example, Hatch and Shiu (1998), have argued strongly for teachers to research their practice, but the acceptance of teachers-as-researchers is not axiomatic. Some, for example, Cochran-Smith and Lytle (1999), are concerned about whether the knowledge created by teacher-researchers belongs in the same category as traditional academic research knowledge. This debate appears to hinge largely on the nature of the evidence offered in support of teachers' narratives, which seems to be a dominant form for reporting teacher research. Malone (2000) has responded to this viewpoint by saying that there is ample evidence to demonstrate that teachers' research is having considerable impact locally, even if it does not have a high profile when viewed from outside the profession. This concern about the status of knowledge from teachers-as-researchers reflects the view that reform should come from the expert rather than being part of an evolutionary process in which teachers play a major role. This view reinforces technical rationality and authoritarianism rather than a community of practice. If teachers feel excluded, they may consider research an academic game of no consequence, which does not engender the desirable collaborative relationship that teachers and researchers need in a democratic educational environment.

Teacher-researchers usually focus on their own classrooms and acknowledge that their findings are specific to their contexts and classroom participants. Thus, their findings are not necessarily seen as applicable to other situations, but the findings slowly permeate the educational system when other teachers are encouraged to test the findings in their own classrooms. Although such a process may seem slow, it would have the advantage of encouraging ownership of findings and adaptation to suit other contexts, and these advantages could well compensate for any disadvantages.

Another aspect of research for development is the focus of the research. Academic research is often concerned with specific foci and is context specific, which is understandable in view of the limits put on many researchers. Policy makers, however, claim to want research that informs them about desirable trends and ways to put the findings into operation to achieve these trends. Such research is available (from feminist, Marxist, psychoanalytic, poststructural, and other critical perspectives), but unfortunately it tends to be ignored because it demands too great an accommodation by policy makers, as it tends to critique existing policies.

Related to research is the researcher. Most research is done by graduate students and by people with research grants. Both these groups seem reluctant to report failure. They naturally choose topics that interest them, and they work hard to ensure that their interests are portrayed positively. Their efforts are not usually likely to be replicated by ordinary teachers in any follow-up study, and the recognised 'halo' or 'Hawthorne' effect that occurs with new initiatives is generally ignored. This is one aspect of the statement that 'all research is subjective' and needs consideration when researchers suggest that their findings are significant.

2. DEVELOPMENT – RESEARCH, POLICY, AND PRACTICE

One way that the results of educational research are disseminated is through development activities.[2] These are typically associated with educational policy, curriculum, assessment, resources, and teachers. Thus, the relationship between development, research, policy, and practice needs to be understood when considering obstacles to dissemination.

Bobbitt and Tyler were early curriculum theorists who influenced curriculum in the English-speaking world. With associationism, an early form of behaviourism, the influence of Thorndike was evident, and then with behaviourism and constructivism, that of Gagné, Bruner, Dienes, and Piaget grew. The traditional research-development-dissemination (RDD) model fitted well with the ideas of behaviourism, and in the 1960s with the product orientation of the so-called new math, it continued to be seen as suitable. Later, however, in the context of curriculum development, Howson, Keitel and Kilpatrick (1981, p. 128) claimed that research, development, and dissemination could no longer be regarded as three distinct phases. Despite considerable research on other models for development (e.g., see Aichele & Coxford, 1994, on professional development), we believe that the RDD model continues to dominate development practices in many regions, not only for curriculum development but also for policy, assessment, and resource development. This dominance is likely to change only when other models become accepted. Alternative models may include more interrelated components, they may be totally integrated, or they may arise by considering alternative relationships between research and practice.

2.1. *The Traditional Development Model*

In the RDD model, the three stages are usually posited as a linear sequence of activities (see Figure 1), with separate groups of people being responsible for each stage. As such it is evident that 'development' comes between research and dissemination and this positions it as either a catalyst or an obstacle in the change process.

In more cynical moments, the RDD model for development activities has been described as the PHUT model because politics, hunches, underfunding, and totalitarianism seem to be the dominant factors influencing development. The RDD model has also sometimes been labelled as rDD and rDd because the various components are often small. Examples from curriculum development occur when the 'research' consists only of an unsystematic consideration of what

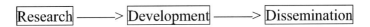

Figure 1. RDD model for development.

nearby regions are doing, comments from lead teachers, and feedback on draft documents by teachers. The influence of considerations of changes in neighbouring regions is evident in spite of statements such as that by Bishop (1996) in the introduction to the first edition of this handbook:

> One can never transplant an idea or a practice from one country to another, but one can certainly learn from the experiences of colleagues elsewhere who do use a different practice or follow a different philosophy. Other countries', and other colleagues', experiences always offer potentially interesting contrasts to one's own. (p. 3)

We would agree with what Bishop has said. At the same time, because of the cost of research and development activities and because these are supported by aid agencies and experts from overseas, the educational systems of many developing countries are under colonial-like pressures to at least partially adopt solutions from other countries. This phenomenon is particularly obvious in countries round the world that use overseas qualification systems to certify the satisfactory completion of schooling. In addition, with pressures of globalisation, internationalisation, and international comparisons, there seems to be even more pressure to consider adopting the practices of others.

When the RDD model is being used, the assumption is usually made that the development personnel are very familiar with the relevant research findings. When they are not, the development phase would seem to be an obstacle to dissemination. This separation of the three stages seems therefore to be a difficulty, yet with a concern about 'provider-capture', new right bureaucracies are increasingly separating them. This concern about separation was highlighted by Robinson (1989) in the context of work on teacher change (which had often been initiated in the past to help in the implementation of new curriculum, assessment, and resources). Robinson indicated that to be successful a number of conditions need to be satisfied, two of these were as follows:

1. Ownership of the change needs to be established by those involved at all stages; familiarity is not enough, and imposition by an external authority is not useful.
2. An ethos for change needs to be established within an empowerment paradigm in which participants decide to make changes rather than have managerial decisions imposed.

The fragmentation of the RDD model (with different groups taking responsibility for the three stages), however, does not allow for ownership to be established, nor does it empower the people affected by implementation to make decisions regarding the development. Thus, it is likely to impede dissemination and consideration may need to be given to alternative models for developing policies and practice.

Unfortunately, there seems to be little research on such models for policy development, which could well provide a focus for some valuable research in the future. There is, of course, a logical (and ironical) flaw in the suggestion that further research is needed on this matter. Can such a recommendation be taken up within the research model itself? We highlight the issue because of the assumption of linearity and causality that infuses the model (along with the assumptions that stakeholder groups can be tidily categorised). It is not clear how such a model could be aware (much less critical) of its own assumptions. Lacking such mindfulness, the recommendations of such research may extend little beyond the "We must all work harder" sorts of suggestions that typify the genre.

2.2. *Interrelated and Integrated Models for Development*

Introducing the section on 'Curriculum, Goals, Contents, Resources' in the first edition of this handbook, Kilpatrick (1996) said

> An appreciation of the distance between theory and practice, between goal and realisation, between intentions and consequences pervades the chapters in this section. The curriculum is inevitably both plan and result. The authors of these chapters have shown, in various ways, that the mathematics curriculum keeps its form even as it moves forward. (p. 9)

This statement implies that a gap or distance exists. In seeking alternative development models, one aim is to close this gap between research and the interrelated forms of development, namely, policy, curriculum, teacher, and resource development – with these five components being envisaged as being mutually dependent. Bringing them together changes the focus for dissemination of research, and it becomes an ongoing process of sharing rather than being something done to participants. This view may dishearten researchers who see the communication of their findings as being vital, but such a model may benefit research by keeping it more grounded in practice and by building the research community by having more teachers involved. This model for development requires the four components of development to be interrelated as illustrated in Figure 2. Such a model requires considerable communication between the people involved with the four aspects.

If the interrelationship of components is thought of as 'being connected' rather than as 'having connections made', then the model for development would become an integrated one as seen in Figure 3. In this model the communication would be automatically improved, as the same people would be involved in all four aspects of the process.

With an interrelated or an integrated model for development decisions would still need to be made about levels of consultation and the degree of consensus required. These models do not overcome such problems but are offered as alternatives that reduce the separation caused by the various stages in the RDD model that seem to be one obstacle to dissemination.

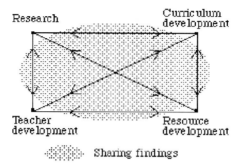

Figure 2.   Interrelated components of development.

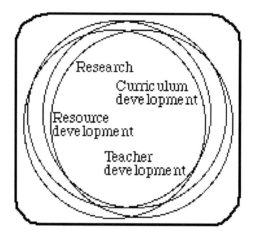

Figure 3.   Integrated components of development.

2.3. *Relationship Between Research, Theory, Policy, and Practice*

Rather than think about research, development, and dissemination as the model, one may consider the relationships between research, theory and policy, and practice and the implications they have for change. Such a model is often thought of in a similar linear way (Figure 4).

The model in Figure 4 emphasises research informing theory and policy, which in turn inform practice. It implies that the researcher and the theoretician have expert roles at the expense of the practitioner, and it reinforces the rhetoric of technical rationality. In putting theory and policy between research and practice,

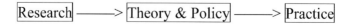

Figure 4.   The research-practice gap.

it simultaneously creates a research-to-practice gap and ignores the practice-to-research connection. These four aspects are better conceptualised as being interdependent and related to each other. In such a situation, it is more appropriate to consider a model such as in Figure 5.

Lampert (2000) has written of "the value of presenting the problems of practice from inside that practice". Her suggestion acknowledges the professionalism of teachers, the value of their knowledge, and the idea that teachers are just as capable as researchers in identifying problems. Such problems may well provide a more effective stimulus for change because of the ownership of the problem. It is desirable therefore to reconceptualise our model in a less hierarchical way by making the arrows two-way so that the reciprocity is clearer with practical theory (or perhaps practical wisdom) informing policy, theorising, and research. It does not avoid the gaps between the four components; to do that, one would need to bring them even closer together to form an integrated model.

Although the linear (RDD) model suited a behaviourist view, and the alternative model is relevant from a constructivist perspective with an emphasis on making connections, it becomes problematic from those points of view that draw on ecological and complex sensibilities. Across these perspectives, particular practices are understood as arising from and being infused with particular habits of seeing – that is, etymologically speaking, with particular 'theories'. So understood, the popular separation of theory and practice implies a pervasive realist attitude, a tacit assumption that established habits of perception are somehow atheoretical and that they reveal the world as it actually is. In contrast, within emergent epistemologies (such as enactivism), knowledge is seen as being in-action, and making connections is replaced with being connected; from this perspective a much more integrated model with the components connected would be desirable. When one is considering aspects of action that belong in a change process, the separation of researching, theorising, reflecting on practice, developing policy, growing professionally, developing assessment, developing resources, and developing curriculum (or the separation of research, development, and dissemination) is part of an analytic stage. This stage needs to be accompanied by a synthetic stage at which the parts are considered together and co-emerging as a whole; such interconnectedness is illustrated in Figure 6, although the notion of all the aspects co-emerging together is not so easy to

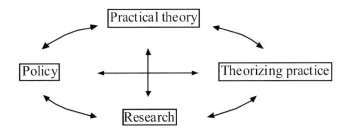

Figure 5. An interrelated model for research, theory and practice.

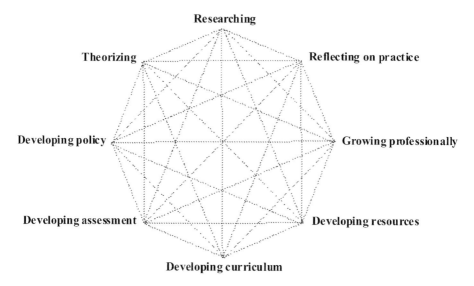

Figure 6.   The eight co-emerging activities in the educational change process.

illustrate. In addition, each of the eight activities can be occurring at many levels (individual teacher, school, and education system), and the eight activities can also be stimulated further by outside sources, which adds further to the complexity of the model. An excellent example that shows how one change influences all the others has been the emergence of calculators and computers. This one new resource has influenced and is influencing, to various degrees, all eight activities in most educational systems.

The initial motivation for change is usually dissatisfaction with what is currently in place, but before one begins to make changes one needs to be reasonably confident that such changes are intelligible, seem plausible, and are likely to be fruitful (Posner, Strike, Hewson, & Gertzog, 1982). Thus, apart from when change is imposed, the role of research is likely to be only suggesting or legitimating alternative approaches. Teachers' reflections on practice, which develop from their personal experience and prior knowledge, will be seen by them to be more important. One way these two aspects can be brought more closely together is through 'teaching experiments', which are a form of research discussed in five chapters of the *Handbook of Research Design in Mathematics and Science Education* (Kelly & Lesh, 2000), through the improvement of "rich mathematical activities" in line with the ideas from Ahmed (1987), or through "substantial learning environments" from Wittmann (2000).

2.4. *Other Pressures*

Howson, Keitel, and Kilpatrick (1981, pp. 2–5), in the context of curriculum change, wrote of the pressures to initiate change as including societal and political pressures, mathematical pressures, educational pressures, and rewards of innovation. Because of the interrelated nature of policy, curriculum, resources, and professional development, we see similar pressures affecting most development activities. Although researchers are part of the educational pressure group in the development process through their input into both mathematics and education, they are not the only part. And although some might wish for a greater influence from research, the need to identify the other pressure groups is also important. One reason is to provide an awareness of alternative concerns that may focus some future research activity; another is to ensure that the other groups are aware of relevant research. Making research findings accessible to these different groups through publications and meetings requires a conscious commitment to communication and often a different language register than that used when communicating with fellow researchers.

The pressure subgroups belong to three main groups: community, professionals, and schools (see Table 3). The people in these groups bring a variety of perspectives to development, they have their own agendas, their perceived needs sometimes conflict, but in democratic societies it would be expected that these voices should be heard.

Although the input from these groups could be collected using research (questionnaires, comparative studies, etc.), it more often will come because of positions of power or authority, or from lobbying. The input from professionals is likely to arise from professional reading, from considering what is happening elsewhere, and from reflecting on changes in the discipline. Although these inputs may have originated from formal research by others, only comparatively few are likely to be the direct result of participation in research. With community and school groups, the likelihood of research influencing their views is quite small.

Researchers need to acknowledge that people are not generally convinced by research from others; they usually rank their own practical wisdom based on

Table 3.   Sources of influence on policy and development

Community	politicians (regional and local)
	community groups (such as employers)
	parents and caregivers
Professionals	professional associations (lobby groups)
	educational researchers
	mathematicians (and statisticians)*
	mathematics educators*
	general educators*
	bureaucrats and educational administrators
School	school managers
	mathematics teachers
	nonspecialist teachers
	students

*These groups may also be doing research.

experience as being more valuable. Although research may not convince, it may provide contrasting ideas that conflict with current views and get people thinking about related issues.[3] More importantly, research findings may resonate with what the people already suspect or believe and provide support for their views. The importance of persuasion and resonance rather than conviction is one way that research can contribute. This indirect mode seems particularly reasonable with the increased recognition that research is closely linked with the researcher and is context specific.

2.5. *An Alternative View of Development*

What does development mean? If development is thought of as growth and change within classrooms, then it becomes learning and knowing. Student development is learning. Teacher development is learning, growth as an adult, or professional development. The development of practice and curriculum is the manifestation of learning and knowing that results from the involvement of the participants. From this perspective, development would be considered a lifelong process, which is summed up from an enactivist perspective with the phrase "to live is to know" (Maturana & Varela, 1987). From such a perspective, the development process cannot be thought of as a stop-start process with stimuli provided by occasional research reports, new curriculum documents, and so on. It becomes an ongoing process that is inevitable – a process in which these stimuli are minor inputs compared with the development and valuing of the professional knowledge that teachers have traditionally relied on and put much trust in but that professional curriculum developers have too often ignored.

3. SOME VARIABLES THAT INFLUENCE CHANGE

As well as the people involved and the eight activities shown in Figure 6, other variables influence the change process and need to be considered. There has been considerable research about development in general but comparatively little that is specific to mathematics education and that considers the variables that influence change and development. Begg (1994) summarised some general education research findings about these variables with respect to professional development, and we see these variables as being relevant to other development activities because of the interrelationship between such activities. The variables were approaches, purposes, responsibility, and leadership; outsiders; time; affective influences; and resource and economic considerations.

3.1. *Approaches, Purposes, Responsibility, and Leadership*

The development process has generally been approached in two ways. On the one hand, reform is imposed with centralised control through regulations, curriculum, and assessment, and on the other, teachers work towards improving their practice. Although the centralised approach with the RDD model fitted with behaviourism and with the introduction of the product-oriented new math in the 1960s, it is no longer appropriate. Teacher-centred approaches fit better with the emphasis on teacher learning and growth, with constructivism, and with emerging ideas about evolutionary learning and enactivism. With this approach, change is conceptualised as continuous, local, and ongoing. Being local enables development to consider local factors such as the culture, background, prior experience, and knowledge of all involved in a development activity.

With the RDD approach, the researcher's task is to ensure that the development team are aware of relevant research findings. With a teacher-centred local approach, it is much harder for researchers to identify who requires what findings. In addition, when researchers foster local initiatives by working on specific projects with a cluster of schools, the benefits usually go no further than those schools. If the benefits of this research are to go further, then researchers have to communicate and be involved with other groups outside the cluster.

Related to both approaches and goals is the question of responsibility for development and leadership. The question is confused, as Douglas (1991) said, because

> people are both extolling the virtues of teachers as experts, and speaking the rhetoric of ownership, and yet at the same time using position power and resource power to exercise hierarchical or managerial control. (p. 105)

Both position and resource power are linked with who controls the development budget and the purposes and approaches being used. The options for responsibility and leadership range from centrally controlled regional initiatives through locally controlled ones to school initiatives, groups of teachers such as a mathematics department, groups of peers, and individual teachers. If the initiative is that of a single school or one involving a cluster of schools, then a designated teacher or an external person such as a researcher may be in charge. In the case of a teacher, access to research findings may be a problem, although a researcher may be involved in the project as a critical friend and expert. If a researcher leads the project, the problem is communication of the findings rather than access, but to be successful the researcher needs to take a facilitative rather than the traditional leadership role, which fits with Robinson's (1989) distinctions between a managerial and an empowerment metaphor.

Linked to leadership and responsibility is ownership, that is, a personal or group understanding that development activities belong to the group rather than being imposed. This notion of ownership involves active initiation and participation (Fullan with Stiegelbauer, 1991). Ownership is not always created at the beginning of a project; it builds and develops over time with involvement. The importance placed on the desire to increase ownership is evident from the way management makes time available, treats dissent, shares information, and responds to suggestions. The development of a sense of ownership with research findings might come about by the project members doing their own research, it may involve working with a researcher, or it may involve reading research reports. If it is developed through reading reports, then considerable time will be needed for discussions about relevance, trustworthiness, generalisability, and related issues before a sense of connection and ownership is established.

Vanier (1998) has highlighted some problems of individuality and community that relate to responsibility, leadership, ownership, and change. It is useful to reflect on these problems as they help us understand some of the anguish of researchers and practitioners in change situations. He wrote:

> Maturity comes through working with others, through dialogue, and through a sense of belonging and a searching together. In order to evolve to a greater maturity and wholeness, we humans need a certain security; only when we have attained this can we advance in insecurity with others towards the new. ... This touches on a real paradox: as humans, we crave belonging, we need the connectedness to others that brings security, but this connectedness can prevent the natural movement and evolution that we need in our lives. It can also get in the way of creativity and stifle the natural loneliness that pushes us to discover something new. ... So here is the paradox: as humans we are caught between competing drives, the drive to belong, to fit in and be a part of something bigger than ourselves, and the drive to let our deepest selves rise up, to walk alone, to refuse the accepted and the comfortable, and this can mean, at least for a time, the acceptance of anguish. (pp. 14, 18)

Recognition of this individual/community tension shifts the emphasis from leader, facilitator, expert, and manager to cooperation, connectedness, creativity, and discovery. This tension can be envisaged as part of the dialogic relationship between self and other. It can also be seen, from an enactivist viewpoint, as resulting from a false dichotomy because belonging and fitting in do not need to be in conflict with being alone and refusing to accept the comfortable; instead, they can be envisaged as being coexisting and complementary aspects of one's being.

3.2. Who Influences Change?

The leaders and providers of change initiatives related to curriculum, policy, or practice can come from within the organization or system or from an external source. They are usually acceptable to other project participants if they have expertise about the initiative, are familiar with the situation, and take an empowering rather than a managerial role, although even that can be problematic. Empowerment can mean different things to different people. One can consider that the empowerment/managerial dichotomy might result from too much dominance of Marxist attitudes and that both might arise from discourses that are obsessed with issues of control – either imposing it or acquiring it. Discourses such as those of critical hermeneutics and enactivism seem more concerned with 'enabling' or 'playful expansion of the realm of the possible', and that can involve cooperating, empowering, and managing together rather than being concerned with control.

Outsiders can influence change through reporting research, developing resources, and providing feedback and reactions. Such influences are not usually high pressure. No one 'loses face' if the ideas in them are rejected, and the ideas are likely to be accommodated if they are seen as desirable. Ideas from such sources are likely to need the support from insider change agents if they are to influence change. From the point of view of researchers as outsiders, the concern is which researchers' findings will be made available and whose responsibility is it to ensure that they are available.

In the past, we have heard it said, "One can change oneself, but one cannot change others". This maxim does not quite 'fit' with the complex ecological sensibilities that suggest something more like, "One is always changing, prompting, and prompted by, changes in others". Thus, in our efforts aimed at transformation, the changes that others undergo cannot be *determined* by what we do, but they are always *dependent* on what we do. Such a shift demands a new ethic, as Varela (1999) elaborates in his book. Unfortunately, change agents and researchers who are involved with developments that have implications for how teachers see themselves and their practices often ignore the demand. They present 'solutions' rather than 'possibilities' that might influence the direction of change.

3.3. *Time Factors Influencing Change*

Change or development usually occurs through activities that require a considerable number of meetings, and four aspects related to time influence such activities and affect researchers. These four are timing (when should meetings occur?), duration (how long should the time period be between first and last meeting?), frequency (how often should the meetings occur?), and rate of change (what rate of change is desirable?)

At the local level, the timing is usually linked to emerging or perceived needs, but people beyond the local environment are often unaware of these needs. The timing of activities related to change has often made it difficult for many people to participate. In particular, researchers who are unaware of the activities are therefore unable to provide input that they believe might be relevant. Such timing issues may be part of deliberate power struggles associated with the professionals' view that their ideas are more important and relevant than those of others.

The question of duration is linked to the desirability of establishing an ethos for change rather than the provision of 'quick-fix' solutions. Even the development of specific new policies and practices requires time, which may be two or three years if the change process involves trials, discussion, reflection, adoption, and institutionalisation of significant changes. When the duration is longer, then it will be more likely that ideas from researchers can be considered, but researchers have other commitments and cannot always make themselves available for extended periods.

If decisions require a number of meetings, what should be their frequency? To allow for experimenting (trialling with support) with new curriculum, policies, or practices, a significant period needs to be sandwiched between sessions. This accommodation fits with the idea of researchers being involved, but again they have other commitments.

Many professionals are concerned about the rate at which changes of practice are expected to be implemented. Society is changing at an ever-increasing rate, however, and curriculum policies and practices are seen as needing to keep abreast with societal changes. Perhaps no choice exists; change is inevitable. A careful examination of suggested initiatives is needed, however, to ensure that time is not wasted on reforms that do not fit with the aims of education. Unfortunately, there is often little preliminary exploration or trialling of alternatives prior to implementation. Research more often follows and evaluates change. This practice suggests a need for a change of focus to emphasise preliminary work, but research may then be seen as causing delays and holding up the inevitable.

The resistance of teachers to changes, including some suggested by research, is usually linked to their concerns about time. In the United Kingdom, Williams, Wilson, Richardson, Tuson, and Coles (1998) and Bramald, Miller, and Higgins (2000) have shown how they see their time and that of their students as obstacles even when they acknowledge that the suggestions made by the research are likely to be beneficial.

3.4. *Affective Influences*

People's reactions to changes in curriculum, policy, and practice are influenced both by their rational consideration of the situation and by their feelings about it. Feelings also influence their reactions to the research that may be informing proposed developments. Little research about this dimension is evident in mathematics education, although Black and Atkin (1996) have reported from one study in the USA how not only teachers have feelings of resistance to change but so do students. Lortie (1975) is more specific; he suggests that teachers resist change if it does not address directly what they perceive in their work situation. With any project there is likely to be some resistance. One cannot assume that this resistance is outright rejection of the values embodied in the change or hardcore resistance to all change (Fullan with Stiegelbauer, 1991). Resisting change may be irresponsible obstinacy or conservatism, but it may also be the responsible rejection of a project that is undesirable or is unlikely to succeed; in other words, it may be the only way to maintain sanity and avoid complete cynicism (Fullan, 1989). It could also reflect important value or power conflicts and give a number of 'signals' to reformers (Dalin, 1986).

Researchers such as Fullan with Stiegelbauer (1991) have listed some of the feelings, fears, and associated beliefs. These include:

- feelings about change and risk taking in general and in relation to a particular change

- feelings of personal insecurity, lack of confidence, and fear of failure
- fear of losing control while making a change
- cultural beliefs that might conflict with change
- behavioural norms that might conflict with change
- trust (or lack of trust) in management, unions, or colleagues
- historical events relevant to the change
- intensity of threat inherent in the change
- manner in which the change is introduced and implemented

One strategy suggested to help reduce the impact of these feelings and fears is ensuring that participants understand the change process itself and are involved in all its aspects: initiating, planning, control, and so on.

3.5. *Resources and Economic Considerations in the Change Process*

People are the most important resource in education, and their development and growth are often the purpose for change. This was recognised by Fullan (1982), who stressed:

> The implementation process has frequently overlooked people (behaviours, beliefs, skills) in favour of things (e.g., regulations, materials) and this is essentially why it fails more times than not. (p. 249)

Although people are one resource, time is another, and both relate to funding. The most significant cost in many initiatives is the payment for the hours of work by the participants, and it is immaterial whether that payment is funded from within an institution, from a central source, or by some other means. Generally with educational reform, a confusing picture emerges in terms of the economic considerations. Proposals to devolve decision making or to centralise it seem not to have been considered in terms of measures such as cost, effectiveness, and cost-effectiveness but have been made for ideological reasons. At both the macro and micro level, administrators seem keen to implement discrete, and often prepackaged, programmes so that they can appear to have satisfied some perceived need for change rather than looking for what may in the long term be considerably more effective and therefore cost effective.

Little research seems to have been undertaken to explore the effectiveness and the cost effectiveness of various development models. Low-cost options are easy to identify, but cost alone is of little use. Planners need to be concerned with cost-effectiveness. Measuring or estimating effectiveness is difficult, however, because the goals of development are complex, they are achieved over a considerable time period, and many other factors are likely to influence change at the same time. In this situation, researchers, most reasonably, have concentrated on identifying the factors that influence change rather than attempting to quantify their impact.

4. SOME OBSTACLES

In discussions of models for change and variables that influence change, a number of obstacles to the dissemination of research have been identified. These generally appear in the literature on change because they are related to change in all subjects as well as mathematics education. In this section, we discuss some of these under three headings: research and researchers as obstacles, teachers and schools as obstacles, and system obstacles.

4.1. *Research and Researchers As Obstacles*

Although mathematics education research occurs within four domains – what mathematicians know and do, mathematics pedagogy, general education, and the nature of learning – researchers usually undertake research within only one of them. This concentration means that the complexity of mathematics education is partially disregarded. In this situation, two paradoxical obstacles emerge. First, when teachers are interested in only one domain, they tend to ignore the other domains in spite of the boundaries being fuzzy and the intersection considerable. Second, the findings may be rejected because they are narrowly focused and ignore the complexity. This issue of complexity can be thought of in terms of analysis and synthesis. Although a need exists to analyse and look at details, there is at the same time a need to look at the details as part of a whole; these two are complementary, and neither is adequate by itself.

In looking at only one aspect of a topic, researchers can be perceived as being obstacles because they are thought of as doing the wrong research. For example, they may seek to find the extent to which a particular group is not achieving in mathematics, whereas finding ways to increase their participation might be seen as more useful. Researchers may also be seen as obstacles when their research is conducted in specific contexts in terms of culture, location, or socio-economic class. Policy makers and teachers may quite reasonably assume that the results are not generalisable to broader or different contexts.

When researchers, and teacher-researchers in particular, are trying new innovations as part of research projects, they spend considerable time planning and preparing the innovation, much more time than normally spent on lesson planning. In addition, students in the classes often react favourably because the innovations are novel compared to what they are used to. There is likely to be a desire for positive outcomes by funding agencies and by the researchers themselves, who might be seeking academic qualifications. All these 'halo' factors are likely to contribute to the success of the project. In such instances, potential users of the results may be sensibly cynical in believing that there is no guarantee for success in the future when such factors are not present.

One aspect of researching is communication, which can be an important obstacle. Researchers do not always communicate their findings to the relevant people or in an appropriate form. Sowder (2000) has expressed her concern about this phenomenon and has suggested that research reports are often a turnoff for teachers, perhaps because researchers tend to write in academic journals for peers and less frequently in teacher journals for practitioners. In presentations, they often communicate their finding as results, whereas an emphasis on the strategies that might lead to solutions may be perceived as more useful for practitioners. Worse than poor communication is a lack of communication, which can occur when researchers are encouraged to quickly move from one project to another as soon as the first is completed. Perhaps a significant communication component that includes teacher journal reports could be built into contracts by funding agencies, and more could be done to extend the impact of projects beyond the original site rather than encouraging movement to new projects.

In improving communication, the first consideration is the audience one is writing for. The culture of the audience varies, not only in nationality or ethnicity but also depending on whether they are teachers, academics, researchers, curriculum officers, textbook authors, or parents. Culture is often seen to comprise three main components – language, beliefs and customs – and these are as significant with work-related cultures as with ethnic cultures. Language is particularly important because the technical terms that academics and researchers may take for granted will often make research findings inaccessible to practitioners. The second consideration is beliefs, which can influence the valuing of research. When teachers work in cultures where research is not held in high esteem or is ridiculed by those in authority, they are unlikely to value it in the way that those who live in more open-minded societies might. Such ridicule and other forms of aggression between the educational system and the teachers are unfortunately too common, and many examples are evident from politicians grandstanding at the expense of teachers. The third consideration is that customs make a difference. If it is not customary to read research, then teachers are unlikely to be directly influenced by it. When considering problems of communication, one should recognize that it is relatively simple to make the language of research reports more appropriate but that to overcome the influence of beliefs and customs is more difficult.

In efforts to communicate, not only the minds of practitioners need to be convinced but also their hearts. Communication, like teaching, has an affective domain as well as a cognitive one, and teachers and other audiences have strong feelings about their practice and beliefs. Suggested changes often challenge not only what people know but also what they do and how they see themselves, which can be difficult for them. Thus, communications have to appeal at a number of levels – something that neither researchers nor intermediaries reporting research seem to have done well in the past.

One audience for communication is politicians, and part of such communication involves political lobbying. This needs to be acknowledged if educators and researchers wish to ensure their voices are heard by decision makers. The preferred 'army' may not be victorious in the 'math wars' in the USA, but they do show how lobbying influences policy.

4.2. *Teachers and Schools As Obstacles*

Few teachers have done formal research or been involved in it apart from perhaps at a superficial level as part of their pre-service education. Most have experienced new ideas that did not work in the past and are justifiably reluctant to accept someone's word that some new practice will be any better than what they already do. Nor do they want change for the sake of change. Generally they have not been provided with evidence that change works before it is imposed upon them, nor have they been given opportunities to trial a change and decide for themselves whether it is worthwhile. Having had these experiences, teachers are naturally somewhat conservative; their reaction has been learnt, and this conservatism can be valuable. It means that school systems do not jump from fad to fad and that the momentum of the educational system is such that fads are usually adapted into current practice rather than adopted as a change of practice. This observation suggests that researchers need to work in collegial ways with teachers if they wish to convince them. Developing ways to conduct such work will take time because in many countries there has not been a culture of involving the teachers *in* research; for too long it has been something that has been done *to* them. Without involvement there has been no ownership of the problems addressed by the research and no investment in the implications of the findings. The situation is changing, however. For example, in the United Kingdom, under the Teacher Training Agency teacher research grants (see <http://www.canteach.gov.uk/>), each grant requires a practising teacher to apply in partnership with an existing higher education partner. Similarly, to be eligible for the Australian Research Council 'Linkage' grants (see <http:// www.arc.gov.au/ncgp/linkage/projects/default.htm>), the researcher must have an industry (i.e., a school) partner.

Teachers are as concerned about behaviour, generic skills and the aims of their school as they are about mathematics. Concerns about behaviour and skills are likely to be related to communication, cooperation, work habits, information seeking, autonomous learning, self-management, and study, whereas the aims for education might link with a concern for others, the desire for self-respect, emotional and moral development, preparation for citizenship, and attributes such as creativity and free spiritedness, sociality and generosity, and responsibility and self-discipline. The consequence of this array of concerns is that they may ignore specific research findings that do not consider such broader educational issues and aims. Some research does of course address these broader concerns, for example, Noddings's (1984, 1992) work on caring. Examples where broader issues may not be considered arise in technology, where research is often linked to specific problems. In this situation, teachers may feel concerned about the influence of technology and the purposes of education and may agree with the philosophic notion that mechanistic or technological explanations render redundant the humanity that technology supposedly serves. If teachers agree with such notions, they are likely to reject research findings that focus on specifics. Researchers disseminating their findings may need to very clearly indicate their assumptions and to accept that with other assumptions a different conclusion might be reached. And in acknowledging different conclusions, it would be inappropriate to use the word *obstacle* as a descriptor of these teachers.

Another example occurs because some conflicting aims in education are not being made explicit. These aims relate to reinforcing the status quo in society versus transforming society and are visible in mathematical activities that reinforce militarism rather than pacifism, individualism instead of cooperation, or consumption versus regard for the environment. When research seems to support activities based on one of these assumptions, teachers may be faced with a moral question. They would be reluctant to implement research findings that worked in ways that contradicted their personal philosophy. Such conflict was evident and some teachers were resistant to change when the SMILE (Secondary Mathematics Individualised Learning Experiment, 1986) project was being implemented in some English schools. This project was based on the notion that individual children needed individual programmes of study. Accordingly, a database of thousands of separate workcards was gradually developed. Each pupil was given a weekly or fortnightly programme of work based upon a particular and unique selection of cards. The development work was done mainly in London, where issues related to gender and race were to the fore. Such issues were seen as high profile and were used to vet illustrations on cards. For example, if an illustration was of a child helping another or was of a sporting event, it was most unlikely to show someone who was obviously white and Caucasian. Such policies were, however, seen as 'not relevant' by many teachers in other parts of England.

Some mathematics teachers are very well qualified in mathematics but may not feel secure with educational theory. In a similar way, nonspecialist teachers who teach younger children are often well qualified in education but not comfortable with some mathematical knowledge or with mathematics specific pedagogical knowledge. When research addresses issues in an area in which one is not confident, a natural reaction is to stay with what one is used to and feels comfortable with. Thus high school and tertiary level teachers may resist change based on research in education, whereas teachers of younger children may resist changes derived from research in mathematics education. For example, teachers of younger children might be unaware of possibilities such as introducing geometry using topology or introducing patterning with simple fractal drawings. Reluctance to change by nonspecialist teachers is also due to the considerable pressure exerted on them to also make changes in other areas of the curriculum. In such situations, it is reasonable for them to prioritise their development activities and resist particular pressures even though they may have some sympathies for the changes. Although this resistance may be only a temporary postponement, it may still be viewed as an obstacle. Such reluctance to change may also reflect a desire for the status quo and the values of the past. These teachers should not be ignored; they usually have a genuine concern both for the system and for their students. If researchers want to make changes, they do not need to convince all teachers of the values of their proposals; instead, researchers need to provide space so some teachers can continue with the status quo for a time, while others prove the success or otherwise of the policies being introduced.

Perhaps an even more important problem or obstacle that many mathematics teachers have encountered in their own work and with colleagues as they work to revise professional practices has been 'overcoming the momentum of habit'. Most of us have repeatedly found ourselves engaging in teacherly behaviours that we know to be ineffective, such as posing questions that are not really questions or setting tasks that have little educational value. Such troublesome actions are not matters of conscious choice; they seem to be more about being caught up in a flow of established ways of acting. These habits are tied to our long history with traditional schooling practices and are supported by such things as curricula, evaluation regimes, and student expectations. At issue is the notion that changes in practice involve more than conscious decisions to do things differently. Just like the old habits that are to be replaced, new habits require repetition, rehearsal, and reflection. Instructional change is not merely about doing things differently but also about enacting different sensibilities around such matters as individual knowing and collective knowledge. Moreover, to be sustained, new habits require a supportive 'culture' (a term that should be considered as much in the bacterial sense as the social sense). Teachers need to be immersed in a different medium. These lessons have been well learned by organizations that are dedicated to helping people overcome personally or socially destructive habits, such as Alcoholics Anonymous groups, Weight Watchers clubs, and support groups for sexual offenders. In changing teacher practice, however, the belief seems to be that a well-presented argument and a little empirical evidence should be all that is required to enable teachers to change what they are doing, and if that does not work, then the teacher is probably assumed to be resisting. Changing both what and how one teaches is much more complex than that, and some details of this complexity can be found in Davis and Sumara (1997). In this situation, the teacher seems to be the obstacle but in fact the problem is the complexity of the change process. When this complexity is not recognised, information from research may be passed on, but that will not be enough. An appropriate and supportive dissemination and implementation process needs to exist if the teacher is to be immersed in a culture with the possibility for shared action.

In the process of becoming more experienced, teachers are often expected to consider research findings, but researchers need to acknowledge that these teachers have had time to develop their ideas about teaching that have stood the test of time. Gravemeijer (2000) carefully discriminated between *episteme*, or scientific understanding, and *phronesis*, or practical wisdom; these can be thought of as research evidence and teacher knowledge. For many teachers, practical wisdom appears more relevant than research. This preference occurs because practical wisdom is personal, takes local issues into consideration, recognizes the complexity of teaching and learning, and is based on the context in which each teacher works and her or his particular circumstances. Thus, when a researcher looks at some aspect of education and interprets what is seen, an experienced teacher may identify a lack of awareness concerning some realities of the classroom. That is not to say that teachers cannot find research relevant. If the research recognises the complexity of education and the results resonate with the teachers' ideas, or if they are involved and find similar results, then the research will gain relevance. This complexity refers to 'organised' (or emergent) complexity rather than 'disorganised' complexity. Whereas the latter is an appropriate target for statistical analysis, the former, which includes human cognition and social systems, refers to things that have a habit of changing. Such things belong to a category of phenomena that need to be studied at the levels of their emergence rather than by statistical analysis, which tends to 'freeze' things rather than consider their dynamic nature.

School mathematics as currently perceived is an obstacle to change. This perception arises because of the pervasive set of assumptions concerning the following:

- The nature of mathematics (instrumental knowledge)
- A refusal to acknowledge the increasing irrelevance of many traditional curriculum topics
- One's reasons for studying it (which seem to amount to preparing oneself to take more of it)

To make matters worse, these beliefs are supported by resilient and institutionalised structures such as

- Standardised examinations (whereby mathematics becomes both a gatekeeper for students and a means of checking up on teachers)
- Commercially produced textbooks (from a profit-oriented industry that would see it unwise to push against the grain of commonly held beliefs)
- A barrage of flattened insights through the media (e.g., movies about mathematics – which are usually romance tales with rarely any suggestion of creative or novel mathematical insights)

In the face of such beliefs and structures, it is hard for school mathematics to embrace such insights as von Glasersfeld's (1995) observation that, because constructivism is *descriptive* rather than *prescriptive*, it cannot tell teachers what to do, it can only tell them what cannot be done. Such insights emerge from researchers who articulate different perspectives on mathematical knowledge (e.g., Ernest, 1991) and from investigations into the relationship between teacher beliefs about mathematics and their instructional methods (e.g., Thompson, 1984). We believe that teachers in schools can embrace such insights if there is an acceptance that *what* one teaches and *how* one teaches cannot be separated. Unfortunately, by the time the research reaches teachers, this insight is often stripped to some thinly masked condemnation of existing practice. In other words, teachers are often under the impression that researchers are keen to influence how they teach even while what they teach is firmly held in place by official (assessment, curricula, and textbooks) and unofficial (popular media) forces.

A further possible school obstacle involves technology. In terms of technology innovations being researched, the problem of the keen researcher has already been identified. In terms of the changes technology is causing in both the subject mathematics and in the way research data are handled, there is no doubt that the influence of technology is inevitable. We know, however, that people who lack confidence with the technology need time to overcome their reluctance and in the short term are likely to be resistant to change involving technology. Primary teachers in England reported that time, equipment, and pupils' reactions were the three major barriers to their implementing recently proposed government sponsored changes to their teaching styles (Moseley et al., 1999). These barriers involved various aspects already alluded to in this chapter. They effectively prevented the teachers from adopting the new teaching style and, as a result, caused unnecessary anguish for the teachers, who knew they would be assessed and measured against the proposed criteria for teaching in forthcoming inspections.

Another perceived obstacle in schools relates to the curriculum and assessment. This obstacle arises when, although the curriculum is seen as 'overfull', there is an acceptance of a need to ensure that all topics are taught because of the demands of assessment. Consequently, when a new idea is mooted, a common reaction from teachers is to ask what will be removed from the curriculum to make way for the additional material. Often, change seems to be resisted and research findings ignored because of these expectations to 'finish the curriculum' and prepare for assessment. Indeed, assessment is often the 'tail that wags the dog'. Unfortunately, acceptable implications from emerging theories of learning have not yet been adequately developed for curriculum and assessment. Assessment continues to exercise a conservative influence on education and tends to pull practice back towards the behavioural objectives approach of the 1970s and 1980s. If assessment is envisaged as a tool for learning rather than a way of measuring the learning that has occurred, then further investigation is needed of other forms of assessment that reflect the aims of courses. These include the use of portfolios, project-based assessment, group assessment, and assessment tasks involving technology. When tests or examinations are used, they need to reflect not only the balance of topics in courses but also the conceptual rather than procedural focus and the emphasis on problem solving, reasoning with uncertainty, and communication.

4.3. *System Obstacles*

One aspect of change that needs to be considered is its nature. The model for change that we introduced in section 2 emphasises complexity, and the question "What causes change?" cannot be answered simply. Inasmuch as research is an influence, one could ask, "Why was that particular aspect researched?" Perhaps it arose from 'hunches', and these need to be considered – hunches are often the result of experience and reflection that might be thought of as informal research that has not been written up. New creative ideas that are considered for implementation in a curriculum can be thought of as part of research, but that is not a definition that most people use. Related to this change process, it is heartening to note the recent international growth in the acceptance of 'discipline education research' as a legitimate form of research within tertiary education. Now at universities, where an expectation to do research exists, it appears that more staff will be able to become involved in researching mathematics and statistics education. This development is unlikely to be as evident with teachers in schools and other tertiary institutions, as the research culture is not well developed, although with degree inflation and more teachers working towards higher degrees, some increase in research in mathematics education is likely to happen.

We would contend that although change is inevitable, it takes time. Although some in the mathematics education community are concerned about the obstacles to dissemination, there are others who see progress occurring, albeit slowly. The two groups have different time scales in mind. Whereas those in the first group hope for rapid change, the others accept the complex interaction of the influences on change within the evolutionary process. For those who hope to accelerate the rate of change occurring, there is a need to influence more of the eight activities in the model and not merely to emphasise research. For example, changes in content may arise from changes in professional practise, as we have seen with the introduction of stem-and-leaf and box-and-whisker plots into some statistics courses as a result of the change in the work of practising statisticians. Other changes in practice may have occurred because of perceived needs created by new problems, perceived inadequacies of current approaches, the possibilities offered by new technology, or an idea suggested by a local or overseas colleague. Changes usually originate with and are developed by people who are willing to think about alternatives. If the changes are researched at the early stages, then the person directly involved usually does the research, and it may therefore be considered to be biased. Such a bias is not a problem; indeed, it is natural and reflects the commitment of the person. In fact, research at this stage is usually informal and limited to collecting evidence that supports or critiques the change so that strengths and weakness can be discerned and modifications made to take account of criticisms. This process involves the originator in exploration, trialling, discussion with colleagues, perhaps a conference paper, feedback, improvements, more discussion, and so on. The more important and often missing role for research comes later, after the changes have been refined. Ideally, someone who can retain as much objectivity as possible but who is familiar with the development and able to see both what it offers and what it does not offer will do this research, and it will involve evaluation. An example of this form of research is provided from 'developmental research' by the Dutch project in realistic mathematics education (Beishuizen, Gravemeijer, & van Lieshout, 1997).

Policy makers at the system level can be seen as obstacles to research and research dissemination. They are obstacles usually because they are constrained to work to externally imposed timelines that may make new research impossible and may even make reviews of the literature very difficult. In many countries, these people are not encouraged to facilitate 'blue sky' research that may guide future policy. Their work is increasingly done within tight financial restraints and with short-term objectives to be met. In addition, when policy makers at the system level or teachers in schools are making changes to policies or curriculum, they often do not have the authority to make decisions about those changes. The changes are often imposed rather than being self- or jointly initiated; they are often made for political or societal reasons, and they are rarely based on formal research findings. An example is the imposition of the National Numeracy Strategy on all the schools of England (Department for Education and Employment, 1998), just a year after the National Literacy Strategy had been imposed on the same schools. These changes are sometimes couched not in a discourse of discontent that might imply a need to consider possible changes but rather in a discourse of domination that implies superiority, disdains critique, and causes teacher resentment.

In addition, although policy makers at school, local, and regional level have usually been teachers, few of them have been immersed in a research culture. They have often had many years of teaching, and they, like teachers, tend to value their own experience over formal research findings. Nonetheless, policy makers are more likely than teachers to have access to and to read about developments in mathematics education, and many of these developments are at least indirectly influenced by research. Thus, although policy makers may appear to be obstacles to specific research, they may be quite significant users of research results without being particularly aware of doing so.

When Glass, McGaw, and Smith (1981) published their book on meta-analysis, it was generally welcomed in the social sciences, but within mathematics education, meta-analyses are comparatively rare. One example, in the context of 'assessment for learning', is from Wiliam and Lee (2001). Although meta-analyses of research in mathematics education may be rare, research syntheses are common. They are often useful for policy makers partly because, as isolated results are put with others to form a bigger picture and as teacher research complements academic research, the results seem to become more relevant. Thus, although researchers may see a need to disseminate findings from isolated studies, it is often better to have them synthesised with other studies in the same area and presented as a body of research. For example, when a number of different people were working in the area of teachers-as-researchers, their findings made more impact when presented as a single volume (Zack, Mousley, & Breen, 1997) than they had previously. Such compilations of research are evident in the various handbooks such as the present series and others (e.g., Grouws, 1992; Kelly & Lesh, 2000), in other education-focused handbooks, and in some thematic yearbooks of professional associations.

Only limited resources are available for research from the budget of any educational system, and existing researchers see the paucity of resources as a major obstacle to their doing more research. Many researchers also teach at universities, and the increasing demands on their time create a further obstacle that limits the amount of research they can do. Similarly, most countries have only limited funds for teachers and others interested to pursue post-graduate courses, which usually have a significant research component. Limited funds mean that the number of new researchers is limited and that the directors of research projects often find it hard to build up and retain a team to help them with a larger project by having others doing ancillary research. This situation seems to be exacerbated by the current culture within the research community, which involves offering research team members short-term contracts. In this situation, the contracted researcher is always on the look out for new, longer lasting contracts and problems of retention and continuity arise.

Education practice in most countries is guided by policies and regulations, and teacher practice is similarly constrained by curriculum. The words *policy* and *politics* are derived from the same root, and both have connotations of authoritarian or representational rather than participatory governance. Although some see advantages in teachers participating in all decision making that affects them, in the current political situations in most countries the best that can be hoped for is general guidelines rather than tight prescriptive regulations and detailed curriculum documents. Unfortunately, politicians and bureaucrats have taken little notice of notions of co-emergence; instead, the influence of politics and the compulsory curriculum has discouraged experimentation, which seems to be a barrier to both research and the dissemination of research findings.

5. STRATEGIES FOR THE FUTURE

In the previous section, we have considered a number of obstacles. In looking to the future, one needs to consider how the negative effects of these obstacles might be minimised. Some possibilities are presented below under the headings 'communication and complexity', 'changing the development model', and 'broadening research boundaries'. Each is only briefly considered, as they follow from the earlier sections.

5.1. *Communication and Complexity*

Research has the potential to help practitioners become mindful of their circumstances and to adapt accordingly. To facilitate that adaptation is not a matter of talking louder about research; what is needed is a rethinking regarding the contexts and nature of our communications. This, for us, implies that research needs to be anchored in the immediate realities of the classrooms – it is working in classrooms and with teachers that informs publications that are relevant to teachers. From such research, one can still find different ways of saying particular things to different audiences; for example, academics, teachers, and policy makers (although this communication would be fostered if academia had reward structures that recognised different audiences).

Teachers and policy makers are not the only ones who need to become mindful of their circumstances and adapt accordingly; researchers do too. We need to be attentive to the consequences of our efforts to report. For example, rather than condemning people who we think have got it wrong, we should be trying to find what or who has caused these people to come to their current understandings. Thus, to develop communication as a two-way process, researchers should be prompted to listen rather than simply encouraged to speak more clearly.

The communication of research may need to concentrate more on synthesising components: perhaps a number of research projects on related topics or alternatively research findings together with teacher articles in response to the findings and ideas about learning and assessment activities that fit with them. This focus is part of recognising the complexity of the change process. Another aspect that may similarly need to be addressed is the valuing of aims and philosophy of education when they may be in conflict with a change that is being considered. This aspect involves balancing philosophical ideas, the practical wisdom of teachers, the research findings, and the need to work together for solutions. It means being explicit about assumptions and valuing what people bring to the debate from their past experiences, their motivation for change, their apparent conservatism, and their concern that changes are relevant. Associated with these complexities is understanding the significance of the time needed for people to consider new ideas and then for any educational change to be adopted or adapted as appropriate.

5.2. *Changing the Development Model*

A second strategy involves working to replace the models used for the development of policy, curriculum, resources, assessment, and teachers by more democratic and inclusive ones. This replacement could result in policy makers becoming colleagues rather than authorities and teachers being involved in all stages of development and decision making. Change would be seen as continuous and evolutionary rather than stop-start, and voluntary rather than imposed. Such a transformation is likely to be facilitated by ensuring that regulations, curriculum, and assessment policies are flexible enough to allow experimentation by teachers and researchers without causing difficulties for the students involved. It is also likely to be helped by the development of 'flatter' administration systems that encourage people affected by decisions to have a voice in them. Experimentation could be encouraged by the provision of space in the curriculum, by the initiation of programmes of exploratory studies, and through the provision of teacher-leave policies linked to qualification upgrades after some years of teaching – such study including a research component.

5.3. *Broadening Research Boundaries*

Research findings may be more acceptable to teachers if they are congruent with how the teachers perceive mathematics, mathematics education, general education, and associated areas such as technology. The boundaries between these domains are fuzzy and artificial for teachers; they depend on the teachers' own experiences. For research to be appealing to a broad spectrum of teachers, however, these boundaries need to be further de-emphasised. Also, the concept of what is accepted and valued as research (or equivalent to research) needs to be broadened, perhaps by giving more recognition to scholarship that involves literature studies instead of data collection. Such scholarship will include developmental research involving the trialling of resources for use with technology, new learning activities for the curriculum, and alternative assessment activities. It seems desirable to make haste slowly and to acknowledge that a development needs space for the exploration of alternative approaches and topics. A first step might be 'exploratory studies' that are a form of research but that are not written up in full and may initially have connotations of merely dabbling. Such explorations need to take into account the diversity of teachers and students and the local needs. They need to begin with local trialling and slowly grow to involve others and build up a feedback process. After the initial stages, the studies might move to an extended trialling phase and external review. If they are seen as worthwhile, they may later be considered as either an alternative within or as part of a curriculum. Such a process would incorporate the development of ownership, it would take place over an extended time period, it would naturally include professional, resource, and assessment development, and it would involve empowerment rather than imposition. With such a model, change within the community of practice might be envisaged in the same way as learning by an individual. An evolutionary approach would be assumed and considerable time provided "to establish an ethos for change" that Rice (1992) identified. The lack of such an ethos may be a fundamental barrier to be overcome. Such an ethos assumes what Robinson (1989) has called 'empowerment' and Davis and Sumara (1997) have called "the possibility for shared action". In such a culture, the developer's role shifts from expert to facilitator in much the same way as the teacher's role is shifting for learning in the classroom. Unfortunately, we have what has been called 'contrived collegiality', which may involve people working together but with the control and power remaining firmly with the developer. In this circumstance, the collaboration may be a form of 'working traitorously with the enemy' rather than working towards a goal agreed upon by all the participants.

CONCLUSION

In this chapter, our focus has been on offering possibilities for consideration in the same way that researchers offer their findings: open to question and with the mathematics education community obligated to question them. By communicating in this tentative way, we hope that some things will resonate with readers and assist their movement by legitimating and supporting them in their decision making and future action.

In addition, although we have discussed issues related to the nature of the subject matter, the processes of learning, the purposes of schooling, the possibilities for teaching, and so on, we would want to emphasise the complex interrelationships that link such issues. Although there is no shortage of articles dealing with one or two of these matters, little is published that deals with three or more. This deficiency is critical. It is frustrating to read an article informed by, say, radical constructivism that speaks only to implications for teaching. Such an article needs to consider the backdrop of that teaching, the taken-for-granted rationales for schooling, and the assumed nature of the subject matter. It is likely to simply contribute to the conventional obsession with doing more effectively whatever one is doing now rather than with trying to make sense of what it is one thinks one is doing when one claims to be teaching mathematics.

NOTES

[1.] For further information on these discourses, the following references may be useful:
Phenomenology: Merleau-Ponty (1962)
Radical constructivism: von Glasersfeld (1995)
Social constructivism: Cobb (1994); Lave and Wenger (1991); Steffe and Gale (1993)
Enactivism: Davis (1995, 1996); Davis, Sumara, and Luce-Kapler (2000); Maturana and Varela (1987); Sumara & Davis (1997); Varela (1999)
Ecology: Abram (1996); Bateson (1979)
Systems theory: Bateson (1972/2000, 1991); Bertalanffy (1968); Capra (1996)
Complexity theory: Capra (1996); Casti (1994); Cohen and Stewart (1994).

Associated with enactivism are notions about the following:
Cartesian dichotomies: Damasio (1994)
Unformulated knowing: Davis (1996); Maturana and Varela (1987)
Embodiment: Johnson (1987); Lakoff and Johnson (1999); Varela, Thompson, and Rosch (1991)
Mindful awareness: Batchelor (1998); de Mello (1990); Krishnamurti (1956); Nhất Hanh (1975/1987)
Emotional knowing and intuition: Atkinson and Claxton (2000); Claxton (1999, chapter 9); Damasio (2000); Goleman (1996)
Neural biological work: Calvin (1996); Edelman (1987); Plotkin (1998); Sacks (1995); Varela, Thompson, and Rosch (1991)
Autopoietic systems: Maturana and Varela (1980); Mingers (1995).

[2.] *Development*, unless qualified, is intended to mean policy, curriculum, resource, assessment, and teacher or professional development. Although these are interrelated, we see: (a) *policy development* as related to both the regional (or national) and local administration of education (and it can be interpreted as including curriculum and assessment policy) and also occurring within schools; (b) *curriculum development* as relating the planned activities for classes (at regional level as well as at school and class level) and including both subject content and subject pedagogy; (c) *resource development* as the development of textbooks, videos, technology resources, and other material that interprets or influences the curriculum (and may even become the 'de facto' curriculum); (d) *assessment development* as related to regional (and in-school) assessment schemes; and (e) *teacher* or *professional development* as related to the in-service education and growth of teachers during their professional life (with particular reference to system-led development related to implementation of curriculum and assessment).

[3.] Although this chapter is about the obstacles to the dissemination of research, one must keep in mind that research also serves other purposes. In addition to stimulating thinking of other issues, Bishop (1977) has argued that there are many things that people can use from research apart from the results; these include the procedures, the data, and the constructs.

REFERENCES

Abram, D. (1996). *The spell of the sensuous: Perception and language in a more than human world.* New York: Pantheon Books.

Ahmed, A. (1987). *Better mathematics: A curriculum development study based on The Low Attainers in Mathematics Project.* London: Her Majesty's Stationery Office.

Aichele, D., & Coxford, A. (Eds.). (1994). *Professional development for teachers of mathematics* (1994 Yearbook of the National Council of Teachers of Mathematics). Reston, VA: NCTM.

Assessment Performance Unit. (1985). *A review of monitoring in mathematics 1978 to 1982* (Parts 1 & 2). London: Department of Education and Science.

Atkinson, T., & Claxton, G. (2000). *The intuitive practitioner: On the value of not always knowing what one is doing.* Buckingham: Open University Press.

Batchelor, S. (1998). *Buddhism without beliefs: A contemporary guide to awakening.* London: Bloomsbury.

Bateson, G. (1979). *Mind and nature: A necessary unity.* New York: E. P. Dutton.

Bateson, G. (1991). *A sacred unity: Further steps to an ecology of mind* (R. E. Donaldson, Ed.). New York: Harper Collins.

Bateson, G. (2000). *Steps to an ecology of mind* (New ed.). Chicago: University of Chicago Press. (Original work published 1972 by Ballentine Books, New York)

Begg, A. (1994). *Professional development of high school mathematics teachers.* Unpublished D.Phil. thesis, University of Waikato, Hamilton.

Beishuisen, M., Gravemeijer, K., & van Lieshout, E. (Eds.). (1997). *The role of contexts and models in the development of mathematical strategies and procedures.* Utrecht: Freudenthal Institute.

Bertalanffy, L. von. (1968). *General system theory: Foundations, development, applications.* New York: Braziller.

Bishop, A. (1977). *On loosening the constructs.* Plenary presentation at the annual conference of the Mathematical Association of Victoria, Melbourne.

Bishop, A. (1988). *Mathematical enculturation: A cultural perspective on mathematics education.* Dordrecht: Kluwer Academic Publishers.

Bishop, A. (1992). International perspectives on research in mathematics education. In D. Grouws (Ed.), *Handbook of research on mathematics teaching and learning* (pp. 710–723). New York: Macmillan.

Bishop, A. (1996). Introduction. In A. Bishop, K. Clements, C. Keitel, J. Kilpatrick, & C. Laborde (Eds.), *International handbook of mathematics education* (pp. 1–4). Dordrecht: Kluwer Academic Publishers.

Black, P., & Atkin, J. (Eds.). (1996). *Changing the subject: Innovations in science, mathematics and technology education.* London: Routledge.

Bramald, R., Miller, J., & Higgins, S. (2000). ICT, mathematics and effective teaching. *Mathematics Education Review, 12,* 1–13.

Calvin, W. (1996). *How brains think: Evolving intelligence, then and now.* New York: Basic Books.

Cambridge Institute of Education. (1985). *New perspectives on the mathematics curriculum: An independent appraisal of the outcomes of APU mathematics testing 1978–82* (Report for the Department of Education and Science). London: Her Majesty's Stationery Office.

Capra, F. (1996). *The web of life: A new scientific understanding of living systems.* New York: Anchor. (Also published as *The web of life: A new synthesis of mind and matter,* London, Harper Collins)

Casti, J. (1994). *Complexification: Explaining a paradoxical world through the science of surprise.* New York: Harper Collins.

Claxton, G. (1999). *Wise up: The challenge of lifelong learning.* London: Bloomsbury.

Cobb, P. (1994). Where is the mind? Constructivist and sociocultural perspectives on mathematics development. *Educational Researcher, 23*(7), 13–20.

Cochran-Smith, M., & Lytle, S. (1999). The teacher research movement; A decade later. *Educational Researcher, 28*(7), 15–25.

Cohen, J., & Stewart, I. (1994). *The collapse of chaos: Discovering simplicity in a complex world.* New York: Penguin Books.

Dalin, P. (1986). From leadership training to educational development: IMTEC as an international experience. In E. Hoyle & A. McMahon (Eds.), *The management of schools* (World Yearbook of Education, pp. 297–309). London: Kogan Paul.

Damasio, A. (1994). *Descartes' error: Emotion, reason, and the human brain.* New York: G P Putnam's Sons.

Damasio, A. (2000). *The feeling of what happens: Body and emotion in the making of consciousness.* New York: Harcourt & Co.

Davis, B. (1995). Thinking otherwise and hearing differently: Enactivism and school mathematics. *Journal of Curriculum Theorizing, 11*(4), 31–58. (Reprinted in Pinar W. (Ed.). (1999). *Contemporary curriculum discourses: Twenty years of JCT* (pp. 325–345). New York: Peter Lang Publishing)

Davis, B. (1996). *Teaching mathematics: Towards a sound alternative.* New York: Garland.

Davis, B., & Sumara, D. (1997). Cognition, complexity, and teacher education. *Harvard Educational Review, 67*(1), 105–125.

Davis, B., Sumara, D., & Luce-Kapler, R. (2000). *Engaging minds: Learning and teaching in a complex world.* Mahwah, NJ: Lawrence Erlbaum Associates.

Davis, P., & Hersh, R. (1981). *The mathematical experience.* Boston: Birkhaüser.

Dawson, S. (1999). The enactivist perspective on teacher development: 'A path laid while walking'. In B. Jaworski, T. Wood, & S. Dawson (Eds.), *Mathematics teacher education: Critical international perspectives* (pp. 148–162). London: Falmer Press.

De Mello, A. (1990). *Awareness.* London: Fount.

Department of Education and Science and the Welsh Office. (1982). *Mathematics counts* (Report of the Committee of Inquiry into the Teaching of Mathematics in Schools under the Chairmanship of Cockcroft, W.). London: Her Majesty's Stationery Office.

Department for Education and Employment. (1998). *The implementation of the national numeracy strategy: The final report of the numeracy task force.* London: Author.

Douglas, B. (1991). 'Teachers as experts': A case study of school-based staff development. In L. Bell & C. Day (Eds.), *Managing the professional development of teachers* (pp. 88–109). Buckingham: Open University Press.

Edelman, G. (1987). *Neural Darwinism: The theory of neuronal group selection.* New York: Basic Books.

Ernest, P. (1991). *The philosophy of mathematics education.* London: Falmer Press.

Fullan, M. (1982). Research into educational innovation. In H. Gray (Ed.), *The management of educational institutions* (pp. 245–261). Lewes: Falmer Press.

Fullan, M. (1989). Planning, doing, and coping with change. In B. Moon, P. Murphy & J. Raynor (Eds.), *Policies for the curriculum* (pp. 183–211). London: Hodder and Stoughton.

Fullan, M., with Stiegelbauer, S. (1991). *The new meaning of educational change.* New York: Teachers College Press.

Gadamer, H.-G. (1990). *Truth and method.* New York: Continuum.

Gallagher, S. (1992). *Hermeneutics and education.* Albany: State University of New York Press.

Giorgi, A. (1970). *Psychology as a human science: A phenomenologically based approach.* New York: Harper and Row.

Glass, G., McGaw, B., & Smith, M. (1981). *Meta-analysis in social research.* Beverley Hills: Sage.

Goleman, D. (1996). *Emotional intelligence: Why it can matter more than IQ.* London: Bloomsbury.

Gravemeijer, K. (2000). *Didatical phenomenological analysis as a design heuristic: Early statistics as an example.* Paper presented in Working Group 8 'Research, Theory and Practice' at the Ninth International Congress on Mathematical Education, Makuhari, Japan.

Grouws, D. (Ed.). (1992). *Handbook of research on mathematics teaching and learning.* New York: Macmillan.

Hart, K., Johnson, D., Brown, M., Dickson, L., & Clarkson, R. (1989). *Children's mathematical frameworks 8–13: A study of classroom teaching.* Windsor: NFER/Nelson.

Hart, K., Kerslake, D., Brown, M., Ruddock, G., Küchemann, D., & McCartney, M. (1981). *Children's understanding of mathematics: 11–16.* London: John Murray.

Hatch, G., & Shiu, C. (1998). Practitioner research and the construction of knowledge in mathematics education. In A. Sierpinska & J. Kilpatrick (Eds.), *Mathematics education as a research domain: A search for identity* (pp. 297–315). Dordrecht: Kluwer Academic Press.

Hiebert, J. (Ed.). (1986). *Conceptual and procedural knowledge: The case for mathematics.* Hillsdale, NJ: Lawrence Erlbaum Associates.

Howson, G., Keitel, C., & Kilpatrick, J. (1981). *Curriculum development in mathematics.* Cambridge: Cambridge University Press.

Johnson, M. (1987). *The body in the mind: The bodily basis of meaning, imagination and reasoning.* Chicago: University of Chicago Press.

Kelly, A., & Lesh, R. (Eds.). (2000). *Handbook of research design in mathematics and science education.* Mahwah, NJ: Lawrence Erlbaum Associates.

Kieren, T. (1995). *Teaching in the middle: Enactivist view on teaching and learning mathematics.* Invited plenary at Queens/Gage Canadian National Mathematics Leadership Conference: Queens University.

Kilpatrick, J. (1996). Introduction to Section 1. In A. Bishop, K. Clements, C. Keitel, J. Kilpatrick, & C. Laborde (Eds.), *International handbook of mathematics education* (pp. 7–9). Dordrecht: Kluwer Academic Publishers.

Krishnamurti, J. (1956). *Education and the significance of life.* London: Victor Gollancz.

Lakoff, G., & Johnson, M. (1999). *Philosophy in the flesh: The embodied mind and its challenge to Western thought.* New York: Basic Books.

Lampert, M. (2000). Knowing teaching: The intersection of research on teaching and qualitative research. *Harvard Educational Review, 70*(1), 86–99.

Lave, J., & Wenger, E. (1991). *Situated learning: Legitimate peripheral participation.* Cambridge: Cambridge University Press.

Lortie, D. (1975). *Schoolteacher: A sociological study.* Chicago: University of Chicago Press.

Malone, J. (2000). Bridging the gap: A challenge for the dual community. In J. Bana & A. Chapman (Eds.), *Mathematics education beyond 2000* (Proceedings of the 23rd Annual Conference of the Mathematics Education Research Group of Australasia, pp. 27–36). Fremantle: MERGA.

Mason, J. (1998). Researching from the inside in mathematics education. In A. Sierpinska & J. Kilpatrick (Eds.), *Mathematics education as a research domain: A search for identity* (pp. 357–377). Dordrecht: Kluwer Academic Press.

Maturana, H., & Varela, F. (1987). *The tree of knowledge: The biological roots of human understanding.* Boston: Shambhala Press.

Maturana, H., & Varela, F. (Eds.). (1980). *Autopoiesis and cognition: The realization of the living.* Dordrecht: Reidel.

Merleau-Ponty, M. (1962). *Phenomenology of perception.* London: Routledge & Kegan Paul.

Mingers, J. (1995). *Self-producing systems: Implications and applications of autopoiesis.* New York: Plenum Press.

Moseley, D., Higgins, S., Bramald, R., Hardman, F., Miller, J., Mroz, M., Tse, H., Newton, D., Thompson, I., Williamson, J., Halligan, J., & Bramald, S. (1999). *Ways forward with ICT: Effective pedagogy using information and communications technology for literacy and numeracy in primary schools* (Report for the Teacher Training Agency, London). Newcastle: University of Newcastle upon Tyne.

National Council of Teachers of Mathematics. (1989). *Curriculum and evaluation standards for school mathematics.* Reston, VA: Author.

National Council of Teachers of Mathematics. (2000). *Principles and standards for school mathematics.* Reston, VA: Author.

Nhãt Hanh, T. (1987). *The miracle of mindfulness: A manual on meditation* (Rev. ed.). Boston: Beacon Press. (Original work published 1975 as *Phép la cua su tinh thuc,* translated by Mobi Ho).

Noddings, N. (1984). *Caring: A feminine approach to ethics and moral education.* Berkeley: University of California Press.

Noddings, N. (1992). *The challenge to care in schools.* New York: Teachers College Press.

Nørretranders, T. (1998). *The user illusion: Cutting consciousness down to size* (J. Sydenham, Trans.). New York: Viking.

Plotkin, H. (1998). *Evolution in mind: An introduction to evolutionary psychology.* Cambridge, MA: Harvard University Press.

Posner, G., Strike, K., Hewson, P., & Gertzog, W. (1982). Accommodation of a scientific conception: Toward a theory of conceptual change. *Science Education, 66*(2), 211–227.

Rice, M. (1992). *Towards a professional development ethos.* Paper presented at the 15th Annual

Conference of the Mathematics Education Research Group of Australasia, University of Western Sydney, Nepean.

Robinson, I. (1989). The empowerment paradigm for the professional development of teachers of mathematics. In N. Ellerton & M. Clements. (Eds.), *School mathematics: The challenge to change* (pp. 269–283). Geelong: Deakin University.

Sacks, O. (1995). A new vision of the mind. In J. Cornwell (Ed.), *Nature's imagination: The frontiers of scientific vision* (pp. 101–121). Oxford: Oxford University Press.

Secondary Mathematics Individualised Learning Experiment (SMILE). (1986). *GCSE aims and objectives*. London: SMILE/Inner London Education Authority.

Sowder, J. (2000). Editorial. *Journal for Research in Mathematics Education, 31*(1), 2–4.

Steffe, L., & Gale, J. (Eds.). (1993). *Constructivism in education*. Hillsdale, NJ: Lawrence Erlbaum Associates.

Sumara, D., & Davis, B. (1997). Enactivist theory and community learning: Towards a complexified understanding of action research. *Educational Action Research, 5*(3), 403–422.

Thompson, A. (1984). The relationship of teachers' conceptions of mathematics and mathematics teaching to instructional practice. *Educational Studies in Mathematics, 15*(2), 105–127.

Vanier, J. (1998). *Becoming human* (CBC Massey Lecture Series). Toronto: Anansi.

Varela, F. (1999). *Ethical know-how: Action, wisdom and cognition*. Stanford, CA: Stanford University Press.

Varela, F., Thompson, E., & Rosch, E. (1991). *The embodied mind: Cognitive science and human experience*. Cambridge, MA: MIT Press.

Von Glasersfeld, E. (1995). *Radical constructivism: A way of knowing and learning*. London: Falmer Press.

Walkerdine, V. (1987). *The mastery of reason: Cognitive development and the production of rationality*. London: Routledge.

Wiliam, D., & Lee, C. (2001, September). *Teachers developing assessment for learning: Impact on student achievement*. Paper presented at the 27th annual conference of the British Education Research Association, University of Leeds, Leeds.

Williams, D., Wilson, K., Richardson, A., Tuson, J., & Coles, L. (1998). *Teachers' ICT skills and knowledge needs: Final report to SOEID*. Retrieved September 26, 2002 from http://www.scotland.gov.uk/library/ict/append-title.htm

Wittmann, E. (2000). *Developing mathematics education in a systemic process*. Plenary lecture presented at the Ninth International Congress on Mathematical Education, Makuhari, Japan.

Zack, V., Mousley, J., & Breen, C. (Eds.). (1997). Developing practice: Teachers' inquiry and educational change, Geelong: Deakin University Press.

Section 4:

Professional Practice in Mathematics Education

Introduction

KEN CLEMENTS
Universiti Brunei Darussalam

In the foreword to an edited collection providing international perspectives on mathematics teacher development, Ellerton (1999) identified what she regarded as the major, over-riding concern in mathematics teacher education by asking the question: "What should teachers do to make mathematics more meaningful for an ever-widening spectrum of students?" That seems to be the nub of issues surrounding the preservice and inservice professional development of teachers of mathematics: in many mathematics classes, in most nations, methods of teaching and learning stem from mathematics classrooms of a bygone era.

It was only in the twentieth century that secondary education became readily available to ordinary students in most nations (and, even today in some nations relatively few students attend secondary schools). For much of the twentieth century, patterns of teaching and learning mathematics derived from what had taken place in classrooms in Europe and North America in the nineteenth century, when mathematics curricula were designed for 'bright' children within a middle-class elite. Much attention continued to be given to teaching and learning rules, and it was accepted that the role of the pen-and-paper mathematics test or examination should be one of checking whether the rules had been fully committed to memory. Such were the inertial forces in education – and one might say, *especially* in school mathematics – that, during the past 100 years, these established traditions proved to be very difficult to change, even when there was a will to change them.

Mathematics teachers everywhere became used to behaving in certain ways, and their students, and indeed whole school communities, became used to accepting how the teachers behaved. But, although accepted, there is now overwhelming evidence that in some countries, probably in most countries, the 'normal' modes of teaching and learning are not efficient. In fact, they are destroying many students' self-concepts with respect to mathematics, and contributing to the propagation of values about mathematics and mathematics education which are not consistent with contemporary theories and ideals in education.

If the premise put forward in the last paragraph is accepted, then there is an urgent need to change school mathematics and mathematics teacher education in fundamental ways. Many believe that the main challenge lies with mathematics teacher educators, who need to revise their own ways of operating so that persons involved in designing, implementing, and evaluating preservice and

Second International Handbook of Mathematics Education, 637–641
A.J. Bishop, M.A. Clements, C. Keitel, J. Kilpatrick and F.K.S. Leung (eds.)
© 2003 Dordrecht: Kluwer Academic Publishers. Printed in Great Britain.

professional development programs for mathematics teachers at all levels will be *empowered* to generate new ways of operation.

Although the word 'empowered' is overused in teacher education literature, I believe it was appropriate to use it in the last paragraph. Old patterns and methods are so deeply entrenched in many schools and teacher education institutions, and particularly in the minds of teachers, lecturers, and students, that there is an urgent need to problematise existing practice, and equip and empower practitioners to achieve change.

Section 4 begins with Chapter 18, which is concerned with strategies for challenging and changing teaching practices in mathematics classrooms. The authors, Dina Tirosh and Anna Graeber, use evidence from the literature to identify two major sources of impetus for teacher change: (a) changes in values and beliefs, and (b) technological advances. They then discuss those issues that the literature suggests are important considerations for implementing planned change in mathematics teaching. They focus their subsequent discussion on the nature of the professional development, and on different organizational approaches to changing teacher classroom practices.

Throughout the chapter, Tirosh and Graeber refer to numerous examples drawn from a range of countries. These examples tend to reinforce the authors' caution that those seeking to change mathematics teaching classroom practices, and mathematics teacher education practices, need to remember that it is unwise to over-generalize conclusions reached in one culture to another. Curricula, or teaching approaches, or examination regimes, which are being successfully used in one cultural setting, may not be at all suitable in another cultural setting. That is to say, those seeking change need to recognize the force and importance of culturally based views on the goals, content and availability of professional development.

Chapter 19, which is concerned with assessment design in mathematics education, asks the question whether standardized tests have been, and continue to be, too widely used in mathematics education. In answering this question, Marja van den Heuvel-Panhuizen and Jerry Becker reflect on the aims of mathematics education, and especially on the role of assessment in the teaching and learning of mathematics. The authors compare and contrast the didactic and psychometric models of assessment design which, they point out, reflect different, even conflicting, ways of thinking about mathematics education.

The crucial issue of the chapter is the need to *extend* assessment design in mathematics education based on a didactic model, so that assessment is in line with the main objectives of achieving understanding in mathematics. Van den Heuvel-Panhuizen and Becker discuss how mathematics teachers and teacher educators can overcome certain misconceptions that inhibit an approach to assessment which is aligned with new ways of thinking about mathematics education. They close their chapter with examples of assessment problems that represent a didactic model of assessment design.

In Chapter 20, Alan Bishop, Wee Tiong Seah, and Chien Chin argue that practices in mathematics education, and in mathematics teacher education in particular, reflect the values of mathematics teachers and teacher educators with respect to the nature of mathematics and the ways mathematics should be taught and learnt. The authors seek to address gaps in research on values in mathematics education by drawing together the various research and theoretical fields that bear upon the values dimension of mathematics education. After distinguishing between values, beliefs and attitudes, they review the literature relating teachers' values to their decisions and actions in the classroom.

The second half of Chapter 20 focuses on the roles of values in mathematics teacher education, both preservice and inservice. It summarizes findings of two projects, one based at Monash University, Australia and the other at the National Taiwan Normal University in Taipei. The first project explored the relationship between teachers' intended and implemented values, and the second teachers' values in relation to their pedagogical identities. The chapter finishes by outlining the research difficulties inherent in this area, and offers a set of challenges designed to carry the research agenda forward.

In Chapter 21, Max Stephens draws attention to the contemporary crisis in mathematics teacher education in many countries. More and more students are studying school mathematics, yet in many nations there are simply not enough qualified young people choosing to become mathematics teachers to meet the demand. Therefore, those responsible for staffing school systems have to devise creative solutions in order to meet the demand for qualified and competent mathematics teachers. That raises important mathematics teacher education questions.

Stephens' analyses of the structures of preservice teacher education in different nations make clear that there are qualitative and quantitative differences in the approaches different nations are taking to the preparation of future teachers of mathematics, especially in relation to practicum experience during teacher education courses. In some nations, great emphasis is placed on giving student teachers as much time as possible in front of real classes of students, but in other nations (e.g., Japan), more emphasis is given to the quality of lesson planning and less to the amount of time actually spent in classrooms. There are also differences in the extent to which preservice teachers collaborate with their peers in their practicum experiences.

In Chapter 22, Tom Cooney and Heide Wiegel examine the place of 'mathematics' in mathematics teacher education. They maintain that central to the preparation of mathematics teachers is their preparation in mathematics, and therefore a careful examination of the nature of teachers' mathematical experiences is warranted. The authors explore factors that influence the teaching of mathematics, including the historical development of mathematics with its inherent formalism. They also review research on teachers' beliefs and knowledge of mathematics, arguing, like the authors of Chapter 20, that beliefs and knowledge relate to teacher change.

Cooney and Wiegel's review of the literature draws attention to three principles for teaching preservice teachers mathematics: (a) treating mathematics as a pluralistic subject, (b) providing teachers with opportunities to understand and reflect on school mathematics, and (c) enabling teachers to experience mathematics as a process. Their conclusion is that the research suggests that teachers are not always well positioned to adopt more reform- and process-oriented teaching styles that move beyond the usual formalism in the teaching of mathematics.

In Chapter 23, Barbara Jaworski and Uwe Gellert describe attempts, in different parts of the world, to achieve an integration of theory and practice in the education of new teachers of mathematics. Through a proposed hierarchy of levels of integration, Jaworski and Gellert discuss elements of the teacher education process and a range of associated issues. They show how student teachers, practising teachers and teacher educators can be brought together powerfully in the designing, implementing, and evaluation of programmes which are not only research- and theory-based, but also contingent on what is going on in schools. They show the extent to which successful integration is dependent on interpersonal relationships in schools and between school and university, and the practical constraints which might be seen to make integration an only partially realisable ideal.

Section 4 concludes with Chapter 24, which surveys international trends in the professional development of mathematics educators. It offers examples of powerful tasks that have been used to assist teachers and other mathematics educators to look beyond current concerns to a more reflective stance so far as mathematics and mathematics teaching are concerned. The authors, Orit Zaslavsky, Olive Chapman, and Roza Leikin, consider the professional growth of mathematics educators – including teachers, teacher educators, and educators of teacher educators – to be an ongoing lifelong process. They focus on trends in the thinking about, and practices within, inservice professional development programmes for mathematics educators – inservice teachers as well as inservice teacher educators – and offer a unifying conceptual framework that takes into account interrelations between the different groups covered by the term 'mathematics educators'. Their framework also facilitates thinking about the complexities and underlying processes involved in professional development in mathematics education.

Zaslavsky, Chapman, and Leikin close their chapter by drawing attention to the central role of tasks and programmes in which participants engage. Examples of tasks with special potential for enhancing the professional development of both teachers and teacher educators are discussed.

Over the past ten years or so, it has been recognized in almost every nation that reforms in mathematics teacher education are needed. Mathematics teacher professional development issues are increasingly being placed on agendas seeking to globalize school curricula, assessment procedures, and teaching methods (see, e.g., Ellerton, 1999). That being the case, it is important that nations do not rush headlong into schemes of operation that could jeopardize the rightful place of research-based cultural, ethical, linguistic, and pedagogical considerations in mathematics teacher education. The impressive group of international scholars who contributed to Section 4 have, collectively, demonstrated in the seven chapters which follow that there is now an emerging, coherent research base which can inform the beliefs and practices of teachers of mathematics and mathematics teacher educators. The seven chapters in Section 4, therefore, can serve as a guide to all educators concerned with ensuring that the highest levels of professionalism underpin the on-going development of those vitally concerned with improving the teaching and learning of mathematics.

ACKNOWLEDGEMENTS

The authors of Section 4, and I, would like to thank the following colleagues who assisted by either reviewing chapters in Section 4 or by providing authors with answers to particular questions.

Harrie Broekman	Masataka Koyama	Tom Romberg
Tom Carpenter	Fou-Lai Lin	Tim Rowland
Phil Clarkson	Tom Lowrie	Yoshinori Shimizu
Raven Deerwater	Olwen McNamara	Rob Sieborger
Nerida Ellerton	Meg Meyer	John Suffolk
Peter Fensham	Wil Oonk	Pongchawee Vaiyavutjamai
James Hartwick	Robert Peard	Merlyn van Voore
Toshikazu Ikeda	Andrea Peter-Koop	Julia Whitburn
Eric Knuth	Margie Probyn	

REFERENCE

Ellerton, N. F. (Ed.) (1999). *Mathematics teacher development: International perspectives*. Perth, Australia: Meridian Press.

18
Challenging and Changing Mathematics Teaching Classroom Practices

DINA TIROSH
Tel-Aviv University

ANNA O. GRAEBER
University of Maryland

ABSTRACT

This chapter summarizes general factors influencing change, and discusses matters which need to be considered by those working to achieve change in mathematics teaching practices. In the first section, we discuss two major sources of impetus for teacher change: (1) values and beliefs, and (2) technological advances. In the next two sections we explore the question: What important considerations in implementing planned changes in mathematics teaching are suggested by the existing body of knowledge? We focus on two seemingly essential dimensions of any planned effort to change teacher classroom practices: organizational approach and the nature of the professional development. Examples presented in the text are drawn from a variety of countries. We conclude with comments on the role of the specific goals of the planned change in framing the professional development and in assessing the change effort, and on the impact of culturally based views on the goals, content and availability of professional development. We acknowledge, throughout this chapter, that when considering research on either challenging or changing mathematics teaching classroom practices, readers should remember that care needs to be exercised in generalizing conclusions reached in one culture to another.

1. OVERVIEW OF THE CHAPTER

Teaching is widely recognized as a complex process involving the interaction of the teacher, the students and the subject matter (National Research Council, 2001, p. 313). This chapter focuses on changes in one aspect of teaching, mathematics classroom practice. Although some changes do occur in a teacher's practice over time, in a naturalistic way (Richardson and Placier, 2001) this chapter concentrates on planned change.

In our discussion we view teaching as a 'cultural activity' (see for example, Stigler & Hiebert, 1999). As such it "evolves over long periods of time in ways that are consistent with the stable web of beliefs and assumptions that are part

Second International Handbook of Mathematics Education, 643–687
A.J. Bishop, M.A. Clements, C. Keitel, J. Kilpatrick and F.K.S. Leung (eds.)
© 2003 Dordrecht: Kluwer Academic Publishers. Printed in Great Britain.

of the culture" (p. 87). There are several implications of this for any consideration of planned changes in classroom practice. First, planned change is apt to be difficult. This is true because of both the tacit way in which cultural practices are learned and the supports for existing practice within the larger school/culture context. A second implication is that some perturbation must occur, some energy added to the existing scheme, if change is to be prompted.

The chapter presents general factors influencing change and considerations in carrying out change. In the first section, we discuss two major sources of impetus for teacher change. Next we examine issues in the organizational approaches to change and in professional development. We conclude with comments on goals and evaluation, and on cultural influences on teacher change. Examples presented in the text are drawn from a variety of countries. When considering research on either challenging or changing mathematics teaching classroom practices, readers should remember that care needs to be exercised in generalizing learnings from one culture to another.

2. CHALLENGES TO TEACHERS' CLASSROOM PRACTICE

When people are asked "What might lead to changes in mathematics teaching classroom practices?" the response that is often unhesitatingly offered is: achievement on international, national or local tests. Respondents explain that achievement on such tests attracts the attention of various sectors of a society (for example, politicians, mathematicians, parents) and dissatisfaction with results often prompt calls for reform of both the content and the form of mathematics instruction. Other 'global factors' (i.e., factors that promote calls for changes in a given system) that are often mentioned are: attempts to provide *all* students (including minorities, females, students with special needs and students with poor socio-economic background) with equal opportunities to succeed in mathematics, demands from workplaces, new knowledge about the learning and teaching of mathematics; and emerging learning theories. Some people address 'local factors' (i.e., factors that encourage teachers in a school or a single mathematics teacher to change classroom teaching practices) that might stimulate changes. Local factors that are typically mentioned are: consistent, low achievement of the students in a particular mathematics teacher's classes, teacher participation in a professional development program, or teacher observation of mathematics teaching by a colleague or on a video.

The above list of factors is clearly not exhaustive. There are a variety of sources of calls for change in mathematics teaching classroom practices and they could be categorized in different ways. We recognize, and the text will support the notion, that different forces for or against change often converge to form an even more powerful force for or against change. And, that the force that represents a press for change for some educators may represent a force against change others.

The discussion below focuses on global factors that lead to calls for change in mathematics teaching classroom practices and describes forces related to two major aspects of culture: (1) values and beliefs, and (2) technological advances. Some members of a culture may press to adopt new values or beliefs or to return to values that they perceive have been lost. Or, the development of new technologies may lead to new conditions that stimulate a call for change. In fact, values and beliefs may also interact with technological advances to provide an impetus for change.

2.1. *Values and Beliefs*

Changes in cultural beliefs concerning who should learn mathematics and what mathematics should be learned may result in calls for changes in teachers' classroom practices. The notion of mathematics-for-all stems from societal movements espousing greater equality as well as from economic considerations. Stances taken by individuals from business and industry about what abilities and dispositions workers need also create a press for change. Changes in beliefs about what mathematics should be learned and how it should be learned are reflected in standards for school mathematics, curricula, and tests. These artifacts serve as major, cultural tools to promote changes in classroom practices.

2.1.1. Reactions to social and economic beliefs

Sensitivity to injustice has led many countries to strive for giving more, indeed all, students access to a better education, including the learning of mathematics. The end of the apartheid era in South Africa placed new demands on education and on teachers' practice. South African curriculum documents, such as Curriculum 2005 (South Africa Ministry of Education, 1997) emphasize that "all people have a right to access to these [mathematical literacy, mathematics and mathematical sciences] domains and their benefits" (1997, Section on Rationale for Mathematical Literacy). The report of a formal review committee on Curriculum 2005 suggested preferable classroom practices: "group work rather than directive teaching, and community participation" (Chisholm, Ndholvu, Mahomed, Lubisi, Ngozi, & Mphahlete, 2000, p. 3). Skovsmose and Valero (2001) argue that the massive calls for 'mathematics for all' in the new era of democracy in South Africa must result in dramatic changes in classrooms. The shifts must be from classrooms in which the authority resides in the teacher or the textbook and there is a transmission notion of teaching to classrooms where deliberation and reflection can occur.

Although the change in South Africa may represent an extreme case in which the majority of a population was denied basic rights, other countries where democratic forms of government have long been in place are attempting to change the classroom practices in an attempt to provide women, minorities and other traditionally underachieving groups with greater opportunities to succeed in mathematics and to increase their representation in careers using science and technology (e.g., Leder & Sampson, 1989; Kaiser & Rogers, 1995; Secada, Fennema, & Adajian, 1995; Trentacosta & Kenny, 1997). Explicit suggestions for changes in classroom practices are listed in the literature. A glance at just one of the listed texts, *Multicultural and Gender Equity in the Mathematics Classroom: The Gift of Diversity* (Trentacosta & Kenney, 1997), reveals that most of the authors (teachers and researchers in mathematics education) who shared their related beliefs and experiences with the readers argued that females and minorities benefit from small-group, cooperative-learning classroom practices. Croom (1997), for instance, wrote: "group interaction or cooperative learning promotes female and minority students' self esteem, motivation and achievement" (1997, p. 7). Khisty (1997, pp. 97–99) specified some essential conditions for effective group learning for specific minorities, and Jacobs and Becker (1997) discuss the preferable nature of small groups from a viewpoint of "gender-equitable multicultural classrooms" (pp. 110–111).

The calls for creating just societies in which all members of a given culture enjoy a fair chance to succeed in mathematics coincide with the economic necessity for more literate workers. Voices from business and industry argue that the economics of today demand that a greater proportion of people must be more mathematically literate. Kearns (1995) once a chief executive officer for Xerox Corporation; and McHenry (1992), a senior vice president at the Amoco Corporation, argued that all students must learn mathematics and that teachers' practice must change to allow them to adapt instruction to a wider range of students. In fact, organizations and business leaders not only argue for a more mathematically literate public, but also for specific changes in teaching practice that they view as more closely aligned with the abilities and attitudes needed by workers in the immediate and foreseeable future. Individuals with this perspective argue that future workers will need greater adaptability, as well as communication, problem solving, cooperation, and technological skills (Pollak, 1987, as cited in National Council of Teachers of Mathematics, 1989, p. 4; National Science Foundation, 1996; Educational Resource Information Center, 1997). A major concern is that traditional classroom practice emphasizes individual work and does not foster cooperative work at job sites. Accordingly, we have call for teaching practices that foster working with others on problems and that create an atmosphere of cooperation in classrooms.

The Organization for Economic Co-operation and Development (OECD) (2000) has developed a Program for International Student Assessment (PISA) in an attempt to assess the extent to which students near the end of compulsory education have acquired some of the knowledge and skills that are deemed essential for full participation in society (OECD, 2000). Results from PISA 2000 assessment indicate that in one-half of the 32 participating countries "there remains a measurable disadvantage for females" (OECD, 2000, p. 10), that home background influences educational success and that school socio-economic status may reinforce the home's effect. In the OECD (2000) report, specific suggestions for classroom practice are identified as factors that interact to influence student performance. These factors are included in a list of "things that schools can do that are associated with student success" (p. 22). The second phase of PISA (PISA 2003), in which mathematical literacy is a major domain (in PISA 2000 reading literacy was the major domain and mathematical literacy was a relatively minor element) the interrelations between social and economic mathematically-related values and beliefs and mathematics teaching classroom practices will be explored further.

2.1.2. Beliefs about the nature of mathematics and the nature of teaching and learning

Conceptions of a discipline are apt to influence what is taught and the manner in which it is taught. Thompson's (1984) classical work describes the relationship of teachers' conceptions of mathematics and mathematics teaching and learning to instructional practices. Thompson reported on substantial differences in the instructional practices of secondary school teachers that she observed, and she noted that "much in the contrast in the teachers' instructional emphases may be explained by differences in their prevailing views of mathematics" (p. 119). She further explained that while Lynn, the instrumentalist, taught in a prescriptive manner, emphasizing teacher demonstration of rules and procedures, Kay, who held a problem solving view of mathematics, emphasized activities aimed at engaging students in the generative processes of mathematics.

Thompson's assertions, which are based on three extensive case studies within the United States, are comparable to those of Stigler and Hiebert (1999) that are based on international comparison. Stigler and Hiebert (1999) argued that differences in classroom practices are at least partially explained by different views of mathematics. U.S. teachers' emphasis on practice of previously modelled solution strategies reflects their procedural view of mathematics. In contrast, Japanese teachers' provision of opportunities for students to develop their own strategies and to seek alternative strategies reflect their belief that mathematics is "a set of relationships between concepts, facts, and procedures" (p. 89). Thus, changes in beliefs about the nature of mathematics might prompt substantial changes in instructional practices. We shall return to this issue of the interconnections between beliefs and practice in the second section.

Likewise, assumptions about the nature of learning influence teaching practice. As different learning theories emerge, they are often interpreted as suggesting certain classroom practices. For example, during the past two decades proponents of constructivist learning theories have proposed implications for classroom practices including rejection of the notion that 'simply telling' will result in long term understanding. Rather, they argue that teachers must first understand the student's understanding and then construct tasks or questions that enable the student to build on that understanding (Confrey, 1990, p. 109). This perspective seems to have gained considerable acceptance and is reflected in mathematics reform documents such as the *National Statement on Mathematics for Australian Schools* (Australian Education Council, 1991), *Principles and Standards for School Mathematics* (National Council of Teachers of Mathematics, 2000), *Matematik faghoefte 12* (Undervisningsministeriet, 1995), and *Tomorrow 1998* (Ministry of Education, 1993).

A fundamental implication of constructivist theory is that instruction must take into account the student's current understandings. An example of research which has taken this implication very seriously and which has had an impact on teacher practice is that conducted by the *Cognitively Guided Instruction (CGI) Program* at the University of Wisconsin. The researchers have reported changes in the practices and beliefs of teachers who were provided with knowledge, derived from research, about the development of children's mathematical thinking (Fennema, Carpenter, Franke, Levi, Jacobs, & Empson, 1996; Franke, Fennema, & Carpenter, 1997). Franke, Fennema and Carpenter (1997), for instance, report that focusing inquiry on children's mathematical thinking encourages teachers to reflect on which pedagogical practices which will enable them to involve their students in problem-solving tasks which are especially likely to reveal their thinking. The teachers then also consider ways to change their mathematics teaching classroom practices along three dimensions: (1) providing opportunities for children to solve mathematical problems in their own ways; (2) listening to children's mathematical thinking, and (3) using children's mathematical thinking to make instructional decisions.

While we have addressed changes in beliefs about learning and about mathematics, little has been said about changes in beliefs about teaching. Stigler and Hiebert (1999) argue that "the widely shared cultural beliefs and expectations that underlie teaching are so fully integrated into teachers' world views that they fail to see them as mutable" (p. 100). In this case, beliefs about teaching are apt to be quite implicit. Stigler and Hiebert argue that changes in beliefs about the choices of activity in teaching can come from comparisons of teaching across cultures. And, indeed the video projects related to TIMSS have been used to stimulate thinking about alternative teaching practices (e.g., Office of Educational Research and Improvement, 1997). However, Stigler and Hiebert caution that all efforts to change teaching practice must be consistent with ways of changing cultural activities.

Planned attempts to change classroom practices to reflect a particular conception of mathematics or a particular learning theory often do involve new curricula or new tests designed to be supportive of particular conceptions or theories. Thus it is in this section that we discuss new curricula and tests as challenges to existing practice.

2.1.3. Values and beliefs reflected in the new curricula

In the past, changes in the curriculum were viewed as attempts to change the content of instruction more than the teacher's classroom practices. While the reform curricula emerging in the last decade of the twentieth century do include changes in content, they also emphasize teacher practices – practices that may be new to many teachers. Most current reform curricula that attempt to promote students' understanding of mathematics require that teachers ask questions that evoke students' thinking, and listen to students' thinking. That, it is assumed, helps them to plan next steps, spend increased amounts of time on single tasks, seek alternative methods of solution, connect mathematical ideas and representations. The aim is to connect mathematical ideas to 'real world' situations and to orchestrate small group learning (Australian Educational Council, 1991; National Council of Teachers of Mathematics, 2000).

2.1.3.1. The influence of the national mathematics curriculum in England.   A somewhat conflicting trend is observed in England. The National Numeracy Strategy, a government-funded initiative (Department of Education and Employment, 1998a, 1998b, 1999), has been mandated for all primary schools in England. The documents provided a detailed description of the program of study for each primary school year. An important aspect of this strategy is the emphasis on whole class teaching: "Overall there should be a high proportion of work with the whole class" (1998b, p. 15). Formal, related documents recommended a 'three-part' lesson structure: the 'introduction, oral and mental starter' (about 10 minutes); the 'main teaching activity' (30–40 minutes); and the 'plenary' (about 10 minutes) (Department of Education & Skills, 2002). In the introduction, the teacher is to work with the entire class. The teacher should provide the students an opportunity to rehearse the skills that are needed in, or that link to, the main part of the lesson; reinforce and develop correct use of mathematical vocabulary, or provide practice of the skills that children find difficult. In the main part of the lesson, the organization may be whole class, small groups, or independent work. The teacher might introduce a new topic or extend previous work with the whole class. In the small group option, the teacher might work with one of the groups (each of which might be working on a different task but all tasks are to be related to the same mathematical topic). Alternatively, in this main part of the lesson, the students might work individually on the same task while the teacher works with a particular individual. The plenary is to involve reflection on what has been learned with a summary of key ideas and vocabulary, or it can be used to hear short reports from groups that have been working individually.

This National Numeracy Strategy challenged beliefs about the nature of instruction, practices and routines in England. Traditionally, curriculum development in England tended to be more process- than product-oriented, and teachers were involved in making the decision to change the curriculum (see, for instance, Howson, Keitel, & Kilpatrick, 1981). Previously, students in primary schools worked in small groups, and it was quite unusual for a teacher to address the entire class. The new curriculum is more product- than process-oriented. Children in England are currently often tested formally in mathematics, and it seems that the teachers have been cast in the role of actor in, rather than that of director of, their classroom. That is, their classroom practices are now largely specified. These dramatic changes were to have occurred rapidly, over the last couple of years. The various, educational implications of this new reform will be studied in the coming years.

It is important to note, in respect to these recommended vast changes in classroom practices in England, that researchers who have attempted to implement curricula changes along with changes in classroom practices have noted that teachers are products of the very system they are expected to reform. As such they tend to incorporate practices that they themselves encountered as learners (Schifter & Fosnot, 1993; Ball, 1997; Fennema, Sowder, & Carpenter, 1999). For instance, a curriculum that focuses on discourse and conjecture requires teachers who experienced learning which emphasized memorization to engage in teaching practices that they themselves never experienced as students.

2.1.4. Values and beliefs reflected in tests and in reactions to test results

Tests are more than a simple instrument for measuring achievement. They communicate to teachers and students values about what students should learn. We discuss two ways in which assessment may serve to prompt changes in teachers' practice. Test content and format may impel teachers to change their practices to those that they view as most likely to lead to student success on the tests. Also, test scores that are low or that indicate a low ranking are often the cause of calls for change in classroom practice.

2.1.4.1. *Test content and format.*   Ideally, decisions about what is to be taught should result in curriculum and assessments that are aligned. However, tests are frequently mandated by educational agencies, sometimes in response to political pressure. In those cases the tests may or may not measure what is actually valued by the teacher. Often, in such cases, the content and the practice is changed to be compatible with the tests. Hence, tests often drive the content and teaching practice in classrooms (Webb, 1992).

Teachers are often compelled to teach to the knowledge tested on tests used in high-stakes assessment programs. This is true both because achievement on tests is often conceived as an important indication of the quality of the teacher and because test results could have far-reaching consequences for the students' future. Thus, teachers are often induced to modify both the content and their methods of instruction to match the tests' content and format. For example, commenting on the 1998 introduction of a new national system of examination in England and Wales, Morgan (2000) argued that "both the content and the method of teaching have been deliberately engineered through the introduction and shaping of national tests" (p. 228). Similarly, Miyake and Nagasaki (1997, p. 224) discussed the examinations for admission to private and national universities in Japan and noted that "there is a strong and growing belief that these examinations exert a powerful negative influence on the implemented and attained curriculum" of the upper secondary schools. Kim (1997) made the following comments about the college admissions examinations in Korea: "These examinations have definite effects on the implementation of curriculum, particularly in the final years of secondary school. Most secondary teachers, for example, emphasize lectures instead of laboratory activities in order to help students pass the college entrance examinations" (p. 233).

Romberg, Zarinnia, and Williams (1989), in a large-scale study of teachers, found that over 80% of the 500 respondents indicated that they made some instructional changes because of district or state mandated tests. A large percentage of the teachers from districts with mandated tests reported that they examined the tests to plan instruction. They also reported that the testing had an impact on how they allocated instructional time and that they emphasized the most basic skills and paper and pencil computations that are on those tests. Romberg et al. concluded that mandated tests wielded a direct influence on what a large number of eighth-grade mathematics teachers teach. Other researchers have also noted that teachers are concerned about changing their practice to those more closely aligned with current reforms because they feared that their students' scores on standardized tests might fall (Ferrini-Mundy & Johnson, 1997, p. 113).

2.1.4.2. *Test results.*   Achievement data which indicate that students in a class, school, or larger community are doing less well on some measure of student knowledge than some other class, school or community may prompt educators or the general public to question and examine classroom practice. Servant (1997) noted that in France the results of annual regional assessments in grade 3 and 6 are used "to enable teachers to adapt their pedagogy to the class" (p. 137).

   Reaction in the United States to the National Assessment of Educational Progress results and results from certain international tests [e.g., the Stevenson and Stigler studies of mathematics achievement in the United States, Japan, Taiwan (Stevenson, Lee, & Stigler, 1986; Stigler & Baranes, 1988) and the Third International Mathematics and Science Study] indicated the extent to which test results can provoke calls for changes. The statements which follow are but a sampling of the rhetoric surrounding the U.S. test results. "It is no secret by now that American education is in crisis" (Stevenson & Stigler, 1992, p. 13). The U.S. Glenn Commission report introduces its title, *Before It's Too Late*, with the following commentary. "The reports of the performance of our country's students on both the Third International Mathematics and Science Study and the National Assessment of Educational Progress echo a dismal message of lackluster performance, ..., it's time the nation heeded it – *before it's too late*" (National Commission on Mathematics and Science Teaching for the 21st Century, 2000, p. 7). Reactions are accompanied by numerous suggestions to improve the situation, and calls for change in teaching practice are prominent. For example, the Glenn Commission Report's first recommendation is a call to "establish an ongoing system to improve the quality of mathematics and science teaching" (p. 5). Specific recommendations addressed to teachers include "work with your peers ... to improve your skills and take full advantage of the professional development opportunities offered" and "incorporate educational technology into your learning and teaching" (p. 33).

   We previously mentioned PISA (Program for International Student Assessment) 2000. The results of this international student assessment indicated that 15-year-olds in Japan and Korea gain the highest mean scores in mathematical literacy (OECD, 2000, p. 11). The report acknowledged that PISA 2000 does not provide causal links between what schools do and how their students perform. Nevertheless in a section titled "What can schools do to make a difference?" the report identified some aspects of classroom practice that were associated with better student performance. It specified three such factors:

teacher-student relations, disciplinary climate of the classroom and the extent to which teachers emphasize academic performance and place high demands on students. The report encouraged schools to adopt these classroom practices.

Concerns about test scores not only led to calls for changes in practice but also to increased interest in how classroom practices differed across countries. Examples include the Stevenson and Stigler studies of classrooms in Japan, Taiwan and the United States (Stigler & Baranes, 1988) and the TIMSS case studies and videos (Stevenson & Nerison-Low, 2000). Stigler and Baranes (1988) noted that in Japanese classrooms, much time was spent discussing one or two problems from many perspectives, whereas in U.S. classrooms many problems were considered and little time was spent discussing any one of them. In the late 1990s the TIMSS video and case studies showed that classroom practices in Germany, Japan and the U.S. differed on dimensions such as number of topics considered in one lesson, the ratio of time spent in whole class discussion to time spent on individual work, amount of class time spent on homework, the ratio of teacher talk to student talk, teacher collegiality in planning for instruction, and the type of task (National Research Council, 1997; Stevenson & Nerison-Low, 2000).

When information about classroom practices in other countries became available through the TIMSS case studies and videos, some of those who were already critical of mathematics instruction on the basis of the test results suggested classroom practices as the cause of the low achievement scores. Schmidt et al. (1999) pointed out that some have criticized U.S. classroom practice and suggested that U.S. teachers imitate practices from countries that scored at the highest levels on the TIMSS tests (p. 202). Yet other voices called for using the information as a "mirror that can be used to examine ourselves" (Stigler & Hiebert, 1997, p. 14). Vastly different opinions have been proffered as to the needed direction of change. For example Schmidt, McKnight, Cogan, Jakwerth, and Houang (1999) noted that the release of TIMSS scores prompted some to call for getting "back to the basics," not only in terms of content but also for the concomitant approaches to teaching (p. 206). However, others called for using techniques closely associated with constructivist theories, for example, the use of collaborative groups (p. 207).

Critical analyses of this kind have led to radical changes in classroom practices in some schools, districts, states or countries. For example, some schools in Israel and some districts in the United States have run pilot tests using the Japanese 'Kumon' method or 'Singapore Math' (students in Singapore and in Japan score at the top of the international mathematics comparisons). A chief goal of both Kumon and Singapore math is to ensure mastery of basic skills. Students typically work on their own and repeat solving the same problems until they achieve 'mastery' – no errors within a certain time period (Strauss, 2000). While other mathematics manipulatives are commonly not used, students are trained to use the ancient abacus. They can use calculators, but before seventh grade, calculators cannot be used on examinations (Colvin, 1997). In other settings, the Japanese 'research lesson' or 'lesson study' has been adopted as a means of staff development designed to enhance specific classroom practice (e.g., special attention to the problem with which the lesson would begin, careful planning of questions that can promote students' thinking, attention to anticipated students' solutions and thought processes, observation of the lesson by other teachers, and a process of several rounds of lesson revision based on experiences in implementation).

2.2. *Technological Advancements*

Advanced technologies are both a result of and an influence on culture. As new technologies find their way into mathematics classrooms they may serve as stimuli to change teaching practice. Calculators and computers are probably the most common technologies currently in widespread use in mathematics classrooms. In addition to changing *what* is taught (although, with much debate), the introduction of new technology also may change *how* a topic is taught.

Many researchers provide evidence that classroom practices can be changed by the introduction of calculators and computers. In the United States, Waits and Demana (2000), for instance, claim "we have learned that calculators cause changes in the way we teach and the way students learn" (p. 56). They illustrate how access to graphing calculators has made it easier for teachers to demonstrate the roles of a and b in equations in the form $y = ax + b$; introduce non-linear functions earlier in algebra; link functions, graphs, and tables; explore the influence of changing one piece of data on a measure of central tendency, test propositions about geometric relationships, etc. Yerushalmy, Chazan, and Gordon (1993) noted that while inquiry teaching was rare in U.S. high schools, the introduction of the *Geometric Supposer* software prompted high school teachers to pose problems that led to much greater inquiry. Teachers using the *Geometric Supposer* observed that the agenda for a class could no longer be controlled as students' investigations took them in different directions (Lampert, 1993). The *Supposer* environment also resulted in the teachers encouraging students to work together and to communicate their ideas to one another.

Examples of the impact of calculators and computers on classroom practices can be drawn from experiences in various countries, including Australia (e.g., Groves & Stacey, 1998), England (e.g., Noss & Hoyles, 1996; Ruthven, 1999), France (e.g., Laborde, 2001), Israel (e.g., Hershkowitz & Schwarz, 1999), Italy (e.g., Bottino & Furinghetti, 1998) and Singapore (e.g., Yingkang, 2002). It is often argued, however, that the recent development of Information Communication Technologies (ICT) in general, and of the Internet, in particular, would lead to major changes in the educational systems and in classroom practices (e.g., Nachmias, Midouser, & Shemla, in press; Pelgrum & Anderson, 1999; Tapscott, 1998).

Nachmias, Midouser and Shemla (2001) claimed that the rapid development of ICT would result in a change in the perception of schooling and learning from the idea of a formally defined and spatially constrained event (i.e., a formal curriculum to be learnt in a school place) to the idea of lifelong learning, anywhere at anytime. Consequently, much of children's learning would take place in an other-than-school setting. Hence, a major challenge that educational systems will face in the coming years is to develop classroom practices that will ensure that the within-school processes maintain strong linkages with outside-school processes, in particular with the varied forms of learning related to the ICT culture. This is just one challenge. The various ways in which the ICT will (or will not) change the classroom practices are still unknown, but ICT's rapid development and the extensive usage could clearly serve as an impetus for dramatic changes in classroom practices.

At the beginning of the chapter we mentioned that different forces for or against change often converge to form an even more powerful force for or against change. One such example is provided by D'Ambrosio (1997). He noted the possibility that social beliefs and technological advancements might exert a complementary press on classroom practices. More specifically, D'Ambrosio (1997) argued that the social value of equity in education should be combined with high technology to create learning environments that foster the learning of females and minorities:

> It is a mistake to believe that the only resources available for introducing cultural issues into mathematics classroom are practices and objects related to popular culture. ... Of course, no possible motivation should be over-looked. Students' major motivation nowadays is high technology. Is it possible to integrate culture with technology? Multicultural education can be instrumental in meeting this major challenge for the mathematics educa-tor. Teacher educators will have to pay more attention to preparing teachers to assume their role as facilitator of a learning environment in which the teacher is no longer the main provider of knowledge. Authentic learning environments, using networks, CD-ROMS, and future technologies, are necessarily multicultural. (p. 247)

In other instances, however, some forces for change work against each other. A case in point is the direction taken by a calculator-aware number curriculum and the UK's new standards for numeracy. In England, as in other countries, the availability of calculators challenges both the curriculum and the practices of the primary schools. Ruthven (1999) described a pioneering project, Calculator-Aware Number (CAN) that was sponsored by the government curric-ulum agency. In the first stage of the project, the project team formulated a set of basic working principles, most of which challenge traditional, classroom practices.

These principles called for classroom activities that would be practical and investigative, emphasizing language and ranging across the curriculum. The importance of mental calculation would be emphasized, and children would be encouraged to share their methods with others. A major principle was that traditional pencil-and-paper algorithms for column addition or subtraction, multiplication and division would not be taught; children would use calculators for those calculations that they could not do mentally. During the first years of the project, the project team reported favourable findings (Shuard, Walsh,

Goodwin, & Worcester, 1991) and observed that the participating teachers began to develop an exploratory and investigative style of working that allowed the children the freedom to take responsibility for their own learning. Thus, the availability of the calculators resulted in changes in the classroom culture. Moreover, calculators continue to develop and to encompass more possibilities for meaningful use in primary classes.

However, the new standards for numeracy that were introduced in England's primary schools carefully defined what is valued in the curriculum and established national assessments (documented in Department of Education and Employment, 1998a, 1998b, 1999). These new standards required children in the first years of primary school to master paper-and-pencil algorithms for calculating the basic operations. These requirements encouraged practices that are quite different from those advocated by the CAN project. Subsequently, poor test results on numeracy in English primary schools resulted in the calculator being "cast as scapegoat despite evidence that it was little used" (Ruthven, 1999, p. 70). Thus, although the CAN project worked toward greater use of technology and a de-emphasis on standard algorithms for multi-digit operations, the National Council Curriculum, related assessments, and the interpretation of some test results, were seen as countering the direction of the CAN project.

We have discussed a number of factors that might serve to spark calls for change in teacher classroom practice. However, such calls do not always prompt change. From successful and unsuccessful reform efforts researchers have attempted to glean insight into the issues that are involved in making change.

3. CHANGING TEACHERS' CLASSROOM PRACTICES

Many recent publications in mathematics education deal, in one way or another, with issues related to changing teacher practices (see, for instance, Elmore, Peterson, & McCarthey, 1996; Fennema & Romberg, 1999; Grant, 1998; Stigler & Hiebert, 1999). Often, these publications discuss the theoretical and practical complexities involved in such changes. Our aim, in this section of the chapter, is to examine such publications from the perspective of a mathematics educator who is about to become engaged in planned efforts to change teachers' classroom practices. This section explores the question: What important considerations in implementing planned changes in mathematics teaching are suggested by the existing body of knowledge? What follows is by no means an attempt to list all of the ideas. We chose to focus on two seemingly essential dimensions of any planned effort to change teacher classroom practices: organizational approach and the nature of the professional development.

3.1. *Organizational Approach Issues*

Many decisions need to be made concerning the scope and strategies to be used in attempting to change teachers' classroom practice. Issues that warrant consideration include: Who will give direction to the change? Who should be involved? and Will the participation be voluntary or mandatory?

3.1.1. Who will initiate the change?

In the past some commentators have argued for a bottom-up approach to change whereas others have preferred top-down approaches. Top-down approaches are generally characterized by decisions made by someone in authority over teachers (for example, a school head, principal, or ministry of education). Top-down approaches involve little teacher participation in either selecting the innovation or in planning how to implement it. This approach was often viewed as an efficient means of getting something done (e.g., implementing a new curriculum) while minimizing interruptions and resistance by those who might not share the values embedded in the proposed change (Fullan & Pomfret, 1977). However studies of teachers' reactions to top-down innovation suggested that teachers were often uninterested in exploring outside interventions, especially those not perceived as addressing immediate needs (e.g., Lortie, 1975). In the United State some also argued that the 'loose coupling' (i.e., the lack of powerful means of enforcing authority from district to principal to teacher) of U.S. school districts meant that innovations were delayed or distorted as they traveled down the system (e.g., Weick, 1976).

Two influential studies in the United States, Bentzen, Bishop, Lieberman, and Seeman (1974) and Berman and McLaughlin (1978), suggested that the local school should be the site for locus of change and that there was a need for 'grass roots' ownership of the change activity – 'grass roots' in the present context means those who are expected to enact the change, the teachers. These researchers, who had studied numerous innovations in the 1960s and early 1970s, argued that implementation was most likely to be successful in instances in which participants were involved in the decisions concerning selection and implementation. In other words, the chances of success were greatest if change were allowed to perk upwards.

Success in implementing top-down approaches are most often reported in educational systems that are centralist in nature and in cases where the curriculum is mandated, students are frequently tested, and their scores are viewed as important by those who are requested to implement the changes. That has been the case, for example, with the new curriculum in Singapore and the National Numeracy Project in England). However, Howson, Keitel and Kilpatrick (1981) noted that a top-down approach is almost doomed if teachers are not involved in making the decision to change:

> The school culture of any country is highly resistant to change and especially to change introduced from outside the school. When 'outsiders' are able to institute curriculum changes without the cooperation and collaboration of teachers, such changes seldom go smoothly or last long. (p. 65)

A classic example of such a failure is the attempt of the mathematics supervisor and members of the board of education to introduce a 'New Math' curriculum program in grades 4 to 6 in one district in the United States. Teachers were not involved in making the decision – they were informed of the intended change.

Sarason (1971) noted that the teachers were anxious, angry and frustrated, and that, in the end, there was little evidence that the goals of the reform had been met.

The frustration of teachers who are to implement the changes but who are not treated as partners is vividly described by Ponte, Matos, Guimarães, Leal, and Canavarro (1994). Ponte and his colleagues describe a case study of an attempt to implement a new curriculum, initiated by the Ministry of Education in Portugal. Although the implementation had a markedly top-down nature, the more enthusiastic teachers took some of the intended changes further than planned and actually brought about much change in their classroom practice. However, these teachers wanted to have a much greater level of participation in the process. Sensing that they were given just a minor role and feeling somewhat ignored in some stages of the work, they limited their responsibility for and sense of ownership of the larger process. Consequently the teachers were caught in a contradictory position, in sympathy with the new approaches, but strongly critical of the process of implementation. Obviously, such feelings do not promote the implementation of changes.

Although the teachers in the Ponte et al. (1994) study felt that the top-down mandate did not involve them enough, such mandates may also leave teachers feeling that too much is being asked of them. Valero and Jess (2000) explained that the *Curricular Guidelines in Mathematics* (Undervisningministeriet, 1995) required a strong shift in teachers' practices and described it as a policy that "supposes that teachers participate actively as curriculum designers" (Valero & Jess, 2000, p. 249). The teachers regarded this new role not as an opportunity to play an important part in curriculum decision-making but as a new set of demands put on them as part of a new and slightly more sophisticated top-down strategy for educational development. Valero and Jess observed that "this situation of forced autonomy" (Skott, 2000) makes reform attempts vulnerable and critical because "teachers do not know well how to cope with the new requirements" (Valeo & Jess, 2000, p. 249).

Bottom-up approaches typically occur when teachers determine the need for change and participate meaningfully in designing or planning the change. The teachers recruit and, if successful, win the support of and resources from the principal and district. Lubinski and Jaberg (1997) describe a school-based change effort that began as a result of the efforts of one teacher. The teacher had attended a summer workshop on teaching mathematics. Upon returning to her school in September and talking with her principal, the teacher persuaded the other teachers in the building to participate in a school staff development project to create the type of mathematics classroom that was envisioned in the *Curriculum and Evaluation Standards for Teaching School Mathematics* (National Council of Teachers of Mathematics, 1989) and the *Professional Standards for Teaching Mathematics* (National Council of Teachers of Mathematics, 1991). Although almost all of the funding came from a state agency, the principal secured the support of the school board by presenting a rationale for the work. The principal also persuaded the school board to give some financial support to the school for the purchase of manipulative materials and printed resources for the teachers. The principal's communication with the school board also meant that parents who read school board notes or the local paper were informed of the project. The researchers conducted classroom observations and administered belief surveys before and after a series of spring and summer professional development sessions. Changes were observed in teachers' beliefs and practices, although the amount of change differed from teacher to teacher.

What is not clear from the report (Lubinski & Jaberg, 1997) is the extent to which all the teachers participated in planning the professional development. Nevertheless, this example illustrates a change process that was essentially bottom-up. It was initiated by a teacher who drew in the other teachers, and the project was then endorsed by the school principal. Subsequently the principal sought the approval and support of those even further up in the hierarchy, the local school board.

In their description of types of planned change strategies, Chin and Benne (1969) also attended to the issue of who initiated the change. They identified three strategies: empirical-rational, normative-re-educative, and power-coercive. In the empirical-rational approach an outside agent brings an innovation that is deemed of value for teachers to receive and implement. Such an implementation is somewhat consistent with a top-down approach, as the outside agent generally has the support of the school hierarchy, while not having their authority.

In the normative-re-educative strategy the intended participants study their beliefs and knowledge and determine whether and how to change them. Such a strategy is more consistent with a bottom-up approach. An example of a program that comes close to the normative-reductive strategy is that of *SummerMath* (Schifter & Fosnot, 1993). Teachers engage in two weeks of workshops that expose them to novel ways of thinking about and doing mathematics. They are left with "in some respects crude, yet compelling, visions of a new kind of mathematics class" (p. 40). *SummerMath* provides a stimulus and a vision that facilitates questioning of beliefs and practice, it offers follow-up support, but the press for change must come from the individual teacher.

In the power-coercive strategy, forces outside the official school hierarchy (e.g., citizen activists) work to use political influence to change practice. The recent press in the United States for school choice (usually involving the use of public funds to defray all or some of the cost of tuition in private schools) and for public 'charter schools' (schools freed from many district and state policies) would be an example of power-coercive strategies. The force for change comes not from the established educational hierarchy or from an agent whom the hierarchy has helped to secure, but from citizens groups. Moses, Kamii, McAllister and Howard's (1989) argument that the taking of algebra by middle school students in the United States is akin to a 'civil right', and their call for community action to assure that algebra is made available to minority students, is another example of a power-coercive strategy.

These strategies or approaches are differentiated by who initiates and attempts to direct the change. Newer literature tends to accept the need for both widespread agreement on change and leadership for change along with acknowledgment of the fact that a variety of leadership and support-building models may be effective. Fullan (1993) argued that "what is required is a different two-way relationship of pressure, support and continuous negotiation. It amounts to simultaneous top-down bottom-up influence" (p. 38).

3.1.2. Who should be involved in the change?

Changes in mathematics classroom practices should be evident in the practices of teachers in their own classes. Hence, in considering how to go about initiating such changes, one must weigh the costs and benefits of attempting to reform teacher-by-teacher with those of initiating reform in some larger community. Some related questions are: Could one teacher in one school succeed in changing his or her classroom practices while others do not? Is it essential to work with each teacher on an individual basis or is it possible (and perhaps preferable) to work with groups of teachers? In either event there are issues of support and collaboration that need to be considered.

In the research literature there are several descriptions of individual teachers who succeeded in changing their classroom practice. A striking example is that of Barbara (Koch, 1997). Barbara, a teacher in a U.S. school involved in a district studied by the R[3]M (Recognizing and Recording Reform in Mathematics Education Project[1]) project, was successfully able to implement changes in her own classroom. However, her colleagues argued against her and noted that the students' program lacked continuity from grade to grade because of her approach. The other teachers resisted change for a considerable period of time causing Barbara to experience alienation and isolation. Barbara, nevertheless, continued her own implementation of reform practices.

The case of Barbara indicates that although a teacher can dramatically change his or her own teaching, successful change is more likely to occur when simultaneous attention is given to changing the system within which teachers work. Loucks-Horsley, Hewson, Love and Stiles (1998) noted that "in the early waves of the reform, impact studies reported the disturbing finding that many teachers who had experienced exemplary professional development returned to their schools to find no support for the kinds of changes they wanted to make, and therefore no change ultimately occurred" (p. 40). This explains why so much attention has been given, in the United States, and in other countries to 'systemic change' efforts.

Systemic change is based on the premise that effective changes in teaching and learning will occur only when all elements involved, including content, teaching, and assessment, are aligned to achieve a compelling vision of high standards that have the support of those involved (Knapp, 1997). Additionally, because school culture is highly resistant to change and change is recognized as difficult, support for teacher change is important. It is clear that if the school environment is supportive, change can be easier for individual teachers. Moreover, in a systemic effort those involved include not only the teachers and immediate school staff, but also parents, students and other members of the community. The support of each of these parties is essential for the change process. On the other hand, each of these parties has the potential to introduce obstacles that could delay or block the change process. We shall briefly describe some of the impacts these different parties can have on a teacher's attempt to adopt new, classroom practices.

First, we consider the teachers' colleagues. A growing number of researchers argue, from a social-cultural view of learning, that participation in a teachers' learning community is of great importance (Stein & Brown, 1997; Cobb & McClain, 2001). Many studies have noted the value derived from sympathetic colleagues who are experiencing similar concerns and can provide ideas for solving the problems encountered in change (Krainer, 1999, 2001). Krainer (2001) described the involvement of Gisela, an Austrian mathematics teacher who was also a vice-principal, in an evolving series of professional development activities in her secondary school. Krainer maintained that the staff moved from an assembly of 'lone fighters' to a 'network of critical friends' (2001, p. 287). He argued that although the growth of individual teachers is important, there is much to be gained from mutual participation. Indeed, Krainer also noted the need for systemic involvement to stimulate and support the growth of teachers.

In addition to the support of colleagues, school level leadership is important in providing the conditions, resources, and at least some of the leadership in the reform effort (Ferrini-Mundy & Johnson, 1997, p. 119). Jones (1997), in a chapter that described the relevance of context to teacher change, reported on a study of eight elementary schools participating in a statewide education reform in Kentucky. Researchers from Appalachia Educational Laboratory found vast differences in the success of the program implementation. One of the two major factors found to be important to successful implementation of the program was the extent to which the principal provided support (the other factor was teacher workload). Jones stated that the supportive principals were well versed in the program, provided direction for the teachers, modelled appropriate instructional practices, and found resources and released time for teachers. The released time was important for collaborative planning for their classes and for alternative assessments. Unsupportive principals tended to avoid workshops on the program, stayed away from the area of the school building in which the program was to be implemented, failed to provide resources for collaborative planning, and discouraged parental involvement in the program.

However, as mentioned previously, the community in which change takes place is larger than the school. Romberg (1997) reported on studies of schools where the entire school staff had agreed to work toward reform via the adoption of a particular National Council of Teachers of Mathematics standards-based curriculum, *Mathematics in Context*. Even in these schools, where the faculty was united in their goal, barriers to change were encountered. One source of opposition came from parents who were concerned that their children might not be adequately prepared to succeed in high school algebra. (In the United States, Algebra was traditionally taken in ninth grade, although there are currently many calls to move Algebra to eighth grade. Algebra has been seen as the first of a series of college preparatory mathematics courses.) Parents were concerned that the new middle school program might prevent their children from obtaining the status ascribed to those who could take Algebra in 8th grade, an early sign of their ability to enter college. Graham and Johnson (1998) also described the need for parental and community support and the ways in which community support was garnered in a number of high school reform projects. Graham and Johnson describe how one district in the R^3M project[1] acted to overcome parental objections and how another involved all stakeholders in initial planning as a strategy for preventing community resistance.

Other, obvious but often overlooked participants in the change process are the students. Students too must be involved in understanding that change is underway, and where appropriate, the rationale for the changes that have an impact on them. Students who have been successful in one type of classroom and who have learned the types of behaviours that are expected and rewarded, may find that a reform classroom demands other and different skills. Such changes in the student-teacher game are considered by students to be a breaking of what Brousseau (1997) has described as a didactical contract. For example, justification of answers and alternative methods of solution may be required (Yackel & Cobb, 1996). Writing about mathematics and working in groups may also be strange to students who are used to providing only short numerical answers and to working alone.

Teachers need to be aware of students' perspectives, prepare students for the change, and support them as they experience new expectations and new classroom values. One example is the story of Fred (Brown, 1985; Cooney, 1985), a teacher who wished to give his general mathematics[2] class students experience with problem solving. The students in the class interpreted the activities as 'games' that did not provide them with what they viewed as the real learning of basic arithmetic and algebraic facts. The students' resistance increased to the point that, despite a supportive principal, Fred felt that he had to discontinue use of the problems that he considered motivational.

We have previously discussed the mixed feelings of the secondary school teachers towards innovative curriculum development programs in Portugal, as described in Ponte et al. (1994). These researchers observed major differences between the 7th and 10th grade students' attitudes about the new innovation (the paper deals with the implementation of the curriculum in these two grades). The 7th graders were satisfied with the new practices: more group work, reports, investigations, more discussions and interdisciplinary activities. The 10th graders felt insecure throughout the year. Most of them, concerned about a possible negative effect on their future success and their application to a university, did not like the supporting materials, felt unsure about the appropriateness of group work in mathematics, and expressed negative feelings toward the interdisciplinary activities. Ponte et al. suggested that these differences are rooted in the more general attitudes of students in these two grades toward school: "It seems that younger students still have an interest in what the school may offer them, while the older ones appear to be driven mostly by personal or career interests, either immediate or long term" (p. 361).

Even at the university level, students' beliefs and attitudes can frustrate attempts to enact changes in teaching. Schuck (1999) writes of Australian student teachers' beliefs that constrained their willingness and ability to learn in new ways. She described her teaching of these students as "driving ... unwilling passengers" (p. 1).

3.1.2.1. *Should the only participating teachers be volunteers?* A longstanding debate about what fosters successful implementation and change has to do with whether participation in change should be voluntary or mandatory. Many reform projects begin with teachers who volunteer. An exception to this practice is found in the elementary school reform project IMPACT (Increasing the Mathematical Power of All Children and Teachers). This project focused on improving the quality of the content and pedagogy of elementary mathematics in several urban schools in the United States. The project sought to support and enhance teachers as they attempted to change their teaching practices (Campbell & White, 1997).

Because the project viewed the school as the critical unit for change, one of the major demands was that all teachers within a school participate. With district level support, the schools involved were notified that teachers had a choice of either agreeing to participate in the associated staff development and changes or transfer to other schools in the district. Some of the participants were clearly reluctant. Yet, Campbell and White reported that initial reluctance did not necessarily imply resistance (p. 348). The inclusion of teachers who were not outwardly interested did provide those teachers with "crucial beginnings for eventual change" (p. 348). After the summer inservice portion of the project, one-third of the teachers indicated that given the choice at the outset, they would not have volunteered. Nevertheless, at the end of the four-year program, 80% of the teachers indicated that the program would have been negatively affected if not all the teachers in the school had been involved. In commenting on her response about the importance of school-wide participation, one teacher noted that:

> I think it (not including all teachers) would make implementation difficult. If all students are not included it could be a nightmare in terms of parents' attitudes. Some may feel that their child is being excluded because of intellectual ability or included because of some lack of ability
>
> (Campbell & Robles, 1997, p. 182)

Campbell and White (1997) note that the school-wide aspect of the program made them "unique for an NSF project" (p. 346). It is our sense that the project's insistence on the participation of all teachers was not just unique among National Science Foundation (NSF) projects, but unique in an era where professional development is largely a voluntary endeavour.

This last example of the success of the mandatory approach to participation in a planned change raises a set of questions. Mandated participation does not, by itself, result in success – in fact, we have noted that teachers often do not cooperate with imposed attempts to change their classroom practices. Thus, how could the success of the mandatory approach, in the case of IMPACT, be explained? A factor that seems critical to the success of this non-voluntary effort is that the principals and the mathematics coordinators of the participating schools had not succeeded in enhancing achievement in previous improvement efforts in which participation by teachers had been voluntary. This led them to strongly believe that all the teachers in a school must be involved in the project and to adopt an uncompromising stance on this issue. This stance is compatible with that of Haberman (1991), in the sense that voluntary professional development efforts have not had an impact on practice in difficult urban situations. Thus, in terms of systemic changes, the school district strongly supported mandatory participation. Additionally, the project focused on a school as the unit of change, it addressed innovations in both curriculum and instructional practice, it was grade-level focused so that curricular challenges and accountability as well as the social context for teaching and learning were considered, and there was continued support from the mathematics specialists placed in the schools as well as from other project staff. These are only some of the characteristics of IMPACT. It is also possible that other factors which are often overlooked, including the personalities of the researchers and their collaboration with the teachers, best explain the success of this mandatory approach.

In this case, as in many other cases in mathematics education, success (or failure) is not unidimensional. A web of factors and their interrelations need to be considered. One such factor is the nature of the professional development.

4. PROFESSIONAL DEVELOPMENT ISSUES

Change, even conceptual change, requires not only a desire to change, but also knowledge of an alternative, an appreciation of the alternative as beneficial, and reflection on the efficacy of the new concept (Posner, Strike, Hewson, & Gertzog, 1982). Thus, bringing about teacher change requires attention to knowledge. Professional development and preservice teacher training are the chief, formal venues for teacher knowledge growth.

As noted above, our intention in this section of the chapter was to examine the publications related to changing mathematics teaching practices from the perspective of a mathematics educator who is about to engage in planned efforts to change teachers' classroom practices. The main focus is the question: What important considerations about implementing such planned changes could a mathematics educator gain from the existing literature on the issue? Whereas the previous section discussed organizational approaches, this section reports on considerations for professional development.

We first note that knowledge of instructional practices is widely recognized, nowadays, as crucial for teaching (e.g., Shulman, 1986) and that prompting and sustaining changes in teaching classroom practices is a major goal of many current, professional development programs (Grant, 1998). This, however, was not always the case. In fact, for many generations, teacher development programs were often confined to learning about content. Professional development typically consisted of a summer course with an expert who taught mathematics courses or of one-time presentations. Lanier and Little (1986), in writing about professional development across content areas, noted that "professional development programs have been found to be programmatically isolated. Staff development is not tied to the central obligations, opportunities, and rewards of work" (p. 562). Cuban (1988) argued that many professional development efforts result in minor, surface 'first order changes'. Second order changes, involving significant changes in thinking, teaching and learning, were rarely achieved and even more rarely sustained.

Over the last 30 years, the profession has begun to look at professional development in a more disciplined manner. Teaching was acknowledged as a demanding occupation, and planned change as complex and difficult (e.g., Fullan, 1993; Schifter & Fosnot, 1993). It is now widely recognized that professional development programs that attempt to achieve second order changes in classroom practices must address the participating teachers' knowledge, beliefs and practices (Ball, 1997; Fullan, 1993). The growing awareness of the importance of attention to classroom practices in professional development programs is reflected, for instance, in the recent publication, *Adding It Up: Helping Children Learn Mathematics* (National Research Council, 2001). In this publication, it is argued that proficient teaching of mathematics requires five interrelated components. Some elements of classroom practices are mentioned and discussed in each of these components. These components are:

1. *Conceptual understanding* of the core knowledge required in the practice of teaching (including integrated knowledge of mathematics, knowledge of how students' mathematical understandings develop, and a repertoire of pedagogical practices) (p. 381);
2. *Fluency* in carrying out basic instructional routines;
3. *Strategic competence* in planning effective instruction and solving problems that arise during instruction;
4. *Adaptive reasoning* in justifying and explaining one's instructional practices and in reflecting on those practices so as to improve them; and
5. *Productive disposition* towards mathematics, teaching, learning and the improvement of practice (p. 380).

Since systematic attention to professional development programs is relatively recent, there is little research on the effectiveness of different, 'modern' professional development strategies. Even less is known about differing strategies' effectiveness in promoting specific, teaching classroom practices. However, some lessons can be gleaned from the existing literature. In what follows, we deal in a general manner with the characteristics of effective professional development strategies. We shall attempt to restrict ourselves to examples of professional development that provide some indications of their effectiveness in changing teaching classroom practices.

4.1. *What Characterizes Effective Professional Development?*

Using the literature on professional development, change and teacher learning, several authors have attempted to identify important principles that can be used to guide the planning and the implementation of professional development programs. Clarke (1994), for instance, listed 10 'key principles' for professional development programs that focus on 'improving the individual teacher's practice' (p. 37). Loucks-Horsley and her colleagues (Loucks-Horsley, Stiles, & Hewson, 1996; Loucks-Horsley, Hewson, Love, & Stiles, 1998) identified seven indicators of effectiveness for teacher development programs in science, mathematics and technology and described a framework to help guide and inform the design work of professional developers. Even more recently, Schwan Smith (2001) described ten features of professional development initiatives that are designed to increase teachers' capacity for change in classroom practice and improve student achievement in mathematics. Not surprisingly, the lists of 'key principles', 'indicators', and 'features' include similar components. In what follows we focus on two main aspects of effective professional development: content and process. Admittedly, these two interact and thus the distinction between them is somewhat artificial. Nevertheless, we find this organization helpful in reflecting on the literature related to professional development.

4.2. *The Content of Effective Professional Development*

Much discussion about the content of professional development has recognized that knowledge of student learning, mathematics and instructional practices are central to proficiency in the teaching of mathematics (e.g., Jaworski, 1994; Even & Tirosh, 1995; National Research Council, 2001). These three foci are also among the features cited by Schwan Smith (2001). In fact, some of the features listed by Schwan Smith (2001) can be viewed as related to the content of effective professional development. Namely that professional development should be: (1) focused on student learning as a goal, (2) grounded in mathematics, (3) designed to support the teacher's day-to-day practice, and (4) appropriate to the participants' context (e.g., resources, students, state mandates). In order to be successful, a professional development activity should exhibit all of these features. Clearly, different professional development programs emphasize these characteristics to lesser or greater degrees. The professional development programs we discuss below generally did attend to all of these characteristics. However, we have elected to emphasize certain characteristics for certain programs in order to provide readers with references to a wider variety of programs.

4.2.1. Focus on student learning

In discussing focus on student learning, Schwan Smith emphasized the need to have student learning as the goal. However, she cautioned that the professional development must keep teachers' attention on *how* students learn not just how a specific technique or tool might be used. Knowledge of students' learning includes both the knowledge of how students' generally learn and knowledge about the learning of each student. One example of a program that clearly includes such a focus is CGI (Fennema et al., 1996). In a paper that described a longitudinal study of students' mathematical thinking, Fennema et al. (1996) explained:

> The goal of CGI teacher development has always been to help teachers develop an understanding of their own students' mathematical thinking and its development and how their students' thinking could form the basis for the development of more advanced mathematical ideas. (p. 406)

The professional development program associated with CGI was designed with two chief goals: (1) to familiarize teachers with an overall framework for the development of elementary school students' ability to solve addition and subtraction problems, and (2) to encourage teachers to describe each of their student's progress in terms of the framework.

The CGI program did not directly prescribe either pedagogy or curriculum for teachers. The program used carefully chosen videotapes showing an interviewer who asked individual children to solve word problems, observed each child solve the problem, and asked questions such as "Could you show me what you did?" These videos served as the stimulus for encouraging new classroom practices. The researchers reported on fundamental changes in the participating teachers' beliefs about learning and teaching and in their classroom practices. Additionally, significant improvements were observed in the students' achievements (Fennema et al., 1996).

Students' conceptions were the main focus of the *Manor Project* (Even, 1999a, 1999b), a project that sought to enhance a professional group of secondary school mathematics teacher-leaders and inservice teacher educators. In contrast to the approach of the *CGI*, participants in the *Manor Project* were not provided with explicit research-based models of children's thinking in specific mathematical topics. Instead, a large part of the program included reading relevant research literature along with presentations and discussions of research articles on students' mathematical conceptions and ways of thinking. The participants were then directed to examine the theoretical knowledge acquired from reading and discuss research in the light of their practical knowledge. They were then asked to choose one of the studies presented in the course, replicate it with their own students, write a report that describe their students' ways of thinking and the difficulties their students experienced, and then compare their results with those of the original study.

Even (1999a) reported that this type of introduction to student conceptions expanded the participants' theoretical knowledge and helped them to develop a better understanding of the issues raised and discussed in the articles. In some cases the teachers found that their students could work successfully with sophisticated mathematical ideas that the teachers originally assessed as too difficult for their students. Even reported that although her study was intended to investigate intellectual restructuring and change in knowledge and beliefs and not actual change in teaching practices, the findings suggest that "acquaintance with theoretical knowledge contributed to the actual change in teaching practice and student learning" (Even, 1999a, p. 250).

We have briefly described two professional development programs that focused on student learning as a component. The list of professional development programs that attend to this component is not short (see, for instance, Simon & Schifter, 1991; Cobb, Wood, Yackel, & McNeal, 1993; Becker & Pence, 1996; Klein, Barkai, Tirosh, & Tsamir, 1998). Most of these professional development efforts have reported some indications that their programs were effective in changing teachers' classroom practices.

4.2.2. Grounded in mathematics

Increasing attention is given to improving teachers' knowledge of the mathematics they teach. This does not necessarily imply learning advanced mathematics but rather learning school mathematics in a more "deep, vast and thorough manner" (Ma, 1999, p. 120). The premise is that an increased understanding of mathematics will result in changes in classroom practice (National Research Council, 2001).

It is quite unusual for a professional development program to focus only on this aspect of teacher knowledge. Nevertheless, some programs focus, more than others, on enhancing teachers' subject matter knowledge. *Project LINCS*, a professional development program for grade 4–8 teachers in the mid-western United States, was designed to enhance teachers' knowledge of geometry and their knowledge of research on student cognition in geometry (Swafford, Jones & Thornton, 1997). The program involved a four-week summer course in geometry and a seminar on van Hiele Theory. Predictably, teachers' scores on a post-course assessment were higher than they had been on a pre-course assessment. Further, classroom observations of four of the strongest and four of the weakest scorers on the geometry course final examination indicated that changes in classroom practice did in fact take place: Teachers spent more time on geometry instruction, they were more willing to try new ideas and instructional approaches and provoke students to higher levels of geometrical thinking. The teachers attributed these changes to increased geometrical content knowledge and research-based knowledge of student cognition.

In describing their work with a number of middle school teachers in California, Sowder, Phillips, Armstrong, and Schappelle (1998), point out that the research was undertaken to answer the question, "How does teacher understanding of rational number, quantity, and proportional reasoning influence the manner in which teachers teach?" (p. 1). Thus, they identified mathematical understanding as central to their work and wanted to relate teacher knowledge to classroom practice. The researchers conducted professional development sessions and semi-nars over a two-year period. Since the sessions were designed to enhance teachers' knowledge, they were indeed focused on how changes in teacher knowledge might change teacher practice. The majority of their report is in the form of case studies.

One of the teachers, Tom, was a respected teacher whose students scored well on standardized tests. Tom was a highly procedural teacher who provided his students with easy rules. The authors note that as Tom increased his conceptual understanding of topics such as the multiplication of fractions, he slowly relinquished his reliance on rule giving. The authors suggest that part of the reason for the slow evolution in his teaching process may be linked to the fact that there are still topics within rational numbers that he does not understand.

Sowder et al's (1998) professional development program also serves as a useful illustration of the way in which such programs combine the characteristics of effective professional development that are noted in this section. The authors reported that in reviewing the presentations and papers prepared for use in the seminars they "noted that the presenters consistently used student work to help teachers understand the mathematics" (p. 30). Thus while the goal was to enhance teacher knowledge of mathematics, student work and thus student thinking became a vehicle for teaching mathematics to the teachers. Mathematics, student learning, and the analysis of student work (a teacher practice) were all evident in this professional development program.

4.2.3. Supportive of teacher practice

Schwan Smith (2001) argued for a "practice-based approach to professional development," one that is "deeply rooted in the practice of teaching" (p. 41). Activities such as lesson planning, observing students, analyzing students' responses to assessments, etc., are among those that teachers routinely engage in and as such can become a focus of professional development. A number of professional development efforts emphasize the use of teachers' everyday practice. Two such examples are 'lesson study' and the use of 'case studies'.

The Japanese 'lesson study' is a commonly used vehicle for professional development that is now being implemented in countries other than Japan. Lesson study involves collaborative groups of teachers, and frequently a content expert, planning a series of lessons, trying them out, analyzing student reaction and student work, revising the lessons, trying the lessons out again, etc. The attention to content and to student thinking means that this form of professional development attends to the two content characteristics described above – that is to say, it is grounded in mathematics and is focused on student learning. The fact that teachers are planning lessons that they will actually use, and are implementing those lessons means that lesson study is a form of professional development that is, indeed, rooted in the practice of teaching.

Although there are many testimonials to the effectiveness of lesson study, there are fewer reports of observation of change in classroom practice. An example of such research is that of Hino and Shigematsu (2002). Although this research was partially situated in a university graduate program, the lesson study portion was conducted in a teacher's own school setting. The university portion of the program was designed to enable teachers to question and characterize their current practice and to consider whether they might usefully incorporate alternative approaches in their own teaching practices (p. 38). Observers visited a teacher's class prior to his work in the program and after he had completed the second year of his university work. They observed lessons on similar topics related to triangles. At both of these observation points, three perspectives were elicited: those of the observers, those of the students, and those of the teacher. All three perspectives indicated that after the lesson study the teacher had increased discussion in the classroom and that his attention to students' thinking was accompanied by a relaxation in his past strict adherence to the textbook. Although the changes were deemed 'not dramatic', the data from the three perspectives signalled an actual change in practice. This particular report (Hino & Shigematsu, 2002) describes the work of one teacher. However, the researchers noted that they have seen similar changes in other participants.

The case study approach consists of presenting teachers with narratives that focus on classroom episodes. These narratives are designed to provoke discussion on mathematical ideas, students' learning and classroom practices. Cases, whether in print or in another medium, present 'whole stories' or short descriptions of discrete instances. Often, the cases are introduced to teachers to invite both private and public reflections.

An example of a project that has developed, implemented and investigated case study as a vehicle for professional development and teacher change is the *Mathematics Case Methods Project* (Barnett & Friedman, 1997). Barnett and Friedman explain that the mathematics case method is designed "to build the capacity of teachers to make informed strategic decisions that draw on and anticipate student thinking" (p. 381). This case study method employed by Barnett, involves a trained facilitator leading a group of teachers through a case study written by a teacher. The cases themselves are written accounts of classroom experiences. In a case there is something surprising or puzzling about the student work. The teacher explains an instructional sequence and then presents information about student work or discussion.

In this way, reflection on cases from the actual work of teaching is facilitated. The sessions involve trust building (if there are new members), individual work on a mathematical problem drawn from or related to the case, a whole group activity that provides a chance to make explicit the facts of the case, pair wise and group identification of issues in the case (posed as questions), discussion, and an evaluation of the process used in the sessions. Another project that has used a case study approach is the *Mathematics Classroom Situations Project* (Markovits & Even, 1999). This project involved inservice teachers in discussions of written, real and hypothetical situations that included students' questions or ideas. The situations highlighted common school students' ways of thinking and their misconceptions. Teachers were first asked to respond to open-ended questionnaires that included eight situations. They were then invited to comment on written, real and hypothetical responses from other teachers (some responses were deliberately contrived by Markovits and Even, to represent particular views and to encourage debate). Finally, the teachers read and discussed related articles and conducted interviews with pairs of students to find out about their conceptions and ways of thinking.

The case method is often viewed as providing a stimulus for change. Yet, there are some indications that a consistent use of this method has some impact on teachers' classroom practices. Barnett and Friedman (1997), for instance, noted that "recent studies trace the influence of case discussions on teaching practice" (p. 382), and Markovits (in press) reported that a most common reaction of the participating teachers was "an increased interest in the students' thinking and consequently, allotting more time in class to listening to the students."

4.2.4. Appropriate to context

Professional development programs should also be reflective of the teachers' context (Schwan Smith, 2001). Moreover, the content of the program should be appropriate and relevant to the participants. For instance, a staff development program that is centred around the use of a computer program is not sensible for a district in which there are few computers in a school and budget constraints suggest the situation will not be reversed in the near term. The discussion below that draws on the work of Ferrini-Mundy and Johnson noted that in their case studies of ongoing reform initiatives, those sites that elected to make changes that were consistent with other ongoing efforts in the context succeeded to a greater degree than sites which did not make such connections. This lends credence to the notion that professional development should be appropriate to the context. The next example, from on a report on the QUASAR Project, notes that the QUASAR staff acknowledged, from the outset, the importance of context and provides an indication of how context differences in two sites led to differences in the activities and outcomes.

Ferrini-Mundy and Johnson (1997) describe highlights of their findings related to the *Recognizing and Recording Reform in Mathematics Education Project*. The R^3M *Project*[1] studied the reform efforts at sites which were recognized as making progress toward implementing the 1989 National Council of Teachers of Mathematics *Curriculum and Evaluation Standards*. The authors identified their most striking finding: "For whatever reason, given that the sites clearly chose different threads of the *Standards* as their initial emphasis, the better those choices seemed to fit with other trends in the community or context, the further the efforts seemed to go" (p. 116). Fit between efforts and contexts are important both for reform efforts as a whole and for the staff development portion.

The QUASAR Project directed by Edward Silver was an effort to help urban middle schools develop mathematics programs that were both consistent with the National Council of Teachers of Mathematics' (1989) *Curriculum and Evaluation Standards for School Mathematics* and were aligned with the local context (Stein & Brown, 1997). The project helped the mathematics teachers and school administrators identify and collaborate with resource partners (local mathematics educators). Stein and Brown describe two contrasting sites. At one site, the mathematics teachers formed a cohesive group that was interested in working on the reform program. At the other site, the teachers tended not to rely on one another, but rather to turn toward the resource partners. The authors describe the differences in those sites and how these contexts influenced the project's work with the two sites.

In this section we have discussed a number of considerations about the content of the professional development. Many researchers have reflected on what matters most in professional development programs (e.g., Loucks-Horsley et al., 1998; Kennedy, 1999; Schwan Smith, 2001). Schwan Smith (2001), for instance, argued "it is the content of the programs that matters most" (p. 40). However, she also noted the importance of the manner (or in our words, the process) of professional development.

> A central consideration in designing professional development experiences for teachers should be determining what one wants teachers to learn, both in short-term and long-term goals. A course, for example, can be a significant learning opportunity or a dreadful experience, depending on the content and the manner in which the course is conducted. (p. 40)

In the next section we focus on three major issues surrounding the process of effective professional development.

4.3. *The Process of Effective Professional Development*

Having in mind the mathematics educator who is about to become engaged in a planned effort to change teachers' classroom practices, we have decided to structure the remaining part of this section around three, process-related issues:

1. What is known about the nature and form of effective professional development?
2. What is known about stages in the change process? and
3. What is known about time allocation for the change efforts?

4.3.1. What is known about the nature and form of effective professional development?

Here we consider what researchers have reported on the manner in which professional development is conducted. Experienced professional-developers who have studied the field (see, for instance, Clarke, 1994; Loucks-Horsley et al., 1998; Schifter & Fosnot, 1993; Schwan Smith, 2001) list a number of characteristics associated with the conduct of satisfactory professional development programs. These authors agree that effective professional development models should reflect the pedagogy that teachers are expected to use with their students, should build teacher collaboration, and should make use of the knowledge and expertise of teachers.

A decision about the form of professional development is made on the basis of various factors (e.g., the cultural context, local context, individual conditions and preferences of all the involved parties). Clearly, such decision should not be made on the basis of one factor. A number of sources list forms of or strategies for professional development (e.g., Loucks-Horsely et al., 1998, National Research Council, 2001). Indeed, Loucks-Horsley et al. (1998) list 15 strategies that have also been logically related to the purposes (developing awareness, building knowledge, reflection, etc.) that they may best serve. For example, case discussions are seen by these authors as best serving to provoke teacher reflection, while immersion in the world of mathematics is seen as serving the purpose of building knowledge. While such classification schemes may help the educator consider a wider array of strategies, there is little research on which we can currently rely in selecting a format or strategy which will be maximally effective. As was noted above, in the discussion of content, even immersion in mathematics coupled with analysis of student work gives some evidence of changing teacher practice. The field is missing a body of research that assesses, in a systematic manner, the impact of various forms of professional development programs on changing teaching classroom practices. It would also seem reasonable that certain combinations of these forms would enhance professional development.

4.3.2. What is known about stages in the change process?

We noted at the beginning of this chapter that teaching is a cultural activity and as such any consideration of planned changes in classroom practices requires some perturbation. Thus, it seems that the first stage in a planned change should consist of creating some dissatisfaction with those teaching classroom practices or teaching outcomes that signal a need for change. Creating some disequilibrium for teachers is, according to Schwan Smith (2001), one of the key features of high-quality professional development experiences.

A question that this assertion immediately raises is: How is such disequilibrium prompted? This in turn raises the long-debated issue of whether changing teacher's beliefs should come before attempts to change their practice or vice-versa. Those who believe that beliefs must be changed before practice will change, base their reasoning on constructivist theories of learning, arguing that practice will not change until related beliefs are changed (Clark & Peterson, 1986; Shulman, 1986; Putnam, Lampert, & Peterson, 1990; Pajares, 1992; Thompson, 1992). Loucks-Horsley et al. (1998) noted that "the conventional wisdom has been that changing teacher beliefs should be the primary work of professional development because when one believes differently, new behaviors will follow" (p. 38). On the other hand, researchers who have studied change efforts have noted that changes in teachers' practice led to changes in teachers' beliefs when the changes in practice resulted in benefits to students (e.g., Guskey, 1986; Sparks, 1988; Prawat, 1992; Mevarech, 1995; Ferrini-Mundy, 1997; Schifter, 1998).

The Franke et al. (1997) data suggested that the relationship between change in teachers' instructional practices and change in their beliefs is complex. They found that there was no consistency in whether a change in beliefs preceded a change in instruction or vice versa. Of the 21 teachers studied over the course of four years, 17 changed both their beliefs and their classroom practice in the direction suggested by the professional development. Of these 17, six teachers changed their beliefs before their instruction changed, five teachers changed their instruction before their beliefs changed, and for six teachers the changes in beliefs and practice occurred simultaneously. However, the authors found that teachers whose practice changed first, often did not make profound changes in their practice. Changes in beliefs needed to accompany or proceed substantial changes in practice.

These studies suggest that changes in beliefs and changes in practices occur in a mutually interactive process. Teachers' thoughts influence their classroom practices. Their reflections on these activities and the outcomes of changed practice influence the teachers' beliefs about mathematics learning and teaching. Changes in attitudes and behaviours are iterative. Therefore, well conceived professional learning experiences should consistently address both, knowing that change in one brings about and then reinforces change in the other.

Several attempts to challenge teachers' beliefs and practices simultaneously are described in the literature. Loucks-Horsley et al. (1998) and Schwan Smith (2001) have argued that engaging teachers in learning that models the desired practices, and reflecting on those experiences, provides teachers with an opportunity to experience and observe the type of practice they are expected to implement. They can also re-examine their beliefs about teaching and learning and their classroom practices. An example of a professional development program that was intentionally designed to raise questions about beliefs and practices by engaging the participants in learning that models a reform practice is SummerMath for teachers (Schifter & Fosnot, 1993). This program was designed to immerse teachers in experiences with mathematics that would give them opportunities to reflect on their own understandings of mathematics and also of teaching. This is done so that teachers have an opportunity to analyze learning, the nature of mathematics and to reflect on and envision the kinds of classroom practices that will promote their goal.

The SummerMath program was based on the idea that the summer sessions must "provide experiences powerful enough to challenge 16-plus years of traditional education" (p. 16). Schifter and Fosnot (1993) noted that "teachers were frequently frustrated, at times angered, by program experiences that created disequilibrium, thereby challenging their professional identities ... some teachers have considerable difficulty coming to terms with the clash of perspectives" (p. 19). They recognized that this provocation and visioning is but a first step. The program encourages collaboration among teachers and provides follow-up with classroom visits.

The notion that disequilibrium is needed to prompt learning and change is the perspective of Piagetian-based learning theories (e.g., constructivism). Disequilibrium is known to be accompanied by discomfort (Flavell, 1977). Indeed, SummerMath is described by Schifter and Fosnot (1993) as "committed to the principles of constructivism" (p. xiii). SummerMath includes stories of success – cases in which the experience of discomfort stimulated some teachers to implement new classroom practices. However, discomfort may also lead to rejecting new ideas and in some cases even to abandoning the professional development.

This raises the issue whether this step is essential: Is the creation of disequilibrium with current beliefs, classroom practices, or student outcomes an essential, first step in professional development? Is it even a desirable step? Or even more radically, could a professional development program result in effective changes in teachers' classroom practices without creating dissatisfaction with existing beliefs, practices or outcomes? Lerman (2001) argued for defining teacher change as a learning process. Although adult's learning, especially learning about their work, is different in some aspects from children's learning, basic assumptions about learning seem to hold for this type of learning as well. Cognitive conflict is a 'must' in Piagetian-based learning theories, but not in others (e.g., situated learning theory). Our search for research that examined the role of disequilibrium in professional development programs that attempt to change teaching classroom practices led us to conclude that this is another area in need of further research.

We have so far discussed a first stage of professional development programs which aspire to change teaching classroom practices. We concluded that more research is needed before it can be concluded that cognitive conflict is an essential stage in the teacher change process. We also noted that changing teacher's beliefs is no longer regarded as a prerequisite to changing teaching classroom practices. This assertion seems to reflect a recent, broader approach to change processes: Change processes are non-linear. Fullan (1993), for instance, argued that although change is a gradual process that does not happen in one step but is progressive, "change is non-linear, loaded with uncertainty, and sometimes perverse" (p. 24). A similar stance was recently expressed in a major survey of teacher change in which a number of developmental stage theories of change were described and discussed (Richardson & Placier, 2001).

A Concerns Based Adoption Model (CBAM) for staff development, developed by Hord and Loucks (1980), outlined the developmental process experienced by teachers who are implementing an innovation. Hord and Loucks defined two critical concepts for diagnosing the individual needs of such teachers: first, the concerns teachers have about the innovation (awareness, informational, ... and refocusing); and second, the level at which they actually use the innovation in their classrooms. Three major sets of questions that reflect the major developmental stages of concerns are described.

These concerns develop from questions which are more self-oriented (e.g., What is it? How will it affect me? and What will I have to do?) to those which are task oriented (e.g., How can I get more organized? Why is it taking so much time? And, How can I best manage the materials and schedules? And, finally, when these concerns begin to be resolved, to more impact-oriented concerns (e.g., How is this affecting students? and How can I improve what I am doing so all students can learn (Loucks-Horsley et al., 1998).

Although the stages of concern may help the professional developer anticipate questions and select forms of professional development that seem 'right' for a particular stage in a change process, we draw the reader's attention to Fullan's (1993) comment that "change is a journey not a blue print" [sic.] (p. 24). Events will not always follow prescribed plans or ideals. Personal concerns that were addressed and appeared to disappear at one point in the change process may reoccur later. To quote Fullan, "We know that early difficulties are guaranteed. The perverse part is that later stages are unpredictable as well" (p. 25). Thus, acquaintance with research on 'stages of change' is important as it illuminates various concerns that professional developers should be aware of and ready to deal with. Recent research has revealed that these concerns are to be expected at various points of a development programme, and not just at one specific episode.

4.3.3. What is known about time allocation for the change process?

Time is a critical factor in change processes. In fact, decisions concerning scheduling and the total amount of time can have a large impact on the success or failure of professional development programs. Yet, the importance of garnering support and time for professional development programs is often overlooked.

Should professional development take place before school, after school, on non-school days, during students' vacation period? Is participation in professional development viewed as a part of teachers' work? How such questions are answered reflects the values and beliefs of the specific culture. In some countries, the traditional view is that teachers' work is governed by the idea that time with students is of singular value, that teachers are primarily deliverers of content, that curricular planning and decision making rest at higher levels of authority, and that professional development is unrelated to improving instruction (Castle & Watts, 1992, p. 2).

This conception does not encourage support for professional development activities. In other countries, teachers are given responsibility for the improvement of classroom practice and are awarded the time to facilitate change. For example, "participation in school-based professional development groups is considered a part of the teachers' job in Japan" (Stigler & Hiebert, 1999, p. 110). Clearly, these conceptions might have a large impact on the commitment and the motivation of the participants.

Another dimension of the time factor is the duration of the professional development program. The complexity of creating second order change suggests that professional development support is needed over a long period. Research shows that sustained professional development is more apt to result in significant change in classroom practices (e.g., Sparks, 1988; Fullan, 1993; Little, 1993). Thus, expecting change in a short period of time can lead to abandonment of practices that might have been beneficial had more time been allowed. Moreover, some researchers identify an 'implementation dip' phenomenon, that is, that outcomes targeted for improvement may actually drop at initial implementation as teachers return, in a sense, to being novices (Richardson & Placier, 2001). And, it is not unusual for researchers to report that three to five years are required before teachers become proficient in new practices (Ferrini-Mundy & Schram, 1997; Loucks-Horsley et al., 1998). Schwan Smith's (2001) comment on the crucial role of the duration of the professional development is relevant:

> Although merely increasing the amount of time available for professional development is unlikely to make a difference, it is equally unlikely that, without being allotted more time, even the best professional development will be effective in accomplishing the ambitious reform agenda. (p. 48)

A third, related dimension is the time allotted for professional development of teachers over their entire teaching career. This dimension, like the first, is not related to a specific professional development program but involves a more general policy toward the professional growth of teachers. Now more than ever, teachers are faced with the challenge of teaching new and familiar mathematical topics in new ways. This is primarily due to swift innovations in technology. Effective teaching of a given mathematical topic demands that the teacher understand the topic to such an extent that he or she will be able to explain and unpack ideas in ways not needed in ordinary life, have solid knowledge of students' ways of thinking about the topic, and be capable of implementing effective instructional practices.

In light of these observations, some researchers argue that professional development should be seen as an ongoing process that should "continue over the course of a teacher's career" (Schwan Smith, 2001, p. 48). In order for this to come about, it would seem that school systems, the public, and teachers need to accept the idea that teachers will attend professional development programs throughout their careers, that such attendance be viewed as an essential part of a teacher's work, and that time away from teaching be allotted for such activity.

At the beginning of this section we posed three questions about the process of effective professional development. In our discussion, we have taken the approach that professional development programs are a major vehicle for changing classroom teaching practices. Recent literature, however, raises theoretical concerns about the potential of some strategies that are often used for initiating, enhancing, and sustaining such changes (e.g., Adler, 1996; Jaworski, 2001; Lerman, 2001). Adler (1996), in a paper on Lave and Wenger's social practice theory and teaching and learning school mathematics, noted that:

> For Lave and Wenger, social practice, and not learning, is their starting point ... Learning is increasing participation in communities of practice and concerns the whole person acting in the world. This is in sharp contrast to dominant learning theory which is concerned with internalization of knowledge forms and their transfer to and applications in a range of contexts. Knowing [in Lave and Wagner's social practice theory] is thus an activity by specific people in specific circumstances ... knowing about teaching is not acquired in courses about teaching, but in ongoing participation in the teaching community in which such courses might be a part. (1996, p. 4).

Jaworski (1999, 2001) suggested that addressing the issue of knowledge growth in teaching from a social practice theory viewpoint may imply an even more extreme position towards some professional development strategies. In Jaworski's (2001) own words:

> Seeing growth of teaching knowledge as a fundamental part of participation has implications for educators working with teachers to develop teaching: and this raises questions about certain approaches to teaching development, courses for teachers being one such approach. To what extent, for example, are teaching development programs a part of the community of practice of teaching. (p. 297)

These comments raise the issue of the complex relationship between theoretical perspectives and empirical results. It seems that the theoretical perspectives on learning and teaching that a professional developer subscribes to are a major factor in determining the chosen professional developments strategies. Thus, to express it in an extreme way, professional developers (or, at least some professional developers) who hold a social practice perspective of learning and teaching would be reluctant to use courses as a strategy of professional development either in general or as a means of changing classroom practices. As noted by Loucks-Horsley et al., 1998), "it is the combinations of strategies that enriches the professional learning of teachers" (p. 48). To the best of our knowledge, there is not enough empirical evidence to confirm either the stand that courses, per se, are ineffective for such purposes or alternatively, that they are effective.

We have noted, previously, that although the argument that beliefs must be changed before practice will be changed has been based on constructivist perspectives, contrary to this assertion, research provides evidence that changes in practices might lead to changes in beliefs. This further illustrates the complex interrelation between learning and teaching theories and empirical research. Conclusions that are drawn from a given theory must be re-examined in the light of solid empirical, research. Theoretical considerations create issues in need of research. Sometimes some adaptations or changes need to be made in the 'core body' of the theory. Thus, we cannot overemphasize the importance of the need for solid evidence for the development of the field of teacher change. Decisions regarding the efficiency of certain professional development strategies for changing teaching classroom practices and other decisions regarding the change endeavour should be based on the results of research.

5. DISCUSSION AND FINAL COMMENTS

The discussion above has addressed prompts for change and what constitutes effective development to support second order, planned change. Specific goals, beyond that of changing classroom practice, were not assumed. But clearly goals play an important role not only in framing the professional development, but also in assessing the change effort. Another issue that deserves some attention is the way in which different cultures' views of the teaching profession have an impact upon teachers' planning and implementation of change.

5.1. *Goals and Evaluation*

As noted above, a change effort needs to have a clear focus and goals. However, in this chapter we have not assumed any specific changes or specific directions for changing classroom teaching practice. This was a considered decision as the changes to be undertaken will vary from classroom to classroom, from country to country, and from one time to another. Some reforms encourage teaching practices that are more supportive of a constructivist theory of learning while others foster teaching practices that support a more behaviourist theory of learning. For example, Hong Kong has attempted efforts to reduce the amount of rote learning in the curriculum and increase the role of higher order thinking, creativity, and critical thinking (Calderhead, 2001, p. 789). By contrast, recent reforms in England have attempted to focus on a basic skills curriculum (Department of Education and Employment, 1998a, 1998b, 1999). Whatever the image of the desired classroom practices, the change effort requires clear goals and a way of assessing both the short-term and longer-term outcomes.

Evaluation of attempts to change classroom practice is important at a number of levels. Those attempting to implement a change should know if change has occurred before assessing the more important but longer-term outcomes such as increased student achievement or increased student enrolment in higher mathematics. If classroom practices are to be changed, then information about the desired practices should be available prior to the change effort. As the effort begins, periodic readings of classroom practices can guide the participants (teacher, administrators, staff developers, etc.) in ongoing planning of the content and process. Baseline data and routine monitoring of data on the more distal outcomes is also important. However, as noted above, participants need to be sensitive to the fact that second level changes require time. If positive changes in student achievement or student persistence in mathematics do not result immediately, calls to abandon the effort may not be appropriate. In fact, all involved in change should be made aware of the fact that steady or declining scores in the initial years of a change effort may be due to the 'implementation dip' phenomenon described above.

Careful evaluation of such efforts can also lead to increased knowledge about the characteristics of successful professional development and successful change in teacher classroom practice. As noted above, some researchers (e.g., Fullan, 1993) now consider the top-down versus bottom-up implementation as a false dichotomy (claiming a combination of these strategies is needed). However, relatively little is known about how such advice is put into practice. Further, student achievement is undoubtedly the main goal of the vast majority of efforts to change classroom practice. Yet, there are few studies that link amount or type of professional development to improved student achievement. This information is important not only to individual schools or districts, but also to policy makers and government officials who have responsibilities related to funding planned change efforts.

There are relatively few research reports on professional development that link participation in professional development programs designed to change teacher practice to the impact of those changes on students' understanding of and beliefs about mathematics. Exceptions include studies by Cobb, Yackel, and Wood (1992), Fennema et al. (1996), and Sowder et al. (1998). Although these reports generally contain accounts of relatively positive results, it is also important that details of unsuccessful ventures be made known to teachers and professional developers. For 'failures', 'mistakes', and 'errors' are important sources of data. The need for data is critical. As Cohen and Hill (2001) have stated, "if research on teacher learning and professional development does not improve ... pressure either to radically reframe or to do away with professional development will undoubtedly mount" (p. 189).

5.2. *Different Cultures' Views of the Teaching Profession*

In a global economy that fosters competition to attract business and industry among countries, international assessments in mathematics have prompted many countries to make serious efforts to improve student achievement (Calderhead, 2001). This has certainly been one reaction to the TIMSS study. How a country attempts to go about improving student achievement reflects the county's view of teachers and the profession of teaching. For example, although some countries have made efforts to improve education by increasing funding for professional development, others have reacted by increasing government policy and regulation without significant input from teachers.

Calderhead (2001) reported that some countries (e.g., Slovenia and Spain) have tended to rely on teacher professionalism and have increased support for preservice teacher training and professional development activities, while other countries (e.g., England, New Zealand) have issued highly prescriptive directives not only about what is to be taught but also how it should be taught. These culturally based views impact the goals, content and availability of professional development. Thus we again see how classroom teaching practice is enmeshed in the culture and how changes in perspectives on the nature of teaching, the role, status and autonomy of the teacher in a given culture can challenge and eventually change classroom teaching practices.

NOTES

[1.] The R^3M *Project, Recognizing and Recording Reform in Mathematics Education,* involved detailed study of 17 sites working to implement reforms consistent with the National Council of Teachers of Mathematics (1989) *Curriculum and Evaluation Standards for School Mathematics.* The grade levels included kindergarten through grade 12. A 'site' varied from one school to an entire district. A description of the project and its findings can be found in Ferrini-Mundy and Schram (1997).

[2.] General mathematics classes usually include those students who have not done well in mathematics and are not likely to continue taking mathematics beyond the minimum high school requirement.

REFERENCES

Adler, J. (1996). Lave and Wenger's social practice theory and learning school mathematics. In L. Puig & A. Guttierrez (Eds.), *Proceedings of the Twentieth Conference of the International Group for the Psychology of Mathematics Education* (Vol. 2, pp. 3–10). Valencia, Spain: University of Valencia.

Australian Educational Council. (1991). *A national statement on mathematics for Australian schools.* Carlton, Victoria, Australia: Curriculum Corporation.

Ball, D. (1997). Developing mathematics reform: What we don't know about teacher learning – but would make good hypotheses. In S. Friel & G. Bright (Eds.), *Reflecting on our work* (pp. 77–111). Lanham, MD: University Press America.

Barnett, C., & Friedman, S. (1997). Mathematics case discussion: Nothing is sacred. In E. Fennema & B. Nelson (Eds.), *Mathematics teachers in transition* (pp. 381–399). Mahwah, NJ: Lawrence Erlbaum Associates.

Becker, J. R., & Pence, B. J. (1996). Mathematics teacher development: Connections to change in teachers' beliefs and practices. In L. Puig & A. Guttierrez (Eds.), *Proceedings of the Twentieth Conference of the International Group for the Psychology of Mathematics Education* (Vol. 1, pp. 103–118). Valencia, Spain: University of Valencia.

Bentzen, M., Bishop, J. Lieberman, A., & Seeman, A. (1974). *Changing schools: The magic feather principle.* New York: McGraw-Hill.

Berman, R., & McLaughlin, M. (1978). *Federal programs supporting educational change, Vol. viii: Implementing and sustaining innovations.* Santa Monica, CA: Rand Corporation (ERIC Document Reproduction Service No. ED159289).

Bottino, R. M., & Furinghetti, F. (1998). The computer in mathematics teaching: Scenes from the classroom. In D. Tinslet & D. Johnson (Eds.), *Information and communications technologies in school mathematics* (pp. 131–139). London: Chapman and Hall (IFIR Series, 16).

Brown, C. (1985). *A study of the socialization to teaching of a beginning secondary mathematics teacher.* Unpublished doctoral dissertation, University of Georgia, Athens, Georgia.

Brousseau, G. (1997). *Theory of didactical situations in mathematics: Didactique des mathématiques, 1970–1990.* Dordrecht, The Netherlands: Kluwer Academic Publishers.

Calderhead, J. (2001). International experiences of teaching reform. In V. Richardson (Ed.), *Handbook of research on teaching* (4th ed.) (pp. 777–802). Washington, D. C.: American Educational Research Association.

Campbell, P. F., & Robles, J. (1997). Project IMPACT: Increasing the mathematical power of all children and teachers. In S. Friel & G. Bright (Eds.), *Reflecting on our work* (pp. 173–178). Lanham, MD: University Press America.

Campbell, P. F., & White, D. (1997). Project IMPACT: Influencing and supporting teacher change in predominantly minority schools. In E. Fennema & B. Nelson (Eds.), *Mathematics teachers in transition* (pp. 309–355). Mahwah, NJ: Lawrence Erlbaum Associates.

Castle, S., & Watts, G. D. (1992). The tyranny of time. *A Forum on School Transformation from the NEA National Center for Innovation,* 7(2), 1–4.

Chin, R., & Benne, K. (1969). General strategies for effecting changes in human systems. In W. Bennis, K. Benne & R. Chin (Eds.), *The planning of change* (2nd ed.) (pp. 32–59). New York: Holt, Rinehart, and Winston.

Chisholm, L., Ndholvu, J., Mahomed, E., Lubisi, J., Ngozi, P., & Mphahlete, B. (2000). *A South African curriculum for the twenty-first century: Report of the Review Committee of Curriculum 2000.* Retrieved, August 2002, from the World Wide Web: http://www.polity.org.za

Clark, C. M., & Peterson, P. L. (1986). Teachers' thought processes. In M. C. Wittrock (Ed.), *Handbook of research on teaching* (3rd ed.) (pp. 255–296). New York: Macmillan.

Clark, D. (1994). Ten key principles for research for the professional development of mathematics teachers. In D. B. Aichele & F. Coxford (Eds.), *Professional development for teachers of mathematics* (1994 Yearbook of the National Council of Teachers of Mathematics) (pp. 37–48). Reston, VA: National Council of Teachers of Mathematics.

Cobb, P., & McClain, K. (2001). An approach to supporting teachers' learning in social context. In

F. Lin & T. J. Cooney (Eds.), *Making sense of teacher education* (pp. 207–232). Dordrecht, The Netherlands: Kluwer Academic Publishers.

Cobb, P., Wood, T., Yackel, E., & McNeal, E. (1993). Mathematics as procedural instruction and mathematics as meaningful activity: The reality of teaching for understanding. In R. Davis & C. Maher (Eds.), *Schools, mathematics and the world of reality* (pp. 119–134). Needham Heights, MA: Allyn & Bacon.

Cobb, P. Yackel, E., & Wood, T. (1992). Interaction and learning in mathematics classroom situations. *Educational Studies in Mathematics, 23,* 99–122.

Cohen, D., & Hill, H. C. (2001). *Learning policy: When state education reform works.* New Haven, CN: Yale University Press.

Colvin, R. L. (1997, February 23). Why tiny Singapore is at the top of the class. *Los Angeles Times.*

Confrey, J. (1990). What constructivism implies for teaching. In R. B. Davis, C. Maher & N. Noddings (Eds.), *Constructivist views on the teaching and learning of mathematics* (*Journal for Research in Mathematics Education* Monograph #4) (pp. 107–124). Reston, VA: National Council for Teachers of Mathematics.

Cooney, T. (1985). A beginning teacher's view of problem solving. *Journal for Research in Mathematics Education, 16,* 324–336.

Croom, L. (1997). Mathematics for all students: Access, excellence and equity. In J. Trentacosta & M. J. Kenney (Eds.), *Multicultural and gender equity in the mathematics classroom: The gift of diversity* (1997 Yearbook of the National Council of Teachers of Mathematics) (pp. 1–9). Reston, VA: National Council of Teachers of Mathematics.

Cuban, L. (1988). Constancy and change in schools (1980s to the present). In P. Jackson (Ed.), *Contribution to educational change: Perspectives on research and practice* (pp. 85–106). Berkeley, CA: McCutchen.

D'Ambrosio, U. (1997). Diversity, equity, and peace: from dream to reality. In J. Trentacosta & M. J. Kenney (Eds.), *Multicultural and gender equity in the mathematics classroom: The gift of diversity* (1997 Yearbook of the National Council of Teachers of Mathematics) (pp. 243–348). Reston, VA: National Council of Teachers of Mathematics.

Department of Education and Employment. (1998a). *Numeracy matters: The preliminary report of the Numeracy Task Force.* London: Department of Education and Employment.

Department of Education and Employment. (1998b). *The implementation of the National Numeracy Strategy: The Final Report of the Numeracy Task Force.* London: Department of Education and Employment.

Department of Education and Employment. (1999). *The National Numeracy Strategy: Framework* for teaching mathematics from Reception to Year 6. London: Department of Education and Employment.

Department of Education and Skills. (2002). *Organizing the daily mathematics lesson in Mixed Reception/Year 1 Classes.* Retrieved August 2002 from the World Wide Web: http://www.srandards.dfes.gov.uk

Educational Resources Information Center. (1997). *Striving for excellence: The national educational goals, Vol. III.* (ERIC Document Reproduction Service No. ED414633).

Elmore, R. F., Peterson, P., & McCarthey, S. (1996). *Restructuring in the classroom.* San Francisco, CA: Jossey-Bass.

Even, R. (1999a). Integrating academic and practical knowledge in a teacher leaders' development program. *Educational Studies in Mathematics, 38,* 235–252.

Even, R. (1999b). The development of teacher-leaders and in-service teacher educators. *Journal of Mathematics Teacher Education, 2,* 3–24.

Even, R., & Tirosh, D. (1995). Subject-matter knowledge and knowledge about students as sources of teacher presentations and subject matter. *Educational Studies in Mathematics, 29,* 1–20.

Fennema, E., Carpenter, T., Franke, M., Levi, L., Jacobs, V, & Empson, S. (1996). A longitudinal study of learning to use children's thinking in mathematics instruction. *Journal for Research in Mathematics Education, 27,* 403–434.

Fennema, E., & Romberg, T. (Eds.) (1999). *Mathematics classrooms that promote understanding.* Mahwah, NJ: Lawrence Erlbaum Associates.

Fennema, E., Sowder, J., & Carpenter, T. (1999). Creating classrooms that promote understanding. In E. Fennema & T. Romberg (Eds.), *Mathematics classrooms that promote understanding* (pp. 185–199). Mahwah, NJ: Lawrence Erlbaum Associates.

Ferrini-Mundy, J. (1997). Reform efforts in mathematics education: Reckoning with the realities. In S. Friel & G. Bright (Eds.), *Reflecting on our work: NSF teacher enhancement in K-6 Mathematics* (pp.113–132). Lanham, MD: University Press America.

Ferrini-Mundy, J., & Johnson, L. (1997). Highlights and implications. In J. Ferrini-Mundy & T. Schram (Eds.), The recognizing and recording reform in mathematics education project: insights, issues and implications (*Journal for Research in Mathematics Education,* Monograph #8) (pp. 111–128). Reston, VA: National Council of Teachers of Mathematics.

Ferrini-Mundy, J., & Schram, T. (Eds.) (1997). The recognizing and recoding reform in mathematics education projects: Insights, issues, and implications (*Journal for Research in Mathematics Education,* Monograph #8). Reston, VA: National Council for Teachers of Mathematics.

Flavell, J. (1977). *Cognitive development.* Englewood Cliffs, NJ: Prentice Hall.

Franke, M., Fennema, E., & Carpenter, T. (1997). Changing teachers: Interactions between beliefs and classroom practice. In E. Fennema & B. Nelson (Eds.), *Mathematics teachers in transition* (pp. 255–282). Mahwah, NJ: Lawrence Erlbaum Associates.

Fullan, M. (1993). *Change forces: Probing the depths of educational reform.* London: Falmer Press.

Fullan, M., & Pomfret, A. (1977). Research on curriculum and instruction implementation. *Review of Educational Research, 47,* 335–397.

Graham, K., & Johnson, L. (1998). What is the role of parents and community members? In J. Ferrini-Mundy, K. Graham, L. Johnson & G. Mills (Eds.), *Making change in mathematics education: Learning from the field* (pp. 73–86). Reston, VA: National Council of Teachers of Mathematics.

Grant, S. G. (1998). *Reforming reading, writing, and mathematics: Teachers' responses and the prospects for systemic reform.* Mahwah, NJ: Lawrence Erlbaum Associates.

Groves, S., & Stacey, K. (1998). Calculators in primary mathematics: Exploring numbers before teaching algorithms. In L. J. Morrow & M. J. Kenney (Eds.), *The teaching and learning of algorithms in school mathematics* (1998 Yearbook of the National Council of Teachers of Mathematics) (pp. 120–129). Reston, VA: National Council of Teachers of Mathematics.

Guskey, T. R. (1986). Staff development and the process of teacher change. *Educational Researcher, 15,* 5–12.

Haberman, M. (1991). The pedagogy of poverty versus good teaching. *Phi Delta Kappan, 73,* 290–294.

Hershkowitz, R., & Schwarz, B. (1999). Reflective processes in technology-based mathematics classrooms. *Cognition and Instruction, 17,* 65–91.

Hino, K., & Shigematsu, K. (2002). A study of teacher change through inservice mathematics education programs in graduate school. In National Research Council, H. Bass, Z. Usiskin & G. Burrill (Eds.), *Studying classroom teaching as a medium for professional development* (pp. 35–45). Washington, D. C.: Proceedings of a U.S.-Japan Workshop, Mathematical Sciences Education Board, Division of Behavioral and Social Sciences and Education, and U.S. National Commission on Mathematics Instruction, International Organizations Board. Press.

Hord, S., & Loucks, S. (1980). *A concerns-based model for the delivery of inservice.* Austin: Texas University at Austin, Research and Development Center for Teacher Education. (ERIC Document Reproduction Service No. ED 206620).

Howson, G., Keitel, C., & Kilpatrick, J. (1981). *Curriculum development in mathematics.* Cambridge, UK: Cambridge University Press.

Jacobs, J. E., & Becker, J. R. (1997). Creating a gender-equitable multicultural classroom using feminist pedagogy. In J. Trentacosta & M. J. Kenney (Eds.), *Multicultural and gender equity in the mathematics classroom: The gift of diversity* (1997 Yearbook of the National Council of Teachers of Mathematics) (pp. 107–114). Reston, VA: National Council of Teachers of Mathematics.

Jaworski, B. (1994). *Investigating mathematics teaching: A constructivist enquiry.* London: Falmer Press.

Jaworski, B. (1999). The plurality of knowledge growth in mathematics teaching. In B. Jaworski, T. Wood & S. Dawson (Eds.), *Mathematics teacher education: Critical international perspectives* (pp. 180–209). London: Falmer Press.

Jaworski, B. (2001). Developing mathematics teaching: Teachers, teacher educators and researchers as co-learners. In F. Lin & T. J. Cooney (Eds.), *Making sense of mathematics teacher education* (pp. 295–320). Boston: Kluwer Academic Publishers.

Jones, D. (1997). A conceptual framework for studying the relevance of context to mathematics teachers' change. In E. Fennema & B. Nelson (Eds.), *Mathematics teachers in transition* (pp. 131–154). Mahwah, NJ: Lawrence Erlbaum Associates.

Kaiser, G., & Rogers, P. (1995). *Equity in mathematics education: Influences of feminism and culture.* London: Falmer Press.

Kearns, D. (1995). Business and industry perspective. In I. M. Carl (Ed.), *Prospects for school mathematics* (pp. 323–328). Reston, VA: National Council of Teachers of Mathematics.

Kennedy, M. (1999). *Form and substance in mathematics and science professional development.* Madison, WI: University of Wisconsin at Madison, National Institute for Science Education (ERIC Document Reproduction Services, No. ED 435552).

Kim, J. (1997). Republic of Korea. In D. Robitallile (Ed.). *National contexts for mathematics and science education* (pp. 226–234). Vancouver: Pacific Educational.

Khisty, L. L. (1997). Making mathematics accessible to Latino students: Rethinking instructional practice. In J. Trentacosta & M. J. Kenney (Eds.), *Multicultural and gender equity in the mathematics classroom: The gift of diversity* (1997 Yearbook of the National Council of Teachers of Mathematics) (pp. 92–101). Reston, VA: National Council of Teachers of Mathematics.

Klein, R., Barkai, R., Tirosh, D., & Tsamir, P. (1998). Increasing teachers' awareness of students' conceptions of operations with rational numbers. In A. Olivier & K. Newstead (Eds.), *Proceedings of the Twenty-Second Conference of the International Group for the Psychology of Mathematics Education* (Vol. 3, pp. 120–127). Johannesburg, South Africa: University of Stellenbosch.

Knapp, M. (1997). Between systemic reforms and the mathematics and science classroom: The dynamic of innovation, implementation, and professional learning. *Review of Educational Research*, 67, 227–266.

Koch, L. (1997). The growing pains of change: A case study of a third-grade teacher. In J. Ferrini-Mundy & T. Schram (Eds.), Recognizing and recording reform in a mathematics education project: Insights, issues and implications (*Journal for Research in Mathematics Education* Monograph 8) (pp. 87–109). Reston, VA: National Council of Teachers of Mathematics.

Krainer, K. (1999). Guest editorial: Teacher growth and school development. *Journal of Mathematics Teacher Education, 2*(3), 223–225.

Krainer, K. (2001). Teachers' Growth is more than the growth of individual teachers: The case of Gisela. In F. Lin & T. J. Cooney (Eds.), *Making sense of teacher education* (pp. 271–294). Boston: Kluwer Academic Publishers.

Laborde, C. (2001). The use of new technologies as a vehicle for restructuring teachers' mathematics. In F. Lin & T. J. Cooney (Eds.), *Making sense of teacher education* (pp. 87–110). Boston: Kluwer Academic Publishers.

Lampert, M. (1993). Teacher's thinking about students' thinking about geometry: The effects of new teaching tools. In J. Schwartz, M. Yerushalmy & B. Wilson (Eds.), *The Geometric Supposer: What is it a case of?* (pp. 143–177). Hillsdale, NJ: Lawrence Erlbaum Associates.

Lanier, J. E., & Little, J. W. (1986). Research on teacher education. In M. C. Wittrock (Ed.), *Handbook of research on teaching* (3rd ed.) (pp. 527–569). New York: Macmillan.

Leder, G., & Sampson, N. (Eds.) (1989). *Educating girls: Practice and research.* Sydney: Allen and Unwin.

Lerman, S. (2001). A review of research perspectives on mathematics teacher education. In F. Lin & T. J. Cooney (Eds.), *Making sense of teacher education* (pp. 33–52): Boston: Kluwer Academic Publishers.

Little, J. K. (1993). Teachers' professional development in a climate of educational reform. *Educational Evaluation and Policy Analysis*, 19, 325–340.

Lortie, D. C. (1975). *Schoolteacher: A sociological study.* Chicago: University of Chicago Press.

Loucks-Horsley, S., Stiles, K., & Hewson, P. (1996). *Principles of effective professional development for mathematics and science education: A synthesis of standards.* Madison, WI: University of Wisconsin at Madison, National Institute for Science Education.

Loucks-Horsley, S., Hewson, P. W., Love, N., & Stiles, K. S. (1998). *Designing professional development for teachers of science and mathematics*. Thousands Oaks, CA: Corwin.

Lubinski, C., & Jaberg, P. (1997). Teacher change and mathematics K-4: Developing a theoretical perspective. In E. Fennema & B. Nelson (Eds.), *Mathematics teachers in transition* (pp. 223–254). Mahwah, NJ: Lawrence Erlbaum Associates.

Ma, L. (1999). *Knowing and teaching mathematics: Teachers' understanding of fundamental mathematics in China and the United States*. Mahwah, NJ: Lawrence Erlbaum Associates.

Markovits, Z., & Even, R. (1999). Mathematics classroom situations: An inservice course for elementary school teachers. In B. Jaworski., T. Wood & S. Dawson (Eds.), *Mathematics teacher education: Critical international perspectives* (pp. 59–67). London: Falmer Press.

Markovitz, Z (in press). *Analyzing mathematics classroom situations*. Tel-Aviv, Israel: Mofet (in Hebrew).

McHenry, K. (1992). Mathematics education: An industrial view. In I. Wirzup & R. Streit (Eds.), *Developments in school mathematics education around the world* (Vol. 3, pp. 14–24). Reston, VA: National Council of Teachers of Mathematics.

Mevarech, Z. (1995). Teachers' paths on the way to and from the professional development forum. In T. R. Guskey & M. Huberman (Eds.), *Professional development in education: New paradigms and practices* (pp. 151–170). New York: Teachers College Press.

Ministry of Education. (1993). *Tomorrow 1998*. Jerusalem, Israel: Ministry of Education.

Miyake, M., & Nagasaki, E. (1997). Japan. In D. Robitallile (Ed.), *National contexts for mathematics and science education* (pp. 218–225). Vancouver: Pacific Educational.

Morgan, C. (2000). Better assessment in mathematics education: A social perspective. In J. Boaler (Ed.), *Multiple perspectives on mathematics teaching and learning* (pp. 225–242). Westport, CT: Ablex.

Moses, R., Kamii, M., McAllister, S., & Howard, J. (1989). The Algebra Project: Organizing in the spirit of Ella. *Harvard Educational Review, 59*(4), 423–443.

Nachmias, R., Midouser, D., & Shemla, A. (2001). Information and communication technologies usage by school students in an Israeli school: Equity, gender, and inside/outside school learning issues. *Education and Information Technologies, 6*(1), 43–53.

National Commission on Mathematics and Science Teaching for the 21st Century. (2000). *Before it's too late*. Jessup, MD: Education Publications Center.

National Council of Teachers of Mathematics (1989). *Curriculum and evaluation standards for school mathematics*. Reston, VA: National Council of Teachers of Mathematics.

National Council of Teachers of Mathematics (1991). *Professional standards for school mathematics*. Reston, VA: National Council of Teachers of Mathematics.

National Council of Teachers of Mathematics. (2000). *Principles and standards for school mathematics*. Reston, VA: National Council of Teachers of Mathematics.

National Research Council (1997). *Learning from TIMSS: Results of the Third International Mathematics and Science Study*. Washington, D. C.: National Academy Press.

National Research Council. (2001). Adding it up: Helping children learn mathematics. In J. Kilpatrick, J. Swafford & B. Findell (Eds.), *Mathematics Learning Study Committee*. Washington, D. C.: Center for Education, Division of Behavioral and Social Sciences and Education, National Academy Press.

National Science Foundation (1996). *Shaping the future: New expectations for undergraduate education in science, mathematics, engineering, and technology*. Washington, D. C.: National Science Foundation, Directorate for Education and Human Resources (ERIC Document Reproduction Service No. ED404158).

Noss, R., & Hoyles, C. (1996). *Windows on mathematical meanings: Learning cultures and computers*. Dordrecht, The Netherlands: Kluwer Academic Press.

Office of Educational Research and Improvement (1997). *Moderator's guide to eighth-grade mathematics lessons: United States, Japan, and Germany*. Washington, D. C.: US Department of Education.

Organization for Economic Co-operation and Development (OECD) (2000). *Knowledge and skills for life: First results from PISA 2000*. Paris: OECD.

Pajares, M. F. (1992). Teachers' beliefs and educational research: Cleaning up a messy construct. *Review of Educational Research, 62,* 307–332.

Pelgrum, W., & Anderson, R. (Eds.) (1999). *ICT and the emerging paradigm for lifelong learning: A worldwide educational assessment of infrastructure, goals and practices.* Amsterdam, The Netherlands: International Evaluation Association (IEA).

Ponte, J. P., Matos, J. F. Guimarães, H. M., Leal, L. C., & Canavarro, A. P. (1994). Teachers' and students' views and attitudes towards a new mathematics curriculum: A case study. *Educational Studies in Mathematics 26,* 347–365.

Posner, G., Strike, K., Hewson, P., & Gertzog, W. (1982). Accommodation of a scientific conception: Toward a theory of conceptual change. *Science Education, 66,* 211–227.

Prawat, R. (1992). Are changes in views about mathematics teaching sufficient? The case of a fifth-grade teacher. *The Elementary School Journal, 93*(2), 195–211.

Putnam, R. T., Lampert, M., & Peterson, P. L. (1990). Alternative perspectives on knowing mathematics in elementary schools. In C. Cazden (Ed.), *Review of research in education* (Vol. 16, pp. 57–150). Washington, D. C.: American Educational Research Association.

Richardson, V., & Placier, P. (2001). Teacher change. In V. Richardson (Ed.), *Handbook of research on teaching* (4th ed.) (pp. 905–947). Washington, D. C.: American Educational Research Association.

Romberg, T. (1997). Mathematics in context: Impact on teachers. In E. Fennema & B. Nelson (Eds.), *Mathematics teachers in transition* (pp. 357–380). Mahwah, NJ: Lawrence Erlbaum Associates.

Romberg, T., Zarinnia, E., & Williams, S. (1989). *The influence of mandated testing on mathematics instruction: Grade 8 teachers' perceptions.* Madison, WI: University of Wisconsin, National Center for Research in Mathematical Sciences Education.

Ruthven, K. (1999). Constructing a calculator-aware number curriculum: The challenges of systematic design and systematic reform. In O. Zaslavsky (Ed.), *Proceedings of the Twenty-Third Conference of the International Group for the Psychology of Mathematics Education* (Vol. 1, 56–71.). Haifa, Israel: Technion Printing Center.

Sarason, S. B. (1971, *The culture of the school and the problem of change.* Needham Heights, MA: Allyn & Bacon.

Schifter, D. (1998). Learning mathematics for teaching: From a teachers' seminar to the classroom. *Journal of Mathematics Teacher Education 1,* 55–87.

Schifter, D., & Fosnot, C. (1993). *Reconstructing mathematics education.* New York: Teachers College Press.

Schmidt, W., McKnight, C., Cogan, L., Jakwerth, P., & Houang, R. (1999). *Facing the consequences: Using TIMSS for a closer look at US Mathematics and Science education.* Dordrecht, The Netherlands: Kluwer Academic Publishers.

Schuck, S. (1999, April). *Driving a mathematics education reform with unwilling passengers.* Paper presented at the annual meeting of the American Educational Research Association, Montreal, Quebec, Canada. (ERIC Document Reproduction Service No. ED431734).

Schwan Smith, M. (2001). *Practice-based professional development for teachers of mathematics.* Reston, VA: National Council of Teachers of Mathematics.

Secada, W., Fennema, E., & Adajian, L. (Eds.) (1995). *New directions for equity in mathematics education.* Cambridge, UK: Cambridge University Press (in collaboration with the National Council of Teachers of Mathematics).

Servant, A. (1997). France. In D. Robitallile (Ed.), *National contexts for mathematics and science education.* Vancouver: Pacific Educational.

Shuard, H., Walsh, A., Goodwin, J., & Worcester, V. (1991). *Calculators, children and mathematics.* London: Simon and Schuster.

Shulman, L. S. (1986). Those who understand: knowledge growth in teaching. *Educational Researcher, 15*(2), 4–14.

Simon, M., & Schifter, D. (1991). Towards a constructivist perspective: An intervention study of mathematics teacher development. *Educational Studies in Mathematics 23,* 309–331.

Skott, J. (2000). The forced autonomy of mathematics teachers. In T. Nakahara & M. Koyama (Eds.),

Proceedings of the Twentieth Conference of the International Group for the Psychology of Mathematics Education (Vol. 4, pp. 169–176). Hiroshima, Japan: Nishiki.

Skovsmose, O., & Valero, P. (2001). Breaking political neutrality: The critical engagement of mathematics education with democracy. In B. Atweh, H. Forgasz & B. Nebres (Eds.), *Socio-cultural research on mathematics education: An international perspective* (pp. 37–55). Mahwah, NJ: Lawrence Erlbaum Associates.

South Africa Ministry of Education. (1997). *Curriculum 2005*. Retrieved August 2002 from the World Wide Web: http://www.polity.org.za.

Sowder, J. T, Phillips, R. A., Armstrong, B. E., & Schappelle, B. (1998). *Middle-grade teachers' mathematical knowledge and its relationship to instruction*. Albany, NY: State University of New York.

Sparks, G. M. (1988). Teachers' attitudes toward change and subsequent improvements in classroom teaching. *Journal of Educational Psychology, 80*(1), 111–117.

Stein, M., & Brown, C. (1997). Teacher learning in a social context: Integrating collaborative and institutional processes with the study of teacher change. In E. Fennema & B. Nelson (Eds.), *Mathematics Teachers in Transition* (pp. 155–191). Mahwah, NJ: Lawrence Erlbaum Associates.

Stevenson, H. W., Lee, S., & Stigler, J. (1986). Mathematics achievement of Chinese, Japanese, and American children. *Science, 231*, 693–699.

Stevenson, H. W., & Nerison-Low, R. (2000). *To sum it up: TIMSS case studies of education in Germany, Japan and the United States*. Philadelphia, PA: U.S. Department of Education.

Stevenson, H. W., & Stigler, J. W. (1992). *The learning gap*. New York: Summit Books.

Stigler, J., & Baranes, R. (1988). Culture and mathematics learning. In E. Rothkopf (Ed.), *Review of research in education* (Vol. 15, pp. 253–306). Washington, D. C.: American Educational Research Association.

Stigler, J., & Hiebert, J. (1997). Understanding and improving classroom mathematics instruction: An overview of the TIMSS Video Project. *Phi Delta Kappan, 79*, 14–21.

Stigler, J., & Hiebert, J. (1999). *The teaching gap*. New York: Free Press.

Strauss, V. (2000). *Looking East for math techniques*. Retrieved August 2002 from the World Wide Web: http://www.washingtonpost.com.

Swafford, J. Jones, G., & Thornton, C. (1997). Increased knowledge in geometry and instructional practice. *Journal for Research in Mathematics Education, 28*, 467–483.

Tapscott, D. (1998). *Growing up digital: The rise of the NET-generation*, New York: McGraw-Hill.

Thompson, A. (1984). The relationship of teachers' conceptions of mathematics teaching to instructional practice. *Educational Studies in Mathematics, 15*, 105–127.

Thompson, A. (1992). Teachers' beliefs and conceptions: A synthesis of the research. In D. A. Grouws (Ed.), *Handbook of research on mathematics teaching and learning* (pp. 127–146). New York: Macmillan.

Trentacosta, J., & Kenney, M. J. (Eds.) (1997). *Multicultural and gender equity in the mathematics classroom: The gift of diversity* (1997 Yearbook of the National Council of Teachers of Mathematics). Reston, VA: National Council of Teachers of Mathematics.

Undervisningsministeriet (1995). *Matematik faghoefte 12*. Kobenhavn: Undervisnings-ministeriet.

Valero, P., & Jess, K. (2000). Supporting change through a mathematics team forum for teachers' professional development. In T. Nakahara & M. Koyama (Eds.), *Proceedings of the Twentieth Conference of the International Group for the Psychology of Mathematics Education* (Vol. 4, 249–256). Hiroshima, Japan: Nishiki.

Waits, B., & Demana, F. (2000). Calculators in mathematics teaching and learning: Past, present and future. In M. Burke & F. Curcio (Eds.), *Learning mathematics for a new century* (pp. 51–66). Reston, VA: National Council of Teachers of Mathematics.

Webb, N. L. (1992). Assessment of students' knowledge of mathematics: steps toward a theory. In D. A. Grouws (Ed.), *Handbook of research on mathematics teaching and learning* (pp. 661–683). New York: Macmillan.

Weick, K. (1976). Educational organizations as loosely coupled systems. *Administrative Science Quarterly, 21*, 1–19.

Yackel, E., & Cobb, P. (1996). Sociomathematical norms, argumentation, and autonomy in mathematics. *Journal for Research in Mathematics Education, 27,* 458–477.

Yerushalmy, M., Chazan, D., & Gordon, M. (1993). Posing problems: One aspect of bringing inquiry into the classroom. In J. Schwartz, M. Yerushalmy & B. Wilson (Eds.), *The Geometric Supposer: What is it a case of?* (pp. 117–142). Hillsdale, NJ: Lawrence Erlbaum Associates.

Yingkang, U. (2002). The impact of Excel on the school mathematics curriculum. In D. Edge & Y. Hap (Eds.), *Knowledge education for a knowledge-based era* (pp. 479–485). Singapore: The Association of Mathematics Educators.

19
Towards a Didactic Model for Assessment Design in Mathematics Education

MARJA VAN DEN HEUVEL-PANHUIZEN
Freudenthal Institute, Utrecht University

JERRY BECKER
Southern Illinois University, Carbondale

ABSTRACT

In this chapter we compare and contrast the didactic and psychometric models of assessment design. We begin with background information and an introduction to assessment, and then the relationship between the goals of mathematics education and assessment is presented. This relationship is made explicit by exhibiting two assessment problems, each reflecting a different way of thinking about mathematics education. The primary objections to the current way of assessing students, and alternatives that have been developed for it, are next presented. We then present a theoretical perspective on the psychometric approach, followed by some recent developments regarding this assessment model. Here we arrive at the crucial issue in this chapter, namely, the need to extend assessment design in mathematics education via a didactic model. The consequences of the psychometric requirements and assumptions for mathematics education are presented and discussed. Importantly, we discuss how we can overcome certain misconceptions that inhibit an approach to assessment which is aligned with the new way of thinking about mathematics education. Finally, we present examples of assessment problems that represent a didactic model of assessment design. The chapter concludes with a reference to Freudenthal and his concept of mathematics as a human activity. The approach to assessment in the chapter, and the examples that exemplify it, are identified as consistent with Freudenthal's thinking.

1. BACKGROUND AND INTRODUCTION

Assessment has a long history in education. Tests have been used in schools for a very long time and their use has increased enormously since the turn of the last century (Haney & Madaus, 1989; Romberg, 1992; Kilpatrick, 1993). The dramatic growth in school testing was no doubt stimulated by the development and popularization of ability and intelligence testing. In fact, following this trend, the use of tests in schools became very common in many countries over the years.

Second International Handbook of Mathematics Education, 689–716
A.J. Bishop, M.A. Clements, C. Keitel, J. Kilpatrick and F.K.S. Leung (eds.)
© 2003 *Dordrecht: Kluwer Academic Publishers. Printed in Great Britain.*

In recent years, in particular, we have witnessed a great increase in the use of standardized testing, especially for mathematics students. A generation ago it was common in many countries for a classroom teacher to construct and implement her or his own assessment, and then make decisions concerning the evaluation of students based on the results. But today, these same classroom teachers are subjected to an enormous focus on standardized testing, often determined by their local, state, regional or national government agencies. Since the test results are then published, teachers, schools, and whole school districts are being assessed, and students as well.

Haney and Madaus (1989) described the leaps in the use of tests in the United States up to the 1990s. The first occurred in the period of the 1920s-1930s when the achievement-testing movement was motivated by a desire to study students' learning in more systematic and objective ways. This was perceived as a remedy to the inconsistencies in classroom teachers' evaluation or grading practices (Kilpatrick, 1993; Shepard, 2000a). Perhaps this movement represented the early beginnings of a focus on standardization. The next leap occurred during the 1950s-60s when national legislation promoted testing in the schools. And shortly after that, in the 1970s, test-driven instruction, in association with the criterion-referenced tests that assessed whether the students had achieved particular attainment objectives, became very common. Teachers and testing specialists alike were convinced that such instruction could improve learning (Popham, 1978, 1987). One consequence was that 'teaching to the test' became common, and further, a positive connotation was attached to it. According to Haney and Madaus (1989), however, the *main leap* in testing began in the 1980s, which coincided with the launching of reform movements in education.

In the 1980s numerous scholars were aware of the serious flaws and inaccuracies of many standardized tests (e.g., the narrow outcomes measured by the tests and the potentially unhealthy consequences for students' learning – c.f., Wassermann, 2001). Even before the 1980s, Oscar Buros, editor of the Mental Measurements yearbooks, had serious concerns about these tests. He wrote:

> Many of you know that I consider that most standardized tests are poorly constructed, of questionable or unknown validity, pretentious in their claims, and likely to be misused more often than not.
>
> (Buros, 1977, p. 9)

Buros (1997) expressed strong views with respect to the inadequacies of standardized tests and his concern about the unwarranted optimism about the values of standardized tests in general, and more specifically about certain kinds of tests.

On a slightly different, but related theme, Buros (1977) advised teachers not to "mistake statistical significance for educational significance, which results in a great deal of sloppy thinking not only in testing but in all areas of research in the behavioral sciences." (p. 13). He further pointed out:

> Standardized tests rarely correspond closely to local instructional programs;

they are greatly influenced by instructional materials closely resembling the test items, and they cannot be used to measure the attainment of specific growth over short periods of time. (p. 14)

In a similar vein, Salmon-Cox (1981) reported that her research revealed that "student scores on standardized tests are not very useful to the classroom teachers" (p. 631). She asserted that rather than relying on the results of standardized tests, teachers would rather use their own judgement regarding student weaknesses and needed areas of help. Sproull and Zubrow (1981) further maintained that education administrators were not significant users of information from tests, and that in fact such test results were not very important to school administrators.

Although we recognize that there are many ramifications of this trend to outside testing, we want to place a focus on the widely accepted view that 'teachers teach to the test'. Although this view is often expressed in negative or derisive tones, there can be little doubt that it has always been true. Whether teachers have constructed their own tests or have had tests imposed upon them by outside agencies, almost all of them nevertheless try to teach content so their students will be able to demonstrate what they know.

From the early 1990s onwards, possible disadvantages of the testing approach have been emphasized by many other scholars (e.g., Shepard, 1988, 2000a; Resnick & Resnick, 1992; Casas & Meaghan, 2001). One of the most widely repeated 'disadvantages' was 'teaching to the test', which often meant teaching to *standardized tests*. The practical consequence of this was a narrowing of the curriculum to the domain of mathematical content encompassed by the tests. Many mathematics educators believe that in the present reform movement in education, designers of tests overly use items which assess only the basic levels of mathematical content knowledge, and rarely include items which assess complex levels of students' understanding (see, e.g., McLean, 1982; Fiske, 1997).

Given the commonly accepted view that "what is tested is what gets taught" (National Research Council, 1989, p. 69), it is not surprising that the consequences of this view of testing are often promoted in the reverse way. Such an optimistic view towards the pervasive influence of standardized testing was, for instance, taken by De Lange (1992) when he noted that if teachers teach to the test, educators then have the opportunity to create tests to which teachers will teach. De Lange (1992) argued:

If the trend towards more open examinations continues it will have definitive effects on the teaching of mathematics. As in many other countries, the teacher (or school) is judged by how well the students perform on their final exam. This leads to test-oriented learning and teaching. However, if the test is made according to our principles, this disadvantage (test-oriented teaching) will become an advantage. The problem then has shifted to the producers of tests since it is very difficult and time consuming to produce appropriate ones. (p. 320)

This same kind of inverse reasoning, by which the scheme of 'teaching to the test' has been put forward as a potential tool for innovation, has also been articulated by other scholars (see, e.g., Wiggins, 1989a; Resnick & Resnick, 1992; Stephens, Clarke, & Pavlou, 1994).

The difficulty with this 'reversed' approach is that, despite the objections raised about standardized tests, important educational decisions are nonetheless still based mainly on the scores on these tests. Thus, classroom practice is subjected to standardized testing determined by regional or national governmental agencies. Since the test results are published, teachers, schools, and school districts are assessed as well as the students. Elmore (2002) argued that so far as school improvement is concerned, internal accountability should precede external accountability. That is to say, school personnel need to share a coherent, explicit set of norms and expectations about what a good school looks like before they can respond to signals from outside their school in an attempt to improve student learning. According to Elmore, giving test results to an incoherent, atomized, badly run school does not mean it will become a better school, for a school's ability to make improvements is fundamentally related to the beliefs and practices that people within it share. School improvement is less related to the kind of information school personnel receive about their performance.

Elmore (2002) argued that, typically, low-performing schools are not coherent enough to respond to external demands for accountability. He went on to say:

> The work of turning a school around entails improving 'capacity' (the knowledge and skills of teachers) – changing their command of content and how to teach it – and helping them to understand where their students are in their academic development. Low-performing schools, and the people who work in them, don't know what to do. If they did, they would be doing it already. You can't improve a school's performance, or that of any teacher or student in it, without increasing the investment in teachers' knowledge, pedagogical skills, and understanding of students. Test scores don't tell us much of anything about these important domains; they provide a composite, undifferentiated signal about students' responses to a problem. (p. 35)

The increase in the use of tests during the twentieth century was enormous. In 1917 (when the United States of America entered World War I), there were 11 arithmetic tests available in the United States (Resnick, 1982). Nowadays, there is a much larger body of standardized tests from which to choose. Aside from the fact that decisions about education are based on scores that do not cover the richness of the present goals and teaching methods of mathematics education (cf., Becker & Selter, 1996), there are also some more silent influences that could be even more harmful.

First, external testing can assist in the twin processes of de-skilling and de-professionalizing teachers (Shepard, 2000b). A dominance of so-called 'objective' tests in classroom practice can shape beliefs about the nature of evidence and principles of fairness (Shepard, 2000a). Moreover, overuse of standardized tests provides a poor model for informal classroom assessment by teachers and for the development of teacher-made tests (Black & Wiliam, 1998; Wilson & Sloane, 2000) that can be used to find evidence bearing on teachers' judgements about students and their decisions regarding further instruction.

We believe that, especially for this last purpose, current standardized tests consisting primarily of multiple-choice items are too limited, in at least two ways: They are limited in both their mathematics and the opportunities they provide to classroom teachers to access students' understanding. This belief stems from a theoretical viewpoint. Currently, standardized tests are based on a psychometric model of assessment design in mathematics education, and this model differs markedly from a model of assessment design that is more closely connected to a domain-specific theory of education, or what we call a 'didactic' model. We judge that such a model needs to be added to assessment design in order to acquire a more acceptable and productive system for educational assessment.

2. APPROACH TO MATHEMATICS EDUCATION AND ASSESSMENT

2.1. *Relationship Between Mathematics Education and Assessment*

According to Pipho (1985), "nearly every large education reform effort of the last few years has either mandated a new form of testing or expanded uses of existing testing" (p. 19). It was not surprising, therefore, that the world-wide reform in mathematics education that commenced during the 1980s was accompanied by proposed reform in assessment (e.g., De Lange, 1987; Romberg, 1995; Van den Heuvel-Panhuizen, 1996; Becker & Shimada, 1997; Hashimoto & Becker, 1999; Nagasaki & Becker, 1999). The strong and close relationship between assessment and instruction has great potential for improving classroom practice. We share Leder's (1992) view that our current approach to mathematics teaching and assessment cannot be separated. According to Leder, assessment is intrinsic to the very act of teaching.

But in what different ways can mathematical learning be assessed? Our response is demonstrated in the following two examples, both of which belong to the content domain of measurement. The examples are meant for fifth-grade students.

2.2. *A Measurement Problem with Multiple Solutions*

In the first assessment problem (see Figure 1), which we call the *Flag* problem (Van den Heuvel-Panhuizen, 1995), students have to answer the following question: "What do you think the size of the flag on the top of this apartment building is in reality?"

The piece of paper that appears on the test sheet is meant for the students' convenience. They may use this scrap paper to jot down their notes and models to support their thinking.

Student work on the scrap paper area of this problem has revealed a rich

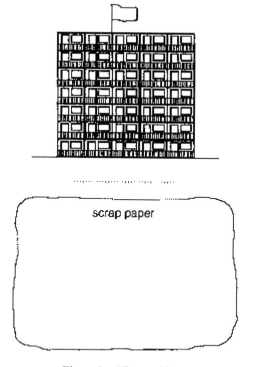

Figure 1.   Flag problem.

variety of responses (see Figure 2). Judging the correctness of answers depended, in part, on what daily-life knowledge those assessing the responses assumed the students had, and how rigorous the assessors were in judging the responses. In this case, the fifth-grade students were not familiar with problems like this, and an answer between, say, 6 and 18 square metres was considered acceptable. Starting from this criterion, among the answers in Figure 2, only #4 would be assessed as correct. But, we should ask, are all the other responses wrong?

Apart from the number aspect, the responses to the *Flag* problem included several other indicators of students' achievement. First, although Students #3 and #5 did not come up with a number between 6 and 18, they did, without any hints, choose square metres as the unit of measure to express size. Student #1 used a very clear informal notation instead of a unit of measure, and Student #4 showed quite clearly that the size of a door could be used as a frame of reference. Student #2 used ratios with the size of the picture as starting point.

It is evident that the assessment of the students' responses on the *Flag* problem is a tricky task. Beyond assessing the students' appreciations of the numbers involved in the problem, there are several other contextual aspects to be considered, including the use of measures of reference. Does a student know the height between two floors? What is the student's visual interpretation of the problem? Does a student recognize the flag to be a rectangle? What was the procedure

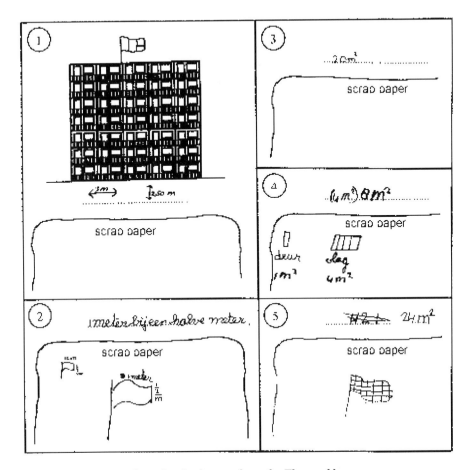

Figure 2.   Student work on the Flag problem.

applied by a student for estimating the answer, and how was this procedure described? How were models used by a student to support his or her reasoning when making estimations?

Students' responses to the *Flag* problem revealed something about their knowledge of measurement (e.g., did the students know how to calculate the area of a rectangle?) and geometry (e.g., did the students identify the flag as a rectangle? Did they realize that where the flag is anchored to the roof matters?). As noted, the problem was also connected to the topic of ratio (e.g., can students use the area of a door to estimate the area of the flag?). In a very real sense, then, there are several mathematical ideas or aspects of content that are evident in this problem.

In the *Flag* problem, students are asked to apply their mathematical thinking ability, knowledge and skills to solve a problem that, although presented on paper, can easily be connected to their daily lives. Such context problems have the characteristic that when students are given freedom to apply their mathematical knowledge, they are not necessarily limited to the structure of mathematics. In other words, here students are asked to integrate their knowledge and not focus on a particular skill. In fact, we think the *Flag* problem is typical of problems that can reveal the way students mathematize in resolving a problem situation. Moreover, problems that require students' mathematical thinking ability may even call for students to generate missing information.

As can be seen in the *Flag* problem, students need not always be provided with all the data for solving a problem. Notice that no actual data are given, nor is it even clear whether the building is of a normal size as opposed to one in a miniature village. This, of course, makes it challenging to determine the correct answer, though in reality no one knows it (or them).

2.3. *A Measurement Problem with Multiple Choices*

All the characteristics of the *Flag* problem are in stark contrast to problems on standardized tests that assess measurement. For example, Figure 3 shows an item from the U.S. California Achievement Test (CAT) for grade 5.

This problem, like the *Flag* problem, also asks students to determine area. But here the length and width of the rectangle are both given (in meters), and the student has only to select one of the four choices. Notice also that the unit of measure (square meters) is given. Thus, all the information needed to solve the problem is given. The student is even given the operation that must be performed. This problem only requires that a certain mechanical procedure be carried out to get an answer. It is consistent with teaching based on step-by-step procedures that focus on number operations, far removed from the real-life situations of the students.

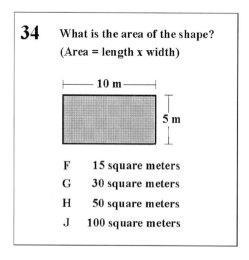

Figure 3.   Measurement problem from CAT (grade 5).

2.4. *What is Good Assessment?*

We note that the CAT test item is quite consistent with the requirements for assessment problems used on traditional standardized tests. But we certainly could not claim this for the *Flag* problem. On the contrary, from the point of view of traditional assessment, serious objections could be raised to the *Flag* problem. For example, a broad range of knowledge is assessed, and it is actually not known in advance what will be assessed; not all the needed data are given; and objective scoring is not possible, because no one knows the correct answer.

In spite of the objections cited above, many mathematics educators would judge the *Flag* problem to be appropriate for assessment because it has rich potential to provide a lot of information about the students' thinking, understanding, and knowledge. Moreover, the problem is consistent with what many think is important for students to learn. Instead of writing out prescribed mechanical procedures, an opportunity is provided for students to apply flexibly their mathematical knowledge and understanding in a manner which makes sense to them in this particular problem situation.

As the above discussion makes clear, appropriate assessment problems depend very much on how one thinks about the goals of mathematics education: What mathematical ideas are important, how is mathematics learned, and how is mathematics taught? That is, a new approach to mathematics education evident in many parts of the world calls for a new approach to assessment (see e.g., Niss, 1993; Clarke, 1996; Van den Heuvel-Panhuizen, 1996; Hashimoto & Becker, 1999). A consequence of this thinking is that as mathematics content and teaching is reformed, assessment also needs to be reformed. This is not an altogether new idea for, more than ten years ago, Romberg, Zarinnia and Collis (1990) predicted a new future world-view of assessment in mathematics.

2.5. *Objections to Standardized Tests*

In some nations it is often alleged that teachers in schools are overloaded with standardized tests that are not consistent with the new approach to mathematics education. Some North American commentators have maintained, for example, that standardized test regimes in the 1980s and 1990s wrought havoc on school mathematics environments (see, e.g., Stake et al., 1994; Apple, 1995).

Stake (1995) pointed to the dangers in school reform which over-emphasized student performance on statewide pencil-and-paper tests. According to Stake, this invariably induced "overstandardization, oversimplification, over-reliance on statistics, student boredom, increased numbers of dropouts, a sacrifice of personal understanding and, probably, a diminution of diversity in intellectual development" (p. 213). In a series of illuminative studies of Chicago's schools and teacher education programs, Stake et al. (1994) pointed to the negative effects that the ever-present reality of standardized examinations had on the classroom practices of some schools.

Occasionally, teachers were prepared to stand up and be counted against multiple-choice assessment regimes mandated by local authorities and governments. According to Clements (1999), in 1993 almost the entire teaching force in England and Wales broke the law in upholding a boycott of national curriculum assessment.

The National Center for Fair and Open Testing (2001), in the United States, claimed that overuse of standardized tests is damaging education, and Kohn (2000, 2001) asserted that not only are such tests a serious threat to good teaching, they also have the potential to ruin schools. Other specific complaints have also been raised, among them, that standardized tests focus on low level skills and take away valuable instruction time from the fundamental purposes of teaching (Casas & Meaghan, 2001). It has been claimed that they have a negative influence on equity (Froese-Germain, 2001), and have an adverse effect on job satisfaction (Rotberg, 2001). Writing with some authority, Popham (2001) declared that measuring what students have learned in school is not the measuring function of traditional achievement tests.

2.6. *Alternatives to Standardized Testing*

Are there feasible alternatives to standardized tests and if so, what are they? We believe there are new assessment tools that have been developed which provide worthwhile alternatives. Furthermore, new approaches to enhancing classroom teachers' assessment abilities have also been developed.

Several new approaches to assessment provide teachers with new *tools* for assessment – examples are portfolio assessment (Wolf, 1989; Mummé, 1990; Herman & Winters, 1994), performance assessment (Linn, Baker, & Dunbar, 1991; Collison, 1992; Baker, O'Neil, & Linn, 1993) and authentic assessment (Wiggins, 1989b; Lajoie, 1995).

The second aspect of the development of alternatives to standardized tests is the recent emphasis placed on recognizing and enhancing the assessment *abilities* of teachers. The idea is that assessment be placed back into the hands of teachers, which is described by terms such as 'informal assessment' (Watson, 1999; 2000), 'instructionally embedded assessment' (Webb, 2001) or 'didactical assessment' (Van den Heuvel-Panhuizen, 1996), 'formative assessment' (Wiliam & Black, 1996) and 'classroom assessment' (De Lange, 1999). All of these descriptive phrases refer to assessment which is intended to support the teaching and learning process. It is closely linked to the instruction and to the subject matter – in this case school mathematics – and, in principle, is part of the teacher's daily educational practice.

Of the terms mentioned in the last paragraph, we prefer the last, 'classroom assessment', which includes everything from informal to formal assessment and also includes an ongoing collection of evidence. This term can be used with respect to the teacher *or students* as the assessor. Its purpose is clear, namely to support learning and teaching, and it is strongly connected to the domain of the school subject and the way it is taught.

Several comprehensive review studies have been published drawing attention to the roles of classroom assessment in raising students' achievement levels (Scheerens & Bosker, 1997; Black & Wiliam, 1998). Advocates of this alternative to standardized tests emphasize that assessment should play an integral role in teaching and learning, and that instruction and assessment should be epistemologically consistent (Shepard, 2000b).

2.7. *Need for a Different Design Model*

Notwithstanding the professional attractiveness of alternatives that have been developed to standardized tests, they are not the only answer to objections raised to and about standardized tests. We need to wonder whether changing assessment formats, as a way to develop new tools, is sufficient to align assessment with the new goals and teaching methods of mathematics education. The same can be asked with respect to enhancing teachers' abilities to design and implement assessment, that is, if teachers are responsible for assessing students' learning, from what frame of reference will they design and develop problems? Until now, more or less the only models they have are the standardized tests.

On its own, neither alternative, however, creates problems like the *Flag* problem. In order to conceptualize assessment in a manner which provides teachers with information about students' achievement, in such a way that it provides direct clues for making didactical decisions, it is necessary to develop a design model that is closely linked to mathematics teaching. In other words, we believe a model is needed that is based on the didactics of mathematics.

The reason for this is that the prevailing psychometric approach utilizes the huge class of mathematics problems that lead to a single, correct answer. This class forms the basis of standardized, multiple-choice exam questions, which has been used for assessment for a very long time. Even if there are multiple ways to get the correct answer to a multiple-choice question, usually it is only the answer which is assessed.

Within newer approaches to assessing school mathematics, however, there is a huge class of mathematics problems that do not lead to a single, correct answer. There are also problems that have a single, correct answer but have multiple ways to obtain it and the assessment approach is interested in both the procedure *and* the answer. The assessment of multiple solutions or multiple paths to a single solution, will occur only when we have an approach to assessment that has the same principles as contemporary approaches to mathematics education. Or, put differently, using the words of Shepard (2000b), assessment design in mathematics education should be 'epistemologically consistent' with the philosophy or the didactics of mathematics education. An assessment design model that has this quality we call a 'didactic model'.

Our tack is to consider the shortcomings of problem design that are bound to the psychometric framework, not so much for the purpose of being negative but more with a view to establishing a need for a new assessment model – one that is tied to the goals of mathematics education.

3. THE PSYCHOMETRIC APPROACH TO ASSESSMENT

3.1. *Psychometric Criteria for Test Item Construction*

The psychometric model for test design assumes certain prerequisites for an assessment problem to be acceptable. Nearly all handbooks on test item construction accept these criteria. Much of the material for this section comes from Osterlind (1998) in his book *Constructing Test Items*.

The following list gives objectives for good item construction under the psychometric model:

1. There must be a high level of congruence between a particular item and the key objective of the whole test.
2. The key objective must be defined clearly and unambiguous.
3. The contribution to measurement errors should be minimized.
4. The format of the test items must be suitable to the goals of the test.
5. Each item must meet specific technical assumptions.
6. The items should be well written and should follow prescribed editorial standards and style guidelines.
7. The items should satisfy legal and ethical questions.

As Osterlind (1998) pointed out, these criteria are generally accepted within the psychometric community. Further, most of the criteria are also valid even beyond the psychometric domain. There are two criteria, however, where, to us, the approaches diverge. These are the criteria mentioned in points 5 and 6 above: the technical assumptions and the editorial standards and style guidelines. A major aspect of editorial standards and style is the call for no ambiguity. A closer scrutiny of these criteria will make clear why they might be, or are, in conflict with assessment problems like the *Flag* problem.

According to Osterlind, there are three fundamental assumptions that apply to all test items, regardless of whether they are included in tests developed under classical test theory or modern test theory design (like item response theory). These three assumptions relate to the need for unidimensionality, for local independence, and for suitable item characteristic curves.

The assumption of *unidimensionality* incorporates the notion that an examinee's response to a test item is a function of a single trait or ability. Osterlind (1998) stated:

> For example, a test item that is designed to assess the trait quantitative ability measures only that trait and does not also assess other traits or abilities, such as verbal ability. (p. 45)

This assumption is important because without an assumption of unidimensionality, it would be very difficult to attempt reliable interpretations of responses that are keyed as correct.

Although the assumption of *local independence* bears some similarity to the foregoing, it is distinct from it. Osterlind formulated the practical consequences of this assumption in the following way:

> Local independence means that an examinee's response on any particular test item is unaffected and statistically independent from a response to any other test item. In other words, local independence presumes that an examinee approaches each test item as a fresh, new problem without hints or added knowledge garnered from responding to any other test item. (p. 48)

The third assumption underlying test item construction concerns the *item characteristic curve* (ICC). An ICC represents the regression of item scores on the attribute or ability variable. An optimal situation, in which an item measures an attribute in a perfectly reliable way, is illustrated in Figure 4.

This implies 'low-ability students' should have only a small probability of responding correctly to a valid test item that measures the attribute. Osterlind pointed out, however, that in practice the relationship between ability and probability of a correct response to an item is more complex.

According to Osterlind (1998), item writers should also *avoid ambiguity*. This requirement plays a prominent role in his judgment of the quality of test items that are discussed in his book, and is true for both multiple-choice items and items for which students are asked to construct their answers. In Osterlind's words:

> In creating short-answer and sentence-completion items, the item writer should be certain that the beginning portion of the sentence will logically lead an examinee to one – and just one – correct response. (p. 239).

The following is an example given by Osterlind to illustrate the requirement:

"The commonly accepted value for pi is _____ " (p. 239).

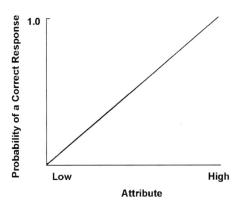

Figure 4.   Example of item characteristic curve (from Osterlind, 1998, p. 51).

Osterlind views the item to be flawed because the number of decimal places expected in an answer is not specified. According to Osterlind (1998) unless a specific direction, such as "decimals should be carried out two places" (p. 239) is clearly stated, examinees will be confused.

3.2. *AERA/APA/NCME Guidelines for Educational Testing and Assessment*

The recently published *Standards for Educational and Psychological Testing* (AERA/APA/NCME, 1999) support the psychometric approach to item, and test, development mentioned above. For instance the *Standards* requires that assessment items should be reviewed for content quality, clarity and lack of ambiguity. In no way is the possibility considered that the criterion for 'lack of ambiguity' could be in conflict with the criterion of educational 'content quality'.

The following statement appears in the *Standards* chapter which addresses educational testing and assessment:

> This chapter concerns testing in formal educational settings from kindergarten through post-graduate training. Results of tests administered to students are used to make judgments, for example, about the status, progress, or accomplishments of individuals or groups. Tests that provide information about individual performance are used to (a) evaluate a student's overall achievement and growth in a content domain, (b) diagnose student strengths and weaknesses in and across content domains, (c) plan educational interventions and to design individualized instructional plans, (d) place students in appropriate educational programs, (e) select applicants into programs with limited enrollment, and (f) certify individual achievement. (p. 137)

The authors of the chapter went on to say that they would not explicitly address issues related to tests constructed and administered by teachers for their own classroom use, or provided by publishers of instructional materials. They added that although "many aspects of the *Standards*, particularly those in the areas of validity, reliability, test development, and fairness are relevant to such tests, this document is not intended for tests used by teachers for their own classroom purposes" (p. 137). Thus, it was made clear that classroom assessment – not to mention the contribution the didactic perspective has to offer – even in a chapter on educational testing and assessment, would more or less be neglected.

The 'non-ambiguous' requirement implies that in the psychometric tradition only those problems having one correct answer are to be valued as assessment items, and it is assumed that *the* correct answer can always be identified without question. It is also assumed that a good assessment problem needs to provide all the information needed to solve it. In this connection, extra or redundant information is considered confusing to students and should be avoided. In other words, problems such as the *Flag* problem would never have a chance for use in assessment, or even to be developed!

3.3. *Educational Assessment Dominated by the Psychometric Tradition*

Although assessment in mathematics education has changed over the years and alternatives have been developed, it continues to be dominated by the psychometric approach (Kilpatrick, 1993). According to Keitel and Kilpatrick (1999), many major international comparative studies have been designed and controlled by psychometricians. Almost all of the people with primary responsibility for conducting the Third International Mathematics and Science Study (TIMSS), for example, were "empirical researchers in education, psychometricians or experts in data processing" (p. 245). Keitel and Kilpatrick (1999) went on to say that "in such studies, questions of content – in all its aspects – have usually been seen as secondary" (p. 245).

Shepard (2000a) commented that "historically, because of their technical requirements, educational tests of any importance were seen as the province of statisticians and not of teachers or subject matter specialists" (p. 1). She has made that point over a sustained period of time (see, e.g., Shepard, 1991, 1993, 2000a). Her plea for more influence of subject matter expertise in educational assessment was the core of a discussion she started in the early 1990s (Shepard, 1991, 1993; Cizek, 1993a, 1993b). The appeal by Berlak et al. (1992) for a new science of educational testing and assessment can be seen in the same light.

Others have emphasized the need to develop a theory of assessment in mathematics education (see, e.g., Glaser, 1986; Grouws & Meier, 1992; Collis, 1992; Webb, 1992, 1993). Notwithstanding the fact that serious efforts have been made to develop such theory and investigate a domain-based approach to assessment (e.g., Webb, 1992; Van den Heuvel-Panhuizen, 1996; Shafer & Romberg, 1999), it cannot be denied that mathematics educators are presently more than ever facing the reality of standardized tests. As Clements and Ellerton (1996) aptly pointed out, in the absence of expressly articulated educational principles for the purpose of guiding assessment policies and practices, "technical and pragmatic criteria became de facto ruling principles" (p. 158).

Clements and Ellerton (1996) also pointed out that the mathematics education community has an important role to play in claiming and accepting responsibility in the domain of assessment. If the goal of mathematics education is mathematization, then assessment problems have to make this process visible. We are arguing, here, that the psychometric model for assessment design literally separates mathematics educators from problems that are crucial for making this process visible. In our view, the foregoing clearly points towards a need to augment the psychometric model for test design and assessment with a didactic model for designing assessment tools. But before working this out we should mention that within the psychometric approach there are some new developments as well.

3.4. *New Developments in the Psychometric Approach*

There are some new developments in the psychometric field. In this community, the need to devise new approaches and techniques compatible with contemporary cognitive, developmental, and educational theories has been accepted (De Corte, Greer, & Verschaffel, 1996). Two examples of these new developments are the BEAR Assessment System (Wilson and Sloane, 2000) and an assessment system designed by Baxter and Junker (2001) aimed at the development of a cognitive developmental map on proportional reasoning in which age-appropriate skills and knowledge competencies can be specified.

Examples like these apparently cause the National Research Council (NRC), in the United States, to be optimistic about the alleged shortcomings of the psychometric-based assessment. In *Knowing What students Know: The Science and Design of Educational Assessment,* published by the NRC's Committee of the Foundations of Assessment (Pellegrino, Chudowsky, & Glaser, 2001), the NRC maintains that the dissatisfaction might disappear if some of the less common models in the psychometric toolkit were more widely used. In particular, reference was made to multidimensional and multi-attribute models. Pellegrino et al. (2001) further maintained that psychometricians are the ones who are supposed to solve, and will solve, the experienced shortcomings in assessment.

Thus, it would appear to be the case that NRC believes that there is little or no room for didacticians to contribute to the challenge. The discussion in the NRC publication concentrates on determining how competencies are composed. If it is known what kind of sub-competencies together make a competency, then how the responses of the students should be analyzed will be known. Little or nothing is mentioned about the kind of problems that have to be presented to students for assessing their competencies.

Similar comments could be made regarding other recommendations in the NCR report. Thus, even though the report makes a strong appeal for rethinking the nature of assessment, doubts linger about who should do this, and how it can be achieved. The NRC argued that this state of affairs has arisen because although the principles and practices of educational measurement have changed over the last century, the changes have not kept pace with the substantial developments that have accrued in the understanding of learning and its measurement. It is the NRC's view, however, the understanding of learning should come from the *sciences of cognition.* The authors of this present chapter, however, are among those who have a preference for a stronger link to *didactics* instead, including both the theories of learning and teaching mathematics and its practice.

3.5. *Departing from the Psychometric Model of Assessment Design*

We would maintain that assessment reform in mathematics education is not possible while there is an allegiance to the psychometric model of test item design. Other conceptualizations of assessment are needed in order to enhance assessment practices in mathematics education. Let us be clear – we are not abandoning standardized tests altogether; rather, we propose to extend the assessment domain to include a model for designing and developing assessment tools and problems that is based on the didactics of mathematics.

To begin, we will present and discuss some misconceptions about mathematics problems that are found in psychometric-based tests. For example, here are some beliefs about assessment:

1. Mathematics problems always have only one correct answer.
2. The correct answer can always be determined.
3. All the needed data should be provided to students.
4. Good mathematics problems should be locally independent.
5. Knowledge not yet taught cannot be assessed.
6. Mathematics problems should be solved in exactly one way.
7. The answer to a problem is the only indicator of a student's achievement level.

Although these beliefs about assessment are closely aligned with the assumptions underlying the psychometric model of tests discussed earlier in this chapter, they are incorrect.

If the issues are to be clarified, it is important that both mathematics and assessment in mathematics education be adequately conceptualized. Although this idea has been mentioned in critiques of standardized tests spanning, say, the last decade, the critics commonly focus on low-level skills. Rarely mentioned, however, is our view that these tests reflect some severe misconceptions about the nature of mathematics and mathematics problems.

Every mathematics item on a standardized test should have exactly one answer. If an item contrary to this belief is inadvertently included on a test, there will likely be a large commotion in the testing community. For example, in 1997 a student discovered that one SAT item had two possible answers. Consequently, the tests of 15,000 students had to be re-scored and the scores revised, in accordance with testing policy (National Council of Teachers of Mathematics, 1997).

Items with more than one correct answer – not to mention problems for which *the* correct answer *cannot be determined* – are not included in standardized tests of mathematics. But, this does not imply they should not be used in assessing students' mathematical learning. On the contrary, a decision not to include such problems would imply that problems that can provide the teacher with valuable instructional information to benefit students' learning are not permitted. We think the *Flag* problem, for example, is a prime example of a problem that can potentially provide a lot of useful information to teachers.

4. NEW ALTERNATIVES FOR ASSESSMENT PROBLEMS

A generation ago, Krutetskii's (1976) classic *The Psychology of Mathematics Abilities in Schoolchildren* challenged mathematics teachers and educators to embrace assessment models which lay outside the psychometric tradition. Now, finally, mathematics educators are rising to this challenge and considering the education possibilities of classes of assessment problems that can provide insight into the significant mathematical thinking of which students are capable. We now elaborate on that statement.

4.1. *Problems with Multiple Solutions*

We begin with the *Candle* problem (Van den Heuvel-Panhuizen, 1996) (see Figure 5). This problem is about a collection of packages containing candles. The number of candles in each box is shown.

This problem was administered to a class of first-grade students. The teacher read the instructions, and then students were asked to 'buy' twelve candles and indicate the cost of their purchase by putting a mark over the chosen packages. As an aside, the *Candle* problem has much in common with a multiple-choice test item – the difference is that the children now *really have multiple choices*. To put it differently, in order for the problem's potential to be realized, it is necessary that the children make *their* choice(s), guided by their own natural mathematical thinking and knowledge. One student might select two packages of six while another student might add small numbers of candles repeatedly until twelve is reached (e.g., 3 and 3 makes 6, and 1 makes 7, and 1 makes 8, and 2 makes 10, ...). If several such items are included in assessment, relevant information can be collected regarding familiarity with numbers and operations.

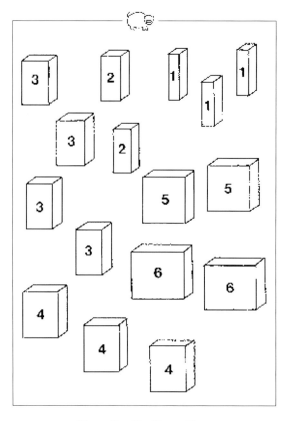

Figure 5.   Candle problem.

The *Whistle and Watch* problem (Van den Heuvel-Panhuizen, 1996) (see Figure 6), which was designed for second-grade students, is a similar problem. Students imagine they are at a fair. They are asked to indicate how much they will have to pay for both the watch and whistle toys shown in Figure 6.

Inherent in problems that have several or many correct answers is what we call a "zone of free construction" (Van den Heuvel-Panhuizen, 1996). That is to say, such problems provide an opportunity for students to think using what-ever natural thinking abilities they choose (see also Becker & Shimada, 1997; Hashimoto & Becker, 1999; Shimada, 1977). This characteristic has potential for revealing many dimensions of students' learning. Here, marking two 25-cent coins is a quite different response from, say, marking a 10-cent coin and 5-cent coin, and then marking three 10-cent coins and a 5-cent coin, though both are correct.

Notwithstanding the revealing capacity of these problems, teachers and researchers should always be alert and check their interpretations and conclu-sions. This is as true for these new problems as it was for the traditional ones. The difference, however, is that these new problems are not exclusively focused

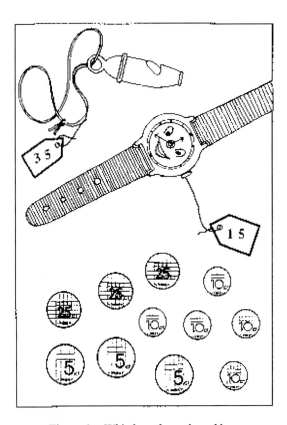

Figure 6.   Whistle and watch problem.

on certainty, but instead allow more uncertainty in order to make the problems more revealing and thereby create opportunity for an assessment practice on a human scale (see also Streefland & Van den Heuvel-Panhuizen, 1999).

Although a portion of the assumed certainty is indeed lost with the introduction of 'elasticity', such problems with latitude provide a wealth of information – particularly for daily classroom practices. In this respect we agree with Wassermann (2001) that we need to help parents, students, teachers and school administrators to have more comfort in a world of uncertainty.

4.2. *Dependent Problems*

The *Ice Cream* problem (Van den Heuvel-Panhuizen, 1996) (see Figure 7) was designed for fifth-grade students. The students are asked to determine what the cost will be, in Dutch guilders, for each of the two Italian ice cream treats.

In this problem, one can use the solution of the first part of the problem to solve the second part. These kinds of problems, sometimes called 'twin problems', violate local independence (which is a requirement of the traditional psychometric model).

Students record their work in the space provided on the test. Thus, there is useful information available about students' strategies in solving the problem – that is, in converting the price from Lires into Dutch guilders (see Figure 8).

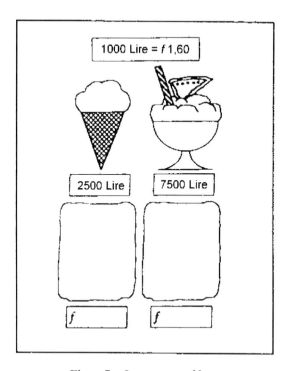

Figure 7.   Ice cream problem.

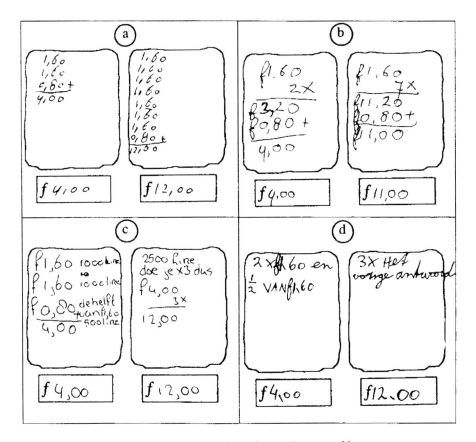

Figure 8. Student work on the Ice Cream problem.

The power of including dependent problems on a test is that the assessment reveals whether the students have insight into the relationship between the two problems, and whether they can make use of it. In the *Ice Cream* problem, the second treat costs three times the first treat which students can determine by using their knowledge of ratios (done by students c and d, but *not* by students a and b).

Below is another example of a dependent problem, the *Banana* problem. But here the presentation is altered – the related problem uses only numbers (Van den Heuvel-Panhuizen, 1997) (see Figure 9).

The two problems are concerned with the same mathematics content, that is to say, "1.49 × 0.740 is about _____". A difference in results between two estimations can be very revealing. For example, in a Dutch fifth-grade class with 29 students, only one student found the correct answer for the problem with the numbers only, whereas 12 students achieved a correct answer in the context version. This illustrates that two problems apparently assessing the same mathematical content may assess quite different things.

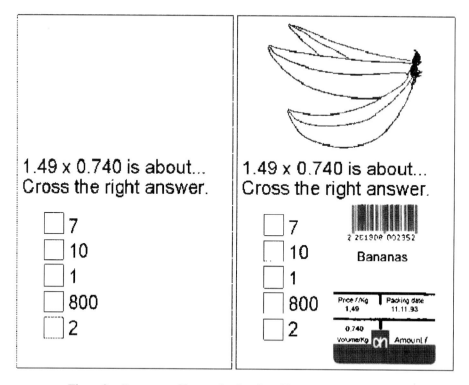

Figure 9.   Banana problem and related problem with only numbers.

A related analysis revealed that if the students' results in the two versions were compared, nearly 75% of the students showed some degree of progress in estimation. However surprising the difference is between the students' responses to the two versions, *what lies behind these differences* is important, rather than the differences themselves. It appears that the 'context' version elicited strategies which were different from those elicited by the problem with only numbers.

Knowledge acquired by teachers in this approach to assessment can provide important information for further instruction. Beyond this, this kind of assessment can determine the approach or method of teaching to be used and also that knowledge can be assessed before the content has been taught. From that perspective, it could be argued that these examples exhibit assessment approaches that seemingly turn the rules of traditional assessment upside-down!

4.3. *Strategy as Assessment Output*

Redefining assessment output to include students' solution strategies may be helpful in diagnosing students' learning difficulties or errors, as well as indicating achievement in its own right. This idea was tried out in an evaluation of the students' achievement in a teacher enhancement project. Students' achievement with non-project teachers was compared with students' achievement with project

$$38 + 39 + 40 + 41 + 42 =$$

Figure 10.   Long addition.

teachers (see Van den Heuvel-Panhuizen & Fosnot, 2001). For this comparison, problems were used that had potential for revealing students' processes of mathematizing. All the problems were written on a sheet of paper on which the students also wrote their solution methods.

The most important requirement for assessing mathematizing is, however, that there *is something to mathematize.* This means that in the case of problems that involve numbers, the students have opportunities to process the numbers in different ways. Also, the numbers need to be chosen in such a way that the students can exhibit their ability to apply smart strategies that bring into play their knowledge of the properties of operations and numbers. An example of such a problem is the long addition problem in Figure 10, intended for third grade students.

The problem appears to be an ordinary addition problem that could trigger a column algorithm or – as it was called in this study – 'ciphering' (see Figure 11).

A student with number sense, however, would be likely to recognize how nicely the numbers can be fit together and link a strategy to this knowledge, that is, use a smart calculation strategy or – as it was called in this study – 'tinkering' (see Figure 12).

Ciphering was the strategy of choice for the majority (62%) of the non-project students ($n = 61$). For the project students ($n = 75$), only 20% applied a ciphering strategy. In contrast, the project students used their number and operation knowledge by tinkering (17%) or decomposing (45%). For the non-project students these percentages were remarkably lower (5% and 15%, respectively).

Overall, the study's results made it clear that assessment loses much if it is

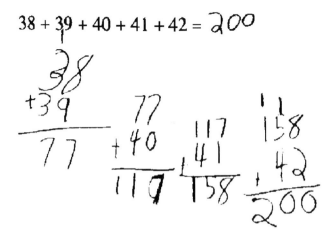

Figure 11.   Ciphering strategy.

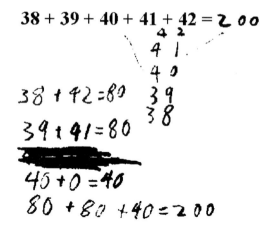

Figure 12.   Tinkering strategy.

restricted to 'answers only' and that the applied strategies should not be overlooked as a direct indicator of student achievement.

5. CONCLUDING REMARKS

There is a common thread running through the alternatives to standardized test problems that have been presented in this paper – they are all grounded in broad ideas on mathematics and mathematics teaching. Each provides a 'rich environment' in which students have an opportunity to demonstrate what they know; that is, to use their natural thinking abilities and apply their knowledge. The problems get to the heart of applying mathematics – that is, mathematics as a human activity (Freudenthal, 1973). In each case, the students have to organize the data, develop or select a model, and select a manner of notation by which they can deal with the data, make use of their knowledge of daily-life measures, reason in order to find ways for combining information, and select or develop adequate and efficient solution strategies.

Assessment in mathematics education should make these processes explicitly clear. This is particularly true for classroom assessment. Classroom teachers need detailed information on their students' mathematical thinking in order to tailor lessons appropriate for them. These requirements cannot be easily met, however, by only using results from standardized tests. By utilizing only the psychometric model for assessment design, we are depriving teachers of problems that are crucial for informing them about their students' mathematization abilities. Therefore, it seems clear that we need to augment significantly the psychometric model with a didactic model for assessment design. If this is achieved we believe that it will generate better assessment and better instruction – they are the two sides of the same assessment coin (Becker & Selter, 1996).

Finally, we acknowledge that there are some aspects of assessment that have not been addressed in this chapter. For example, we have not dealt with examples used in international assessments and in national assessments in some countries. Nor have we discussed the multiple and varied realities of classroom teachers who, in most countries, are spending nearly all their teaching days with students, and find it difficult to get the time required to learn, implement, and apply new approaches to assessment. Further, assessment is, really, a political issue and this implies that teachers, parents, administrators and political decision makers need to be enlightened about proposed changes.

REFERENCES

American Educational Research Association/American Psychological Association/National Council on Measurement in Education (1999). *Standards for educational and psychological testing.* Washington, D. C.: American Educational Research Association.

Apple, M. (1995). Taking power seriously: New directions in equity in mathematics and beyond. In W. G. Secada, E. Fennema & L. B. Adajian (Eds.), *New directions for equity in mathematics education* (pp. 329–348). Cambridge, UK: Cambridge University Press.

Baker, E. L., O'Neil Jr, H. F., & Linn, R. L. (1993). Policy and validity prospects for performance-based assessment. *American Psychologist, 48*(12), 1210–1218.

Baxter, G. P., & Junker, B. (2001, August). *Designing cognitive-developmental assessments: A case study in proportional reasoning.* Paper presented at the annual meeting of the National Council for Measurement in Education, April, Seattle, Washington.

Becker, J. P., & Selter, C. (1996). Elementary school practices. In A. J. Bishop, K. Clements, C. Keitel, J. Kilpatrick & C. Laborde (Eds.), *International handbook of mathematics education* (pp. 511–564). Dordrecht, The Netherlands: Kluwer Academic Publishers.

Becker, J. P., & Shimada, S. (1997). *The open-ended approach – A new proposal for teaching mathematics.* Reston, VA: National Council of Teachers of Mathematics.

Berlak, H., Newmann, F. M., Adams, E., Archbald, D. A., Burgess, T., Raven, J., & Romberg, T. A. (1992). *Toward a new science of educational testing and assessment.* Albany, NJ: SUNY Press.

Black, P., & Wiliam, D. (1998). Inside the black box: Raising standards through classroom assessment. *Phi Delta Kappan, 80*(2), 139–148.

Buros, O. (1977). Fifty years in testing: Some reminiscences, criticisms, and suggestions. *Educational Researcher, 6*(7), 9–15.

Casas, F. R., & Meaghan, D. E. (2001). Renewing the debate over the use of standardized testing in the evaluation of learning and teaching. *Interchange, 32*(2), 147–181.

Cizek, G. J. (1993a). Rethinking psychometricians' beliefs about learning. *Educational Researcher, 22*(4), 4–9.

Cizek, G. J. (1993b). The place of psychometricians' beliefs in educational reform: A rejoinder to Shepard. *Educational Researcher, 22*(4), 14–15.

Clarke, D. (1996). Assessment. In A. J. Bishop, K. Clements, C. Keitel, J. Kilpatrick & C. Laborde (Eds.), *International handbook of mathematics education* (pp. 327–370). Dordrecht, The Netherlands: Kluwer Academic Publishers.

Clements, M. A. (1999). Education policy, education research, and the development of mathematics teachers. In N. F. Ellerton (Ed.), *Mathematics teacher development: International perspectives* (pp. 217–246). Perth, Western Australia: Meridian Press.

Clements, M. A., & Ellerton, N. F. (1996). *Mathematics education research: Past, present and future.* Bangkok: UNESCO.

Collis, K. F. (1992). Curriculum and assessment: A basic cognitive model. In G. C. Leder (Ed.), *Assessment and learning of mathematics* (pp. 24–45). Hawthorn, Victoria: Australian Council for Educational Research.

Collison, J. (1992). Using performance assessment to determine mathematical dispositions. *Arithmetic Teacher, 39*(6), 40–47.

De Corte, E., Greer, B., & Verschaffel, L. (1996). Mathematics teaching and learning. In D. C. Berliner & R. C. Calfee (Eds.), *Handbook of educational psychology*. New York: Simon & Schuster/ Macmillan.

De Lange, J. (1987). *Mathematics, insight and meaning*. Utrecht, The Netherlands: OW&OC, Utrecht University.

De Lange, J. (1992). Critical factors for real changes in mathematics learning. In G. C. Leder (Ed.), *Assessment and learning of mathematics* (pp. 305–329). Hawthorn, Victoria: Australian Council for Educational Research.

De Lange, J. (1999). *Framework for classroom assessment in mathematics*. Madison, WI: NICLA/ WCER.

Elmore, R. F. (2002). Testing trap: The single largest – and possibly most destructive – Federal intrusion into America's public schools. *Harvard Magazine (Alumni), 105*(1), 35.

Fiske, E. B. (1997, May 1). America's test mania. *New York Times (Education Supplement)*, 19.

Freudenthal, H. (1973). *Mathematics as an educational task*. Dordrecht, The Netherlands: Reidel Publishing Company.

Froese-Germain, B. (2001). Standardized testing + High-stakes decisions = Educational inequity. *Interchange, 32*(2), 111–130.

Glaser, R. (1986). The integration of instruction and testing. In *The redesigning of testing for the 21st century. Proceedings from the 6th Annual Invitational Conference of the Educational Testing Service*, 26 October 1985.

Grouws, D. A., & Meier, S. L. (1992). Teaching and assessment relationships in mathematics instruction. In G. C. Leder (Ed.), *Assessment and learning of mathematics* (pp. 83–106). Hawthorn, Victoria: Australian Council for Educational Research.

Haney, W., & Madaus, G. (1989). Searching for alternatives to standardized tests: Whys, whats, and whithers. *Phi Delta Kappan, 70*, 683–687.

Hashimoto, Y., & Becker, J. P. (1999). The open approach to teaching mathematics – Creating a culture of mathematics in the classroom: Japan. In L. J. Sheffield (Ed.), *Developing mathematically promising students* (pp. 101–119). Reston, VA: National Council of Teachers of Mathematics.

Herman, J. L., & Winters, L. (1994). Portfolio research: A slim collection. *Educational Leadership, 52*(2), 48–55.

Keitel, C., & Kilpatrick, J. (1999). The rationality and irrationality of international comparative studies. In G. Kaiser, E. Luna & I. Huntley (Eds.), *International comparisons in mathematics education* (pp. 241–256). London: Falmer Press.

Kilpatrick, J. (1993). The chain and the arrow: From the history of mathematics assessment. In M. Niss (Ed.), *Investigations into assessment in mathematics education: An ICMI study* (pp. 31–46). Dordrecht, The Netherlands: Kluwer Academic Publishers.

Kohn, A. (2000). *The case against standardized testing*. Portsmouth, NH: Heinemann.

Kohn, A. (2001). Learning is threatened by specific, measurable, uniform mandates. *Education Week, 21*(4), 38 and 52.

Krutetskii, V. A. (1976). *The psychology of mathematics abilities in schoolchildren* (translated by J. Teller and edited by J. Kilpatrick). Chicago: University of Chicago Press.

Lajoie, S. P. (1995). A framework for authentic assessment in mathematics. In T. A. Romberg (Ed.), *Reform in school mathematics* (pp. 19–37). Albany: NY: SUNY Press.

Leder, G. C. (1992). Curriculum planning + assessment = learning? In G. C. Leder (Ed.), *Assessment and learning of mathematics* (pp. 330–344). Hawthorn, Victoria: Australian Council for Educational Research.

Linn, R. L., Baker, E., & Dunbar, S. B. (1991). Complex, performance-based assessment: Expectations and validation criteria. *Educational Researcher, 20*(8), 15–21.

McLean, L. (1982). Achievement testing – Yes! Achievement tests – No!. *e + m Newsletter*, Ontario Institute of Education, Fall, p. 1.

Mummé, J. (1990). *Portfolio assessment in mathematics*. Santa Barbara, CA: University of California.

Nagasaki, E., & Becker, J. P. (1993). Classroom assessment in Japanese mathematics education. In

N. Webb (Ed.), *Assessment in the mathematics classroom* (pp. 40–53). Reston, VA: National Council of Teachers of Mathematics.

National Center for Fair and Open Testing (2001). *How standardized testing damages education.* Published on the website of the National Center for Fair and Open Testing.

National Council of Teachers of Mathematics (NCTM) (1997). Student catches SAT Math problem error. *NCTM News Bulletin,* March, 4.

National Research Council (NRC) (1989). *Everybody counts.* Washington, D. C.: National Academy Press.

Niss, M. (Ed.) (1993). *Cases of assessment in mathematics education. An ICMI study.* Dordrecht, The Netherlands: Kluwer Academic Publishers.

Osterlind, S. J. (1998). *Constructing test items.* Dordrecht, The Netherlands: Kluwer Academic Publishers.

Pellegrino, J. W., Chudowsky, N., & Glaser, R. (Eds.) (2001). *Knowing what students know: The science and design of educational assessment.* Washington, D. C.: National Academy Press,

Pipho, C. (1985). Tracking the reform, part 5: Testing – Can it measure the success of the reform movement? *Education Week,* 22 May, 19.

Popham, W. J. (1978). *Criterion-referenced measurement.* Englewood Cliffs, NJ: Prentice-Hall.

Popham, W. J. (1987). The merits of measurement-driven instruction. *Phi Delta Kappan, 68,* 679–682.

Popham, W. J. (2001). Standardized achievement tests: misnamed and misleading. *Education Week, 21*(3), 46.

Resnick, L. B. (1982). History of educational testing. In A. K. Wigdor & W. R. Garner (Eds.), *Ability testing: Uses, consequences, and controversies, part 2: Documentation section* (pp. 173–194). Washington, D. C.: National Academy Press.

Resnick, L. B., & Resnick, D. P. (1992). Assessing the thinking curriculum: New tools for educational reform. In B. R. Gifford & M. C. O'Connor (Eds.), *Changing assessments: Alternative views of attitude, achievement and instruction* (pp. 37–75). Dordrecht, The Netherlands: Kluwer Academic Publishers.

Romberg, T. A. (1992). Evaluation: A coat of many colors. In T. A. Romberg (Ed.), *Mathematics assessment and evaluation: Imperatives for mathematics educators* (pp. 10–36). Albany, NY: SUNY Press.

Romberg, T. A. (1995). *Reform in school mathematics and authentic assessment.* Albany, NY: SUNY Press.

Romberg, T. A., Zarinnia, E. A., & Collis, K. F. (1990). A new world view of assessment in mathematics. In G. Kulm, *Assessing higher order thinking in mathematics* (pp. 21–38). Washington, D. C.: AAAS.

Rotberg, I. (2001). A self-fulfilling prophecy. *Phi Delta Kappan, 83*(2), 170–171.

Salmon-Cox, L. (1981). Teachers and standardized achievement tests: What's really happening? *Phi Delta Kappan, 62*(9), 631–634.

Scheerens, J., & Bosker, R. (1997). *The foundations of educational effectiveness.* Oxford, UK: Elsevier Science Ltd.

Shafer, M. C., & Romberg, T. A. (1999). Assessment in classrooms that promote understanding. In E. Fennema & T. A. Romberg (Eds.), *Mathematics classrooms that promote understanding* (pp. 159–183). Mahwah, NJ: Lawrence Erlbaum Associates.

Shepard, L. A. (1988, April). *Should instruction be measurement-driven? A debate.* Paper presented at the meeting of the American Educational Research Association, April, New Orleans.

Shepard, L. A. (1991). Pychometricians' beliefs about learning. *Educational Researcher, 20*(7), 2–16.

Shepard, L. A. (1993). The place of testing reform in educational reform: A reply to Cizek. *Educational Researcher, 22*(4), 10–13.

Shepard, L. A. (2000a). *The role of assessment in teaching and learning.* Santa Cruz, CA: CRESST/CREDE, University of California, Los Angeles.

Shepard, L. A. (2000b). The role of assessment in a learning culture. *Educational Researcher, 29*(7), 4–14.

Shimada, S. (1977) (Ed.). *The open-ended approach in arithmetic and mathematics – A new proposal toward teaching mathematics,* Mizuumishobo, Tokyo, Japan (in Japanese).

Sproull, L., & Zubrow, D. (1981). Standardized testing from the administrative perspective. *Phi Delta Kappan, 62*(9), 628–631.

Stake, R. E. (1995). The invalidity of standardised testing for measuring mathematics achievement. In T. A. Romberg (Ed.), *Reform in school mathematics – and authentic assessment* (pp. 173–235). State University of New York, New York.

Stake, R. E., Cole, C., Sloane, F., Migotsky, C., Flores, C., Merchant, M., Miron, M., & Medley, C. (1994). *The Burden: Teacher professional development in Chicago school reform.* Urbana-Champaign: University of Illinois.

Stephens M., Clarke, D. J., & Pavlou, M. (1994). Policy to practice: High stakes assessment as a catalyst for classroom change. In G. Bell, B. Wright, N. Leeson & J. Geake (Eds.), *Challenges in mathematics education: Seventeenth Annual Conference of the Mathematics Education Research Group of Australasia* (pp. 571–580). Lismore, Australia: Mathematics Education Research Group of Australasia.

Streefland, L., & Van den Heuvel-Panhuizen, M. (1999). Uncertainty: A metaphor for mathematics education. *Journal of Mathematical Behavior, 17*(4), 393–397.

Van den Heuvel-Panhuizen, M. (1995). Toetsen bij reken-wiskundeonderwijs. In L. Verschaffel & E. de Corte (Eds.), *Naar een nieuwe reken/wiskundedidactiek voor de basisschool en de basiseducatie* (pp. 196–246). Brussels, Deel 1, StOHO.

Van den Heuvel-Panhuizen, M. (1996). *Assessment and realistic mathematics education.* Utrecht, The Netherlands: Freudenthal Institute, Utrecht University, CD-ß Press.

Van den Heuvel-Panhuizen, M. (1997). *Bananentoets. een onderzoek naar het schattend vermenigvuldigen met kommagetallen* (internal publication). Utrecht, The Netherlands: Freudenthal Institute, Utrecht University.

Van den Heuvel-Panhuizen, M., & Fosnot, C. T. (2001). Assessment of mathematics achievements: Not only the answers count. In M. van den Heuvel-Panhuizen (Ed.), *Proceedings of the 25th Conference of the International Group for the Psychology of Mathematics Education* (Vol. 4, pp. 335–342). Utrecht, The Netherlands: Freudenthal Institute, Utrecht University.

Wassermann, S. (2001). Quantum theory, the uncertainty principle, and the alchemy of standardized testing. *Phi Delta Kappan, 83*(1), 28–40.

Watson, A. (1999). Paradigmatic conflicts in informal mathematics assessment as sources of social inequity. *Educational Review, 51*(2), 105–115.

Watson, A. (2000). Mathematics teachers acting as informal assessors: Practices, problems and recommendations. *Educational Studies in Mathematics, 41*, 69–91.

Webb, D. C. (2001). *Instructionally embedded assessment practices of two middle grades mathematics teachers.* Unpublished dissertation, University of Wisconsin, Madison, WI.

Webb, N. L. (1992). Assessment of students' knowledge of mathematics: Steps toward a theory. In D. A. Grouws (Ed.), *Handbook of research on mathematics teaching and learning* (pp. 661–683). NCTM/Macmillan, New York.

Webb, N. L. (1993). Visualizing a theory of the assessment of students' knowledge of mathematics. In M. Niss (Ed.), *Investigations into assessment in mathematics education: An ICMI study.* Dordrecht (pp. 31–46). The Netherlands: Kluwer Academic Publishers.

Wiggins, G. (1989a). Teaching to the (authentic) test. *Educational Leadership, 46*(7), 41–47.

Wiggins, G. (1989b). A true test: Towards more authentic and equitable assessment. *Phi Delta Kappan, 70*(9), 703–713.

Wiliam, D., & Black, P. (1996). Meanings and consequences: A basis for distinguishing formative and summative functions of assessment? *British Educational Research Journal, 22*, 537–548.

Wilson, M., & Sloane, K. (2000). From principles to practice: An embedded assessment system. *Applied Measurement in Education, 13*(2), 181–208.

Wolf, D. P. (1989). Portfolio assessment: Sampling student work. *Educational Leadership, 46*(7), 35–39.

20
Values in Mathematics Teaching – The Hidden Persuaders?

ALAN BISHOP and WEE TIONG SEAH
Monash University

CHIEN CHIN
National Taiwan Normal University

ABSTRACT

Values are at the heart of teaching any subject, but are rarely explicitly addressed in the mathematics teaching literature. In particular, research on values in mathematics education is sadly neglected. This chapter addresses these gaps by drawing together the various research and theoretical fields that bear upon the values dimension of mathematics education. It begins with a theoretical reflection on the distinctions between values, beliefs and attitudes, and continues with reviewing the literature relating teachers' values to their decisions and actions in the classroom. Moving to the limited research on values in mathematics education, there is discussion of values in the increasingly researched area of socio-cultural aspects of mathematics education. The second half of the chapter is devoted to issues regarding research approaches to studying values in our field, and presents two projects, one based in Monash University, Australia and the other at the National Taiwan Normal University in Taipei. The first project focused on the relationship between teachers' intended and implemented values, and the second explored teachers' values as constituting their pedagogical identities. Implications of this research for teachers' professional development are drawn, and the chapter finishes by outlining the research difficulties inherent in this area, and offers a set of challenges designed to carry the research agenda forward.

1. INTRODUCTION

This chapter is concerned with a crucial yet neglected aspect of mathematics education, namely values and, more specifically, values education and teaching in mathematics. Although many recommendations have been made, and articles written, about teaching for the development of mathematical knowledge, there is a surprising dearth of literature about mathematics teaching in the values area. In recent times, however, it has been increasingly recognized that to neglect

Second International Handbook of Mathematics Education, 717–765
A.J. Bishop, M.A. Clements, C. Keitel, J. Kilpatrick and F.K.S. Leung (eds.)
© 2003 Dordrecht: Kluwer Academic Publishers. Printed in Great Britain.

values is no longer sensible, given the variety of and weight of those recommendations. Any recommendation for changing teaching invariably carries with it the implication of a change in the values being taught. Whether the recommendations concern the need for greater use of technology, or for the development of critical thinking, or for creating multicultural awareness, or for promoting flexible learning, a change in values is implied. Any significant development in mathematics education probably implies a change in values.

It could be argued that one of the main reasons why mathematics teaching today appears to be so similar to how it was 40 years ago is because so few of the recommendations put forward for changing teaching have been adopted. This, we would maintain, is largely due to ignorance about the need to take value changes into account in any move to achieve reform. That is one of the reasons why it is so important to take values into account when considering research and professional development in mathematics education. Many mathematics educators with whom these ideas have been discussed believe that the values which teachers of mathematics bring to various aspects of their work profoundly affect what and how they teach, and therefore what and how their students learn. Furthermore, they recognize that those values influence the next generation on matters such as the nature of mathematics and how it is best taught and learned.

Many national curricula and related documents do contain statements about intended values, with some countries taking these more seriously than others. In that sense, there seems to be much tacit agreement that mathematics classrooms can be regarded as places where values are expressed, communicated and learned. At the bottom line, there is widespread agreement among writers about values in education that whenever and wherever any teaching takes place, values are being taught and learned (e.g., Kohlberg, 1981; Gudmundsdottir, 1990; Eckermann, 1994; Neuman, 1997; Veugelers & Kat, 2000; Alexander, 2002).

Why then have mathematics education researchers and mathematics teachers largely ignored the topic? There appear to be two main reasons. Firstly, there are lingering beliefs about mathematics being culture-free and, therefore, value-free knowledge. The universalism of mathematics, whereby any mathematical idea can be shown to be true no matter where the researcher is located or what language the researcher speaks, fuels this belief, as does the universal and powerful applicability of mathematical ideas. What is usually not realized is that this universalism has been and continues to be one of the prime values underlying the development of 'western' mathematics (see Bishop, 1988). It is one of the reasons that this mathematics has achieved its pre-eminence in all parts of the world, underlying and formatting so much of our lives.

The second main reason for ignorance about the importance of values in mathematics education relates to long-held beliefs that mathematics teachers do not need to take 'human' or 'social' aspects of mathematics education into account in their teaching. Mathematics teaching in most countries of the world is still based on a technique-oriented curriculum, with skill teaching and learning being the main diet in the mathematics classroom (Bishop, 1988). This uniformity of practice is of course fuelled by large-scale international 'comparisons' such as the Third International Mathematics and Science Study (TIMSS) and other so-called international comparative studies, which of necessity focus on the similarities between countries and their educational activities rather than on the much more significant educational differences. If human and social variability is ignored by these types of studies, and this approach is supported in large measures by governments, then many teachers can feel justified in believing that there is little point in their attempting to address such aspects of education as human values.

The 'East Asia' region, made up of countries such as China, Indonesia, Taiwan, Singapore, Malaysia, Brunei, and the Philippines, is one of the most active regions in the world in terms of incorporating values in mathematics teaching and learning. Asian schools generally "promote learning and ... strengthen public morality and hence social order" (Cummings, 1996). The provision of general education, including mathematics education, in Southeast Asia over the last 30 to 40 years has been instrumental in creating economic wealth and maintaining socio-politico stability in the region. Together, with other school subjects, the mainly cognitive developments in mathematics education have opened many windows of knowledge, and equipped many people in this region with the latest scientific/technological know-how.

Lim-Teo (1998) cited the case of Singapore. School mathematics reforms in Singapore in the late 1990s – which included a reduction of curricular content by up to 30% (Singapore Ministry of Education, 1998) and a well-defined statement for IT-based learning and teaching (Teo, 1997) – reflected the Singapore government's aim to actualize the concept of 'thinking schools, learning nation' in the looming knowledge and information age. Likewise, in 1983 Malaysia's KBSR primary school curriculum included a new topic 'commercial practices', which aimed "to acquaint pupils with the elements of commercial practices, hence stimulating their interest in business and commerce" (Wong, 1993, p. 97). The timing was appropriate for a country moving from an agriculturally-based economy to an industrial economy.

Indonesia's 'Panca Sila', Malaysia's 'Nilai-Nilai Murni', and Singapore's 'Shared Values' are examples of documents and policies which reflect some Asian governments' efforts to maintain a sense of national identity and social cohesion amid the challenges of Western cultures and values. Each of these governmental documents encourages the inculcation of desirable values through school subjects (Singapore Government, 1991; Swadener & Soedjadi, 1988; Tan, 1997). Interestingly, the objectives statement in Thailand's current education reform is entirely affective in nature (Thailand Ministry of Education, 1999). Swadener and Soedjadi (1988) establish the link among the five fundamental principles of the 'Panca Sila', values in mathematics education, and pupils' affective development. Tan (1997) shows how the 16 values embodied in Malaysia's 'Nilai-Nilai Murni' may be explicitly harnessed in the science classroom in the nurturing of the 'compassionate scientist'.

National mathematics curriculum statements also echo the role of school mathematics in general education. For example, as stated in Singapore's lower secondary mathematics syllabus, "the primary aim of the [Singapore] mathematics curriculum is to enable pupils to develop their ability in mathematical problem-solving" (Singapore Ministry of Education, 1990, p. 3). While this focus on problem-solving deals with the cognitive dimension, it also reflects the activist view (see Dormolen, 1986) of mathematics learning, promoting pupil valuing of intuitive reasoning and discovery learning. On the other hand, deductive reasoning remains a useful skill to prepare pupils for the future, and therefore the syllabus encourages the fostering of this skill as one of the thinking and heuristics processes for effective problem-solving. Implied here is the mathematical value of *rationalism* (see Bishop, 1988). The syllabus also promotes *relational understanding* (see Skemp, 1979): lower secondary pupils are to be able to "recognize the relationships between topics ... [and to] become aware of the application of mathematics in other subjects" (Singapore Ministry of Education, 1990, p. 5).

For countries, such as Australia, which do not have in place a formal statement of national values, school mathematics curriculum statements can nevertheless include statements pertaining to the inculcation of desirable values in students. For example, the 'Curriculum and Standards Framework' of Victoria, Australia, states that the fulfilment of mathematics learning goals will require student engagement in activities that promote a set of abilities and values. In particular, students are expected to develop "logical reasoning and a conception of the nature of proof" (Board of Studies, 2000, p. 6), which is one of the six mathematical values identified by Bishop (1988). Also, student practical ability in "making sensible use of calculators and computers" (Board of Studies, 2000, p. 6) in their respective mathematics learning experiences also reflects underlying values, one of which may be *technology* generally.

Thus, instead of being a value-free and impersonal school subject, mathematics (like other subjects) provides teachers with opportunities to inculcate desirable values in their pupils. In scholarly education research however, attention to values, beliefs and attitudes has more often been a focus of other subjects than mathematics. See, for example, papers on values in the languages, literature studies, history, and physical education (e.g., Lee & Cockman, 1995; Aplin & Saunders, 1996) and the sciences (see e.g., Proctor, 1991; Tan, 1997; Allchin, 1999). This is perhaps because these other subjects deal more directly and explicitly with 'natural' phenomena and life experiences, and values, beliefs and attitudes are thought of as being embedded in them, and as being important factors in students' future encounters with them. For example, learning about the Second World War illustrates how values, beliefs and attitudes contribute to the shaping and interpreting of events. At the same time, there is an intentional inculcation of relevant values, beliefs and attitudes related to this event in students. The same may also be said of discussion/teaching in science classes concerning energy sources, or of stem-cell research and development in some language classes.

This chapter aims to redress this balance by firstly summarizing existing research and then theorizing. This research and theorizing has been situated within three domains: the affective domain and values education, affective aspects of mathematics education, and socio-cultural aspects of mathematics education. Following this description and analysis, two sets of studies will be presented that focus specifically on teachers' values in mathematics education. There are implications from these sets of studies both for research practices in this area and for professional development for teachers

2. VALUES, BELIEFS AND ATTITUDES

Values, more than any other, is the core concept across all the social sciences. It is the main dependent variable in the study of culture, society, and personality, and the main independent variable in the study of social attitudes and behavior.

(Rokeach, 1973, p. ix)

Theories related to values are not new, and the notion of values has been explored in fields as diverse as anthropology (e.g., Kluckhohn, 1962), philosophy (e.g., Rescher, 1969; Rokeach, 1973; Kohlberg, 1981; Unger, 1990), psychology (e.g., McConatha & Schnell, 1995), religion (e.g., Kwast, 1992), organisational theory (e.g., Hall, 1994; Hofstede, 1997), and education research (e.g., Raths, Harmin, & Simon, 1987; Hill, 1991; Nixon, 1995; Halstead, 1996; Tan, 1997; Allchin, 1999). It will be instructive, here, to explore similarities shared by a number of the conceptions of values within these different domains.

Discussions of values are almost always culturally referenced. In fact, culture can be considered to be "an organized system of values which are transmitted to its members both formally and informally" (McConatha & Schnell, 1995, p. 81). In perceiving values as cultural products, Jurdak (1999) demonstrated that they may be considered as "shared meanings which had captured in certain periods in history the collective experience of a culture" (p. 42). Values arise from an individual's experience in – and relationships with – the world (Raths et al., 1987).

To Hofstede (1997), visible practices such as rituals and symbols are but external manifestations of culture; values form the core of the different manifestations at the deepest level. In turn, "values mediate a human being's inner and outer worlds, and enable us to express our inner selves outwardly in our daily activities" (Hall, 1994, p. 35). It would be expected too that this interaction between culture and values is an ongoing and cyclical one. Hofstede's (1997) transcultural empirical study of values in the 1970s revealed dimensions of cultures which were found consistently within a number of different countries. The survey data were based on a sample size of more than 100,000 people in over 50 countries around the world. These countries included Western cultures (e.g., Australia, Canada, Great Britain, Sweden, and USA), Eastern cultures (e.g., India, Indonesia, Iran, Singapore, and Taiwan), developed nations (e.g., France, Japan, and Switzerland) and developing countries (e.g., African nations, Colombia and Malaysia). Hofstede (1997) proposed that five values continua could be used to provide unique, holistic summaries of the cultures within the individual nations. The first continuum related to power distance, "the extent to which the less powerful members of institutions and organizations within a country expect and accept that power is distributed unequally" (Hofstede, 1997, p. 28). Along this continuum, the country registering the largest power distance relative to the other countries in the survey data was Malaysia, while Austria was at the other end of the scale.

The next value dimension examined the degree of individualism in different countries. According to (Hofstede, 1997), where "the ties between individuals [in relatively individualistic countries] are loose: everyone is expected to look after himself or herself and his or her immediate family" (p. 51). Along this dimension, USA was the most individualistic country, and Guatemala was the most 'collectivist'.

The third value dimension regards the degree to which countries are masculine or feminine. "Masculinity pertains to societies in which social gender roles are clearly distinct" (Hofstede, 1997, p. 82). Among the countries surveyed, Japan is the most masculine, and Sweden the least.

Countries were also found to differ according to the "extent to which the members ... feel threatened by uncertain or unknown situations" (Hofstede, 1997, p. 113). Here, Greece ranked top as a country with the strongest uncertainty avoidance, and at the other end of the scale, Singapore had the lowest uncertainty avoidance index.

The fifth, and last continuum, which related to the orientation perspective of different countries, was proposed by Michael Bond and added to the value dimensions by Geert Hofstede. Countries with a long-term orientation in this Confucian dynamism continuum embrace values which are more oriented to the future (e.g., thrift, persistence), whereas those with a short-term orientation are associated with values which are more oriented towards the past and present (e.g., tradition, personal stability). Although only 23 countries were surveyed here, these also included Eastern and Western cultures, as well as developed and developing nations. China exhibited the highest long-term orientation index, and Pakistan has the lowest score.

These culture-specific value dimensions remind us that the multicultural (mathematics) classroom represents a space wherein different values meet, sometimes in conflict. Certainly, the degree to which cooperative group discussions is an effective learning activity for students is partly dependent on the degree to which students subscribe to collectivist values (this is not to say, however, that students from individualistic countries will not gain anything from group discussions in class). Even if classrooms in different countries are treated as being homogenous in their cultural composition, the value dimensions outlined above provide another way of interpreting and understanding cross-cultural comparative studies such as those associated with the TIMSS projects.

2.1. *Values and Value Indicators*

That any value may be regarded differently in different cultures is attributed to the subjective nature with which members of the different cultures perceive it. A value is a construct (McConatha & Schnell, 1995), an ideal (Hall, 1994) which refers to the desirability (Kluckhohn, 1962; Raths et al., 1987), preference (Rokeach, 1973, Hofstede, 1997), worthiness (Raths et al., 1987; Swadener & Soedjadi, 1988; Hill, 1991; Tan, 1997), priority (Hill, 1991), moral rightness (Raths et al., 1987; Nixon, 1995; Tan, 1997), or the potential benefit (Rescher, 1969) of particular objects, phenomena, actions or goals. Obviously, what is desirable, preferable, worthy, important, right, or beneficial in one culture may not be equally so in another.

Another idea relevant to mathematics education is that although values can be defined in terms of other affective states, such as attitudes and beliefs, nevertheless, values represent something much more significant or at a deeper level. Thus, Raths et al. (1987) referred to these affective states as 'value indicators'. Where values were perceived to be the more significant representations of value indicators, Hofstede (1997) regarded values as "feelings with an arrow to it: they have a positive and a negative side" (p. 8). Rescher's (1969) definition referred to a significant set of attitudes: "a value represents a slogan capable of providing for the rationalization of action by encapsulating a positive attitude toward a purportedly beneficial state of affairs" (p. 9). Hill (1991) also linked values with a subset of beliefs, values being "those beliefs held by individuals to which they attach special priority or worth, and by which they tend to order their lives" (p. 4).

Another perspective evident in the research literature sees values as occupying a more internalized and deep-seated position within the human psyche. Rokeach's (1973) reference to values as enduring beliefs (p. 5) is an example. Krathwohl, Bloom, and Masia's (1964) second set of "taxonomy of educational objectives", which pertains to the affective domain, adopts a stage-learning perspective and positions the learning of values at the apex. Values development is seen as a process involving different affective objectives located along a multidimensional internalization continuum. The most basic stage is 'receiving (attending)', when the individual's attention is drawn to a phenomenon. Successive stages – the rest being 'responding', valuing', organization', and 'characterization (by value or value complex)' – involve increasing levels of internalization, greater levels of internal control over the ownership of affective objectives, and increasing complexities and abstraction of these variables.

Raths et al. (1987) perceive values as the end-result of value indicators (e.g., attitudes, beliefs and interests) going through valuing processes. Satisfaction with respect to all of the following seven criteria must be achieved for a successful valuing process to occur:

- choosing
  - freely
  - from alternatives
  - after thoughtful consideration of the consequences of each element

- prizing
  - acting
  - cherishing
- acting
  - with choice being available
  - repeat, as part of a pattern of life.

The relevance to mathematics education of some of these seven criteria is open to debate (see, e.g., Stewart, 1987; Seah, 1999). For example, certain life experiences may create such deep impressions and have such strong impacts on an individual that they will shape or alter his/her outlook and attitudes to life, and personal values forever. In that case, the criteria of values being the outcome of choosing "after thoughtful consideration of the relevant consequences" may not apply. After all, the formulation of value systems of toddlers and young children are determined to a large extent by their life experiences and by the significant others with whom they come into contact. These children may not have much control over 'choosing' their own values. Thus, while there are certainly values which are internalized within us through a conscious process (and which may satisfy the seven criteria listed in the valuing process), some values – and the processes through which they become values – may be subconscious to us (Schlöglmann, 2001).

The key point from the valuing process, though, is that value indicators are subjected to 'trials and tests' before emerging as values. This is consistent with the assumption of increasing internalization inherent in Krathwohl et al.'s (1964) *Taxonomy*. Indeed, the valuing process corresponds to the mid-level of the *Taxonomy*, i.e. the valuing level, at which values are accepted and committed to.

In his review of research on beliefs, attitudes and emotions, McLeod (1992) distinguishes between these affective constructs in terms of "the degree to which cognition plays a role in the response, and in the time that they take to develop" (p. 578). According to McLeod, "we can think of beliefs, attitudes, and emotions as representing increasing levels of affective involvement, decreasing levels of cognitive involvement, increasing levels of intensity of response, and decreasing levels of response stability" (p. 579). Thus, McLeod postulates an increasing level of internalization, from beliefs, attitudes, emotions, to values and this corresponds to an increasing level of cognitive involvement and a decreasing level of affective involvement.

Although values may derive from interests, attitudes, beliefs and the like, they also exert "a direct or indirect influence on attitudes, beliefs, feelings, and the perception of the social and political world" (McConatha & Schnell, 1995, p. 80). "Values form the basis of a person's ... attitudes toward others and toward the world at large" (Tan, 1997, p. 559). They play a role in one's subsequent response to social stimuli in a general sense, that is to say, in one's affective notions in the forms of interests, attitudes and beliefs. Senger (1999) alluded to this when she acknowledged the presence of underlying values in beliefs.

Thus, although attitudes and beliefs may be internalized to become values, these values subsequently foster the continual and wider adoption of related attitudes and beliefs. As different value indicators and values are activated in new and wider areas of personal experience such as mathematics education, new values may be fostered as well, thereby leading to an increasingly complex and intertwining system of personal affective-cognitive reference systems.

2.2. *Values and Beliefs*

Although beliefs have been well studied in mathematics education, the difference between values and beliefs is not always made clear. That values represent a more internalized form of affect, with a greater cognitive involvement, than beliefs does not necessarily lead to any *observable* difference between the two. In fact, the terms 'values' and 'beliefs' are often used interchangeably in mathematics education documents, as if they are different labels for the same construct. However, it is important to distinguish these because of research findings which have shown that teachers' classroom behaviours often reveal inconsistencies between stated beliefs and values which might be inferred from classroom practices.

The seven criteria in the valuing process proposed by Raths et al. (1987) represents a systematic approach to distinguishing values; according to Raths et al., a belief evolves into a value only when it satisfies *all* seven criteria of the valuing process. The anthropologist Kluckhohn (1962) made the point that values differ from beliefs "by the commitment to action in situations involving possible alternatives" (p. 432). According to Kluckhohn, if one is committed to act on a belief, then there is a value element involved. Clarkson and Bishop (1999) see values as beliefs in action, thus also emphasising the notion of observable, behavioural aspect of values, similar to the acting element in the valuing process mentioned above.

Although values are "expressed through views and behavior" (Veugelers & Kat, 2000, p. 11), not all personally held values may manifest themselves as observable behaviour over any specified period of time. Hill (1991) cautioned that the volitional aspect of values need not necessarily follow from the cognitive and affective. There may be contextual factors which prevent strong, personally held values from being demonstrated publicly. For example, a teacher whose current school expects staff members to propagate a set of institutional values may find that it is in his/her professional interest (to survive, so to speak) consciously to suppress the display of particular personally-held values. Hence, it may be said that another personally held value has over-ridden other relevant values of the teacher. Immigrant teachers who experience racism in their own classrooms may also exhibit particular values because they feel the need to 'act mainstream'. The value of *humility*, for example, may even prompt a teacher to refrain from executing particular values in the immediate context of a particular situation.

Kluckhohn (1962) has attached beliefs to the dichotomies 'true/false' and 'correct/incorrect', and values to 'good/bad'. This reference to values as indicative of one's notion of what is good has also been referred to in later years in definitions of values offered by Nixon (1995) and Tan (1997). Rokeach (1973) introduced an additional dichotomy 'desirable/undesirable'. Reference to research literature as well as school and national value statements may also hint at how these categories may be manifested symbolically. The judgement of the truth or falsity of any phenomenon is only possible and meaningful when it is made with reference to something. A belief that 'mathematics is fun' reflects a true/false judgement, one which is made on an object, specifically, the subject mathematics. Holding this belief does not mean believing that any other subject, or any other thing, is necessarily fun. On the other hand, in the case of values, the notion of what is or is not desirable does not necessarily require any specific target object. A person who subscribes to the value of *fun* will look for it and emphasize it in his/her daily life. It is a personally desirable quality in a somewhat universal way. This is also evident in values listed in curriculum statements and in national documents. Thus, values are invariably context-free. In Rokeach's (1973) words, values are transcendental (across objects and situations). Similarly, Krathwohl et al. (1964) refer to values in the personal value system to be "broadest with respect both to the phenomena covered and to the range of behavior which they comprise" (p. 185).

Similarly, research by Chin, Leu and Lin (2001) in Taiwan differentiates between 'pedagogical identities' (which are expressed in the form of words) and 'pedagogical identifications' (which are expressed in sentences). Pedagogical identities are identified with the notion of values, and pedagogical identifications with decontextualized beliefs. This also proposes the idea that each value develops from an interaction amongst several beliefs, reflecting the internalization continuum in the taxonomy of Krathwohl et al. (1964), and the seven criteria valuing process of Raths et al. (1987).

Nixon (1995) and Tan (1997) also introduce a moral dimension into their definitions of values. As suggested in the beginning of this section, virtues are values as well. However, the morality dimension may not be generalisable to all values. Valuing student *regular practice* in problem solving, for example, is not a moral activity, but one which merely reflects a particular teacher's preference and desirability in terms of a student's responsibility towards his/her own learning processes.

The discussion above has also differentiated values from value indicators with respect to the affect versus cognition perspective. "Values may be looked at as psychological constructs that students and teachers have formed as a result of cumulative individual and collective contextualized experiences" (Jurdak, 1999, p. 41). However, Kluckhohn (1962) referred to values as 'conceptions' and Krathwohl et al. (1964) related the corresponding categories in their cognitive and affective taxonomies. In a similar vein, McConatha and Schnell (1995) linked values to 'constructs', and Raths et al. (1987) perceived valuing as involving the activities of choosing, prizing and acting. Thus, there seems to be some agreement that internalization of values is a highly cognitive activity.

"The fact that we attempt to analyze the affective area separately from the cognitive is not intended to suggest that there is a fundamental separation. There is none" (Krathwohl et al., 1964, p. 45). Schlöglmann (2001) and Seah (2001) put forward similar propositions about the human psyche being made up of inseparable affective-cognitive facets. Schlöglmann (2001) demonstrated how the operations of Jean Piaget's adaptation strategies (i.e. assimilation and accommodation) involve interplay between cognitive and affective processes. Drawing on the Eastern perspective on being and relating, and the associated concepts of equilibrium and harmony, Seah (2001) saw the human affective-cognitive system as being made up of interlocking components of thinking about thinking, feeling about thinking, feeling about feeling, and thinking about feeling. In this model of the human affective-cognitive system, values make up the thinking about feeling component, reflective of the increased role that cognition plays in what is essentially an affective variable.

3. VALUE DECISIONS AND ACTION

The notion of values and beliefs as internal perspectives to an individual is important for both teachers and learners. Equally important for teachers of mathematics are the decisions and actions that flow from the values to which they personally subscribe. Values play a crucial role in shaping our interpretative schema. They provide "abstract frames of references for perceiving and organizing experience" (McConatha & Schnell, 1995, p. 80), and are essentially "a form of conceptual and emotional goggles" (Tan, 1997, p. 559). However, the relationship between values and subsequent action may not be causal. Values influence rather than determine the choice of possible actions available to an individual (Kluckhohn, 1962; Raths et al., 1987; Hill, 1991; Nixon, 1995; Hofstede, 1997; Tan, 1997). In fact, situations often generate several possible and often incompatible responses (Raths et al., 1987), and "rational choice must not be random but guided by considerations of comparative merit, considerations in which values must play a pivotal role" (Rescher, 1969, p. 45; see also McConatha & Schnell, 1995).

Hall's (1994) categorization of values into phases and stages also means that "generally speaking, the phase and stage of the value given first priority determines the world view of an individual or group" (p. 67). Hill (1991) appears to have had this in mind when he remarked that the volitional element of values need not follow from their cognitive and affective elements. The consideration of infringement of personal rights implied by any expectation of conformity to actions is in fact a demonstration of the weighing against the value of *personal rights*. Seen in this perspective, we can understand better Hall's (1994) assertion that "we act on [values] consistently and repeatedly" (p. 21) as alternative choices of actions are weighed against one another. The values that an individual holds are called upon whenever necessary, but such consistent and repeated acts do not always imply observable behavioural forms representing the eventual actions.

In other words, individual values alone do not determine the nature of human decisions, actions and responses. Rather, it is the role of the value system, a learned organization of principles and rules, which "help one choose between alternatives, resolve conflicts, and make decisions" (Rokeach, 1973, p. 14). As Rokeach (1973) explained, it is "through experience and a process of maturation [that] we all learn to integrate the isolated, absolute values we have been taught in this or that context into a hierarchically organized system, wherein each value is ordered in priority or importance relative to other values" (p. 6).

By considering value systems/complexes – named variously as 'values schemas' (Hamberger & Moore, 1997), and 'affective-cognitive reference systems' – we may be in a better position to explain the inconsistencies between individual beliefs and actions observed in several studies. Possible relationships between individual beliefs (which could well be values!) and subsequent actions are discussed in numerous references (see, for example, Schoenfeld, 1989; Schraw, Olafson, Bendixen, & Klockow, 2002; Sosniak, Ethington, & Varelas, 1991; Thompson, 1992; Tirta Gondoseputro, 1999).

Complexities associated with any decision-making situation may invoke several values within one's value system. In fact, "since a given situation will typically activate several values within a person's value system rather than just a simple one, it is unlikely that he [sic.] will be able to behave in a manner that is equally compatible with all of them" (Rokeach, 1973, p. 14). For example, a mathematics teacher may value opportunities to stimulate his/her pupils to develop breadth in the mathematics content taught in class by relating particular mathematics theorems/formulae to their historical or cultural evolution. The same teacher might help pupils see applications in society, and to challenge pupils to establish novel applicational links. Yet, the teacher may also value the importance of pupil academic excellence in mathematics, especially in tertiary entrance examinations. How is this teacher going to plan for a particular topic within the limited amount of time allocated to mathematics in the school teaching plan? Time constraints do not afford this teacher with the luxury of emphasising both enrichment and practice. 'Competing' values are involved here, and the teacher has to prioritize among 'competing' values underlying spending time enriching pupils' knowledge breadth, utilizing the same period of time drilling pupils for examinations, or even incorporating a bit of both. Pressure from 'competing' values in classroom interactions also come about as teachers and students negotiate over and within the parameters of a working consensus – a set of understandings which allows for mutual survival (Pollard, 1982).

For any teacher, it is unlikely that the priorities among 'competing' values will remain the same across situations and contexts. These values override one another differently at different decision points. After all, in different situations, constraints and goals can be different, and thus the choice of actions reflect such differences through the interaction of different 'competing' values.

It is worthwhile noting that the notion of 'competing' values is not entirely novel in the research literature. Hofstede (1997) talked of conflicting values within people, which made it "difficult to anticipate their behavior in a new situation" (p. 11). An example quoted was one in which students in masculine cultures may be characteristically vocal in class and compete openly with peers, but such characteristics may not always be observed when the same students enter another masculine society, one which also subscribes to collectivist values. The science teacher participant in a study by Lewis-Shaw (2001) experienced "tension between ... [the] sometimes competing priorities" (p. 186), between communication of subject content and interest/concern for students, due to such factors as time constraints.

The notion of teacher negotiation among these 'competing' values certainly applied in what Bishop and Whitfield (1972) considered as classroom situations, each of which required teacher decision-making, and which involved multiple decision areas. Orlich, Harder, Callahan, Kauchak, Pendergrass, Keogh, and Gibson (1990) quoted research which concluded that elementary teachers are involved in as many as 1000 interactions daily, most of which involve minor or major decision-making. "The problem then for the teacher is basically a *priority* decision concerning the decision areas. Here the teacher's own value system is fundamental" (Bishop & Whitfield, 1972, p. 16). Decision-making certainly involves a significant amount of cognition, a point which was discussed earlier in this chapter. That "the teacher's own value system is fundamental" also implies that the negotiations among 'competing' values are not made with reference to any individual personally-held values alone.

Decisions are made within the ambit of an entire value system, so that different values within the system act on one another according to the situation at hand. Also, although the teacher's own value system may be of fundamental importance, that does not imply the existence of a static personal value system guiding decisions and choices among the 'competing' values. Rather, although the teacher's value system helps in weighing 'competing' values as a unit, the result modifies the value system in return. In a broader sense, any individual's value system interacts with his or her daily experiences so that it is continually being refined and modified.

Another factor behind observed inconsistencies between beliefs, attitudes and values on the one hand, and teacher practices on the other, may be due to what Tripp (1993) calls second-hand values (or what Lewis-Shaw (2001) refers to as 'reflected values'). In the context of education, these are values which have been articulated by more experienced colleagues and peers for example, and which may be implemented by a teacher in need of an immediate on-site response at a particular critical incident. Second-hand values do not normally form part of a teacher's value system, however. The reflective teacher, having executed a decision based on some second-hand values, normally appraises the action. "The processes of review and evaluation provide for on-going assessment of the effects of particular forms of action on self and on specific interests" (Pollard, 1982, p. 35). Nevertheless, the teacher's personal value system may be fine-tuned in the process, beginning with a positive attitude to, or belief in, the desirability of the second-hand value. In time, this can provide a person, through his or her ongoing developing value system, with new insights into the surrounding world.

Such second-hand influences have been documented, sometimes as 'beliefs', and observed in students. For example, Carpenter, Lindquist, Matthews, and Silver (1983) reported that student inconsistencies in stated beliefs "reflect the beliefs of their teachers or a more general social view rather than emerge from their own experience with school mathematics" (p. 657).

As will be seen below, Lin and Chin's (1998) study with an experienced senior high school mathematics teacher revealed a similar sequence in the teacher's professional development in this area. For this teacher, experts' (textbooks') values were accepted and portrayed to the pupils wholesale, before these interacted with the teacher's own values to bring about further development of his own unique teaching style. In this instance, then, teacher reflection – as part of the teacher's three-stage personal professional development (i.e. accepting experts' values, reflecting with own views, developing own unique style) – was based on second-hand values (in this case, values espoused in textbooks).

The apex of the Krathwohl et al's (1964) *Taxonomy of Educational Objectives (Affective Domain)* refers to an individual's characterization by his/her value system. At this level, values are so internalized within the individual that one expects "a persistent and consistent response to a family of related situations or objects" (p. 166). They can therefore be termed 'overriding values'. Due in part to the fact that they are so much a part of the person who owns them, overriding values may be activated without conscious forethought (Krathwohl et al., 1964). Examples from the VAMP Project which illustrate this point will be presented in Section 7 of this Chapter.

3.1. *Value Change*

That values are deeply internalized qualities within humans does not rule out the fact that an individual's values may – and can – undergo changes. Krathwohl et al.'s (1964) taxonomy of educational objectives in the affective domain, as well as Senger's (1999) model, both identify human awareness as the basis upon which affective variables gain stability and are increasingly internalized. Thus, unless an individual ceases to be aware of what is around him or her, life experiences will continue to shape the individual's attitudes, beliefs and other value indicators, thereby putting pressure on the nature of the individual's existing value system. Value change brought about by this fine-tuning process is thus inevitable. The views of Raths et al. (1987) are similar:

Since we see values as growing from a person's experiences, we would expect that different experiences would give rise to different values and that any one person's values would be modified as those experiences accumulate and change ... And a person who has an important change in awareness or in patterns of experience might be expected to modify his or her values. Values may not be static if a person's relationships to the world are not static. As guides to behavior, values evolve and mature as experiences evolve and mature. (p. 198)

In fact, causal factors underlying value change were examined by Rescher (1969) around the same time that David Krathwohl's team constructed the different taxonomies of educational objectives. Rescher (1969) categorized value change as either derivative or direct. Derivative value change applies to a subsidiary or means value when the corresponding higher-order or end value undergoes a change itself. On the other hand, direct value change may be induced by newly discovered or acquired factual information, ideological/political change, a reaction to boredom/disillusionment, and most relevant for his discussion in the book, value change caused by changes in the society's operating environment. That is to say, direct value change may be induced by "the whole range of social, cultural, demographic, economic, and technological factors that comprise the way of life in that society" (p. 177).

Despite the possibility that one's values can undergo change, the fact that values are more internalized than other affective variables implies that value changes may not be as dramatic, easy, or as frequent as, say, attitude or belief changes. Value changes tend to be evolutionary (as opposed to revolutionary), and many values (such as virtues) have actually withstood the test of time to remain stable, resilient and cherished by generations of the human race (Rescher, 1969; Nixon, 1995).

Similar observations have been made in regard to mathematics education, and some will be discussed in the two case projects summarized in sections 7 and 8 of this chapter. The two immigrant teachers of mathematics in Australia reported by Seah (2002) provide another example of the resilience of personal and pedagogical values. Although both of these teachers employed different strategies to negotiate value differences/conflicts that, they perceived, arose in mathematics classes in their new cultural contexts, the feelings and actions of each teacher were continually guided by values associated with their views on the nature of mathematics. One teacher regarded mathematics as *culture-free* and the other as *lifelong applicational*, and each had developed the value before having migrated to Australia.

4. RESEARCH ON VALUES IN MATHEMATICS EDUCATION

McLeod's (1992) chapter in the *Handbook of research on mathematics teaching and learning* (Grouws, 1992) is one of the most significant reviews of mathematics education research in which affective issues were important. Drawing on the work of cognitive psychologist George Mandler, McLeod (1992) reconceptualized the affective domain in mathematics education into three categories, i.e. emotions, attitudes and beliefs. According to McLeod (1992) "we can think of beliefs, attitudes, and emotions as representing increasing levels of affective involvement, decreasing levels of cognitive involvement, increasing levels of intensity of response, and decreasing levels of response stability" (p. 579). His concern has been that although

affect plays a significant role in mathematics learning and instruction ...

[and although it] is a central concern of students and teachers, research on affect in mathematics education continues to reside on the periphery of the field. If research on learning and instruction is to maximize its impact on students and teachers, affective issues need to occupy a more central position in the minds of researchers.

(McLeod, 1992, p. 575)

Although the reader may have noticed a growing number of papers related to affect in mathematics education being presented in academic conferences during the past few years, the situation has not 'improved' in the most authoritative mathematics education research journals. The percentages of articles or reports explicitly dedicated to the study of affective factors in mathematics education to have been published in the *Journal for Research in Mathematics Education* in 1980 and 2000 were 9.1% (2 out of 22) and 9.7% (3 out of 31), respectively. For *Educational Studies in Mathematics*, the figures for 1980 and 2000 were 4.2% (1 out of 24) and 8.3% (1 out of 12), respectively.

In fact, there still exists relatively little knowledge on the portrayal and teaching of values in the mathematics classroom. Two possible reasons for that state of affairs were given at the beginning of this chapter. Yet,

they [i.e., values] seem to have a deep influence on how, why and what we learn. Hence, depending on the values learnt in mathematics classrooms, students may be helped in their life long learning, or may sadly learn values that inhibit their in-built creative potential.

(Clarkson, Bishop, FitzSimons & Seah, 2001, p. 44)

Similarly, Dossey (1992) cited research which demonstrated that different conceptions of the nature of mathematics "have an influence on the ways in which both teachers and mathematicians approach the teaching and development of mathematics" (p. 39). According to Jurdak (1999), the relatively recent research focus on values in mathematics education has been brought about partly by a shift from macro-descriptions of mathematics education (e.g., goals, content, pedagogical methods and evaluation) to more micro-descriptions (e.g., the breaking down of 'pedagogical methods' into units such as classroom furniture layout, teacher-student roles). In such circumstances, the value-laden nature of each of the smaller building blocks of mathematics education is more evident.

Bishop (1988), who considered values in relation to cultural influences on mathematics, provided one of the first analyses of values relating to mathematics teaching and learning. As Kroeber and Kluckhohn (1952) stated "values provide the only basis for the fully intelligible comprehension of culture, because the actual organisation of all cultures is primarily in terms of their values" (p. 340). Bishop (1988) argued that 'western' mathematical values can be conceived as three pairs of complementary values, i.e. *rationalism* and *objectivism*, *control* and *progress*, *openness* and *mystery* (see Bishop, 1988, chap. 3 for details). The two values in any pair are complementary in the sense that both are portrayed in mathematical knowledge, and yet they seem to contradict each other. For example, in discussing the complementary nature of *openness* and *mystery*, Bishop (1988) noted that "one of the paradoxes of Mathematics is that even though Mathematical culture brings with it the values of 'openness' and accessibility, people still feel very mystified about just what Mathematics is" (pp. 77–78).

In a later analysis, Bishop (1991) discussed these values as the 'qualities' associated with western mathematical knowledge. He went on to focus on three aspects of the teaching/learning situation relating to the education of values through mathematics. The first aspect concerns the *asymmetrical* nature of the teaching/learning process, which focuses on the role of the teacher in educating the values of the learners. The second aspect refers to the *intentional* nature of teaching and learning, linking values to educational goals and aims. The third aspect is the *ideational* quality of values in mathematics education, the fact that the values are related to mathematical ideas.

In exploring values encountered in the mathematics classroom, Bishop (1996, 1998, 2001a) identified three categories of values of interest – general educational, mathematical, and specifically mathematics educational:

> For example, when a teacher admonishes a child for cheating in a test, the values of 'honesty' and 'good behaviour' derive from the *general educational* and socialising demands of society. Then when a teacher proposes and discusses a task such as the following: 'Describe and compare three different proofs of the Pythagorean theorem' the *mathematical* values of 'rationalism' and 'openness' are being conveyed. However there are other values being transmitted which are specifically associated with the norms of the institutions within which *mathematics education* is formally conducted. For example, consider the following instructions from the teacher: 'Make sure you show all your working in your answers'). Don't just rely on your calculator when doing calculations, try estimating, and then checking your answers', the values implied are all about 'examination-wisdom' and 'efficient mathematical behaviour'.
>
> (Bishop, 1998, p. 34)

Another analysis, by Chin and Lin (1999b) related values in the mathematics classroom to teacher identity, reflecting Halstead's (1996) association between values and personal identity. According to Chin and Lin (1999b):

> Values as social and individual phenomena, therefore, are conceived ... as teachers' pedagogical identities concerning mathematics, teaching, learning, and curriculum. They reveal the principles or standards of teacher selections and judgements on the importance or worth of using certain pedagogical identifications in his or her classroom teaching of mathematics. (p. 317)

Chin and Lin (2001b) elaborated further their view that mathematics teachers' values are their *pedagogical identities* concerning mathematics and pedagogy, and these develop through a dialectical relationship between the varieties and complexities of individual pedagogical identifications. Here, 'pedagogical identities' referred to teachers' underlying principles which are normally expressed in short words (like, for example, 'individual thinking'). By contrast, 'pedagogical identifications' referred to teachers' propositions about mathematics and its teaching, and these were usually longer and expressed in complete sentences (such as 'there is no learning if students do not think'). This is consistent with the idea, discussed earlier, that values develop from beliefs. In addition, values transcend across objects and situations but beliefs are contextualized.

Seah and Bishop's (2001) description of values in mathematics education reflected an amalgamation of the various definitions of values in the different disciplines:

> Values in mathematics education represent one's internalization, 'cognitisation' and decontextualisation of affective variables (such as beliefs and attitudes) in one's socio-cultural context. They are inculcated through the nature of mathematics and through one's experience in one's socio-cultural environment and in the mathematics classroom. These values form part of one's ongoing developing personal value system, which equips one with a pair of cognitive and affective lenses to shape and modify one's way of perceiving and interpreting the world, and to guide one's choice of course of action. They also influence the development of one's other beliefs and one's needs in mathematics education and in life. (p. 444)

Mathematics educational values, too, may be conceptualized as complementary pairs. In his textbook-analysis study, Seah (1999) identified the following pairs with respect to mathematics learning:

- *formalistic* versus *activist* views (see Dormolen, 1986);
- *instrumental* versus *relational understanding and learning* (see Skemp, 1979);
- *relevant* versus *theoretical* nature of mathematics teaching and learning;
- *accessibility* versus *specialism* of mathematics knowledge; and
- mathematics as *process* versus mathematics as *product*.

Brown (2001) used similar categories in his examination of values in mathematics assessments, which he classified as being essentially either pedagogical or cultural.

It can be argued that general educational, mathematical, and specifically mathematics educational, values do not exist mutually exclusive of one another. Some values fit into two or all three of the categories. For example, *progress* and its associated value of *creativity* is as much a mathematical and mathematics educational value as a general educational value. When Taplin (2001) wrote about ways by which teachers can integrate values education into existing mathematics lessons, she was referring to a range of human values – such as *perseverance, teamwork* and *truthfulness* – being both general educational and mathematics educational in nature.

Of course, since culture and values are closely related, the nature of any given value in the mathematics classroom is relative to the socio-cultural setting. The value of *rationalism*, with its characteristic promotion of logical thinking and deductive reasoning, may belong to each of the three categories of values discussed in the context of Western society. On the other hand, it may not be a socially desirable value in some other cultures.

In the mathematics classroom, general educational, mathematical and mathematics educational values are operationally portrayed by teachers, textbooks, syllabi, etc. These are usually also accompanied by a range of (more implicit) supporting values, which include the implicit message portrayed by, for example, teacher dress (Neuman, 1997), and the physical design of textbooks. Drawing on Billett's (1998) five levels of knowledge genesis, Seah and Bishop (2000) posited values in the mathematics classroom within increasingly larger contexts of personal, institutional, epistemological and societal values. In particular, 'epistemological values' refer to those values which are continually being constructed and modified by mathematicians and mathematics education scholars. Similar categories have been discussed with reference to science education variously as "epistemological and supporting values" (Tan, 1997) and "values of science and research ethics" (Allchin, 1999).

5. VALUES AND SOCIO-CULTURAL ASPECTS OF MATHEMATICS EDUCATION

Our foregoing discussion on the affective aspects of mathematics education has been conducted with close reference to socio-cultural factors. After all, culture has been defined as "an organized system of values which are transmitted to its members both formally and informally" (McConatha & Schnell, 1995, p. 81). Thus, values are attributed to and by members of cultural groups – that is to say, by each and every one of us. In a sense, then, values are social phenomena as well. From that perspective, this section will look more closely at social and cultural aspects of mathematics, as a discipline of scientific knowledge, and of mathematics education.

Rather than being a body of objective knowledge which exists 'out there' waiting to be discovered, as it is often perceived, mathematics can be regarded as socialized knowledge which has been developed as a response to human needs (Cai, 1986; D'Ambrosio, 1990). In fact, socio-cultural dimensions of mathematical knowledge have gained increasing prominence over the last few decades, with one significant area of development being 'ethnomathematics', a field of enquiry which has been researched by scholars like Alan Bishop, Ubiratan D'Ambrosio, Gelsa Knijnik, Marcia Ascher, Paulus Gerdes, Rik Pinxten, and Robert Ascher.

D'Ambrosio (1985) distinguished between academic mathematics and ethnomathematics. Bishop (1988) refers to them as M and m respectively. Walkerdine

(1997) considered each class of knowledge as being produced within their respective discursive practices. In this context, Pinxten (1994) attributed the rise of M and the corresponding decline of m to the popularity of absolutist/formalist views on the nature of mathematical knowledge. He urged that steps be taken to bridge the gap between a pupil's m and the academic M, arguing that mathematical knowledge has its foundation in the contextual and cultural knowledge of everyday mathematics. One outcome of this is that pupils' understanding can actually be strengthened if contrasts are highlighted.

Society not only helps define the form and development of different mathematical systems, it also shapes the ways in which mathematical knowledge is applied and thus valued. It often serves the interest of particular social groups, via the sociology of mathematical knowledge and through the production and application of this knowledge (Martin, 1997), and through defining its role in society. Martin (1997) identified the availability of research funding and applications, socio-politico correctness, and values of dominant social groups as factors affecting the development and prestige of particular branches of mathematics. He quoted the example of operation research, the development of which was closely related to military applicational needs during World War II. The construction of the mathematical theory of games reflected embedded socio-cultural values. In game theory,

> the values of the modelers are incorporated into the game theoretical formulation, which usually ensures that the game gives results which legitimate those very same values. Game theory in this situation provides a 'mystifying filter': values are built into an ostensibly value-free mathematical framework, which thus provides 'scientific' justification for the decision desired.
>
> (Martin, 1997, p. 161)

Financial funding sources extend their values influence into this aspect as well (Martin, 1997). The concerns for the self-interests of the community of increasingly professional, full-time mathematicians has also led to the conception and promotion of 'pure' mathematics to establish "exclusive claim to control over the discipline" (Martin, 1997, p. 164). It has also led to the specialization of a body of mathematical knowledge (Martin, 1997). If we agree that the value systems of individual mathematicians are built into the mathematical frameworks they conceive, then the fact that the international community of mathematicians consists mainly of males makes it unsurprising that mathematical applications reinforce or reflect values more commonly associated with men.

The roles played by mathematical knowledge within societies are also socially constructed. The fact that since the ascendancy of the Greeks, over 2000 years ago, mathematical knowledge and skills have been regarded as the basis for the development of new knowledge has allowed mathematics to be widely used as a social and educational filter (D'Ambrosio, 1990). From that perspective,

Skovsmose (1992) has explained how mathematics has been used by people to modify behaviour through colonising parts of reality and re-arranging them.

Moreover, whenever and wherever mathematics is taught, the ways in which it is learnt and taught are subject to socio-cultural influences. In fact, education in general (Veugelers & Kat, 2000), and mathematics education in particular (Cobb, 1996; Munro, 1996; Horwood, 1999), are themselves socially-referenced activities. Insofar as mathematics learning and teaching are also personally referenced (Munro, 1996), the individual differences of actors involved in the teaching and learning of mathematics are culturally determined as well. Thus, mathematics education is culturally referenced. Schmidt, McKnight, Valverde, Houang, and Wiley (1997) arrived at the same point, arguing that "school mathematics is mathematics as it is conceptualised, represented, structured, and sequenced to share with the next generation through the formal schooling experience" (p. 4).

When Joseph (1993) discussed three approaches to mathematics education, he considered that the utilitarian approach was one in which mathematics is essentially dissociated from society, and acquired for its own sake and/or aesthetic value. However, the mathematical knowledge involved also has its own cultural dimension. Thus, whichever approach or approaches to mathematics education is/are adopted or adapted, school mathematics curricula reflect relationships between mathematics and the society in which it is situated.

Even if the 'intended' mathematics curricula appear to be similar in different cultures, teachers and schools can teach the content according to different approaches or perspectives. For example, in their comparative study of Asian and American sixth-graders, Brenner, Herman, Ho and Zimmer (1999) cited studies in the 1990s which showed how manipulatives were used to establish linkages with abstractions in Asian classrooms, whereas the same manipulatives were utilized in more concrete ways in American classrooms.

Fasheh (1982) advocated the teaching of mathematics in such a way as to relate to culture, to enable pupils to know more about reality, culture, society and themselves, so that the level of awareness, criticism, appreciation and self-confidence among pupils will be raised. Yet, in many countries, the culture of schooling encourages conformity and discourages criticism. There are therefore cultural and social aspects of values in mathematics teaching and learning.

In fact, the price of 'ignoring' the cultural aspect of mathematics education can be huge, as some developing countries have discovered. Nebres (1995) noted the influence of mathematics education systems of developed nations in some Southeast Asian nations, and Orton (1992) referred to 'meticulous translations' of 'Western' mathematics in some developing countries around the world. That these countries continue to produce disappointing mathematics results is due to what Orton (1992) asserts to be a misfit between 'Western' mathematics and pupils' own cultures.

Decisions by almost all developing nations to adopt the mathematics education systems of developed nations reflect the influence of prevailing socio-cultural forces and values which existed in each of these developing nations in the first place. In Bishop's (1994) words, "all formal mathematics education is a process of cultural interaction, and every child experiences some degree of cultural conflict in that process" (p. 16). Bishop acknowledges that these conflicts are concerned with, among other things, affective qualities like values, beliefs and attitudes. Over the years, the school mathematics classroom has become increasingly multicultural, to the extent that these cultural conflicts now apply to almost all teachers of mathematics, including immigrant teachers.

Bishop (1994) argued for research to be directed towards exploring the nature and implications of cultural dissonance within mathematics classrooms. Drawing on related research across mathematics education, Bishop (1994) listed approaches to cultural conflicts as culture-blind (traditional view), assimilation, accommodation, amalgamation, and appropriation. This provided a useful framework for examining possible ways in which education policy makers, teacher educators, and teachers might respond to culture conflicts in mathematics classrooms.

As demographic movements across geopolitical boundaries increase in both intensity and variety, the socio-cultural aspects of mathematics education are likely to assume greater prominence in host countries' attempts to optimize the learning experiences of migrant/international students and the professional socialization/growth of immigrant teachers. These students and teachers' cultural perspectives will inevitably be brought into school mathematics classrooms thereby generating important and far-reaching implications for more responsive mathematics curricula and pedagogical approaches. Inherent in this consideration is the assumption that more emphasis be given to the roles of mathematical and mathematics educational values. This, in turn, will require the mathematics education research community to understand and harness these values in order that they will be in a position to assist in the development of more effective mathematics education programs.

6. RESEARCH APPROACHES TO STUDYING VALUES

Most, if not all, of empirical research studies into values in mathematics education have been carried out within the last five years. Following this brief introduction, we shall, in the next two sections, summarize and discuss two sets of recent studies.

Some studies have analyzed the values portrayed by the various textual materials involved in mathematics teaching. For example, Seah (1999) compared the mathematical and mathematics educational values inherent in lower secondary mathematics textbooks in Australia and Singapore. He found that four chosen popular textbook series in Victoria, Australia and in Singapore emphasized the same mathematical and mathematics educational values over their corresponding complementary values. Cao, Seah and Bishop (2001) extended this study by analyzing the treatments of comparable topics in Chinese textbooks.

Using a similar approach, Brown's (2001) textual analysis study explored and compared the mathematical and mathematics educational values found in three different high-stakes school mathematics assessment programs. In particular, the focus was on the values underlying decisions related to the kinds of mathematical knowledge to be assessed. Lim and Ernest (1997), who conducted a textual analysis of the Malaysian primary and secondary curriculum statements, identified values which were explicitly and implicitly portrayed. Analysis was also carried out, through teacher questionnaires, to elicit a list of values which teachers believed characterized their professional behaviour. A comparison of the two categories of values revealed that "not all intended values are mentioned by the teachers and not all values mentioned by the mathematics teachers are explicitly or implicitly expressed in the curriculum" (Lim & Ernest, 1997, p. 7).

Other studies have focused on teachers of mathematics in classrooms and on the values-related activities in classrooms. A series of three 'Values In Mathematics Teaching' (VIMT) projects from Taiwan will be described in some detail in section 8. These projects covered the primary (Leu, 1999; Leu & Wu, 2000, 2001), junior high (Chang, 2000, 2001) and senior high levels (Chin & Lin, 1999b, 2000a, 2000b). They were initiated in 1997 in Taiwan to investigate and document mathematics teachers' mathematical and mathematics educational values, to investigate the extent to which these teachers were able to clarify their own value positions, and to investigate and document forms of teacher-student values interaction in the mathematics classroom. Data were gathered through questionnaire surveys, lesson observations, and interviews.

Chin and Lin (2000b) extended their values research with one of the teacher participants by administering test items and questionnaires to his students. They then interviewed six selected students from the class for the purpose of investigating the values revealed by their decisions to answer some questions and not others among the test items. When these values were compared with the values of their mathematics teacher, the correspondence was not consistent. Chin and Lin (2000b) explained this observation in terms of the differing identities of the teacher and his students. Nonetheless, each identity was related to the values upheld by the individual teacher or by an individual student.

The 'Values And Mathematics Project' (VAMP), described in greater detail in section 7 of this chapter, is another study which focused on values in the mathematics classroom. It was a three-year research study (conducted from 1999 to 2001) based in Australia. Utilising a range of methods, including teacher focus groups, questionnaire analysis, lesson observations and semi-structured interviews, VAMP attempted to investigate and document mathematics teachers' understanding of their own intended and implemented values. This was done in order to investigate the extent to which mathematics teachers could gain control over their own values teaching, and to increase the possibilities for more effective mathematics teaching through values education of practising and of preservice teachers.

Seah (2002) reported on some preliminary findings of an investigation into the range of cultural, mathematical, and mathematics educational value conflicts experienced by immigrant teachers in Australia. Like the textbook comparative studies mentioned above, this research project highlighted the similarities and differences among mathematical, mathematics educational, and general educational values across cultures. Further, the study also relates value conflicts to teachers' professional socialization experiences (Seah & Bishop, 2001).

The next two sections of this Chapter offer descriptions of two research studies on values in teaching mathematics, one based in Australia and the other in Taiwan. Although the focus of both is the mathematics teacher, they illustrate different aspects of the researching of values, as well as the range of values which can be found in mathematics classrooms.

7. CASE STUDY 1: THE VALUES AND MATHEMATICS PROJECT (VAMP)

The three-year *Values and Mathematics Project* (VAMP) was funded by the Australian Research Council. It began in 1999 with the organisation of a teacher focus group and a series of professional development sessions. During these sessions, primary and secondary mathematics teachers were encouraged to discuss both the actual and intended values that were part of their teaching of mathematics. The purpose of these discussions was to identify and understand the positions taken by mathematics teachers on value issues. These discussions also helped in the formulation of survey questions, and to identify teachers who would be willing to participate further in the project. The greatest difficulty initially faced by the project team was the recruitment of practising teachers. The researchers believed that this was due primarily to anxieties about having their value positions on mathematics and mathematics teaching analyzed.

7.1. *Clarifying Teachers' Intended and Implemented Values*

In the first stage of the VAMP research, knowledge gained from the focus group phase of the study was used to create questionnaires. These were disseminated to mathematics teachers across the state of Victoria in order to explore in detail the values held and taught by respondents. The results from the survey indicated that primary teachers, at least, considered values teaching an important part of mathematics education. They generally preferred mathematics' logical and creative aspects over its societal gate-keeping role. Pedagogically, they preferred *process/understanding* to *product/result*, with *testing* preferred least.

The surveys indicated the considerable influence of the teacher's own personal value framework, but perceived inconsistencies in the results suggested the possibility of competing sets of values, heavily dependent on context. The results also strongly indicated the absence of a common language within mathematics education with which to discuss values, retarding progress towards teacher awareness and control, and increasing the researchers' difficulties in researching this complex area (see FitzSimons, Seah, Bishop & Clarkson, 2000, for further details in relation to the survey data).

The emphasis in the next phase of the research was on working with eight volunteer teachers to clarify the relationships between their intended and implemented values. Throughout this process, teachers were encouraged to identify the role that values teaching plays in their classrooms, and how they were implementing these values.

To clarify the discussions of 'implemented values' for each teacher participant, classroom observations took place during three mathematics lessons. The teacher participants mostly chose the lessons for which they would be observed, and observations were generally conducted weekly. These lessons were videotaped with the researcher taking field notes of critical incidents and decision points. Following each classroom observation, an interview was held in which the observer suggested, using video clips as prompts, a description of the classroom which highlighted those values that were perceived as being implemented, and the behaviours associated with them. The focus of the interview was on comparisons between the 'intended values' planned by the teacher, and the 'implemented values' noted by the observer. The interview continued until consensus was arrived at between the teacher and observer concerning both the values taught in the lesson, and appropriate language with which to describe them.

The discussion below draws on the notes and data from that fieldwork of case studies in primary and secondary classrooms in order to illustrate the tensions teachers experienced between their intended and implemented values when teaching mathematics – an overview of which is provided by Table 1.

An important point which arose was whether the teachers nominated particular values that they were intending to teach and how these nominations related to whether the teachers were observed to be teaching the values explicitly or implicitly. The labels used to represent the values were either articulated (and justified) by teacher participants, or agreed upon during the discussions between individual teacher participants and their respective researchers. What follows in this section are examples of teachers' actions corresponding to five of the six cells in Table 1. The sixth cell, referring to values which were neither nominated nor observed, is necessarily blank.

7.1.1. Nominated explicitly/taught explicitly

The following is an example of a teacher explicitly nominating a value which was then observed to be explicitly taught in the classroom. Anna was a Year

Table 1. Categories of intended and implemented values observed

		Implemented/Observed		
		Taught explicitly	Taught implicitly	Not observed
Intended/ Nominated	Nominated	*Co-operation* (Anna)	*Self-esteem* (Ben)	*Creativity* (Colin)
	Not Nominated	*Individual differences* (Diane)	*Inclusiveness* (Edward)	—

1/2 classroom teacher in an outer suburban, middle class, co-educational Catholic school in Melbourne, the capital city of Victoria, Australia. In the pre-lesson interview, she nominated the value of the children *working co-operatively* in small groups. She mentioned that some children had found it difficult to select themselves into a group (for example, when she said: "make a group of five") due to their difficulty in counting and also for developmental reasons. She felt that students should be respected if they choose not to work in groups, and that teachers needed to weigh up the situation. She said that she knew, from past experience, that lessons could be 'sabotaged' by behavioural issues in *co-operation*.

Observation of the class revealed that Anna discussed the task at hand (measurement of students' heights with unmarked paper strips), including relevant vocabulary for comparison of heights. Time was given over for the students to form small groups of various sizes, including 'one'. After students had made groups of five, she asked each group to nominate one member as leader/reporter. She then spent time discussing the process of election, particularly as one student appeared to have usurped control of his group. Students then carried out the task of measuring each other's heights by marking a strip of paper with a coloured pen. It became apparent that one group of five boys was having trouble co-operating – it seemed they were in dispute over who was taller than whom! Following the measuring, the whole group reassembled to discuss group *co-operation* and the difficulties encountered.

In the post-lesson interview, Anna observed that *co-operation* and small group work "probably took up far more time than I had expected – it's what happens". She continued by saying that when children choose their own groups,

> you've got all those power relationships, whereas with the 'table groups' [teacher-selected groups] ... you probably get more 'on-task'. But I can't rescue you [the children] from that all the time. You have to be able to experience that stuff, you know.

Co-operative group work was an integral part of Anna's teaching in every subject area, not just mathematics. It appeared that other classes at this age-level operate similarly, and this may be a reflection of the ethos of the school which had a general 'Value of the Fortnight' programme in operation. The relative time spent in this lesson on *co-operation* compared to the actual task of measurement reflected the importance placed by Anna upon this particular value.

7.1.2. Nominated explicitly/taught implicitly

This category pertains to values which were explicitly nominated by a teacher, but which were implicitly taught in class. The following example involves Ben, who had had nine years of secondary mathematics teaching experience. He was head of the mathematics department at an independent boys' secondary college in an affluent inner, southeastern suburb of Melbourne.

The class observed was a small, Year 11 Further Mathematics class (average

age 17 years). He had chosen to teach this class of ten 'under-achieving' boys "partly to challenge myself to do something with the boys, and partly because I know that I could relate well with them".

A value, which Ben explicitly nominated to emphasize with his students, was student *self-worth/self-esteem* – one of two main values identified in the school's philosophy. He said that with this class, especially,

> the thing that I will really try to push is to – hopefully – get them to build their self-esteem up. Anybody who gets anything, even if it is not even close, will get a really huge pat at the back. That will really pump them up because they have had so many years of failure, of not doing well, getting poor results in tests, they really need building up, attending to.

Over the three lessons observed, it became evident that the value of *self-esteem* was often emphasized, although its portrayal was implicit in Ben's behaviour. That is, he neither introduced nor discussed the value with the students. As an example, one of the ways in which Ben picked students to answer a particular question in class was to 'target' those whom he believed might know the answer, but were too shy to speak out. Giving these students opportunities to demonstrate to themselves (and to the class) that they could "do it right", Ben felt, would be good for their self-esteem.

Another notable illustration took place when the students were having an in-class test. Ben moved among the students, commenting to individuals that they were doing particular questions well, and that their solutions were looking really good. For him, these personal remarks were good for the students' self-esteem. In fact, for a few students, he went so far as to tell them that "this is the formula", so that these students might have a chance to experience success. However, as the situation was an assessment, Ben confessed that he did not really feel comfortable with such an act (suggesting, perhaps, an unresolved personal conflict between competing values).

Ben felt that the value of *self-esteem* could be successfully portrayed without his stating it explicitly to the students. In fact, to attempt to promote *self-esteem* any more than he did might have explicitly reminded students that their self-esteem was low. This is an interesting point concerning the relative effectiveness of values being taught implicitly as opposed to explicitly, which was happening in Anna's case. There may also be an important aspect arising from the age of these students. Whatever the reason for the difference, Ben's top priority was to provide as many opportunities as possible for the students to experience success personally. In his own evaluation, Ben felt that his effort with this class over the last nine months had been rewarded. One particular example was a student named Ron:

> Ron in front was fantastic. He worked today. And, he would never, ever, at the start of the year, have said anything that might contradict what I was saying just because he had a different way of doing the same question.

He would sit there, with his head down, and never said anything. Now he is confident enough to say this is how he did it, and it is okay, and that is really good for him.

7.1.3. Nominated explicitly/not observed

In this category, values were nominated but were not observed in the actions of the teacher concerned. An example of the (non-)portrayal of such values was provided by Colin, who taught Year 7 (average age 13 years) mathematics in a state secondary college in a large country town north of Melbourne. According to Colin, most of the students in his school came from middle- and upper-class families.

Colin was a chemist in the local dairy centre before entering the teaching profession 14 years ago. Among the values he nominated and personally embraced was the value of *creativity* in doing mathematics. In his response to a hypothetical contextualized situation, in which he was asked if he would adhere to curriculum guidelines and thus show linkages between different mathematical topics, Colin remarked that the underlying value guiding his actions would be that which reflected *creativity*) "looking for and at alternative solutions".

However, the promotion of this value was not observed during the researcher's visits to the class. Moreover, Colin was aware of this. According to him, the reality of the class prevented him from portraying the value of *creativity*: few students had normally responded to his invitation. At the same time, Colin had to consider the less able students in the class too so that they would not get confused in the process.

Thus, Colin neither encouraged nor discouraged students to come up with alternative solutions. Colin felt that although he would compliment any student who provided an alternative solution, he was concerned that the weaker students did not get confused and lose interest in the context of a general discussion of the alternative solution in class. For him, it was a difficult situation. Often, there appeared to be an internal, personal conflict between values related to *creativity* and *confidence* and, as far as the three lessons observed were concerned, the latter seemed to have prevailed.

7.1.4. Not nominated/taught explicitly

In the example below, the teacher did not nominate that she was going to teach a certain value in the following lesson, but nevertheless did teach that value explicitly in the classroom.

Diane was an experienced primary teacher with a composite Year 3/4 class in a Catholic school, located in a small country town. In the preliminary interview she emphasized and nominated values of (a) *relating the mathematics to real-life*, (b) *strength of character*, and (c) *co-operation*. During the lesson on making three-dimensional shapes, however, one value that was observed being taught and also frequently explicitly addressed was *individual differences*. Despite not having nominated this value, she was continually celebrating individual differences in the lesson:

Remember the Lego activity? Who did it one way, who did it another? What works for one doesn't work for another, ...

In some way this was linked with other implicit ideas she had about mathematical *creativity*:

I hope I'm not going to get all cubes! ... Well done Mary, no-one's made that shape before!

In discussion after the lesson it was clear to Diane that she had been engaged in explicit values teaching. She also agreed that it was an important value for her:

They all get the same answer but there are different ways ... I need them to know that it doesn't matter which way you do it you come to the same conclusion ... to make them realize that there isn't a set pattern, and maths is the place to do it ... It doesn't matter which way you do it, it's correct if it works for you. ... We all see things differently ... but what comes from the parents is the (demand for) one right answer, meaning also one right way!

It was unclear why Diane had not explicitly nominated this value in her pre-lesson interview. One interpretation might be that it is such an integral part of her teaching that she didn't even recognize it as being important. However, in the subsequent observed lesson, Diane decided to nominate *individual differences* explicitly, and in this case she was looking for students' ways of estimating the results of calculations. As she said in the pre-lesson interview:

What I'm looking for (today) is what sort of strategies they use ... I'll be trying to make them realize that everyone's going to use different types of strategies. ... So what sort of strategies they use for estimating.

Again in this lesson phrases such as the following appeared:

Good ... any other way? Each of you might do it differently ... Did anyone else get anything different?

7.1.5. Not nominated/taught implicitly

The following is an example of a teacher who did not nominate particular values in the pre-lesson interview, but nevertheless taught them, albeit implicitly. Edward was an experienced teacher, with tertiary mathematics education lecturing experience, teaching in a substantial, private, co-educational secondary school in a regional city. The class observed was a Year 8 class, average age 14 years, described as a 'mixed ability' group, with 11 girls and 7 boys. The topic to be taught was 'Chance and Data: Comparison of world times in athletics for men and women'.

In the pre-lesson interview Edward identified the following values that he intended to teach in the following lesson: (a) *co-operation* – sharing of ideas for growth, (b) *valuing the individual* by taking 'this' approach to teaching, (c) showing mathematics as a *tool* – utilitarian, (d) clear *communication* through (i) effectiveness of graphing, (ii) verbal communication in small groups, and (iii) written summaries by students, and (e) a systematic approach – *logic*.

However, there were other values that seemed to be taught through the lesson, which were not planned, or nominated. One in particular became evident through Edward's frequent questioning that focused on the students having to clarify exactly what they were saying to him on a one-to-one basis, or when responding in a whole class situation. This was different from, and additional to, the notion of *communication* that Edward had planned to teach. There was a pattern to the questioning and to the requests for students to respond which seemed to the observer to be a valuing of *understanding, encouraging*, and *including*.

Edward agreed with this observation in the post-lesson interview. He explained that he did not attempt to close off the lesson at the point which was planned, but was content to let the students continue on – since the students had not been able to progress as fast as he had anticipated.

7.2. *Discussion*

The examples given in this section demonstrate that not only are different values taught in mathematics classrooms but these values may also be categorized according to the teachers' degrees of awareness of their own intentions to teach particular values. Another factor influencing categorization is the degree of teacher explicitness in teaching values. Nevertheless, it appears from the examples above that regardless of teacher intention and of the ways in which the values were implemented, all the teacher participants (except Colin, of course) felt that their respective identified values were taught effectively.

None of the teacher participants portrayed their values in any one of the five ways consistently during the lessons observed. It was not clear, however, why some intended values were not nominated explicitly by the teachers concerned. The most likely interpretation is that such values were so much a part of the teachers' pedagogy (e.g., with Edward and Diane) that the teacher had not assumed it necessary to mention them.

The examples also illustrate some of the factors influencing the implementation (or not) of intended values, and whether the teaching was to be carried out explicitly. There were influences at the institutional macro-level (Anna and Ben), at the institutional micro-level of classroom interactions (Ben and Colin), and even at the individual level of trying to resolve personally held competing values (Edward, Ben, and Colin). Other fieldwork data suggested the possible influence of other factors too, such as socio-cultural and systemic aspects.

The reader is cautioned not to infer from the data above that female and/or primary school teacher participants portrayed values explicitly, whereas the male and/or secondary school teachers would either portray values implicitly or choose not to teach selected values. That is an accidental result, as the same teachers were all observed to teach values associated with multiple cells in Table 1, and the values listed in Table 1 are not the only values associated with each individual teacher.

8. CASE STUDY 2: THE VALUES IN MATHEMATICS TEACHING (VIMT) PROJECTS

8.1. *Background to the VIMT Research*

All members of the VIMT team believed that values should be an integral part of any mathematics teaching in the classroom. The two preliminary assumptions of the study were:

1. The more mathematics teachers understand about their own value positions, the more flexible they will be in their thinking about – and practice in – their classroom teaching of mathematics; and
2. The more persons engaged in the various facets of mathematics education understand the processes, features, and mechanisms of teacher values clarification, the better position they will be in to develop effective programs for educating mathematics teachers about values.

Each of the three 'Values In Mathematics Teaching' (VIMT) projects, funded by the Taiwanese National Science Council, focused on different contexts of schooling in Taiwan, namely primary, junior high, and senior high levels. These three projects shared the goals of:

1. investigating and documenting mathematics teachers' values about mathematics and pedagogy,
2. investigating the extent to which mathematics teachers can clarify their own value positions, and
3. investigating and documenting forms of teacher-student values interaction in mathematics teaching.

The VIMT projects (Chang, 2000; Chin & Lin, 2000a; Leu & Wu, 2000) began in 1997. The investigation had three main foci: (a) to explore the intended and implemented values of groups of seven experienced teachers of mathematics; (b) to identify the activities of teacher-student values interaction; and (c) to examine the extent to which the teachers could clarify/change their own values. There were 2, 2, and 3 teacher participants for each level from primary to senior high. In the first phase of the studies, teachers' values and value clarification processes were identified in terms of one teacher case from each study, and the classroom teacher-student values interactions were recorded and analyzed. To extend the researchers' understandings of the nature and content of teacher values, the projects then went on to examine the stability of the methodologies used. The researchers tried to extend the results found in the previous stage by

adopting the same research procedure but focusing on another group of participant teachers. There were 2, 1, and 1 teacher participants for each level from
senior high to primary.

8.2. *Theoretical Base of the VIMT Research*

A statement of a mathematics teacher's values can be regarded as a carrier of
values, containing that teacher's principles for selecting and judging certain
identifications about issues of mathematics teaching in terms of whether they
are important or worthy of being adopted in his or her classroom teaching. A
core value statement contextualizes a teacher's values into a concise sentence
summarizing that teacher's major principles for instruction. Such a statement
describes a set of values that the teacher endorses. A values statement for a
school, as Taylor (2000) pointed out, is a goal-directed description indicating
the values by which that school intends its practices to be guided, and setting
out the values the school intends to promote and which it intends to demonstrate
through all aspects of its life. An example of a secondary teacher's values
statement might be: "We want our school to be caring and Christian, disciplining,
encouraging, happy". Such a statement then includes the values of *care*, *discipline*,
encouragement and *happiness* that the secondary school has chosen to emphasize
across the curriculum.

   In the VIMT projects, values were conceived and analyzed from three different
perspectives: social, psychological, and word meaning.

8.2.1. Values as pedagogical identities

In the VIMT projects, social and individual phenomena contributed to values
which were conceived as teachers' identities in relation to mathematics and
mathematics teaching. These identities underpinned the teachers' instructional
standards for classroom teaching (Chin & Lin, 2000a). They were personal
testable propositions about values. It was assumed that individuals as members
of a society or group strive to achieve satisfactory concepts or images of themselves (Tajfel, 1978). This self-concept constitute and individual's identity as a
unique entity within a society. When answering the question "who am I as a
mathematics teacher?" a teacher is invited to recognize the self by reflecting on
elements of that self. Such an identity is likely to refer to traits which are not
only characteristic of the self but also specifically distinguish the self from others
(Jarymowicz, 1998). The VIMT researchers especially considered values with
respect to mathematics classroom situations, for those values were likely to guide
their behaviour when teaching mathematics.

   Fereshteh (1996) defined teaching as an activity concerned with *intellectual*
and *knowledge acquisition*, *guidance* and *evaluation of learning processes*, and
artistic scientific discovery. In pursuit of these values, a teacher is expected to
play the role of a manager, a creator and organizer of lessons, a motivator who
fulfils students' needs, and a professional who is enjoying and developing his or
her career.

In a mathematics lesson the teacher's social-personal nature of identity is converted into the pedagogical realm, reflecting how and in what ways that teacher believes he or she should think in accord with such an identity. In this case, values are an integral part of the teacher's pedagogical content knowledge, for they affect such matters as the restructuring of content knowledge, the use of the textbook, the choice of pedagogical strategies, and perceptions of students' needs (Gudmundsdottir, 1990). These elements therefore reflect basic features of a teacher's identity with respect to mathematics teaching in the classroom. According to Kerr (1981), there can be no excellence in teaching unless teachers bring into their classrooms what they value and cherish about their subject matter, in particular, and about life, in general.

Individual mathematics teachers' values about mathematics and pedagogy, then, are seen as expressions of their pedagogical identities; they guide the orientation of the means and ends of specific actions of teaching and learning. They also serve as criteria by which objects, actions or events are evaluated in the context of situations which arise in mathematics classrooms. They underlie standards by which teachers see themselves as beings, concerning the rightfulness and desires for modes of conduct and the end-states of existence. For example, Schwartz (1992) attests to the centrality of the self in the value system; Rokeach (1973, 1979) suggests that values are integral to the self-identity whereby people strive to be authentic, moral beings by acting on the basis of values tied to their desired self-conceptions. Lydon (1996), in developing a theory of commitment, compared the roles of the self in terms of values, beliefs, and identities, and argued that these roles provide standards for the self and the basis of specific self-conceptions. Erikson (1963) maintained that value systems properly reflect those features of the development of eight identity development stages, and Chickering and Reisser (1993) offered a seven-vector model in which identity formation was tied to individuals' values development.

8.2.2. Values and the concept of worthiness

Chang (2000) regarded values in mathematics education as the ideas or concepts about the worth of something which is to be taught or thought about. His analysis was in terms of dictionary terminology, and referred to conceptions associated with something to be worthy of, something which is important, or desirable, for the value possessor. Based on a recognition of values which are inferred in its nature from value indicators involving cognitive, affective, and conative components, a three-step examination procedure is used which follows the steps of "to investigate what teacher participants says", "to check the consistency of a teacher's sayings with doings", and "to test the teacher's preferences".

8.2.3. Values as the products of valuing

Conceiving values as the products of the process of valuing, Leu and Wu (2000) adopted another theoretical approach, introduced by Raths et al. (1987), to identify teacher values. From the perspective of Raths et al's theory, values are defined as sets of indicators such as beliefs, attitudes, or feelings, meeting the requirements of the choosing, prizing, and acting procedures. What teachers talk about as meeting each of the three grouped criteria (that is to say, seven criteria) are considered as fulfilling the standards of a value. In this case, values are conceived of as teachers' beliefs, attitudes, and feelings, satisfying all the major criteria of choosing, prizing, and acting procedures.

8.3. *Research Approaches Used in the VIMT Projects*

Case study approaches, including classroom observations and pre- and post-lesson interviews, were used as the major mode of inquiry for exploring the values and value interaction activities of the mathematics teachers in the VIMT Project. There were three phases of investigation in the VIMT studies, the teacher phase, the interview phase, and the change/clarification phase.

In the teacher phase, teachers' responses to a pilot questionnaire survey and data from a pre-study classroom observation enabled the researchers to examine features of the teacher participants' teaching activities and planning, and this analysis generated criteria for the selection of cases. Case study teachers had all taught mathematics in public schools for between 10 and 30 years. In general, the type of classroom teaching they used was characterised by the teacher standing in front of the class and talking to the class, with all students grouped or working together as an intact class. That type of classroom environment is very common, and well accepted for teaching mathematics in Taiwan. As a result, the teachers' pedagogical thinking and teaching patterns revealed consistent salient features.

Pre- and post-lesson dialogue interviews, recommended by Chin and Lin (2000a), were adopted in all three VIMT studies. They were developed and used for interviews in which teachers play an active role in the conversation while researchers act as listeners and inquirers. The VIMT interviews with teachers allowed for reflective and introspective discussion and recursive probing procedures. The teachers were asked questions like: "What would you consider the most important things in your teaching? And why?" and "What kinds of message did you try to pass on to your students through mathematics teaching (for example the topic of mathematical induction)? And why?" and "For what reason did you teach mathematics like this?" The researchers edited certain critical events from the participants' teaching activities for use as probes in the post-lesson interviews. In the classroom interactive phase, several whole teaching topics were videotaped during one academic year for each teacher. All data were collected before and at the end of each of the taught topics.

Finally, in the change/clarification phase, teachers were required to reflect on their own teaching activities. The interviewers assisted them in this process, with special attention being given to issues identifying any changes in or clarifications of values by the teachers.

One conclusion reached by the VIMT researchers was that people's values cannot be fully uncovered by questionnaire surveys. The researchers tried to do that at the beginning of the projects, using several different questionnaire formats, but were not satisfied with data generated. The researchers then used questionnaire items as probes in interviews for the purpose of identifying, and examining, value indicators. In fact, the interview processes followed a dynamic and cyclic format of predicting, testing, and reflection (Wu & Lin, 1999). It was not always easy for an interviewer to grasp immediately what a teacher meant. In such cases, the use of a 'recursive probing approach' (Chin, Leu, & Lin, 2001) proved to be helpful.

Classroom observation was another important component of the study. The videotaping procedures were such that some important aspects of the teaching could have been lost. It was often difficult to predict which activities would be particularly important, and once a potentially interesting episode did begin to emerge, it was sometimes difficult to zoom in on key aspects of that episode.

Overall, the data-gathering procedures were successful in that they provoked teachers to attempt to clarify their values. For example, Ming (Chin & Lin, 2001b), a senior high school teacher who had taught mathematics for over 20 years, stated that after working with the researchers, his classroom teaching had become more sensitive to student needs about mathematical knowledge, student feelings about mathematics, and student language used in describing mathematical concepts. In another case, it seemed that a primary school teacher changed her values from being committed to predominantly 'telling' to becoming committed to 'listening' more to students during lessons (Leu & Wu, 2000). However, it should not be assumed that such successes demonstrated that mathematics teachers' values are easily changed.

Nor should it be assumed that value changes are permanent. In one case (that of teachers White and Wang) at the junior high school level (Chang, 2000), the teachers moved from being committed to the values of 'telling' and 'demonstrating' to 'listening' and 'discussion', and then back again to 'telling' and 'demonstrating'. The teachers explained that they developed a serious concern about the practicality of 'listening' and 'discussion' so far as school learning and assessment were concerned. For them, there were three more central values which practical teachers needed to acknowledge and operationalize: these were 'score-ism' in general education (where score-ism refers to the importance of getting high scores on the regular tests); 'specialism' in mathematics education; and 'absolutism' about mathematics.

8.4. *Teachers' Values and Values Research*

Three provocative conclusions in relations to teacher values emerged out of the projects which have been described. The first was that although the content of teachers' values varies, the values are social-individual in nature. For example, the mathematics teaching of Ms Chen, an elementary school teacher, was framed by the values of 'original enlightenment', listening', and 'self-awareness' (Leu, Wu & Wu, 1999). These were all closely related to her experiences with Buddhism (Leu, 1999). Her classroom teaching moved from a teacher 'chalk and talk' format, in which teacher posed and solved questions from the textbook and students listened, to one of addressing student autonomy, by asking for student inspiration and enlightenment, student articulation as well as silent work.

Two junior high teachers, White and Wang (Chang, 2000) although having been involved in an inservice training program in which a constructivist philosophy was expounded, were still committed to the values of 'score-ism' in education, 'specialism' in mathematics education, and 'absolutism' in mathematics. Thus, 'teaching by the syllabus' and 'raising student test scores' were the two most important and prevalent aims for them as junior high school teachers. In fact, those aims remain the two societal and parental requirements that almost all the schools and teachers in Taiwan have to face. However, some teachers in senior high schools, for instance Ming (Chin & Lin, 2000a), are particularly concerned about values related to the nature of mathematical knowledge and the affective aspects of mathematics learning. In Ming's teaching, the values of potential infinity, formality, and generality were central and important. The need for students to learn mathematical concepts and the need for students to experience pleasure in doing mathematics were used as a source for promoting intrinsic student motivation (Chin & Lin, 2001a; Chin, Leu & Lin, 2001).

The values revealed in the separate projects pointed to the existence of a set of varied yet deeply loaded values that mathematics teachers have. The revealed values also reflected the complexity of the task of teaching mathematics at different levels of schooling, as well as the social and individual constraints which exist within Chinese society so far as school education is concerned.

On the other hand, to clarify one's own values is not an easy thing to achieve, for either a researcher or a teacher. In the studies described, the researchers were stimulated by the act of comparing values identified in the Wang, Ming, and Chen's cases, in which different degrees of value clarification were related to different shifts of classroom teaching activities for the three teachers. Ming had a relatively high degree of value clarification and his classroom teaching was modified so that it took into account student needs and language. Chen had a lower value clarification but nevertheless attempted to teach mathematics through Buddhist values. Wang, on the other hand, seemed to be unaware of the values that she taught, and did not think that she was teaching any values in the mathematics classroom. Therefore, the researchers argued, the relationship between teacher's awareness of their values and the values that they actually taught in the classrooms was dialectical. Some teachers believed that they taught some kinds of values and were willing to try to modify their classroom teaching so that their practices would reflect their own values more fully. Others could neither clarify what their values were nor recognize how values influenced their own teaching. Some did not even believe in the existence of values in relation to mathematics teaching.

The above discussion draws attention to two important issues: first, "how can mathematics teachers be helped to become aware of, and clarify, their own values?" And second, "are there processes available which are likely to assist teacher educators who work with practising teachers to help the teachers become willing to engage in values identification and clarification?" These issues are discussed below.

Clearly, issues arising from attempts to change the values of teachers of mathematics are complex, and likely to vary from teacher to teacher. For example, although Lin, a primary school teacher in the VIMT Project, was able to identify, clarify, and modify her values (Leu & Wu, 2000), in the cases of the secondary teachers Ming and Wang value change was not so simple (Chang, 2000; Chin & Lin, 2001b). This might have been because of different ethos in the schools concerned, including the levels of autonomy each teacher had in the different schools. It might be advantageous for issues associated with achieving values changes to be considered within broader social-cultural contexts. In particular, with teaching there would appear to be a need to take practical classroom contexts into account.

The proposition put forward earlier, that "values should be an integral part of mathematics teaching", was supported by the analyses of data from classroom teachers, which revealed the hidden and to some extent subconscious nature of values which affect classroom teaching of mathematics. More effort, aimed at encouraging mathematics teachers to articulate and clarify their own values, is needed. For mathematics teacher educators, more effort should be put into developing values-related activities which will assist teachers to establish learning environments which will facilitate greater teacher and student communication and reflection in relation to the teaching and learning of specific mathematics content areas (Chin & Lin, 2001b).

9. IMPLICATIONS FOR PROFESSIONAL DEVELOPMENT

What are the practical outcomes and ideas of the values research which teachers of mathematics may find professionally useful and personally empowering? Earlier in this chapter we observed that the very act of teaching inevitably involves the explicit and implicit portrayal of values. This is as much the case in mathematics education as it is in any other area of education. Bishop (2001a) and Bishop, Clarkson, FitzSimons and Seah (2000) have explained how teachers' decisions in the mathematics classroom are shaped by their own values. What are needed, though, are proven strategies for raising teachers' consciousness of their constantly developing values systems.

9.1. *Teacher Awareness of, and Willingness to Teach, Values*

The general approach taken in the VAMP Project in Australia and in the VIMT Project in Taiwan was one of promoting teachers' conscious awareness of their mathematical, mathematics educational, and general educational values, by helping them clarify the relationship between their intended and implemented values. This assisted the teachers to exert greater control over their portrayal of professional values in mathematics classroom situations. That teachers' values portrayal underlies the majority of events taking place in any particular mathematics lesson is demonstrated by the range of classroom situation listed, such as lesson/curriculum planning, selection of textbooks and teaching aids, homework/assessment setting, as well as student grouping. Action research strategies put forward by Bishop (2001b) were based on the premise that teachers examine their professional decisions and actions, as well as their teaching materials, in terms of six mathematical values (see also, Bishop, 1996, 1998, 2001b).

Two affective issues associated with teachers' values have emerged. The first is concerned with the extent of consciousness associated with personal values. Being unaware of the reality of classroom values teaching, it took quite a long time for six of the seven Taiwanese teachers from primary to senior high schools to realize the roles that values play in their mathematics teaching (Chang, 2000; Leu & Wu, 2000). The one exception was a senior high school master teacher who, in a short period of time, passed through five stages of values clarification and moved from being a value carrier to being a value communicator. This teacher described the significant features of his values teaching to others in terms of his own classroom incidents (Chin & Lin, 2000b). This notion is also supported by research findings in Australia (see FitzSimons, Seah, Bishop & Clarkson, 2001) that different values were taught by different teachers according to the degree of awareness of the teachers' intentions to teach particular values.

The second issue is about teachers' willingness or conation to teach particular values. Varying degrees of explicitness of values teaching were examined in the Australian research (Bishop, FitzSimons, Seah & Clarkson, 2001; FitzSimons et al., 2001), and it was found that the number of values explicitly taught by the teachers, either consciously or subconsciously, was greater than the number of implicitly taught values. However, in the research carried out by Chang (2000), Leu and Wu (2000), and Chin and Lin (2001b), not only were fewer teachers aware of the values being taught, but also teachers were often unwilling to teach certain values. They even refused to teach values that they had taught before.

Thus, there are pedagogical tensions associated with the extent of explicitness, willingness, and awareness of teachers' classroom values teaching. In short, there appear to be varying pedagogical and social tensions for mathematics teachers in different cultures. For the Australian teachers, the tensions of values teaching were more about personal consciousness and explicitness of engaging in some particular values. However, for Taiwanese teachers the tensions seem more to do with conative aspects than with individual awareness of values teaching.

Taplin (2001) offered three ways of integrating values education into school mathematics programs: (a) influencing teachers' approaches to teaching; (b) using mathematics as a tool with which to practise values; and (c) discussions of values exemplified in the lives of great mathematicians. In relation to the first approach, Taplin (2001) discussed the kinds of values implied by teacher approaches such as problem-solving, cooperative learning, and valuing individual differences. Although Taplin suggested ways by which teachers could explore the integration of values education into existing school mathematics programs without the need to change those programs, the degree to which this would be successful is unknown. Successful values education would depend on the extent to which there is match between the teacher's own values and those implied by the particular process which is being applied.

Taplin's (2001) second approach, that of introducing activities and thereby using mathematics as a tool to relate to values, provided the context for Chin and Lin's (2001a) paper. Mathematics teacher values and identities were discussed based on a 'value-loaded activity' (the 'Tower of Hanoi') used by a teacher participant to develop student ideas of 'potential infinity'. Chin and Lin (2001a) argued that "to inform classroom practices, the practitioners need more supports on learning and constructing value-loaded activities that might be useful ... [where the] means of planning and enacting values are the foci" (p. 255)

9.2. *Value Transition and Identity Development*

Three approaches to value transition and identity development can be found in the literature on teacher development. With the first approach the process is conceived as professional knowledge growth/change – for example, growth or change occurs in relation to pedagogical content knowledge or teachers' knowledge about students. Some researchers (e.g., Even, Tirosh & Markovits, 1996) have worked from the assumption that teacher possession of certain pedagogical knowledge is necessary for a useful activity for a teacher education programme to be developed.

Another approach might be to assist teachers to identify and shape their own beliefs. For instance, they might be assisted to identify their beliefs in relation to the role of 'authority' in mathematics classrooms. In such a case, one growth indicator could be the conceptualization of a process by which a teacher can become a reflective person (see, e.g., Cooney, Shealy, and Arvold, 1998). This could use a theoretical framework of change in beliefs to set up activities in educational programmes for individual teachers. The third approach might be to consider the process of values change as an intertwined web of conceptual changes, including knowledge, beliefs, and context, using a situated learning model to monitor the professional growth of a group of prospective elementary teachers (see, e.g., Llinares, 1996). This approach combines knowledge and beliefs into the situated context, as a means for promoting teachers' development.

Although these approaches have been productive it could be argued that they have not recognized sufficiently that teachers of mathematics are all in the process of pedagogical identity development through which they are learning to see themselves as becoming the teachers that they value most. Therefore, a fourth aspect of conceiving teacher professional development is to draw attention to their identity development and value transition.

Some explicit ideas have been developed concerning the role of identity and value in education and learning. For example, Chickering and Reisser (1993) identify a seven-vector model, in which one vector is *establishing identity*, which addresses the development of a person from confusion about 'who I am' to clarification of self-concept through roles and lifestyle in the process of education.

According to Furlong and Maynard (1995), in order that student teachers can develop and maintain their self-images as teachers, they need to identify four interconnecting dimensions. First, they need to establish suitable professional relationships by which awareness of self to the notion of '*me-as-a-teacher*' comes to be related to the idea of individual teacher identity. Another vector of the Chickering and Reisser (1993) model is '*developing integrity*', which concerns the process of humanizing and personalizing individuals' values through education. In discussion of a continual development of values from early youth to old age, Erikson (1963) indicated that the value systems properly reflect those features of the development of eight identity stages. Loevinger's (1976) nine-stage model of ego development also stresses the unity of personality by contending that "what one perceives and understands bears the imprint of the ego" (p. 9) and "it is close to what the person thinks of his self" (p. 67). The stages of conscientious, autonomous, and integrated are more aligned with values transition and identities development. These are stages concerning the search of one's standards, uniqueness, and integrity.

Researchers in mathematics education have also called for attention to the problem of unravelling the complex relationships which exist between identity formation and values (see e.g., Bishop et al., 2000; FitzSimons et al., 2000). Bishop (2001a) suggested several ways of clarifying and educating student teachers with respect to values in mathematics teaching. He recommended approaches such as developing sensitivity towards value issues, engaging in values clarification and values-related activities, and providing and analyzing critical teaching incidents. Lerman (2001), in a review of research perspectives on mathematics teacher education, also argued for a focus on the development and articulation of teacher identities. Based on the results of two case studies, Chin, Leu, and Lin (2001) described activities that could be used to educate mathematics teachers about pedagogical values through values articulation and values clarification.

In the process of teacher professional development, five transitional stages in identity development can be theorized. At the *student* teacher stage, a teacher sees his or her identity as 'a student' in which learning and thinking different ethos and ideas are of importance for a learner. In the *probationary* teacher stage, one might see oneself as 'a classroom practitioner' who has the task of integrating theory with practice. In the following *induction* stage, the teacher becomes a novice in the teaching community, being considered as 'a newcomer'. Later, teachers gradually reach the *experienced* teacher stage and begin to regard themselves as 'old-timers'. Then, finally, teachers approach the fifth *expert teacher* stage, when they are considered as 'master' teachers within the teaching community.

This five-stage development sequence defines a possible path for a teacher's identity transition, for being a mathematics teacher can normally be associated with having certain values compatible with that identity. Ming, a teacher studied by Chin and Lin (1999b), recollected his own professional growth in terms of his developing through a three-stage procedure, from a textbook *follower*, to an *own-style builder*, to a *value characterizer*. Ming's pedagogical identities moved from a knowledge transmitter, to a mathematics tutor, to a contextual knowledge initiator. At each stage there were accompanying salient values, such as being committed to the values of mathematical structure and knowledge, to values associated with educational realities, and pleasure. Therefore, different teacher identities incorporated different pedagogical identities and values.

10. RESEARCH CHALLENGES AND DIFFICULTIES

We finish this chapter by briefly considering several research challenges and difficulties unique to the nature of the research topic of values. In empirical research involving human participants, "the subject of 'values' seems to immediately provoke in many teachers notions of judgement and finding fault" (Clarkson, Bishop, FitzSimmons & Seah, 2000, p. 158; see also, Chin & Lin, 1999a). This is perhaps because values have often been associated with virtues, which in turn provides a gauge of the goodness and worthiness of a person (see also, FitzSimmons et al., 2001). At the same time, it may be due to the relatively new research notion of values adopted by researchers in the field of mathematics education. It could also be a consequence of the internalized and personalized nature of values, or the lingering assumption held by many teachers that it is dangerous to discuss one's own values with others for by so doing one can expose one's inner self.

There are implications of all of this for evaluating the quality of values research, requiring as it does teachers who feel comfortable enough to participate in such research. Indeed, it may be the case that teachers who volunteer to take part in such research studies usually possess a set of common values. Even among teacher participants, the personal nature of values may well affect their individual willingness to share honestly their thoughts and views during interviews with researchers. One strategy in response to this latter research concern, adopted by one of the VIMT projects in Taiwan, was to conduct the interviews with a "recursive probing approach" (Chin & Lin, 1999a).

Another methodological challenge in conducting research on values with teachers of mathematics is "the lack of an appropriate and shared vocabulary to discuss the types of values ... based in mathematics and mathematics education" (Chin & Lin, 2000b; Clarkson, Bishop, FitzSimons & Seah, 2000; Clarkson, Bishop, Seah & FitzSimons, 2000). This may be construed to affect the quality of communication between researchers and teacher participants; indeed, it may in part account for the failure of teacher participants in the VAMP project to nominate values which were subsequently observed in their respective lessons (see, Seah, Bishop, FitzSimons & Clarkson, 2001).

The paradox here for the VAMP project was that:

> In a very real sense, this problem of language was inescapable ... [A] central feature of this project is to explore together the linguistic framework that we as researchers and teachers will use to try and share our understanding

of the values that they teach in their mathematical classrooms. Thus it was decided that a set lexicon to be made available to teachers involved in the project was neither possible nor practicable.

(Clarkson, Bishop, FitzSimons & Seah, 2000, p. 157)

This lack of appropriate lexicon with which to discuss values may be due to the fuzzy boundaries which exist between definitions of values and definitions of value indicators. In itself, this difficulty in differentiating between values and value indicators also poses practical problems when interpreting written responses, observed actions and recorded interviews of teacher participants (Chin & Lin, 1999a, 2000a).

However, perhaps the greatest challenges in documenting values during research comes from the fact that researchers themselves inevitably belong to different (ethnic, institutional, etc.) cultures, and are not value-free as individuals; thus, it is expected that different researchers place different significance and interpretations on the same phenomenon. Of course, this is always a challenge to any researcher, but it seems to have particular significance in research on teachers' values. With non-reactive studies this may perhaps be addressed with the use of a checklist of observable value signals, such as in the textbook analysis in Seah (1999). With studies involving lesson observations and participant interviews, however, a possible strategy is the regular 'checking-back' confirmations and clarifications with the participants by the researchers, which the VAMP and VIMT projects have found to be useful.

As was stated at the start of this chapter there is very little research which is focussed on values in mathematics teaching, although the two cases of research studies described in this chapter can perhaps indicate how research can be done in this field. They have certainly helped to clarify the kinds of research that should now begin to be explored if the task of professional development concerning the values education of teachers of mathematics is to progress. The research challenges therefore include the following:

1. To clarify and theorize the principal values which teachers of mathematics have with respect to mathematics, mathematics teaching, and mathematics learning, and how these develop.
2. To clarify and theorize the relationship between teachers' values, their values when teaching, and students' learning of values.
3. To identify differences between implicit and explicit values teaching in mathematics, and the significance of these differences.
4. To clarify whether explicit values teaching is more effective than implicit values teaching in changing student values towards mathematics.
5. To investigate whether it is important for teachers' development to help them change subconscious value decisions into conscious value decisions.
6. To discover ways to help mathematics teachers develop their values teaching.

REFERENCES

Alexander, R. (2002, April). *French pedagogy*. Paper presented at the 83rd Annual Meeting of the American Educational Research Association, New Orleans, LA.

Allchin, D. (1999). Values in science: An educational perspective. *Science and Education, 8*, 1–12.

Aplin, N., & Saunders, J. (1996, March). *Values and value priorities of Singaporean and Australian swimmers* [Online]. Australian Association for Research in Education. Available: http://www.swin.edu.au/aare/conf96/APLIN96.422 [1999, May 20].

Billett, S. (1998). Transfer and social practice. *Australian and New Zealand Journal of Vocational Education Research, 6*(1), 1–25.

Bishop, A. J. (1988). *Mathematical enculturation: A cultural perspective on mathematics education*. Dordrecht, The Netherlands: Kluwer Academic Publishers.

Bishop, A. J. (1991). Mathematical values in the teaching process. In A. J. Bishop, S. Mellin-Olsen & J. van Dormole (Eds.), *Mathematical knowledge: Its growth through teaching* (pp. 195–214). Dordrecht, The Netherlands: Kluwer Academic Publishers.

Bishop, A. J. (1994). Cultural conflicts in mathematics education: Developing a research agenda. *For the Learning of Mathematics, 14*(2), 15–18.

Bishop, A. J. (1996, June). *How should mathematics teaching in modern societies relate to cultural values – some preliminary questions*. Paper presented at the Seventh Southeast Asian Conference on Mathematics Education, Hanoi, Vietnam.

Bishop, A. J. (1998). Culture, values and assessment in mathematics. In H. S. Park, Y. H. Choe, H. Shin & S. H. Kim (Eds.), *Proceedings of the ICMI-East Asia Regional Conference on Mathematics Education* (Vol. 1, pp. 27–37). Seoul, Korea: Korea Society of Mathematical Education.

Bishop, A. J. (2001a). Educating student teachers about values in mathematics education. In F.-L. Lin & T. J. Cooney (Eds.), *Making sense of mathematics teacher education* (pp. 233–244). Dordrecht, The Netherlands: Kluwer Academic Publishers.

Bishop, A. J. (2001b). What values do you teach when you teach mathematics? *Teaching Children Mathematics, 7*(6), 346–349.

Bishop, A. J., Clarkson, P., FitzSimons, G., & Seah, W. T. (2000). Why study values in mathematics teaching? Contextualising the VAMP project. In W. S. Horng & F.-L. Lin (Eds.), *Proceedings of the HPM 2000 International Conference on History in Mathematics Education* (Vol. 2, pp. 147–154). Taipei: National Taiwan Normal University.

Bishop, A. J., FitzSimons, G., Seah, W. T., & Clarkson, P. (2001). Do teachers implement their intended values in mathematics classrooms? In M. van den Heuvel-Panhuizen (Ed.), *Proceedings of the 25th Conference of the International Group for the Psychology of Mathematics Education* (Vol. 2, pp. 169–176). Utrecht, The Netherlands: Utrecht University.

Bishop, A. J., & Whitfield, R. C. (1972). *Situations in teaching*. Berkshire, UK: McGraw-Hill.

Board of Studies (2000). *Mathematics: Curriculum and standards framework II*. Carlton, Victoria, Australia: Board of Studies.

Brenner, M. E., Herman, S., Ho, H.-Z., & Zimmer, J. M. (1999). Cross-national comparison of representational competence. *Journal for Research in Mathematics Education, 30*(5), 541–557.

Brown, R. (2001, September). *Educational values and summative assessment: A view across three educational systems*. Paper presented at the British Educational Research Association 2001 Annual Conference, Leeds, UK.

Cai, J. (1986). Aesthetic education in mathematics education [in Mandarin]. *Bulletin of Mathematics* [in Mandarin], *86*(2), 14–19.

Cao, Z., Seah, W. T., & Bishop, A. J. (2001). *A comparison of mathematical values conveyed in mathematics textbooks in Australia and China*. Unpublished manuscript, Monash University, Melbourne.

Carpenter, T. P., Lindquist, M. M., Matthews, W., & Silver, E. A. (1983). Results of the third NAEP mathematics assessment: Secondary schools. *Mathematics Teacher, 76*(9), 652–659.

Chang, C. K. (2000). Score-ism as their pedagogical value of two junior high mathematics teachers. In W. S. Horng & F.-L. Lin (Eds.), *Proceedings of the International Conference on History in Mathematics Education* (Vol. 2, pp. 172–177). Taipei: National Taiwan Normal University.

760 *Bishop, Seah and Chin*

Chang, C.-K. (2001). The Taiwanese teachers' beliefs and values in mathematics education. In M. van den Heuvel-Panhuizen (Ed.), *Proceedings of the 25th Conference of the International Group for the Psychology of Mathematics Education* (Vol. 1, p. 294). Utrecht, The Netherlands: Freudenthal Institute.

Chickering, A. W., & Reisser, L. (1993). *Education and identity.* San Francisco: Jossey-Bass.

Chin, C., & Lin, F.-L. (1999a). Interpreting mathematics teachers' pedagogical values. In F.-L. Lin (Ed.), *Proceedings of the 1999 International Conference on Mathematics Teacher Education* (Vol. 1, pp. 326–331). Taipei: National Taiwan Normal University.

Chin, C., & Lin, F.-L. (1999b). One mathematics teacher's pedagogical values: Intended, implemented, and self phases. In F.-L. Lin (Ed.), *Proceedings of the 1999 International Conference on Mathematics Teacher Education* (Vol. 1, pp. 315–324). Taipei: National Taiwan Normal University.

Chin, C., & Lin, F.-L. (2000a). A case study of a mathematics teacher's pedagogical values: Use of a methodological framework of interpretation and reflection. In *Proceedings of the National Science Council, Part D: Mathematics, Science, and Technology Education, 10*(2), 90–101.

Chin, C., & Lin, F.-L. (2000b). Values and values statements emerged in students' preferences on test items: A case study from mathematical induction. In W. S. Horng & F.-L. Lin (Eds.), *Proceedings of the International Conference on History in Mathematics Education.* Taipei: National Taiwan Normal University.

Chin, C., & Lin, F.-L. (2001a). Value-loaded activities in mathematics classrooms. In M. van den Heuvel-Panhuizen (Ed.), *Proceedings of the 25th Conference of the International Group for the Psychology of Mathematics Education* (Vol. 2, pp. 249–256). Utrecht, The Netherlands: Utrecht University.

Chin, C., & Lin, F.-L. (2001b). Mathematics teacher's pedagogical value clarification and its relationship to classroom teaching. In *Proceedings of the National Science Council, Part D: Mathematics, Science, and Technology Education, 11*(3), 114–125.

Chin, C., Leu, Y.-C., & Lin, F.-L. (2001). Pedagogical values, mathematics teaching and teacher education: Case studies of two experienced teachers. In F.-L. Lin & T. J. Cooney (Eds.), *Making sense of mathematics teacher education* (pp. 247–269). Dordrecht, The Netherlands: Kluwer Academic Publishers.

Clarkson, P. C., & Bishop, A. J. (1999, July). *Values and mathematics education.* Paper presented at the 51st Conference of the International Commission for the Study and Improvement of Mathematics Education, University College, Chichester, UK.

Clarkson, P. C., Bishop, A. J., FitzSimons, G. E., & Seah, W. T. (2000). Methodology challenges and constraints in the VAMP project. In W. S. Horng & F.-L. Lin (Eds.), *Proceedings of the HPM 2000 Conference: History in Mathematics Education: Challenges for a New Millennium* (Vol. 2, pp. 155–162). Taipei: National Taiwan Normal University.

Clarkson, P. C., Bishop, A., FitzSimons, G. E., & Seah, W. T. (2001). Lifelong learning and values: An undervalued legacy of mathematics education?' In G. E. FitzSimons, J. O'Donoghue & D. Coben (Eds.), *Adult and lifelong education in mathematics: Papers from the Working Group for Action (WGA) 6, 9th International Congress on Mathematics Education (ICME9)* (pp. 37–46). Melbourne: Learning Mathematics, and Language Australia.

Clarkson, P. C., Bishop, A. J., Seah, W. T., & FitzSimons, G. E. (2000, December). *Methodology challenges and constraints in the Values and Mathematics Project.* Paper presented at the Australian Association for Research in Education Conference, Sydney.

Cobb, P. (1996, July). *Accounting for mathematical learning in the social context of the classroom.* Paper presented at the 8th International Congress on Mathematical Education, Seville, Spain.

Cooney, T. J., Shealy, B. E., & Arvold, B. (1998). Conceptualizing belief structures of pre-service secondary mathematics teachers. *Journal for Research in Mathematics Education, 29*(3), 306–333.

Cummings, W. K. (1996). Asian values, education and development. *Compare, 26*(3), 287–303.

D'Ambrosio, U. (1985). Ethnomathematics and its place in the history and pedagogy of mathematics. *For the Learning of Mathematics, 5*(1), 44–48.

D'Ambrosio, U. (1990). The role of mathematics education in building a democratic and just society. *For the Learning of Mathematics, 10*(3), 20–23.

Dormolen, J. von (1986). Textual analysis. In B. Christiansen, A. G. Howson & M. Otte (Eds.),

Perspectives on mathematics education (pp. 141–171). Dordrecht, The Netherlands: D. Reidel Publishing,

Dossey, J. A. (1992). The nature of mathematics: Its role and its influence. In D. A. Grouws (Ed.), *Handbook of research on mathematics teaching and learning* (pp. 39–48). New York: Macmillan Publishing Company.

Eckermann, A.-K. (1994). *One classroom, many cultures: Teaching strategies for culturally different children.* Sydney: Allen and Unwin.

Erikson, E. H. (1963). *Childhood and society.* New York: Norton and Company.

Even, R., Tirosh, D., & Markovits, Z. (1996). Teacher subject matter knowledge and pedagogical content knowledge: Research and development. In L. Puig & A. Guitierrez (Eds.), *Proceedings of the 20th Annual Conference of the International Group for the Psychology of Mathematics Education* (Vol. 1, pp. 119–134). Valencia, Spain: International Group for the Psychology of Mathematics Education.

Fasheh, M. (1982). Mathematics, culture, and authority. *For the Learning of Mathematics, 3*(2), 2–8.

Fereshteh, H. (1996). The nature of teaching, effective instruction, and roles to play: A social foundation's perspective. *Contemporary Education, 68*(1), 73–75.

FitzSimons, G., Seah, W. T., Bishop, A. J., & Clarkson, P. (2000). Conceptions of values and mathematics education held by Australian primary teachers: Preliminary findings from VAMP. In W. S. Horng & F.-L. Lin (Eds.), *Proceedings of the HPM 2000 International Conference on History in Mathematics Education* (Vol. 2, pp. 163–171). Taipei: National Taiwan Normal University.

FitzSimons, G., Seah, W. T., Bishop, A., & Clarkson, P. (2001). Beyond numeracy: Values in the mathematics classroom. In J. Bobis, B. Perry & M. Mitchelmore (Eds.), *Numeracy and beyond: Proceedings of the Twenty-Fourth Annual Conference of the Mathematics Education Research Group of Australasia* (Vol. 1, pp. 202–209). Turramurra, Australia: Mathematics Education Research Group of Australasia.

Furlong, J., & Maynard, T. (1995). *Mentoring student teachers.* London: Routledge.

Grouws, D. A. (Ed.) (1992). *Handbook of research on mathematics teaching and learning.* New York: Macmillan.

Gudmundsdottir, S. (1990). Values in pedagogical content knowledge. *Journal of Teacher Education, 41*(3), 44–52.

Hall, B. P. (1994). *Values shift: A guide to personal and organizational transformation.* Twin Lights, MA.

Halstead, J. M. (1996). Values and values education in schools. In J. M. Halstead & M. J. Taylor (Eds.), *Values in education and education in values* (pp. 3–14). London: Falmer Press.

Hamberger, N. M., & Moore, R. L. (1997). From personal to professional values: Conversations about conflicts. *Journal of Teacher Education, 48*(4), 301–310.

Hill, B. V. (1991). *Values education in Australian schools.* Hawthorn, Victoria: Australian Council for Educational Research.

Hofstede, G. (1997). *Cultures and organizations: Software of the mind.* New York: McGraw-Hill.

Horwood, J. (1999). Cultural aspects of the definition of the secondary mathematics curriculum. In M. A. Clements & Y. P. Leong (Eds.), *Cultural and language aspects of science, mathematics, and technical education* (pp. 326–334). Gadong, Brunei Darussalam: Universiti Brunei Darussalam.

Jarymowicz, M. (1998). Self-we-others schemata and social identification. In S. Worchel, J. F. Morales, D. Páez & J.-C. Deschamps (Eds.), *Social identity: International perspectives* (pp. 44–52). London: SAGE.

Joseph, G. G. (1993). A rationale for a multicultural approach to mathematics. In D. Nelson, G. G. Joseph & J. Williams (Eds.), *Multicultural mathematics* (pp. 1–24). Oxford, UK: Oxford University Press.

Jurdak, M. (1999). The role of values in mathematics education. *Humanistic Mathematics Network Journal, 21*, 39–45.

Kerr, D. (1981). The structure of quality in teaching. In J. Soltis (Ed.), *Philosophy and education* (pp. 61–93). Chicago: University of Chicago.

Kluckhohn, C. (1962). Values and value-orientations in the theory of action: An exploration in definition and classification. In T. Parsons & E. A. Shils (Eds.), *Toward a general theory of action* (pp. 388–433). New York: Harper and Row.

Kohlberg, L. (1981). *The philosophy of moral development: Moral stages and the idea of justice.* Los Angeles: Harper and Row.

Krathwohl, D. R., Bloom, B. S., & Masia, B. B. (1964). *Taxonomy of educational objectives, the classification of educational goals: Handbook 2: Affective Domain.* New York: Longmans.

Kroeber, A. L., & Kluckhohn, C. K. M. (1952). Culture: A critical review of concepts and definitions. *Papers of the Peabody Museum of American Archaeology and Ethnology* (Vol. 47). Cambridge, MA: Harvard University.

Kwast, L. E. (1992). Understanding culture. In R. D. Winter & S. C. Hawthorne (Eds.), *Perspectives on the world Christian movement: A reader* (C3–C4). Pasadena, CA: William Carey Library.

Lee, M. J., & Cockman, M. (1995). Values in children's sport: Spontaneously expressed values among young athletes. *International Review for the Sociology of Sport, 30,* 337–349.

Lerman, S. (2001). A review of research perspectives on mathematics teacher education. In F.-L. Lin & T. J. Cooney (Eds.), *Making sense of mathematics teacher education* (pp. 33–52). Dordrecht, The Netherlands: Kluwer Academic Publishers.

Leu, Y.-C. (1999). The influences of Buddhism on an elementary mathematics teacher's professional development. In F.-L. Lin (Ed.), *Proceedings of the 1999 International Conference on Mathematics Teacher Education* (Vol. 1, pp. 332–353). Taipei: National Taiwan Normal University.

Leu, Y.-C., & Wu, C.-J. (2000). An elementary teacher's pedagogical values in mathematics: Clarification and change. In W. S. Horng & F.-L. Lin (Eds.), *Proceedings of the International Conference on History in Mathematics Education* (Vol. 2, pp. 178–194). Taipei: National Taiwan Normal University.

Leu, Y.-C., & Wu, C.-J. (2001). Mathematics pedagogical value system centering on mathematics knowledge acquisition in elementary school. In M. van den Heuvel-Panhuizen (Ed.), *Proceedings of the 25th Conference of the International Group for the Psychology of Mathematics Education* (Vol. 1, p. 336). Utrecht, The Netherlands: Freudenthal Institute.

Leu, Y.-C., Wu, Y.-Y., & Wu, C.-J. (1999). A Buddhistic value in an elementary mathematics classroom. In O. Zaslavsky (Ed.), *Proceedings of the 23rd PME Conference* (Vol. 3, pp. 233–240). Haifa, Israel: Israel Institute of Technology.

Lewis-Shaw, C. P. (2001). Measuring values in classroom teaching and learning. In D. Clarke (Ed.), *Perspectives on practice and meaning in mathematics and science classrooms* (pp. 155–196). Dordrecht, The Netherlands: Kluwer Academic Publishers.

Lim, C. S., & Ernest, P. (1997, March). *Values in mathematics education: What is planned and what is espoused?* Paper presented at the Conference of the British Society for Research into Learning Mathematics, Nottingham, UK.

Lim-Teo, S. K. (1998). Seeking a balance in mathematics education – The Singapore story. In H. S. Park, Y. H. Choe, H. Shin & S. H. Kim (Eds.), *Proceedings of the ICMI-East Asia Regional Conference on Mathematical Education* (Vol. 1, pp. 315–329). Seoul, Korea: Korea Society of Mathematical Education.

Lin, F.-L., & Chin, C. (1998). *Study on values in mathematics education in Taiwan.* Unpublished manuscript, National Taiwan Normal University and National Tsing Hua University, Taiwan.

Llinares, S. (1996). Improving knowledge, professional growth and monitoring the development of mathematics teachers: A necessary integrating of theoretical frameworks. In L. Puig & A. Guitierrez (Eds.), *Proceedings of the 20th Annual Conference of the International Group for the Psychology of Mathematics Education* (Addenda, pp. 23–31). Valencia, Spain: International Group for the Psychology of Mathematics Education.

Loevinger, J. (1976). *Ego development: Conceptions and theories.* San Francisco: Jossey-Bass.

Lydon, J. (1996). Toward a theory of commitment. In C. Seligman, J. M. Olson & M. P. Zanna (Eds.), *The psychology of values: The Ontario Symposium* (Vol. 8, pp. 191–213). Mahwah, NJ: Lawrence Erlbaum Associates.

Martin, B. (1997). Mathematics and social interests. In A. B. Powell & M. Frankenstein (Eds.), *Ethnomathematics: Challenging Eurocentrism in mathematics education* (pp. 155–171). Albany, NY: State University of New York Press.

McConatha, J. T., & Schnell, F. (1995). The confluence of values: Implications for educational research and policy. *Educational Practice and Theory, 17*(2), 79–83.

McLeod, D. B. (1992). Research on affect in mathematics education: A reconceptualisation. In D. A. Grouws (Ed.), *Handbook of research on mathematics teaching and learning* (pp. 575–594). New York: Macmillan.

Munro, J. (1996). Cognitive styles and mathematics learning. *Australian Journal of Remedial Education, 27*(5), 19–24.

Nebres, B. F. (1995, May). *Mathematics education in an era of globalisation: Linking education, society, and culture in our region.* Paper presented at the Regional Collaboration in Mathematics Education Conference, Monash University, Victoria, Australia.

Neuman, W. L. (1997). *Social research methods: Qualitative and quantitative approaches* (3rd ed.). Boston, MA: Allyn and Bacon.

Nixon, J. (1995). Teaching as a profession of values. In J. Smyth (Ed.), *Critical discourses on teacher development* (pp. 215–224). London: Cassell.

Orlich, D. C., Harder, R. J., Callahan, R. C., Kauchak, D. P., Pendergrass, R. A., Keogh, A. J., & Gibson, H. (1990). *Teaching strategies: A guide to better instruction* (3rd ed.). Lexington, MA: D. C. Heath.

Orton, A. (1992). *Learning mathematics: Issues, theory and classroom practice.* London: Cassell.

Pinxten, R. (1994). Ethnomathematics and its practice. *For the Learning of Mathematics, 14*(2), 23–25.

Pollard, A. (1982). A model of classroom coping strategies. *British Journal of Sociology of Education, 3*(1), 19–37.

Proctor, R. (1991). *Value-free science? Purity and power in modern knowledge.* Cambridge, MA: Harvard University Press.

Raths, L. E., Harmin, M., & Simon, S. B. (1987). Selections from 'values and teaching'. In J. P. F. Carbone (Ed.), *Value theory and education* (pp. 198–214). Malabar, FL: Robert E. Krieger.

Rescher, N. (1969). *Introduction to value theory.* Englewood Cliffs, NJ: Prentice-Hall.

Rokeach, M. (1973). *The nature of human values.* New York: The Free Press.

Rokeach, M. (1979). *Understanding human values: Individual and social.* New York: The Free Press.

Schlöglmann, W. (2001, June). *Affect and cognition: Two poles of a learning process.* Paper presented at the 3rd Nordic Conference on Mathematics Education, Kristianstad, Sweden.

Schmidt, W. H., McKnight, C. C., Valverde, G. A., Houang, R. T., & Wiley, D. E. (1997). *Many visions, many aims* (Vol. 1). Dordrecht, The Netherlands: Kluwer Academic Publishers.

Schoenfeld, A. H. (1989). Explorations of students' mathematical beliefs and behavior. *Journal for Research in Mathematics Education, 20*(4), 338–355.

Schraw, G. J., Olafson, L. J., Bendixen, L. D., & Klockow, J. (2002, April). *Teachers' epistemological beliefs and classroom practices.* Paper presented at the 83rd Annual Meeting of the American Educational Research Association, New Orleans, LA.

Schwartz, S. H. (1992). Universals in the content and structure of values: Theoretical advances and empirical tests in twenty countries. In M. P. Zanna (Ed.), *Advances in experimental social psychology* (Vol. 25, pp. 1–64). New York: Academic Press.

Seah, W. T. (1999). *The portrayal and relative emphasis of mathematical and mathematics educational values in Victoria and Singapore lower secondary mathematics textbooks: A Preliminary Study.* Unpublished Master of Education project, Monash University, Melbourne.

Seah, W. T. (2001, September). *Soul, mind, ... action!: Partnership between affect and cognition in human awareness.* Paper presented at the Annual Conference of the Monash University Educational Research Community for Students and Staff, Clayton, Australia.

Seah, W. T. (2002). The perception of, and interaction with, value differences by immigrant teachers of mathematics in two Australian secondary classrooms. *Journal of Intercultural Studies, 23,* 189–210.

Seah, W. T., & Bishop, A. J. (2000, April). *Values in mathematics textbooks: A view through two Australasian regions.* Paper presented at the 81st Annual Meeting of the American Educational Research Association, New Orleans, LA (ERIC Document Reproduction Service No. ED 440 870).

Seah, W. T., & Bishop, A. J. (2001). Teaching more than numeracy: The socialisation experience of a migrant teacher. In J. Bobis, B. Perry & M. Mitchelmore (Eds.), *Numeracy and beyond: Proceedings of the Twenty-Fourth Annual Conference of the Mathematics Education Research Group of Australasia* (Vol. 2, pp. 442–450). Turramurra, Australia: Mathematics Education Research Group of Australasia.

Seah, W. T., Bishop, A. J., FitzSimons, G. E., & Clarkson, P. C. (2001, December). *Exploring issues of control over values teaching in the mathematics classroom.* Paper presented at the 2001 Annual Conference of the Australian Association for Research in Education, Fremantle, Australia.

Senger, E. S. (1999). Reflective reform in mathematics: The recursive nature of teacher change. *Educational Studies in Mathematics, 37*(3), 199–221.

Singapore Government (1991). *Shared values* (White paper). Singapore: Government of Singapore.

Singapore Ministry of Education (1990). *Mathematics syllabus: Secondary 1 to 2 (Special/Express Course), Secondary 1 to 2 (Normal Course).* Singapore: Ministry of Education.

Singapore Ministry of Education (1998, June 25). Content reduction in the curriculum' *Press release EDUN N25-02-004* [Online]. Singapore Ministry of Education. Available: http://www1.moe.edu.sg/Press/980716.html [1999, November 23].

Skemp, R. R. (1979). *Intelligence, learning, and action.* Chichester, UK: John Wiley and Sons.

Skovsmose, O. (1992). Democratic competence and reflective knowing in mathematics. *For the Learning of Mathematics, 12*(2), 2–11.

Sosniak, L. A., Ethington, C. A., & Varelas, M. (1991). Teaching mathematics without a coherent point of view: Findings from the IEA Second International Mathematics Study. *Journal of Curriculum Studies, 23*(2), 119–131.

Stewart, J. S. (1987). Clarifying values clarification: A critique. In J. P. F. Carbone (Ed.), *Value theory and education* (pp. 215–224). Malabar, FL: Robert E. Krieger.

Swadener, M., & Soedjadi, R. (1988). Values, mathematics education, and the task of developing pupils' personalities: An Indonesian perspective. In A. J. Bishop (Ed.), *Mathematics education and culture* (pp. 193–208). Dordrecht, The Netherlands: Kluwer Academic Publishers.

Tajfel, H. (1978). Social categorization, social identity and social comparison. In: H. Tajfel (Ed.), *Differentiation between social groups: Studies in the social psychology of inter-group relations.* London: Academic Press.

Tan, S. K. (1997). Moral values and science teaching: A Malaysian school curriculum initiative. *Science and Education, 6,* 555–572.

Taplin, M. (2001). Integrating values education into the mathematics classroom. *Education Horizons, 6*(5), 5–8.

Taylor, M. J. (2000). Values education: Issues and challenges in policy and school practice. In M. Leicester, C. Modgil & S. Modgil (Eds.), *Education, culture and values, Vol. II, Institutional issues* (pp. 151–168). London: Falmer Press.

Teo, C. H. (1997, August). *Opening new frontiers in education with information technology: Speech by R. Admiral Teo Chee Hean, Minister for Education, at the launch of the masterplan for IT in education* [Online], Singapore: Singapore Ministry of Education. Also available: http://www1.moe.edu.sg/Speeches/280497.htm [1999, November 23].

Thailand Ministry of Education (1999). *Education reform at the Ministry of Education (1996–2007),* [Online]. Bangkok: Thailand Ministry of Education. Also available: http://www.moe.go.th/nu/reform.htm [1999, November 22].

Thompson, A. G. (1992). Teachers' beliefs and conceptions: A synthesis of the research. In D. A. Grouws (Ed.), *Handbook of research on mathematics teaching and learning* (pp. 127–144). New York: Macmillan.

Tirta Gondoseputro, T. (1999). The cross-cultural perspective of teachers' beliefs and their influence on teaching practices: A case study of two teachers teaching secondary mathematics in Australia and Indonesia. In J. M. Truran & K. M. Truran (Eds.), *Making the difference: Proceedings of the Twenty-Second Annual Conference of The Mathematics Education Research Group of Australasia* (pp. 494–501). Sydney: The Mathematics Education Research Group of Australasia.

Tripp, D. (1993). *Critical incidents in teaching: Developing professional judgement.* London: Routledge.

Unger, P. (1990). *Identity, consciousness and value.* Oxford, UK: Oxford University Press.

Veugelers, W., & Kat, E. d. (2000, April). *The teacher as a moral educator in secondary education: The student perspective.* Paper presented at the 81st Annual Meeting of the American Educational Research Association, New Orleans, LA.

Walkerdine, V. (1997). Difference, cognition, and mathematics education. In A. B. Powell & M. Frankenstein (Eds.), *Ethnomathematics: Challenging Eurocentrism in mathematics education* (pp. 201–214). Albany, NY: State University of New York Press.

Wong, K. Y. (1993). Overview of mathematics education in Malaysia. In G. Bell (Ed.), *Asian perspectives on mathematics education* (pp. 90–110). Lismore, Australia: Northern Rivers Mathematical Association.

Wu, C.-J., & Lin, F.-L. (1999). The dichotomizing views of research methodology on the study of values: Dynamic interview and reflective construction. *Proceedings of the National Science Council Part: Mathematics, Science, and Technology Education, 9*(3), 89–98.

21
Regulating the Entry of Teachers of Mathematics into the Profession: Challenges, New Models, and Glimpses into the Future

MAX STEPHENS

The University of Melbourne

ABSTRACT

This chapter draws attention to different methods being used in the preservice training of teachers of mathematics in the United States of America, Australia, Japan, and the Netherlands. The analysis presented reveals that there are qualitative and quantitative differences in the approaches the nations are taking to the preparation of future teachers of mathematics, especially in relation to practicum experience during teacher education courses. In some nations, great emphasis is placed on giving student teachers as much time as possible in front of real classes of students, but in other nations (e.g., Japan), more emphasis is given to the quality of lesson planning and less to the amount of time actually spent in classrooms. There are also between-nations differences in the extent to which preservice teachers collaborate with their peers in their practicum experiences.

By focusing on two U.S. reports issued in the year 2000, the chapter makes clear that there is a contemporary crisis in preservice and inservice mathematics teacher education in the United States. It is argued that many other countries are already experiencing, or are likely to experience, a similar crisis. In many nations, more and more students are studying school mathematics in classes taught by unqualified teachers, or partly qualified teachers. There are simply not enough qualified young people choosing to become mathematics teachers, and various temporary 'solutions', some of them quite creative, are being hastily trialled. But those responsible for staffing school systems urgently need to devise long-term strategies for solving the problem, and also decide what new teachers should be expected to learn during their initial training. There is also a need to decide what is non-negotiable for the ongoing professional development of practising teachers of mathematics.

The chapter closes with a glimpse into the mathematics department of a typical secondary school in the year 2010.

1. DEMAND FOR MORE, AND BETTER PREPARED, MATHEMATICS TEACHERS

Two reports published in the United States of America in the year 2000 drew attention to issues associated with the preparation of teachers of mathematics

Second International Handbook of Mathematics Education, 767–793
A.J. Bishop, M.A. Clements, C. Keitel, J. Kilpatrick and F.K.S. Leung (eds.)
© 2003 Dordrecht: Kluwer Academic Publishers. Printed in Great Britain.

in that country. Both reports were widely reported, both in the United States and abroad. The first report, prepared by the National Commission on Mathematics and Science Teaching for the 21st Century, was entitled *A Report to the Nation: Before It's Too Late*. The Secretary of Education commissioned the report and, because Commission meetings were chaired by US Senator John Glenn, it is referred to as the 'Glenn Report' in this chapter. It deals especially with the shortage in the United States of qualified teachers in the mathematical sciences, and makes recommendations for the recruitment of new teachers and for supporting those currently in the field.

The second report, published by the College Board for the Mathematical Sciences (CBMS) for its *Mathematics Education of Teachers Project*, dealt directly with the mathematical preparation of teachers for the elementary, middle and senior years of school. Its focus was squarely on the mathematical content that CBMS believes teachers at each stage should possess. Its recommendations were directed primarily at those in Departments of Mathematics in US colleges and universities who are responsible for the mathematical preparation of new teachers, as distinct from those who teach Mathematics Education.

Both of the above-mentioned reports can be regarded as responses from within the United States to the perception that North American students did relatively poorly on the Third International Mathematics and Science Study (TIMSS). There were many reactions within the United States to the TIMSS results (see, e.g., Schmidt, McKnight & Raizen, 1997; Stigler & Hiebert, 1999; Martin & Mullis, 2000). Teaching methods, teachers' mathematical knowledge and teacher preparation in the USA have been compared unfavourably to the teaching of mathematics in those countries, especially Japan, Singapore and Korea, whose students did much better on the TIMSS tests. Although some scholars have questioned aspects of the design of TIMSS (see, e.g., Keitel & Kilpatrick, 1999), in general the findings have been accepted as indicative of the need for fundamental changes in the intended, implemented and attained mathematics curricula in North American schools.

Numerous accusations and counter-accusations have been made with respect to where the blame should be placed. Those who have followed the *Math Wars*, as they have been commonly called, in the State of California, would know of the often bitter and public attacks made by some mathematicians on the quality of work done by mathematics educators. The mathematicians have drawn attention to what they see as a lack of mathematical clarity and depth in some current textbooks and a failure by the mathematics educators as a whole to address these weaknesses.

Issues arising from the various interpretations given to TIMSS results are now viewed as issues of public concern, and have moved well beyond being matters on which mathematicians and mathematics educators alone should offer opinions. A section in the Glenn Report urged parents and community members to ask at their local high school, for example, how many of those currently teaching mathematics were strictly 'out of field' – that is lacking the formal courses of college mathematics required to receive a state licence in that subject.

In some urban districts, it is said that in some high schools there may be no teacher with a licence to teach mathematics.

The rhetoric of the Glenn Report echoed concerns which are familiar to readers outside the USA. The debate is not restricted to relative rankings on TIMSS or to differences in curricular intentions among those countries that participated in TIMSS (Schmidt, McKnight, Valverde, Houang & Wiley, 1997; Schmidt, McKnight, Houang, Wang, Wiley, Cogan & Wolfe, 2000). Education in the mathematical sciences is now regarded as a fundamental basis for scientific, technological and economic development. In developed countries, employment in agriculture and manufacturing occupations has decreased as a result of the nature of work in those traditional areas becoming dramatically less labour intensive. By contrast, those areas of greatest expansion, in information technology and services, require people to be mathematically literate at least, and often require a high level of mathematical sophistication. The Glenn Report argued that common features of labour markets in many countries, heightened by the impact of increased global competition, have made it essential for the majority of students to complete high school with a sound background in mathematics. Many more young people need to proceed to college and university where further studies in the mathematical sciences are either explicitly required or assumed.

The root of the problem addressed by the Glenn Report is that growth in occupations requiring a strong grounding in the mathematical sciences typically exceeds the supply of suitably qualified graduates. Many positions in these occupations are located in the private sector, which is able to offer high financial rewards for new graduates. Whereas a generation ago, teaching mathematics in a public school may have been a financially rewarding career for young graduates, it is no longer able to compete financially with what these young people can obtain working in the private sector. The supply of suitably qualified graduates seeking to become teachers of mathematics is diminishing, and a state of crisis has been reached in developed countries where school enrolments continue to rise. Nor is it likely to improve, without targeted government intervention, since the education sector, left on its own, is unable to compete for scarce human resources with private industry. The current crisis in the supply of suitably qualified graduates in the mathematical sciences to enter teaching is likely to become even worse over the next 10 years, as many of those who became teachers of mathematics 25 years ago resign or retire in the next ten years.

In 'developing' countries, the supply of qualified people to become teachers of mathematics has always been in a state of crisis. In some nations the full impact of the crisis is masked by the restricted access of students to secondary education. In general, though, the supply of suitably trained mathematics graduates is never enough to meet the needs of industry. Expanding the access of students to secondary education is the key to economic improvement in all developing countries. Achieving this goal, however, is doubly difficult when developing countries have to deal with increasing the number of suitable qualified teachers at the same time as they are establishing a new infrastructure for economic development. Achieving the latter requires people with high levels of training in the mathematical sciences – economists, computer specialists, scientists and engineers. Few with these qualifications can be spared to enter teaching, even if they have a desire to teach. Until the number of qualified teachers of mathematics increases, and the quality of the teaching of mathematics improves, economic improvement will be hampered and unevenly distributed.

Increased demands for mathematical literacy for all young people completing high school have a flow-on effect for the teaching of mathematics in the preceding years of school. As a result, teachers of mathematics in the middle years of school are expected to provide a solid background in mathematics for all students. Similarly, higher expectations are made for teachers of mathematics in the elementary years. Typically these teachers have been generalists responsible for teaching *all* subjects, sometimes with the exception of some specialist subjects such as music, art and physical education. As a result, the training of elementary teachers has been based on an assumption that they are trained to teach all subjects. Increasing requirements for the teaching of mathematics in the elementary school years has implications for the length of training needed by prospective elementary teachers, the mathematical competence of teachers, and for their continuing professional development. It is to the credit of the Glenn Report that it directed attention both to the preparation and recruitment of new teachers of mathematics and to the continuing professional development of those who are currently teaching.

In this chapter it will be important therefore to describe typical courses of preparation of new teachers of mathematics in several countries, and to make some comparisons between different patterns of preparation. It will also be necessary to examine common problems and issues concerning the preparation of teachers of mathematics in a range of countries. Indeed, if the issues of supply and demand for qualified teachers of mathematics, as identified in the Glenn Report, are common to many countries, it will be necessary to consider how patterns of recruitment, certification, school staffing and professional development need to change to take account of these complexities.

This chapter should not be confined to describing what currently takes place. Nor should it be content to make a list of recommendations which, however fine and worthy, are not likely to be feasible. It will need to look at emerging patterns and possibilities and consider how in practical terms the preparation of new teachers of mathematics might respond to changing circumstances generated by increased expectations of schools – despite the crisis in the supply of well-trained graduates to enter teaching. This chapter is not intended to set forth compromised expectations; rather, its aim is to explore what needs to change, what is feasible, and how to maintain high quality mathematics education in the difficult years that lie ahead.

2. TO WHAT EXTENT ARE THESE ISSUES INFORMED BY RESEARCH?

The extent to which teacher education issues are informed by research is a complex and somewhat controversial matter. Although various national documents refer to research findings in mathematics education, and to current and projected employment data, the positions these reports adopt are fundamentally policy statements about what teachers *ought* or *need* to receive as part of their initial and continuing professional development. Findings from different types of research are used to support these policy positions and accompanying political agendas. There appear to be several areas where research findings are used to inform these policy directions.

First, in all developed countries there is intense public interest in strengthening school mathematics, and in many countries equally intense debate about how well mathematics is being taught. For example, one of the conclusions reached by Stigler and Hiebert (1999), from their videotape analyses of eighth-grade mathematics classes in the United States of America, France and Japan, was that in the United States teaching practices in mathematics tend to follow a common recipe (Stigler & Hiebert, 1999). According to the Glenn Report (2000) the predominant approach adopted by teachers consisted of the following sequence of events:

1. A review of previous material and homework;
2. A problem illustration by the teacher;
3. Drill on low-level procedures that imitate those demonstrated by the teacher;
4. Supervised seatwork by students, often in isolation;
5. Checking of seatwork problems; and
6. Assignment of homework.

Stigler and Hiebert (1999) and Olsen (1999), in reporting on the findings of the TIMSS video study, pointed out that when the 81 videotapes of mathematics classes in the USA were analyzed, no student was found to have been engaged in constructing a mathematical proof. The Glenn Report (2000) contrasted the style of teaching found in U.S. schools with what appears to take place in Japanese schools, where "closely supervised, collaborative work among students is the norm" (p. 20). The Report continued:

Teachers [in Japan] begin by presenting students with a Mathematics problem employing principles they have not yet learned. They then work alone or in small groups to devise a solution. After a few minutes, students are called upon to present their answers, the whole class works through the problems and solutions, uncovering related mathematical concepts and reasoning. The students learn through reasoned discovery, not lecture alone. (p. 20)

These depictions of conceptually rich teaching in classrooms outside the U.S. are strongly featured in other research studies such as those carried out by Stevenson and Stigler (1993), and by Stigler, Gonzales, Kawanaka, Knoll and Serrano (1999). TIMSS results now feature widely in public discussion, as much in countries like the United States, whose international rankings are disappointingly low, as in countries such as Singapore that achieve at much higher levels (Teo, 2000).

Second, research findings are used to inform policy documents such as the *2000 NCTM Principles and Standards for School Mathematics* (NCTM, 2000). Although research findings certainly do not dictate the content of these professional documents, they are used to give strength or credence to certain recommendations. For example, the emphasis in the *Standards* document on the need to strengthen algebraic teaching and learning in the elementary school years was informed by a long line of research into the capacities of young children to engage in algebraic thinking (see, e.g., Davis, 1964; Kaput, 1998; Schifter, 1999; Carpenter & Levi, 2000). That emphasis was buttressed by assumptions about the importance of algebra in the curriculum. Given concerns about poor algebraic understanding among students in the middle and high school years (Matz, 1982; Kieran, 1992), the specific recommendations about the inclusion of algebraic thinking in the elementary school appear to be justified. However, other proposals concerning the teaching of algebra could be justified using the same premises (see, e.g., Silver, 1997).

Third, these raised expectations about the content of school mathematics have clear implications for the training of teachers and how their entry to the profession should be regulated. We need to recognize the profound changes that have taken place over the past one hundred years in the preparation of teachers and how the entry of teachers to the profession is regulated. The CBMS (2000) report aptly summarized these vastly changed expectations when it stated:

> Until 1900, teachers of mathematics were largely seen as drill masters, training students to perform numerical computations. Beyond the eight primary grades, most teachers had at best a year or two at a special high school, called a normal school. The introduction of universal high school(-ing) around 1900 gave rise to secondary level subject specialists who majored in their subject at teachers' colleges. Teachers for earlier grades also were required to go to college, but focused their education on the psychological and social development of children. It was largely assumed, and still is by some today, that prospective elementary teachers, and perhaps middle school teachers, had adequately learned during their own schooling all the mathematics that they would need to teach mathematics well. (p. 3)

This assumption, as the Report says with considerable understatement, is now 'seriously questioned'. It is now recognized that prospective teachers in the elementary school need a strong understanding of the mathematics they are to teach, not just a knowledge of the procedures to be followed. Many of those who aspire to become elementary teachers have not received sound mathematical instruction at school. Many enter teachers' college with negative experiences drawn from their own schooling. Research studies such as that by Ball (1993) point to major conceptual strands of the elementary school curriculum that are not sufficiently well understood by teachers.

Fourth, it is now agreed that teachers at all levels need more than a conceptually correct understanding of the mathematics they are to teach. Sometimes, this additional kind of understanding is referred to as 'deep understanding' (Ma, 1999) or as 'pedagogical content knowledge' (Shulman, 1987). In either sense, sound conceptual knowledge needs to be complemented by an understanding of how these concepts are to be presented to students. Also important is the knowledge that some contexts are especially powerful for most students in illustrating these concepts. Furthermore, teachers need to know how to connect new concepts to what students already know. They need to know how to draw out students' own conceptual frameworks so these can be further developed and where appropriate modified and challenged.

Although these areas are at the centre of the mathematical preparation of teachers, the CBMS (2000) report commented that these very areas sometimes 'fall between the cracks'. Often teacher education specialists think that they have been addressed in mathematics courses, and those teaching mathematics courses think that they will be taken up in education courses. One remedy proposed is the provision of 'capstone' courses, which explicitly aim to link mathematical content knowledge with methods by which that content can be taught effectively. Although this calls for greater coherence in the delivery of teachers' initial training, it also points strongly to a further issue.

It is unrealistic to expect that 'deep understanding' or 'pedagogical content knowledge' can be achieved by the conclusion of initial training. That kind of knowledge is sometimes referred to as case knowledge or situated knowledge. It is the sort of knowledge that cannot be learned from textbooks or at best is poorly learned from textbooks. It is knowledge that grows out of reflective practice by a professional over a number of years.

In their initial training, teachers need to be introduced to what many see as the heart of mathematics teaching. But a deeper appreciation only comes with experience working with students and with the opportunity to reflect and build on that experience. Research studies, such as Stigler and Hiebert's (1999), point to the fundamental importance of providing for the continued professional growth of teachers. These opportunities need to be based in the first instance in a teacher's home school where colleagues need time to meet to discuss how best to teach and how children learn. Drawing on these studies, the CBMS (2000) report commented that "in many countries where TIMSS scores were high, teachers alone or in groups spend time every day refining their lessons and studying the underlying mathematics ... They observe each others' classes. Beginning teachers have extensive mentoring. The teacher's manuals accompanying their textbooks have chapters to educate them further about the mathematics being taught" (pp. 3–4).

Findings of the international comparative studies support the view that initial preparation should be seen as a starting platform for career-long learning about the teaching of mathematics. The following section draws briefly upon current practices and emerging trends in teacher preparation in Australia, Japan and the Netherlands. These accounts provide a backdrop for further discussion for regulating entry to the mathematics teaching profession.

3. REGULATING ENTRY INTO THE PROFESSION – AUSTRALIA AND JAPAN

In Australia, the mathematical requirements for prospective primary (elementary) teachers are quite diverse. They vary between states and territories, and even between systems of education. Most universities require applicants to have completed several mathematics courses in their final two years of high school. However, since almost all students study mathematics in the junior year of high school, and given the range of courses offered, this requirement is easily met. Most universities require students to complete a semester-length course in mathematics covering mathematics concepts in number, space, measurement, chance and data. Such courses typically serve as review courses of key ideas relevant to primary and early secondary school. In addition, students are required to take one or two courses in Mathematics Education. A few universities do not require students to take a course in mathematics, relying entirely on courses in mathematics education to prepare new teachers of mathematics.

In Australia, attention is often focussed on the high level of approved school practice that preservice teacher education students need to complete in order to be eligible for registration as teachers. In the State of Victoria, for example, persons who wish to qualify for registration as secondary teachers are required to have 45 days supervised practice, and primary teachers are required to have 80 days. In Queensland, the number of supervised days of practical teaching for prospective secondary teachers is now 60 days. The robust level of school practice required for prospective primary teachers, across all teaching subjects, needs to be contrasted with the often slender amount of time on mathematics and mathematics education subjects that students experience within their initial training. Registration to teach is regulated by respective State government bodies. There is no subject-specific registration for high school teachers. However, when appointing teachers, employing bodies and individual schools do take teachers' academic qualifications into account.

Contrast this with the Japanese system, where the practicum is comparatively short for both primary and secondary teachers, as illustrated in the interviews reported below. This relatively short period of practicum experience in Japan is offset by the fact that prospective elementary teachers, for example, are required to take ten semester-length courses in mathematics. In addition, they are required to take at least three semester-length units of mathematics education, including a semester course dealing with Mathematics and Information Science. Each course corresponds to 2 credits and usually involves a class of 90 minutes each week for the semester (Shimizu, 2001).

In their first year, teachers will typically take five such courses in areas such as algebra, geometry, calculus or statistics. A typical second year might involve four mathematics courses, a course in information science, and two courses in mathematics education. In the third year, a prospective elementary teacher might do one more mathematics course and one more course in Mathematics Education. These requirements, which are more demanding than those applying in many other developed countries, are based on national regulations for elementary and secondary teacher certification. Prospective elementary teachers undertaking a course of training in a junior college may take fewer units. However, many prospective elementary school teachers in Japanese universities take sufficient additional courses for them to obtain a teaching certificate as a secondary teacher. They can do this by taking at least four additional courses in mathematics education.

According to Shimizu (2001), many prefectures today prefer to hire teachers with multiple certificates. To some extent this reflects a wish to be able to place teachers flexibly in schools where enrolments may be decreasing. The following procedures for the selection and appointment of teachers in Japan reflect a current, but possibly short-term, oversupply of teachers. Students in their fourth and final year of training undergo an extensive selection programme at prefectural (local government) level organized by its board of education. With the exception of Hokkaido, the northernmost island, the first step consists of a written test held on the same day so that students have to make a decision about the prefecture to which they will apply. The test covers general knowledge of education in Japan and students' knowledge of the national course of study. Prospective teachers of mathematics need to be able to place topics according to the year level specified in the national course of study and be able to elaborate on what treatment of topics is recommended. Essentially, this is a test of book knowledge. Those successful in the first round, held in July, are invited back for a second round in August. This round involves an interview, students' writing a paper on a current topic, and possibly some microteaching.

Selection for employment is finalized in the following February. In their first year of teaching, new teachers are given an equivalent 0.8 teaching load and are assigned to a mentor teacher in their home school. Prior to taking up their appointment they will have attended seminars and workshops conducted by their prefecture on school operations. Within their school, they will have extended periods of supervised teaching. In this way, the gap between the Australian model and that of Japan may be evened out. New teachers may also have opportunities to engage in team teaching. They will certainly participate with other colleagues in what the Japanese call *kenkyu jugyo*, best translated as 'lesson study', by which an experienced teacher prepares a lesson on a given topic which is then observed by other members of the lesson study circle, and refined. It may in fact go through several cycles of refinement.

Stigler (1999) has estimated that almost all elementary school teachers and half of middle school teachers in Japan participate in lesson study groups that operate for several hours each week. These teachers are provided with time in their weekly schedule that allows them to meet for collaborative planning as well as individual preparation of lessons. In addition, teachers in their first year of teaching will have a one-month summer excursion provided by the prefecture (although a Japanese academic described this excursion as being more of a 'junket' than any serious training). From the commencement of their second year, teachers' allotments increase to full-time. New teachers in Australia in their first year of employment may be given a slightly reduced teaching allotment, but there are no formal mentoring programs like those in place to support young teachers in Japan.

3.1. *Four Young People Entering Teaching in Japan*

Four students (here referred to as R, T, K and D) were interviewed at Yokohama National University. All were completing their fourth and final year of teacher training. Three were prospective elementary teachers and one a prospective secondary teacher. During their third and fourth years, the three prospective elementary teachers spent four weeks in an elementary school, two weeks in a junior high school and two weeks in a special education school. During their four weeks in an elementary school, two weeks were spent observing.

When asked how many lessons they had taught the following information was given. Student R had taught at second grade only for a total of 20 lessons, including three 'full days' in which he had taught four to five lessons. Student T had taken 17 lessons at first grade only, including one full day. Both students had completed their teaching practicum at a public school. A third student, K, had completed four weeks at an elementary school attached to the university. Student K had taught between six and seven lessons in the second grade. Two lessons had been taught in mathematics; two lessons, using team teaching had been taught in *seikatsu* (a combination of social studies and science); one lesson in national language; and one lesson in physical education. The remainder of the time was spent observing classes. Student K reported that her supervising teacher required very detailed lesson plans, with each lesson requiring about five hours of preparation time.

The secondary teacher trainee, Student D, had spent four weeks (22 days) at a junior high school, with the first week being spent in observation. Student D had also spent two weeks at an elementary school. In all, he had taught seven lessons in junior high school, teaching ninth-grade mathematics only. Other days were spent observing students in mathematics, science and music classes. During this time, lesson plans were prepared. Student D also participated in the school soccer club. Two lessons were also taught in *doutoku* (moral education). During his time at an elementary school Student D had taught approximately ten lessons – four in mathematics, two in social studies, one in physical education, one in national language, with time also spent attending class meetings. The selection of subjects had been arranged in discussion between Student D and his supervising teacher.

There appears to be a marked difference between teaching practice undertaken in a university attached school, where many student teachers in training are likely to attend, and in a public school, where students may have more opportunity to teach. The Yokohama School District, for example, requires prospective teachers to take at least eight lessons across a range of subjects. Student K also reported that in her second year she was able to visit a primary school for games and for some practical work assisting teachers. She had also been able to visit the school on Saturdays when classes were in session.

In the recently reorganized Faculty of Education, the number of students has decreased. Under new arrangements, students in their first year will visit a school. In their second year, they will also undertake school visits and will be expected to prepare a limited plan for some teaching. In their third year, practical teaching in the elementary school will take place, followed by practical teaching in a junior high school in the final year.

Having been appointed to a teaching position, new teachers are required to attend a monthly meeting organized by the Yokohama School District. Their teaching load in first year is equivalent to 80% of a regular allotment. During a teacher's first year, an advisory teacher will observe teaching and provide detailed feedback on lesson planning, classroom management and school responsibilities. Having met selection requirements for their initial appointment, no further interviews are required for first-year teachers to be confirmed in their position for the Yokohama School District. In some other prefectures, beginning teachers may need to undertake further testing before being confirmed in their position. This, however, is more the exception than the rule.

4. REGULATING ENTRY INTO THE PROFESSION – THE NETHERLANDS

For upper secondary teachers, the traditional mode of preparation in the Netherlands, as in many other developed countries, has been a university degree with a major study in mathematics and possibly with a minor study in another subject. This is taken over five years, and is followed by a one-year course of teacher preparation. In this year, half of the time (about 820 hours) is spent on "a lengthy period of supervised teaching practice" (National Office of Overseas Skills Recognition, 1992, p. 13). In addition to this model, prospective teachers can become qualified at higher vocational colleges that offer a part-time program with evening classes. Prospective teachers who have followed this program get a professional degree instead of an academic degree in mathematics. About half of the mathematics teachers in upper secondary schools have followed this part-time trajectory.

In recent years the number of students who choose to study mathematics has decreased and, in addition, courses of teacher preparation have also become less popular, as demand for people with substantial qualifications in mathematics has risen among other sectors of the economy. Salary prospects for graduates in teaching in the Netherlands lag behind what is available in business and industry. Moreover, the working environment at school is considered to be less attractive. This feature is now common to many industrialized nations. It cannot be denied that those who have come through this preparation pathway have a strong discipline base. In addition, they have opportunities to develop their pedagogical and didactical knowledge in a year-long post-graduate training course. However, with greater responsibility being asked of teachers in course development and assessment, a one-year end-on model is seen, by many, to have shortcomings.

Teacher training colleges, known as higher vocational colleges, on the other hand, have provided a continuous training program over a four-year period for new teachers in primary and junior secondary schools. Separate colleges train prospective primary and secondary teachers.

In colleges preparing those to teach in lower secondary school, students generally study one academic subject, together with integrated courses in didactics and pedagogy. After one year in the college, they enter classrooms initially as observers, leading in later years to periods of supervised practice teaching. In general, 20 to 25 per cent of the total program time is spent on supervised teaching.

For those who are preparing to become teachers in primary schools there is a 4-year trajectory consisting of a 3-year college program and 1-year inservice training. Colleges offer general training for all subjects in the primary school curriculum up to Year 6, that is, for children up to about 12 years of age. Mathematics is an integrated part of the mathematics education course. As in many other countries, the focus has been on preparing generalist teachers. Some colleges allow prospective teachers to specialize in mathematics in their third year, but again the focus is on mathematics education.

According to van den Heuvel-Panhuizen and Broekman (2002), all prospective teachers get only a limited number of courses in mathematics education. Van den Heuvel-Panhuizen and Broekman reported that courses at the colleges range from an average of 20 minutes a week to one hour a week during the three-year period. In addition to these lecture and workshop hours, the prospective teachers are expected to engage in relevant reading and coursework for between 40 minutes and two hours a week.

The minimal amount of formal mathematics required of beginning primary teachers is a problem in many countries including the Netherlands, with relatively few prospective primary teachers specializing in mathematics. Compulsory courses in mathematics vary across teachers colleges. Usually, time spent on mathematics education is not included in this calculation. It should be noted that in the Netherlands prospective primary school teachers take mathematics education courses in which some mathematics is included. There has, however, been a recent development towards job differentiation in elementary schools, with teachers undertaking courses, usually after graduation, in order to become a specialist in a particular area, such as information technology, language or mathematics. Again, these 'mathematics' courses are within 'mathematics education' strands in which some mathematics is included. It should be noted that the provision of specialist teachers of mathematics in elementary schools is yet to be formalized, and that suitable programs of preparation are just beginning.

In recent years, in many countries, including the Netherlands, there has been a national shortage of primary school teachers and mathematics teachers, and new models of professional entry have emerged. These models allow qualified people with an academic or higher vocational degree and suitable industry or other experience to teach in primary and junior secondary schools after taking a different program of professional entry. For prospective primary school teachers there are two new models. The first one is called the 'compacted program' in which the regular 4-year teacher preparation is compacted into a 2-year trajectory. This program is meant for people who finished a higher vocational or university study for a different profession. The other new model is called a 'side-in stream' by which prospective teachers consisting of people with various backgrounds, ranging from parents (mostly mothers) interested in the education of their children to those who have worked in business, industry, nursing or social work, can start directly as a teacher, after passing an assessment of their readiness to teach. Those who enter the profession by this pathway are required to teach under supervision for a period of two years.

For secondary school there is only one model for 'side-in stream'. Prospective mathematics teachers are required to undergo a formal assessment of their knowledge of mathematics and pedagogy and didactics. Based on the results of this assessment, a personal training trajectory is then set up that generally takes one to two years, while they work in schools under supervision.

Although these models are relatively new in the Netherlands, they have parallels in the United States where some school districts, particularly, in larger cities, are searching for new ways to attract new people to teach in what are often seen as difficult areas. Teacher education for this group is largely school-based, that is, completed under the direction of colleagues in schools.

5. REGULATING ENTRY INTO TEACHING OF MATHEMATICS IN THE UNITED STATES OF AMERICA

In the United States, high school teachers of mathematics need to hold a certificate or licence to teach in that area of the curriculum. The terms of the licence are set down by each State's Department of Public Instruction. Typically, these require teachers to have studied a major sequence in mathematics at a recognized university *and* to have completed certain education courses and a period of supervised practical teaching. Teachers are usually licensed to teach in one area of the curriculum. High school mathematics certification covers the years 6 to 12, entitling a teacher to teach both in the high school (Years 9–12) and the middle school (Years 6–9). Elementary teachers hold a generalist certification, which entitles them to teach in both elementary and middle school programs. At present, there is no licence specific to the middle school years.

5.1. *High School Teachers*

In the United States, certification as a secondary mathematics teacher normally takes at least five years to achieve – a first degree normally taking four years. The two principal components of mathematics teacher certification are content area specialization and required education studies accompanied by a professional sequence of at least 2 semesters. In some cases the professional sequence will be 3 or 4 semesters. For example, the Bachelor of Science (Education) at the University of Wisconsin-Madison is a five-year course. It requires students to complete 34 credits of a mathematics major. The major consists of 3 sequences of calculus (13 credits), linear algebra (3 credits), geometry (3 credits), statistics, taken in the Department of Statistics, (3 credits), combinatorics (3 credits), probability (3 credits), modern algebra (3 credits), and Foundations of Mathematics, with a special focus on proof, (3 credits).

As well as completing a major study in mathematics, Bachelor of Science (Education) students at the University of Wisconsin-Madison are required to take additional courses in a liberal arts programme in order to meet graduation requirements for the University. For example, they may complete six credits of history or nine credits of science. In addition to those courses taken in University Departments of Mathematics or Statistics, students at the University of Wisconsin-Madison are required to pass a 3-credit sequence dealing with technologies in secondary school mathematics. This course is offered by the Department of Curriculum and Instruction, and deals with the use of computers, graphic calculators, the Internet, data probes and software as these relate to school mathematics.

Those who have completed a first degree, for example, in Engineering, and who wish to obtain certification as teachers of mathematics, are required to complete an equivalent set of sequences in mathematics. Engineering graduates are unlikely to have completed a required course in geometry. In general, those seeking to be certified as teachers of mathematics after having completed another first-degree programme are required to complete a minimum of one semester's coursework.

At the University of Wisconsin-Madison, the professional sequence is taken over four semesters and is fully prescribed. During the first semester, students take courses in inclusive schooling, offered by the Department of Curriculum and Instruction, which focus on working with students of special needs. Additional courses will be taken in adolescent development, offered by the Department of Educational Psychology, as well as a third course, School in Society, offered by the School of Education. It is expected that these three courses will be taught in an integrated way.

During the first semester of their junior year, the year before they graduate as teachers, all students undertake an initial school practicum. They are assigned to a particular teacher in their content area. This may be in mathematics, science, social studies, or foreign languages. The practicum requires students to work in a school two mornings a week for 11 weeks, observing, and providing help for the classroom teacher – such as reviewing homework or assisting in the preparation of student materials. The school practicum will be integrated with student's academic studies during the semester.

In the second semester students are assigned to full-time student teaching. A typical semester for a school district is usually longer than that for a university, and lasts for about 18 weeks. During this teaching practicum, the aim is to have students undertake roughly half the workload of a regular teacher. This will usually require them to teach three periods a day on average, whereas a regular teacher would typically teach five of the seven periods in a school day. Supervised lessons are usually undertaken with one teacher, sometimes two teachers, and are spread across year levels. After school hours, students undertake a concurrent methods course in mathematics at the University.

In the third semester, students return to campus to complete three courses. One required course is in educational psychology, dealing with theories of learning. There is a second course dealing with reading and writing across the curriculum, and a third course, which focuses on individual differences. During this semester, students at the University of Wisconsin-Madison undertake a second practicum, which complements that undertaken in the first semester. Like the first practicum, it requires students to spend two mornings each week in school observation. If the first practicum was undertaken in a high school, the second practicum will be undertaken in a middle school, or vice versa. This second practicum is intended to be one of observation, although it may involve some classroom teaching. However, during this practicum, any teaching a student does is supervised, for students are not expected to be given primary responsibility for a class.

Semester 4 follows the pattern of semester 2 and involves a full semester of student teaching, with three lessons being taught per day. During this practicum students are assumed to have a teaching load of no more than one half of a regular teacher. Where possible, this semester of teaching practice introduces students to working in the middle school years, a practice that may not be matched in other states. The practicum is concurrent with a continuing methods course in mathematics that focuses on Curriculum and Assessment. The practice of alternating experience in the middle school and high school is a distinctive feature of the University of Wisconsin-Madison program.

In other states, certification requirements are typically completed in three semesters. The middle school practicum experience sometimes influences students to opt for middle school mathematics teaching. It is intended to provide all certified graduates with a knowledge of the middle school, and therefore with greater flexibility in the job market. Alongside these formal requirements, realities in schools can take different forms. Unregulated entry into mathematics teaching is, nevertheless, a serious issue with many teachers in urban and rural schools teaching 'out of field' – that is to say, teaching high school mathematics without certification. The extent of this problem will be discussed later in this chapter.

Alternative pathways to certification are likely to be needed for 'second career' people, or for those who are currently teaching out-of-field and who wish to obtain certification as teachers of mathematics. Requiring people with extensive experience in industry or already in the profession to complete a three or four semester sequence for certification would be quite likely to discourage suitably qualified people from considering teaching mathematics as a second career. The first practicum, essentially a programme of school observation, although entirely appropriate for young graduates who have no experience in the workforce, may not be so important for those with accumulated professional experience. Academic studies for second career people need to include courses in adolescent development, learning and a study of school and society, as well as a course in teaching methods.

A key issue is whether all these courses need to be completed before a 'second career' teacher takes responsibility for classroom teaching. There are several models for regulating entry, which are quite strict over a more extended period of time. New York City, for example, requires newly certified teachers of mathematics to have completed a masters degree after five years of teaching. Other models that are more flexible allow 'second career' people to undertake an intensive summer programme before receiving permission to teach, and to undertake additional studies concurrent with employment. The latter model is especially attractive to those school districts which find it difficult to attract suitably qualified teachers of mathematics. Inner urban schools and rural schools appear to have greatest difficulty in that regard.

Some schools in large urban districts may not have a single licensed teacher of mathematics on staff. Some school districts may be forced to hire people from 'outside' to teach hard-to-staff courses in mathematics or physics. These 'outside' employees or specialists may have no other school duties apart from teaching the class for which they are hired. They may be engineers, for example, and may not be fully certified teachers. In view of these problems, it is recognized that new models of regulating entry into the profession, including the entry of experienced professionals, will need to be developed. These are currently being explored in a number of US cities. One well established model is incorporated into the programme known as *Teach for America* (TFA) to be discussed later in this chapter.

5.2. *Elementary Teachers*

The mathematics component of training of an elementary school teacher in the United States is much more difficult to pin down. At the University of Wisconsin-Madison, prospective elementary teachers are required to take nine credits of Mathematics, equivalent to three semester-length courses in their third and fourth year. These courses, provided by the Department of Mathematics, cover number systems; measurement, geometry and space; and probability and statistics. The teaching practicum is completed in the fifth year. In the first semester of this year, practice teaching is combined with courses in teaching methods. In the second semester, practice teaching is carried out across three different year levels. Other universities in the United States have less demanding mathematical requirements for prospective primary teachers.

6. REACHING CBMS STANDARDS

6.1. *Varying Requirements in Different Nations*

Current practices in the preparation of elementary teachers in the United States and in most other countries fall well short of the recommendations of the College Board for Mathematical Sciences (CBMS, 2000). The report recommended that elementary grade teachers "should be required to take at least nine semester-hours of mathematics courses on fundamental ideas of elementary school mathematics" (General Recommendations, p. 1). This recommendation is met by the current University of Wisconsin-Madison program, but not by many other U.S. universities. Nationally regulated teacher preparation courses in Japan currently exceed this requirement. Few Australian universities meet this requirement.

One programme in Australia which exceeds the requirement is that offered within the Department of Science and Mathematics Education at the University of Melbourne. In that program, prospective primary teachers are required to take a year-long course in mathematics in each of their first and second years, and one semester of mathematics education in each of the third and fourth year of training. Some other Australian universities require only one semester of mathematics followed later by a course or courses in mathematics education.

Equally challenging to current practice in the USA, and to many other countries, is the CMBS report's recommendation relating to teachers of mathematics in the middle grades:

> Middle grade teachers of mathematics should be required to take at least 21 semester hours of mathematics that includes at least 12 semester-hours on fundamental ideas of school mathematics appropriate for middle school teachers. (*General Recommendations*, p. 1)

This requirement broke new ground in delineating specific requirements for teachers of the middle grades. In the United States, for example, those who hold a licence as an elementary school teacher are able to teach middle school. In countries where high school covers Years 7–12, it is desirable for the junior years to be taught by fully qualified teachers in mathematics. In view of the shortage of qualified teachers of mathematics in high schools in many nations, out-of-field teachers often teach Mathematics classes in the early years of high schools. Creating a special category for teachers of mathematics in the middle years may be one way of addressing this current problem.

For high school teachers of mathematics, the CMBS report confirmed the importance of holding an undergraduate major in mathematics. However, it added that the major should include "a 6-hour capstone course connecting their college mathematics courses with high school mathematics" (*General Recommendations*, p. 1). Such a course in algebra, or number, for example, could aim to "provide teachers with valuable insight into the structure of high school mathematics, its modern uses, and the conceptual difficulties in learning number and algebraic concepts" (*General Recommendations*, p. 1). On the other hand, it "could trace the development of key number and algebra ideas from early secondary school through contemporary applications" (p. 1).

6.2. *The CBMS Report on the Need to Develop Professional Knowledge*

When reading the CBMS (2000) report it is important to distinguish between those recommendations which focus on knowledge of essential mathematical ideas and those which focus on knowledge of effective ways of using mathematics. For example, in detailing what should be known by those well prepared to teach high school algebra, the report drew attention to having an "understanding of the ways that basic ideas of number theory and algebraic structures underlie rules for operations on symbolic expressions, equations, and inequalities" (Chapter 10, p. 4). In the same section, the report stated that well-prepared teachers should have an "understanding of ways to use graphing calculators, computer algebra systems, and spreadsheets as tools for exploring algebraic ideas and extending calculation skills" (Chapter 10, p. 4).

The report emphasized the need for prospective mathematics teachers not only to acquire content knowledge but also to develop the capacity to apply this knowledge effectively in teaching. But whereas the first might be comprehensively taught in any undergraduate program, the second requires teaching experience, familiarity with the mathematics curriculum, and a practical knowledge of how students think about mathematics. This kind of knowledge appears to be closer to Shulman's (1987) description of 'pedagogical content knowledge'. It cannot be established, other than in a basic sense, in a programme of teacher preparation. Groundwork established in such a programme needs to be built upon in subsequent professional formation.

The same distinction was made quite clearly in the report's recommendations concerning the need for teachers to be well prepared to teach geometry in high school. The report drew attention to the importance of having an "understanding of trigonometry from a geometric perspective and skill in use of trigonometric relationships to solve problems" (Chapter 10, p. 10). In the same section, the report referred to having an "ability to use dynamic computer drawing tools to conduct geometric investigations emphasizing visualization, pattern recognition, and conjecturing" (Chapter 10, p. 10). The first element could reasonably be expected to form part of a student's undergraduate academic program, and may become refined through later teaching. The second element, on the other hand, draws much more deeply on knowing how to design a good investigation, and to know what one's students are capable of visualizing, and how they recognize patterns and engage in conjecturing.

The same distinction was also evident in the report's recommendations for being well prepared to teach elementary school mathematics. In setting out its recommendation for teaching arithmetic with understanding, for example, the report stated that teachers need to understand 'place value'. They need to appreciate how place value permits efficient representation of numbers; that the value of each place is ten times as large as the value of the next place to the right. They also need to know the implications of place value for ordering numbers, estimation, and approximation (see Chapter 8, p. 5).

Soon after the section on place value, the report referred to the importance of students having a thorough understanding of 'multi-digit calculations', including standard algorithms, 'mental math', and *"non-standard methods commonly created by students: the reasoning behind the procedures"* (my emphasis). They also need to know "how the base-10 structure of number is implicated in all multidigit computation" (Chapter 8, p. 5). To teach standard algorithms and place value as used in whole numbers and decimals, teachers clearly need sound conceptual knowledge. Further experience is likely to be needed for a teacher to appreciate the many different problems that can arise for children as they move from whole-number thinking to fractions and decimals, and how these misconceptions can be identified and best treated. This requires content-specific pedagogical knowledge that comes from working insightfully with children over a number of years. Likewise, although an appreciation of students' use of non-standard methods is likely to be developed during practice teaching, knowing how to respond to those non-standard methods and to utilize them in moving children towards formal algorithms requires substantial experience as a teacher.

These important distinctions between what might be broadly classified as academic content knowledge and pedagogical content knowledge are not intended, here, to diminish the importance of the recommendations made by the CBMS (2000) report. Similar emphasis on the pedagogical content knowledge needed by teachers of mathematics is embedded in *Principles and Standards for School Mathematics* (NCTM, 2000) in its conception of effective teaching as "understanding what students know and need to learn and challenging and supporting them to learn it well" (p. 11).

Having made such a distinction, it is important to consider what might reasonably be accomplished during courses of initial teacher preparation. By and large, this is the time when sound conceptual knowledge needs to be consolidated and the foundations laid for pedagogical content knowledge. Content knowledge is invariably refined as a result of initial teaching experience. Pedagogical content knowledge is in a different category. Those completing initial teacher preparation can, at best, be viewed as novice holders of such knowledge. Such knowledge typically develops as a result of professional practice and opportunities to reflect upon that practice. It is sometimes called situated or case-specific knowledge. It cannot be taught or imparted in the same way as conceptual knowledge. The more seriously one takes this latter kind of knowledge as fundamental to the profession of teaching, the more seriously one has to view regulating entry to the profession as a process that commences with initial training but necessarily must continue well beyond that stage.

7. AN EMERGING CRISIS

Demographic factors and changing employment patterns in the U.S. and in many other countries have made it urgent to find new ways not only of recruiting new teachers of mathematics but also of regulating their entry to the profession. Old models are unlikely to work under these changing conditions. Delineating these factors for the United States can help to illuminate issues common to many other countries. There are acute shortages in specific subject areas such as mathematics, and it is estimated that by 2010 the United States will require 2.2 million new teachers. Why should this be a problem when one considers that 200,000 new teachers graduate from U.S. universities and colleges each year?

A range of factors by no means peculiar to the United States can be cited to explain what might be regarded as an emerging crisis. First, enrolments are growing in schools. Birth rates fell during the seventies and levelled out during the eighties, but are now rising again. Second, nearly half of those currently employed have been teaching for 25 years or more. The Glenn Report (2000) predicted that two-thirds of the current teaching force would be replaced in the next 10 years.

The major component of these losses will be retirements of those members of the baby-boomer generation who entered teaching when it was still seen by many as a lifelong profession. Those who now enter the profession are no longer expected to make a lifelong career of teaching. Other causes of a massive impending replacement are attrition and job changes. One-fifth of those who start off as teachers can be expected to leave the profession within three years of starting.

Third, although these statistics apply nationally across the USA, many urban and rural areas have even more difficulty in attracting and retaining new teachers. To this list, one could add the rising expectations for teaching competence and student achievement in mathematics and science (CMBS, 2000).

7.1. *Teacher Shortage in Mathematics*

The U.S. Department of Education has estimated that over the next ten years 240,000 middle and high school mathematics and science teachers will be needed. Of these, nearly 70% will be new to the profession. This critical shortage is compounded by what the Glenn Report (2000) referred to as "the diffuse and therefore uneven quality of the education delivered by teacher preparation institutions" (p. 30). The Report added:

> The sad fact is that many teacher preparation programs do not build an adequate knowledge base in their graduates. An aggressive recruitment program, therefore, must be accompanied by an equally aggressive, and simultaneous, effort to improve teacher preparation. (p. 30)

In making these criticisms of current practices in teacher preparation, the Glenn Report drew on recommendations made by the National Research Council (NRC) in its report, *Educating Teachers of Science, Mathematics and Technology: New Practices for the New Millennium* (NRC, 2000).

Early in 2001, the U.S. weekly, *Time* magazine (April 2, 2001) reported that

"States and school districts are aggressively recruiting new teachers from among the ranks of accountants, doctors, lawyers, retired military officers and other career switchers, who now represent about 5% of the nation's 2.8 million public-school teachers" (p. 68). The same article reported that New York City, in its accelerated certification in the year 2000, hired 350 new teachers after receiving more than 2500 applications, and expected to hire an additional 1500 teachers in 2001. Accelerated teacher certification programs, together with bonuses of the order of $20,000 for those selected, were being offered in Massachusetts, and were being planned for several large city districts in a number of States, including California, Colorado, Louisiana and Missouri.

Clearly such fast-track programs of entry to the profession lack the depth and breadth of the professional sequence offered over four semesters in the University of Wisconsin-Madison programme or of the even shorter programs offered by other colleges and universities. Those completing fast-track training in New York City, for example, are required to pass State examinations before receiving full certification. Their is no temporary or provisional certification. These intensive programs necessarily focus on basic methods of teaching, lesson planning, legal responsibilities of teachers, and techniques for maintaining classroom control. Teachers completing these intensive programs are often required to accept employment in hard-to-staff or low-performing schools in return for a bonus payment.

It should be noted that teachers completing fast-track certification are typically people of considerable experience in professions. Placed in schools which are often experiencing severe problems with student discipline and truancy, there is understandable concern that many will find it hard to cope with full responsibility for classroom teaching. Teacher educators feel that formal mentoring programs during their initial year of teaching should be considered, and ongoing professional education should also be provided. Those responsible for introducing the fast-track certification programs seem to assume that subject matter expertise is of primary importance, especially if those who are recruited are able to fill vacancies in the mathematical sciences and physics. There is an assumption that these second-career teachers will be able to pick up educational knowledge and experience of school operations *on site*, so to speak.

An assumed commitment to teaching in difficult schools is reflected in the call, "Sign up for the most important job in New York City" (cited the *Time* magazine article). The head of the New York City schools was quoted as saying, "Urban education has the same moral force as the civil rights movement". A similar sense of idealism, seriousness of moral purpose and altruism were inherent in *Teach for America* (TFA), a programme which, over a decade ago, pioneered a precedent for fast-track certification. Popkewitz (1998) provided a brief account of the origins of TFA in the following passage:

In 1989, a senior at Princeton University proposed in her thesis that a private organization be created to find a solution to the shortage of teachers

for urban and rural schools through an alternative teacher education programme that would bring liberal arts graduates into teaching. After she
graduated, funds were solicited from private businesses and foundations in
order to develop an organization that would provide an alternative
certification/teacher education program. By the end of the year following
her graduation, the program was functioning with its first 500 recruits from
the finest private and public universities in the nation. After an eight-week
training session at the University of California, the students were placed as
full-time teachers in rural Georgia and North Carolina; Baton Rouge and
New Orleans, Louisiana; New York City; and the metropolitan areas of
Los Angeles. (p. 8)

The recruits were expected to teach for two years working with students in
disadvantaged schools. Like the fast-track certification programs described in
the *Time* magazine article, TFA sought to provide solutions to longstanding
problems faced by disadvantaged urban and rural schools. Popkewitz (1998)
emphasized that the TFA Program "intended to change the way in which
teachers were recruited and attacked what was seen to be the entrenched inept-
ness of government bureaucracy" (p. 8). The emergence in more recent years of
alternative certification programs for second-career teachers has likewise been
intended to channel scarce resources in ways that are more efficient than the
traditional method of employing graduates of schools of education.

Recruitment procedures instituted by TFA, as Popkewitz (1998) described
them, were "modelled on the Peace Corps – active recruitment, short time
commitment, selective and centralized application process, intensive training,
placement and a support mechanism" (p. 13). Popkewitz (1998) also provided
details of the 8-week Summer Institute held at the University of Southern
California. According to Popkewitz, the Institute provided for an intensive
15-hours-a-day, 6-days-a-week, 8-week training programme aimed at assisting
recruits to acquire teaching skills and cross-cultural understanding as well as
providing them with intensive experience in schools as student teachers. Each
corps member was placed in a Los Angeles Unified School District classroom
to work with an experienced cooperating teacher for six weeks. There, they spent
the mornings in classrooms, with the afternoons being assigned, in most instances,
to teacher education classes that corresponded with the subject area they would
teach in the Fall (pp. 13–14).

7.2. *Difficult Times Call for New Measures*

As we have seen, the Glenn Report (2000) drew attention to specific and urgent
problems confronting the teaching of mathematics and science. According to
Darling-Hammond (1999), more than 25% of high school mathematics teachers
lacked a major sequence in their subject area and did not possess even a minor
sequence; and 27% of students taking high school mathematics were taught by
out-of-field teachers. More than 12% of newly recruited teachers entered the

classroom without any formal professional training and about 14% entered the profession without meeting the teaching standards of their states. Darling-Hammond (1999) pointed to an even bleaker situation in those schools with the highest proportion of minority enrolments. Only 50 per cent of the Mathematics and Science classes in those schools, which are usually in high poverty areas, were being taught by teachers with both a licence and a degree in the field being taught.

The Glenn Report (2000) was clear that unregulated entry into the profession has left the U.S. school system with serious problems. The same Report was also clear that the causes of these deficiencies were likely to remain unless substantial reforms occurred. These reforms would be needed in patterns of teacher preparation, the recruitment of new teachers, support for those who are currently teaching out-of-field, and in the provision of support within district and within schools for those who teach mathematics and science.

The primary criterion by which a programme of teacher preparation is judged effective, according to the Glenn Report, rests in its capacity to impart a deep understanding of subject content. The Report argued that there could be no substitute for a deep knowledge of the subject matter being taught. Both it and the Report of the College Board for Mathematical Sciences (2000) clearly articulated the view that content knowledge should embrace more than listing what subject content knowledge students are expected to acquire. It should also include effective teaching methods on how to teach the key concepts of school mathematics. The terms 'pedagogical content knowledge', as used by Shulman (1984, 1987), or 'deep understanding' as used by Ma (2000), to which reference has previously been made, seem to come close to capturing the applied or situated content knowledge that is at the heart of teaching mathematics.

The Glenn Report (2000) maintained that rigorous performance criteria needed to identify exemplary programs of teacher preparation which went well beyond those that were currently being used by those bodies that accredit programs of teacher preparation. Faced with the pressing issues discussed above, teacher preparation institutions in the United States, and elsewhere, will be under pressure to devise new courses and pathways for certification. Any search for 'rigorous criteria', as envisaged by the Glenn Report, will be undertaken in rapidly changing circumstances.

The Glenn Report is to be commended on seeing entry to the profession not as a single transition point in a teacher's career but as an ongoing process of professional development. It pointed to the responsibilities of authorized certificating bodies for:

[carrying out] needs assessments and publishing data on mathematics and science teaching that emerge from these assessments; helping schools and schools districts consider ways to align their state curricula, teaching guidelines, performance standards and assessment frameworks; disseminating models for restructuring the school day and teachers' responsibilities to

provide sufficient time to support a system of ongoing professional development; collecting and disseminating research on improving mathematics ...
teaching; [and] measuring progress and making the results of implementing
these action strategies widely known to the public. (pp. 28–29)

The language used in these recommendations reflected the division of responsibilities peculiar to the governance of schools in the United States. Indeed, it may
be argued that the fragmentation of responsibility for schools among 15,000
school districts in the United States makes the possibility of reform very difficult.
It is therefore not surprising that new initiatives for teacher certification appear
to have come from large city districts which have the necessary infrastructure
to undertake these reforms and to liaise effectively with state governments, city
administrations and universities. The Glenn Report sought to deal with problems
caused by fragmentation in school governance by setting up coordinating coun-
cils and partnerships between schools and industry.

7.3. *Ongoing Professional Development*

The implementation of recommendations in the Glenn Report, such as the
establishment of two-week summer institutes to support the professional development of teachers, and providing subject matter training for out-of-field teachers
as well as workshops for already certified teachers, will require funding from
government and school districts. Federal and state government backing will also
be needed to establish 15 Mathematics and Science Teaching Academies across
the nation to coordinate exemplary teacher preparation in mathematics and
science, even if these academies are not expected to require new buildings and
plant. The role of these Academies is to provide a one-year intensive course in
effective teaching, as distinct from a fast-track programme of certification, for
up to 3000 prospective teachers, either college graduates or mid-career candidates
(both holding a degree in mathematics or science). Those in the former category
would be competitively selected for teacher training, and the fast-track programme enrollees would be supported during the programme, involving a school-
based internship and supervised teaching, by a $30,000 stipend.

Graduates from such programs would, it is assumed, be targeted for school
districts that suffer a chronic shortage of suitably qualified teachers in mathematics and science. In addition, the Glenn Report proposed that such districts be
offered a federal grant of $10,000 to hire graduates of these Mathematics and
Science Teaching Academies (p. 32). The strategies proposed by the Glenn
Report were similar to those described earlier in fast-track programs of certification for second career teachers: financial rewards for those selected and for
districts prepared to hire new certified teachers.

To its credit, the Glenn Report recognized that sound professional preparation
is less likely to be achieved in an intensive 6-week or 8-week summer program.
The Report also recognized that schools where new graduates are most urgently
needed are least likely to offer opportunities for continuing school-based professional development to cover the inevitable gaps left by a fast-track program. On

the other hand, those cities which have embarked on fast-track certification recognize that a 1-year 'deluxe' programme of teacher preparation will not be sufficient to attract many second-career or other mature-age candidates unless they are offered a substantial stipend during their course of training. Nothing short of a nationally coordinated and well-funded strategy is needed if the recommendations of the Glenn Report are to be implemented.

Establishing, in each school, 'inquiry groups' intended to provide time for teachers to work together on common issues – similar to the teacher study groups in Japan – will require a review of school roles and teaching responsibilities. It will also require a shift in a school culture which has seen teachers as sovereign in their own classrooms. Those needed to lead summer institutes and local inquiry groups will need some form of advanced certification such as that provided by the National Board for Professional Teaching Standards (NBPTS, 2000). New roles for these leading teachers will need to be devised in their home schools, along with suitable changes to promotion structures, salary scales, and a capacity for such teachers to work across schools and in some cases across districts.

8. WHAT MIGHT THE STAFFING OF A MATHEMATICS DEPARTMENT IN A SCHOOL LOOK LIKE IN THE FUTURE?

In ten years' time, what might be expected of the typical profile of staff in a mathematics department in a high school? This glimpse at a possible future may well apply to any one of many countries currently experiencing an acute shortage of well-prepared graduates and the imminent loss, through retirement, of many who are currently holding the profession together.

Given the almost inevitable slowness of governments to respond to mathematics teacher shortages, a high school mathematics department in 10 years time is unlikely to have a full complement of fully certified teachers of mathematics. Out of 10 or so teachers engaged in teaching mathematics, a minority – at most three or four – might be fully certified. In an ideal situation, one of these might hold advanced certification in mathematics, such as provided by a national board (c.f., NBPTS, 2000), and would be responsible for providing and coordinating on-site training and professional development for other members of the faculty. There might be three or four other teachers who have minor certification in mathematics but lacking either a major study in mathematics or have not experienced supervised teaching in mathematics as part of their training. Some of these teachers may be working towards certification in mathematics. Another group of teachers, three or so, could be expected to hold a limited-term or provisional licence, having been recruited with a mathematics major or equivalent academic study, and needing to complete professional training and other requirements for full certification within a specified period following employment.

In this future scenario, school-based professional development and training will be an essential component of regulating entry into the profession. Those pathways of entry that have more or less sufficed in the past will not be able to provide sufficient graduates. Ongoing professional training will be an essential component of the work of teachers and to improving the quality of teaching Mathematics. Stigler (1999) has remarked that the key to this improvement "is to figure out how to generate and share professional knowledge" among all those who teach. This may not only be the key to improvement but to the very survival of the profession in the immediate future.

REFERENCES

Ball, D. L. (1993). With an eye on the mathematical horizon: Dilemmas of teaching elementary school mathematics. *Elementary School Journal, 93*(4), 373–397.

Carpenter, T. P., & Levi, L. (2000). *Developing conceptions of algebraic thinking in the elementary grades. Research report.* Madison, WI: National Center for Improving Student learning and Achievement in Mathematics and Science (see also www.wcer.wisc.edu/ncisla/publications/index.html)

College Board for the Mathematical Sciences (CBMS) (2000). *Mathematical Education of Teachers Project* (draft report). Washington, D. C.: Author.

Darling-Hammond, L. (1999). *Supply, demand and quality in mathematics and science teaching.* Briefing for the National Commission on Mathematics and Science Teaching for the 21st Century, National Commission for Mathematics and Science Teaching, Washington, D. C.

Davis, R. B. (1964). *Discovery in mathematics: A text for teachers.* Palo Alto, CA: Addison-Wesley.

Kaput, J. (1998). Transforming algebra from an engine of inequity to an engine of mathematical power by 'algebrafying' the K-12 curriculum. In National Council of Teachers of Mathematics, *The nature and role of algebra in the K-14 curriculum.* Washington, D. C.: National Academy Press.

Keitel, C., & Kilpatrick, J. (1999). The rationality and irrationality of international comparative studies. In G. Kaiser, E. Luna & I. Huntley (Eds.), *International comparisons in mathematics education* (pp. 241–256). London: Falmer Press.

Kieran, C. (1992). The learning and teaching of school algebra. In D. Grouws (Ed.), *Handbook of research on mathematics teaching and learning* (pp. 390–419). New York: Macmillan.

Martin, M. O., & Mullis, I. V. S. (2000). International comparisons of student achievement: Perspectives from the TIMSS International Study Center. In D. Shorrocks-Taylor & E. W. Jenkins (Eds.), *Learning from others* (pp. 29–47). Dordrecht, The Netherlands: Kluwer Academic Publishers.

Matz, M. (1982). Towards a process model for school algebra errors. In D. Sleeman & J. S. Brown (Eds.), *Intelligent tutoring systems* (pp. 25–50). New York: Academic Press.

National Board for Professional Teaching Standards (2000). *A distinction that matters: Why national teacher certification makes a difference.* Arlington, VA: Author.

National Office of Overseas Skills Recognition (NOOSR) (1992). *Country education profiles: Netherlands – A comparative study.* Canberra: Department of Employment, Education and Training (DEET), Australian Government Publishing Service.

National Research Council (2000). *Educating teachers of science, mathematics and technology: New practices for the new millennium.* Washington, D. C.: National Academy Press.

Olsen, S. (1999, May/June,). Candid camera. *Teacher Magazine on the Web.*

Popkewitz, T. S. (1998). *Struggling for the soul: The politics of schooling and the construction of the teacher.* New York: Teachers College Press.

Schmidt, W. H., McKnight, C. C., Valverde, G. A., Houang, R. T., & Wiley, D. E. (1997). *Many visions, many aims, Volume 1: A cross-national investigation of curricular intentions in school mathematics.* Dordrecht, The Netherlands: Kluwer Academic Publishers.

Schmidt, W. H., McKnight, C. C., & Raizen, S. A. (1997). *An investigation of U.S. science and mathematics education.* Dordrecht, The Netherlands: Kluwer Academic Publishers.

Schmidt, W. H., McKnight, C. C., Houang, R. T., Wang, H. C., Wiley, D. E., Cogan, L. S., & Wolfe,

R. G. (2000). *Why schools matter: A cross-national comparison of curriculum and learning.* San Francisco: Jossey-Bass.

Seago, N. (1999). *Eighth-grade mathematics lessons: United States, Japan, and Germany* (videotape). Washington, D. C.: U.S. Department of Education.

Shifter, D. (1999). Reasoning about algebra: Early algebraic thinking in Grades K-6. In L. V. Stiff & F. R. Curcio (Eds.), *Developing mathematical reasoning in Grades K-12* (pp. 62–81). Reston, VA: National Council of Teachers of Mathematics.

Shimizu, Y. (2001). *Personal communication.*

Shulman, L. S. (1984). The practical and the eclectic: A deliberation on teaching and educational research. *Curriculum Inquiry, 14*(2), 183–200.

Shulman, L. S. (1987). Knowledge and teaching: Foundations of the new reform. *Harvard Educational Review, 57*(1), 1–17.

Silver, E. A. (1997). Algebra for all – Increasing students' access to algebraic ideas, not just algebra courses. *Mathematics Teaching in the Middle School, 2*(4), 204–207.

Stevenson, H. W., & Stigler, J. W. (1992). *The learning gap: Why our schools are failing and what we can learn from Chinese and Japanese education.* New York: Simon and Schuster.

Stigler, J. W. (1999). *Briefing for the National Commission on Mathematics and Science Teaching for the 21st Century.* Washington, D. C.: United States Department of Education.

Stigler, J. W., Gonzales, P., Kawanaka, T., Knoll, S., & Serrano, A. (1999). *The TIMSS Videotape Classroom Study: Methods and findings from an exploratory research project on eighth grade mathematics instruction in Germany, Japan and the United States.* Washington, D. C.: National Center for Educational Statistics.

Stigler, J. W., & Hiebert, J. (1999). *The teaching gap: Best ideas from the world's teachers for improving education in the classroom.* New York: The Free Press.

Teo, C. H. (2000 May). *21st century education: Embracing change yet remaining constant and timeless.* Keynote address by Radm Teo Chee Hean, Minister for Education and 2nd Minister for Defence of Singapore, to the 30th International Management Symposium, University of St. Gallen, Switzerland (see www1.moe.sg/speeches/sp26052000c.html).

United States Department of Education (2000). *Before it's too late: A report to the nation from the National Commission on Mathematics and Science Teaching for the 21st Century* (Glenn Report). Washington, D. C.: Author.

Van den Heuvel-Panhuizen, M., & Broekman, H. (2002). *Personal communication.*

22
Examining the Mathematics in Mathematics Teacher Education

THOMAS J. COONEY and HEIDE G. WIEGEL

The University of Georgia

ABSTRACT

Central to the preparation of mathematics teachers is their preparation in math-ematics. Consequently, a careful examination of the nature of teachers' mathemati-cal experiences is warranted. There are many factors that influence the teaching of mathematics including the historical development of mathematics with its inher-ent formalism. This linkage will be explored along with a review of research on teachers' beliefs and knowledge of mathematics as beliefs and knowledge relate to teacher change. We conclude that this research suggests that teachers are not always well positioned to adopt a more reform- and process-oriented teaching style that moves beyond the usual formalism in the teaching of mathematics. Grounded in this review of the literature, three principles for teaching preservice teachers mathematics will be presented. These principles are: (a) treating mathematics as a pluralistic subject, (b) providing teachers with opportunities to understand and reflect on school mathematics, and (c) enabling teachers to experience mathematics as a process. We will discuss and illustrate these principles using a specific mathe-matical problem solved from a variety of perspectives.

INTRODUCTION

It seems obvious to suggest that mathematics is an integral part of mathematics teacher education. But the word *mathematics* has many meanings and inter-pretations. We speak of the mathematics courses teachers take in order to be certified as teachers of mathematics. Here, it would seem, mathematics refers to a subject consisting of fixed objects that, more or less, are consistent across teacher education programs. For example, most high school mathematics teach-ers will have studied calculus, abstract algebra, and other elements of advanced mathematics. Most of their elementary school counterparts will have studied number systems and certain aspects of geometry and measurement. Although there are differences across cultures in what is regarded as mathematics, nonethe-less, there is more consistency than diversity.

But there is also the mathematics of the mind, both the teacher's mind and

Second International Handbook of Mathematics Education, 795–828
A.J. Bishop, M.A. Clements, C. Keitel, J. Kilpatrick and F.K.S. Leung (eds.)
© *2003 Dordrecht: Kluwer Academic Publishers. Printed in Great Britain.*

the student's mind. Constructivists would argue that mathematics is of the mind for where else could it be. Even when we agree that mathematics is what the mind makes it to be, in our teaching we often act as if the mathematics to be taught is of the fixed variety and not of the constructed variety. Indeed, one of the goals of teacher education is to enable teachers to see the mathematics that is in the minds of their students, perhaps by first exploring the mathematics in their own minds.

Our chapter focuses on several aspects of mathematics in the hope of elucidating how teachers' mathematical experiences can provide a foundation for their teaching of mathematics that honours both the canon of school mathematics and the mathematics constructed by teacher and students. We will begin by examining various historical perspectives about mathematics and what we know about teachers' conceptions of mathematics. We conclude with three illustrated principles for developing a mathematical perspective for mathematics teacher education.

1. THE RELEVANCE OF HISTORICAL PERSPECTIVES

The history of the development of mathematics is long and deep. Plato believed that the objects of mathematics have a real, objective existence in some ideal state beyond the human experience. Plato's student, Aristotle, allowed that our senses constitute a source of mathematical ideas: "In Aristotle's view, the construction of a mathematical idea comes through idealizations performed by the mathematician as a result of experiences with objects" (Dossey, 1992, p. 40).

The contrast between Plato and Aristotle centred on whether mathematical objects are abstractions from our experiences or whether those abstractions are independent of human experience. At issue is whether mathematical understanding comes about "through the collection and classification of empirical results derived from experiments and observations and then by deduction of a system to explain the inherent relationships in the data" (Dossey, 1992, p. 40).

About 2000 years after Plato, Descartes also strove to divorce mathematical thinking from experience rooted in the senses and emphasized a separation between rationalism and experimentalism. By assuming the position of a skeptic, Descartes allowed that there were certain things that could be known with certainty, things that could not be deceived by our senses. This emphasis on developing knowledge based on reason rather than our senses led to what is sometimes referred to as Cartesian philosophy.

The tension between mathematics as pure reason, the *sine qua non* of science, and mathematics as a subject grounded in the senses has been an issue throughout the history of mathematics. The schools of thought developed by Frege, Brouwer, and Hilbert generated debates among philosophers of mathematics. Frege, a developer of the logician school of thought, saw mathematics as a special instance of logic. Whitehead and Russell revealed the difficulty of this approach in the various paradoxes they identified. Brouwer, who was credited with founding the intuitionist school of thought, viewed mathematics as a set of objects that arose from valid demonstrations. Unlike the logician school, the intuitionalist school saw logic as a subset of mathematics. Hilbert developed a third school of mathematical thinking that became known as the formalist school. This school was based on the notion that mathematics is the product of formal axiomatic systems. This attempt to characterize mathematics was largely discredited by Gödel (1931) – see Benacerraf and Putnam (1964) and Dossey (1992) for more complete analyses.

Each of these different schools has contributed to the advancement of mathematics. Each has attempted to establish the notion of mathematical truth, thus freeing mathematics from possible fallibility that characterizes the human condition. By contrast, Lakatos (1976), in his classic work *Proofs and Refutations*, directly assaulted the notion of mathematics as an infallible science. Lakatos perceived mathematics as the bastion of dogmatisms, a circumstance he challenged with his heuristical approach.

Others addressed the notion of science, truth, and fallibilism (or infallibilism) as well. Born (1968), in his self-reflective analysis, concluded that "the belief in the possibility of a clear separation between objective knowledge and the pursuit of knowledge has been destroyed by science itself" (p. 190). Davis and Hersh (1981) argued that the search for an infallible foundation for mathematics was not a productive line of inquiry and focused instead on the notion of mathematics as a fallible subject. These authors described their own transformation of dealing with the different schools of mathematical thought and, through their teaching about these schools, recognized the need for a broader perspective regarding a philosophy of mathematics.

Hersh (1986) further argued that there was little to be gained when mathematicians try to fix any of the three schools of mathematical thought. Rather, the focus should be on current practice in which the fallibility of mathematics is acknowledged and is seen as an opportunity to explore human invention rather than as a curse to be avoided.

In light of the severity of the attacks on the absolutist view of mathematics, Ernest (1991) accepted the fallibilist view of mathematics and considered the implications of such a view for mathematics education. Ernest was quick to note that abandonment of the absolutist perspective does not relegate mathematics to uncertainty. Rather, we must recognize that the absolutist view is an idealization, not a reality. Ernest's perspective, and that of others who adhere to a fallibilistic perspective, reject the Cartesian philosophy and the notion that our knowledge should be grounded in a certain irrefutable logic.

It should be recognized that practising mathematicians and teachers in our schools are seldom paralyzed by the tension between an absolutist and a fallibilistic perspective. As Dossey (1992) noted, the mathematician is less governed by a specific school of thought and more by the specific circumstances of his or her work. Teachers of school mathematics seldom have time for lofty debates on the fallibility of mathematics as their world is far more practical. Nevertheless, one can find traces of the different schools in the teaching of school mathematics.

For example, the so-called modern mathematics of the 1960s had a strikingly formalistic perspective that honoured a highly axiomatic approach to mathematics. By contrast, constructivist perspectives that emerged in the 1980s were grounded in a fallibilistic view of mathematics.

One might argue that whether mathematics is God-given or an invention of the human mind is largely irrelevant in terms of thinking about the teaching and learning of mathematics and the preparation of those who will become teachers of mathematics. Yet, in almost every classroom the authors have observed, across many cultures, the tentacles of these theoretical perspectives reveal themselves in certain unmistakable ways.

Most people still consider mathematics as abstract, formal, and irrefutable. Indeed, this certainty is attractive to many teachers and students. You know when you have the right, usually unique, answer. Yes, there are excursions into the empirical world when young children use manipulatives or when older students use geometric software to explore certain relationships. But the empirical approach is usually seen as a vehicle for realizing the abstractness of mathematics and not as a valid way of thinking.

One of the authors recalls a conversation with a mathematician who had just completed teaching a course to middle school teachers. When asked how the course went, his reply was something like the following, "It went great until we started doing mathematics". He was referring to the fact that the first part of the course provided the teachers with exploratory, empirical mathematical investigations and the second part of the course was devoted to a more formal, abstract mathematical development. It was the latter part of the course that constituted mathematics in the eyes of this instructor.

Wittmann (1992) claimed that the formalistic and structured nature of mathematics carries with it an implied pedagogy that is likewise formalistic and structured. Wittmann's point implies that those who have extensive experience with abstract mathematics may be more inclined to adopt a formalistic and structured approach to teaching. Owens (1987) found that preservice teachers who seemed to handle the abstractness of mathematics best often had a more formalistic view of mathematics and of the teaching of mathematics. All of this is to suggest that should mathematics educators want teachers to have a broader view of mathematics in the sense of seeing mathematics as both a formal system and as an empirical science, then the road to this perspective is likely not through formal training in mathematics itself.

The old adage that "teachers teach as they were taught, not how they were taught to teach" has considerable merit. How is it, then, that the mathematical education of teachers can honour much of the historical development of mathematics yet provide a perspective that enables teachers to teach mathematics as a subject that is more than a formalized set of topics? The evidence suggests that the extent to which mathematics is taught from a pluralistic perspective is to a great extent dependent on what the teacher believes about mathematics and its teaching. Hence, we provide a brief review of what research tells us about teachers' conceptions of mathematics and its teaching. Simultaneously, we shall consider the kinds of mathematical experiences for teachers that can promote the teaching we envisage necessary to promote a broader, fallibilistic view of mathematics.

2. TEACHERS' CONCEPTIONS OF MATHEMATICS

There exists a fairly substantial body of literature on teachers' beliefs and knowledge about mathematics. In this section we will consider teachers' beliefs about mathematics and its teaching and learning and their knowledge of mathematics. The distinction between beliefs and knowledge provides more of an organizational scheme for our review rather than a sharp distinction between the two concepts.

2.1. *Research on Teachers' Beliefs*

It seems fair to say that the common mode of teaching mathematics is rooted in a traditional style of lecture and guided discussion in which teachers present mathematics and students work assigned problems. There are exceptions to this as some teachers have been observed to use a more intuitive discussion mode of presentation and other teachers play a more passive role expecting students to solve problems on their own. Nevertheless, the modal approach is traditional. This is not to say that such teaching is bad. Students can learn from lessons in which the instructor uses appropriate and well-chosen illustrations and clearly demonstrates procedures. It is likely that most of the readers of this volume prospered in such an environment when they were students.

Most reform movements, however, and scholars who support those movements advocate a more student-centred, process-oriented approach which we will refer to as *reform-based* teaching. We will use reform-based teaching and process-based teaching interchangeably. The publication *Principles and Standards for School Mathematics* (National Council of Teachers of Mathematics [NCTM], 2000) represents one attempt to provide direction toward development of a more process-oriented teaching style. Indeed, there are many other documents and movements that similarly emphasize processes such as reasoning, problem solving, and communication. Given teachers' propensity to teach mathematics in a teacher-centred way, to what extent are their beliefs elastic enough to adopt such a teaching style?

Wilson and Goldenberg's (1998) two-year study of Mr Burt, a middle school teacher who welcomed the opportunity to reform his teaching, is a case in point. The authors noted that although Mr Burt's teaching became more conceptually oriented, his basic teaching style remained teacher centred. They concluded that, "Mr Burt's approach generally portrayed mathematics as a rigid subject to be mastered and correctly applied, rather than as a way of thinking or as a subject to be explored" (p. 287). One of the contributing factors to this circumstance appeared to be Mr Burt's weak understanding of the underlying mathematics although this was not the only factor. Left unanswered is the question of whether

Mr Burt's view of mathematics as a formalized, structured subject also contributed to his inability to move toward a more process-oriented approach to teaching.

Schifter (1998) reported that teachers' adopted a reform mode of teaching after they had participated in a professional development program that had focused on the mathematical ideas the teachers were to teach and on how children constructed those ideas. The importance of this approach rests with the teachers interacting with mathematics in such a way that they had to reflect on their own understanding as well as their students' understanding. Schifter concluded that "teachers must come not only to expect, but to seek, situations in their own teaching in which they can view the mathematics in new ways, especially through the perspectives that their students bring to the work" (p. 84). That is, Schifter provided a context in which the teachers could experience mathematics not as a formalized subject but as a subject that resulted from human invention.

Grant, Hiebert, and Wearne (1998) described what teachers see when they observe alternative forms of teaching. As might be expected, teachers see what their beliefs allow them to see, that is, their beliefs act as a filter through which their observations are shaped. Teachers with more traditional beliefs tended to focus on the details of the lessons and the types of materials used by the teachers. The authors provided the following analysis:

> To the extent that these [teachers'] beliefs define mathematics as a series
> of procedural rules and hold the teacher responsible for students acquiring
> these rules, teachers will acquire little from watching demonstrations of
> reform-minded instruction. These teachers are likely to consider the use of
> alternative strategies as confusing and detrimental to their students despite
> the fact that the students were successful on the end-of-the-year test. (p. 233)

By contrast, teachers with more reform-minded beliefs were more likely to focus on children's mathematical thinking and to appreciate more process-based instructional styles. Teachers whose beliefs were more aligned with a process-oriented learning and student responsibility for learning perspective were better able to internalize many of the precepts of reform-minded teaching.

Skott (2001) maintained that teachers' beliefs about mathematics interact with other beliefs or with certain social constituents that involve the school culture more generally and classroom interactions more specifically. Skott argued that we should question "direct connections between teachers' priorities in school mathematics and classroom interactions" (p. 25). In his study of Christopher, a novice teacher, he found that at times Christopher's primary interest was in students' learning of mathematics but at other times his primary interest was couched in more general educational goals such as building students' confidence. Indeed, it seemed that Christopher's dominant belief seemed to be his view of learning and what he considered the organizational consequences of that belief. Skott concluded that "the degree to which other aspects of Christopher's SMIs

[School Mathematics Images] influence the classroom is contingent on their compatibility with the dominant organizational approach" (p. 26).

Gellert's (2000) study of 42 elementary preservice teachers revealed that many of the teachers held the view that their role as teachers of mathematics was to protect their students from the teachers' own frightening mathematical experiences. In order to achieve their goals, the teachers introduced child-centred media for instruction and reduced the mathematical content. Teachers saw as one of their goals the protection of children from that abstractness for which children are not intellectually ready.

Chauvot (2000) studied three secondary preservice teachers (Liz, Brenda, & Stacey) who participated in a reform-oriented teacher education program that was based, to a large extent, on the NCTM Standards. Perhaps because it was a reform-oriented program, the teachers' views of mathematics and mathematics teaching reflected elements of a reform-oriented teaching style. For example, Liz appreciated multiple representations of mathematical concepts and viewed problem solving as a means of enabling students to see connections among mathematical concepts. Nevertheless, their newly acquired reform-oriented beliefs were grounded in rather traditional views of mathematics and its teaching. Brenda, who learned a variety of new techniques for solving problems during her teacher education program, also felt that she had already learned in high school all of the mathematics she needed to know. Stacey saw mathematics as a subject in which "everything fits together" and especially appreciated how mathematics was connected to other school subjects. For Stacey, mathematics was about meaning and not memorization.

Yet Stacey, as did Brenda and Liz, saw mathematics primarily as a subject to be acquired from an external source, that is, an authority who had the responsibility to verify mathematical truths. As learners, they saw their teachers as these authorities. As teachers, they expected to be the authorities. Although they did not envision teaching mathematics in ways which would relegate students to passive roles, they did see themselves developing carefully constructed lessons and activities to promote learning. Their sureness about the certainty of mathematics led them to see their role as teachers as that of clearly laying out the mathematics for their students. Laudable as this may be, it suggests a view of mathematics that is external to the student in the sense that the school's curriculum, not the students' thinking, largely determines what mathematics gets taught. Chauvot's teachers acknowledged much of the reform message yet held it at bay in lieu of the notion that their students would likely learn mathematics much as they had learned it.

Eggleton (1995) provided an in-depth analysis of a single secondary preservice teacher, Ken, as he progressed through his teacher education program. Initially, Ken's view of mathematics was as a set of rules and guidelines that he collectively referred to as 'number crunching'. Ken saw mathematics as certain and made up of absolute truths. His view of teaching was essentially that of telling; learning mathematics consisted primarily of practice, discipline, and memorization.

These perspectives led Eggleton (1995) to interpret Ken's initial view of mathematics education as 'Dualistic-Absolutist' (Ernest, 1991). But Ken allowed that these views were not unquestioned, a circumstance that led to certain changes when he engaged more process-orientated mathematical activities. Once Ken's views were challenged, he underwent a re-examination of his beliefs that led to a view of mathematics not unlike that described by Tymoczko's (1986) description of a quasi-empiricist philosophy of mathematics. It was not that Ken bought into the whole reform notion. Rather, he sorted through the reform philosophy and assimilated, without accommodation, various aspects of reform. He maintained a rather absolutist view of mathematics but allowed that such processes as reasoning and problem solving could facilitate an understanding of that mathematics. It was not so much that Ken reinvented his philosophy of mathematics education but rather that he accepted a broader perspective without denying his initial beliefs. Perhaps this explains why his student teaching performance was rather routine and traditional with only occasional forays into the processes of problem solving and reasoning.

Frykholm (1999) reported that most of the preservice teachers he studied "had never engaged in the type of mathematics experiences advocated by the reform movement" (p. 97). Their secondary experiences had been lecture oriented and void of the kinds of empirical experiences in which they could ground their mathematics. Further, they generally had excelled in high school mathematics. So why should they consider alternative methods of teaching? Reform demands serious thinking and discussion yet university supervisors and mentor teachers seldom engage in such conversations. Frykholm concluded that the preservice teachers recognized new ways of teaching mathematics and generated certain beliefs about those ways but the impact of those beliefs on instruction was weak. Frykholm did note, however, that the students recognized a duality between their beliefs and their teaching, a situation that can foster later reflection.

What we see, then, is that teacher education programs can provide a basis for teachers to appreciate a broader view of mathematics and alternatives to teaching beyond telling. But we cannot expect those beliefs to transform teaching as they may be secondary to other beliefs deemed more fundamental. As noted by Skott (2001), beliefs about mathematics are often buffeted by other more centrally-held beliefs and by circumstances particular to schools and society. Further, as emphasized by Schifter (1998), when teachers engage in process-oriented mathematics and particularly the mathematics of their students, there is an increased likelihood that teachers can experience a kind of paradigm shift in their beliefs about mathematics and mathematics teaching. A question then arises about the quality of teachers' mathematical backgrounds which support these new experiences, the focus of the next section.

2.2. *Teachers' Mathematical Backgrounds*

Although the mathematical preparation for elementary teachers varies across countries and types of teacher education programs, the literature strongly suggests that elementary teachers often lack the kind of mathematical sophistication needed to support a reform-oriented agenda that goes beyond the acquisition of skills and procedural knowledge. Brown, Cooney, and Jones (1990) reviewed a number of studies that demonstrated this lack of mathematical sophistication among elementary teachers. Similarly, Ball (1990 a, b) reported that preservice elementary teachers often are not able to provide explanations for mathematical principles even though they have generated or recognized correct answers to problems. Further, they often fail to recognize connections between mathematical topics. Because of their limited mathematical knowledge, it is difficult for them to appreciate the nature of reform in mathematics teaching and adopt practices that promote that reform.

Stacey et al. (2001) found that about 20% of the 553 elementary preservice teachers they studied had an inadequate knowledge of decimals. About 13% of the teachers made errors when they compared a positive decimal number with zero. The authors concluded that "only 57% of the preservice teachers reported that students might have difficulty with the items of the type that they got wrong themselves, indicating that quite a sizeable proportion of preservice elementary school teachers may not suspect they are making errors" (p. 222). The authors cited a number of other studies that demonstrate the difficulty teachers have with understanding decimal numbers.

Cooney, Wilson, Albright, and Chauvot (1998) studied 15 secondary preservice teachers' understanding of function and other selected secondary school content as the teachers began their training in mathematics education. The researchers found that when asked, "What is a function?" preservice teachers tended to equate functions with equations, formulae, or rules. This is indicated in the following responses:

A function is a formula that can have various items inserted.
A function is an equation or graph in which there are no two *y*'s for every *x*.
Is an algebraic equation of a line in a plane.

The preservice teachers were also asked about the importance of studying functions in high school.

Most of the preservice teachers' responses focused on academic reasons. Thus, for example, they maintained that functions should be studied because of their importance to the further study of mathematics. The preservice teachers were generally vague in identifying applications. When asked, "What is similarity?" the responses were likewise vague and often provided a colloquial definition of similarity. When asked to write the equations that reasonably represented the graphs of quadratic, exponential, and logarithmic functions, about one-third of the teachers were not able to recognize the graphs with reasonable accuracy. When asked to provide real world applications of these functions their answers were again vague albeit appropriate. For example, they mentioned growth of bacteria or the calculation of compound interest as examples of exponential functions.

The Cooney et al. (1998) study demonstrates that secondary preservice teachers' knowledge of secondary school mathematics cannot be taken for granted. Although secondary preservice teachers' training in mathematics is typically extensive, their experiences with school mathematics are often limited to their mathematical experiences as teenagers, with all the immaturity that implies. Mentor teachers of student teachers often note student teachers' inability to locate specific lessons within the context of the school's curriculum as a limiting factor in their teaching. That is, student teachers tend to see lessons as singular events; they fail to see a sequence of lessons as contributing to the greater whole.

One conclusion that could easily be drawn from this research is that teachers at all levels need to study more mathematics. Although we could hardly disagree with this conclusion, the question remains, "What kind of mathematics?" It is not clear that the study of advanced mathematics per se results in a better understanding of school mathematics, although it could provide a better foundation for that understanding. Neither is it the case that more experiences with abstract mathematics necessarily result in a broader view of mathematics. Again, this is not to argue for decreased attention to the rigour of mathematics. But it does call our attention to the fact that study of advanced mathematics does not necessarily lead to the kind of beliefs about mathematics and knowledge of school mathematics that promotes an understanding of students' mathematics and a teaching style that fosters problem solving, reasoning, and making connections.

3. RE-EXAMINING THE NOTION OF MATHEMATICS

Davis (1999) pointed to the irony that when society clamours for mathematics education to return to the *basics*, the most basic question is "What is mathematics?" When he posed this question to 19 preservice secondary mathematics teachers, their responses represented attempts to remember what previous instructors had indicated mathematics to be, such as the study of relationships or the study of patterns. What *they* thought mathematics to be was missing from their responses. Through the study of fractals and an emphasis on reflective thinking, Davis encouraged the teachers to consider what mathematics meant to them and what it meant for something to be basic. He helped the preservice teachers appreciate that there is no clear, decisive answer to the question. In conclusion, Davis identified the following response as typical of the teachers' views about what constitutes mathematics:

> When we started, I knew what math was, and I couldn't figure out why you would ask us that. Now [I] realize that I don't know the answer. The weird [ironic] thing is that I also realize my *not* knowing is going to make me a better math teacher (*emphasis in original*). (p. 43)

Davis found that the preservice teachers were essentially aphilosophical with respect to mathematics. Implicit, however, was the notion that mathematics was abstract and 'out there', distinct from the human experience. What emerged from this circumstance is that teachers, especially preservice teachers, need to experience mathematics in a pluralistic way for otherwise their implicit beliefs about mathematics prevail, a circumstance that works against process-oriented teaching of mathematics.

What constructs can guide our thinking about providing such experiences? Lerman (2001) lamented the fact that although various studies have reported changes in teachers' beliefs, there is a dearth of rationales that might account for that change. The notion of reflection is often offered as a basis for change, but Lerman argued that reflection is seldom analyzed in a critical way. The question arises as to whether the profession is today collectively wiser about educating teachers than was the case, say, 20 years ago. Based on the questions being asked and the sophistication of the studies that have evolved over that period, the answer would seem to be 'Yes' despite our impatience to arrive at a more explicit theoretical grounding for our work.

Sowder et al. (1998), for example, outlined four recommendations for educating teachers on multiplicative structures. Those recommendations were grounded in an extensive body of research on children's constructs of rational numbers and then translated into principles for teacher education. But research on learning certain mathematical constructs is not always sufficiently developed to provide guidelines for educating teachers. There is, as Lerman (2001) suggested, a dearth of constructs to guide our thinking.

Our task is to provide principles that are rooted in what we know about teachers' knowledge and beliefs. Although we share Lerman's concern about the lack of theoretical precepts in mathematics teacher education, we maintain that the body of growing research provides a reasonable rationale for the development of effective teacher education programs. Our review suggests several findings that seem consistent across teacher education programs, namely, teachers' beliefs that mathematics is abstract and not based on human experience, a lack of a broader conception of mathematics, and only secondarily held beliefs about the advantages of reform-based teaching. In some sense, this should not be surprising given the historical development of mathematics itself and the fact that the primary emphasis has been on mathematics as an infallible foundation. It seems rather unreasonable to expect teachers to develop a fallibilistic view of mathematics such as suggested by Lakatos, Davis and Hersh, and other scholars given that their experiences in learning mathematics have largely been contrary to a fallibilistic perspective.

The notion of fallibilism in mathematics is grounded in recognition of the fallibility of human activity. We recognize that humans operate in a very pluralistic, multifaceted way. It is the nature of being human. We now present and illustrate three principles for mathematical experiences that we consider essential if teachers are to have the basis for an enriched approach to the teaching of mathematics. These principles stem from mathematical fallibilism and, consequently, emphasize the notion of pluralism.

4. PRINCIPLES FOR TEACHING TEACHERS MATHEMATICS

In light of the previous analysis, we offer three principles that address the kinds of mathematical experiences that would promote an open and process-oriented approach to teaching. Our principles are stated in terms of preservice teachers, but we believe they apply to teachers at all levels of professional development.

- *Principle 1:* Preservice teachers should experience mathematics as a pluralistic subject;
- *Principle 2:* Preservice teachers should explicitly study and reflect on school mathematics; and
- *Principle 3:* Preservice teachers should experience mathematics in ways that support the development of process-oriented teaching styles.

We will elaborate on each of the principles and offer an example of an activity that we have used with preservice teachers that we believe embraces and illustrates the principles.

4.1. *Mathematics as a Pluralistic Subject*

The first principle is perhaps the most fundamental for it provides the basis for what teachers believe about mathematics and how they construct their vision of teaching mathematics. Although the work of Lakatos (1976) and Davis and Hersh (1981) sparked or at least popularized the debate about the fallibility of mathematics, the fact remains that most mathematicians act as if it is a Platonist subject free of flaws.

It is no wonder, then, that this perspective trickles down to the classroom and leaves teachers and students with the view that mathematics is an abstract subject based on formalistic approaches to its development. There is, of course, much truth in this perspective. Mathematics, by its very nature, can be abstract and is to a great extent grounded on formalized reasoning.

But the work of Lakatos (1976), Davis and Hersh (1981), and Ernest (1991) implies that there are other viable interpretations as well. Nevertheless, the seeds of abstractness and formalism are well sown by the time preservice teachers reach their teacher education programs. It is no wonder that Gellert's (2000) elementary teachers saw their task as one of protecting children against the harsh reality of that abstractness and formalism. Wilson and Goldenberg's (1998) Mr Burt portrayed mathematics as a rigid subject rather than as a way of thinking. This interpretation belies those who see mathematics as an infallible subject for surely they did not see mathematics as a rigid and unchanging subject. But where did Mr Burt develop his conception of mathematics? Perhaps, as suggested by Wilson and Goldenberg, his knowledge of the subject itself was lacking which led to a superficial view of mathematics. But it is also possible that his interpretation stems from his experience of mathematics as a formalistic subject which left him to conclude that the subject was not only Platonist but rigid as well.

What would it mean to teach mathematics from a pluralistic perspective? Here we can take clues, although not direct implications, from the historical development of mathematics. Aristotle allowed that mathematics was a product of our senses. Brouwer's conclusion that mathematics is of the mind and its written record is secondary (see Ernest, 1991) supports the notion that mathematics is a subject not detached from our senses. Lakatos (1976) also maintained that mathematics is the object of the mind's invention. Although it is easy to oversimplify and to trivialize the notions of these scholars, there is, nevertheless, the sense that mathematics is not solely the product of formalization – a perspective that gives rise to mathematical pluralism.

At the pragmatic level, pluralism can include the construction of mathematical ideas based on empirical data. For example, students can construct – from a point inside an equilateral triangle – perpendicular segments to the sides of the triangle and measure those segments. They might then conclude that the sum of the measures equals the length of the altitude of the triangle – an empirical, intuitive approach that leads to a generalization subject to verification by a variety of means. Or students can use empirical means to discover that the sum of the distances from an ellipse's foci to a point on the ellipse is equal to the length of the major axis.

Pluralism can mean that the verification process can consist of a variety of approaches that involve different domains of mathematical knowledge. Pluralism can also mean the use of different representations of concepts as, for example, when we represent a fraction using pictorial representations or decimals. It can also mean different solution methods to problems. Consider how or whether the equations

$$2x - 4 = 5 - x \qquad 2^x + 2^{-x} = 10 \qquad x + \log x = 20$$

could be solved with different approaches such as standard algebraic algorithms, spreadsheets, or graphing calculators.

When teachers are engaged in pluralistic mathematical experiences, they tend to see value in those experiences. For example, Chauvot's (2000) Liz appreciated the value of different representations of the same concept and the value of different problem-solving strategies to solve problems. Brenda did as well. Stacey's experiences enabled her to better understand how different mathematical representations are connected. Yet, Chauvot found that these teachers clung to a rather traditional, formalistic view of mathematics. Similarly, Eggleton (1995) found that Ken, who progressed through essentially the same mathematics teacher education program as did Chauvot's three preservice teachers, revised his beliefs about mathematics and its teaching but not in such a fundamental way that it influenced his student teaching.

Perhaps Ken's pluralistic experiences were not deep enough or extensive enough. Or perhaps the constraints existent in student teaching inhibited or even prohibited the more pluralistic teaching style he professed to value. Chauvot's three teachers and Eggleton's Ken were all willing to value a reform-oriented, pluralistic approach to teaching mathematics but not enough that this value would transform their views of mathematics nor, more importantly, their teaching of mathematics.

Skott (2001) reminded us that a pluralistic view of mathematics in and of itself is not sufficient to produce the kind of teaching that honours problem solving, reasoning, and mathematical communication. Rather, there is a myriad of beliefs about a variety of things which interact to produce a teaching style. It is difficult to see how a teacher could adopt a more process-oriented teaching style while holding to a rigid, formalistic view of mathematics. But Skott's point is well taken that a pluralistic view of mathematics may only be a necessary condition for realizing a reform-oriented teaching style.

It is not difficult to see that the task of enabling teachers to see mathematics as something other than a formalized subject is ominous. The anxiety that surrounds elementary teachers' mathematical experiences is legendary. At the secondary level, teachers are among those who have survived and largely prospered from the abstract terrain of collegiate level mathematics. Indeed, often their models of exemplary teaching stem from those same teachers who demonstrate a formalized approach to mathematics. Those are the models they often come to admire, that is, the perceived brilliance of their professors, which suggests to them that they too can be perceived as brilliant if they perpetuate a formalized teaching style. The viciousness of the circularity that each generation passes to the next the notion of mathematics as formal and abstract is difficult to break. But if our schools' teachers are to adopt a more pluralistic approach to the teaching of mathematics then it will need to be challenged and, ultimately, broken.

We would be remiss if we did not emphasize the point that mathematical pluralism in no way rules out the possibility that students experience the formalism of mathematics. Indeed, one of the beauties of mathematics is that we have a system wherein we can verify in a formal way what our senses tell us must surely be the case. Our quarrel is not with formalism per se but rather with the notion that mathematics is only formalism.

In summary, we submit that a pluralistic approach to the teaching of mathematics includes the presentation of mathematics

- as an intuitive subject in which students use pattern recognition to discover mathematical concepts and generalizations,
- as an empirical subject in which students' investigations give rise to mathematical concepts and generalizations, and
- as a formalized system of logical consequences.

Collectively, these views of mathematics are fundamental to reform and should be manifest in teachers' mathematical experiences.

4.2. *Understanding and Reflecting on School Mathematics*

There is extensive evidence that preservice teachers have an insufficient mathematical background to support a more reform-based or process-oriented teaching style (see Brown, Cooney, & Jones, 1990). Certainly the case can be made that teachers need to study more mathematics. But our second principle addresses the need for teachers to study the mathematics that they will be teaching. That is to say, they need to study and reflect on school mathematics. Schifter (1998) pointed out that much can be gained when teachers engage not only the mathematics that they teach but also how children construct that mathematics. Of course, these two kinds of understandings are integrally connected. Stacey et al. (2001) found that elementary teachers' understanding of decimals was such that many of them were not aware of the errors they were making. It would be difficult for teachers with such understanding to appreciate their students' construction of mathematics when, in fact, their own was fraught with error.

Years ago, one of the authors taught a course designed to acquaint preservice secondary teachers with the various curricular projects existing in mathematics education. In an effort to cover the great variety of projects, the teachers were asked to select a project and report to the class about the type and nature of the mathematics in that project. What became abundantly clear was that many of the preservice teachers struggled with the mathematics and revealed a significant lack of understanding school mathematics. It should be mentioned that the teachers had extensive backgrounds in collegiate level mathematics, some with honours.

In an effort to address this problem in subsequent years, the instructor asked the students to purchase school mathematics textbooks. Selected topics were covered from the books. The course was a smashing success in terms of students' evaluations and the immediate face validity of the course's content. What was troubling, however, was the nature of the praise the students provided. For example, it was not uncommon for them to say something like, "This was a great *review* of what I need to know in student teaching". Laudatory as it might seem, the instructor was troubled by two parts of the message. First, he did *not* see the course as a review course. Second, the purpose of the course was not seen solely as preparation for student teaching albeit this perspective was not unreasonable. The outcome of the course with respect to student teaching seemed quite positive. Students expressed less apprehension in having to teach advanced topics or geometry.

What seemed important, then, was to provide the prospective teachers with opportunities to engage school mathematics in an explicit and reflective way. Two specific kinds of activities were developed.

First, preservice teachers were asked to work in groups and solve a variety of construction problems such as:

- Construct an isosceles triangle given one of the equal sides and the altitude to the base.
- Construct a square given a segment that represents the sum of a diagonal and one of the sides.

Because the prospective teachers worked in groups, mathematical communication was fostered. Assessment of their learning required that each teacher had to know how to solve all of the problems although it was not expected that each teacher solved each problem individually. The activity was popular among the preservice teachers for they liked the idea of group work. Further, they learned a considerable amount of secondary school geometry. No longer did they see the course as a review. Finally, some of the teachers adapted the activity as a means of working with their own students during student teaching and when they had their own classroom.

The second group of tasks focused on functions and involved a number of different activities and approaches (see Cooney, Brown, Dossey, Schrage, & Wittmann, 1999). The purpose, again, was to engage the preservice teachers in the *doing* of secondary school mathematics but from a perspective they had not seen. There were no formal definitions of function presented. Rather, students had to grapple with the characteristics of those functions commonly found in the secondary school curriculum through the 'card sort' activity. This activity was particularly appealing to both the instructor and the students. It served as a vehicle to revisit a secondary school topic from a different perspective with pedagogical implications as well. What became abundantly clear was that the teachers' explicit focus on topics in the secondary school curriculum not only had a positive impact on their understanding of that curriculum but also, through reflection on their own learning experiences, resulted in discussions on how their teaching of that curriculum might be reconceptualized.

The work of Cooney et al. (1999) represents one attempt to engage secondary teachers in selected secondary school topics such as functions, the Pythagorean Theorem, combinatorics, and mathematical processes such as modeling and problem posing and solving. The authors' contribution is rooted in the very notion that teachers, especially preservice teachers, should study topics they will eventually be teaching but in a far more sophisticated way than what they had experienced when they were high school students. The Cooney et al. (1998) study demonstrated that secondary preservice teachers' understanding of school mathematics is fragile when they enter their mathematics teacher education programs but, because of their mathematics background, they are positioned to develop a deep understanding of at least certain topics.

Bromme (1994) identified five types of knowledge teachers should possess: school mathematics knowledge, philosophy of school mathematics, pedagogical knowledge, subject-matter-specific pedagogical knowledge, and cognitive integration of knowledge from different disciplines. All but one of these are grounded in an understanding of school mathematics. This, in itself, points to the need for teachers' in-depth study of school mathematics. An example of what would appear to represent Bromme's notion of subject-matter-specific pedagogical knowledge is found in the work of Sowder et al. (1998). Sowder et al's (1998) principles for educating teachers about multiplicative structures are grounded in the extensive literature on those structures. This research involves a number of theoretical precepts but it also assumes an understanding of the mathematics underlying those structures. It would be difficult to understand the value of those principles if a firm grasp of the underlying mathematics was not obtained.

Given that teachers do not always possess the kind of deep understanding of school mathematics that supports and is necessary for a reform-based teaching style, the question about how teachers acquire such understanding remains. The answer does not lie in the study of more advanced mathematics by itself although this might be an important prerequisite for that understanding. Rather, it must be part and parcel of a teachers' training in mathematics education. Therein lies a problem. Even in the most extensive training in mathematics education, this training pales in comparison to the impact of their training in mathematics. Further, it is not likely that the nature of the mathematics courses will change. Perhaps it shouldn't.

For the most part, collegiate level mathematics is governed by a philosophy of identifying and promoting those gifted in doing mathematics – a laudable goal. As Freudenthal (1973) noted, the inclination of the mathematician is to think of mathematics education as a matter of educating one to become a mathematician. By the time individuals pass through the funnel of doing abstract, collegiate level mathematics, we can be assured that they are among the best of those who study mathematics. But teachers, and especially elementary teachers, have a different orientation. For them, mathematics education is not about just identifying the brightest and most able but allowing all children to prosper mathematically.

Consequently, there is a tension between the purposes of mathematics education at the collegiate level and that at the school level. For the elementary teacher, the result is often fear and trepidation in doing mathematics, a consequence that can be a powerful, negative influence on their teaching of mathematics. For the secondary teacher, who has succeeded in such a system, there is the attitude that what was good for them will surely be good for their students. That is, they teach as they were taught.

This is not to disparage collegiate teachers of mathematics who feel the responsibility to produce the able mathematician. Rather, it is to recognize different orientations that often exist between the collegiate teacher and the school teacher. This recognition can begin to deal with the problem that teachers engage school mathematics at a deeper level than has typically been the case. Perhaps the question of studying school mathematics should be extended to inservice programs where the learning of such content has immediate face validity.

But it needs to be recognized that 'filling voids' as a vehicle for acquiring knowledge is unlikely to solve the real problem; it violates Principle 1. It is not only important for teachers to understand the connections among the mathematical topics they teach and how those topics can be realized in real world applications, but also to have a basis for understanding their students' construction of those ideas. Principle 2 involves not only an understanding of school mathematics but the development of an understanding of how students think about that mathematics. Carpenter, Fennema, and Franke's (1996) *Cognitively Guided Instruction* (CGI) program provides one context for teachers to understand children's construction of mathematical knowledge. Properly used, the work of Sowder et al. (1998) can provide another.

The study of collegiate level mathematics can provide a basis for understanding the intricacies of school mathematics, but the development of this second kind of knowledge cannot be assumed given only the acquisition of the first kind. The understanding of children's mathematics goes beyond the mathematics per se but must necessarily be rooted in a thorough understanding of school mathematics.

4.3. *Experiencing Mathematics as Process*

In some sense, the third principle is a consequence of the first two principles. If teachers have been taught mathematics from a pluralistic perspective and if they have had extensive experiences with school mathematics, then a foundation has been laid for them to develop a process-based teaching style. Chauvot's (2000) teachers had such teaching, at least to some extent, and consequently, they saw value in a process-oriented teaching method. But their teacher education experiences were secondary to other, long-term experiences as students of mathematics in schools and the university.

Perhaps this argues for the creation of a greater number of contexts in which teachers experience school mathematics from a pluralistic perspective. Or maybe it argues that preservice teacher education programs are insufficient in themselves to enable teachers to adopt process-oriented teaching styles. Teacher education programs can, however, provide contexts in which preservice teachers can envision such teaching even though they do not engage in such teaching themselves. Recall that Frykholm (1999) found that some preservice teachers who participated in a reform-based teacher education program could not only recognize new ways of teaching but also realized that their own teaching was in contradiction to those ways.

Grant et al's (1998) observation that teachers see what their beliefs allow them to see highlights the need for preservice teachers to experience school mathematics in a pluralistic way and that they envisage how those experiences can be translated into actions as a teacher. Again, one cannot expect such a translation without explicit direction. Mason (1998) argued that teachers need to develop a layered notion of awareness in that they need to become aware of their awareness-in-action which thereby provides grist for reflective thinking and teaching. Mason used the term *awareness* with reference to teachers being aware of their children's awareness-in-action and to their own awareness-in-discipline so that they can be sensitized to work with their students in a mathematically informed and appropriate way.

Mason's (1998) analysis provided a certain symmetry between being aware of others and being aware of our own awareness of others. But, as Mason pointed out, in order for teachers to develop awareness of the sort to which he referred, teacher education programs should help teachers develop the skills that promote awareness and reflection. We support Mason's attention to awareness but add that it should be couched in the context of a pluralistic view of school mathematics. We cannot assume that awareness void of explicit attention to the subject being taught is likely to lead to teaching in which awareness matters.

Ponte (2001) identified a certain parallelism between the activities of the mathematician and that of the student. Ponte noted that an investigative approach to the learning of mathematics receives significant attention in some countries such as France and England. He pointed to the similarity between Polya's four stages of solving a problem (understanding the problem, designing a plan, carrying out the plan, and looking back) and teachers' investigations and action research.

This similarity gives value to the concept of investigation as a vehicle for knowledge construction – whether the teacher is learning how to teach or the student is learning mathematics. Ponte's (2001) point that teachers' experiences in professional development programs need not be structurally different from the kind of experiences one would like students to have as they learn mathematics is well taken. Although the focus of his analysis was on the construct *investigation* applied to a variety of contexts, the investigations could involve mathematical concepts that both teachers and students investigate albeit at different levels of understanding.

We would be remiss if we did not point out that technology can provide rich environments not only for the first two principles but for the third principle as well. Technology offers a context in which teachers can investigate school mathematics from a perspective not previously appreciated. As Olive (1998) and Laborde (2001) argued, technology can be a catalyst for teachers to restructure their mathematics and to envision new ways of teaching that mathematics. Technology-rich environments provide means for teachers to experience mathematics in a pluralistic way and to expand their existing understanding of school mathematics. In addition, they create contexts in which teachers can appreciate how their mathematical experiences can give rise to teaching strategies that afford their students similar experiences.

Further, as Balacheff (1998) noted, technology allows teachers to maintain control of the learning environment, a circumstance important to teachers, but allows students the autonomy to engage in genuine learning experiences. However, Laborde (2001) cautioned us that even experienced teachers need time and support to integrate technology into their teaching in non-superficial ways. It is not that technology by itself can result in the kind of process-oriented teaching of which we speak but it can provide contexts that have immediate face validity with teachers who are teaching that content. Finally, we have to keep in mind that the central focus "is not on the machine but on the mind, and particularly on the way in which intellectual movements and cultures define themselves and grow" (Papert, 1980, p. 9).

5. AN ILLUSTRATION OF THE PRINCIPLES

As a means of illustrating the principles, we invite the reader to consider the following problem.

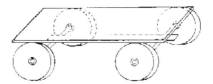

Figure 1.   Cart with cardboard resting on wheels.

As the cart shown in Figure 1 moves forward, the strip of cardboard on top of the wheels also moves forward. What is the relationship between the distance d_c the cart moves and the distance d_s that the strip of cardboard moves? State the relationship and provide a rationale that justifies the relationship beyond the existence of empirical evidence (see House, 1980, p. 10).

When this problem was introduced to a class of preservice teachers, their empirical solution was inconsistent with what they had anticipated the relationship to be. One of the preservice teachers generated a graph (Figure 2) that represented the distance her cart had moved versus the distance the strip had moved. The apparent slope of the line in the graph was 2, which suggested that the strip of cardboard had moved twice as *far* as the cart or, equivalently, that the strip had moved twice as *fast* as the cart. This seemingly counterintuitive result motivated the preservice teachers to analyze the problem more deeply in an effort to account for the empirical result.

It was important to realize that the cardboard did not contribute any movement of its own but moved via friction as fast as the wheels' points of contact moved. Consequently, the problem was changed from "Why does the strip on the wheels move twice as fast as the cart?" to "Why does the highest point of

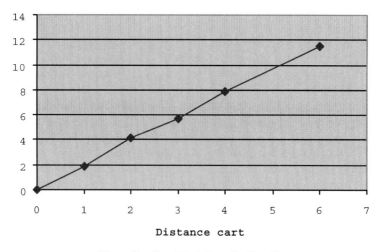

Distance cart

Figure 2.   Empirical data (in Excel).

the wheel move twice as fast as the wheel as a whole?" and, more generally, "How do movement and velocity of a point on a rolling wheel relate to the movement and velocity of the wheel as whole?" The reader is invited to analyze the problem before reading how the investigation, that became known as the 'Ant-on-the-Wheel' investigation, unfolds.

5.1. *Experience: A Basis for Re-Presentation and Reflection*

The investigation began with a hands-on activity in which preservice teachers measured the height of the ant and the wheel's centre and the horizontal distance traveled by ant and centre as they rolled a wheel along a line. The experiment, however, was much more than an opportunity to collect data for the purpose of graphing any of the different relationships (see, for example, Figure 3). The experiment served as an experiential basis and backdrop for the mathematics to be explored. As one student wrote in her reflection on the problem:

> I think that the very first day of the project was by far the best learning day that we experienced while conducting this experiment. The hands-on experience gave me a better understanding of exactly [what] happens to a particular point on a wheel as it rolls. During the rest of the experiment, if I was ever lost, I was able to remember and think back to the first day in order to help my confusion.

The preservice teacher's comment highlights the importance of experience as material for re-presentation and reflection. For example, as preservice teachers interpreted their initial graphs of the distance traveled by the centre of the wheel and the ant on the wheel, they wondered why the ant's distance graph wove back and forth around the centre's distance graph. In re-presenting the experiment they visualized how – at the beginning of each rotation – the ant had

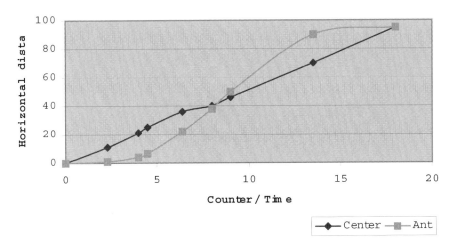

Figure 3.   **Representation of experiential distance data of centre and ant.**

lagged behind the centre and thus had not traveled, horizontally, as far as the centre.

In the graph, the beginning of each rotation is represented by a section of the graph in which the ant's distance curve is below the centre's distance curve. What parts of each rotation are represented by the intersections of the two graphs? When has the ant traveled further than the centre? The mental re-presentation of the rolling wheel, of the ant directly above or below, or in front of the centre provided a basis for making sense of the graph.

5.2. *Mathematical Analysis: Building on Firm Ground*

The experience of observing the ant and of measuring its height above the ground and its horizontal distance from the starting point led to the question of how these movements could be represented mathematically. The mathematical analysis of the ant's position on the rolling wheel had two supporting pillars: the prior investigation and the preservice teachers' prior knowledge of school and college mathematics. This prior mathematical knowledge, however, could not be simply recalled. It had to be remodelled, adapted, and used as a tool in a context that went beyond the standard treatment of trigonometric functions.

The mathematical analysis modelled the experiment and at the same time formalized it. A coordinate system with the origin as the starting point of the wheel's movement provided the initial structure for the analysis. Figure 4 shows the wheel at the starting point and after an initial roll through angle (Ant-Centre-E).

As preservice teachers developed the pictorial representation of the position of the ant after the initial movement of the wheel (Figure 4b), they again needed to build on the experiment, either in repeating part of the actual experience or in re-presenting it. The key insight that evolved from the representation was that the distance the centre had moved horizontally was equal to the length of the arc determined by the angle (Ant-Centre-E). From there, preservice teachers could use their knowledge of trigonometry to develop the position formulae:

$$\text{Height}_{\text{Ant}} = \text{radius} - \text{radius} * \cos(\text{angle})$$

and

$$\text{Distance}_{\text{Ant}} = \text{arc}(\text{AntE}) - \text{radius} * \sin(\text{angle})$$
$$= \text{radius} * (\text{angle}) - \text{radius} * \sin(\text{angle}).$$

The preservice teachers verified that the formulae made sense for all four quadrants as well as for special points determined by the angles $\pi/2$, π, $3\pi/2$, and 2π. However, it was difficult for them to appreciate that the position of the coordinate system was arbitrary and that they could adjust the position formulae for any coordinate system. Their tedious attempts to translate the formulae for differently positioned coordinate systems highlighted their lack of flexibility and deeper understanding of the trigonometric relationships.

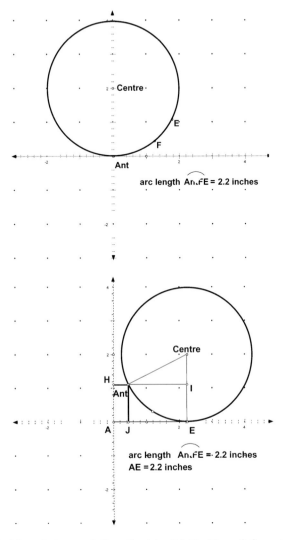

Figure 4. (a)Position of the ant before the trip. (b) Position of the ant after the initial movement.

5.3. *Representation: More Than One Medium*

With the position formulae at hand, the preservice teachers could produce more formal and precise graphs than their rough graphs based on empirical data. Excel provided the environment in which they could view data, formulae, and graphs side by side. Also, with the introduction of a counter, the angle turned could be related to an arbitrary unit of time, e.g., each rotation of 10^0 could represent a fraction of a second. Table 1 and Figures 5–6 show the distance and height data and graphs.

Table 1. Excel data table

Counter/time	Radius = 1				Height		Distance	
	Angle	sin(angle)	cos(angle)	Centre r	Ant r(1−cos(angle))	Centre r*angle	Ant r(angle−sin(angle))
0	0	0	1	1	0	0	0
2	0.34906585	0.34202014	0.9396	1	0.06030738	0.34906585	0.00704571
4	0.6981317	0.64278761	0.7660	1	0.23395556	0.6981317	0.05534409
6	1.04719755	0.8660254	0.5	1	0.5	1.04719755	0.18117215
8	1.3962634	0.98480775	0.1736	1	0.82635182	1.3962634	0.41145565
10	1.74532925	0.98480775	0.1736	1	1.17364818	1.74532925	0.7605215
12	2.0943951	0.8660254	−0.5	1	1.5	2.0943951	1.2283697
14	2.44346095	0.64278761	0.7660	1	1.76604444	2.44346095	1.80067334
16	2.7925268	0.34202014	0.9396	1	1.93969262	2.7925268	2.45050666
18	3.14159265	1.2246E-16	−1	1	2	3.14159265	3.14159265
20	3.4906585	−0.3420201	0.9396	1	1.93969262	3.4906585	3.83267865
22	3.83972435	−0.6427876	0.7660444	1	1.76604444	3.83972435	4.48251196
24	4.1887902	−0.8660254	−0.5	1	1.5	4.1887902	5.05481561
26	4.53785606	−0.9848078	0.1736	1	1.17364818	4.53785606	5.52266381
28	4.88692191	−0.9848078	0.1736	1	0.82635182	4.88692191	5.87172966
30	5.23598776	−0.8660254	0.5	1	0.5	5.23598776	6.10201316
32	5.58505361	−0.6427876	0.7660	1	0.23395556	5.58505361	6.22784122
34	5.93411946	−0.3420201	0.9396	1	0.06030738	5.93411946	6.2761396
36	6.28318531	−2.449E-16	1	1	0	6.28318531	6.28318531
...	...	...	...	...	...	...	...
72	12.5663706	−4.899E-16	1	1	0	12.5663706	12.5663706

Height vs. Angle/Time

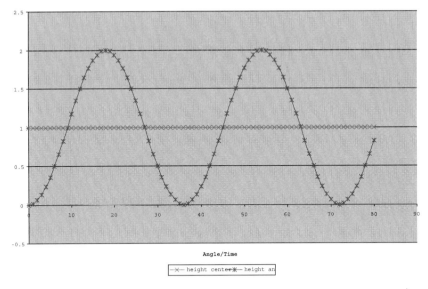

Angle/Time

Figure 5. Height of centre and ant.

Distance vs. Angle/Time

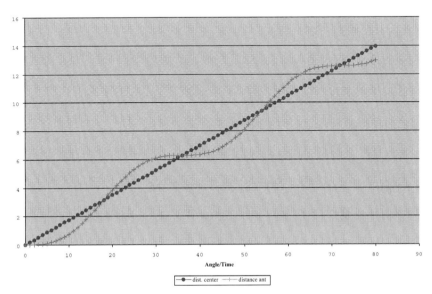

Angle/Time

Figure 6. Distance traveled by centre and ant.

Excel graphs, like hand-produced graphs, are discrete environments and thus provide the opportunity to relate data points and graphs. Although all computer environments are discrete environments, the appearance of continuity was fostered in a graph produced by the Graphing Calculator.[1] In order to graph a function with the Graphing Calculator only the equations were required. Thus, emphasis was placed on the relationship between the formulae and the graphs (see Figure 7).

$$y = x - \sin x \qquad y = 1 - \cos x$$

$$\begin{bmatrix} x \\ y \end{bmatrix} = \begin{bmatrix} t - \sin t \\ 1 - \cos t \end{bmatrix}$$

In Figure 7, the path of the ant – the cycloid – was added as an extension that related the distance traveled by the ant and its height.

5.4. *Velocity: More Than One View*

The investigation of the velocity of the ant in relation to the velocity of the centre provides the answer to the initial problem. A close look at the ant's distance graph provided first insights: The graph is steepest when the ant is at its highest point, and it is flat when the ant touches the ground (see Figures 3, 6, and 7). As mathematics education majors, preservice teachers had all the tools to determine the velocities of the centre and the ant from the distance functions. Under the assumption that the wheel turned 10° or 0.175 radians every unit of time then

$$f(t)_{\text{centre}} = r * 0.175t$$

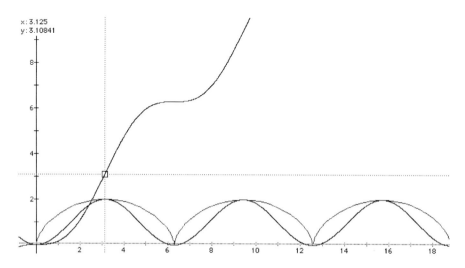

Figure 7.   Distance graph, height graph, and cycloid for $r = 1$.

and

$$g(t)_{\text{ant}} = r*(0.175t - \sin 0.175t).$$

Differentiation gave

$$f'(t)_{\text{centre}} = r*0.175$$

and

$$g'(t)_{\text{ant}} = r*(0.175 - 0.175*\cos 0.175t)$$
$$= 0.175r*(1 - \cos 0.175t)$$

Preservice teachers evaluated f' and g' for different t and investigated the relationship of the two velocities (see Table 2).

The connection between the mathematical interpretation of the velocities and the physics representation enriched the preservice teachers' understanding. Here, the important insight was that the movement of a rolling wheel is composed of two different components, a translational component and a rotational component (Figure 8).

Figure 8a shows the translational component: All points move with the same linear velocity, that is, with the velocity represented by the velocity of the centre. Figure 8b shows the rotational component. All points move with the same angular velocity, but the velocity with respect to the horizontal direction is continuously changing as the wheels turn. Figure 8c shows the superposition of the two velocities.

At the bottom of the wheel the rotational and the translational components cancel each other. That is, if the ant is at the bottom of the wheel her velocity with respect to the horizontal direction is zero (see Table 2, $t = 0$). When the ant

Table 2. **Horizontal velocities of ant and centre (for key points of a rotation)**

Radius $= 1$		Velocity		
Counter	Angle	Ant	Centre	$V_{\text{ant}}/V_{\text{centre}}$
0	0	0	0.17453293	0
3	0.52359878	0.02338298	0.17453293	0.1339746
6	1.04719755	0.08726646	0.17453293	0.5
9	1.57079633	0.17453293	0.17453293	1
12	2.0943951	0.26179939	0.17453293	1.5
15	2.61799388	0.32568287	0.17453293	1.8660254
18	3.14159265	0.34906585	0.17453293	2
21	3.66519143	0.32568287	0.17453293	1.8660254
24	4.1887902	0.26179939	0.17453293	1.5
27	4.71238898	0.17453293	0.17453293	1
30	5.23598776	0.08726646	0.17453293	0.5
33	5.75958653	0.02338298	0.17453293	0.1339746
36	6.28318531	0	0.17453293	0

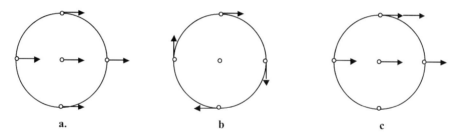

Figure 8.   Components of velocities of a rolling wheel.[2]

is at the same height as the centre ($t = 9$ and $t = 27$), the rotational velocity components do not contribute to the horizontal movement, that is, the points at the centre's height move with the same horizontal velocity as the centre. Finally, at the top of the wheel ($t = 18$), the two components are added, that is, the top of the wheel moves twice as fast as the centre of the wheel or as the wheel as a whole.

In summary, mathematical and physical analysis of the points on a rolling wheel and their velocities at different positions provided the explanation why the cardboard on the wheels of the cart moved twice as fast and twice as far as the cart itself.

5.5. *Consolidation and Communication*

The investigation concluded with two tasks in which the preservice teachers were asked to assemble all the pieces of what they had done and learned. As part of their homework assignments they wrote a report that included the initial experiment and the problem resulting from that experiment, a description of the investigation of the rolling wheel, the experiential data and graphs, development of the position and velocity formulae, and their reflection on the investigation as a whole.

Thus, for the preservice teachers the report served as a record of their learning experiences as well as a reflection on those experiences. For the instructor, the reports served as a basis for an assessment of the teachers' understanding and their proficiency with mathematical communication. The reports also provided the basis for an evaluation and revision of the investigation.

In the second concluding task, the preservice teachers were asked to model the rolling wheel, including a representation of the different velocities, in a dynamic geometry environment (*Geometer's Sketchpad* (1997), Figure 9). For this task they had to use and expand the computer skills they had previously learned and to represent the mathematical knowledge in yet another way.

5.6. *Reflection on the Principles*

The Ant-on-the-Wheel investigation is not necessarily a topic teachers should add unchanged to their high school mathematics curriculum. Rather, the Ant-on-the-Wheel investigation serves as a model that highlights the principles for

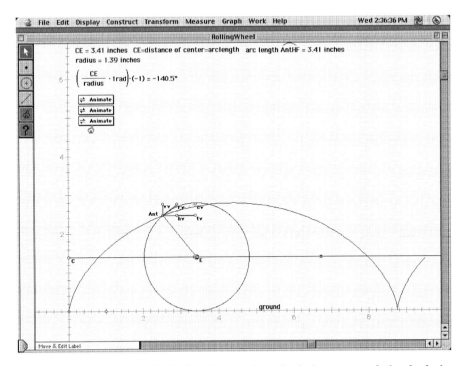

Figure 9.   The ant's path and velocities (hv – horizontal velocity, tv – translational velocity, vv – vertical velocity; Tv – total (rotational) velocity, cv – composite (rotational plus translational) velocity).

mathematics in teacher education. Pluralism is apparent as the problem is approached empirically and from several different perspectives with different tools such as spreadsheets and geometric exploration software.

The underlying mathematics is typical of school mathematics except possibly the approach that involves differentiation. This mathematics is not taken as given, but developed from experience, a critical part of the investigation. The experience is a starting point and basis for formalization, abstraction, and reflection. The development of the position and velocity formulae provides the preservice teachers with opportunities to use concepts and skills from school mathematics in a new context and thus to consolidate and expand their previous knowledge. The representations shed light on different aspects of the mathematics involved in the investigation.

Finally, the Ant-on-the-Wheel investigation also serves as a teaching model for the preservice teachers, and thus illustrates Principle 3. As the teachers reflected on the investigation they were asked to trace the development of the mathematics from experience to representation to abstraction and consolidation. This sequence represents an alternative to the teaching by telling style that dominates so many classrooms. Contexts that model how typical school lessons can be transformed into lessons that invoke experience, formalization, abstraction, and reflection can further reinforce this alternative style. This is not to say that the investigation's teaching sequence is *the* alternative teaching style but it certainly is *one* alternative. When provided with extensive mathematical experiences that embody the principles there is an increased likelihood that preservice teachers will carry the image of those principles into their own teaching.

6. FINAL COMMENT

Jaworski and Wood (1999) identified various themes that emerged in mathematics teacher education from approaches in 11 countries as described in the book *Mathematics Teacher Education: Critical International Perspectives.* One of these themes involves teachers' acquisition of teaching methods that are alternatives to teaching by telling. In short, the various programs sought to promote a pluralistic view of teaching and of mathematics in an effort to make teaching more student centred rather than teacher-centred. Traces of constructivism abounded in these approaches although it was not the case that constructivism was an explicit epistemological foundation that drove the different reform-based approaches.

Another theme identified by Jaworski and Wood (1999) was that of teachers as researchers of their own teaching. Here, reflection was the primary concept as teachers reflected on their own mathematical experiences in solving problems and on their own teaching. Krainer (1999) made explicit the outcomes of reflective practice when he asked teachers to do at least three things that went beyond teachers' normal activities and responsibilities:

- They have to gather data and to reflect on them systematically (and not only take action);
- They have to write down their findings (and not just communicate them orally); and
- They have to formulate these results for other people (and not just practise something within their own classrooms) (p. 108).

As Krainer pointed out, it is not that the findings were significant to the profession, generally speaking, but they were significant to the participating teachers.

Although not all of the themes identified by Jaworski and Wood (1999) were the result of scientific inquiry, they do represent the collective wisdom of mathematics teacher educators from around the world. The theme of pluralism with respect to mathematics (and also mathematics teaching) is consistent with Principle 1. Our focus on mathematics in Principle 1 stems from our belief that what teachers believe about mathematics is fundamental to any other kind of pluralism. As much as one can promote alternative methods of teaching including those that have the appearance of being student centred, that effort is nullified if what is being taught does not reflect mathematical pluralism. In some sense, it is a tautology to say that a student-centred approach is based on mathematical pluralism. Given students' individuality, it follows that teaching based on *their* mathematics is necessarily pluralistic.

But alternative methods of teaching, such as group work, that seemingly are student centred do not in themselves promote the find of mathematics envisioned in Principle 1. One must be vigilant that mathematics is treated pluralistically for much is lost if alternative forms of teaching promote discussion that leads to a predetermined mathematics. Student discussion about a singular solution path predetermined by the teacher gains little in terms of developing processes such as problem solving, reasoning, and communicating mathematically.

Perhaps it could be argued that the three principles previously identified are logical consequences of any movement toward reform-based teaching. Be that as it may, we think the principles are supported by research that clearly points the way toward pluralism, attention to school mathematics, and developing a certain parallelism between the kinds of experiences teachers should have and the kind of teaching we would like to see in the classroom. Perhaps it could be argued that there is not much new in the principles. But then we encounter the recent writing of Hyman Bass, a mathematician, who concluded:

> Somehow, however, in teaching teachers about mathematics, we don't seem to have looked carefully at how the mathematics is actually used in practice. We treat it as a disembodied subject matter to be imported by the teacher, and the very complicated and difficult process of importation, which entails considerable knowledge in its own right, is not part of the picture.
>
> (Mathematical Sciences Education Board, 2001, p. 27)

Bass's perspective emphasizes the complexity that is revealed through the Ant-on-the-Wheel investigation and reflects the depth of understanding school mathematics advocated in the principles. Bass added that "mathematical language is not simply an inert canon inherited and learned from a distant past. It is, as well, a medium in which learners, as mathematicians, act and create" (p. 29). This obviously humanistic, and consequently fallibilistic, orientation toward mathematics highlights the importance of understanding students' mathematics – not a new perspective but one just as relevant today as in yesteryear.

Finally, we would be remiss if we did not mention a moral component inherent in our principles in that we all have an obligation to educate teachers in a manner consistent with the way we envision the teaching of mathematics. Attention to context is of fundamental importance in a democratic society. If education is to be as Dewey (1916) defined it, namely, the "reconstruction or reorganization of experience which add to the meaning of experience, and which increases ability to direct the course of subsequent experiences" (p. 76), then we begin to see the necessity of educating teachers in the full realm of what it means to be educated. This means that teachers must have what Ma (1999) referred to as a *profound understanding of fundamental mathematics*.

It is only from such understanding that the full sense of Dewey's education can be realized – an education that we see as integrally intertwined with our three principles. The evidence that we have examined leads to the inevitable conclusion that teachers will largely teach as they were taught in the absence of intervention. This conclusion, buttressed by the formalism of the subject itself, suggests that in order to break the fetters of teaching by telling, a new order of teacher education is needed. We can begin by examining the mathematics in mathematics teacher education and deciding what it is that is fundamentally important about the knowing and learning of mathematics for teachers and for their students.

ENDNOTES

[1.] Graphing Calculator 3.1, Pacific Tech.
[2.] Adapted from Halliday and Resnick (1988), p. 258.

REFERENCES

Ball, D. L. (1990a). Prospective elementary and secondary teachers' understanding of division. *Journal for Research in Mathematics Education, 21*, 132–144.

Ball, D. L. (1990b). The mathematical understandings that prospective teachers bring to teacher education. *Elementary School Journal, 90*, 449–466.

Balacheff, N. (1998). Construction of meaning and teacher control of learning. In D. J. Tinsley & D. J. Johnson (Eds.), *Information and communication technologies in school mathematics* (pp. 111–120). New York: Chapman and Hall.

Benacerraf, P., & Putnam, H. (1964). *Philosophy of mathematics*. Englewood Cliffs, NJ: Prentice Hall.

Born, M. (1968). *My life and my views*. New York: Charles Scribners Sons.

Bromme, R. (1994). Beyond subject matter: A psychological topology of teachers' professional knowledge. In R. Biehler, R. Scholz, R. Strässer & B. Winkelmann (Eds.), *Didactics of mathematics as a scientific discipline* (pp. 73–88). Dordrecht, The Netherlands: Kluwer Academic Publishers.

Brown, S., Cooney, T., & Jones, D. (1990). Mathematics teacher education. In R. Houston (Ed.), *Handbook of research on teacher education* (pp. 639–656). New York: Macmillan.

Carpenter, T., Fennema, E., & Franke, M. (1996). Cognitively Guided Instruction: A knowledge base for reform in primary mathematics instruction. *Elementary School Journal, 97*, 3–20.

Chauvot, J. (2000). *Conceptualizing mathematics teacher development in the context of reform*. Unpublished doctoral dissertation, University of Georgia, Athens.

Cooney, T., Brown, S., Dossey, J., Schrage, G., & Wittmann, E. (1999). *Mathematics, pedagogy, and secondary teacher education*. Portsmouth, NH: Heinemann.

Cooney, T., Wilson, P., Albright, M., & Chauvot, J. (1998, April). *Conceptualizing the professional development of secondary preservice mathematics teachers*. Paper presented at the American Educational Research Association annual meeting, San Diego.

Davis, B. (1999). Basic irony: Examining the foundations of school mathematics with preservice teachers. *Journal of Mathematics Teacher Education, 2*, 25–48.

Davis, P., & Hersh, R. (1981). *The mathematical experience*. Boston: Birkhäuser.

Dewey, J. (1916). *Democracy and education*. New York: The Free Press.

Dossey, J. A. (1992). The nature of mathematics: Its role and its influence. In D. A. Grouws (Ed.), *Handbook of research on mathematics teaching and learning* (pp. 39–48). New York: Macmillan.

Eggleton, P. J. (1995). *The evolving mathematical philosophy of a preservice mathematics teacher*. Unpublished doctoral dissertation, University of Georgia, Athens.

Ernest, P. (1991). *The philosophy of mathematics education.* London: Falmer Press.

Freudenthal, H. (1973). *Mathematics as an educational task.* Dordrecht, The Netherlands: D. Reidel Publishing Company.

Frykholm, J. (1999). The impact of reform: Challenges for mathematics teacher preparation. *Journal of Mathematics Teacher Education, 2,* 79–105.

Gellert, U. (2000). Mathematics instruction in safe space: Prospective elementary teachers' views of mathematics education. *Journal of Mathematics Teacher Education, 3,* 251–270.

Geometer's Sketchpad 3.06/PPC [Computer software] (1997). Emeryville, CA: Key Curriculum Press.

Gödel, K. (1931). Über formal unentscheidbare Sätze der principiä mathematica und verwandter Systeme I. *Monatshefte für Mathematik und Physik, 38,* 173–198.

Grant, T. J., Hiebert, J., & Wearne, D. (1998). Observing and teaching reform-minded lessons: What do teachers see? *Journal of Mathematics Teacher Education, 2,* 217–236.

Graphing Calculator 3.1 [Computer software] (2001). Woodside, CA: Pacific Tech.

Halliday, D., & Resnick, R. (1988). *Fundamentals of physics* (3rd ed.). New York: John Wiley & Sons.

Hersh, R. (1986). Some proposals for reviving the philosophy of mathematics. In T. Tymoczko (Ed.), *New directions in the philosophy of mathematics* (pp. 9–28). Boston: Birkhäuser.

House, P. (1980). *Interactions of science and mathematics.* Columbus, OH: ERIC Clearinghouse for Science, Mathematics, and Educational Education.

Jaworski, B., & Wood, T. (1999). Themes and issues in inservice programmes. In B. Jaworski, T. Wood & S. Dawson (Eds.), *Mathematics teacher education: Critical international perspectives* (pp. 125–147). London: Falmer Press.

Krainer, K. (1999). PFL-mathematics: Improving professional practice in mathematics teaching. In B. Jaworski, T. Wood & S. Dawson (Eds.), *Mathematics teacher education: Critical international perspectives* (pp. 102–112). London: Falmer Press.

Laborde, C. (2001). The use of new technologies as a vehicle for restructuring teachers' mathematics. In F.-L. Lin & T. Cooney (Eds.), *Making sense of mathematics teacher education* (pp. 87–110). Dordrecht, The Netherlands: Kluwer Academic Publishers.

Lakatos, I. (1976). *Proofs and refutations.* New York: Cambridge University Press.

Lerman, S. (2001). A review of research perspectives on mathematics teacher education. In F.-L. Lin & T. Cooney (Eds.), *Making sense of mathematics teacher education* (pp. 33–52). Dordrecht, The Netherlands: Kluwer Academic Publishers.

Ma, L. (1999). *Knowing and teaching elementary mathematics: Teachers' understanding of fundamental mathematics in China and the United States.* Mahwah, NJ: Lawrence Erlbaum Publishers.

Mason, J. (1998). Enabling teachers to be real teachers: Necessary levels of awareness and structure of attention. *Journal of Mathematics Teacher Education, 1,* 243–267.

Mathematical Education Sciences Board (2001). *Knowing and learning mathematics for teaching.* Washington, D. C.: Mathematical Education Sciences Board.

National Council of Teachers of Mathematics (2000). *Principles and standards for school mathematics.* Reston, VA.

Olive, J. (1998). Opportunities to explore and integrate mathematics with the *Geometer's Sketchpad.* In R. Lehrer & D. Chazan (Eds.), *Designing learning environments for developing understanding of geometry and space* (pp. 395–418). Mahwah, NJ: Lawrence Erlbaum Associates,

Owens, J. (1987). *A study of four preservice teachers' constructs of mathematics and mathematics teaching.* Unpublished doctoral dissertation, University of Georgia, Athens.

Papert, S. (1980). *Mindstorms: Children, computers, and powerful ideas.* New York: Basic Books Inc.

Ponte, J. (2001). Investigating mathematics and learning to teach mathematics. In F.-L. Lin & T. Cooney (Eds.), *Making sense of mathematics teacher education* (pp. 53–72). Dordrecht, The Netherlands: Kluwer Academic Publishers.

Schifter, D. (1998). Learning mathematics for teaching: From a teachers' seminar to the classroom. *Journal of Mathematics Teacher Education, 1,* 55–87.

Skott, J. (2001). The emerging practices of a novice teacher: The roles of his school mathematics images. *Journal of Mathematics Teacher Education, 4,* 3–28.

Sowder, J. Armstrong, B., Lamon, S., Simon, M., Sowder, L., & Thompson, A. (1998). Educating teachers to teach multiplicative structures in the middle grades. *Journal of Mathematics Teacher Education, 1,* 127–155.

Stacey, K., Helme, S., Steinle, V., Irwin K., Baturo, A., & Bana, J. (2001). Preservice teachers' knowledge of difficulties in decimal numeration. *Journal of Mathematics Teacher Education, 4,* 205–225.

Tymoczko, T. (1986). Making room for mathematicians in the philosophy of mathematics. *The Mathematical Intelligencer, 8*(3), 44–50.

Wilson, M. R., & Goldenberg, M. P. (1998). Some conceptions are difficult to change: One middle school mathematics teacher's struggle. *Journal of Mathematics Teacher Education, 2,* 269–293.

Wittmann, E. (1992). One source of the broadcast metaphor: Mathematical formalism. In F. Seeger & H. Steinbring (Eds.), *The dialogue between theory and practice in mathematics education: Overcoming the broadcast metaphor* (pp. 111–119). Bielefeld, Germany: Institut für Didaktik der Mathematik der Universität Bielefeld.

23

Educating New Mathematics Teachers: Integrating Theory and Practice, and the Roles of Practising Teachers

BARBARA JAWORSKI
Agder University College, Kristiansand, Norway[1]

UWE GELLERT
Freie Universität Berlin

ABSTRACT

This chapter addresses issues of integration of theory and practice in the education of new mathematics teachers and tries to achieve an appropriate blend of theory and practice in its approach. Thus, it begins with an episode from practice, proposes a set of theoretical models of 'integration', situates these models in examples from teacher education around the world and follows with a discussion of theoretical issues and the associated literature. A case study from a current programme of initial teacher education in the UK follows, where issues of integration are re-addressed from a practical perspective. We end with a short review of the status quo as we see it currently in terms of relationships between those involved in the educational process.

1. AN INTRODUCTORY VIGNETTE

Imagine a teaching room in the basement of an old Victorian house. Nineteen student teachers and their tutor sit in front of a TV screen. On the screen they see one of themselves introducing a lesson to a class of students. John, the student teacher of the class, has inserted the videotape into the player, and is sitting with his peers and the tutor as they all watch the screen.

The class teacher introduces the student teacher to the class. "Mr Jones will be taking your lesson today. He's borrowed these videotapes from me. I wonder what he's going to do with them."

The student teacher jokes with the class as he removes a set of 12 videotapes from a box, and spins a story about the tapes. They are James Bond tapes, and belong to the class teacher. "I'll have to take good care of them or he'll

829

Second International Handbook of Mathematics Education, 829–875
A.J. Bishop, M.A. Clements, C. Keitel, J. Kilpatrick and F.K.S. Leung (eds.)

murder me", John says. The class giggles. "Let's count them, so that we ensure that none go missing." They count to 12 – there are 12 tapes.

"OK, now, just suppose I was to lose four of these tapes – oh, ..., oh, no I can't do that, that would be terrible! I was going to say, what fraction would I have lost? Look, we'll do it a different way. These four all have the same person playing James Bond. Can you guess who it is?" Various responses from the class: "Yes, Sean Connery! Now what fraction of the videos have Sean Connery in them?"

Various students volunteer answers, not all the same. There is some discussion about which suggestions are right. Four-twelfths is agreed by the class to be acceptable, and so is a third. Then someone suggests two-sixths, which is also agreed. They go on to discuss the relationship between these fractions. When later, the one videotape with George Lazenby as James Bond is withdrawn ("He wasn't very popular, George Lazenby!"), the Sean Connery tapes are now agreed to be four out of eleven. But, no longer one-third!

The lesson continues, and the group sees about 10 minutes of it. Then the video player is switched off, and the student teachers talk about what they have seen. They congratulate John on his relaxed air in the classroom. He says he was very nervous, but he didn't appear nervous. They like his use of the videotapes as a familiar context in which to address equivalent fractions. They are starting to recognise the value of different kinds of questions, and ways of involving students in thinking about mathematics. In sessions at the university, they have all engaged in analysis of the topic of fractions and are familiar with typical errors or misconceptions, so they can analyse students' responses.

The tutor guides discussion into addressing the planning of the lesson, what thinking was involved, where the ideas came from, what guidance was given or sought from experienced teachers, and so on. John responds, and others chip in with questions, or anecdotes from their own school experience. The tutor is using a theoretical model, known as *the anecdoting process*, which emerged from collaborative research between teachers and educators many years previously (Mathematical Association, 1991).

Here we glimpse one university session in which a tutor works with student teachers. On the next day they will all be in school, teaching lessons that they have planned, working with other teachers and their mentor. How will their learning from this university session relate to their work in school? How will this learning influence their interactions with other teachers? How will their ongoing learning be influenced by the teachers with whom they work?

This chapter is about the learning of student teachers to teach mathematics in school and about how theory and practice are related in their learning. It is also about the role of practising mathematics teachers in the student teachers' learning progress. Where and how does this learning take place? Who influences the learning, and how? What elements of knowledge are important to the student teacher's developing practice?

We shall be returning to John and his learning later in the chapter.

2. ISSUES ADDRESSED IN THIS PAPER

The questions asked above just start to open up the complexities of issues that this chapter seeks to address.

What do teachers need to know in order to teach mathematics at any level? We address aspects of mathematical and pedagogical knowledge and how these are related. We consider the knowledge that teachers bring with them to a teacher education course and issues in building on this knowledge. We relate student teachers' knowledge to knowledge of other teachers, particularly those who work as mentors, and consider where this knowledge is tacit or explicit.

How do teachers learn? We contrast notions of learning by imitation, by construction, and through critical reflection and enquiry. We consider the class-room and school as a social setting in which norms are created and teachers and students collaborate to ensure working practices and fulfil expectations. Relationships between student teachers and their mentors are a part of this environment, and contribute critically to student teachers' learning. We go on to address the possibility of co-learning partnerships and ways in which they can lead to greater democracy in the learning process and reduce any deficit views of teachers. Modes of teacher learning such as apprenticeship, critical apprenticeship and critical inquiry are addressed.

The issues above are dealt with at a theoretical level in Section 4 of this chapter. Before that, we consider current practices in initial teacher education in a number of countries, or places. So Section 3 begins by elaborating briefly four models of teacher education with developing degrees of theory-practice integration. These models aim at providing a rough and simple framework for description (and discussion) of current practices. They are constructed in a way that the status quo of initial teacher education fits mainly in models 2 and 3, and, at model 4, we consider the ideals and practicality of a fully integrated model.

The final section (Section 5) of the chapter offers a case study of a model that tries currently to achieve as full an integration as possible, and looks in some depth at issues that arise from this model from certain of its participants. Here we return at a practical level to some of the issues raised in Section 4, and look at ways in which integration is associated with co-learning, and through which educators themselves can develop alongside student teachers and mentors in the integrated programme.

In the title of the chapter as well as in its issues outlined above we used the notions of theory/theoretical and practice/practical – without clarification of what we consider as theory and as practice. In order to acknowledge a multiplic-ity of meanings, we differentiate between two uses of the word 'theory'. First, theory can be thought of as a system of ideas explaining a concept, particularly based on general principles independent of the phenomena to be explained. And second, theory can be regarded as speculative thought, as in: "This is all very well in theory, but how will it work in practice?" In terms of Mason and Waywood (1996), the first perspective is "accepted knowledge that applies in a variety of circumstances" (p. 1055), while the latter displays the more constructive component of theoretical thought. Thus, where we referred to Section 4 as operating on a theoretical level, we took theory as a body of knowledge that is acknowledged and (more or less) accepted in our scientific community. Compared with this, theory in Section 5 is more related to the ideas that teachers have in planning for lessons and conceptualising classroom approaches. One important question, relating to the latter perspective on theory, addresses how student teachers can bridge the gap between the (theoretical) idea of an activity and its realisation (in practice).

We believe it is valuable to consider theory and practice not as distant poles but as reflexively connected elements of knowledgeable activity. Psychological, sociological and educational theory, even if not explicitly empirically grounded, is a human reflection on practice. In a way it is rooted in experience. On the other hand mathematics education practice, as long as it is purposeful, is always resting on theories of mathematical content, teaching and learning. Hence, our interest is in the relationships between theory and practice rather than in any dichotomous approach.

3. PRACTICES OF INITIAL TEACHER EDUCATION

Before situating our theme in its theoretical roots, in Section 4, we turn to the status quo of initial teacher education. In the face of an enormous variety of practices of mathematics teacher preparation around the world, we have taken as a focus the theory-practice interface, and begin by introducing four crude descriptors or 'models' for initial teacher education:

- Model 1: No specific teacher preparation at all
- Model 2: Teacher preparation in which theory and practice are treated separately (i.e., theory $>-<$ practice mode)
- Model 3: Teacher preparation in which theory and practice start to be integrated (i.e., theory $<->$ practice mode)
- Model 4: Teacher preparation in 'theory/practice/theory/practice/ ...' mode

Of course, this hierarchy of models is for analytical purposes and, thus, may appear to be exaggerated or too clear-cut. Nevertheless, it serves as a device for gaining access to issues which can then be discussed with respect to real situations. We shall do this by offering selected examples of mathematics teacher preparation practice from around the world and looking at some of the particular issues that prevail and how they are addressed.

3.1. *Four Models of Initial Teacher Education*

The proposed four models of initial teacher education relate to a controversial debate over the extent to which practising teachers of mathematics should be involved in the preparation of future teachers of mathematics. There are those who allege that if practising teachers are allowed too much influence then in most cases the status quo of mathematics teaching will be reinforced. By contrast, others criticise much of the teacher preparation done in tertiary institutions as being too theoretical and not helpful for the novice teachers trying to cope with curriculum and classroom realities. We recognise that this summary of the debate, so far, is a rather polarised one, but we will stay with it for the moment.

One assumption, in the debate, is that increasing the involvement of practising mathematics teachers will inevitably reduce the influence of theory within teacher education. Theory and practice are seen as competing for dominance rather than as different modes of thought and experience that might fruitfully support teaching development. Other conceptions of initial teacher education try to link theory and practice in mutually supportive ways. Within such models, theory can be used as a lens to reflect on practice, and practice can develop from theoretical reflections. Different ways of linking theory and practice result in different consequences for professional development, both for individual professionalism and for a professionalization of mathematics teaching.

3.1.1. Model 1: No Specific Teacher Education

Because of the tradition of teacher education, in some parts of the world, that teacher education is not particularly important, and/or the inadequate provision of financial resources for teacher education, some mathematics teachers do not pass through any programme of teacher preparation. The reasons for this are often different for elementary teachers from those for secondary mathematics teachers. One tendency is to consider elementary teaching as similar to bringing up one's children and to take this occupation as a common sense activity that does not require specific preparation, or just a short period of observation of teaching practice. For secondary teaching, a focus on specific academic subjects often assumes that those highly qualified in the subject are ideally placed to pass on their knowledge to learners. In both phases, without explicit teacher preparation, teachers follow the predominant practices in the school where they teach and mostly teach the way they were taught. Thus, "no specific teacher education" tends to result in the perpetuation of existing practices (Brown & McIntyre, 1993; Lortie, 1998)

3.1.2. Model 2: Teacher Preparation in 'Theory $>-<$ Practice' Mode

In model 2, theory and practice are two largely separate aspects of teacher education. Generally, here, theoretical knowledge is 'imparted' to prospective teachers in higher education institutions before they are exposed to school practice. Once student teachers have entered the practical phase of teacher preparation, the theoretical knowledge acquired beforehand can be little more than an academic background bearing no direct relation to teaching practice. Although much theoretical knowledge about teaching and learning is empirically grounded, many practitioners criticise it as being far from the reality of mathematics classes.

Within this model, the student teacher is virtually the only person to link theory and practice. The student teachers' tutors in higher education institutions may try to relate theory to practice as part of their teaching, but they do not operate in, or confront, real school practice. Theory is something to be learnt and to be traced back to its origins, but its relation to current practice is often a matter of hope, or chance. On the other hand, the student teachers' mentors in schools may not relate their own practice, or their comments and hints to student teachers, explicitly to theory. Practice can appear to be following its own rules which are often practically situated rather than theory-based. We refer to the conflict that is inherent in the missing link between theory and practice as *the placement dilemma*.

In the long run, because the pressures of practice and the role of routines are often dominating factors, the enaction of this model results largely in a perpetuation of existing practices: New teachers generally follow the predominant practices in the school where they teach.

3.1.3. Model 3: Teacher Preparation in 'Theory <-> Practice' Mode

In this model theory and practice are no longer separated. There exists some overt linkage of theory and practice but the linkage can range from being minimal to something approaching integration. As linkage moves towards integration of theory and practice, mathematics teacher preparation provides more opportunity to the student teachers to be thoughtful reflective practitioners, to develop overtly their own knowledge, to question existing practices and routines, but also to learn from valued aspects of existing practice. For the student teacher, integration of theory and practice might be less a struggle to put theory into practice, and more an adjustment of theory to and through practice with help and support from educators and teachers who guide their progress.

In order to accomplish such integration and to avoid what we called the placement dilemma, the student teachers' tutors in higher education institutions and the mentoring teachers in school share, to differing degrees, their theoretical and practical knowledge with each other. In this way, a linked programme might be established. It is implicitly or explicitly part of the programme that mentoring teachers develop their own knowledge and practice alongside their role in teacher education by reflecting on their own practice in relation to student teachers and tutors from higher education institutions.

3.1.4. Model 4: Teacher Preparation in 'Theory/Practice/Theory/Practice ...' Mode

This is a fully integrated model between theory and practice – an ideal that probably does not exist, although some educators and institutions are working towards it. It assumes that higher education institution tutors, mentor teachers and student teachers work together in mutually supportive ways, albeit with differing roles and goals. All are reflective practitioners, all are learners. Power and responsibility go with knowledge and experience. Accordingly, making the model work is the greater responsibility of the more powerful.

3.2. *Examples from Around the World*

On a first view, it would seem to be a straightforward matter to discuss examples of mathematics teacher preparation practices from around the world. Unfortunately, the selection of the most interesting, wide-ranging and convincing examples is an activity that is not only difficult but also limited in its results.

The variety of the social, cultural, political and economical frames within which teacher preparation around the world is organised is enormous. Moreover, there is only little evidence of how this frame affects the ways in which professionalization and professionalism of mathematics teaching develop. We are just starting to get an idea about possible implications of religion, economic and geographical situations, knowledge distribution, academic traditions, and so on, for the specific modes of teacher preparation in different countries. In order to write this section we have talked with colleagues from a number of different countries, and acknowledge that we have learned a lot from doing so. There is clear value in sharing methods, experiences and issues. We have included below references to our own two countries, Germany and England, and to two other countries, Japan and South Africa for which we acknowledge gratefully the assistance of colleagues well versed with education in these countries. We conclude this section with reference to a number of initiatives in teacher education around the world that use hypermedia as a central factor in the education of mathematics teachers.

3.2.1. Germany – Dualism of a Theoretical and a Practical Phase

The predominant characteristic of the German teacher preparation system is that it is separated into two successive blocks: a first (theoretical) and a second (practical) phase. The first 4 to 6 years of teacher preparation at universities or similar higher education institutions (*Pädagogische Hochschulen*) provide, among other things, theoretical studies of the one or two subjects the prospective teacher will be teaching. They also provide, typically, a differing range of studies in educational and social sciences, in particular in pedagogy and psychology, as well as didactics of the subjects.

This first period, or phase, of teacher preparation is followed by two years of practical training in schools guided by experienced teachers and under the authority of the state administration. Preparing and teaching mathematics lessons makes up the core of the practical preparation of prospective mathematics teachers. The main cornerstones of these two years, the second phase, are lessons that prospective teachers have to perform periodically and which are central and crucial for the experienced teachers' evaluation of the work done by the prospective teachers.

Although the terminology of 'theoretical' and 'practical' phases suggests that the phases are completely separated in mathematics teacher preparation (as in model 2) there exist well-defined links between theory and practice (as in model 3) in both the first and second phases. Three periods of practical placement in schools are included in the first phase, in which student teachers firstly observe and reflect on mathematics teaching and, then, gradually take the responsibility for teaching a complete mathematics lesson. Most of the student teachers consider these periods to be the most fruitful experiences within the first phase. Many universities try to increase the value of this experience for linking theory with practice.

During the second phase of teacher preparation, the main link between theory and practice is constituted by the *Fachseminar*, that is a joint meeting of about 10 prospective teachers who, although at different schools, are teaching the same subject (mathematics) and one experienced teacher. The role of the experienced teachers is to foster, evaluate and assess the prospective teachers' progress. In the context of secondary school mathematics, the main task of *Fachseminar* is to turn mathematical knowledge into school mathematics; for prospective primary teachers the central aim is to relate educational and psychological theory to the realm of the *mathematics* classroom. In that sense, the person in charge of a *Fachseminar* is crucially important in the process of facilitating linkages between theory and practice.

There seems to be agreement that the second phase of teacher preparation provides the base for the socialisation of prospective mathematics teachers into the traditions and rituals of teaching mathematics (Keitel, 1992; Seeger & Steinbring, 1992). This second phase has traditionally been based on an apprenticeship model of learning in which the apprentice internalises and reproduces standard routines and norms of mathematics teaching and, in that sense, perpetuates its practices. It is well recognised that this model is limited, since the prospective teachers' placement dilemma of integrating innovations, rather ambitiously suggested at the university, with the content of traditional lectures also offered at the university, and with the practices of experienced teachers in schools, still remains. The challenge facing young teachers interested in relating theory and practice urgently requires a greater degree of integration between the theoretical and practical phases than has traditionally been offered in German teacher education programmes (Keitel, 1992; Seeger & Steinbring, 1992).

3.2.2. England: The 66% School Factor Leading a Shift to Integration

Over the last 20 years there have been two main routes into teaching in England. Those routes are the BEd (Bachelor of Education) route – a four-year degree course including both subject studies and studies in education, and the BA/BSc + PGCE (Bachelor of Arts or Science in an academic subject + Post Graduate Certificate of Education) route. The former route is now used only with the professional preparation of primary teachers, and even in that context is becoming less common than the latter.

For both primary and secondary teaching, the second route has involved students in an undergraduate degree in an academic subject at a university leading to a Bachelor's degree qualification. This is followed by a one-year course in education providing QTS (qualified teacher status). For secondary teaching, a major part of the PGCE course would be a study of the pedagogy of the subject or subjects the teacher is being 'trained' to teach. In addition there would be a programme of wider study of issues in schooling: for example, pastoral work and form tutoring; differentiation for pupils with special needs and of differing experience and ability. A PGCE for primary teaching would include subject studies in the main teaching subject and also an introduction to the teaching of other subjects in the school curriculum beyond the specialised subject. This would include, for all prospective teachers, attention to mathematics, particularly as one of the core subject areas (along with English and Science). However, it is recognised that preparation in mathematics as a subject is a serious problem for the majority of primary teachers, and issues concerned with how this situation might be improved are strenuously debated.

For all secondary PGCE courses, since 1994, there has been a statutory requirement that 66% of the course be taught in school, with a minimum of two schools being used during the course. This requirement has emphasised the importance of teachers' learning in the practical setting. Although there are a few courses that are delivered entirely within schools, or consortia of schools, most courses involve relationships between a higher education institute (usually a university education department) and a number of schools. Thus, there has been 'encouragement' from policy makers to reduce the theoretical input of such a course and increase the practical – a shift from versions of model 2 to versions of model 3 as outlined above. This has had both negative and positive effects. Firstly, it has seemed to undervalue theory as an important component of learning to teach. However, secondly, it has pressured educators to reflect on ways in which theory has been taught, and what theory is fundamental to learning to teach. As a result, courses have shifted towards a greater degree of integration of theory and practice, with theory taught at the university being made more directly relevant to teaching practice, and teaching practice being used as a source of issues on which to base theory.

A consequence of the more obvious importance of schools to the education of teachers is that schools now have designated mentors, teachers in the schools, who have taken on an educator role in working with student-teachers. Mentoring has become a feature of the roles of certain teachers, and a significant part of teachers' professional development.

There are considerable variations in the roles of mentors in primary and secondary schools. In secondary schools, mentors are mainly teachers within subject areas such as mathematics, and so can focus their thinking on issues in mathematics teaching. In primary schools, where teachers teach all subjects, mentors need to develop understandings of teaching across the range of subjects, a demanding task. Although still in its infancy, as far as explicit knowledge of the professional activity and thinking of mentors is concerned, there is a growing body of research and professional literature in mentoring in English schools (McIntyre, Hagger, & Wilkin, 1993; Jaworski & Watson, 1994; Haggarty, 1995; Smith, 2001).

Some issues and outcomes of current shifts in teacher education in England can be seen in the case study discussion in Section 5 of the present chapter.

3.2.3. South Africa: A Time of Innovation and Change

Post-apartheid education in South Africa has been guided since 1997 by an outcomes-based education and training system and a new National Qualifications Framework (NQF), both of which are still in the process of development. Interested readers are referred to *Norms and Standards for Educators* which can be found via the site *www.polity.org.za* or more specifically *http://education.pwv.gov.za/*. The NQF is structured in eight levels, from early schooling to doctoral level qualifications. School education to Grade 9 is included within level 1, and teacher education programmes and qualifications are located at levels 5 to 7.

Within these levels there are a number of routes to teacher education, training and certification. These include a four-year BEd degree (at level 6), with staging posts of Certificate and Diploma in Education (at level 5); a Post Graduate Certificate in Education which 'caps' an undergraduate qualification; and an Advanced Certificate in Education that accredits further study in specialised areas. The post-graduate certificates operate at level 6, and lead to study at level 7; the BEd honours, with advanced studies leading to the Post Graduate Diploma in Education, masters and doctoral degrees, at level 8. The new system can be characterised as one that is centrally regulated with de-centralised participation and implementation.

The integration of theory and practice is specified as a key strategic objective of a 'Norms and Standards' document which states:

> In order for qualifications and their associated learning programmes to be recognised for employment in education, providers must ensure that the roles and applied competence specified in the exit level outcomes of the qualification meet the requirement of learners to demonstrate their ability to integrate theory and practice.

(Norms and Standards for Educators, 2000, p. 24)

Policy indicates that school experience should be integrated into the programme, rather than being a separate 'add-on', and be a structured teaching and learning experience with some form of observational assessment.

There is, therefore, a requirement for school-based practice, but no prescribed model or period of time for its implementation. Existing teacher education programmes interpret the requirements in differing ways, including a model of university-based theory and school-based practice, and other models that are starting to include training for mentoring. In one Post Graduate Certificate programme of one year full time, students have two weeks before registration and two periods of four or five weeks teaching practice in schools during the academic year. In another university's programme, information suggests that attempts have been made recently to integrate theory and practice, using a school-based mentoring approach, but this is not yet fully implemented. It seems that integration of theory and practice is widely desired, but institutions are still in the process of implementation. However, one of our correspondents identified some of the constraints in mentoring provision:

> The constraints that exist (in my opinion) are largely lack of funding for such mentor training and practice. Teachers acting as mentors in schools are not given any time off to fulfil these duties, largely because there is no funding to do so. In my own experience while initiating a trial mentor programme in '99 in [one university] ... there was a general lack of awareness amongst members of the Ed Dept about mentoring per se, a certain amount of scepticism, and a reluctance to change the status quo which they felt was working pretty well; also there was a reluctance to impose on teachers in schools, in terms of asking more time from them for training, as there is no obligation on the part of schools to take student teachers; there is no formalised agreement. Students are taken as a favour. Nevertheless ... teachers in schools who were given some training really appreciated having their role clearly framed and understood, and all said they found the experience of working closely with university-based tutors and student teachers a fruitful and satisfying one – a big improvement on being 'dumped' with student teachers (personal communication).

In the less than 10 years of transition from an apartheid era when black teachers had different levels and quality of teacher education from white teachers, and black schools were able to deliver only a limited curriculum, much time, money and effort has gone into making better provision for all. Many teachers study part time, through distance education and through contact courses at universities, to get degrees or to upgrade qualifications in other ways. Part of the provision for educating new teachers seems to be directed towards integration of theory and practice in teacher education, and mentoring approaches in linking university and schools. However, it is clear from our sources that the scale of the need and the multiplicity of issues involved make achievements slow and patchy.

3.2.4. Japan: Teacher Education Modelling Classroom Approaches

In Japan the main route by which to qualify as a teacher is through a four-year undergraduate course at a university or university college. This qualifies teachers for elementary and lower secondary teaching, and extra courses can be taken as a qualification for higher secondary teaching. According to the Ministry of

Education (*Monbukagakusho*), 82% of teachers qualify through this route. Having obtained a teaching certificate in this way, sometimes referred to as a 'common certificate', teachers must then sit the recruitment examination held annually by the Prefectural Board of Education of the area in which they want to teach. Results of this examination are placed in order of merit, and teaching posts are allocated to the most successful candidates. As there is an oversupply of qualified teachers, those not successful in any year must sit the examination and compete again another year.

In Japan, then, teacher education is largely provided by universities, and *Monbukagakusho* determines its content. The number of courses to be taken by any student is prescribed. Teacher Training institutions must provide *Monbukagakusho* with structured syllabuses that clearly meet the specified conditions. However, the content of courses is determined by the providing institution. Thus, institutions retain a degree of academic autonomy and are free from restrictive curriculum and assessment practices that are pervasive in some other countries (for example, in England).

Unlike many countries (as has been seen in the TIMSS results), subject knowledge in the case of mathematics is rarely a problem in Japan, even for those teachers qualifying to teach in elementary school, because of the importance placed on mathematics in schooling. Thus, rather than needing to focus on improving students' subject knowledge in mathematics, as in, say, England, elementary teacher education in Japan is able to concentrate more on teaching methods and pedagogical issues. There is, however, a big difference between the mathematical knowledge required for elementary teaching in Japan and that required for secondary teaching; since elementary teachers teach almost all school subjects, they are not required to learn as much mathematics during ITE (initial teacher education) as those who teach (only) secondary mathematics.

In the Japanese system, a whole-class approach is common, at least in the early years of schooling, and involves a high level of pupil participation and interaction. Student teachers are familiar with this kind of approach as they themselves have learned mathematics in this system, so their needs are chiefly to learn how to implement it in the classroom.

In initial teacher education programmes, professors present lectures and seminars in model format. Student teachers are expected to present seminars (usually jointly) and to reflect on their presentation performance. A high level of professionalism is expected and sought. Discussion of learning points for both student teachers and pupils is encouraged; learning difficulties are identified and discussed. Considerable attention is given to the construction of lesson plans.

More recently, greater emphasis is being given to the value of a small-group, differentiated approach to learning in mathematics. As this is currently outside the experience of student teachers whose own learning in schools was largely through whole-class approaches, it creates difficulties while the student teachers strive to develop awareness of the nature and characteristics of such an approach.

In the programme as a whole, courses spent in school-based teaching practice are relatively few (less than 10 percent of the total time of the teacher education programme). As students often defer a decision on the type of school in which they will teach until late in their programme, it is common for elementary and lower secondary students to be following the same set of courses. Indeed, since 2001, students at certain universities have been required to take courses which will qualify them for both elementary and lower secondary teaching. In such programmes, school-based teaching practice is spent in both types of school. While in school, trainees work alongside practising teachers who act as mentors in enabling them to implement the models of teaching they have addressed in detail in the university.

Thus it can be seen that Japanese teacher education strives to integrate theory and practice through the modelling approaches described. However, student teachers comment on the difficulties that arise during school based practice in dealing with the behavioural problems they encounter, and also with slower learning pupils. These aspects are beginning to be addressed during ITE, but there is a feeling that they are given insufficient attention at present.

3.3. *Investigations of Recorded Practice – Mathematics and Teaching Through Hypermedia*

We include examples of certain uses of computer technology in the preparation of teachers as such examples provide interesting experiences relating to the theory-practice interfaces of teacher education.

The MATH project, conducted by Ball, Lampert and colleagues (Lampert & Ball, 1998) in Michigan, can be regarded as an attempt to link theory and practice within a methods course by benefiting from developments of information and communication technology. It is one answer to the question of how class-room practice can be taken as a starting point in teacher preparation, and how theoretical knowledge about learning and teaching can contribute. This principle has been taken as the basis of a second project MILE developed in the Netherlands (Dolk, Faes, Goffree, Hermsen & Oonk, 1996). MATH and MILE tried to use classrooms as sites for inquiry into practice; hence they are examples of teacher education in mode 3.

One of the main resources used in the MATH project is a selection of videotaped classroom sessions, with attached written reflections of the lessons' teachers, theory-based commentaries of teacher educators as well as examples of pupils' work. This makes it possible for student teachers "to investigate how ideas travelled from one part of the room to another" and to access everything "at a few mouse clicks for printing and projection". Both the teacher educator and the student teacher record their reflections on these materials and, thereby "produce the sort of multiple journeys across the same terrain that we imagined could represent the study of teaching from the perspective of practice" (Lampert & Ball, 1998, p. 55). An important task of the teacher educator is to help the student teachers to see the acquired, context-based knowledge in a broader theoretical context. The videotapes bring to student teachers real issues and problems that have arisen in real contexts, and invite intellectual engagement with these issues. Student teachers work in small groups and lecturers listen in and assess how to use the issues effectively, asking what understandings can be built on and what knowledge is lacking (Mousley, 1999).

In a similar environment for future primary teachers, the Multimedia Interactive Learning Environment (MILE), developed in the Netherlands, recordings of lessons were arranged into video fragments with an average of one to two minutes each and completed with transcripts and a search engine. The fragments were considered as separate narratives. Whereas in MATH the video-tapes served as impetus for teacher preparation, in MILE they were used as enriched orientation for subsequent analyses of student teachers' own classroom observations (Goffree & Oonk, 1999).

Similar work has taken place in Australia in the 'Learning About Teaching' project, led by Sullivan and Mousley (1996), which developed exemplars to support student teachers' learning about teaching mathematics. The exemplars were delivered by interactive computer media, integrating video, graphics and text. Investigations of their use with groups of teacher education students indicated that students could move beyond merely describing events to detailed analysis and explanation. In that sense bridges between theory and practice were built.

MATH, MILE, and 'Learning About Teaching' are examples of what has been called the case methodology, in particular for the stimulation of reflection on practice (c.f., Merseth, 1996; Walen & Williams, 2000). The design or the selection of cases is guided by specific values that give the professional development programme its structure (Barnett, 1998). Therefore, theory and practice are not just linked by the student teachers' and teacher educators' reflections on the cases but already by the teacher educators who adjust the videotapes according to their theoretical orientation.

4. THEORETICAL FOUNDATIONS OF INITIAL TEACHER EDUCATION

This section situates the theme of the chapter in its theoretical roots. It serves as a theoretical foundation and opens up the complexity of issues involved in the theme. The first focus is on preconceptions of student teachers and on the professional knowledge that they acquire. Thereafter, various purposes of teacher preparation are identified, after which selected social aspects of teacher preparation and the role of mentor teachers are discussed. Some of these issues receive a more practice-oriented consideration in Section 5.

4.1. *Preconceptions and the Knowledge Required for Mathematics Teaching*

4.1.1. Student-teacher Preconceptions and the Need of Reflection, Enquiry and Investigation

When students enter initial mathematics teacher education they already have extensive knowledge about mathematics teaching. There is no *tabula rasa* situa-tion. They know something about how teachers teach, how pupils learn, and have views, even if implicit, on the nature of mathematics. Of course, this knowledge is limited because it is based mainly on their experience as students. There is a wealth of literature on student teachers' knowledge about mathematics education (e.g., Davis, 1999; Gutiérrez & Jaime, 1999; Gellert, 2000).

Although such reports are often (mis-)interpreted as pointing to student teachers' deficits, they allow us a view of student teachers' sense-making within their specific situation as a mathematics teaching newcomer. Gellert (2000), for instance, reported on prospective elementary teachers' attempts to change mathematics classes from being frightening and subject-matter-oriented to friendly and what might be called 'child-centred' safe spaces for learning. These student teachers introduced 'child-centred' media for instruction (e.g., radio play cassettes), and reduced the mathematical content to fundamental arithmetic operations as the only useful and necessary content in mathematics. Not being confident in mathematics, the prospective teachers selected the teaching material and the mathematical problems more with respect to the pupils' fun and motivation than to the mathematical substance of students' learning.

The knowledge base for the newcomers' sense-making can be described as everyday knowledge or common sense and, thus, within mathematics teacher preparation it turns out to be quite superficial. Some newcomers, especially those in elementary teaching, have strong educational ambitions, such as to care for and motivate the pupils, but use only mathematically weak conceptions that can conflict with their educational ambitions. By contrast, newcomers in secondary teaching often tend to value mathematics as important and beautiful but lack a critical attitude to mathematics and to teaching itself. They are prone to regard mathematics as a culturally and socially neutral discipline, as a game within mind. At the same time, and due to being able mathematicians, they tend to over-emphasise the value and beauty of mathematical applications for everyday situations, and overlook the possibility that these are not necessarily of interest to many students (Gellert, Jablonka, & Keitel, 2001).

Such preconceptions, as with most common sense and everyday knowledge, normally remain tacit. It is one of the main challenges to initial mathematics teacher educators to make preconceptions and tacit knowledge explicit – in and through whatever ways their initial teacher education programmes are framed. Without explication of the knowledge base, purposeful and ambitious teacher preparation is difficult. There seems to be agreement among researchers of mathematics education that the process of explication of knowledge is adequately termed reflection, although it needs to be recognised that this notion has the advantage of being multi-faceted (c.f., Schön, 1983; Cooney, 1996; Clarke, 2000) and of a broad conceptual variety.

Reflection might facilitate a process by which explicit knowledge about mathematics education gradually becomes based on enquiry and investigation. Research with preservice and inservice teachers has made clear that reflection often stimulates them to analyse in more detail their own teaching practices. In addition, it can stimulate them to use research reports or educational theory in order to make their enquiries and reflections more focused, conscious and systematic (e.g., Krainer & Posch, 1996; Jaworski, 1998). Nicol (1999) compared 'pedagogy of presentation' with 'pedagogy of investigation' for teacher education. While a pedagogy of presentation of methods or visions construes teaching as a matter of applying principles and procedures in practice, a pedagogy of investigation "attempts to bring learning to teach more in line with the practice of teaching as a complex activity" (p. 47). To view mathematics teaching as complex – and not as 'pretty basic stuff' (c.f., Bobis & Cusworth, 1995, p. 113) – is a first step towards an enquiry-based understanding of mathematics education.

4.1.2. Mathematical and Pedagogical Knowledge

What kinds of knowledge are important to the teaching and learning of mathematics? The seminal work of Shulman and colleagues in the 'knowledge growth in teaching' project is well known, particularly the so called 'missing paradigm' of *pedagogical content knowledge* (PCK) as one of the seven elements proposed as a basis of professional knowledge for teaching (Shulman, 1986, p. 8):

- Content knowledge, both 'substantive' and 'syntactic';
- General pedagogical knowledge: generic principles of classroom management;
- Curriculum knowledge: materials and programmes;
- Pedagogical content knowledge: for a given subject area, this includes forms of representation of concepts, useful analogies, examples and demonstrations;
- Knowledge of learners;
- Knowledge of educational contexts, communities and cultures;
- Knowledge of educational purposes and values.

For mathematics teaching, the subject matter, or the *content*, is *mathematics*. That mathematics teachers need to know mathematics is uncontested; however, the claim is that mathematical knowledge alone is not sufficient. As Wilson, Shulman and Richert (1987) wrote, "while a personal understanding of the subject matter may be necessary, it is not a sufficient condition for being able to teach" (p. 115).

Content knowledge itself is declared to be 'both substantive and syntactic'. Briefly, substantive knowledge can be seen to include knowledge of the facts and concepts of the subject, and the ways that they are organised. Syntactic knowledge concerns the nature of enquiry in the field, how new knowledge is introduced and accepted in that community; it includes knowledge about proofs and rules of structures (Shulman, 1986).

The distinction between content knowledge and PCK in mathematics is at best fuzzy. For example, in 'representation of concepts' we need to ask how the notion of 'concept' is perceived, and what a 'representation' of a concept means. Mathematics subject matter itself can be seen as a form of representation (McNamara, 1991). For example, consider the notion of 'function' in mathematics. If we consider function to be a concept, do we think of its representations (such as algebraic, graphical, mapping) to be parts of the concept, or additional to it? Seeing a fraction as a number, a ratio or as a part of a whole may be thought of as seeing different representations of the concept of fraction, or may be considered as fundamental to the concept of fraction. In the experience of the authors, beginning teachers whose mathematical knowledge includes concepts of fractions and functions do not distinguish between concept and representation, and are very surprised when a multiplicity of representations are pointed out. Understanding of such concepts seems to include an unremarked ability to shift readily between representations.

It seems to us that the importance for teaching a concept lies rather in the recognition that our understanding of the concept includes a variety of representations, than a distinction between concept and representation. We need to be aware of the richness of any concept in order to conceptualise ways of offering it to students. Research into relationships between concepts and their representations is an important part of the discipline of mathematics education, and is especially important for teacher education (see e.g., Even & Tirosh, 1995; Cooney, Shealy & Arvold, 1998). Where prospective teachers themselves do not have ready manoeuvrability within such concepts, part of their educational needs in learning to teach are similar to those of students learning the concepts in the classroom. Certain research in teacher education has worked with this principle; see for example the cognitively guided instruction (CGI) project (see, e.g., Fennema, Sowder, & Carpenter, 1999), and the work of Deborah Schifter and colleagues (see, e.g., Schifter, 1998).

Debating the respective importance or delineation of subject matter and pedagogy for the learning of teachers seems less important than conceptualising ways in which they are related and interdependent. Research shows inadequacies in the mathematical knowledge of teachers (both novice and established teachers), and this includes both factual and relational knowledge (e.g., Askew, Brown, Rhodes, Johnson, & Wiliam 1997; Aubrey, 1997; Ma, 1999; Rowland, Martyn, Barber, & Heal, 2000; Goulding & Suggate, 2001). Some researchers have suggested that there are relationships between quality of mathematical knowledge and effective classroom teaching (e.g., Rowland et al., 2000) while others have suggested that no such links are discernible (e.g., Askew et al., 1997). Although effective teaching as a concept is hard to define, research has suggested that teachers who offer a *relational* or *connected* view of concepts are more effective than those who offer a mainly *instrumental* perspective (e.g., Askew, 1997) – following here Skemp's (1978) seminal distinction between relational and instrumental views of mathematics.

How mathematics itself is perceived, whether in terms of conceptual understanding or a relational perspective, emerges as central to the way it is taught. Research and experience over decades reports teaching that is stereotypically 'traditional' in the sense that it "relies heavily on the textbook and the traditional teaching patterns of exposition-examples-exercise" (Howson & Wilson, 1986). The patterns of 'direct instruction' reported by Romberg and Carpenter (1986) are still much in evidence across the world (Askew et al., 1997; Ma, 1999). It should be recognised, however, that the Third International Mathematics and

Science Video Study demonstrated departure from that in the case of Japan (Stigler & Hiebert, 1999).

In recruitment interviews for candidates for a current teacher education programme, we find many examples of mathematically-well-qualified teacher candidates who, asked to divide one fraction by another, obtain a correct answer quickly and readily by using a 'turn it upside down and multiply' approach. Asked to explain this approach, many are unable to do so and suggest this approach was the way they were taught, that they were never asked for, or given, a reason for the approach. It would be unlikely that such knowledge would enable a relational or connected approach to teaching division of fractions. Moreover, many of these candidates have not thought of teaching as more than passing on such methods, procedures or rules to enable students to gain a desired facility with the mathematical process. That this has been the basis of much teaching in England is reflected in a report from Her Majesty's Inspectors (HMI) in which they said that the work was predominantly teacher controlled (HMI, 1982). The report went on to say that teachers explained, demonstrated, and perhaps gave notes on procedures and examples, and that pupils were led deductively through small steps and closed questions to the principle being considered. Recent doctoral research in England shows such teaching still to prevail (Norman, 2000).

4.2. *Purposes of Teacher Preparation*

When people talk about teachers' work they often describe it using metaphors. Teachers' work becomes construed as that of technicians, executives, workers, evaluators, or intellectuals (cf., Smyth, 1998). Each metaphor communicates a specific social function of teaching. For instance, when teachers are identified as minor technicians within an industrial process they become classified as human manpower in terms of national needs, and it becomes the curriculum expert's task to equip them with pre-packaged materials. Such a view trivialises the work of teachers and, thus, denies its complexity. Smyth called this phenomenon "proletarization of teachers' work" (p. 1250) alluding to what happened to factory workers in the nineteenth century when they came increasingly under factory control. Although proletarization of teachers' work may appear to be an attractive administrative solution to the social destiny of teachers and the question of an appropriate preparation, it fails to acknowledge the fact that it is essentially the teacher who is shaping and determining the educational process.

However, even if teaching is considered to be a highly complex activity, varied perspectives on teacher preparation account for diverse purposes that teacher preparation is meant to serve. These various purposes, which we describe in the following section, range from 'training for the job' via 'reflection of teaching practice' to an understanding of teacher preparation as 'school development'. Of course, this classification is analytical. Most conceptualisations of teacher preparation include all three purposes, at least partly.

4.2.1. Teacher Preparation as Training for the Job

Although classroom life is certainly different in many ways from life outside the classroom it is part of teachers' day-to-day lives. From a sociological point of view, we can talk of mathematics classes as the space in which teachers and pupils plan, act, experience, and mutually adjust to each other. It is a milieu which teachers and pupils construct and yet are part of (c.f., Soeffner, 1989).

Within this space, teachers and students develop a set of ingrained actions – for instance, how to introduce an activity or how to respond to a teacher's question. These actions develop from experience, with actions deemed to have been 'successful' becoming candidates accepted for future replication. The actions corroborate the reciprocal expectancy of the interacting partners within mathematics classes. They tend to become economical and relieve pressure with respect to decisions that have to be taken in classrooms. At the same time, they are not usually subject to reflection and scrutiny.

In short, classroom interactions form part of teachers' and pupils' day-to-day lives, and these are highly constrained by norms and routines (see e.g., Mehan, 1979; Wood, Cobb, Yackel, & Dillon, 1993; Voigt, 1995; Krummheuer, 2000). Teaching develops a 'normal desirable state' (Brown & McIntyre, 1993), and the meanings that are negotiated during interactions are 'controlled' by didactical contracts (Brousseau, 1986). Although norms and routines may differ from country to country (Stigler, Gonzales, Kawanaka, Knoll, & Serrano, 1999) there seems to be reason to take them as consistent for communities of larger extent, and not as particularities that are bound to specific teachers and pupils. For instance, we refer to the way in which the multiplication table often is taught: by chanting or other forms of rote memorising.

With respect to teacher preparation, an acknowledgement of the importance of norms and routines for mathematics teaching may give rise to a conception of preparation that we want to call 'apprenticeship'. It might be possible to learn how to teach mathematics by doing what mathematics teachers do. Within a teacher apprenticeship, a first task of apprentices is to observe the routines of experienced teachers as well as the norms that structure the processes of teaching and learning (e.g., Brown & McIntyre, 1993). After that, apprentices may start to teach some selected sections of a lesson under the guidance and control of experienced teachers. They can attempt to learn to motivate the pupils, to sequence learning activities, to control effectively a mathematics classroom etc.

In the course of the preparation process, apprentices gradually take over the control for the lessons from the experienced teachers and also take the responsibility for successful teaching and learning upon themselves. Through this procedure apprentices both internalise and reproduce the routines and norms that are characteristic for mathematics classes. That way, the practice of mathematics teaching is perpetuated. This specific style of preparation has been called 'training', where the mere performance of educational techniques is the central goal of the preparation process (c.f., Bishop, 1988; Freudenthal, 1991).

In order to avoid possible misunderstanding, the concept of apprenticeship within the field of mathematics education in general, and mathematics teacher education in particular, needs further exploration. A theoretical base for this 'entrance' to learning has been formulated for children and adults learning mathematics by Jean Lave (see Lave, 1988; Lave & Wenger, 1991). Lave's formulation offers a socio-mathematical perspective by arguing that learners should engage in serious mathematical activities instead of internalising mathematical facts. Seriousness of activities corresponds to dilemma-motivation: mathematics "will be problematic in substantive ways only when the central dilemmas of ongoing activity are mathematical ones" (Lave, 1997, p. 31).

This view of apprenticeship within mathematics learning suggests that teacher preparation should search for serious activities in which the central dilemmas derive from problems of mathematics teaching. As a matter of course, such problems may be observed in normal classroom interactions. But, in the apprentice model for teacher education, when beginning teachers observe the routines of many experienced teachers they can be assisted to reflect on, rather than merely accept as something to be replicated, what they observe. In other words, their primary focus is not to acquire the ability to act routinely according to the traditional classroom norms, but rather to accept the invitation to problematise what they observe, and to reflect on what might be done to improve things. We may refer to this extended apprenticeship approach as 'critical apprenticeship'. Critical apprenticeship is substantively different from what beforehand has been termed apprenticeship, and is strongly related to the teacher-preparation-as-reflection approach.

4.2.1.   Teacher Preparation as Reflection on Teaching Practice

One aim of the 'normal desirable state' of mathematics classes is a reduction of the unusual and an extinction of doubts, so that an unproblematic and thus economic co-ordination of teaching can be realised. In order to accomplish this state, teachers try to typify new and unknown situations and actions as if these were part of the normal and well known. It is this very mode of thinking and acting which generates 'normal lessons' and regulates the course of most mathematics classes.

A conception of teacher preparation as reflection on teaching practice gives the routines and patterns of interaction special emphasis. Contrary to the familiar approach of dealing with routines within the teacher-preparation-as-apprenticeship mode, the aim becomes one of facilitating processes by which 'apprentice' teachers examine closely and critically the routines and patterns of interaction they observe. What are the mechanisms and consequences of the routinized mathematics teaching, and what are the arguments for and against continuing to regard such practices as 'normal'?

In short, the contingency of classroom interaction comes to the fore. That kind of reflection requires a certain distance or, more precisely, a relief of the pressure of ongoing actions within the classroom situation. Therefore, reflection on teaching practice demands a safe space in which the practitioner and one or more observers can trustingly discuss and evaluate the teaching experience. Such a reflecting practice might gradually develop the ability of self-evaluation and lead to a deeper and more differentiated understanding of the ways in which classroom interaction proceeds. Teaching practice becomes less straightforward, and classroom situations are demonstrated to be much more open than on a first view. Together with the opening-up of classroom situations goes an extension of the teacher's scope for arrangement and realisation of mathematics teaching and learning processes. This may cause a feeling of uncertainty and unease – there is no secure path to follow – but, according to Krummheuer (1999), it seems to be a precondition for the development of self-confident and self-determined teaching.

It is an implicit assumption of the reflection-on-teaching-practice approach that there is an urge to develop and improve approaches to the practices of mathematics teaching. This may sound like undue attention is being paid to a deficit model, with proven qualities of current mathematics instruction being placed in danger of being disregarded, or discounted. But that is, in fact, not the case. Two arguments may help to clarify this point.

Firstly, all routines and patterns in the interaction between teachers and pupils, or among pupils are, despite existing power differentials, socially negotiated and, thus, dependent on the confirmation of their aptness and validity. Changes within the socially shared understanding of mathematics teaching and learning and developments of theoretical perspectives in mathematics education may call this confirmation into question. Moreover, whenever a routine is abandoned and a new way of acting is introduced or tested, then this new way itself needs to become a routine in order to maintain the everyday character of mathematics classes. Therefore, reflection on teaching practice is not aiming at abolishing routines, but rather at sensitizing teachers to their consequences and a need for their periodical social verification.

Secondly, when practitioners and observers reflect jointly on teaching practice they are able to operate with a language which avoids a deficit approach. It is part of the responsibility of tutors and mentors to take care of the establishment of such language. As Dawson (1999) put it, there is nothing wrong with newcomers that needs 'fixing' by teacher educators. Rather, it is a case of both drawing mutually on their respective knowledge and experience to enable growth of knowledge that is necessary for effective mentoring and effective teaching.

With this focus on joint reflection on teaching practice, the social relationships that are negotiated within teacher preparation practice gain particular importance. On the one hand, often, there is an institutional separation between those who learn to teach and those who show how to teach. This relationship can be characterised as highly hierarchical not only with respect to its institutional constitution but often also to its situational realisation. There can be no doubt that hierarchies affect the relationships within teacher preparation: some participants try to achieve a qualified teacher status and others control the access to it. On the other hand, the mentor-mentee relationship is open to negotiation and may range between the two poles of criticism and support (Watson, 1994).

Nolder, Smith and Melrose (1994) encouraged mentees to regard mentors as 'listening friends', 'supportive critics', 'gatekeepers and guides' and 'link agents'.

Moreover, teacher-educators as well as experienced teachers do learn while educating new teachers. Practising mathematics teachers can improve their knowledge about teaching by reflecting with the newcomer on their teaching. Teacher-educators are themselves learners who try to adjust their knowledge about educational theories to the educational practice (Even, 1999; Jaworski, 2001). So, a clear-cut distinction between learners and demonstrators within teacher preparation is fictitious.

According to our experience, the willingness and openness of practising teachers and teacher educators for *joint* reflection is critical. Particularly when formal assessment is part of the mentors' contract, the hierarchies of the system can exert a constraining influence on the establishment of trustful relationships and safe spaces for joint reflection (see Haggarty, 1995).

4.2.2. Teacher Preparation as School Development

Whenever international comparative studies of students' achievements report on the differences between the participating countries, the less successful within the ranking cry for improvement and development of schooling in their country (Keitel & Kilpatrick, 1999). This call might generate a rise in governmental funds for research on school change and development of innovations – or just a drive back to the basics of fundamental arithmetic. Unfortunately, in most cases the greater part of these funds ends up in the development of instruments for more precise measurement of the deficit, or in (over) hasty and uncoordinated supply of new technological equipment. That could be observed, for instance, in Germany after publication of results of the Third International Mathematics and Science Study (Keitel & Kilpatrick, 1999).

Attempts to innovate schooling from the perspective described at the end of the last paragraph often focus on the need for new teaching aids and media. They can also generate calls for a change in external factors, such as the ingredients and composition of the students' timetables, or the ways in which final examinations are organised.

In fact, such changes are concerned merely with conditions associated with the teaching and learning and of themselves do not problematise the ways in which teachers teach and students learn. But it could be argued (see, e.g., Bauer & Rolff, 1978) that what really makes the difference is the teachers' understanding of teaching and learning, their corresponding conceptions of mathematics classes, and their realisations of mathematics education in their classrooms.

Central to educational change and school development is the sociological question (c.f., Giacquinta, 1998; Stigler and Hiebert, 1999): "What new patterns of interaction in the classroom, explicitly stated or embedded in planned change, need to be enacted, and what old routines need to be abandoned?" Seen from this perspective, teacher preparation is not just the technology that equips future teachers with knowledge and proficiency. It rather lays the foundations for novice teachers' enacting of new or modified patterns of interaction. Essentially, it is these modifications that bring about school development. However, our discussion on mutually reflective mentoring approaches, above, indicates that such change needs to happen as part of ongoing reflective practice rather than external imposition.

4.3. *Social Meaning of Teacher Preparation*

In order to deepen our understanding of teacher preparation as a social practice and to concentrate on the social consequences that grow out of different models of it, two traditional sociological categories may be considered (cf., Luhmann & Schorr, 1979; Noddings, 1992). First, we ask how the autonomy of the teacher and the collegiality among teachers can be addressed, not as contrasting aims but in a relationship that proves fruitful. Second, we ask how teacher preparation can cope with the structural problem of providing a safe space for the novice teacher's development of specific professional knowledge and, at the same time, be responsible for the social selection of new teachers.

In this Section we will discuss theoretical aspects of these issues. We will come back to some of the issues in Section 5, when we look in our case study at social relationships between mentors and mentees. Section 5 draws attention to how autonomy, collegiality and selection can be organised in practice.

4.3.1. Autonomy – Collegiality

Although the practice of mathematics teaching is framed by institutional circumstances, nevertheless, individual teachers act according to their sense making of classroom processes. Their autonomy as teachers is based on a specific rationality gained during the preparation period. For example, in some countries teachers are free to choose the teaching methods, aids and, at least partly, the content of instruction. In many European countries there is a tradition of giving teachers considerable freedom to develop syllabuses from skeletal frameworks and guidelines (Clarke, Clarke, & Sullivan, 1996). In some countries, teachers are responsible for the construction of final examination tasks. In others, a central agency takes the burden and control of it. This point is somewhat condensed in the concept of *Didaktik* and the (German) *didaktical* tradition (see, e.g., Klafki, 1995a, 1995b). That tradition gives teachers "substantial leeway to develop their own intentions, interpretations and critiques of both the objectives and content of the state syllabi" (Keitel & Hopmann, 1995, p. 1; see also Clarke et al., 1996). In other countries, teaching is more regulated, and a good teacher may be thought to be one who follows the teachers' guides to the letter.

We want to define the term 'autonomy' not just negatively as the absence of external constraints or restrictions but positively as the independence of self-determination. Consequently, autonomy does not necessarily aim at a reduction of dependence. It rather indicates that a self-determined choice of particular interdependence is desirable. The term autonomy does not mean the isolated single teacher in front of the classroom. It describes the freedom of committing oneself to a consciously selected teaching style as well as the independence for determination of interdependent relationships with colleagues, pupils, parents and headteachers.

Thus, autonomy is not a counterpart of collegiality but a precondition for the achievement of it. Moreover, research on teacher preparation and teacher development suggests that the concept of autonomy ought to include within its ambit the notion of being critical for the development of professionalism (Cooney & Shealy, 1997; Artzt, 1999).

In the context of notions of autonomy and collegiality we raise two questions which need to be discussed when models of teacher preparation become the objects of evaluation and judgement. The first is: "How does teacher preparation prepare for autonomy and collegiality?"

In most teacher education programmes, autonomy and collegiality are issues that remain not specifically included in official goals and assessment tasks. Pragmatically, it is hoped that autonomy will develop with increasing teaching practice, and so will collegiality, because in schools, teachers, to some extent, are obliged to work with other teachers. But when we consider the situation with John and the Bond-videotapes (at the start of this chapter), it becomes obvious that both collegiality and autonomy are crucial points when student teachers, their tutors and mentoring teachers enquire into teaching practice. John demonstrates his introduction to a lesson on fractions to his peers, which, in the very situation of teacher preparation, are potentially his colleagues.

Organising teacher preparation in this way offers student teachers a space in which they may develop a sense of what collegiality could be: a joint reflection and support, a safe space with empathetic atmosphere in which personal and professional development is possible (van Zoest & Bohl, 2002). Thus, joint reflection within teacher preparation is not restricted to a method by which student teachers shall acquire teaching proficiency – although this has much value of its own. It also intends to introduce student teachers into fruitful relationships with peers – now student teachers, later on other teachers in the school in which they will teach. The introduction of student teachers into collegiality with their teaching peers is complemented by the particularities of mentor-mentee relationships (Jaworski & Watson, 1994a).

Collegiality of teachers in schools includes relations among teachers of different teaching and life experience. On one hand, such differences make collegiality fruitful but, on the other, they sometimes result in simmering conflicts. Mentor-mentee relationships are similar to this in many ways. There also is a gap of experience and, of course, in some cases mentors and mentees co-operate and in others they do not. One can argue that in the beginning of a mentor-mentee relationship the responsibility for establishment of fruitfulness is more on the side of the mentor, and slowly becomes more balanced. This implies that mentors should be aware that they also participate in the introduction of student teachers into collegiality, and are willing to do so. Such characteristics of mentor-mentee relationships can influence future headteacher-teacher relationships, too (see McIntyre et al., 1993; Haggarty, 1995).

The development of autonomy is strongly linked to the ways in which peer interactions of student teachers and mentor-mentee relationships occur. This seems to be a very delicate point, particularly for the co-operation between student teachers and their mentors. The teacher's autonomy is, among other issues, characterised by the development of a critical perspective towards the teaching practice of others and of self. This implies that mentors should be sufficiently able, and self-conscious, to encourage students to be in a position to criticize the teaching practice of the mentors. In order to facilitate this, mentors have to develop ways in which they offer critique on the teaching of their mentees so that a joint reflection can be started, including the acceptance of and esteem for diversity of mathematics teaching. Autonomy and the acceptance of autonomy of others are only possible when diversity within teaching practice is considered not only as fruitful but as a fundamental requirement of the development of this very practice (Nolder et al., 1994).

This leads to our second question: "What are the effects of hierarchies within teacher preparation for the development of autonomy and collegiality?" It is not clear at all whether the ideal of joint generation of collegiality and autonomy is successful in practice. There are numerous studies which describe how student teachers do exciting, reflective work within high-quality preservice courses (see, e.g., Artzt, 1999; Skott, 2001; van Zoest & Bohl, 2002). On the other hand, there are a lot of reports about rather traditional teaching practice of full-time employed teachers (e.g., Askew, 1997, Ma, 1999; Norman, 2000).

Apparently, most young teachers do not exercise sufficient autonomy to resist levelling which is done by the 'cultures' of the schools. It seems to be highly questionable whether the relationships of student-teachers with peers and mentors actually foster the development of a critical perspective towards the teaching practice of others and of self. There is the distinct possibility that relationships often increase the tendency to avoid conflicts with mentors and tutors and to adjust their teaching practice to what is perceived as desired. That could be why many young teachers, when they become fully employed, are not able to contribute the results of their high-quality preparation into the culture of their schools and to make use of diversity. Instead, they cannot resist the conservative power exerted by most experienced teachers, and as a result they adjust themselves to the rather traditional practices. Without sufficient autonomy the development of challenging collegial relationships is problematic (see, e.g., McIntyre et al., 1993; Calderhead & Shorrock, 1997).

If mentors of student-teachers are obliged to give reports on the work of their mentees then this can be a major constraint on the development of a fruitful, challenging collegiality – particularly within times when good marks are necessary for future employment. Even in situations where mentors do not judge their mentees, hierarchies may affect the mentor-mentee relationship. It should always be more the responsibility of the person that is 'higher' within the hierarchy to be sensitive and constructive with respect to the developing relationship.

4.3.2. Criteria for Selection

In the field of teacher preparation, 'selection' has a double meaning. One meaning is concerned with the characteristics of a 'successfully prepared' novice teacher.

What are standards required of a beginning teacher in order to be considered for employment? Who sets the standards? Who is in charge of the selection process?

The second meaning relates to the situation when selection is applied to persons in charge of teacher preparation. What, particularly, qualifies teachers for selection as mentors? Who selects them? Unlike the situation with the beginning teacher who obviously is the subject of selection, in some countries the selection of mentors often comes down to the problem of having enough experienced teachers volunteering to accept a beginning teacher. In other countries, 'volunteering' seems to be the wrong term when teachers are just told to be mentors. This may cause frustrations among beginning teachers when, sometimes, the teaching they are exposed to contradicts what they have been taught by their university tutors. This issue, which has been termed the 'placement dilemma', takes into account the potentially enormous impact experienced teachers have in what elsewhere has been called the socialisation of beginning teachers. Mentoring teachers have been attributed the most significant influence on the development of beginning teachers' thinking and teaching strategies (Zeichner & Gore, 1990; Jaworski & Watson, 1994; Haggarty, 1995; Frykholm, 1999).

In many countries, teacher preparation has ignored or has underestimated the fact that mentors may not only be subject to selection but also to qualification. It is probably not sufficient for a mentor to be an experienced teacher who, in the best case, demonstrates mathematics lessons which fit to the current state of the art. In addition, awareness, knowledge and proficiency are required for co-operation with mentees. Of course, some mentors succeed in generating both challenging and empathetic relationships with their mentees, without providing any support. But others fail, not because they are unwilling to assist the mentees in their professional development but because of lack of particular qualification for this demanding task. Thus, there is a need to qualify adequately the very persons who exert so much influence on the development of student teachers.

5. A CASE STUDY

Having located our theme in its theoretical roots, we now offer an account of a case study which raises issues relating to models 3 and 4 of initial teacher education/training and, in doing so, addresses in practice many of the issues raised in Section 4 above. In the case study we look at an example of integrated practice which fits well within model 3, and moves to some extent into model 4. This location allows us to highlight issues we see as being fundamental to such integration, without necessarily favouring a fully integrated model.

The case is from a schools-university partnership scheme, of 17 years' standing in the United Kingdom. In this scheme a one-year (36 weeks) Post Graduate Certificate of Education (PGCE) course for training secondary teachers is offered. Schools have moved in and out of partnership over the years. Within the partnership, university tutors in curriculum areas (mathematics is one example) work closely with teachers in the schools to enable the growth and development of student teachers and their teaching. Student teachers are called 'interns', according to a medical model of internship whereby new practitioners work alongside experienced practitioners in the field. Interns are placed in groups of at least six in a school in various subject areas. Where possible, two interns are placed together in any subject area. Every intern, or pair of interns, has one teacher of their subject designated as their mentor, guiding their activity within the subject department of the school. The internship scheme is research-based in that, over the years, critical evaluation of all aspects of the programme, undertaken jointly by schools and university, have fed back into its developing practice. In addition, several university education tutors (in different subject areas) have completed doctoral degrees researching aspects of internship. From one of these, Haggarty (1995) offered a severe critique of mentoring processes within the scheme, some of which have developed more positively since the time of her study.

The course takes place over three university terms. Interns are placed in two schools for extended school work. The first two weeks are orientation weeks in a primary and a secondary school chosen by the intern. There are then 11 weeks of joint activity involving two days in School 1 and three in the university. This is followed by 15 weeks full time in School 1 with a 55% teaching programme. Finally there are six weeks full time in School 2 with a similar teaching load. During the year two weeks are spent wholly in the university.

Where subject teaching, in our case mathematics teaching, is concerned, the key relationships, are between interns, their mathematics education tutors in the university and mathematics teachers (one of whom is their mentor) in their partnership school. The case focuses on a small group of people who work together to effect interns' learning in mathematics teaching. The group consists of one mathematics education tutor working with interns, mentors and other teachers in three established partnership schools: thus, three mentors and their associated (five) interns are involved.

5.1. *Relationships as Exemplified in this Case Study*

In order to write this case study, the interns and teachers concerned were selected and asked by the tutor (Jaworski) to comment on aspects of interns' learning, ways in which the partnership contributed effectively to this learning, and issues that impede an integrated approach to learning. Data were collected by the tutor through half-hour interviews with each mentor, towards the end of the first term of a three-term course, and a short questionnaire, with open-ended questions, which the interns completed during the Christmas break. The tutor recognised that her asking of the questions was a factor in the responses she received from interns and teachers, and this had to be taken into account in offering an analysis of comments and issues emerging.

The three schools were selected as examples in which the partnership was seen to be at its best in terms of integrated practice for developing mathematics teachers. This was deliberate since we wanted the case to raise issues related to achieving integrated practice. Our judgment of 'best' refers to well-developed relationships between schoolteachers and university tutors involving considerable degrees of shared knowledge and understanding of mathematics learning and teaching and its development. Relationships have developed through joint research projects and participation in university Diploma or Master's courses, as well as through the internship scheme. The sketches which follow are intended to paint a picture of ongoing partnership between university and schools – teachers, tutors and interns. Table 1 summarises these relationships.

In School A, George has been a mentor for eight years, not always active. During this time he has worked in research projects with two doctoral students from the university. He has contributed to the University sessions of the PGCE course for several years, focusing on learning mathematics using graphical calculators and computer algebra packages. He teaches in the mathematics department of School A in which his Head of Department is a former mathematics intern (nine years ago) and another member of the department was also an intern (four years ago). The Head of Department currently has a 'Best Practice' scholarship from the Department for Education and Employment (DfEE),[2] to enhance his teaching through research in collaboration with the university. Interns in the department this year are Laurinda and John (John was discussed in the vignette at the beginning of the Chapter).

In School B, Sally is a new mentor this year. The mathematics department in which she teaches has had close links with the university in a variety of ways over many years. The Head of Department is a teacher who has contributed to university sessions in the PGCE course, focusing on A Level mathematics teaching.[3] She is currently completing a 2-year diploma course in Developing Mathematics Teaching, at the university. Another teacher in the department completed his MSc in Mathematics Education at the university seven years ago. He has also been a mentor and a *Professional Tutor* (PT) in the Internship

Table 1.   **Personnel involved in the case study**

School	Mentor	Years	Teacher links with University	Interns
A	George	8	1. Mentor: PGCE teaching; research participant 2. HoD: former intern; Best Practice researcher 3. Former intern	Laurinda John
B	Sally	1	1. HoD: former PGCE teaching; Diploma student 2. MSc graduate; former mentor; former PT 3. Former PGCE supervisor/tutor 4. Former intern	Judith
C	Jeanette	9	1. Mentor: research participant; MA student; former PGCE teaching 2. HoD: PT 3. NQT: former intern	Geoff Andrew

Scheme – the PT's role is to organise professional development study and activity for all the interns in the school. Another teacher has acted as a university tutor, supervising interns in schools, and yet another teacher was an intern (seven years ago). There is just one intern in this department, Judith.

In School C, Jeanette has been a mentor over a 9-year period, not always active. During this time she has participated in two research projects at the university, in one of them conducting research into her own teaching. She has recently been studying for her MA at another university, and is just completing her dissertation. For three years, she contributed to university sessions of the PGCE course, focusing on gender, multicultural and anti-racist issues. She teaches mathematics in the mathematics department at School C. The Head of Department is also a Professional Tutor in the partnership scheme. Currently, there are two newly qualified teachers (NQTs) who were interns last year. Interns in the department this year are Geoff and Andrew.

The relationships described here are not intended to be representative either of this particular scheme or of such schemes in the UK widely. However, subject departments in many of the internship schools would fit these patterns, and there would be similar patterns in schemes throughout the UK. They illustrate how an integrated scheme can develop, and emphasise the importance of shared knowledge and experience between tutors and teachers in university and schools. The issues discussed below arise because of, or in spite of, such shared knowledge and experience.

5.2. *Examples of Interns' Learning*

5.2.1. Case for Perceptions

For the case study, mentors were asked, first, to identify a significant aspect of their interns' learning during the past term (October to December) – the first one of the PGCE year. George talked about John's developing teaching. According to George, John is good at having ideas for lessons – for example, his idea for using the videotapes as a context in which to address equivalent fractions. However, he lacks experience in turning such an idea into a lesson: how to introduce it to the class; how to get students involved and thinking; how to sustain thinking and activity to enable mathematical ideas to be addressed and understood. George sees his task as mentor to enable John to turn his good ideas into sustainable activity – "fleshing it out a bit: they (interns) don't have the experience at that stage to turn them [the ideas] into full blown lesson plans". In John's earlier lessons, such ideas had been lost in a very quick initial delivery, leaving him short of further material and ideas and at a loss as to how to proceed with the lesson.

George helped John to "increase the mathematical content of his good idea – varying the activity to get a bit more out of it". For example, George encouraged John to vary the number of tapes from 12 to some other number, such as 11, thereby enabling a new set of fractions to be considered, and compared with those with denominator 12 and their equivalents. Discussion between George and John led to the 'story' (contextualizing the videotapes activity) being enhanced to fit with the mathematical concepts the class needed to understand.

Thus, mentoring activity here involved mentors being prepared to build on interns' ideas and enable interns to see what else, beyond the idea, is needed for a successful lesson. This might be seen as bridging the gap between the *idea* (theory) of activity and the *realisation* (practice) of activity in the classroom. In that sense, George's role became one of acting as link agent. George drew attention to a variety of aspects of the PGCE course which contributed to interns' learning, with emphasis on the shifting between school and university. Among these aspects were:

- Intern working with peers at the university to analyse a mathematical topic and suggesting classroom activities around the topic;
- Tutors providing input concerning topic analysis (for example, consideration of factors such as imagery and language patterns, valuable contexts and resources; use of computers and calculators to develop mathematical ideas);
- Intern working with mentor and another intern in mentor sessions in school, planning with a particular class in mind; and
- Intern putting ideas into practice in the classroom, with feedback from a teacher.

Sally's response to the same question was to speak of Judith's recognition of the importance of building on students' prior experience. Judith put a lot of time into planning lessons. Initially her focus was on clear objectives regarding "where she wanted to lead them (the students), whether they get there or not", that is to say, being clear about the mathematics she wanted students to learn and understand. However, as she gained experience with the students – "she's taught short 15-minute pieces, so has got to know the group" – her confidence grew. "Originally it [her focus] was on what she had to teach them, but now it's more listening to them and getting from them; her personality is coming through; she has more of a bond – not exactly jokey, but ... there's more flexibility – she's more aware, using names a lot, using commands, making clear that she expects them to be quiet, developing her personal authority". Sally added: "We've spent quite a bit of time together, planning beforehand, discussing how thing are going to work. A lot of it is down to self-confidence, happy when she goes in there".

Thus, we see the mentor role being interpreted by both these mentors in terms of giving time to interns for talking through potential lessons, enabling interns to build their own classroom images, to see how to introduce and sustain activity and to manage the classroom effectively, thereby building confidence. Sally noticed that Judith was learning to *build on her knowledge of the students* in planning activities. It seemed to the tutor, analysing the words of Sally and George, that they were similarly *building on interns' knowledge*, in order to enable interns' teaching to develop. Just as Judith was getting to *know her students*, George and Sally showed considerable personal *knowledge of the interns* they were working with, and their own development of this knowledge. Time for working together seemed an essential resource.[4]

For this research, squeezing interviews with mentors into their busy professional lives was not always easy. So the tutor's interview with Jeanette took place as part of another meeting with another colleague present: this teacher, Sam, is Head of Mathematics at another school, not one of the chosen three. Jeanette and Sam had worked in two research projects with the university tutor and the three were used to reflecting together on teaching (Jaworski, 1998; Potari & Jaworski, 2002). Sam said he felt it was a privilege to have "dedicated time to talk about mathematics with interns"; he felt 'envious' of Jeanette who was given such time as part of her mentoring role. Jeanette indicated that for her the most valuable use of this time was to encourage intern reflection: "If we don't start the reflective process in their first year ... [she implied, it might never develop, otherwise] – thinking deeply about their practice, and how they can make it better. This year is the start of it all". She continued:

> The way I run a mentor session, I always start with a reflection on what's happened between the last session and this one; which is invariably a discussion of lessons they've [interns have] taught. Because they've been able to take very few of *my* lessons, I'm relying on feedback from colleagues,[5] and also on feedback the interns bring to mentor sessions – tell me about this lesson – you told me last week what you were going to do; how did it go? What sort of things came up? What have you learnt from there? What can you put into practice? How could you have made it better?

Thus, Jeanette requires interns to reflect overtly; she provides opportunity for this reflection and gives feedback within the mentor session. Reflection is emphasised in both school and university.

The episode described in the vignette, at the beginning of this chapter, was from a type of university session called 'Episodes and Issues' (Jaworski & Watson, 2001). In such sessions, interns bring significant episodes (or anecdotes) from their teaching to share with the intern group. Each intern decides what is significant and shares this with the group and the group then discusses issues raised by the intern's account of the episode. Interns are encouraged by tutors to take a positively critical stance towards such issues, relating the questions that arise to teaching situations they have personally experienced.[6] In that way, interns take the role of supportive critics.

Thus, for example, during discussion in the episode in the vignette, one issue which was raised concerned the use of real world contexts (for example, James Bond films) as a basis for considering mathematical concepts. What if the students' attention stays with the context, rather than grappling with the mathematics? For example, what if students were fantasising about James Bond so that equivalent fractions were only peripheral to their attention? An expectation of the course, is that such issues, and their analysis, will be taken by interns back to their schools, and reappear in some metamorphosis in intern-mentor reflections, and subsequently be manifested in classroom action. Current research is exploring interns' emphasis on such issues in their developing practice (Burn, Hagger, Mutton, & Everton, 2000).

5.2.2. Interns' Perceptions

Interns' perceptions of their learning were revealing and fascinatingly different. For example, Judith wrote, "This term I have learnt how to find/create and evaluate resources". She continued, "I have learnt to ask appropriate questions to modify ideas, or create new ones to make activities that are moulded and suited to my classroom and my pupils". She spoke of evaluating activities in terms of the needs of her students. She said that activities should provide support with a mathematical topic, enable students to work independently, and offer something that is easier or harder according to perceived needs. She indicated that she seems to have internalised such evaluative activity to the extent that she now engages subconsciously in it whenever encountering a 'potential resource'. She concluded by saying, "this first term has sown a seed of 'resource study' in my mind that I intend to cultivate."

Andrew pointed to his realisation that being good at mathematics was not enough to make a good teacher – "it takes much more than that". He had recognised that "some of the mathematics that are and always have been obvious for us are not easy for everybody". He pointed to the need to "become aware of the different perceptions pupils, and people, have in mathematics (whether correct or not)"; and to the importance of becoming knowledgeable about common mistakes and misconceptions. Although school mathematics can "seem so basic and obvious", once one has identified what pupils do not understand, it can be "tricky to explain it in simplest terms".

Geoff focused on his own personal presence and presentation. "If I don't feel so in control, my teaching suffers." He had had previous experience of teaching and had felt fairly confident in becoming a teacher. However, the many factors to consider meant that perhaps he was not always as confidently in control as he would like to be. He said, "The constantly changing classes, unfamiliarity with procedures and names of pupils, all contribute to the problem". However, he acknowledged that his range of experiences in the first term had enabled him to feel prepared for the weeks of teaching that would follow, especially through observation of experienced professionals. "Observing how other teachers deal with pupils, whether it be good or bad, gives new ideas and prevents mistakes".

Laurinda focused on her developing thinking: "the need to think through in depth the topics that I plan to teach in school", and "the different types/levels of thinking that I need to master". Like Andrew, she emphasised the importance not only of knowing the mathematics herself, but also of "thinking around the area and considering issues such as common misconceptions". She highlighted areas of classroom management/practical considerations; learning objectives for pupils and whether these are achieved; and implications of what occurs in one lesson for future lessons. She concluded with, "I have begun to appreciate how emotionally demanding teaching is. I have learned that when a lesson goes well it is extremely satisfying and when it does not go as planned it is frustrating and disappointing."

Interns had been asked to express *briefly* significant aspects of their learning, and there was probably much more that each one could have said. The above remarks were revealing for the tutor in terms of what the interns chose to express from their complex experiences up to this point. They were also fascinating in terms of the particular focuses and ways in which key concepts of the course were reflected back. It was pleasing to see the emphasis on pupils' alternative conceptions, and on the importance of monitoring pupils' learning and providing appropriate resources to foster that learning. These remarks, albeit brief, provide evidence of a critically reflective stance to developing teaching which is emphasised in the course. Although there might have been an element here of interns giving the tutor what they felt she wanted to hear, it would not have been possible to achieve this so eloquently without an associated quality of thinking and understanding of the issues. The course requires interns to write a short set of 'Friday Reflections' each week. These allow tutors to tap into what students are thinking and what is concerning them, and to respond individually to the issues that are revealed.

5.3. *Interns, Mentors and Other Teachers*

5.3.1. Mentors' Perceptions

In Jeanette's interview, she indicated her reliance on feedback from colleagues in following her interns' progress. "They always take time to give feedback to both me and the intern". Teachers complete standard observation sheets (developed within the partnership and centrally produced). Typically, they write a log of the observed lessons on the back of the sheet, discuss this with the intern, and summarise the main issues on the front of the sheet, relating these to the *Standards* for QTS.[7] When Sam asked what sorts of comments had been made, Jeanette responded:

> They [teachers] invariably try to be positive. Interns can only see the things that go wrong. Colleagues point out things that went well; often from a mathematics point of view, rather than just class control; they might offer some advice – next time you might try this – or an extension idea.

Jeanette indicated that many of her colleagues in School C have a lengthy experience of internship; they know how to work at it – "you can't just go to the staffroom and put your feet up!" Sam was sceptical of this, suggesting that not all teachers are so committed. This works well in a team where teachers are interested in their own improvement, and pass this attitude on to interns. However, some teachers speak of throwing an intern "in at the deep end, sink or swim". It can be hard to convince them that an alternative approach is more effective. Here Sam raised a practical issue related to the theoretical idea we discussed earlier regarding autonomy and collegiality not being seen as opposite poles.

George was realistic about what he might expect from some of his colleagues. As a mentor he is expected to give time to interns, and some dedicated time is provided for this on his timetable. The same is not true for other teachers, so finding time for interns is harder and can be less of a commitment – "the quality of feedback [from other teachers] is not what a mentor can give, although colleagues who have been interns can help". However, a mentor has to be careful since colleagues not designated to work with interns feel 'singled out'.

As a mentor, George tries to have both interns working with his own classes for part of their teaching time, so that he can keep close observation of their progress. As this is not possible for Jeanette, she has to rely more on her colleagues. Sally, who is a new mentor, spoke to her Head of Department about her mentoring role. The Head of Department indicated colleagues in the department who would be particularly effective in working with the interns. These colleagues had all been mentors in the past and had considerable knowledge of internship. Sally commented that Judith communicated well with a number of teachers who were "a great help and so enthusiastic". One colleague, approached by Sally about the interview questions (which had been provided in advance of the interview), had said that the links between school and University had been built up over many years, and she could not see how they would be bettered.

These indications from the three schools suggest that many teachers have a deep commitment to working with interns, give their time generously to do so, and learn over the years from their experiences. The issues involved are delicate ones. Mentors have to work with their colleagues, and while wanting to persuade them to contribute to interns learning in a positive way, have to accept the quality of input that results. The overall commitment of the school, often through the Professional Tutor, is also an important influence. The University works hard at developing relationships with Professional Tutors.

However, tutors know there are teachers who have little understanding of the principles of the internship scheme, and little sympathy with its practices. Sometimes, encouraging such teachers to work with internship aims and principles has positive results for both the teachers and others. Sometimes, working with such teachers is avoided. In one case, in Mathematics, work with one particular school was discontinued: although the mentor was very knowledgeable and committed, colleagues in his department were unsupportive and to some extent antagonistic with respect to what he was asking of them. Such decisions are taken jointly between university and schools. Where there are differences of view or expectation, these are negotiated, not always totally comfortably, but with the chief aim of optimising the quality of provision for interns. A serious factor in such negotiating is the time it takes. All the professionals involved are being seriously challenged regarding the time it is possible to give, despite the best aims of all concerned.

5.3.2. Interns' Perceptions

Interns reflected on what each of the professionals with whom they were associated contributed to their learning, focusing on ways in which they saw these contributions being linked to their overall learning to teach. With tutors, interns had addressed issues in learning and developed a deeper understanding of the processes involved; they paid attention to learning objectives, and developed an analytical approach to planning lessons. Their teaching became based more solidly in the theoretical roots of the domain. This occurred despite, as Laurinda said, "the more artificial setting" of the university. Mentors helped interns to turn planning into practicality, "looking critically with me at what I had planned" and providing assistance with ideas and practicalities. Work in school was about 'getting experienced oneself'.

Mentors and teachers acted as role models in the classroom, teaching interns 'by example', and critical observers of interns' teaching, "causing me to think in greater depth". Andrew observed that although the praise offered by teachers was appreciated, he valued their constructive criticism. Teachers were also essential in enabling interns to deal with the emotional demands of learning to teach.

It is clear that interns value greatly the support from teachers, mentor and tutor, and none offered any criticisms of the kinds or quality of support they were offered. This is unsurprising, given they were writing for their tutor. However, there was a sophisticated sense from their brief remarks that they could see the enterprise being about their learning, that it was of value to get the different kinds of input from different people, and that ultimately it was their own responsibility to make sense of it all in their own developing experience.

5.4. *The Effective Nature of the Internship Partnership*

5.4.1. Mentors' and Tutor's Contrasting Perceptions

It is hard for mentors to see the partnership at work in its more global sense as they are based in their school with their own interns. They see something of other mentors in the school: cross-subject mentors' meetings in school are often officially organised by the Professional Tutor. They see something of mentors from other schools when they attend officially organised mathematics mentors' meetings at the university. However, they rarely see other interns, and they get only peripheral insights into practices within other schools.

Interns move between the university and their own school. They spend 11 weeks part-time and 15 weeks full-time in their first school and six weeks full-time in their second school. However, they do not gain experience of other schools except peripherally through their intern peers.

Tutors, on the other hand, visit and get to know mentors, teachers and practices across partnership schools. Thus the tutoring role, as well as to present the university programme for the interns, must provide insights into a wider experience of schooling as well as into national issues and the research literature relating to teaching.

By contrast, mentors bring specialised knowledge of their school and the education of their students within that school. In complementary ways, both tutors and mentors aim to support and challenge interns to engage critically with learning to teach from both local and more global perspectives. This is the theory and it works out in particular ways in particular schools.

The wider understandings of the tutor, in this case study, draw on relationships with the mentors and many of the teachers within the three schools. These include engagement with teachers in research, supervision of teachers in university courses, and association with the research of doctoral students working with these teachers. Thus, in visiting an intern in one of the schools, the tutor has expectation of how that intern might be learning from certain teachers, and where there are valuable associations to foster. For the tutor, entering a school staffroom or department team room, there are many colleagues to greet and talk with. Informal conversations provide important insights into interns' progress from a number of perceptions.

When asked about the contributions, to interns' learning, of relationships in the partnership, mentors were much less clear in their responses than when discussing interns' activity and progress. One reason is obvious: interns' activity is fundamental to the knowledge of a mentor and experienced mentors are confidently pleased to discuss interns' progress. Their knowledge of wider relationships in partnership is less clearly defined. However, there are also sensitivities, both to other colleagues and to the tutor. Mentors might be deliberately vague in cases where delicate issues are concerned. There is obviously a potential difficulty when questions about relationships which involve the tutor are being asked by the tutor.

Sally talked overtly of the help and support both she and Judith received from certain experienced members of the mathematics department. She emphasised the very good relationship between herself and Judith, and it seemed clear that she welcomed the contributions of these other colleagues to Judith's growth in teaching. This fitted with the tutor's perceptions of this department, the ways in which teachers work together within it, and the support they would provide for a new mentor.

George, while extremely circumspect, implied reservations about the support for interns that some of his colleagues might be able or willing to provide. Given her own current or past relationships with certain of his colleagues, the tutor felt unable to probe further. An independent researcher may have been able to glean more in this situation.

Jeanette was fulsome in her praise of colleagues and their commitment to interns' learning. She said, "I spend a certain amount of time with them in department meetings, just talking to them about working with interns and the sort of feedback I expect. They always take time to give feedback to me and the intern." It was clear that Jeanette saw part of her role to be the encouragement and informing of her colleagues. The nature and structure of a mathematics department and relationships between teachers in it are likely to be influencing forces of such possibility, but can be a sensitive area for a tutor to probe. Where departmental relationships seem important to the learning and progress of an intern, the tutor would engage in a confidential discussion with the Professional Tutor.

5.4.2. Interns' Perceptions: Ensuring Partnerships Meet their Needs

Like mentors, interns find it difficult to see the 'partnership' in any objective sense, especially after just one term of working within it. They tend to see it as it affects them, and recognise the interrelationships of its key people – tutors, mentors and teachers – for their own learning. They value the 'learning, doing and sharing', the continuity provided by strong links between teachers and the university tutor, and the opportunity to build up their experiences in both academic and practical ways in the early weeks. As one intern put it, this enables "your personal 'partnership' between the two environments to grow".

If relationships with teachers and tutors are helpful and fruitful, then partnership is working well. If there are conflicts, inconsistencies, or unsupported needs, then there are problems. It is the responsibility of tutors to be alert to problems as they visit schools, as they have the privilege of seeing beyond the local situation. Mentors' meetings held twice a term at the University allow tutors and mentors to share their perceptions of interns' development and whether provision is meeting needs.

Course evaluations each year, consisting of detailed questionnaires to interns which can be completed anonymously, alert course leaders to places where the system is not working as well as it should. However, interns are almost unanimous in their praise of mentors, recognising the very considerable time given to them by most mentors and the invaluable forms of advice, help, critical questioning and emotional support. There are of course areas that receive a less positive response from interns, often to do with their learning about wider school issues such as pastoral work with pupils, and the heavy demands of assessment. They are encouraged to critique the detail of their curriculum courses and the mathematics course has taken very seriously over the years the criticisms interns have directed at it. Such criticisms are taken up as sensitively as possible in meetings with mentors and professional tutors.

5.5. *Problematic Issues*

The above sections have begun to highlight some of the issues and sensitivities of developing an integrated programme for interns' learning involving university and schools, tutors and teachers. The issues so far have been largely to do with relationships between people within schools and between school and university.[8]

When asked about problems that they perceived, both mentors and interns focused very specifically on the tasks that interns are asked to complete in school as part of the joint programme in the first term. This focus is unsurprising given that the question was asked at the end of this term and before interns moved into being full-time in the school. Had the questions been asked at the end of their second term, the focus might have been different. A second problem or tension, for interns particularly, concerned the diversity of experience needed before interns could settle down to steady teaching of classes. Gaining this experience can be unsettling; as one intern put it, "it has enabled me to see many classes and experience many different styles of teaching, but it has also meant that I have been flitting around, not on quite firm ground."

The early weeks of the course are spent jointly between university and school. University sessions address a complex curriculum related to learning to teach mathematics, and school sessions provide a range of experiences to introduce practical issues and to relate ideas to classroom realities. Interns work with teachers and with small groups of students, starting to put ideas into practice, and feed back their experiences to university sessions. They gradually grow into whole-class teaching through the range of tasks they are asked to undertake. However, these experiences lack a stability of regular teaching of the same classes. This is delayed until the second and third terms of the course by which time interns have a wide range of experiences to bring to their planning and teaching. One intern expressed the situation as follows, "Occasionally there have been conflicting demands between school and the university, but I think that is probably inevitable. Also, at the start of the course, I did feel that I was being pulled in different directions because of the different demands on my time. It was hard to decide how to prioritise my work between school and university. However, as I have become settled, this has eased."

The programme of tasks is tightly constructed, so that university sessions are followed up with activity in school, and activity in school feeds into university sessions. Thus, certain tasks are constrained by the university timetable, and may be difficult to accomplish in school at the specific time required. In addition, the nature of a task may not always be clear to all concerned; this might lead to difficulties in its interpretation. Although the programme has developed over the years, with input from mentors and interns, the programme leaders are the university tutors. They have ultimate responsibility for the effective delivery and monitoring of the programme. They also teach the sessions at the university, with occasional help from colleagues in the schools (e.g., George & Jeanette).

The course recruits interns who have good degrees in Mathematics or closely related areas (e.g., Engineering or Physics). Interns have to audit their own mathematical understanding against the requirements of the National Curriculum, and update it where there are gaps. However, as indicated by one of the interns above, although interns' own mathematical knowledge is strong, their ability to translate their knowledge into classroom activity through which students will learn mathematics is neither obvious nor straightforward. It is therefore essential that interns learn to analyse mathematical topics, both in terms of their content and the processes that are valuable in working and thinking mathematically.

Early in the programme, interns are introduced to a framework for analysing a mathematical topic for teaching it to students. This framework includes elements of imagery, language patterns, situative contexts, standard techniques, root questions, and common errors or misconceptions (e.g., Griffin, 1988). In the course, it is first used in the context of analysing the topic of *decimals*. Although interns 'know' decimals very well indeed, there are nevertheless aspects of decimals, about which they have given little thought, but which are central to considerations of teaching decimals to other learners (we might see this as PCK relating to learning and teaching decimals). An intensive session is spent at the university focusing on such aspects. This is related to the relevant research literature.

Interns are asked to undertake a number of tasks associated with their developing knowledge of teaching decimals. The first is to conduct interviews with students of varying age and ability to seek their decimal understanding. A second is to construct a lesson on decimal understanding for a designated small group of students. The learning from the interviews should feed into the lesson. Thus these tasks are necessarily sequenced, and they need to be fitted in before interns proceed to a planning task on fractions involving group activity with other interns. There is, therefore, little room for manoeuvre in school, especially given that interns are there for only two days per week at this stage. Mentors thus have quite a difficult task in planning the timetable for interns to do the work on decimals with appropriate groups of students at the required times.

Another session at the university involves a focus on *imagery* in mathematics learning and teaching. As the university curriculum is extremely demanding, with a lot to be achieved in a small amount of time, sessions have to be very concentrated, with many objectives to be achieved in a single session. Thus the focus on imagery includes many examples of what imagery might entail, across a number of topic areas. To a certain extent, interns are bombarded for 90 minutes by a kaleidoscope of topics, images and approaches to addressing imagery. This is done in a workshop environment with whole group activity, small group activity, discussion, questioning and critique.

Modelling of classroom approaches is a major part of such activity. Providing ideas for classroom work is also central. However, these strands of a university session are interwoven and interns need to analyse and extract from it to use the material in their school work. They have one school task designated to plan and deliver a lesson with a focus on imagery; the mathematics of the lesson is not prescribed. Jeanette reported that interns believed they had to pack into this lesson all that had been included in the university session, and were unsurprisingly confused by this. Thus, before they could plan their task in school, a translation task was necessary – translating the kaleidoscope of ideas into the practical reality of a lesson on a given topic with given students. As an experienced mentor, Jeanette was able to aid this translation knowledgeably.

However some mentors in the past have themselves been confused by what is required of interns from such a task. Mentors do not see the session at the university. From the timetable of university sessions, they see that a session on imagery takes place. However, they have little insight into its nature and content except what they hear from interns. If interns are confused as to what is expected, this confusion can translate into a perception of ridiculous expectations on the part of university tutors, with little relevance to the needs of students in classrooms. Thus a theory-practice dichotomy can arise with interns feeling they are in the middle of two parts of a system that do not communicate or make sense together.

Tutors are aware of these issues, and there is a compelling pressure to simplify the complexity and state clearly what interns should expect to do in school. However, such simplification and direction works counter to a declared objective of the course to develop critically reflective teachers, able to analyse, synthesise and choose knowledgeably the dimension of any lesson they teach. Over the years, the apparent dichotomy resolves itself into practical compromise, knowledge within the system (such as that of mentors) aids its effective progress, and recruitment of able interns ensures that the prospective teachers are able to cope with the high demands the system places on them. Nevertheless, all three mentors spoke of the difficulty of fitting in the multiplicity of tasks; also, feedback from interns in previous years has indicated the pressure it places on interns and mentors. A demanding course generates such pressures, and it is up to tutors, who have the ultimate responsibility, to understand, support, clarify, encourage, stimulate and inspire interns and mentors, as well as maintain their own confidence and knowledge growth.

5.6. *Concluding the Case Study*

The partnership scheme strives for an integrated approach to the learning of student teachers. From the sections above can be seen the complexity of knowledge, professional traditions and practical wisdom to which student teachers need access, and opportunity to learn. We have discussed some of the approaches taken in the scheme, and some of the issues arising. Through the words of interns and mentors we have tried to bring some of these issues alive, to offer a depth of insight into the complexity.

It is important to recognise the very particular nature of the case study discussed here. It is not presented as typical of practice in the United Kingdom, or indeed anywhere else. However, it is a real example of what is possible in seeking for integration of theory and practice, and the inter-related roles played by teachers, mentors and tutors in the education of beginning teachers. It provides examples of some ways of approaching integration, and a range of issues associated with these practices. There is no claim that integration is in any sense fully achieved. Some of the issues highlighted make clear that this is not so.

6. INTEGRATION IN TEACHER EDUCATION

The complexity of any teacher education system is evident, not least in the layers of knowledge that it encompasses. While the inter-relatedness of this knowledge is fundamental, it is worth identifying some of its components. In the case presented in Section 5, interns are recruited with good mathematical knowledge, evidenced by their earlier degree studies.[9] As indicated in the discussion of the decimals activity above, this subject knowledge does not include knowledge necessary for translating the subject into learning activities for students.

Such knowledge we believe is a part of what is meant by Shulman's (1986) concept of Pedagogic Content Knowledge, PCK[10] discussed in Section 4 above. This has to be learned by interns. We might refer to it as Mathematical Knowledge for Teaching (MKT). It is part of the knowledge, tacit or explicit (e.g., Polanyi, 1967; Schön, 1987), of practising teachers. It needs to be explicitly evident in the knowledge of university tutors, as it is part of the curriculum that tutors are required to teach. As mentors become more experienced in mentoring, this MKT becomes more obvious (less tacit) to them as reported many times by mentors in the internship scheme. We refer to a quotation from a mentor reported by Jaworski and Watson (1994b):

> One thing that I've found valuable, once I got over the initial feeling of being threatened by it, is that when a student-teacher asks me why I do something, I have to try to explain something which I've never really thought about before. I have to ask myself, "why do I do that?" And struggling to answer the question makes me learn something about myself which can make me a more effective teacher. (p. 126)

In addition, knowledge in mathematics mentoring as exemplified above has to be developed by mentors, and knowledge of mathematics tutoring has to be developed by tutors. There is just starting to be attention to tutors' knowledge and learning in the literature. For example, Jaworski (2001) has suggested the following three levels of knowledge necessary to the experienced teacher-educator:

Level 1. Mathematics and provision of classroom mathematical activities for students' effective learning of mathematics;
Level 2. Mathematics teaching and ways in which teachers think about developing their approaches to teaching;
Level 3. The roles and activities of teacher-educators in contributing to developments in (1) and (2).

We would now extend Level 1 to include also socio-cultural knowledge of mathematics education – the wider influences on pupils' learning and the reasons why pupils need to learn mathematics, and Level 3 to include constraints on teacher educators and how they can be tackled.

Presented in this way, these levels seem to imply a linear process, but in fact each higher level encompasses those below it. The teacher-educator as learner is operating at Level 3, which involves dealing directly with issues at Level 2, which requires attention at Level 1. Teachers work mainly at Level 1, with some engaging in thinking at Level 2 (Jaworski, 2001).

Mentors, who are also teachers, work largely at Levels 1 and 2, and the quotation from Jaworski and Watson above is evidence of a shift from Level 1 to Level 2. It is part of the internship scheme to provide opportunities for mentors and mentoring to develop through mentors and tutors working explicitly on the issues involved. Zaslavsky and Leikin (1999) and Even (1999) wrote about courses through which teacher educators are themselves educated explicitly. Tzur (2001) analysed his own development as a teacher educator, offering a complex set of steps that fit well with the three levels above. Prestage and Perks (2001) developed a model to relate the complexities of these levels to the forms of knowledge highlighted by Shulman. This is a multi-dimensional model working from the learner of mathematics to the teacher-educator (or tutor) in recognition of the inter-related processes and practices in which all participants engage.

It is clear that, for the learning teacher to teach effectively, the different kinds and layers of knowledge need to be well integrated, both for the individual and between all those who interact for the learning to take place. We have seen knowledge being mediated between university and school, between interns and their tutors, mentors and other teachers, and between theory and practice. The partnerships involved constitute a dynamic learning enterprise that is constantly developing and changing to meet demands and tackle issues. It seems important to see integration, not as an unreachable ideal, or an imperfect transitional state, but rather as a growing organism. All the people involved, including the student teachers themselves, contribute to this overall growth and most are committed to professional and personal development. Reflection and enquiry are central elements, manifested at a variety of levels. All participants are learners, their roles developing in relation to their critical evaluation of them. We have here something that looks very like a research programme whose purpose is development of the programme as well as the practices of all those working within it.

NOTES

[1.] This chapter was written while Barbara Jaworski worked at the University of Oxford, and draws on her work there in teacher education.

[2.] The Department for Education and Employment (a UK Government Department) introduced (in 2000) 'Best Practice' scholarships for teachers who would undertake research in their own class-rooms. This research has to provide evidence for improvement of practice (known as 'evidence-based' practice). It has to be undertaken with the support of an educational institution with expertise in research, such as a university department of education.

[3.] Specialist studies in mathematics at 16+ in preparation for university or other careers in industry or commerce.

[4.] Time is a problem. Mentors receive from half an hour to one hour per week per intern for such collaboration with interns. They usually give much more time than this, finding it from their own personal planning time, or outside school hours. Consultation between interns and other teachers is given no dedicated time; it is squeezed into minutes between lessons or in tea breaks.

[5.] Interns teach lessons initially with the class teacher present. Later, as expertise develops, they will be left alone with the class. Teachers observe the teaching at regular intervals and provide written, and short oral, feedback after observation. In the very early days of a course, interns work *with* teachers in the classroom, and develop expertise with small groups or half classes.

[6.] See Mathematical Association (1991), for an account of a process that uses vignettes (or 'anec-dotes') to raise issues relating to teaching, and hence to enable development of thinking and teaching.

[7.] The Standards for QTS, Qualified Teacher Status are issued by the Teacher Training Agency in the UK and are statutory for the assessment of new teachers. (http://www.canteach.gov.uk/home.htm)

[8.] See Nolder, Smith and Melrose (1994) for a consideration of such roles

[9.] Such recruitment has become more difficult over the years as is shown in research nationally. This course recruits fairly well compared to many in the UK However, the Government has realised the necessity to recruit persons with the best chance of becoming good mathematics teachers and now offers a number of financial incentives to attract teachers of shortage subjects like mathematics.

10. The case study has focused on secondary teachers. The concept of Pedagogical Content Knowledge has been discussed with focus on primary mathematics teachers by Marks (1990).

REFERENCES

Artzt, A. F. (1999). A structure to enable preservice teachers of mathematics to reflect on their teaching. *Journal of Mathematics Teacher Education, 2*(2), 143–166.

Askew, M., Brown, M., Rhodes, V., Johnson, D., & Wiliam, D. (1997). *Effective teachers of numeracy.* London: King's College.

Aubrey, C. (1997). *Mathematics teaching in the early years: An Investigation of teachers' subject knowledge.* London: Falmer Press.

Barnett, C. S. (1998). Mathematics case methods project. *Journal of Mathematics Teacher Education, 1*(3), 349–356.

Bauer, K.-O., & Rolff, H.-G. (1978). Vorarbeiten zu einer theorie der schulentwicklung [Towards a theory of school development]. In K.-O. Bauer & H.-G Rolff (Eds.), *Innovation und schulentwicklung* [Innovation and school development] (pp. 219–266). Weinheim: Beltz.

Bishop, A. J. (1988). *Mathematical enculturation: A cultural perspective on mathematical education.* Dordrecht, The Netherlands: Kluwer Academic Publishers.

Bobis, J., & Cusworth, R. (1995). Attitudinal shifts towards mathematics of preservice teachers. In B. Atweh & S. Flavel (Eds.), *Proceedings of the 18th Annual Conference of the Mathematics Education Research Group of Australasia* (pp.109–114). Darwin: Mathematics Education Research Group of Australasia.

Brousseau, G. (1986). Fondements et méthodes de la didactique des mathématiques. *Recherches en Didactique des Mathématiques, 7*(2), 33–115.

Brown, S., & McIntyre, D. (1993). *Making sense of teaching.* Buckingham, UK: Open University Press.

Burn, K., Hagger, H., Mutton, T., & Everton, T. (2000). Beyond concerns with self: The sophisticated thinking of beginning student teachers. *Journal of Education for Teaching, 26*(3), 259–278.

Calderhead, J., & Shorrock, S. B. (1997). *Understanding teacher education: Case studies in the professional development of beginning teachers.* London: Falmer Press.

Clarke, B, Clarke, D., & Sullivan, P. (1996). The mathematics teacher and curriculum development. In A. J. Bishop, K. Clements, C. Keitel, J. Kilpatrick & C. Laborde (Eds.), *International handbook of mathematics education* (pp.1207–1234). Dordrecht, The Netherlands: Kluwer Academic Publishers.

Clarke, D. (2000). Guest editorial: Time to reflect. *Journal of Mathematics Teacher Education, 3*(3), 201–203.

Cooney, T. J. (1996). Conceptualizing the professional development of teachers. In C. Alsina, J. M. Alvarez, B. Hodgson, C. Laborde & A. Pérez (Eds.), *Selected lectures, 8th International Congress on Mathematical Education* (pp. 101–117) Sevilla, Spain: SAEM Thales.

Cooney, T. J., & Shealy, B. (1997). On understanding the structure of teachers' beliefs and their relationship to change. In E. Fennema & B. N. Nelson (Eds.), *Mathematics teachers in transition* (pp. 87–110). Mahwah, NJ: Lawrence Erlbaum.

Cooney, T. J., Shealy, B. E., & Arvold, B. (1998). Conceptualizing belief structures of pre-service secondary mathematics teachers. *Journal for Research in Mathematics Education, 29*(3), 306–333.

Davis, B. (1999). Basic irony: Examining the foundations of school mathematics with preservice teachers. *Journal of Mathematics Teacher Education, 2*(1), 25–48.

Dawson, A. J. (1999). The enactive perspective on teacher development: A path laid while walking. In B. Jaworski, T. Wood & A. J. Dawson (Eds.), *Mathematics teacher education: Critical international perspectives.* London: Falmer Press.

Dolk, M., Faes, W., Goffree, F., Hermsen, H., & Oonk, W. (1996). *A multimedia interactive learning environment for (future) primary school teachers with content for primary mathematics teachers education programs.* Utrecht: Freudenthal Instituut/NVORWO.

Eraut, M. (1995). Schön shock: A case for reframing reflection-in-action? *Teachers and Teaching: Theory and Practice, 1*(1), 9–22.

Even, R. (1999). The development of teacher leaders and inservice teacher educators. *Journal of Mathematics Teacher Education, 2,* 3–24.

Even, R., & Tirosh, D. (1995). Subject-matter knowledge and knowledge about students as sources of teacher presentations and subject matter. *Educational Studies in Mathematics, 29,* 1–20.

Fennema, E., Sowder, J., & Carpenter, T. (1999). Creating classrooms that promote understanding. In E. Fennema & T. Romberg (Eds.), *Mathematics classrooms that promote understanding* (pp. 185–199). Mahwah, NJ: Lawrence Erlbaum Associates.

Freudenthal, H. (1991). *Revisiting mathematics education: China lectures.* Dordrecht, The Netherlands: Kluwer Academic Publishers.

Frykholm, J. A. (1999). The impact of reform: Challenges for mathematics teacher preparation. *Journal of Mathematics Teacher Education, 2*(1), 79–105.

Gellert, U. (2000). Mathematics instruction in safe space: Prospective elementary teachers' views of mathematics education. *Journal of Mathematics Teacher Education, 3*(3), 251–270.

Gellert, U., Jablonka, E., & Keitel, C. (2001). Mathematical literacy and common sense in mathematics education. In B. Atweh, H. Forgasz & B. Nebres (Eds.), *Sociocultural research on mathematics education: An international perspective* (pp. 57–73). Mahwah, NJ: Lawrence Erlbaum.

Giacquinta, J. B. (1998). Seduced and abandoned: Some lasting conclusions about planned change from the Cambire school study. In A. Hargreaves, A. Lieberman, M. Fullan & D. Hopkins (Eds.), *International handbook of educational change* (pp. 163–180). Dordrecht, The Netherlands: Kluwer Academic Publishers.

Goffree, F., & Oonk, W. (1999). Educating primary school mathematics teachers in the Netherlands: Back to the classroom. *Journal of Mathematics Teacher Education, 2*(2), 207–214.

Goulding, M., & Suggate, J. (2001). Opening a can of worms: Investigating primary teachers' subject knowledge in mathematics. *Mathematics Education Review, 13,* 41–54.

Griffin, P. (1988). Preparing to teach ratio. *Project Mathematics Update, PM753B.* Milton Keynes, UK: The Open University.

Gutiérrez, A., & Jaime, A. (1999, Preservice primary teachers' understanding of the concept of altitude of a triangle. *Journal of Mathematics Teacher Education, 2*(3), 253–275.

Haggarty, L. (1995). *New ideas for teacher education: A mathematics framework.* London: Cassell.

HMI (1982). *The new teacher in school.* London: HMSO.

Howson, A. G., & Wilson, B. J. 1986). *School mathematics in the 1990s.* Cambridge, UK: Cambridge University Press.

Jaworski, B. (1998). Mathematics teacher research: Process, practice and the development of teaching. *Journal of Mathematics Teacher Education, 1*(1), 3–31.

Jaworski, B. (2001). Developing mathematics teaching: Teachers, teacher-educators and researchers as co-learners. In F-L Lin & T. J. Cooney (Eds.), *Making sense of mathematics teacher education.* Dordrecht, The Netherlands: Kluwer Academic Publishers.

Jaworski, B., & Watson, A. (Eds.) (1994a). *Mentoring in mathematics teaching.* London: Falmer Press.

Jaworski, B., & Watson, A. (1994b). Mentoring, co-mentoring and the inner mentor. In B. Jaworski & A. Watson (Eds.), *Mentoring in mathematics teaching.* London: Falmer Press.

Jaworski, B., & Watson, A. (2002). *PGCE Mathematics: Mathematics course handbook.* Oxford: University of Oxford Department of Educational Studies.

Keitel, C. (1992). The education of teachers of mathematics: An overview. *Zentralblatt für Didaktik der Mathematik, 24*(7), 265–273.

Keitel, C., & Hopmann, S. (1995). Editorial. *Journal of Curriculum Studies, 27*(1), 1–2.

Keitel, C., & Kilpatrick, J. (1999). Rationality and irrationality of international comparative studies. In G. Kaiser, I. Huntley & E. Luna (Eds.), *International comparative studies in mathematics education* (pp. 241–257). London: Falmer Press.

Klafki, W. (1995a). Didactic analysis as the core of preparation of instruction. *Journal of Curriculum Studies, 27*(1), 13–30.

Klafki, W. (1995b). On the problem of teaching and learning contents from the standpoint of critical-constructive didaktik. In S. Hopmann & K. Riquarts (Eds.), *Didaktik and/or curriculum* (pp. 187–200). Kiel: Institute für die Pädagogik der Naturwissenschaften.

Krainer, K., & Posch, P. (Eds.) (1996). *Lehrerfortbildung zwischen prozessen und produkten* ['Teacher inservice education between processes and products', reviewed by A. Peter, in *Journal of Mathematics Teacher Education 1*(1), 113–116]. Bad Heilbrunn: Klinkhardt.

Krummheuer, G. (1999). Die analyse von unterrichtsepisoden im rahmen von grundschullehrerausbildung' ['The analysis of classroom episodes in the frame of primary teacher education']. In F. Ohlhaver & A. Wernet (Eds.), *Schulforschung – Fallanalyse – Lehrerbildung* ['Research on schools – Case method – Teacher education'] (pp. 99–120). Opladen: Leske + Budrich.

Krummheuer, G. (2000). Mathematics learning in narrative classroom cultures: Studies of argumentation in primary mathematics education. *For the Learning of Mathematics, 20*(1), 22–32.

Lampert, M., & Ball, D. L. (1998). *Teaching, multimedia and mathematics: Investigations of real practice.* New York: Teachers College Press.

Lave, J. (1988). *Cognition in practice: Mind, mathematics and culture in everyday life.* Cambridge, UK: Cambridge University Press.

Lave, J. (1997). The culture of acquisition and the practice of understanding. In D. Kirshner & J. A. Whitson (Eds.), *Situated cognition: Social, semiotic, and psychological perspectives* (pp. 17–35). London: Lawrence Erlbaum.

Lave, J., & Wenger, E. (1991). *Situated learning: Legitimate peripheral participation.* Cambridge, UK: Cambridge University Press.

Lortie, D. C. (1998). Unfinished work: Reflections on schoolteachers. In A. Hargreaves, A. Lieberman, M. Fullan & D. Hopkins (Eds.), *International handbook of educational change* (pp. 145–162). Dordrecht, The Netherlands: Kluwer Academic Publishers.

Luhmann, N., & Schorr, K.-E. (1979). *Reflexionsprobleme im erziehungssystem* ['Issues for reflection within the system of education']. Stuttgart, Germany: Klett-Cotta.

Ma, L. (1999). *Knowing and teaching elementary mathematics: Teachers' understanding of fundamental mathematics in China and the United States.* Mahwah, NJ: Lawrence Erlbaum Associates.

Marks, R. (1990). Pedagogical content knowledge: From a mathematical case to a modified conception. *Journal of Teacher Education, 41*(3), 3–11.

Mason, J., & Waywood, A. (1996). The role of theory in mathematics education and research. In A. J. Bishop, K. Clements, C. Keitel, J. Kilpatrick & C. Laborde (Eds.), *International handbook of mathematics education* (pp. 1055–1089). Dordrecht, The Netherlands: Kluwer Academic Publishers.

Mathematical Association (1991). *Develop your teaching.* Cheltenham, UK: Stanley Thornes.

McIntyre, D., Hagger, H., & Wilkin, M (Eds.) (1993). *Mentoring: Perspectives on school-based teacher education.* London: Kogan Page.

McNamara, D. (1991). Subject knowledge and its application: Problems and possibilities for teacher educators. *Journal of Education for Teaching, 17*(2), 113–128.

Mehan, H. (1979). *Learning lessons.* Cambridge, MA: Harvard University Press.

Merseth, K. K. (1996). Cases and case methods in teacher education. In J. Sikula, T. J. Buttery & E. Guyton (Eds.), *Handbook of research on teacher education* (2nd ed.) (pp. 722–744). New York: Macmillan.

Mousley, J. (1999). Bringing teaching to teacher education. *Mathematics Education Research Journal, 11*(2), 149–153.

Nicol, C. (1999). Learning to teach mathematics: Questioning, listening, and responding. *Educational Studies in Mathematics, 37,* 45–66.

Noddings, N. (1992). Professionalization and mathematics teaching. In D. A. Grouws (Ed.), *handbook of research on mathematics teaching and learning* (pp. 197–208). New York: Macmillan.

Nolder, R., Smith, S., & Melrose, J. (1994). Working together: Roles and relationships in the mentoring process. In B. Jaworski & A. Watson (Eds.), *Mentoring in Mathematics Teaching* (pp. 41–51). London: Falmer Press.

Norman, N. (2000). *The use of television for the teaching and learning of mathematics in secondary school.* Unpublished PhD Thesis, University of Oxford.

Polanyi, M. (1967). *The tacit dimension.* New York: Doubleday.

Potari, D., & Jaworski, B. (2002). Tackling complexity in mathematics teaching development: Using the teaching triad as a tool for reflection and analysis. *Journal of Mathematics Teacher Education*, 5(4), 351–380.

Prestage, S., & Perks, P. (2001). Models and super models: Ways of thinking about professional knowledge. In C. Morgan & K. Jones (Eds.), *Research in Mathematics Education, Volume 3: Papers of the British Society for Research into Learning Mathematics* (pp. 101–114). London: British Society for Research into Learning Mathematics.

Romberg, T. A., & Carpenter, T. P. (1986). Research on teaching and learning mathematics: Two disciplines of scientific enquiry. In M. C. Wittrock (Ed.), *Handbook of research on teaching* (3rd ed.) (pp. 850–873). New York: Macmillan.

Rowland, T., Martyn, S., Barber, P., & Heal, C. (2000). Primary teacher trainees' mathematics subject knowledge and classroom performance. In T. Rowland & C. Morgan (Eds.), *Research in Mathematics Education, Volume 2: Papers of the British Society for Research into Learning Mathematics* (pp. 3–18). London: British Society for Research into Learning Mathematics.

Schifter, D. (1998). Learning mathematics for teaching: From a teachers' seminar to the classroom. *Journal of Mathematics Teacher Education, 1*(1), 55–87.

Schön, D. A. (1983). *The reflective practitioner: How professionals think in action.* London: Maurice Temple Smith.

Seeger, F., & Steinbring, H. (1992). The practical phase in teacher training: Preparing for professional practice under changing conditions. *Zentralblatt für Didaktik der Mathematik, 24*(7), 280–286.

Shulman, L. S. (1986). Those who understand: Knowledge growth in teaching. *Educational Researcher, 15*(2), 4–14.

Skemp, R. R. (1978). Relational understanding and instrumental understanding. *Arithmetic Teacher, 26*(3), 9–15.

Skott, J. (2001). The emerging practices of a novice teacher: The roles of his school mathematics images. *Journal of Mathematics Teacher Education, 4*, 3–28.

Smith, D. N. (Jim) (2001). The influence of mathematics teachers on student teachers of secondary mathematics. *Mathematics Education Review 13*, 22–40.

Smyth, J. (1998). Three rival versions and a critique of teacher staff development. In A. Hargreaves, A. Lieberman, M. Fullan & D. Hopkins (Eds.), *International handbook of educational change* (pp. 1242–1256). Dordrecht, The Netherlands: Kluwer Academic Publishers.

Soeffner, H.-G. (1989). *Auslegung des alltags – Der alltag der auslegung* ['The interpretation of everyday life – Daily routines of interpreting']. Frankfurt, Germany: Suhrkamp.

Stigler, J. W., Gonzales, P., Kawanaka, T., Knoll, S., & Serrano, A. (1999). *The TIMSS Videotape Classroom Study: Methods and findings from an explanatory research project on Eighth-Grade Mathematics instruction in Germany, Japan, and the United States.* Washington, D. C.: U.S. Government Printing Office.

Stigler, J. W., & Hiebert, J. (1999). *The teaching gap.* New York: The Free Press.

Sullivan, P., & Mousley, J. (1996). Learning about teaching: The potential of specific mathematics teaching examples, presented on interactive media. In L. Puig & A Gutiérrez (Eds.), *Proceedings of the 20th Conference of the International Group for the Psychology of Mathematics Education* (pp. 283–290). Valencia, Spain: International Group for the Psychology of Mathematics Education.

Tzur, R. (2001). Becoming a mathematics teacher educator: Conceptualising the terrain through self-reflective analysis. *Journal of Mathematics Teacher Education, 4*(4), 259–283.

Van Zoest, L. R., & Bohl, J. V. (2002). The role of reform curricular materials in an internship: The case of Alice and Gregory. *Journal of Mathematics Teacher Education, 5*, 265–288

Voigt, J. (1995). Thematic patterns of interaction and sociomathematical norms. In P. Cobb & H. Bauersfeld (Eds.), *The emergence of mathematical meaning: Interaction in classroom cultures* (pp. 163–201). Hillsdale, NJ: Lawrence Erlbaum.

Walen, S. B., & Williams, S. R. (2000). Validating classroom issues: Case method in support of teacher change. *Journal of Mathematics Teacher Education, 3*(1), 3–26.

Watson, A. (1994). A mentor's eye view. In B. Jaworski & A. Watson (Eds.), *Mentoring in mathematics teaching* (pp. 1–12). London: Falmer Press.

Wilson, S., Shulman, L., & Richert, A. (1987). 150 ways of knowing: Representations of knowledge in teaching. In J. Calderhead (Ed.), *Exploring teachers' thinking* (pp. 104–124). London: Cassell.

Wood, T., Cobb, P., Yackel, E., & Dillon, D. (Eds.) (1993). *Rethinking elementary school mathematics: Insights and issues.* Reston, VA: NCTM.

Zaslavsky, O., & Leikin, R. (1999). Interweaving the training of mathematics teacher-educators and the professional development of mathematics teachers. In O. Zaslavsky (Ed.), *Proceedings of the 23rd Conference of the International Group for the Psychology of Mathematics Education* (Vol. 1, pp. 143–158). Haifa, Israel: Israel Institute of Technology.

Zeichner, K. M., & Gore, J. M. (1990). Teacher socialization. In W. R. Houston, M. Haberman & J. Sikula (Eds.), *Handbook of research on teacher education* (pp. 329–348). New York: Macmillan.

24
Professional Development of Mathematics Educators: Trends and Tasks

ORIT ZASLAVSKY
Technion – Israel Institute of Technology

OLIVE CHAPMAN
University of Calgary

ROZA LEIKIN
University of Haifa

ABSTRACT

In this chapter the professional growth of mathematics educators – including teachers, teacher educators, and educators of teacher educators – is presented as an ongoing lifelong process. So far as teachers are concerned, it occurs in various stages and contexts, beginning with their experiences as school students, followed by formal preservice preparation towards an academic qualification and teaching certificate. It continues in formal and informal inservice settings and, sometimes, in graduate studies. In this chapter we focus on trends in the thinking about, and practices within, inservice professional development programmes for mathematics educators – inservice teachers as well as inservice teacher educators. We begin by offering a unifying conceptual framework which takes into account interrelations between the different groups covered by the term 'mathematics educators'. This framework, which acknowledges the central role of tasks and programmes in which participants engage, facilitates thinking about the complexities and underlying processes involved in professional development in mathematics education. We describe in detail the main types of programmes reported in the literature. Examples of tasks with special potential for enhancing the professional development of both teachers and teacher educators are discussed.

1. CONCEPTUAL FRAMEWORK

Numerous models have been put forward by scholars attempting to describe the main features of, and interrelationships within, the professional development of teachers. Most of these not only differ in their assumptions, expectations, and beliefs about professional growth, but also in the implicit and explicit demands

Second International Handbook of Mathematics Education, 877–917
A.J. Bishop, M.A. Clements, C. Keitel, J. Kilpatrick and F.K.S. Leung (eds.)
© 2003 Dordrecht: Kluwer Academic Publishers. Printed in Great Britain.

that they make on the individuals involved, and in the orientations for change that they represent.

Historically, professional development programmes in mathematics education have mirrored traditional teaching of mathematics. They have generally focused on transmitting information, providing ideas and providing training in skills and techniques. The objective has been to train teachers to perform in a particular way – specifically, to get them to teach in ways that the teacher educator thought they should (Grant, Hiebert, & Wearne, 1998). Less emphasis has been given to helping them to develop new forms of practice.

Schön (1983, 1991) labelled the traditional approach to professional development of teachers the 'technical rationality' model. The approach assumed that teaching could be improved and at the same time ready-made theory could be transmitted to practitioners: somehow, participants, acting as inert media, would learn how, when and why to do what they were taught.

More recent professional development programmes have invited teachers to reflect on, and initiate, reform-oriented perspectives of learning – such as constructivism (Davis, Maher, & Noddings, 1990; von Glasersfeld, 1995). Those responsible for the design of these reform programmes expect teachers to play an active role in their own professional development. There is tacit agreement that "teachers must make sense of proposed changes in the context of their own prior knowledge and beliefs about teaching, learning, and the nature of the content being taught" (Grant et al., p. 218). It is expected that not only will teachers be offered opportunities to learn challenging mathematics of the kind they are expected to teach, but also will become engaged in alternative modes of learning and teaching (Brown & Borko, 1992; Cooney & Krainer, 1996; Ball, 1997; Grant et al., 1998).

Consequently, the focus of professional development programmes is now on individuals' development levels and the different ways that practitioners make sense of their teaching experiences. The overarching assumption is that professional knowledge cannot be transferred; it is actively constructed individually and socially through personal experiences with the surrounding environment and interactions with others, involving reflection and adaptation. As Cooney (1994) noted, "ultimately, any attempt to reform the teaching of mathematics is an exercise in adaptation from what we are *able to do* to what we *want to do*" (p. 9).

Most programmes rely to some extent on social practice theory, which stems from Vygotsky's theory on the social nature of the learning process, and considers teachers' knowledge as developing socially within communities of practice (Vygotsky, 1978; Rogoff, 1990; Lave & Wenger, 1991; Adler, 1996, 1998; Cobb & McClain, 2001). The two communities of inservice mathematics teachers and inservice mathematics teacher educators are considered as two interrelated communities of practice, which often may not be separable. In this context the most, though not the only, relevant practice of teachers is *providing mathematical learning opportunities for students*, while the most relevant practice of teacher educators is *providing mathematical and pedagogical learning opportunities for teachers*.

A foremost concern in almost all contemporary professional development programmes is the need to foster teachers' reflection on their practice and learning experiences. Theories of reflective practice follow Dewey's emphasis on the reflective activity of both the teacher and the student, as a means for advancing their thinking (Dewey, 1933; Schön, 1983, 1987, 1991; Calderhead, 1989; Jaworski, 1994; Krainer, 1998).

There have been transitions from theoretical perspectives related to the constructs of reflection and action to more practical positions. Consequently, the notions of reflection on-action and reflection in-action emerged and have been recognized as an effective component contributing to the growth of teachers' knowledge about their practice. Lerman (2001), in discussing the concept of reflective practice, argued that "reflective practice offers a view of how teachers act in the classroom as informed, concerned professionals and how they continue to learn about teaching and about learning, about themselves as teachers, and about their pupils as learners" (p. 39). From such a position, it follows that teachers and teacher educators can be seen as learners who continuously reflect on their work and make sense of their histories, their practices, and other experiences.

There is a consensus that a key issue to be addressed in professional development in mathematics education is the *learning of mathematics*. To somewhat simplify our discussion of teachers' growth, we look at two core kinds of knowledge: mathematical and pedagogical. Moreover, we consider most (inservice) professional development activities as problem solving situations – combining mathematics and pedagogy – which engage participants in 'powerful tasks' fundamental for teacher development (see, e.g., Krainer, 1993; Sullivan & Mousley, 2001). This view concurs with Cooney's (1994, 2001) constructs of *mathematical power* and *pedagogical power*, two constructs which deal with a teacher's ability to draw on the knowledge that is needed – mathematical or pedagogical – to solve problems in context. Jaworski (2001) added a third construct, *educative power*, which, she maintained, characterizes the roles that teacher educators may play in the process of enhancing (or 'engendering') teachers' learning. We take the term 'educative power' to encompass the ability of teacher educators to draw on knowledge that is needed for facilitating teachers' mathematical and pedagogical problem solving.

Jaworski (2001) proposed a hierarchy of three levels, each encompassing those below, at which teachers and teacher educators should interact and reflect:

Level 1: Mathematics and provision of classroom mathematical activities for students' effective learning of mathematics;

Level 2: Mathematics teaching and ways in which teachers think about developing their approaches to teaching;

Level 3: The roles and activities of teacher educators in contributing to developments in (1) and (2). (p. 301)

These three levels reflect in many ways the three types of knowledge described above (mathematical, pedagogical, and educative). According to Jaworski (2001), movements from one level to another occur throughout the development process.

Most mathematics educators share the view that teaching is strongly influenced by a teacher's personal experiences as a learner (see, e.g., Zaslavsky, 1995; Stigler & Hiebert, 1999). Ma (1999) argued that professional development occurs at three main stages of a teacher's career: schooling, teacher preparation and teaching. At each of these stages, teachers learn, "through years of participating in classroom life" (Stigler & Hiebert, 1999, p. 1), about learning and teaching mathematics, both directly in a specific designated context and indirectly through their practice. In the context of inservice professional development of mathematics educators, we consider teachers' participation in special professional development programmes as *direct* inservice learning, while teachers' professional development that is embedded in their practice involves *indirect* learning. Clearly, direct and indirect learning are interrelated and depend on each other.

Various trends in professional development programmes may differ with respect to the emphasis the programmes place on a direct learning process as opposed to an indirect learning-through-practice process. We put forward a three-layer model (see Figure 1) that conveys the complexity of mathematics educators' (both teachers' and teacher educators') professional growth, on the one hand, and integrates the various aspects of learning that are involved in inservice professional development settings on the other hand. Our model is an extension of Steinbring's model (1998), and is based on the three-layer model of growth-through-practice of teacher educators, developed by Zaslavsky and Leikin (in press).

Steinbring's (1998) model of teaching and learning mathematics pointed to autonomous systems that further explain the learning-through-teaching process. According to this model, the teacher offers a learning environment for his or her students in which the students operate and construct knowledge of school mathematics in a rather autonomous way. This occurs by subjective interpretations of the tasks in which they engage and by ongoing reflection on their work. The teacher, by observing the students' work and reflecting on their learning processes, constructs an understanding, which enables him or her to vary the learning environment in ways that are more appropriate for the students. Although both the students' learning processes and the interactive teaching process are autonomous, the two systems are nevertheless interdependent. This interdependence can explain how teachers learn through their teaching.

Our model takes account of all persons engaged in mathematics education – students (Ss), mathematics teachers (MTs), mathematics teacher educators (MTEs), and mathematics teacher educator educators (MTEEs). Ss learn mathematics; MTs facilitate students' learning of mathematics, and also participate as learners in inservice programmes; MTEs facilitate the learning of MTs, yet also participate as learners in professional development programmes for MTEs; and MTEEs facilitate the learning of MTEs.

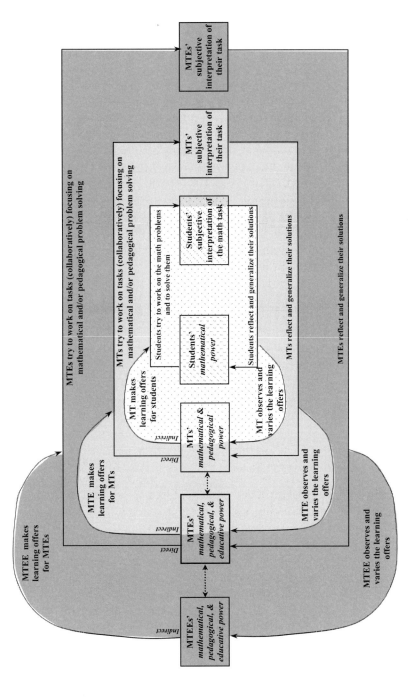

Figure 1. A Three-Layer Model of Growth of Mathematics Educators through Direct and Indirect Learning [Borrowed, with modification, from Zaslavsky & Leikin (in press)].

This three-layer model consists of three interrelated facilitator-learner config-urations (dotted, light shaded, and dark shaded), each of which includes two autonomous systems. One system describes the main actions in which the facilita-tor of learning engages (depicted by circle-like arrows), while the other system describes the main actions in which the learner engages (depicted by rectangle-like arrows). Embedded in the model is the need for the learning facilitators' ongoing awareness, reflection in and on action, and self-analysis.

Our model indicates possible locations of direct and indirect learning as well as the mutual relationships and connections between these two kinds of learning contexts. Additionally, this model explicitly highlights the central role of tasks and reflection in and on action that are characteristic of many professional development settings. Note that the tasks and settings may also enhance social interactions, cooperative learning and other kinds of collaboration, all of which contribute to the development of a community of practice that fosters the professional growth of the individual participants within it.

The model suggests that in any professional development programme there is, or should be, a co-learning component, which fosters the continuous learning of teachers as well as of teacher educators. Jaworski (2001) explicitly addressed this issue by describing her own learning as an MTEE as a result of working with prospective MTEs. Similarly, Halai (1998) provided a reflective account of the learning she encountered through her work as an MTE in mentoring math-ematics teachers.

2. THE CHANGING NATURE OF PROFESSIONAL DEVELOPMENT PROGRAMMES FOR MATHEMATICS TEACHERS

Our conceptual framework suggests that professional development programmes for inservice teachers must be fundamentally different from traditional approaches to professional development to be effective in helping teachers trans-form or enhance their practice. This is reflected in current literature that conveys a variety of non-traditional approaches or programmes aimed at mathematics teachers' growth. In this section, we focus on this changing nature of professional development programmes for mathematics teachers. In particular, we highlight programmes and approaches that are representative of the current landscape for inservice mathematics teacher education and have proved successful in initiating school mathematics reform.

Preparing teachers to teach in reform-oriented ways (e.g., NCTM 1991, 2000) often entails 'unlearning' (Ball, 1997). Some programmes convey this through their focus of aiming at changing mathematics teachers' beliefs, conceptions and actions. The range of these programmes has shown that although there is a shift towards making the teacher the centre of professional development activities, there is no unique way of successfully beginning this process of change. The sequencing or depth of description of the following examples of programmes or approaches is not related to the level of significance of each.

2.1. *Action Research*

Action research provides a basis for teachers to engage in direct and indirect learning (see Figure 1). As a form of professional development activity, action research involves systematic reflection on teachers' actions or professional activities in order to improve them (see, e.g., Crawford & Adler, 1996). For example, a teacher might identify an issue she or he was aware of in the classroom and investigate it.

Holly (1991) distinguished between doing research for actions (according to a prospective orientation) and doing research in/of action (which is largely a retrospective approach). Both can be considered as action research, but the former provides a basis for action planning while the latter focuses on monitoring and evaluating the impact and effectiveness of the changes. Both are valuable in professional development. The choice should depend on what the teacher is interested in, as a basis for improving teaching and dealing with the constraints on a teacher (e.g., time). Holly explained that teachers seem to like the second approach (research in/of action), because it is natural and can be directly related to changes they have to make. The process involves planning, acting, observing and reflecting.

In mathematics education, cases of action research reported in the literature are generally collaborative. Usually a teacher works with a mathematics education researcher (e.g., Miller & Hunt, 1994; Edwards & Hensien, 1999), or under the guidance of an instructor in the context of a university course (e.g., Jaworski, 1998, Krainer, 1998).

Miller and Hunt (1994) were involved in a project in which three teachers worked with two university mathematics educators. They reported on one of the teachers who researched the use of writing in his mathematics classes to enhance the teaching and learning process. The teacher implemented writing activities in an introductory calculus class. He allowed students to respond for five minutes in approximately three out of every five instructional periods to a writing prompt he composed. He kept journals on what he was learning from the students' writings. The teacher claimed that the action-research experience influenced him to change his teaching practices in a way that was more closely aligned with reforms in mathematics teaching.

Edwards and Hensien (1999) described their work as collaborative action research, in the sense that it focused on practical problems of individual teachers as they interacted with university staff on issues that were of interest to both university and school partners. They reported a project involving collaboration between a middle school mathematics teacher and a mathematics teacher educator. The collaboration took a number of forms, including:

- Collaborative planning of team activities, as well as individual lessons;
- Lessons taught by the teacher educator and observed by the middle school teacher;
- Lessons taught by the middle school teacher and observed by the teacher educator;

- Lessons co-taught by the collaborators; and
- Debriefing following each lesson taught as part of the collaborative.

This action research collaboration focused on one of the teacher's efforts to change her practice in the direction of the NCTM *Standards*. Three variables were regarded as critical to the success of the change initiative: (a) providing the teacher with collaborative support; (b) providing the teacher with a non-threatening context within which to examine her beliefs; and (c) generating regular opportunities for the teacher to reflect on her practice.

The teacher wrote a narrative description of the collaboration and of the changes she made in her instructional practice as a result of the collaboration. An interpretive analysis of the teacher's narrative by the teacher educator revealed that the collaboration itself, the support for change inherent in the collaboration, and the teacher's regular reflections on her own beliefs and practices which derived from the collaboration were important to her process of change.

Edwards and Hensien (1999) claimed that the findings indicated instances of change in beliefs and instructional practices – for example, in the increased use of manipulatives, open-ended questions, and self-reflection. The teacher educator concluded that the collaboration involved three features deemed necessary for the enhancement of classroom practices, viz., regular feedback to the teacher concerning her work with students, a place for her voice in curricular decision-making, and a high level of collegial interaction.

These two examples of action research as a basis of mathematics teacher development illustrate the essence of the approach. Most of the chapters in an edited collection of articles on mathematics teacher development written by members of the Mathematics Teacher Development Group of the International Group for the Psychology of Mathematics Education (Ellerton, 1998) described action research efforts which were consistent with the model presented in this chapter. Other studies with this emphasis can be found in Clements and Ellerton (1996) and Bobis (1998).

2.2. Case Inquiry

Case inquiry is another approach that is being adopted in professional development programmes for mathematics teachers. Cases, as Shulman (1992) explained, provide occasions for professionals to gather together for retelling, reflection, and analysis. One version of such cases, for example, provides accounts of how a particular teacher experienced a problem, the analysis and strategies she employed, and the eventual resolution or stalemate that resulted. Drawing on Lampert's (1990) work, Shulman explained that, through cases, one could learn theoretical principles about mathematics and its pedagogy. One could also learn practical maxims for the organization and management of mathematics classrooms, and come to believe that a particular type of classroom represents how mathematics should be taught.

On a more general basis, Richert (1991) described the use of cases in terms of:

- Reflection – teachers learn to be reflective as they learn to think critically about their work and learn to see their work as problematic rather than given.
- Learning – reflection leads to learning, for example, understanding of particular teaching situations.
- Knowledge – an outcome of learning is the construction of knowledge. As learners write and talk about their work, they come to know what they know.
- Collaboration – reflective conversations with colleagues foster a collaborative disposition.

These ways of thinking of cases are reflected in the following examples of work with mathematics teachers.

Stein, Smith, Henningsen and Silver (2000), in strongly advocating the use of cases in inservice mathematics teachers' professional development, produced a set of cases which they described as 'paradigm cases'. These cases, Stein et al. (2000) explained, embody certain principles or ideas related to the teaching and learning of mathematics. They are different from 'dilemma-driven cases', which close with a pedagogical problem to be solved and aim to help teachers realize that teaching is an inherently dilemma-ridden enterprise, and teachers need to learn how to think about the trade-offs involved in selecting one course of action over another.

Stein et al. explained that their cases aim to assist teachers not only to develop an understanding of mathematical tasks and how the cognitive demands evolve during a lesson, but also the skill of critical reflection in their own practice guided by reference to a framework based on these ideas. Their cases are based on the QUASAR ('Quantitative Understanding: Amplifying Student Achievement and Reasoning') project, a national project in the United States. QUASAR was aimed at improving mathematics instruction for students attending middle schools in economically disadvantaged communities in ways that emphasized thinking, reasoning, problem solving, and the communication of mathematical ideas.

The Stein et al. cases were developed for the COMET ('Cases of Mathematics Instruction to Enhance Teaching') project in which practice-based materials for mathematics teacher professional development were created. The materials were intended to provide teachers with opportunities to construct knowledge central to teaching by engaging them in activities along several dimensions that were built around samples of authentic classroom practice. In particular, COMET materials allowed teachers to explore the mathematical ideas associated with tasks that could be used with students, to consider student thinking about important mathematical ideas, and to analyze how teacher and student actions and interactions in the classroom support or inhibit learning. The materials provided sites for teachers and teacher educators to engage in critique, inquiry, and investigation into the practice of teaching.

The unique aspect of the Stein et al. (2000) cases is that each was a case of a research-based pattern of teaching and learning, viewed through the lens of a 'Mathematical Task Framework', which provided a representation of how tasks unfolded during a lesson. Thus the role of the cases was to situate the abstract ideas of the Mathematical Tasks Framework in episodes of classroom practice.

The set of cases represented the most prevalent ways in which cognitively challenging mathematical tasks played out during classroom lessons. Each case featured an instructional episode in the classroom of a teacher in an urban middle school who was attempting to enact standards-based instruction. Each case portrayed the events that unfolded in the classroom as the teacher and students engaged with a cognitively challenging mathematics task. Each case, told from the perspective of the teacher, made salient his/her thoughts and actions as he/she interacted with students and with key aspects of mathematical content. Accompanying each case was an opening mathematics activity, intended to engage readers of the case with some of the key mathematical ideas embedded therein.

The cases were organized into content areas or clusters, such as: Algebra as the Study of Patterns and Functions; Geometry and Measurement in Two and Three Dimensions; and Reasoning with Rates, Ratios, and Proportions. Within each cluster, a set of mathematical ideas thought to be central to the development of solid mathematical proficiency in the middle grades was identified and explored within and across cases. In the algebra cluster, for example, the notions of variable, connections among representations, and mathematical generalizations were woven throughout the set of cases.

Stein et al. (2000) explained that once teachers begin to view their cases as cases of various patterns of task enactment, they can begin to reflect on their own practice through the lens of the cognitive demands of tasks and the Mathematical Task Framework. The ultimate goal was to influence the instructional practice through teacher reflection. Stein et al. pointed out that teachers often report that, without guidance, it is difficult to begin to think about their own instruction. For example, when teachers first view a video of their own practice, they often lack a coherent focus and therefore experience 'reflection' as a frustrating attempt to decipher and bring meaning to the myriad actions and interactions that constitute classroom activity. Stein et al's intention, then, was to help teachers learn a particular way of critically examining classroom activity by viewing it through the lens of the Mathematical Task Framework.

Stein et al. (2000) thought of their cases as important learning tools which could serve as mediating devices between teachers' reflection on their own practice and their ability to interpret their own practice as instances of more general patterns of task enactment. The cases play this mediating function, when facilitators assist teachers to view them through the lens of the Mathematical Tasks Framework. Teachers become sensitive to important cues in the teaching episodes, and learn how to interpret those cues as influences on students' opportunities to engage productively with tasks. This is done in the relaxed, non-threatening environment of the case discussion.

Stein et al. concluded that because teachers naturally compare their own classroom lessons with the cases, they also gain insights into ways of attending to and interpreting events in their own day-to-day instruction. Teachers recognize and resonate with the 'here-and-now' events depicted in the cases, and readily make comparisons with their practice. These conclusions of Stein et al. were based on their witnessing teachers spontaneously comparing specific events in their own lessons with events in the cases.

Stein et al. suggested that facilitators may want to guide teachers' individual reflections on a case by asking them to respond to the following three questions:

1. What are the main mathematical ideas in the case?
2. What evidence is there that the students learned these ideas?
3. What did the teacher do to facilitate or inhibit students' learning of these ideas?

They found that these questions helped orient teachers to key issues and set the stage for productive discussion.

Although Stein et al. (2000) provided the actual cases suitable for use in professional development, others have proposed the writing of cases as a means of accomplishing professional development. Shulman (1992), for example, maintained that case writing may bring special benefits to those who write them, prompting them to reflect on their practice and to become more analytic about their work.

Teacher-written cases played a central role in Walen and Williams' (2000) work with inservice mathematics teachers. They discussed how case methodology could be used to identify areas of concern and to provide opportunities for teachers to engage in discussing and attempting to solve their problems using case methods in a teacher development setting. Walen and Williams' use of cases evolved from a study in which participating teachers implemented an innovative 4-year secondary mathematics curriculum. The cases under consideration were vignettes of problematic situations actually encountered by teachers as they worked towards implementing the new curriculum. Originally, the cases were developed and presented as a way of validating data gathered on the difficulties the teachers faced. However, the teachers' reactions to the cases and the discussions and reflections that followed suggested that the cases had played a surprisingly powerful role in helping the teachers acknowledge their classroom concerns and begin to deal with these concerns.

The teachers involved in this study had chosen to implement the SIMMS IM ('Systemic Initiative for Montana Mathematics and Science Integrated Mathematics') Project curriculum, which was designed to replace traditional 9–12 mathematics courses. SIMMS IM emphasizes student-centred instruction. Four of the cases generated from the implementation were applied with 115 teachers at a 2-day professional development conference for this purpose. The participants worked in small discussion groups with a facilitator. One primary purpose of the meeting was to read and discuss the four cases as part of the project evaluation. The cases were presented as stories for discussion and the teachers were informed that the story ideas came from actual classrooms but did not represent any one classroom in particular.

Walen and Williams (2000) discussed two of the cases in relation to benefits to the participants. For one case, they found that the teachers genuinely enjoyed the opportunity that the case provided for discussion. It also allowed teachers to develop some workable ideas to solve real problems and to view small groups, a focus of the case, as common classroom practice. For the other case, which featured follow-up after the inservice, many of the teachers reported after the conference that they had successfully incorporated other teachers' ideas into their classroom practice.

Overall, the teachers were found to have valued the time spent with their peers in these focused discussions and found the dialogues useful in helping them identify and attempt to solve problems that they had encountered in their own classrooms. Walen and Williams concluded that the case methodology facilitated this outcome in several ways. First, the cases focused on situations that were familiar and practical for the teachers. Second, the cases dealt with breakdowns in practice that called for solutions and made sense within the context of that practice. This oriented teachers toward a contextually reflective mode and enabled more context-sensitive reflection.

Although the problems described in the cases were not their own, the teachers showed considerable engagement with the issues and felt compelled to find solutions. The teachers in the study were able to use the cases to reflect on their own practice, to identify areas of concern and, in large part, to build consensus and to work towards solutions.

2.3. Narrative Inquiry

Narrative inquiry makes a unique contribution to mathematics teacher development particularly in terms of the pedagogical dimension discussed in our conceptual framework. The narrative approach generally focuses on teachers' stories of lived experiences in the classroom as a basis of understanding practice in order to facilitate growth. This use of stories is based on the premise that stories may be more helpful than theoretical expositions to people who need to learn to think in new ways about complex, context-dependent domains like teaching (Witherell & Noddings, 1991; Carter, 1993). Two examples of such use of narratives to foster mathematics teachers development are conveyed by the works of Schifter (1993, 1996) and Chapman (1993, 1999a, 1999b).

Schifter (1993, 1996) promoted the use of stories in mathematics teacher development in which the aim is to get teachers to give voice to new pedagogy. She argued that what teachers are learning in their own classrooms should be communicated to their colleagues and to others with an interest in mathematics education. The success of the movement for reform cannot rest on individual teachers constructing the new practice classroom by classroom, independently of one another and without engaging in many-sided exchanges about their efforts. Schifter went on to say that only through telling stories about their classrooms can teachers convey the richness, the interconnectedness and subtlety of what they have come to understand.

The idea is that teachers, themselves, and others will benefit from their giving expression to matters concerning their students, schools, and communities. As teachers face the challenge of constructing new ways of teaching it is useful for them to talk about the subject matter they teach, and about both established classroom structures and experimental practices. Schifter further explained that current mathematics education literature provide examples upon which such teacher narratives might be modelled. They offer case studies of classroom teachers written by researchers; case studies conducted by university faculty who also teach mathematics and make their own teaching the object of their research; and cases written by full-time classroom teachers. Studies like these provide rich accounts of classroom processes, illustrating the kinds of dilemmas that arise in daily instruction and explicating how teachers experience, think about, and resolve them.

Schifter (1996) provided details of a project designed to support teachers willing to write narratives of classroom processes and professional transformation. The teachers who participated were participants of SummerMath for Teachers, discussed later. Forty-nine narratives – some of which were published in Schifter (1996) – were produced by project participants. The narratives contextualized teaching activities in the life-process of particular classrooms. They included detailed descriptions of classroom events, including dialogue. The authors vividly narrated students' words and gestures, bringing readers into their classrooms to 'see' and 'hear' for themselves. But unlike videotape, this medium presents scenes from the teachers' perspective, complete with their thoughts, doubts, frustrations, and second thoughts. Thus, their audience comes to share the dilemmas they face, the decisions they make, and the satisfaction they experience.

According to Schifter, readers of these narratives learned about the teachers' goals for the lessons, about what was happening before a particular problem was posed, and what happened afterwards. They also learned about the questions students asked, the ideas they suggested, how they interacted with one another and with the teacher, about what students learned, and about what the teacher learned. Other narratives addressed issues that classroom teachers are likely to face as they attempt to implement the new mathematics pedagogy. How does one teach students to listen to one another, work collaboratively, and participate in mathematical inquiry? How does one reach all students? What role can computer technology play in students' construction of mathematical concepts? Through the paper one comes to know individual students, their strengths and weaknesses, their understandings and confusions. One also comes to see how students of diverse abilities can be challenged and supported as they construct mathematical concepts.

Schifter's work focused on narrative as a basis for teaching about teaching, but did not make explicit the nature of narrative in relation to narrative knowing or narrative inquiry. Chapman (1999a), on the other hand, did this in a study of a Problem-Solving Inservice (PSI) programme. She focused on narrative inquiry as a basis of reflecting on experience and changing teaching. The goal of the PSI programme was to provide opportunities that would allow traditional mathematics teachers to focus on personal experience as a way of achieving self-understanding and a way of reconstructing their personal meanings about problem solving and problem-solving instruction.

The PSI programme had a humanistic emphasis based on concepts of lived experience, personal meaning and narrative reflection. In Chapman's (1999a) work, narrative was considered to be a way of knowing essential for understanding human experience. According to Bruner (1986), narrative knowing is concerned with the explication of human intentions in the context of actions. In particular, narrative reflection refers to reflection framed in narrative knowing. It is a way of living out one's story and a way of storying one's experience. It is a process of collaboration that involves mutual storytelling and re-storying among participants. It focuses more on the expression than the analysis of meaning. In the PSI programme, narrative reflection based on self-stories of past, present, and possible future experiences formed the basis for meaning recovery and re-construction of teachers' thinking and actions.

The activities of the PSI programme were organized into four stages: introduction, reflection on personal meaning, problem-solving experiences, and reflection on problem-solving experiences. Stage 1, the introduction, focused on the nature of narrative reflection – for example, writing and sharing self-stories and resonating in stories of peers as a way of becoming aware of and understanding one's thinking. The main activity involved practising narrative reflection in terms of how to facilitate depth in personal reflections, sharing, and collaboration.

Stage 2, which involved reflection on personal meaning, focused on the teachers' histories, actions, and intentions in the context of teaching and learning problem solving prior to entering the PSI programme. The main activity was narrative reflection with a focus on self, content, teaching, and learning.

Stage 3, the problem-solving experience, focused on non-algorithmic problem solving based on three themes: the problem-solving process of an individual, the problem-solving process of a small group, and teacher-student interactions while students solved problems. The key activities allowed the teachers to solve a variety of problems that were non-routine for them and to experience actively each of the three themes. For example, they engaged in role-play, taking turns being student and teacher in different scenarios for the teacher-student interaction theme.

Stage 4, which was concerned with reflection on problem solving experiences, focused on what the teachers learned as a result of the experiences in stage 3. The main activity was narrative reflection on self, content, teaching and learning similar to stage 2.

The approach was found to be effective in allowing the teachers to reconstruct their thinking and reconceptualize their teaching in ways that were consistent with the current reform movement. For example, they came to view themselves more positively as problem solvers, developed a broader view of problems, and adopted a more student-centred approach to problem-solving instruction.

In earlier work with narratives, Chapman (1993) focused on the use of written instead of oral narratives to facilitate teacher development. This work was framed on the premise that the stories we tell reflect who we are and what we may become. In that sense, they provide a basis for meaning recovery and meaning construction of our actions. Chapman (1993) illustrated this perspective based on a project involving inservice mathematics teachers. The focus of the project was self-reflection on autobiographical stories of teaching as a basis of professional development. The process consisted of the following activities:

1. Reflecting on personal experiences of their teaching and selecting and describing a set of specific events, each in the format of a story.
2. Identifying themes underlying their behaviours in the collection of stories, with the assistance of a teacher educator-researcher acting as facilitator.
3. Reflecting on what the themes meant from their perspective in the larger context of their practice.
4. Reflecting on alternative themes suggested by the facilitator.
5. Reflecting on the consequences of their findings on their future classroom behaviours.
6. Sharing and discussing their findings with each other to facilitate further reflection as a group.

The approach allowed the teachers to understand key aspects of their behaviour in ways that affirmed or conflicted with their expectations. The teachers were able to draw on their experiences to make meaningful suggestions for change to enhance their teaching.

2.4. *Student Thinking*

Our conceptual framework highlighted the possible importance of the interdependence between the students' learning processes and the interactive teaching processes as a basis of understanding how teachers learn through their teaching. This also implies that assisting teachers to become more aware of their students' thinking could be a worthwhile approach to achieving professional growth. This perspective is reflected in the Cognitive Guided Instruction (CGI) inservice programme (see, e.g., Carpenter and Fennema, 1992; Chambers and Hankes, 1994; Borko and Putnam, 1995), which was designed to help teachers understand children's thinking and to use this knowledge to make instructional decisions.

Teachers participating in the CGI programme are expected to adapt their own instructional methodologies to include the use of their students' understanding. They either develop their own instructional materials or adapt available materials. The programme uses a problem-solving approach to working with teachers and does not provide ready-made solutions for the problems of instruction. The specific goal of the program is to help elementary teachers understand how addition and subtraction concepts develop in children and to explore the use of this knowledge for instruction. The teachers learn to classify problems, identify solution strategies that children use to solve different problems, and relate these strategies to levels and problems on which they are commonly used. This provided a basis for deciding what questions to ask and offered insights into what to listen for.

Carpenter and Fennema (1992) reported significant difference between CGI classes and control classes on:

- the emphasis on problem solving and low level skills;
- the freedom given to students to construct their own strategies for solving problems;
- the teachers' knowledge of their students thinking; and
- the students' achievement in both problem solving and skills.

They concluded that researchers and educators could bring about significant changes in classroom practice by helping teachers to make informed decisions rather than by attempting to train them to perform in a specified way. However, as Borko and Putman (1995) pointed out, the workshops alone did not change the teachers. It was listening to their own students solving problems that made the greatest difference in their instructional practices. It also took many of the teachers considerable time to adapt their teaching to the principles of CGI, and some only changed their practices to a limited extent.

Chambers and Hankes (1994) offered a follow-up study based on the CGI programme. They summarized characteristics of CGI classrooms – e.g., problem solving, children's understanding, children's talk, multiple strategies, integration – and then presented three case studies which focused on discussing changes in the thinking of participating teachers in regard to classroom behaviour. Chambers and Hankes considered the CGI workshop to be designed to help teachers modify their beliefs about teaching and learning. They concluded that when teachers are equipped with these new beliefs and more structured knowledge, it is no surprise that dramatic changes in their classroom teaching often result.

2.5. *Reform Classroom Context*

We noted earlier that historically, professional development programmes in mathematics education have mirrored traditional teaching of mathematics. One might therefore expect a similar pattern to emerge in relation to current reform perspectives of teaching mathematics. This is reflected in the SummerMath inservice programme for teachers which, like the CGI programme, is well documented (see, e.g., Simon & Schifter, 1991, 1992; Aichele & Coxford, 1994; Borko & Putman, 1995). The programme, which combined course work with ongoing support in the classroom, was designed to stimulate teachers' development of a constructivist view of learning to serve as a basis for mathematics instruction.

It was guided by two principles: first, it is important to teach teachers as you want them to teach; and second, follow-up support and supervision are important in facilitating teacher learning and fostering teacher instructional change.

Teachers participated in a two-week summer institute designed to provide them with an opportunity to learn mathematics in a setting where construction of meaning was valued and encouraged. The teachers were encouraged to reflect on their experiences at the institute and on the roles of teacher and students, and then design instructional sequences that would provide their own students with similar opportunities. The teachers were then provided with extensive support and supervision throughout the year following the summer institute in order to facilitate the integration of new learning into their classroom practices.

The intervention was found to have a substantial impact on the participants' beliefs about learning, and the changes in the teachers' beliefs affected decisions they reported making in the classroom. Almost all teachers adopted new classroom techniques. In particular, they began listening more to students and focusing on their ideas and understandings.

2.6. *Model Lessons/Illustrative Units*

For the most part, the preceding examples of teacher development left it to teachers to convert the inservice experience into instructional strategies and behaviours. Other programmes, however, have been developed which provide model lessons or illustrative units to reflect reform perspectives for teaching mathematics. The Michigan Mathematics Inservice Project (M^2IP) (Laing & Mayer, 1994) is an example of the latter.

M^2IP involved participants in using curriculum materials based on ten teaching principles. These principles were based on research on the teaching and learning of mathematics, new priorities in mathematics education, and the teaching experiences of the project staff. The curriculum materials included model lessons through which the principles would be implemented. Each inservice session involved participating in a model lesson, analyzing the lesson in relation to the ten mathematics teaching principles, and adapting the lesson by grade levels for implementation in the participants' classrooms prior to the next session.

The first activity of the following session presented an opportunity for sharing these classroom-teaching experiences in grade-level groups. The model lessons consisted of rationale, outcomes, materials, teaching/learning procedures and commentary regarding possible teacher action. There were mixed results in terms of change in teaching and attitude, although some teachers showed significant changes on both counts.

Another example of professional development in this category of illustrative units was provided by Borasi, Fonzi, Smith, and Rose (1999), who investigated the nature and results of a professional development programme which introduced middle school teachers to an inquiry approach to mathematics instruction. The programme was characterized by the use of a few illustrative units which provided an integrated context for experiences as learners and experiences as teachers. Project participants consisted of mathematics and special education teachers in school-based support teams led by school facilitators.

Key elements of the professional development programme were 'Summer Institute Experiences' and 'Supported Field Experiences' expectations. The Summer Institute Experiences included:

1. Experiences as learners of illustrative units, each followed by explicit reflections from complementary perspectives;
2. Readings, reflections, and discussions on aspects of mathematics, learning, and teaching;
3. Informative sessions on learning disabilities and their implications for mathematics instruction; and
4. Activities to prepare for the implementation of an illustrative unit as the participants' first experience as teachers.

Expectations of the Supported Field Experiences component of the programme were that each participant would:

1. adapt and implement one illustrative unit in at least one class at the very beginning of the school year.
2. adapt and implement at least one more inquiry unit (either another illustrative unit or preferably a unit designed by the participant).
3. meet regularly with a support team during the school year.
4. attend three to four project-wide, day-long follow-up meetings, scheduled at strategic points during the school year, in order to share experiences and receive further professional development.
5. engage in final reflection on the field experiences.

Overall, feedback from participants suggested that many teachers found the Summer Institute Experiences valuable. Borasi et al. (1999) concluded that the programme was successful in accomplishing its main goal of initiating the process of rethinking beliefs and practices, although the extent of the changes in beliefs and practices that resulted from the participation in the programme varied considerably among individuals. Participants tracked after the programme sustained and even increased the instructional changes observed during the field experiences, even after several years. They all continued to teach most of the innovative units they had developed, in all of the classes in which such units were appropriate.

According to Borasi et al. (1999), their analysis suggested that overall this professional development programme was successful in initiating a long-term process of rethinking one's pedagogical beliefs and practices, as well as in promoting some immediate instructional change, at least for the great majority of the participants. They suggested that the use of illustrative units could enhance the value of established professional development practices – such as engaging teachers as learners in instructional experiences modelling a novel pedagogy, offering a supported field experience component, and providing multiple opportunities for reflection.

2.7. *Other Approaches*

Maher and Alston (1990) focused on two kinds of experiences for teachers in order that they would build their own systems of representations of mathematical ideas and become more attentive to children's mathematical thinking.

Experience 1: Teachers engage in a mathematical exploration. Maher and Alston's (1990) assumption here was that as teachers worked to build greater understanding of some mathematical ideas they would be likely to become more aware of their own mathematical thinking. As they engage in their own problem-solving experiences, opportunities would naturally evolve in which they become more aware of their personal approaches. They would also begin to consider the implications of this experience for their own students' learning.

Experience 2: Teachers conduct a task-based interview with a student. This experience would be analyzed in terms of the teacher's attention to the child's mathematical thinking. Teachers first view video-tapes of children doing mathematics, both in small groups as a part of regular classroom instruction and individually, in task-based interviews. The interview format calls for attention to the process of the child's problem-solving behaviour, to the various representations that are built, and to how the child connects them. The teacher conducts the interview and, using tapes, reflects on it with other teachers.

In studying this approach, Maher and Alston found that participating teachers began to pay greater attention to children's thinking. They moved away from getting students to use given procedures to solve problems by 'the teacher's method', and became more attentive to ways their students thought about problems.

Ball (1996) drew attention to ideas about teacher learning that persistently show up in the literature on effective professional development: prior beliefs and experience; subject-matter knowledge; knowing students; importance of contexts, time, reflection, follow-up; modelling and teacher control. She recommended a stance of critique and inquiry which involved participants in asking and debating, and thereby developing a discourse of conjecture and deliberation. She maintained that appropriate curriculum materials and videotapes provided two means for experimenting with ways to foster a stance of inquiry and critique.

Keiny (1994) reported on the worth of using a teacher-thinking seminar – in the context of a post-graduate course – as a basis of professional development. Teachers started with their own practical knowledge. They identified dilemmas in their teaching situations which, when analyzed, revealed several dimensions – that is to say, they represented a multidimensional reality. The teacher-thinking seminar was based on the teachers' own practical knowledge which they shared in the group. The main strategy was the "dialectical process of reflection in the group", which was used as a means of encouraging participants – who included mathematics teachers – to investigate their own practice and construct their own theories of teaching. Keiny concluded that the approach facilitated construction of meaningful pedagogical knowledge by the teachers.

Other programmes for professional development of mathematics teachers around the world are presented in Ellerton (1999) and Jaworski, Wood, and Dawson (1999).

3. TRENDS IN THE PROFESSIONAL DEVELOPMENT OF MATHEMATICS TEACHER EDUCATORS

An underlying assumption of the various professional development programmes described above is that there are well-prepared mathematics teacher educators ready to facilitate learning opportunities for mathematics teachers. However, this may not be the case, for there are relatively few formal programmes available which provide adequate training for potential mathematics teacher educators. Similarly, there is little research to be found on how and why mathematics teacher educators choose to be mathematics teacher educators.

Until recently, mathematics teacher educators developed their own practices and procedures through their own practice. Tzur (2001) has provided a detailed account of his personal process of becoming a mathematics teacher educator through his practice, at different levels and phases of his life, beginning with his years as an elementary school student who learned mathematics. Tzur's work reflects to a certain extent the kind of development that many mathematics teacher educators (MTEEs in Figure 1) experience in their formal higher education and in their subsequent practices.

Currently, there is a growing interest in the nature of the roles and activities of mathematics teacher educators as well as in ways to enhance their professional development (see, e.g., Halai, 1998; Even, 1999a; 1999b; Krainer, 2001; Jaworski, 2001; Zaslavsky & Leikin, 1999 (in press)). This interest reflects a recognition that mathematics teacher educators' practices represent a complex terrain which needs to be further conceptualized and studied.

We find Jaworski's (2001) levels describing mathematics teacher educators' practice (discussed earlier) useful in thinking about mathematics teacher education. Accordingly, teacher educators should aim to contribute to teachers' development with respect to the opportunities teachers provide their students for effective learning of mathematics (e.g., by providing mathematical challenges) (Level 1). They also contribute to ways in which teachers think about developing their approaches to teaching (i.e., enhancing their pedagogical power) (Level 2). And, in addition to those roles and responsibilities, teacher educators need to reflect continuously and think about developing their own approaches to teacher education (Level 3).

In the context of inservice mathematics teacher education, our conceptual framework (Figure 1) points to different layers in which teacher educators learn and develop. They may enrol in a direct programme for (either prospective or de facto) mathematics teacher educators, in which there is a mathematics teacher educators' educator (MTEE in Figure 1) whose responsibility it is to provide learning opportunities for participants to become qualified teacher educators. This occurs in the external (dark) layer of our model. Direct formal programmes are mostly in the form of university graduate courses (or clusters of courses) or a special M.Ed./M.Sc. programme towards a degree in Mathematics Teacher Education (e.g., the M.Ed programme in Pakistan, described by Jaworski, 2001). Other direct programmes are in the form of extensive inservice courses for mathematics teachers, directed towards a formal certificate or other kind of recognition indicating that those who completed the course requirements qualify to serve as inservice mathematics teacher educators.

An example of the latter is the Manor programme for developing teacher leaders and educators for the role of promoting teachers' learning about mathematics teaching (Even 1999a, 1999b). This programme focused on the development of: (a) teachers' understanding of current views of mathematics teaching and learning, through readings, discussions and replication of relevant research; (b) teachers' knowledge of ways to work with and provide learning opportunities for teachers; and (c) a professional reference group.

Participants in the Manor programme met with their teacher educators on a weekly basis for three consecutive years. The learning opportunities provided for the participants at the weekly meetings addressed ways to combine theoretical and practical issues – like, for example, characteristics of worthwhile tasks for students. These meetings were followed by the participants' implementing the discussed ideas in their own classrooms, conducting a mini-study with the support of the project staff members, and working with other teachers to provide for them similar opportunities to learn.

The Manor programme illustrates how even formal and direct settings can include, as an integral part of the programme, indirect learning experiences for the prospective teacher educators, through implementation in their classrooms and work with other colleagues. Interestingly, Even found that prospective teacher educators were more inclined to deal in depth with issues concerning students' learning of mathematics than with issues regarding teachers' ways of thinking and learning. This point supports the hierarchical nature of Jaworski's (2001) levels describing teacher educators' practice. It seems that teacher educators' concerns regarding their need to know more about how teachers learn is an indication of expertise, as manifested by Jaworski (2001) and Halai (1998). Even suggests that one of the main contributing factors to the successful preparation of inservice teacher educators within the framework of the Manor programme was the numerous occasions interwoven in the programme activities in which connections between theory and practice were explicitly addressed.

Another model for developing teacher educators is the co-learning partnership described by Jaworski (2001), in which 'teachers and educators learn together in a reciprocal relationship of a reflexive nature' (p. 315). This model was implemented in Pakistan within the framework of an M.Ed programme in

Teacher Education which comprised a special 18-month graduate course followed by a three-year period of internship as teacher educators. The programme relied on continuous co-learning between all the participating members, researchers and practitioners: faculty members who acted as experienced teacher educators (MTEEs), the teachers who enrolled in the M.Ed programme, namely the developing teacher educators (novice MTEs), and the teachers (MTs) with whom the MTEs worked during their internship. This model resembles to some extent models of apprenticeship in communities of practice where newcomers learn from old-stagers (Lave & Wenger, 1991). In terms of focus, like Even's model, this co-learning model emphasizes connections between theory, practice, and research. Jaworski's (2001) analysis pointed to the growth of the MTEs' knowledge along several dimensions, including mathematics, mathematical learning, pedagogy of mathematical learning, theories of mathematics education, and issues of schooling.

Programmes that rely more heavily on indirect development of teacher educators through their practice are based on the assumption that teacher educators develop in the same ways as teachers develop. Traditionally, teachers have acquired expertise in their teaching as a result of their own teaching practice. It is often assumed that, likewise, prospective mathematics teacher educators need real experience in facilitating the learning of mathematics teachers (Brown & Borko, 1992; Mason, 1998; Steinbring, 1998; Leikin, Berman & Zaslavsky, 2000; Cobb, 2000; Cobb & McClain, 2001).

Along the same line, Zaslavsky and Leikin (1999) described a model for developing mathematics teacher educators that was embedded in a 5-year reform-oriented teacher professional development project. The project was designed to enhance the development of staff members hand-in-hand with the development of inservice teachers who participated in the programme. Staff members formed a diverse community of practice whose members varied considerably with respect to their knowledge of mathematics, length and level of teaching experience, and extent of practice in aspects of teacher education.

The development of qualified teacher educators in this context was enhanced by integrating several contributing components, such as: shared planning and carrying out of activities with teachers, mutual observations and feedback, written accounts of professional experiences, collaboration and social interactions, encouraging initiatives and ownership, and organizing mini-conferences. In terms of the conceptual model in Figure 1, staff members kept switching roles from learners (MTs) taking part in teachers' activities to facilitators (MTEs) of learning opportunities for teachers.

Leikin, Zaslavsky and Brandon (2002) presented another model of professional development of MTEs that is interwoven with MTs' professional development. It is an exponential model, in which teachers enter a programme for enhancing students' critical mathematical thinking by first enrolling in a preparation course. Then, eventually having gained experience in teaching mathematics according to the special program, coached by a qualified mentor, the more outstanding teachers take over the mentoring of the less experienced teachers first in their own schools and later in other schools.

4. TASKS ENHANCING PROFESSIONAL DEVELOPMENT OF MATHEMATICS TEACHERS AND TEACHER EDUCATORS

In the conceptual framework which was depicted in Figure 1, tasks play a critical role in the learning offers that can be made to participants in professional development programs. On the basis that professional development implies growth in teachers' mathematical and pedagogical powers, and in teacher educators' mathematical, pedagogical, and educative powers, it is assumed that tasks should address these elements in a challenging and engaging way. They should create mathematical and pedagogical problem-solving situations, in which relevant issues are addressed, including sensitivity to learners and reform-oriented approaches to management of learning.

Inservice teacher educators are usually rather flexible and "have a considerable latitude in terms of defining their curricula" (Cooney, 2001, p. 15). Many are relatively free of time and of other constraints that teachers face in their practice. Consequently, tasks enhancing professional growth vary to a large extent with respect to their nature, content, and focus.

In this section we try to conceptualize what could be considered powerful tasks for enhancing the mathematical, pedagogical, and educative power of mathematics educators at the different layers of our model (depicted in Figure 1). We expect powerful tasks to be open-ended, non-routine problems, in the broadest sense, that lend themselves well to collaborative work and social interactions, elicit deep mathematical and pedagogical considerations and connections, and challenge personal conceptions and beliefs about mathematics and about how one comes to understand mathematics. We find particularly worthwhile the use of tasks that can equally present challenges to mathematics educators and to their target learners (even if some modifications and adaptations must be carried out). The use of such tasks allows educators and learners to encounter and reflect on very similar experiences.

Tasks are usually constructed or adapted by a mathematics educator in order to provide learning opportunities for others. We argue that the process of planning and implementing powerful tasks inevitably provides important learning for educators.

In this section we offer examples of what we consider to be 'powerful tasks', and analyze them in terms of their potential contributions for direct learning of teachers and indirect learning of teacher educators. Six types of tasks which have been successfully used in various professional development settings and portray how reform teaching (Cooney, 2001) may be facilitated, are presented. These examples address the following aspects of professional development:

- Dealing with uncertainty and doubt (Task 1);

- Rethinking mathematics (Task 2);
- Engaging in multiple approaches to problem solving (Task 3);
- Identifying mathematical similarities and differences (Task 4);
- Developing a critical view of the use of educational technology (Task 5); and
- Learning from students' thinking (Task 6).

In our analysis we reflect on our personal learning associated with the tasks.

4.1. *Dealing with Uncertainty and Doubt: What Can the Measure of this Angle be?*

Many worthwhile tasks are associated with elements of doubt and uncertainty. The grounds for these elements are rooted in Dewey's (1933) notion of reflective thinking that involves both a state of doubt and an inner drive to resolve the doubt. Cooney (2001) suggested that any change in teachers' current beliefs must stem from a reason to doubt and question them.

Tasks that create a state of doubt and conflict may seem at first rather simple, yet lead to some subtle mathematical issues that often are not addressed. For example, one might consider what remains invariant under change of scale, or in other words, the connections between algebraic and geometric aspects of slope, scale, and angle (Zaslavsky, Sela, & Leron, 2002).

Tasks 1a and 1b (see Figures 2 and 3) provides an example of the way tasks can develop as a result of the continuous co-learning of teacher educators. Zaslavsky (submitted) reports on the way that an informal conversation which she overheard between two prospective mathematics teachers in an undergraduate methods course, regarding a geometric problem that they had solved at

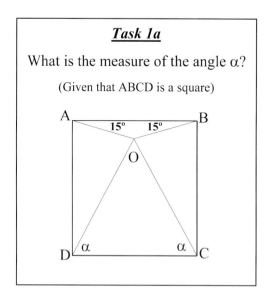

Figure 2.   The original task.

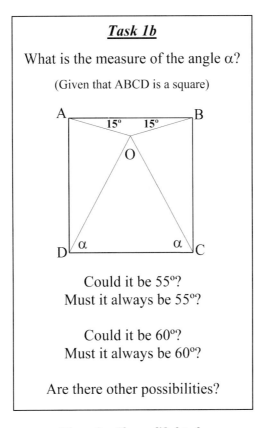

Task 1b

What is the measure of the angle α?

(Given that ABCD is a square)

Could it be 55°?
Must it always be 55°?

Could it be 60°?
Must it always be 60°?

Are there other possibilities?

Figure 3. The modified task.

home (Task 1a) as part of a course assignment, created a moment of uncertainty for her. Her personal experience as a preservice teacher educator drew her attention to the learning potential of the problem for mathematics educators (MTs, MTEs, and MTEEs) as well as for students. Following the uncertainty that arose in her course spontaneously, Zaslavsky altered the original task (see Task 1b) for future use in inservice professional development settings in order to recreate the same kind of learning situation. In response to Task 1a, the preservice teachers were debating whether the measure of α was 55° or 60°. Both answers seemed possible, and thus arose conflict and doubt.

Task 1b created a state of doubt and conflict among many inservice teachers and teacher educators. One of the participants made the following comments in a reflective discussion that followed teachers' collaborative efforts to solve the problem:

At first when I worked on the problem by myself, I felt like a student. I felt unconfident and said to myself: "this can also happen to me. It's not always possible to find the correct answer".

I observed my colleagues struggle with the problem, and that made me feel better about the possibility to hesitate or err. It became legitimate. I felt that I was in the process of learning. I wondered how I, as a teacher, could create such situations in my classroom and how I could change regular questions into questions that stimulate discussion.

This reaction illustrates how, in the context of inservice activities, powerful mathematical problems can become pedagogical problems as well. The mathematical considerations are often inseparable from the pedagogical ones.

It should be noted that following this experience, many teachers decided to try out this task in their classrooms. When sharing with each others the ways in which their students dealt with the problem, the teachers realized once again that meaningful learning situations that they had encountered themselves could be provided for their students as well.

4.2. *Rethinking Mathematics: Considering Alternative Mathematical Definitions*

There is an agreement among mathematics teacher educators that one of the important issues in mathematics teacher education is the development of connected mathematical knowledge. One argument supporting this claim is that the success of reform efforts that include restructuring the mathematical curriculum relies to a great extent on teachers' understanding of alternative structures (see, e.g., Askew, 2001). Another argument rests on the premise that greater teacher flexibility will promote more effective mathematics teaching (Simon, 1995).

One factor that influences the structure of mathematical curricula is the set of definitions used to define basic mathematical concepts included in the curriculum (Brown, 1999; Dörfler, 1999). The set of definitions chosen often influences the sequencing of mathematical concepts. Thus, it is important to address these issues with teachers and teacher educators.

Task 2 (see Figure 4) is part of a larger set of similar tasks that were designed for an inservice course dealing with alternative ways of defining mathematical concepts (Leikin and Winicki-Landman, 2000, 2001). More specifically, the activity focuses on a family of geometric concepts, namely, *Special Quadrilaterals*. A special quadrilateral may be defined in terms of the properties of its angles and/or sides or with respect to its symmetries (see, e.g, Ellis-Davies, 1986; Leikin, 1997; Leikin & Winicky-Landman, 2000). In some cases the definitions are equivalent, but in other cases they are not equivalent.

Task 2 was offered to the inservice mathematics teachers in a cooperative learning setting, in which each group had to present the results of their investigation to the whole group. It stimulated mathematical, meta-mathematical, and pedagogical discussions surrounding the nature of mathematical definitions and communication, the choice of definitions, logical relationships between mathematical statements, didactical sequences of learning, and mathematical connections (Leikin & Winicky-Landman, 2001).

The following excerpt conveys the kind of considerations and connections

---

Task 2

(a) For each card, examine the logical relationships between the two definitions that appear on it.

(b) Which one of the definitions do you prefer? Why?

Card 1

Definition 1: A *Trapezon* is a quadrilateral in which one pair of sides are parallel and the other two sides are equal

Definition 2: A *Trapezin* is a quadrilateral with a symmetry axis that does not include any of the diagonals

---

Card 2

Definition 1: A *Rectangon* is a quadrilateral with four equal angles

Definition 2: A *Rectangin* is a quadrilateral with two symmetry axes that do not include any of the diagonals

---

Card 3

Definition 1: A *Rhombon* is a quadrilateral with four equal sides.

Definition 2: A *Rhombin* is a quadrilateral with two symmetry axes that include the diagonals

---

Card 4

Definition 1: A *Kiton* is a quadrilateral with two pairs of equal adjacent sides

Definition 2: A *Kitin* is a quadrilateral with a symmetry axis that includes a diagonal

---

Figure 4.   Considering alternative definitions.

(e.g., between 'definition' and 'proof') that were triggered by the task. One of the teachers expressed his preferences towards definitions based on symmetry in the following way:

> If you define [quadrilaterals] by symmetry it may simplify proving procedures. For example, the properties of a rhombus defined by symmetry (see definition 2, card 3) become obvious: the diagonals are perpendicular – they are symmetry axes, and they [the diagonals] bisect the angles as symmetry axes.

The workshop opened indirect learning opportunities for Leikin (the MTE who managed the workshop) to deepen her understanding of the potential of the task for teachers' learning. From her perspective, the specific content, namely *Special Quadrilaterals*, served as a vehicle for dealing with more general issues. However, unexpectedly from her point of view, in the whole-group discussion teachers raised the question of hierarchy of the mathematical objects and how defining by symmetry may change the hierarchical structure of quadrilaterals. This part of the discussion was surprising both for the MTs and for the MTE, and gave the MTE an opportunity to model flexible ways to deal with unexpected shifts in the intended learning trajectory (Simon, 1995).

The potential value of considering alternative definitions is reflected also in van Dormolen and Zaslavsky's (in press) account of deep mathematical musing that evoked spontaneously within a community of practice of MTEs surrounding the definition of periodicity. For a number of MTEs it was the first (and somewhat 'shocking') experience they had encountered in considering alternative definitions and accepting the arbitrariness of choice between two possible and reasonable definitions.

Mathematics is often regarded as a discipline in which there is no room for subjective views (Schoenfeld, 1989). This type of task, in which discussions surrounding personal mathematical preferences and choices are encouraged, seems helpful in pointing towards a different view of mathematics. With this different view, mathematics can be seen as a more humanistic discipline, in which results are socially constructed or rejected, and can be driven by personal values (Borasi, 1992; Brown, 1996; Shir& Zaslavsky, 2001).

4.3. *Engaging in Multiple Approaches to Problem Solving: Connecting Geometry, Algebra, and Calculus*

Teachers' problem-solving expertise is considered critical for fostering connectedness of students' mathematical knowledge (e.g., Polya, 1963; Silver & Marshall, 1990; Yerushalmy, Chazan, & Gordon, 1990; NCTM, 2000). In this context, teachers' abilities to employ different strategies to solve a problem in a reflective way is particularly vital (Romberg & Collins, 2000). According to Askew (2001) a 'connectionist orientation' distinguishes some highly effective teachers from others. In her study on teachers' mathematical understanding Ma (1999) found that for Chinese teachers, solving a problem in several different ways seemed to be a significant vehicle for improving their mathematical knowledge. Similarly, Stigler and Hiebert (1999), in their comparative analysis of mathematical lessons in the United States, Germany and Japan, found that encouraging the idea that there could be multiple solutions to problems increases the quality of mathematical lessons. Dhombres (1993) suggested that providing two different proofs for one particular theorem supports the construction of different images in the problem solvers' minds, each of which may be awakened when appropriate.

Based on these arguments, Leikin constructed a program entitled 'Solving Problems in Different Ways' and studied the potential of this program for teacher's professional development (Leikin, 1997, in press). She found that the program did, indeed, develop teachers' inclinations to solve problems in different ways. Task 3 (see Figure 5) illustrates this approach.

The teachers worked on the problem in small groups. At first, most of the teachers thought that the sum depended on the location of point E on the diameter and that "if the length of the chord changes then the sum changes". Some of the teachers suspected that "this can't be so simple" and started to consider the possibility that the sum was constant. Other teachers decided to "check the answer" on the computer screen. In this mode some of them found support for their assumption while others were surprised when they *saw* the

Task 3

Solve the following problem in as many ways as you can.

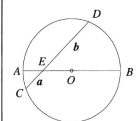

Chord *CD* intersects the diameter of a circle with center *O* at point *E*. The angle between the diameter and the chord is 45°. Does the value of the sum $CE^2 + ED^2$ (i.e., $a^2 + b^2$) depend on the location of *E* on the diameter? Prove your answer.

Figure 5.   A problem with multiple solution strategies.

result. At the next step the teachers turned to proving their conjectures. As they were thinking about different solutions they realized that they differed in their approaches to the problem.

Figure 6 depicts three different approaches to solving the problem. The first two approaches were suggested by teachers, but none of them thought of Approach 3, probably because using a functional approach for a geometric problem was unfamiliar to them. The possibility of using algebraic, geometric and calculus thinking for the same problem led to a discussion about learning sequences and the location of the same problem at different points of the mathematical curriculum.

Task 3 proved to have the potential for enhancing mathematical connections,

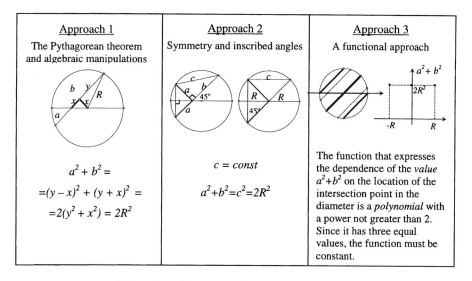

Figure 6.   Three approaches to solving Task 3.

developing the notion of 'elegance' in relation to a mathematical solution, and addressing issues concerning sequencing in the mathematics curriculum.

4.4. *Identifying Mathematical Similarities and Differences: Grouping Mathematical Objects*

Classification of different mathematical objects according to various criteria may enhance awareness of ways in which they are related to each other (Silver, 1979). This process requires the identification of similarities and differences between mathematical objects along several dimensions, which is considered "a basic component of mathematical thinking" (Cooney, 1994, p. 17). Zaslavsky (1989) found that Task 4 (see Figure 7), which is an example of an open-ended sorting task, provided a rich context for eliciting many viewpoints regarding mathematical structures. It generated much discussion on a wide range of issues, including common features of various families of functions (e.g., polynomials of different degrees), different representations of mathematical relations (that are not necessarily functions), and connections between equations and functions.

Task 4 has many correct answers that can be accessible and applicable to various communities of practice (students, teachers, and teacher educators) (Zaslavsky, 1995). Although students usually focus only on mathematical criteria, mathematics educators tend to consider pedagogical criteria also, such as learning sequencing, and likely student difficulties. Thus, Task 4 is consistent with our characterization of powerful tasks for professional development settings.

The design and implementation of these types of task proved to be effective in enhancing professional growth of inservice teacher educators as well as of teachers (Zaslavsky & Leikin, in press). Generally, teachers who were exposed to such tasks (usually in cooperative small group settings) began sorting by what Zaslavsky and Leikin term *surface features* (that is to say, features that can be observed without the need to carry out any mathematical procedures or careful analysis). Only after a while did they begin to consider more *structural features* (that may be identified only after more complex considerations). They then begin to look at other mathematical topics through a classification lens and try to design similar tasks for their students.

Sorting tasks can be used to identify teachers' and students' mathematical and pedagogical thinking, and are therefore helpful in developing educators' sensitivity to learners. Teachers often generated classifications that were not expected by the teacher educator, leading to mathematical and meta-mathematical discussion.

4.5. *Developing a Critical View of the Use of Educational Technology: Searching for a Special Point in a Triangle*

The National Council of Teachers of Mathematics' 'Technology Principle' (NCTM, 2000) stated that "technology is essential in teaching and learning mathematics; it influences the mathematics that is taught and enhances students' learning" (p. 24). However, "the effective use of technology in the mathematics

Task 4

On each card there is a mathematical object. Group the cards in as many ways you can think of, using a different criterion for each grouping. List the sorting criteria in the order they were employed, describe each criterion and specify its corresponding grouping.

(1) $y = 2x - 1$	(9) $(2x+1)^3 = 8$	(17) $y = 2x^2 + 1$	(25) 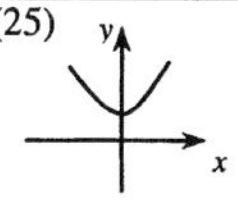
(2) $y = (2x-1)^2$	(10) 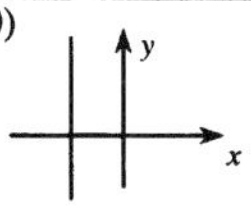	(18) $x^2 + y^2 = 9$	(26) $y = (2x+1)(x-1)$
(3) $y = -x + 1$	(11) $y = 1$	(19) $2x + 1 = 0$	(27) $y = (2x+1)^2$
(4) $y = \frac{1}{x} + 1$	(12) $(2x+1)^2 = 9$	(20) 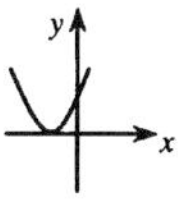	(28) $2x + 1 = 8$
(5) 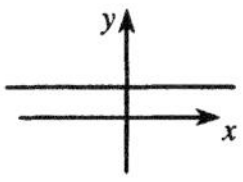	(13) $2x^2 + 1 = 0$	(21) $y = 2x^2 + 3x + 1$	(29) $y = (2x+1)^3$
(6) $x = -\frac{1}{2}$	(14) 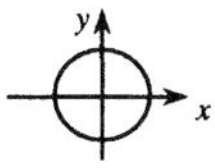	(22) $y = 2x + 3$	(30) $y = 2x + 1$
(7) $(2x+1)^3 = 0$	(15) $y = x^3 + 1$	(23) $(2x+1)^2 = 0$	(31) 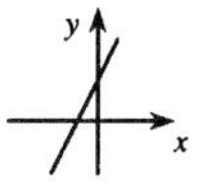
(8) 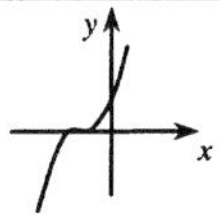	(16) $y = 3x - 1$	(24) $y = 2x - \frac{1}{2}$	(32) $y = (x-2)^2$

Figure 7. A sorting task.

classroom depends on the teacher" (NCTM, 2000, p. 25). The extensive body of research on the use of technology in mathematics teaching (see, e.g., Yerushalmy & Chazan, 1990, 2002; Wilson & Goldenberg, 1998; Hadas, Hershkowitz, & Schwarz, 2000; Laborde, 2001) has revealed that many unexpected difficulties arise when technology is used in mathematics classrooms. Nevertheless, Laborde (2001) found that the use of technology in mathematics teaching can serve as a springboard for restructuring teachers' mathematics.

Thus, we argue that the roles of mathematics teacher educators should include enhancing teachers' awareness of the potential of technology, by offering convincing evidence that it is both possible and worthwhile to use technology in classrooms. Using technology in investigative classroom contexts can foster conceptual understanding. On the other hand, we wish to emphasize at the outset that educators should prepare teachers to be critical and aware of the limitations of such media, so that they will be in a position to make mindful judgments and decisions with respect to their use in teaching and learning.

Task 5 (see Figure 8) addresses the need to develop a critical mindset with respect to technology. It was developed and studied by Zaslavsky and Leikin (submitted) in undergraduate and inservice courses. In fact, the task was first set in the context of geometry problem solving in an undergraduate methods course, with no particular intended use of technology in mind. Over time, through observing and reflecting on preservice and inservice teachers' work on the problem, the two MTEs gained insight regarding different approaches to the problem and the learning opportunities that the task can open.

This task has proved to be challenging for many inservice teachers. Most find it hard to solve the problem without using technology. This in itself is an important feature of the task – it lends itself well for initiating exploration in a dynamic geometry environment (e.g., *Geometric Supposer*, or *Geometer's Sketchpad*). However, once teachers begin working on the task they realize that the environment presents unforeseen challenges in terms of search strategies.

Teachers tend to begin with 'free search' strategies. The first strategy they usually employ is "moving a random point (in the triangle) to fit the condition". However, this strategy does not yield a point that precisely fulfils the condition. Figure 9(a) depicts the position of a very 'close' but not 'exact' point.

Another, more structured 'free search' approach, which some teachers employ, is based on an analysis of the ratio between the distances of the intended point from two sides of the triangle. Teachers try to find a point position for which the ratio of its distances from two of the given triangle sides is inverse to the ratio of the lengths of the respective sides. Although they can prove that for such a point the areas of the two relevant triangles are equal, on the screen this

---

Task 5

In a given Triangle *ABC*, is there a point P in the triangle such that the areas of triangles *ABP*, *ACP*, and *BCP* are equal?

Does your answer depend on the type of the triangle? If it does, how does it?

If it does not (in other words, if such a point exists in any triangle), how many points that fulfil this condition exist in a triangle? Explain your answer.

Figure 8.   Task 5.

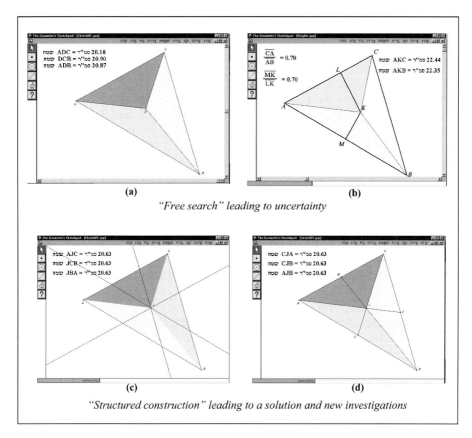

(a)

"Free search" leading to uncertainty

(c)   (d)

"Structured construction" leading to a solution and new investigations

Figure 9.   Different outcomes of the search strategies in Task 5.

still does not yield the intended point. Those who do this often cannot believe their eyes: the ratios are of inverse values, but still the areas are not equal (see Figure 9(b)).

At this point teachers begin to use more structured approaches to find the point. One approach is finding an intersection of the 'level lines', and the other is 'examining special points in the triangle'. Each of these strategies yields a point that exactly satisfies the required condition (see Figures 9(c) and 9(d)). The next question that comes up naturally is: *Do these points coincide?*

Through reflective discussions teachers become aware of the limitations of the media with respect to 'free search' strategies, opposed to its potential with respect to more structured approaches. Thus, they begin to evaluate the strengths and weaknesses of the environment.

4.6. *Learning from Students' Thinking: The Case of Probability and Fair Game*

Developing an awareness of, and sensitivity to, learners' mathematical thinking and preconceptions has been recognized as an important factor in the development of mathematics educators (e.g., Maher & Alston, 1990; Carpenter & Fennema, 1992). In order to incorporate this aspect of professional development the following task, 'A Game for Two Players with Two Dice', was used. It was originally designed by Maher (1995) as part of a larger study at Rutgers University.

Following the favorable outcomes reported by Maher on U.S. students' ways of reasoning with such tasks, Task 6 (see Figure 10) was presented to a pair of 5th grade Israeli students, Shani and Danit, who were videotaped as they worked on the problem. Their session was transcribed, and parts of the transcription were used in an inservice workshop for mathematics teachers. In this workshop teachers were first given the same task (i.e., Task 6) to work on and, after they had done so, were presented with the protocol of Shani and Danit. They were then asked to react to that protocol (Zaslavsky, 1998).

A pair of inservice teachers, Yael and Miriam, who were working on the task, wondered whether (1, 2) was the same outcome as (2, 1), and whether (1, 2) and (3, 3) were equally likely outcomes. (Note that their notation (1, 2) designated that '1' appeared on one die and '2' on the other one, while (2, 1) designated the 'reverse'.)

It was only after several trials and dice tossing that Miriam changed her mind and seemed convinced that there were twice as many outcomes when the numbers were different than when they were the same. They both realized that the tossing of the dice provided supporting evidence that the game was not fair. In fact, Player A got a point in 8 of the 21 possible outcomes whereas Player B got a point in the remaining 13 possible outcomes.

At this point, the teachers were presented with the protocol in which Shani and Danit proposed to change the original game, so that player A would get a point if the sum were 3, 8, 9, 10, or 12 and player B would get a point if the sum were 2, 4, 5, 7, or 11. Yael and Miriam realized right away that this new

---

Task 6

Game Directions: Assign Player A and Player B. Roll two dice.
If the sum of the two dice is 2, 3, 4, 10, 11, or 12, Player A gets 1 point (and Player B gets 0).
If the sum is 5, 6, 7, 8, or 9, Player B gets 1 point (and Player A gets 0).
Continue rolling the dice. The first player to get 10 points is the winner.

1. Is this a fair game? Why or why not?

2. Play the game with a partner. (You can play several games if you need to). Do the results of playing the game support your answer to Question 1? Explain.

3. If you think the game is unfair, how could you change it so that it would be fair?

Figure 10.   A dice game for two players.

game was also not fair, and began to consider ways to convince Shani and Danit that it wasn't fair:

Yael: Did they play their version of the game? Because if they did, they would learn more things – that the sum is not enough.

Facilitator: Why don't you play the game Shani and Danit suggested and see if it's fair?

Yael: We know it is not fair, because they didn't refer to the multiplication of possibilities, so unless it somehow evens up, it is not fair.

They were persuaded to try to play the game, and after a few games realized that this time the tossing did not support their claim.

Miriam: It's almost equivalent.

Yael: Wow, it's even. Now let's count ... it's 15 [possible outcomes] and 16 [possible outcomes], so it's really hard to notice.

Miriam: It's almost the same. This game is sort of fair.

Facilitator: So, what would you suggest to Shani and Danit?

Yael and Miriam began to analyze carefully the mathematical reasoning that led Shani and Danit to their suggestion. They realized that unlike the first game they tried – for the new game that Shani and Danit proposed – playing this game would not be helpful, since there is only a slight difference in favor of Player B (16 compared to 15 possible outcomes). They had to think of a different approach, which they had not considered before. Thus, they decided to try to turn to a simpler case and convince Shani and Danit that outcomes 2 and 3 are not equally likely. They decided on a simple game in which Player A gets 1 point if the sum is 2, and Player B gets 1 point if the sum is 3. They tried it out for a large number of tosses and were then confident that this would better demonstrate the difference between the likelihood of these two outcomes than would the game that was suggested by Shani and Danit. In fact, the need to react to Shani and Danit's way of thinking led the teachers as well as the teacher educator to gain insight into the limitations of using empirical evidence for falsifying a general claim.

The above task as a whole, the setting, and the way it developed in the context of an inservice professional development programme illustrates once again what we consider powerful tasks.

More specifically, it supports the following claims that powerful tasks may:

- be equally challenging mathematically for (5th grade) students as for teachers;
- provide opportunities for teachers to develop their mathematical (in this case, probabilistic) thinking through personal experiences;
- foster teachers' awareness and appreciation of students' creative ways of reasoning and problem solving. Furthermore, such tasks may assist teachers to recognize that they may face similar problems as students do (e.g., in this

case: What constitutes evidence? What is fair? What is an appropriate outcome space?). Thus they are likely to develop sensitivity to students as well as a disposition that acknowledges students' difficulties as legitimate and understandable;
- elicit teachers' pedagogical considerations in an attempt to design a specific task to draw students' attention to the mathematical implications of their suggestions (rather than 'telling' them what the 'right answer' is).

In addition to the task's contribution to the teachers, the facilitator (i.e., teacher educator) developed her own educative power through observations of and reflections on Miriam and Yael's struggle to make sense of the task in ways that she had not anticipated.

5. CONCLUDING REMARKS

The professional growth of mathematics educators – including teachers, teacher educators, and educators of teacher educators – is an ongoing lifelong process of a dual nature. It occurs through direct and indirect learning, often by reciprocally switching from acting as a learner to facilitating learning for others. In this process tasks play a critical role.

The interplay between teaching, learning, and tasks has been an important issue with respect to students' learning (e.g., Leinhardt, Zaslavsky, & Stein, 1990). In our paper we elaborated on the connections between teaching, learning and tasks with respect to mathematics educators. In this context, as portrayed in our model of mathematics educators growth (Figure 1), tasks also have a dual nature: they are the content by which direct learning is facilitated; however, by a reflective process of constructing and implementing them, they become a means for indirect learning of the facilitator.

The duality between 'content' and 'means' can be seen in other aspects and trends of professional development as well. For example, a narrative or case can be used as the object of reflection or a process of reflection. As object, it refers to a product built from the information provided by experience. As process, it is associated with developing the product. The product, in return, may be viewed as both consequence and content of reflective thinking (Chapman, 1999b).

Our framework points to the complexities of the terrain of professional development. We suggest that the intricacy of this domain calls for further study of the interrelations between the various communities of mathematics educators in the processes of their ongoing growth, with particular consideration of both inhibiting and contributing factors.

REFERENCES

Adler, J. (1996). Lave and Wenger's social practice theory and teaching and learning school mathematics. In L. Puig & A. Gutierrez (Eds.), *Proceedings of the 12th Conference of the International*

Group for the Psychology of Mathematics education, (Vol. 2, pp. 3–10). Valencia, Spain: University of Valencia.

Adler, J. (1998). Lights and limits: Recontextualising Lave and Wegner to theorise knowledge of teaching and of learning school mathematics. In A. Watson (Ed.), *Situated cognition and the learning of mathematics* (pp. 161–177). Oxford: Centre for Mathematics Education Research.

Aichele, D. B., & Coxford, A. G. (Eds.) (1994). *Professional development for teachers of mathematics. 1994 Yearbook.* Reston, VA: National Council of Teachers of Mathematics.

Askew, M. (2001). Policy, practice and principles in teaching numeracy: What makes a difference? In P. Gates (Ed.), *Issues in mathematics teaching* (pp. 105–119). London: Routledge.

Ball, D. L. (1996). Teacher learning and the mathematics reforms: What we think we know and what we need to learn. *Phi Delta Kappan,* (March), 500–508.

Ball, D. L. (1997). Developing mathematics reform: What don't we know about teacher learning – but would make good working hypotheses? In S. N. Friel & G. W. Bright (Eds.), *Reflecting on our work: NSF teacher enhancement in K-6 mathematics* (pp. 77–111). Lanham, MD: University Press of America, Inc.

Bobis, J. (1998). Partnerships with practising teachers: Action research in practice. In N. Ellerton (Ed.), *Issues in mathematics education: A contemporary perspective* (pp. 18–40). Perth, Australia: Edith Cowan University.

Borasi, R. (1992). *Learning mathematics through inquiry.* Portsmouth, NH: Heinemann Educational Books, Inc.

Borasi, R., Fonzi, J., Smith, C. F., & Rose, B. J. (1999). Beginning the process of rethinking mathematics instruction: A professional development program. *Journal of Mathematics Teacher Education, 2,* 49–78.

Borko, H., & Putnam, R. T. (1995). Expanding a teacher's knowledge base. In T. R. Guskey & M. Huberman (Eds.), *Professional development in education* (pp. 35–65). New York: Teachers College Press.

Brown, C. A., & Borko, H. (1992). Becoming a mathematics teacher. In D. A. Grouws (Ed.), *Handbook of research on mathematics teaching and learning* (pp. 209–239). New York: Macmillan.

Brown, J. R. (1999). *Philosophy of mathematics: An introduction to the world of proofs and pictures.* London: Routledge.

Brown, S. I. (1996). Towards humanistic mathematics education. In A. J. Bishop, K. Clements, C. Keitel, J. Kilpatrick & C. Laborde (Eds.), *International handbook of mathematics education* (pp. 1289–1321). Dordrecht, The Netherlands: Kluwer Academic Publishers.

Bruner, J. (1986). *Actual minds, possible worlds.* Cambridge, MA: Harvard University Press.

Calderhead, J. (1989). Reflective teaching and teacher education. *Teaching and Teacher Education, 5*(1), 43–51.

Carpenter, T. P., & Fennema, E. (1992). Cognitively guided instruction: Building on the knowledge of students and teachers. *International Journal of Research in Education, 17,* 457–470.

Carter, K. (1993). The place of story in the study of teaching and teacher education. *Educational Researcher, 22*(1), 5–12, 18.

Chambers, D. L., & Hankes, J. E. (1994). Using knowledge of children's thinking to change teaching. In D. B. Aichele & A. G. Coxford (Eds.), *Professional development for teachers of mathematics. 1994 Yearbook* (pp. 286–295). Reston, VA: National Council of Teachers of Mathematics.

Chapman, O. (1993). Facilitating in-service mathematics teachers' self-development. In I. Hirabayashi, N. Nohda, K. Shigematsu & F-L. Lin (Eds.), *Proceedings of the 17th International Conference of the Psychology of Mathematics Education* (Vol. 1, pp. 228–235). Tsukuba, Ibaraki, Japan: University of Japan.

Chapman, O. (1999a). Inservice teacher development in mathematical problem solving. *Journal of Mathematics Teacher Education, 2,* 121–142.

Chapman, O. (1999b). Reflection in mathematics education: The storying approach. In N. F. Ellerton (Ed.), *Mathematics teacher development: International perspectives* (pp. 201–216). Perth, Australia: Meridian Press

Clements, M. A., & Ellerton, N. F. (1996). *Mathematics education research: Past, present and future.* Bangkok: UNESCO.

Cobb, P. (2000). Conducting teaching experiments in collaboration with teachers. In A. E. Kelly & R. A. Lesh (Eds.), *Handbook of research design in mathematics and science education* (pp. 307–333). Mahwah, NJ: Lawrence Erlbaum Associates, Publishers.

Cobb, P., & McClain, K. (2001). An approach for supporting teachers' learning in social context. In F.-L. Lin & T. J. Cooney (Eds.), *Making sense of mathematics teacher education* (pp. 207–231). Dordrecht, The Netherlands: Kluwer Academic Publishers.

Cooney, T. J. (1994). Teacher education as an exercise in adaptation. In D. B. Aichele & A. F. Coxford (Eds.), *Professional development for teachers of mathematics. 1994 Yearbook* (pp. 9–22). Reston, VA: National Council of Teachers of Mathematics.

Cooney, T. J. (2001). Considering the paradoxes, perils, and purposes of conceptualizing teacher development. In F.-L. Lin & T. J. Cooney (Eds.), *Making sense of mathematics teacher education* (pp. 9–31). Dordrecht, The Netherlands: Kluwer Academic Publishers.

Cooney, T. J., & Krainer, K. (1996). Inservice mathematics teacher education: The importance of listening. In A. J. Bishop, K. Clements, C. Keitel, J. Kilpatrick & C. Laborde (Eds.), *International handbook of mathematics education* (pp. 1155–1185). Dordrecht, The Netherlands: Kluwer Academic Publishers.

Crawford, K., & Adler, J. (1996). Teachers as researchers in mathematics education. In A. J. Bishop, K. Clements, C. Keitel, J. Kilpatrick & C. Laborde (Eds.), *International handbook of mathematics education* (pp. 1187–1205). Dordrecht, The Netherlands: Kluwer Academic Publishers.

Davis, R. B., Maher, C. A., & Noddings, N. (Eds.) (1990). *Constructivist views on the teaching and learning of mathematics.* Monograph No. 4, *Journal of Research in Mathematics Education.*

Dewey, J. (1933). *How we think: A restatement of the relation of reflective thinking to the educative process.* Boston: D. C. Heath and Co.

Dhombres, J. (1993). Is one proof enough? Travels with a mathematician of the Baroque period. *Educational Studies in Mathematics, 24*, 401–419.

Dörfler, W. (1999). Mathematics provides tools for thinking and communicating. In C. Hoyles, C. Morgan & G. Woodhouse (Eds.), *Rethinking the mathematics curriculum.* (pp. 63–77). London: Falmer Press.

Edwards, T. G., & Hensien, S. M. (1999). Changing instructional practice through action research. *Journal of Mathematics Teacher Education, 2*, 187–206.

Ellerton, N. F. (Ed.) (1999). *Mathematics teacher development: International perspectives.* Perth, Australia: Meridian Press.

Even, R. (1999). The development of teacher leaders and inservice teacher educators. *Journal of Mathematics Teacher Education, 2*(1), 3–24.

Even, R. (1999). Integrating academic and practical knowledge in a teacher leaders' development program. In D. Tirosh (Ed.), *Forms of mathematical knowledge: Learning and teaching with understanding* (pp. 235–252). Dordrecht, The Netherlands: Kluwer Academic Publishers.

Grant, T. J., Hiebert, J., & Wearne, D. (1998). Observing and teaching reform-minded lessons: What do teachers see? *Journal of Mathematics Teacher Education, 1*(2), 217–236.

Hadas, N., Hershkowitz, R., & Schwarz, B. (2000). The role of contradiction and uncertainty in promoting the need to prove in dynamic geometry environments. *Educational Studies in Mathematics, 44*, 127–150.

Halai, A. (1998). Mentor, mentee, and mathematics: A story of professional development. *Journal of Mathematics Teacher Education, 1*(3), 295–315.

Holly, P. (1991). Action research: The missing link in the creation of schools as centers of inquiry. In A. Liberman & L. Miller (Eds.), *Staff development for education in the 90's: New demands, new realities, new perspectives* (pp. 133–157). New York: Teachers College Press.

Jaworski, B. (1994). *Investigating mathematics teaching: A constructivist enquiry.* London: Falmer Press.

Jaworski, B. (1998). Mathematics teacher research: Process, practice, and the development of teaching. *Journal of Mathematics Teacher Education, 1*(1), 3–31.

Jaworski, B. (2001). Developing mathematics teaching: Teachers, teacher educators, and researchers as co-learners. In F.-L. Lin & T. J. Cooney (Eds.), *Making sense of mathematics teacher education* (pp. 295–320). Dordrecht, The Netherlands: Kluwer Academic Publishers.

Jaworski, B., Wood, T., & Dawson, A. J. (Eds.) (1999). *Mathematics teacher education: Critical international perspectives.* London: Falmer Press.

Keiny, S. (1994). Constructivism and teachers' professional development. *Teaching and Teacher Education, 10*(2), 157–167.

Krainer, K. (1993). Powerful tasks: A contribution to a high level of acting and reflecting in mathematics instruction. *Educational Studies in Mathematics, 24*, 65–93.

Krainer, K. (1998). Some considerations on problems and perspectives of inservice mathematics teacher education. In C. Alsina, J. M. Alvarez, J. Hodgson, C. Laborde & A. Pérex (Eds.), *Eighth International Congress on Mathematics Education: Selected lectures* (pp. 303–321). Sevilla, Spain: S. A. E. M. Thales.

Krainer, K. (2001). Teachers' growth is more than the growth of individual teachers: The case of Gisela. In F.-L. Lin & T. J. Cooney (Eds.), *Making sense of mathematics teacher education* (pp. 271–293). Dordrecht, The Netherlands: Kluwer Academic Publishers.

Laborde, C. (2001). The use of new technologies as a vehicle for restructuring teachers' mathematics. In F.-L. Lin & T. J. Cooney (Eds.), *Making sense of mathematics teacher education* (pp. 87–109). Dordrecht, The Netherlands: Kluwer Academic Publishers.

Laing, R. A., & Mayer, R. A. (1994). The Michigan math inservice project. In D. B. Aichele & A. G. Coxford (Eds.), *Professional development for teachers of mathematics. 1994 Yearbook* (pp. 255–265). Reston, VA: National Council of Teachers of Mathematics.

Lampert, M. (1990). When the problem is not the question and the solution is not the answer: Mathematical knowing and teaching. *American Educational Research Journal, 27*(1), 29–64.

Lave, J., & Wenger, E. (1991). *Situated learning: Legitimate peripheral participation.* Cambridge: Cambridge University Press.

Leikin, R. (1997). *Symmetry as a way of thought – A tool for professional development of mathematics teachers.* Unpublished doctoral dissertation, Technion, Haifa (in Hebrew).

Leikin, R. (in press). Problem-solving preferences of mathematics teachers: Focusing on symmetry. *Journal of Mathematics Teacher Education.*

Leikin, R., Berman, A., & Zaslavsky, O. (2000). Learning through teaching: The case of symmetry. *Mathematics Education Research Journal, 12*, 16–34.

Leikin, R., & Winicki-Landman, G. (2000). On equivalent and non-equivalent definitions II. *For the Learning of Mathematics, 20*(2), 24–29.

Leikin, R., & Winicki-Landman, G. (2001). Defining as a vehicle for professional development of secondary school mathematics teachers. *Mathematics Teacher Education and Development, 3*, 62–73.

Leikin, R., Zaslavsky, O., & Brandon, D. (2002, July). *Development of excellence in mathematics as a springboard for professional development of mathematics teachers.* Paper presented at the 8th Conference of the European Council for High Ability (ECHA), Rhodes.

Lerman, S. (2001). A review of research perspectives on mathematics teacher education. In F.-L. Lin & T. J. Cooney (Eds.), *Making sense of mathematics teacher education* (pp. 33–52). Dordrecht, The Netherlands: Kluwer Academic Publishers.

Leinhardt, G., Zaslavsky, O., & Stein, M. K. (1990). Functions, graphs and graphing: Tasks, learning and teaching. *Review of Educational Research, 60*(1), 1–64.

Ma, L. (1999). *Knowing and teaching elementary mathematics: Teachers' understanding of fundamental mathematics in China and the United States.* Mahwah, NJ: Lawrence Erlbaum Associates.

Maher, C. A. (1995). Children's development of ideas in probability and statistics: Studies from classroom research. *Bulletin of the International Statistical Institute, 2*, Beijing.

Maher, C. A., & Alston, A. (1990). Teacher development in mathematics in a constructivist framework. *Journal for Research in Mathematics Education.* Monograph No. 4, 147–165.

Mason, J. (1998). Enabling teachers to be real teachers: Necessary levels of awareness and structure of attention. *Journal of Mathematics Teacher Education, 1*(3), 243–267.

Miller, L. D., & Hunt, N. P. (1994). Professional development through action research. In D. B. Aichele & A. G. Coxford (Eds.), *Professional development for teachers of mathematics. 1994 Yearbook* (pp. 296–303). Reston, VA: National Council of Teachers of Mathematics.

National Council of Teachers of Mathematics (NCTM) (1991). *Professional standards for the teaching of school mathematics*. Reston, VA: Author.

National Council of Teachers of Mathematics (NCTM) (2000). *Principles and standards for school mathematics*. Reston, VA: Author.

Polya, G. (1963). On learning, teaching, and learning teaching. *American Mathematical Monthly, 70*, 605–619.

Richert, A. E. (1991). Using teacher cases for reflection and enhanced understanding. In A. Liberman & L. Miller (Eds.), *Staff development for education in the 90's: New demands, new realities, new perspectives* (pp. 113–132). New York: Teachers College Press.

Richert, A. E. (1992). Writing cases: A vehicle for inquiry into the teaching process. In J. H. Shulman (Ed.), *Case methods in teacher education*. New York: Teachers College Press.

Rogoff, B. (1990). *Apprenticeship in thinking: Cognitive development in social context*. New York: Oxford University Press.

Romberg, T. A., & Collins, A. (2000). The impact of standards-based reform methods of research in schools. In A. E. Kelly & R. A. Lesh (Eds.), *Handbook of research design in mathematics and science education* (pp. 73–85). Mahwah, NJ: Lawrence Erlbaum Associates.

Schifter, D. (1993). *Reconstructing mathematics education: Stories of teachers meeting the challenge of reform*. New York: Teachers College Press.

Schifter, D. (Ed.) (1996). *What's happening in math class? Envisioning new practices through teacher narratives* (2 vols.). New York: Teachers College Press.

Schoenfeld, A. H. (1989). Explorations of students' mathematical beliefs and behavior. *Journal for Research in Mathematics Education, 20*(4), 338–355.

Schön, D. A. (1983). *The reflective practitioner: How professionals think in action*. New York: Basic Books.

Schön, D. A. (1987). *Educating the reflective practitioner*. Oxford, UK: Jossey-Bass.

Schön, D. A. (1991). *The Reflective Practitioner* (2nd ed.). London: Temple Smith.

Shir, K., & Zaslavsky, O. (2001). What constitutes a (goood) defiition? The case of square. In M. van den Heuvel-Panhuizen (Ed.), *Proceedings of the 25th Annual Conference of the International Group for the Psychology of Mathematics Education* (Vol. 4, pp. 161–168). Utrecht, The Netherlands: Utrecht University.

Shulman, L. S. (1992). Towards a pedagogy of cases. In J. H. Shulman (Ed.), *Case methods in teacher education* (pp. 1–30). New York: Teachers College Press.

Silver, E. A., & Marshall S. P. (1990). Mathematical and scientific problem solving: Findings, issues, and instructional implications. In B. F. Jones & L. Idol (Eds.): *Dimensions of thinking and cognitive instruction* (Vol. 1, pp. 265–290). Hillsdale, New Jersey: Lawrence Erlbaum Associates.

Silver, E. A. (1979). Student perceptions of relatedness among mathematical verbal problems. *Journal for Research in Mathematics Education, 10*, 195–210.

Simon, M. A., & Schifter, D. (1991). Towards a constructivist perspective: An intervention study of mathematics teacher development. *Education Studies in Mathematics, 22*, 309–331.

Simon, M. A., & Schifter, D. (1992). Assessing teachers' development of a constructivist view of mathematics learning. *Teaching and Teacher Education, 8*(2), 187–197.

Simon, M. A. (1995). Reconstructing mathematics pedagogy from constructivist perspective. *Journal for Research in Mathematics Education, 24*, 114–145.

Stein, M. K., Smith, M. S., Henningsen, M., & Silver, E. A. (2000). *Implementing standards-based mathematics instruction: A casebook for professional development*. New York: Teachers College Press.

Steinbring, H. (1998). Elements of epistemological knowledge for mathematics teachers. *Journal of Mathematics Teacher Education, 1*(2), 157–189.

Stigler, J. W., & Hiebert, J. (1999). *The teaching gap: Best ideas from the world's teachers for improving education in the classroom*. New York: The Free Press.

Sullivan, P., & Mousley, J. (2001). Thinking teaching: Seeing mathematics teachers as active decision makers. In F.-L. Lin & T. J. Cooney (Eds.), *Making sense of mathematics teacher education* (pp. 147–163). Dordrecht, The Netherlands: Kluwer Academic Publishers.

Tzur, R. (2001). Becoming a mathematics teacher educator: Conceptualizing the terrain through self-reflective analysis. *Journal of Mathematics Teacher Education, 4*(4), 259–283.

van Dormolen, J., & Zaslavsky, O. (in press). The many facets of a definition: The case of periodicity. *Journal of Mathematical Behavior.*

von Glasersfeld, E. (1995). A constructivist approach to teaching. In L. P. Steffe & J. Gale (Eds.), *Constructivism in education* (pp. 3–15). Mahwah, NJ: Lawrence Erlbaum Associates.

Vygotsky, L. (1978). *Mind and society.* Boston, MA: Harvard University Press.

Walen, S. B., & Williams, S. R. (2000). Validating classroom issues: Case method in support of teacher change. *Journal of Mathematics Teacher Education, 3*(1), 3–26.

Wilson, M. R., & Goldenberg, M. P. (1998). Some conceptions are difficult to change: One middle school mathematics teacher's struggle. *Journal of Mathematics Teacher Education, 1*(3), 269–293.

Witherell, C., & Noddings, N. (1991). *Stories lives tell: Narrative and dialogue in education.* New York: Teachers College Press.

Yerushalmy, M., Chazan, D., & Gordon, M. (1990). Mathematical problem posing: Implications for facilitating student inquiry in classrooms. *Instructional Science, 19,* 219–245.

Yerushalmy, M., & Chazan, D. (1990). Overcoming visual obstacles with the aid of the Supposer. *Educational Studies in Mathematics, 21,* 199–219.

Yerushalmy, M., & Chazan, D. (2002). Flux in school algebra: Curricular change, graphing technology, and research on students' learning and teacher knowledge. In L. English (Ed.), *Handbook of international research in mathematics education* (pp. 725–755). London: Lawrence Erlbaum Associates.

Zaslavsky, O. (1989, April). *Teachers' conceptions of instructional examples: The case of functions and graphs.* Paper presented at the Annual Meeting of the American Educational Research Association, San Francisco.

Zaslavsky, O. (1995). Open-ended tasks as a trigger for mathematics teachers' professional development. *For the Learning of Mathematics, 15*(3), 15–20.

Zaslavsky, O. (1998, April). *Teachers' learning from students' thinking: The case of probability.* Paper presented at a Symposium on 'Classroom Research on Students' Probabilistic thinking', NCTM Research Pre-session, Washington D. C.

Zaslavsky, O. (submitted). *Seizing the opportunity to create uncertainty in mathematics education.*

Zaslavsky, O., & Leikin, R. (1999). Interweaving the training of mathematics teacher educators and the professional development of mathematics teachers. In O. Zaslavsky (Ed.), *Proceedings of the 23rd Conference of the International Group for the Psychology of Mathematics Education* (Vol. 1, pp. 143–158). Haifa, Israel: Technion.

Zaslavsky, O., & Leikin, R. (in press). Professional development of mathematics teacher educators: Growth through practice. *Journal of Mathematics Teacher Education.*

Zaslavsky, O., & Leikin, R. (submitted). *Enhancing and inhibiting factors of problem solving processes in a dynamic geometry environment.*

Zaslavsky, O., Sela, H., & Leron, U. (2002): Being sloppy about slope – The effect of changing the scale. *Educational Studies in Mathematics, 49*(1), 119–140.

List of Principal Authors

Prof. J Adler, School of Science Education, University of the Witwatersrand, Private Bag 3, PO Wits 2050, South Africa. E-mail: adlerj@educ.wits.ac.za

Prof. B Atweh, School of Mathematics, Science and Technology Education, Queensland University of Technology, Victoria Park Road, Kelvin Grove, QLD 4059, Australia. E-mail: b.atweh@qut.edu.au

Dr AJC Begg, CME, M + C, The Open University, Milton Keynes, MK7 6AA, UK. E-mail: a.j.c.begg@open.ac.uk

Prof. AJ Bishop, Associate Dean, Faculty of Education, PO Box 6, Monash University, Victoria 3800, Australia. E-mail: alan.bishop@education.monash.edu.au

Prof. J Boaler, School of Education, 485 Lasuen Mall, Stanford University, Stanford, CA 94305-3096, USA. E-mail: joboaler@Stanford.edu

Prof. C Breen, Department of Education, University of Cape Town, Private Bag, Rondebosch 7701, South Africa. E-mail: cb@education.uct.ac.za

Prof. D Clarke, Department of Science and Mathematics Education, Faculty of Education, The University of Melbourne, Victoria 3010, Australia. E-mail: d.clarke@unimelb.edu.au

Prof. MA Clements, Sultan Hassanal Bolkiah Institute of Education, Universiti Brunei Darussalam, Jalan Tungku Link, Gadong, BE 1410, Brunei Darussalam. E-mail: clements @shbie.ubd.edu.bn

Dr T Cooney, Department of Mathematics Education, The University of Georgia, 105 Aderhold Hall, Athens, GA 30602-7124, USA. E-mail: Proftcooney@aol.com

Dr G FitzSimons, 34 The Boulevard, Warrandyte, Victoria 3113, Australia. E-mail: gail.fitzsimons@education.monash.edu.au

Dr P Gates, University of Nottingham, School of Education, Wollaton Road, Nottingham, NG8 1BB, UK. E-mail: peter.gates@nottingham.ac.uk

Prof. C Hoyles, Mathematical Sciences Group, Institute of Education, University of London, UK. E-mail: choyles@ioe.ac.uk

Dr E Jablonka, Freie Universität Berlin, Fachbereich Erziehungswissenschaften und Psychology, Habelschwerdter Allee 45, 14195 Berlin, Germany. E-mail: jablonka @zedat.fu-berlin.de

Prof. B Jaworski, Department of Educational Studies, The University of Oxford, Oxford, OX2 6PY, UK. E-mail: barbara.jaworski@hia.no

Prof. C Keitel, Freie Universität Berlin, Habelschwerdter Allee 45, 14195 Berlin, Germany. E-mail: keitel@zedat.fu-berlin.de

Dr J Kilpatrick, 105 Aderhold Hall, University of Georgia, Athens, GA 30602-7124, USA. E-mail: jkilpat@coe.uga.edu

Prof. J-B Lagrange, DIDIREM (Paris VII) and Teacher Education Institute of Reims, France. E-mail: lagrange@univ-rennes1.fr

Dr FKS Leung, Faculty of Education, The University of Hong Kong, Hong Kong. E-mail: hraslks@hkucc.hku.hk

Prof. J Mousley, Faculty of Education, Deakin University, Australia. E-mail: j.mousley@deakin.edu.au

Prof. M Stephens, Department of Science and Mathematics Education, Faculty of Education, The University of Melbourne, Victoria 3010, Australia. E-mail: m.stephens@unimelb.edu

Prof. MOJ Thomas, Mathematics Education, Department of Mathematics, The University of Auckland, New Zealand. E-mail: m.thomas@math.auckland.ac.nz

Dr D Tirosh, School of Education, Tel-Aviv University, Tel-Aviv 69978, Israel. E-mail: dina@post.tau.ac.il

Dr M van den Heuvel-Panhuizen, Freudenthal Institute, Utrecht University, Aidadreef 12, 3561 GE Utrecht, The Netherlands. E-mail: M.vandenHeuvel@fi.uu.nl

Dr R Vithal, Faculty of Education, University of Durban-Westville, Private Bag X54001, Durban 4000, South Africa. E-mail: rvithal@pixie.udw.ac.za

Dr D Wiliam, Kings College London, Franklin-Wilkins Bldg, 150 Stamford Street, London, SE1 9NN, UK. E-mail: dylan.wiliam@kcl.ac.uk

Prof. N-Y Wong, Department of Curriculum and Instruction, The Chinese University of Hong Kong, Hong Kong. E-mail: nywong@cuhk.edu.hk

Prof. D Woodrow, Manchester Metropolitan University, Institute of Education, Crewe Green Road, Crewe, CW1 5DU, UK. E-mail: derek.woodrow@ntlworld.com

Dr O Zaslavsky, Technion, Department of Science Education, Haifa 32000, Israel. E-mail: orit@techunix.technion.ac.il

Index of Names

Abboud, M. 550
Adajian, L. 65, 554, 645
Adamson, R. 329
Adda, J. 111
Adler, Jill
  action research 883
  change 676
  ethical issues in research 436, 441–70
  generativity 578
  language 45
  multiculturalism 548
  poverty 550
  social practice 878
  teacher research 525, 529, 531, 539–41
  teaching materials 65
Agherdien, G. 540
Agudelo, C. 221, 555
Ahmed, A. 355, 610
Aichele, D. B. 605, 892–3
Ainley, J. 251, 266–7, 334, 336
Akiba, M. 167–9
Albright, M. 803
Alexander, R. 166, 173, 718
Allchin, D. 720–1, 735
Alston, A. 895, 910
Anderson, A. 477
Anderson, G. L. 575–6
Anderson, J. R. 253–4, 255, 263–4, 326
Anderson, L. W. 168
Anderson, R. 653
Anderson, S. E. 36–7
Anderson-Levitt, K. M. 168
Andrewartha, G. 381
Andrews, P. 59
Ang, K. C. 36
Anthony, G. 115
Anzul, M. 503, 512
Aplin, N. 720
Apple, M. W.
  critical perspectives 568
  inequalities 18
  National Curriculum 207
  power 12, 25, 43
  reflexivity 577
  skill jobs 78
  social class 26–7
  standardized tests 697
Applebaum, P. 17
Appleby, J. C. 384
Arcavi, A. 77, 334, 359, 377

Archer, D. 127
Arias Ochoa, M. 221
Aristotle 471, 480, 482, 796, 807
Armstrong, B. E. 667–8
Armstrong, G. M. 363–4
Arnold, S. 276, 359
Aronowitz, S. 109
Artigue, Michèle
  didactical contract 506
  software games 273
  technology impact on curriculum 301–3, 305–6
  technology research 233, 235, 237–69
  transparency of technology 339
Artzt, A. F. 852–3
Arvold, B. 755, 845
Arzarello, F. 335
Ascher, Marcia 203, 735
Ascher, Robert 735
Asiala, M. 386
Askew, M. 120, 845, 853, 902, 904
Asp, G. 359, 379, 401
Atkin, J. M. 156, 157, 162, 174–6, 616
Atweh, Bill
  drain of expertise 15
  global context 6, 9–11, 14, 185–229
  globalization 106, 565
  social stratification 49
  universal mathematics 38
Au, W. K. 312
Aubrey, C. 845
Aus, B. 276
Ausubel, D. P. 313
Azuma, H. 159–60, 313

Back, K. 212
Bagnall, R. G. 108–9
Bailey, C. 275
Bailey, P. 85, 554
Baker, D. P. 82, 120, 167–9, 177, 553
Baker, E. 698
Balacheff, N.
  calculators 461–2
  Computer Algebra Systems 337, 339
  computer usage 474
  computer-based learning 301
  democratizing effect of software 463
  didactical contract 506
  dynamic geometry 334, 335
  epistemological penetration 475
  graphing software 336

learning situations   257
  student autonomy   813
  teacher/machine partnership   307
Ball, Deborah Loewenberg
  classroom practices   650
  elementary education   772–3, 803
  MATH project   398, 407–8, 841
  professional development   664, 878
  research practices   437, 491–521
  teacher learning   895
  technology in teacher education   399,
      407–8, 410, 423, 425–6
  unlearning   882
Bangert-Drowns, R.   238
Banu, H.   81
Bapoo, A.   456
Barab, S. A.   400–1, 415–16
Baranes, R.   651–2
Barber, P.   845
Barkai, R.   667
Barnes, M.   154, 157
Barnes Wallis, Neville   471–2
Barnett, C. S.   669–70, 842
Barrett, G.   276
Barro, R. J.   20
Barron, L.   410
Bartolini Bussi, M. G.   445
Barton, Bill   7, 12, 84, 203–4, 439, 548
Bass, Hyman   511, 518n1, 825
Bassey, M.   451, 454
Batanero, M. C.   494, 516–17
Battista, M. T.   171
Bauer, K.-O.   850
Baxter, G. P.   704
Beaton, A. E.   149–50, 161, 474
Becher, T.   113
Beck, Ulrich   106
Becker, Jerry R.   7, 145, 638, 646, 667,
      689–716
Begg, Andy   438–39, 533, 593–634
Begle, E. G.   473
Behr, M.   472
Beishuizen, M.   625
Bellah, R. N.   487
Beller, M.   163
Benacerraf, P.   797
Bendixen, L. D.   728
Benn, R.
  adult education   77, 111–13, 115–17, 123,
      128
  radical feminism   118
Benne, K.   658
Bentley, C. B.   103
Bentzen, M.   656
Berg, R.   333
Berger, E. J.   272

Bergsten, C.   368–9
Berlak, H.   703
Berliner, D. C.   173–4, 485
Berman, A.   898
Berman, R.   656
Berne, J.   455–6, 462, 486
Bernstein, Basil
  hierarchical rules   53
  official/pedagogic fields   208
  power relations   446
  recontextualization   501, 570
  research in conflict situations   573
  social class   44–5
  trainability   109
Berry, J. S.   37, 249, 258n4, 359
Bessot, A.   37
Beyer, K.   547
Bickmore-Brand, J.   123
Biddle, B. J.   25, 27–8, 550
Biehler, R.   37
Biggs, J. B.   313
Billett, S.   735
Birch, I.   110
Bird, T.   403, 424
Bishop, Alan J.
  adult education   112, 126
  changing role of teacher   307
  cultural perspective   201–2
  democratization   62–3
  disadvantaged groups   562
  ethnomathematics   299
  Formal/Informal/Non-formal Mathematics
      Education   106, 126–7, 129
  ICME conferences   194
  Introduction   ix–xiv
  journals   567
  mathematics activities   594
  mathematics/education relationship   593
  pan-cultural mathematics   84, 118, 202
  research   439, 472, 601, 606, 630n3
  similarity in research   201
  social enterprise   14
  teacher preparation   847
  technology research   235
  universals   202, 204–5
  values   48, 638–9, 717–65
Bishop, J.   656
Black, Paul J.
  assessment   513–15, 693, 698–9
  communication of research   513–15
  failure of research to impact
      practice   484–5
  international comparative research   156–7,
      162, 174–6
  resistance to change   616
Blackmore, P.   117

Blanchard, Maha 258n1
Bleicher, R. 49
Block, D. 486
Bloom, B. S. 723
Bloor, D. 553
Blum, W. 37, 89
Blume, G. 323
Boaler, Jo
  gender issues 547, 573
  IOWME 193–4
  Mathematics for All 36
  poverty 25–6
  research 437, 439, 491–521
  setting 59–60
  socio-cultural issues 553
  student behavior 562
Bobbitt, F. 605
Bobis, J. 844, 884
Boekaerts, M. 36
Boero, P. 553
Bohl, J. V. 852–3
Bohle-Carbonell, M. 96
Boileau, A. 264–5
Bond, Michael 722
Booß-Bavnbeck, B. 88–9, 96
Bookman, J. 363–4, 385
Booth, Lesley R. 306, 475
Borasi, R. 893–4, 904
Borba, M. C. 13–14, 17, 83, 557, 569–70
Borko, H. 878, 891–2, 898
Born, M. 797
Bosker, R. 699
Bottino, R. M. 653
Boulter, C. 533
Bounigev, M. M. 419
Bourdieu, Pierre 12, 42, 49, 107, 573
Bowers, J. S.
  cognitive/socio-cultural research
    integration 342
  technology in teacher education 398–9,
    403, 405–7
Bracey, G. W. 14, 16, 20, 155, 173, 175, 177
Bradley, J. 385
Bramald, Rod 438, 593–634
Branca, N. A. 276
Brandon, D. 898
Branson, R. K. 308–9
Brauer, K. 366
Breedlove, B. A. 276
Breen, Chris 437, 523–44, 626
Breiteig, T. 37
Brenner, M. 574, 737
Brew, C. 562
Britt, M. 526
Brodie, K. 445, 456, 555
Broekman, H. 778

Bromme, R. 810
Brousseau, Guy 250, 257, 265, 506–8, 661,
  847
Brouwer, L. E. J. 796–8, 807
Brown, A. 376–7, 447, 499
Brown, C. A. 406, 416, 660–1, 670–1, 878,
  898
Brown Claridge, P. 485
Brown, G. 209
Brown, J. R. 902
Brown, Margaret 7
  numeracy 76, 120
  research 439, 594
  setting 60
  SIMS 16
  teachers' knowledge 845
  TIMSS 14, 19–20, 460
Brown, R. 734, 738–9
Brown, S. I. 803, 809–10, 833, 847, 904
Bruce, R. 188
Bruckheimer, M. 377
Bruner, J. S. 244, 605, 890
Bryant, I. 124
Buenfil-Burgos, R. 187
Burkhouse, B. 419
Burn, K. 860
Burn, R. P. 353, 376, 384
Buros, Oscar 690–1
Burrill, G. 277
Burton, L. 7, 36, 193, 554
Bussi, M. B. 484
Butler, D. 361
Butler, E. 106–7, 109
Butler, M. K. 382
Buzan, B. 58
Buzan, T. 58
Bynner, J. 119

Cai, J. 735
Calderhead, J. 678–9, 853, 879
Callahan, R. C. 729
Campbell, Donald 477
Campbell, P. F. 164, 662
Canavarro, A. P. 657
Cao, Z. 738
Capponi, B. 249–50, 254–5, 265–6, 334
Capra, F. 595
Carbone, R. E. 420
Carboni, L. W. 398, 402, 412
Cardenas, ▮–▮ 222
Carey, D. 485
Carlsen, W. S. 509
Carlson, D. 374
Carpenter, T. P.
  algebra 772
  beliefs 730

CGI program   485, 648, 811–12, 845, 891–2
  classroom practices   648, 650
  direct instruction   845
  research practices   494
  student thinking   910
Carr, M.   66
Carraher, D. W.   36–7, 117, 333, 553
Carraher, T. N.   36–7, 117
Carter, K.   888
Casas, F. R.   691, 698
Castells, M.   548–9
Castle, S.   675
Castro, M.   221, 555
Caughey, W.   285
Chaachoua, H.   258n1
Chacon, P.   251, 253, 260–1
Chambers, D. L.   891–2
Chambers, D. P.   404–6, 422
Chanda, N.   117, 120–2
Chang, C.-K.   739, 747, 749, 751–4
Chapman, Olive   640, 877–917
Charles, R. I.   472
Chassapis, D.   14
Chauvot, J.   801, 803, 807, 812
Chazan, D.   333, 335, 653, 904, 907
Cheng, Y. C.   174
Cheung, K. C.   277–8, 311, 500–1
Cheung, W. M.   174
Chevallard, Y.   338
Chiang, C. P.   485
Chiang, Yik-man   146
Chickering, A. W.   749, 755–6
Chin, Chien   48, 638–9, 717–65
Chin, R.   658
Chisholm, L.   645
Chou, S.   275
Christian-Smith, L.   43
Christiansen, F. V.   579
Christiansen, I. M.   554, 579
Chrostowski, S. J.   41
Chudowsky, N.   704
Cizek, G. J.   703
Clark, B. I.   412
Clark, C. M.   672
Clark, J. M.   369
Clarke, B.   278, 555, 851
Clarke, David J.
  assessment   45, 692, 697
  classroom practices   399, 406, 407
  collaborative research project   213–14
  international comparative studies   6, 79, 143–84
  knowledge   843
Clarke, Doug M.   278, 555, 665, 671, 851
Clarkson, Philip C.

global context   6, 11, 38, 185–229
globalization   106, 565
values   725, 732, 740, 753–4, 757–8
Clarkson, R.   594
Clea, F.   65
Clements, D. H.   328, 331, 472, 483
Clements, M. A.   xi
  action research   884
  assessment   703
  Australian context   209
  boycott of national curriculum   698
  community mathematics education programmes   110
  curriculum similarities   200
  journals   567
  National Statement for School Mathematics   226n2
  professional practice   xiii, 637–41
  teacher education   409
  'Western mathematics'   206
Clifford, Geraldine J.   476, 486
Cline, H. F.   573
Cnop, I.   308
Coady, C.   123
Cobb, C. E. Jr.   83
Cobb, P.
  classroom interactions   847
  cognitive/socio-cultural research integration   342
  professional development   667, 679, 878, 898
  research practices   502, 506
  socio-cultural influences   737
  student perspectives   661
  support by colleages   660
Coben, Diana   6, 10, 37, 103–42
Cochran-Smith, M.   528, 530–1, 533, 538–40, 604
Cockman, M.   720
Coffield, F.   104
Cogan, L. S.   652, 769
Cohen, D.   119, 122–3, 177, 679
Coles, L.   616
Colleran, N.   115, 117
Collins, A.   559, 904
Collis, K. F.   697, 703
Collison, J.   698
Colvin, R. L.   652
Colwell, D.   115
Colyn, W.   525, 531
Confrey, J.
  constructivist learning theories   647
  generativity   578–9
  research in conflict situations   559, 564, 566
  technology research   333, 337, 342n3

Constanza, A. 221
Coombs, P. H. 126–9
Cooney, Thomas J.
  information technology 279
  knowledge of pedagogy 122
  mathematical objects 906
  mathematical/pedagogical power 879
  professional development 878
  research 472
  student perspectives 661
  teacher education 639, 795–828, 843, 845,
    852
  teacher educators 899
  teachers' beliefs 755, 900
Cooper, B. 27, 458, 464
Cooper, T. 49, 52–3
Copa, G. H. 103
Copas, J. B. 95
Cornbleth, C. 446
Cornu, B. 370
Costello, J. 48
Cottingham, S. 127
Cotton, T. 58, 554, 573
Cottrill, J. 354, 370
Coubertin, Pierre, Baron de 18
Coxford, A. G. 605, 892–3
Crawford, Kathryn
  action research 525, 883
  teacher research 525, 529, 531, 539–41
Cremin, L. 77
Cribb, P. 285
Croft, A. 123
Cronbach, L. 492
Croom, L. 646
Cropley, A. J. 105
Crosswhite, F. J. 494
Cuban, Larry 475–6, 664
Cummings, W. K. 719
Cundy, H. M. 272
Cunningham, D. J. 400–1, 415–16
Cuoco, A. 334–5, 375
Cushing, K. 485
Cusworth, R. 844
Czarnocha, B. 368

Dahland, G. 494
Dalin, P. 616
Damarin, S. K. 17
D'Ambrosio, Beatriz 439
D'Ambrosio, Ubiratan
  colonialism 202, 547
  conflict 554
  cultural activities 117
  environmental problems 88–9
  equity 654
  ethnomathematics movement 11, 203
  labor groups 82
  mathematical knowledge 735–6
  matheracy/technocracy 47
  social enterprise 14
Damerow, P. 37, 93, 194
Daniel, P. 398–99, 412
Darling-Hammond, L. 14, 788–9
Dautermann, J. 376, 380
Davidson, D. 167
Davis, Brent 438, 534, 593–634, 804–5, 843
Davis, D. 212
Davis, G. 354
Davis, H. 456
Davis, N. 416
Davis, P. J. 91, 94, 599, 797, 806
Davis, Robert B. 405, 772, 878
Davis, S. 207
Dawson, A. J. 849, 896
Dawson, S. 526, 596
De Abreu, G. 553
De Castell, S. 81
De Corte, E. 704
de Laat, M. 123
De Lange, J. 37, 67, 126, 691, 693, 698
de Villiers, M. 335
Degnan, J. 402
Dekkers, A. 383
Delors, J. 46, 104
Delozanne, E. 258n1
Demana, F. 276, 303–4, 312, 653
Dench, S. 21, 78
DeNisi, A. 484
Densmore, K. 50, 58
Denvir, H. 120
Denzin, N. K. 574
Derluguian, G. M. 190
Descartes, René 796
Desrosières, A. 547
Dessart, D. J. 277
Dettori, G. 336
DeVries, D. J. 376–7
Dewey, John
  education definition 825–6
  individual progressive sentiment 108
  lifelong learning 103
  reflective thinking 879, 900
Dhombres, J. 904
Dhunpath, Rubby 439
Dick, T. P. 304, 307, 312, 359
Dickson, L. 594
Dienes, Z. 605
Dikgomo, P. 456
Dillon, D. 847
Dinh Tri, N. 38–9
diSessa, A. A. 325, 327–8, 340, 342n4
Dobbins, M. 405–6
Doerr, H. M.

calculators   359, 380
computers   302
technology in teacher education   398–9,
   403, 405–7, 420
Dolk, M.   398, 413, 841
Dorans, N. J.   278
Dörfler, W.   902
Dormolen, J. von   720, 734
Dossey, J. A.
   Aristotle   796
   discrete mathematics   307
   formalism   797
   personal construct position   117
   researchers   497
   teacher education   810
   values   732
Douglas, B.   613
Dowling, P.   54, 89, 204, 447, 499, 550, 573
Downing, M.   503, 512
Dowsey, J.   359
Doyle, Walter   492
Drake, P.   122
Dreyfus, H.   482–3
Dreyfus, S.   482–3
Dreyfus, T.   88, 333, 338, 358, 368, 371, 373
Drijvers, P.   337, 359, 380
du Plessis, S. A.   398, 414
Duba, N.   570
Dubinsky, E.
   abstract algebra   376–7
   APOS theory   244
   assessment   385
   economic issues   11, 23–4
   linear algebra   374–5
   objects   354–5
   pedagogical innovations   380
   programming   356–7
   Riemann sums   368
DuCette, J.   402
Duffin, J.   123
Dunbar, S. B.   698
Dunham, P. H.   359
Dunne, M.   11, 27, 458, 464

Earl, L.   45
Easley, J. A.   32
Eckermann, A.-K.   718
Edwards, L. D.   329–30
Edwards, P.   382–3
Edwards, R.   109–10
Edwards, T. G.   883–4
Eggleton, P. J.   801–2, 807
Eisenberg, M.   333, 340
Ell, F. R.   37
Ellerton, N. F.
   assessment   703
   Australian context   209

curriculum similarities   200
National Statement on School
   Mathematics   226n2
professional development   640, 884, 896
teacher education   637
Elliott, S.   123
Ellis-Davies, ▌–▐   902
Elmore, R. F.   655, 692
Ely, M.   503, 512
Empson, S.   648
Engeström, Y.   132, 416
English, L. D.   472–3, 484
Ensor, Paula   439, 500–1, 538
Erickson, Fred   506
Erikson, E. H.   749, 756
Ernest, P.
   exclusion   547
   fallibilism   116, 797
   knowledge   623
   pedagogical practices   117
   social constructivism   201, 553, 599
   teacher education   802, 806–7
   values   64, 739
Ethington, C. A.   728
Evans, J.   22–3, 54, 111, 117
Even, Ruhama
   concepts   845
   pedagogical knowledge   755
   professional development   665–7, 669–70
   research practices   437, 491–521
   teacher-educators   850, 869, 896–7
   technology   359
Everton, T.   860

Faes, W.   841
Falbel, A.   336
Falk, ▌–▐   189
Fasheh, M.   547, 737
Feingold, A.   476
Feldman, A.   574
Fenby, B.   285
Fennema, E.
   CGI program   485, 648, 666, 811–12, 845,
      891–2
   classroom practices   645, 648, 650, 655
   culture   65
   equity   554
   gender issues   476
   professional development   679
   student thinking   910
Fenstermacher, G. D.   529
Fereshteh, H.   748
Ferrini-Mundy, J.
   changing teacher practices   651, 660, 672,
      676
   R³M Project   679n1
   reform efforts   670

undergraduate mathematics 369, 370
Feurzeig, S. 328
Fevre, R. 104
Fey, J. T. 77, 303
Findell, B. 79, 82
Fischbeck, S. 276
Fischer, R. 87
Fiske, E. B. 691
FitzSimons, Gail E. 7
  curriculum 20
  everyday mathematics 37
  lifelong mathematics education 6, 10,
    103–42
  numeracy 77, 79
  values 732, 740, 753–4, 756–8
  workplace 82
Flavell, J. 673
Flecha, R. 548
Flyvbjerg, B. 480, 482–3
Foletta, G. 334
Foley, G. 398, 414, 417
Fong, H. K. 36
Fonzi, J. 893
Ford, P. 162
Forgasz, H. 36, 187, 398, 562
Forgione, P. D. 177
Foroni, N. 130
Forrester, K. 106, 108
Fosnot, C. 650, 658, 664, 671, 673, 711
Foucault, Michel 109, 486, 573
Fournier, J. 117
Franke, M. L. 485, 648, 672, 811–12
Frankenstein, M.
  conflict 548, 550, 554
  data measures 91
  ethnomathematics 38, 118, 202–3
  exclusion 85
  statistical literacy 118
Fraser, B. J. 554
Frege, Gottlob 796
Freire, P. 109, 568–9
Freudenthal, Hans
  assessment 689, 712
  international comparative studies 143,
    154
  mathematical tools 80
  mathematicians 811
  Realistic Mathematics Education 67
  research 352
  teacher preparation 847
Friedlander, A. 301
Friedman, C. P. 363–4, 385
Friedman, L. 476
Friedman, S. 669–70
Friel, S. N. 398, 402, 412
Froese-Germain, B. 698

Frykholm, J. 802, 812, 854
Fuchs, S. 530
Fullan, M. 613, 616–17, 656, 659, 664,
  674–5, 678
Fuller, B. 177, 179
Fuller, D. 66
Fung, A. C. W. 308, 310
Fung, C. I. 303, 305
Furinghetti, F. 653
Furlong, J. 104, 756
Fusaro, B. A. 88
Futrell, M. H. 39

Gadamer, H.-G. 534, 601–2
Gafni, N. 163
Gagné, Robert 605
Gagnon, D. 302
Gal, I. 77, 117–18, 120
Galbraith, P. L. 7, 21
Gale, T. 50, 58
Gallagher, S. 603
Gallimore, R. 165, 171–2
Gamoran, A. 61
Ganter, S. L. 363–4
Gao, X. 275
Garancon, M. 264–5
Garden, R. A. 41, 154, 171, 278, 307
Gates, Peter 5, 10, 12, 19, 27, 31–73, 554
Gellert, Uwe 34, 81, 84, 640, 801, 806,
  829–75
Gerdes, Paulus
  Africa 38
  ethnomathematics 11, 117–18, 203–4, 548,
    554, 735
  ICME conferences 194
  indigenous knowledge 83
  social enterprise 14
  subcultural groups 37
Gergen, K. 553, 578
Gertzog, W. 610, 663
Giacquinta, J. B. 850
Giarelli, J. 568
Gibb, E. G. 473
Gibbons, M. 132
Gibson, H. 729
Giddens, A. 106, 188
Gillborn, D. 12, 54–5
Gilligan, Carol 50
Gipps, C. 53
Giorgi, A. 602
Giroux, H. A. 89, 109, 132, 568–9
Glance, N. 94
Glaser, R. 703–4
Glass, G. 626
Glenn, John 768
Godden, G. L. 107, 111, 122–23
Gödel, Kurt 797

Godino, J. D.   494
Goebel, J.   276
Goesling, B.   167–9
Goffree, F.   841–2
Gold, B.   385
Goldenberg, M. P.   325, 334–6, 799, 806, 907
Goldin, G. A.   357
Goldman, E.   410
Goldsmith, L.   336
Goleman, D.   50
Gomes Ferreira, V.   336
Gómez, Pedro   221, 439, 555, 559, 564
Gonzales, P.   771, 847
Gonzalez, E. J.   41, 474
Goodlad, J. I.   278
Goodwin, J.   655
Gorard, S.   104, 107–8
Gordon, M.   653, 904
Gore, J. M.   854
Gorgorió, N.   554
Gough, P. B.   177
Goulding, M.   845
Graeber, Anna O.   638, 643–87
Graf, K. D.   217
Graham, A. T.   248, 252–3, 261–2, 462
Graham, K.   369–70, 661
Grant, S. G.   655, 664
Grant, T. J.   800, 812, 878
Gravemeijer, K.   622, 625
Gray, E.   354, 360–1
Gray, M. W.   547
Greenwood, L.   162–3
Greer, B.   7, 358, 704
Greer, S.   190
Gregg, J.   45
Gregory, K. D.   41
Grenfell, M.   12
Grießhammer, Rainer   271
Griffin, P.   866
Grignon, C.   83
Groman, M. W.   418–19
Grossman, Pamela   509
Grouws, D. A.   472, 567, 626, 703, 731
Grover, B.   491–2
Groves, S.   653
Grugeon, B.   258n1
Guba, E. G.   567, 575
Gudmundsdottir, S.   718, 749
Guedes, E. M.   123
Guimarães, H. M.   657
Guin, D.
    Computer Algebra Systems   380
    handheld calculators   359
    instrumental genesis   339
    meta-study on technology research   258n1
    technology impact on curriculum   302,
        306–8, 311

Gunew, S.   189
Guppy, N.   207
Guskey, T. R.   672
Gutiérrez, A.   843
Guzman, Miguel de   208

Haacke, F.   123
Haberman, M.   663
Hadamard, J.   352
Hadas, N.   334–6, 377, 907
Hadfield, O. D.   402
Hadley, M.   420
Hadley, W. H.   326
Haggarty, L.   838, 850, 852, 854–5
Hagger, H.   838, 860
Haimes, D.   238–9
Haines, C. R.   21
Halai, A.   882, 896–7
Hall, B. P.   721, 723, 727
Hallam, Susan   59
Halliday, D.   826n2
Halstead, J. M.   721, 733
Hamberger, N. M.   728
Hancock, Chris   336, 340, 342n4
Haney, W.   689–90
Hankes, J. E.   891–2
Hanna, G.   36, 193, 554
Harder, R. J.   729
Harding, S.   580
Hardy, T.   573
Harel, G.   358, 372, 374
Harel, I.   244, 262, 266, 328
Hargreaves, A.   45, 200, 207, 224–5
Harlen, W.   26
Harmin, M.   721
Harris, G. A.   417
Harris, M.   32, 36, 119, 554
Harris, Pam   204–5
Harris, S.   17
Harrison, C.   485
Harry, V.   420
Harskamp, E.   359, 379
Hart, K. M.   475, 483, 574, 594
Hartzler, J. S.   94
Hashimoto, Y.   693, 697, 707
Hashweh, M. Z.   509
Hatano, G.   178–9
Hatch, G.   526, 529–31, 604
Hatfield, M. M.   411–12
Haymore, J.   509
Heal, C.   845
Healy, L.
    didactical intervention   342n3
    macros   343n10
    microworlds   331
    software tools   334, 336, 340, 342
    technology research   249–50, 262–3

Heid, M. K.   307, 323, 325, 337
Heintz, G.   314n2
Hembree, R.   277
Henderson, L.   399
Hendrix, L. J.   363–4
Henningsen, M.   491–2, 885
Henry, M.   188–90, 201
Hensien, S. M.   883–4
Herget, W.   91, 385
Herman, J. L.   698
Herman, S.   737
Hermsen, H.   841
Herr, K.   575–6
Herrington, J.   398, 411
Herrington, T.   398, 411
Hersh, R.   94, 599, 797, 805–6
Hershkowitz, R.   335–6, 653, 907
Hess, R. D.   159–60, 313
Hewitt, D.   540–1
Hewson, P. W.   610, 659, 663, 665
Hiebert, James
   beliefs   648, 800
   classroom practices   647, 655
   cultural activity   643
   data analysis   503–5
   international comparative research   159,
      168, 171–2, 175
   Japanese teaching   313
   learning   599
   NCTM   472
   problem-solving   904
   professional development   675, 773
   question framing   499–500
   school development   850
   teacher education   878
   teacher professionalism   297
   teachers' learning experience   880
   TIMSS   527, 652, 768, 846
   US teaching practices   771
   video studies   161, 165–6, 499–500
Higgins, S.   616
Hilbert, D.   796–7
Hill, B. V.   721, 723, 725, 727
Hill, C.   355
Hill, H. C.   679
Hillage, J.   477
Hillel, J.   337–8, 359, 371–4, 386
Hino, K.   668–9
Hirano, Y.   105
Hirsch, C. R.   279
Hitchcock, G.   444
Hite, A.   190–1
Ho, H.-Z.   737
Hofstede, G.   721–3, 727–9
Hollingsworth, S.   538
Holly, P.   883

Holton, Derek   122, 234–5, 351–94
Holton, R. J.   190
Hölzl, R.   334–5
Holzwarth, A.   95
Hong, Y. Y.   359–61, 366, 368, 378, 385
Hopmann, S.   851
Hord, S.   674
Horta, Victor   148
Horwood, J.   737
Houang, R. T.   155–6, 652, 737, 769
House, P.   814
Howard, J.   658
Howe, K. R.   447–50
Howie, S.   458–9
Howson, A. G.
   barriers to change   596, 656
   curriculum   39, 610–11, 649
   information technology   299–300, 304,
      307, 311
   RDD model   605
   research   352
   traditional teaching   845
Hoyles, Celia
   adult education   82, 119, 129
   integration of technology   378
   key skills   21–2
   Logo   467n5
   obstacles to technology
      implementation   383–4
   problem-solving   377
   representation   358
   technology impact on curriculum   272–3,
      300–2, 311
   technology research   234, 249–50, 262–3,
      266, 323–39, 362, 653
Hu, A.   173
Huberman, M.   504, 529
Hubermann, B.   94
Hughes, D.   444
Hughes, M.   45
Hummel, J. A.   275
Hunsaker, D.   276
Hunt, N. P.   883
Hunter-Boykin, H.   39
Huntley, I. D.   37, 197
Husén, T.   436
Hyde, J. S.   476

Illeris, K.   579
Illich, P.   109
Inagaki, K.   178–9
Ireson, Judith   59
Irwin, K. C.   37, 526
Isoun, T.   38

Jaberg, P.   657–8
Jablonka, Eva   7
   anxiety   34

mathematical applications   46, 56, 843
mathematical literacy   5–6, 75–102, 152,
    154
Jackson, A.   282
Jacobs, J. E.   646
Jacobs, V.   648
Jacobsen, E.   10, 15, 195–6, 208
Jaime, A.   843
Jakwerth, P.   652
James, D.   12
Jansen, T.   106
Jarvis, P.   124
Jarymowicz, M.   748
Jaworski, Barbara
    action research   883
    change   676
    educative power   879
    learning   882
    levels of teacher knowledge   879–80,
        896–7
    PME   526
    reflective practice   879
    social practice theory   677
    teacher education   640, 665, 824, 829–75
    teacher educators   896–8
    technology research   235–6
    video studies   398
Jess, K.   657
Jessup, D.   66
Jipson, J.   536
Johnson, C.   374
Johnson, D.   594, 845
Johnson, L.   651, 660–1, 670
Johnson, S.   123
Johnson, W. R.   477
Johnston, B.   117, 121, 123, 195
Johnston, R.   124
Jones, D.   330, 472, 660, 803, 809
Jones, G.   484, 667
Jones, K.   336, 449, 460
Jones, M. G.   36
Jones, P.   196
Jorgensen, L.   382
Joseph, G. G.   84, 554, 737
Julie, C.   550
Jungwirth, H.   105, 120
Junker, B.   704
Jurdak, M.   721, 726, 732

Kahn, K.   329
Kaiser, G.   36, 65, 193, 197, 199–200, 554,
    645
Kaiser-Messmer, G.   37
Kamii, M.   658
Kanes, C.   118–19
Kant, Immanuel   352
Kaphesi, E.   45

Kaput, J. J.
    algebra   772
    calculators   461–2
    Computer Algebra Systems   337
    computer usage   474
    databases   336
    democratizing effect of software   463
    dynamic geometry   334
    epistemological penetration   475
    lack of technology research   324–5
    notation   327
    Palm Pilot   422–3
    portable devices   359
    representation   357–8
    SimCalc project   332–3
    technology impact on curriculum   271,
        279, 299, 301–2, 306–7
Kassem, D.   55
Kat, E.   718, 725, 737
Kauchak, D. P.   729
Kawamura, K.   105
Kawanaka, T.   165, 771, 847
Kawski, M.   386
Kearns, D.   646
Keeves, J. P.   169–71
Keiny, S.   895–6
Keitel, Christine   xi, xii
    barriers to change   596
    collaborative research project   213–14
    critique of TIMSS   14, 174, 458–9, 703,
        768, 850
    culture   65
    curriculum change/development   610–11,
        649
    didaktical tradition   851
    gender   554
    globalization   566
    ICME conferences   193–4
    international comparative research   148,
        174, 200, 566, 703, 850
    IOWME   193
    journals   567
    Mathematics for All   34, 36–7
    policy dimensions   3–7
    power   89, 549
    RDD model   605
    realized abstractions   93
    reflective knowledge   90
    research   439, 472
    resistance to change   656
    secondary teachers   843
    socialization of teachers   836
    stakeholders   149
Keith, S.   385
Kelly, A. E.
    compilations of research   626

journals 567
psychology 558–9
research quality 574
software tools 326
teaching experiments 564, 610
Kelly, D. L. 474
Kemmis, S. 124
Kemp, M. 385
Kendal, M. 257, 307, 338, 369, 384
Kennedy, M. 671
Kennedy, Robert F. 477
Kenny, M. J. 554, 645–6
Kent, Phillip 342
Keogh, A. J. 729
Kerr, D. 749
Kerslake, D. 475, 594
Kessel, C. 399
Keum, J. 41
Khisty, L. L. 646
Khuzwayo, H. 547, 550
Ki-Zerbo, J. 38
Kieran, C.
  algebra 772
  NCTM 472
  technology impact on curriculum 301,
    305–6
  technology research 247–8, 257, 264–5
Kieren, T. 596
Kiernan, C. 385
Kilpatrick, Jeremy xi, xiii
  barriers to change 596
  conflict 559
  critique of TIMSS 14, 174, 458–9, 703,
    768, 850
  curriculum 607, 610–11, 649
  ICME conferences 195
  international comparative research 148,
    174, 200, 566, 703, 850
  journals 567
  Mathematics Learning Study
    Committee 79, 82
  'maths wars' 226n3
  psychology 558
  RDD model 605
  research 112, 435–9, 478–9, 530
    failure to impact practice 472–3, 476
    identity 581
    paradigms 201
    practices 494–5
    quality 574
  resistance to change 656
  spreadsheets 336
  stakeholders 149
  teachers as researchers 523–4, 539
  tests 689–90
Kim, J. 650

Kincheloe, J. L. 532, 575
King, B. W. 276
King, K. D. 365, 438
Kirby, P. 107
Kissane, B. 359, 384–5
Klafki, W. 851
Klein, G. A. 482
Klein, H. A. 482
Klein, M. 117
Klein, R. 667
Klockow, J. 728
Kluckhohn, C. 721, 723, 725–7, 732
Kluger, A. N. 484
Knapp, M. 659
Knapper, C. K. 105
Knijnik, Gelsa
  adult education 83, 113, 115, 118
  conflict situations 554, 566, 568
  knowledge 735
Knoblauch, C. H. 78
Knoll, S. 771, 847
Knowles, M. 108
Koblitz, N. 11, 23–4, 308
Koc, Yusuf 235, 395–432
Koch, L. 659
Koedinger, K. 253–5, 263–4, 326
Kogan, M. 111
Kögler, H. H. 566
Kohlberg, L. 718, 721
Kohn, A. 698
Kong, S. C. 312
König, Gerhard 439
Korsgaard, O. 106
Kotagiri, T. 105
Kotzmann, E. 89–90, 93, 549
Krainer, K.
  action research 883
  professional development 878
  reflective practice 824, 844, 879
  teacher colleagues 660
  teacher educators 526–7, 896
  teacher research 526–7, 530, 532
Krathwohl, D. R. 723–4, 726–7, 730–1
Kreith, K. 88
Krieger, S. 507–8
Kroeber, A. L. 732
Krummheuer, G. 847, 849
Krutetskii, V. A. 705
Küchemann, D. 594
Kuku, A. 11, 201, 206
Kutzler, B. 385
Kvale, S. 574, 578
Kwast, L. E. 721
Kwon, O. 359–60
Kynigos, C. 330, 340

Laborde, Colette
  didactical contract 506

digital technology   333–4, 336–7, 653
journals   567
technology research   233, 237–69, 472,
    813, 907
Laborde, J. M.   333–4
Labov, W.   45
Lacey, C. A.   403, 425
Lagemann, Ellen Condliffe   477–9
Lagrange, Jean-Baptiste
    handheld calculators   338, 359
    limit concept   370
    meta-study on technology research   233,
        237–69
    technology impact on curriculum   301,
        305
Laing, R. A.   893
Lajoie, S. P.   698
Lakatos, Imre   352, 797, 805–7
Lakoff, G.   360
Lam, I.   398, 416
Lambdin, Diana   235, 395–432, 494–5
Lamon, S. J.   476
Lampert, Magdalene
    beliefs   672
    case inquiry   884
    communication of research   515–16
    geometry software   653
    MATH project   398, 407–8, 841
    teachers   604, 609
    technology in teacher education   399,
        407–8, 410, 423, 426
Landvogt, J.   398
Lang, Andrew   172–3
Lanier, J. E.   664
Lappan, G.   497
Lather, P.   180, 575
Laughbaum, E. D.   385–6
Lauten, A. D.   370
Lave, Jean   117, 454, 676, 848, 878, 898
Lawler, Brian R.   439
Lawnham, P.   210
Lay, D.   374
Leal, L. C.   657
Leatham, K.   421
Lebethe, A.   540
Leder, G. C.   36, 194, 398, 562, 645, 693
Lee, C.   485, 626
Lee, L.   337
Lee, M. J.   720
Lee, P. Y.   292
Lee, S.   651
Lee, Wai-Keung   314n1
Lefton, L. E.   363
Leigh-Lancaster, D.   297, 379
Leikin, Roza   640, 869, 877–917
Leinhardt, G.   509, 912

Lelliott, T.   453–4, 456, 467n4
Lennex, L.   161
Lenzo, K.   580
Leonelli, E.   117, 124
Leont'ev, A. N.   416
Lerman, Stephen   7
    beliefs   805
    constructivism   117
    ethical issues in research   436, 441–70
    mental operations   357–8
    reflective practice   879
    social turn   495
    socio-cultural issues   38, 554
    teacher change   674, 676
    teacher identities   756
Leron, U.   328, 357, 376, 380, 900
Lesh, R. A.
    compilations of research   626
    journals   567
    knowledge transfer   484
    psychology   559
    representations   358, 359
    research quality   574
    software tools   326
    teaching experiments   564, 610
Lester, Frank K. Jr.   439, 480, 494–5, 505
LeTendre, G.   167–9, 175
Leu, Y.-C.   726, 739, 747, 749, 751–4, 756
Leung, Frederick K. S.   xi
    East Asia   217
    examinations in China   42, 56
    technological developments   xii, 233–6
    technology impact on curriculum   278–9,
        292, 308
Levi, L.   648, 772
Levin, D.   534
Lewin, P.   354
Lewis-Shaw, C. P.   729
Licón-Khisty, L.   548
Lieberman, A.   656
Lim, C. S.   57, 64, 314n1, 739
Lim-Teo, S. K.   61, 63, 719
Lin, F.-L.
    professional development   755–6
    values   726, 730, 733–4, 739, 758
    VIMTS projects   747–8, 750–4, 757
Linchevski, L.   337
Lincoln, Y. S.   567, 574–5
Lindberg, L.   123
Lindquist, M. M.   730
Lingard, B.   188–90
Lingefjärd, Thomas   236, 336, 494
Linn, M. C.   476
Linn, R. L.   698
Little, J. K.   664, 675
Littleton, C. E.   402

Llinares, S.   755
Llorente, Juan Carlos   115, 126, 128–9
Loch, S.   368
Loef, M.   485
Loevinger, J.   756
Lokan, J.   154–5, 162–3
Lortie, D. C.   616, 656, 833
Loucks, S.   674
Loucks-Horsley, S.   659, 665, 671–4, 676–7
Love, N.   659, 665
Lovitts, B.   559
Lowe, S.   329
Lubienski, S. T.   25–6, 36, 510
Lubinski, C.   657–8
Lubisi, J.   645
Luhmann, N.   851
Luna, E.   197
Lutkus, A.   402
Lydon, J.   749
Lynch, S.   39
Lytle, S.   528, 530–1, 533, 538–40, 604

Ma, L.
   'deep understanding'   667, 773, 789, 825
   professional development   880, 904
   teacher education   845, 853
Maaß, J.
   adult mathematics education   105, 112–13,
      117, 120, 122–3
   readers   90
McAllister, S.   658
McAloon, A.   18
McCall, J.   485
McCarthey, S.   655
McCartney, M.   594
McClain, K.
   learning community   660
   professional development   878, 898
   teacher education and technology   398–9,
      405, 407, 411, 420, 425
McConatha, J. T.   721, 723–4, 726–7, 735
McCoy, L.   402
McCrae, B.   379, 401
McDonald, J.   538
McDonald, M.   354, 365
Macedo, D.   568
McGatha, M.   411, 420, 425
McGaw, B.   626
MacGilchrist, B.   485
McGraw, R. H.   406, 416
McHenry, K.   646
McIntosh, A.   77
McIntosh, J. A.   494
McIntyre, D.   833, 838, 847, 852–3
McIntyre, J.   107
McKenzie, P.   105

McKnight, C. C.   155–6, 157, 652, 737,
   768–9
McLaren, P. L.   132, 548, 568, 575
McLaughlin, M.   656
McLean, L.   691
McLeod, D. B.   36, 438, 724, 731–2
McLuhan, M.   188
Macnab, D. S.   14
McNamara, D.   844
McNeal, B.   506
McNeal, E.   667
Madaus, G.   689–90
Madden, ▮–▮   211
Madsen, R.   487
Maerker, L.   123
Maguire, T.   123
Maher, C. A.   405, 878, 895, 910
Mahomed, E.   645
Makinster, J. G.   415–16
Malcolm, H.   26
Malloy, C. E.   36
Malone, John   238–9, 523–4, 530–2, 604
Mandinach, E. B.   573
Mandler, George   731
Manly, M.   116, 120, 123
Marion, W.   385
Mariotti, M. A.   256, 336
Mark, M. A.   326
Markovits, Z.   669–70, 755
Marks, R.   509, 871n10
Marr, B.   118, 121
Marshall, B.   485
Marshall, S. P.   904
Martin, B.   209–10, 736
Martin, M. O.   41, 474, 768
Martino, A. M.   405
Martyn, S.   845
Masia, B. B.   723
Masingila, J. O.   398, 399, 403, 405–7, 420
Mason, J.   535, 541, 598, 812–13, 832, 898
Matos, J. F.   577, 657
Matras, M. A.   307
Matthews, W.   730
Maturana, H.   534, 612
Matz, M.   772
May, W. F.   449
Mayer, R. A.   893
Mayer, R. E.   475
Mayes, R.   249, 337
Maynard, T.   756
Mbeki, Nomakhaya   525, 531
Meaghan, D. E.   691, 698
Means, B.   299
Mearleau-Ponty, M.   534
Meel, D. E.   363, 364, 369
Mehan, H.   847

Mehrtens, H.   550
Meier, S. L.   703
Meira, ▮-▮   343n13
Mellin-Olsen, S.   118, 550, 553, 573
Melrose, J.   850, 870n8
Merseth, K. K.   403, 425, 842
Merson, M. W.   124
Metz, M.   497, 499, 502
Mevarech, Z.   672
Mezirow, J.   108
Midouser, D.   653
Miles, M.   504
Miller, J.   486, 616
Miller, L. D.   883
Miller-Reilly, B.   115, 117, 123, 126
Millett, A.   120
Minstrell, J.   574
Mirza, H.   54
Mislevy, R. J.   174, 199
Mittag, K. C.   161
Miyake, M.   650
Mohanty, C. T.   132
Mohanty, R.   131
Monaghan, J.   257, 337, 342, 370
Moon, B.   474
Moore, D. S.   280
Moore, J. A.   415–16
Moore, R. L.   728
Moreno-Armella, L.   486
Morgan, A. R.   425
Morgan, C.   327, 650
Morgenstern, O.   91
Moritz, J.   404
Morrison, J. Cayce   476
Moschkovich, J. N.   574
Moseley, D.   624
Moses, M. S.   447–50
Moses, R. P.   83, 658
Moshkovitch, J.   359
Mousley, Judith
    'Learning About Teaching' project   842
    professional development   879
    teacher education   235, 395–432, 842
    teacher research   526, 529, 626
Mphahlete, B.   645
Mueller, W.   379–80
Mukhopadhyay, S.   7, 554
Mullen, J.   117
Muller, E. R.   379, 381–2, 384
Muller, J. P.   530
Mullis, I. V. S.   41, 161, 474, 768
Mummé, J.   698
Munro, J.   737
Murphy, E.   115, 117
Murphy, P.   53
Mutton, T.   860

Mwakapenda, W.   441–2

Nachmias, R.   653
Nagasaki, E.   650, 693
Nanry, W. P.   275
Nardi, E.   336
Nash, K.   189
Ndholvu, J.   645
Nebres, Bienvenido F.
    culture   12
    global context   6, 11, 185–229
    globalization   106
    international comparative studies   458
    universal mathematics   106
    Western influence on Southeast Asia   737
Nekhwevha, F.   548
Nelson, D.   554
Nemirovsky, R.   332
Nerison-Low, R.   652
Neuman, W. L.   718, 735
Newman, K.   127–8, 130
Newton, W.   285
Ngozi, P.   645
Nguyen, D. T.   39
Nichols, D.   354
Nicol, C.   844
Nielsen, L.   19, 85, 89, 569
Nietzsche, F.   486
Niss, M.
    assessment   697
    mathematical experience   545
    Mathematics for All   36–7, 105
    scholarly study of mathematics   112
    undergraduate teaching   121
Nixon, J.   721, 723, 726–7, 731
Noble, T.   332
Noddings, N.   14, 620, 851, 878, 888
Noffke, S.   532
Nohda, N.   67
Nolder, R.   850, 853, 870n8
Norman, N.   846, 853
Nørretranders, T.   597
Noss, Richard   7
    adult education   82, 119, 129
    economic imperialism   11
    ICT   23–4
    key skills   21–2
    National Numeracy Strategy   120
    non-euclidean geometry   377–8
    numeracy   76
    problem-solving   377
    representation   358
    technology research   234, 250, 262, 266,
        323–39, 653
Nunes, T.   82, 117, 553
Nunez, R. E.   360
Nyabanyaba, T.   456

Oakes, J. 61
Oates, G. 379
O'Connor, K. M. 41
O'Donoghue, John 6, 10, 37, 103–42
Olafson, L. J. 728
Oldham, E. 200
Oldknow, Adrian 236
Olds, H. 273
Olive, J. 333, 421, 813
Oliver, R. 411
Olsen, A. 212
Olsen, S. 771
Olson, D. 327
Olson, M. 534
O'Neil, H. F. Jr. 698
Oonk, W. 841–2
Orlich, D. C. 729
O'Rourke, U. 122
Orpwood, G. W. F. 154
Orton, A. 370, 737
Osterlind, S. J. 700–2
Otte, M. 558
Owens, J. 798

Paechter, C. 50–1, 565
Page, R. N. 61, 497
Pajares, M. F. 672
Paley, N. 536
Pallas, A. 497, 503
Palmiter, J. R. 274, 337
Papert, S.
    intellectual movements 813
    microworlds 262, 272, 331, 358
    syntonicity 332
    technology research 244, 266, 328
Park, K. M. 295, 363–4
Parker, L. H. 554
Parsons, S. 119
Pate, G. 96
Paulos, John A. 77
Pavlou, M. 692
Payne, K. J. 25, 27–8, 550
Pea, R. 244, 326, 337, 515
Pearn, C. 562
Pearson, R. 477
Peddiwell, J. A. 314
Pehkonen, E. 463
Pelgrum, W. 653
Pellegrino, J. W. 704
Pence, B. J. 667
Pendergrass, R. A. 729
Penglase, M. 359
Perks, P. 869–70
Perry, P. 221, 555–6
Peter, A. 533
Peterson, P. L. 485, 655, 672
Phillips, R. A. 667–8

Phillips, R. J. 279
Phnuyal, B. 127–8
Piaget, Jean 475, 605, 727
Pickering, A. 493
Pierce, R. 359, 369
Pimm, D. 85–6, 398
Pinnegar, S. 485
Pinxten, Rik 735–6
Pipho, C. 693
Pissalidis, C. 402
Placier, P. 643, 674–5
Planas, N. 554
Plato 796
Plomp, T. 458–9
Poincaré, H. 352
Polanyi, M. 868
Pollak, H. O. 304, 646
Pollard, A. 728, 729
Pólya, G. 352, 813, 904
Pomfret, A. 656
Ponte, J. P. 657, 661, 813
Popham, W. J. 690, 698
Popkewitz, T. S. 568, 787–8
Porter, A. D. 374
Posch, P. 844
Posner, G. 610, 663
Potari, D. 859
Povey, H. 381
Powell, A. B. 38, 85, 202–3, 548, 554
Pozzi, S.
    adult education 82, 119, 129
    Computer Algebra Systems 338
    databases 336
    didactical intervention 342n3
    situated abstraction 341
Prabhu, V. 368
Pratt, D. 251, 266–7, 331, 334, 336
Prawat, R. 672
Prestage, S. 869–70
Proctor, R. 720
Profke, L. 37
Prosser, D. 416
Pun, S. W. 308, 310, 312
Putnam, H. 797
Putnam, R. T. 672, 891–2
Putt, I. 398–9

Rabardel, P. 251, 339
Raby, R. L. 148
Raizen, S. A. 157, 768
Ramanujam, R. 131
Rampal, Anita 131
Ransom, M. 381
Rappaport, J. 12–13
Rasmussen, C. 365–6
Raths, L. E. 721, 723, 725–7, 730, 749
Rav, Y. 84

Ravitch, D.   476
Rawls, John   449
Reddy, V.   573
Reed, Y.   453–4, 456, 467n4
Rees, G.   104
Reese, William   476
Reeves, J.   485
Reisser, L.   749, 755–6
Rennie, L. J.   554
Rescher, N.   721, 723, 727, 731
Resnick, D. P.   691–2
Resnick, L. B.   691–2
Resnick, M.   329, 333
Resnick, R.   826n2
Restivo, S.   14, 89, 550, 553
Reys, B. J.   77
Reys, R. E.   77, 494
Rhodes, V.   845
Rice, M.   629
Richardson, A.   616
Richardson, L. F.   94
Richardson, V.   643, 674–5
Richert, A. E.   844, 885
Ridgway, J.   37
Ritzer, G.   25
Rizvi, R.   188–90
Robbins, Tom   512
Roberts, L. F.   372
Robertson, ▌–▌   188
Robinson, I.   606, 613, 629
Robinson, P.   15–16, 48
Robitaille, D. F.   149–50, 185, 197, 199, 201,
   278, 307
Robles, J.   662
Rochowicz, J. A.   369
Rogers, P.   36, 65, 193, 205–6, 554, 645
Rogoff, B.   878
Rojano, Teresa   306, 336
Rokeach, M.   721, 723, 726, 728, 749
Rolff, H.-G.   850
Rollett, A. P.   272
Romberg, T.
   assessment   689, 693, 697, 703
   changing teacher practices   655, 660
   constructivism   27
   direct instruction   845
   international comparative studies   199
   research in conflict situations   559
   teacher problem-solving   904
   testing   650–1
Rorty, Richard   481
Rosch, E.   534
Roschelle, J.   332–3, 342n3
Rose, B. J.   893
Rose, L. C.   177
Ross, G.   244

Rotberg, I.   698
Rousseau, C.   486
Rowland, T.   845
Roy, D.   244
Ruddock, G.   594
Rudner, L.   238
Russell, Bertrand   796
Ruthven, Kenneth
   Calculator-Aware Number project   654–5
   calculators   276–7, 461–2, 474
   conflict situations   583
   curriculum   280
   data analysis   503
   power relations   446
   technology   339, 359, 653
Ryan, D.   168
Rycraft, M.   115

Saberrs, D.   485
Sacristán, A. I.   330
Safford, K.   123–4
Sakai, A.   167
Salmon-Cox, L.   691
Salomon, G.   326
Samara, J.   331
Sammons, P.   26
Sampson, N.   645
Samuel, M.   439, 549, 573
Santayana, George   474
Santos, A. G. D.   369
Santos-Wagner, V.   533
Sarason, S. B.   657
Saraswati, L. S.   131
Sartre, Jean-Paul   512
Saunders, J.   720
Sawiran, M.   11, 206
Schappelle, B.   667–8
Scheckler, R.   416
Scheerens, J.   699
Scheurich, J. J.   575, 580
Schifter, Deborah
   algebra   772
   beliefs   800, 802
   changing classroom practices   650, 664,
      667, 671–2
   concepts   845
   narratives   888–9
   reflection on school mathematics   809
   SummerMath programme   658, 673, 889,
      892
Schliemann, A. D.   36–7, 117, 119, 333, 553
Schlöglmann, W.   90, 105, 120, 122–3, 724,
   727
Schmidt, M.   45
Schmidt, W. H.
   Characteristic Pedagogical Flow   168
   cultural reference   737

curricular organization 175
TIMSS 14, 155–7, 652, 768–9
Schmitt, M. J. 124
Schnell, F. 721, 723–4, 726–7, 735
Schoenfeld, A. H.
 beliefs 728
 non-subjective nature of mathematics 904
 problem-solving 159
 representations 359
 research practices 494, 497, 499, 502–3,
  505
Schofield, J. W. 302
Scholle, D. 157
Schön, D. A. 110, 843, 868, 878–9
Schorr, K.-E. 851
Schrage, G. 810
Schram, T. 676, 679n1
Schraw, G. J. 728
Schubring, G. 435
Schuck, S. 398, 414, 417, 662
Schwab, J. J. 499, 509–10, 517
Schwan Smith, M. 665–6, 668, 670–3, 676
Schwartz, B. 335–6
Schwartz, J. 273
Schwartz, J. L. 378, 385
Schwartz, S. H. 749
Schwarz, B. 653, 907
Schwendeman, R. 124
Schwingendorf, K. E. 354, 363
Scollon, R. 181n
Scollon, S. W. 181n
Seah, Wee Tiong 48, 638–9, 717–65
Secada, W. G. 36, 65, 554, 645
Seeger, F. 836
Seegers, G. 36
Seeman, A. 656
Seepe, S. 548
Sela, H. 900
Selinger, M. 398
Selter, C. 692, 712
Sendov, B. 328
Sendova, E. 328
Senger, E. S. 724, 730
Serrano, A. 771, 847
Servant, A. 651
Setati, M. 456, 542, 548, 568, 571
Sewell, B. 111
Sfard, A. 328, 354–5
Shafer, M. C. 703
Shaffer, D. 327
Shafrir, U. 359
Shan, S. J. 85, 554
Shapiro, B. 168
Shavelson, R. J. 479
Shaw, C. T. 115
Shaw, V. F. 115

Sheaty, B. E. 755, 845, 852
Sheets, C. 307
Sheingold, K. 420
Shemla, A. 653
Shepard, L. A. 690–2, 699, 703
Sherin, Bruce 331, 342n4
Shigematsu, K. 668–9
Shimada, S. 693, 707
Shimahara, N. 167
Shimizu, Yoshinori 166–9, 213–14, 774–5
Shir, K. 904
Shiu, C. 526, 529–31, 604
Shorrock, S. B. 853
Shuard, H. 654–5
Shulman, L. S.
 case inquiry 884, 887
 classroom practices 663, 672
 communication of research 511, 513–14
 methodology 502
 pedagogical content knowledge 773, 784,
  789, 844, 868
 research practices 492–3, 496, 509
Shumway, R. 277, 279–80
Sierpinska, A.
 conflict 559
 constructivism 117
 journals 567
 linear algebra 371, 374
 research 112, 495, 574, 581
Silver, Edward A.
 algebra 772
 ICME conferences 195
 NAEP achievement data 164
 NCTM research 472
 paradigm cases 885
 QUASAR project 485, 670
 research paradigms 201
 teacher beliefs 730
 teacher education tasks 904, 906
Silverberg, J. 363
Simon, M. A. 667, 892, 902–3
Simon, S. B. 721
Simonsen, L. M. 304, 307, 312
Simpson, A. 123, 354
Singh, S. 547, 573
Siu, Chan Fung Kit 290–91, 314n1
Skemp, R. R. 720, 734, 845
Skott, J.
 beliefs 800–2
 collegiality 853
 forced autonomy 657
 pluralistic view of mathematics 808
 reforms 555, 560
Skovsmose, Ole
 behavior modification 737
 citizenship 120

collectivity   571
critical mathematics education   19–20, 85,
    554, 569, 579
critique of constructivism   117
democratization   62
ethnomathematics   11–12, 84, 204–5, 548
foreground   563
globalization   566
Mathematics for All   645
methodology   570
power   89
power-knowledge   549
psychological perspective   559
public conception of mathematics   17
realized abstractions   93
reflective knowledge   90
research   439, 557, 572
social role of mathematics   32
technology   13–14
Slavit, D.   382–3
Sloane, K.   693, 704
Slonimsky, L.   456, 467n4
Smit, J. H.   398, 414
Smith, C. F.   893
Smith, D. A.   365–6, 378–9, 383, 509
Smith, D. N.   838
Smith, E.   337
Smith, L. T.   547, 568, 577, 582
Smith, M.   626
Smith, M. S.   885
Smith, S.   850, 870n8
Smith, T. A.   41, 474
Smyth, J.   846
Snow, P.   285
Soedjadi, R.   719, 723
Soeffner, H.-G.   847
Sohn-Rethel, A.   92
Sormani, H.   123
Sosniak, L. A.   728
Soto-Johnson, H.   251, 260–1, 370–1
Souviney, R.   196
Sowder, Judith T.
  CGI   845
  classroom practices   650
  communication of research   618–19
  ethical issues in research   447–8, 450,
      452–4
  multiplicative structures   805, 810
  professional development
      programs   667–8, 679
  research   439, 472
  student thinking   812
Sparks, G. M.   672, 675
Sparrow, L.   411
Spindler, G.   167
Sproull, L.   691

Stacey, K.
  CAS active curriculum   379
  elementary teachers   803, 809
  handheld calculators   359, 653
  inter-representational links   369
  teacher education   401, 404, 406, 422
  teacher privileging   307, 384
  technology research   257, 338
Stake, R. E.   32, 697
Stanic, George   56, 439
Stedman, L. C.   178
Steen, L. A.   77, 89, 303, 307, 438
Stein, M. K.   485, 491–2, 660, 670–1, 885–7,
    912
Stein, P.   485
Steinbart, E. M.   363
Steinberg, R.   509
Steinbring, H.   836, 880, 898
Steiner, H. G.   494
Steiner, R. L.   402
Stephens, M.   297, 639, 692, 767–93
Stephens, W. M.   154, 157
Stevenson, H. W.   64, 199, 651–2, 771
Stevenson, I.   330, 377–8
Stewart, J. S.   724
Stiegelbauer, S.   613, 616
Stigler, J. W.
  achievement studies   651–2
  beliefs   648
  classroom practices   647, 655
  cultural traditions   65
  international comparative research   159,
      168, 171–2, 175
  Japanese teaching   313, 775
  lesson study   775
  local community support   64
  norms and routines   847
  problem-solving   904
  professional development   675, 773, 792
  question framing   499–500
  school development   850
  teacher professionalism   297
  teachers' learning experience   880
  teaching as cultural activity   643
  TIMSS   527, 652, 768, 846
  US teaching practices   771
  video studies   161, 165–6, 399, 499–500
Stiles, K.S.   659, 665
Stillman, G.   399
Stodolsky, S. S.   509
Stokes, D. E.   485
Stoll, C.   308, 311
Sträßer, R.   21, 37, 119, 335
Strauss, A. L.   497, 504
Strauss, V.   652
Streefland, L.   708

Strike, K.   610, 663
Stronach, Ian   10, 17–18
Stroup, W. M.   329, 333
Struyk, L.   402
Suggate, J.   845
Suhre, C.   359
Sukhnandan, L.   61
Sullivan, P.
  curricula   278
  knowledge   842
  multimedia resources   403, 409–10, 425
  professional development   879
  reforms   555
  teacher autonomy   851
Sullivan, W. M.   487
Sumara, D.   622, 629
Sun, S.   370
Suppes   492
Sutherland, Rosamund   257, 272, 306, 330–1, 336, 467n5
Suydam, M. N.   276
Suzuki, S.   105
Swadener, M.   719, 723
Swafford, J.   79, 82, 667
Swetz, F.   94
Swidler, A.   487
Sykes, G.   403, 424

Tabach, M.   301
Tabachnik, B. R.   500
Taconis, R.   398, 416
Tajfel, H.   748
Tall, D.
  concept image   354
  embodied objects   360–1
  generic organizers   358
  Graphic Calculus program   365
  graphing software   337
  information technology   299
  limit concept   370
  procept notion   305
  representation   358, 360
  research   352–3
  technology research   244, 247–8, 261, 267–8
  undergraduate teaching   121
Tamkin, P.   477
Tan, S. K.   719, 721, 723–4, 726–7, 735
Tanner, D.   278
Tanner, L.   278
Taole, K.   539
Taplin, M.   734–5, 754–5
Tapscott, D.   653
Tarr, J. E.   161
Tate, William F.   25, 27, 63, 486, 554
Taylor, Keith   382
Taylor, M. J.   748

Taylor, N.   462
Taylor, P. C.   10, 17, 19
Taylor, R.   326
Taylor, S.   188–90, 201
Teese, R.   85
Telese, J. A.   419
Teo, Chee Hean   164, 719, 772
Thomas, K.   376–7
Thomas, Michael O. J.
  IT influence on curriculum   302
  technology research   244, 248, 252–3, 261–2, 462
  undergraduate mathematics   234–5, 351–94
Thomas, R. M.   157
Thompson, A. G.   623, 647, 672, 728
Thompson, E.   534
Thompson, P. W.   358, 360
Thompson, T.   406
Thorndike, Edward L.   605
Thornton, C.   667
Thorsten, M.   147–9, 160, 178
Timmerman, M. A.   419–20
Timmons, R.   190–1
Tipton, S. M.   487
Tirosh, Dina   484, 638, 643–87, 665, 667, 755, 845
Tirta Gondoseputro, T.   728
Tizard, B.   45
Tobin, J.   167
Tobin, K.   574
Toulmin, Stephen   481–2
Tout, D.   116–18, 120–21, 123
Toutounji, Inji   59
Towne, L.   479
Traglova, J.   371
Travers, K. J.   185, 197, 199, 201, 363–4
Travers, R. M. W.   476
Trentacosta, J.   554, 645–6
Trigueros, M.   365
Tripp, D.   532, 729
Trouche, Luc
  Computer Algebra Systems   380
  handheld calculators   359
  instrumental genesis   339
  meta-study on technology research   233, 237–69
  technology impact on curriculum   302–3, 305–8, 311
Tsamir, P.   667
Tsatsaroni, A.   22–3
Tuijnman, A. C.   111
Tung, C. H.   311
Turner, P.   275
Turner, S. E.   550
Tuson, J.   616

Tyack, D. B. 476
Tyler, R. 605
Tymoczko, T. 802
Tzur, R. 869, 896

Uekawa, K. 161
Unger, P. 721
Ursini, S. 331
Usher, R. 124, 451
Usiskin, Z. 195, 205

Valero, Paola
  Colombia 221
  democratization 62
  'disruptions in the data' 443
  Mathematics for All 645
  power relations 446
  research in conflict situations 437–8,
    545–91
  research participants 177
  teacher participation 657
Valverde, G. A. 155–6, 737, 769
Van den Heuvel-Panhuizen, Marja 155, 291,
    638, 689–716, 778
Van der Veen, R. 106
van Dormolen, J. 904
van Duin, S. 123
Van Groenestijn, M. 115, 120, 123
van Lieshout, E. 625
Van Streun, A. 359
Van Voorst, C. 422
Van Zoest, L. R. 852–3
Vanier, J. 614
Varela, F. J. 534, 612, 615
Varelas, M. 728
Veen, W. 398, 416
Veloo, P. 58–9
Verhulst, François 95
Verillon, P. 251, 339
Verschaffel, L. 704
Veugelers, W. 718, 725, 737
Vickers, M. 476
Vidakovic, D. 354, 368
Vinjevold, P. 462
Vinner, S. 354
Vinovskis, M. 476
Vinz, R. 503, 512
Vistro-Yu, Catherine 5, 10, 12, 19, 27, 31–73
Vithal, Renuka
  democratic participatory validity 177, 455
  'disruptions in the data' 443
  ethnomathematics 11–12, 84, 204–5
  power relations 446
  research in conflict situations 437–8,
    545–91
  teacher research 542
Voigt, J. 847
Volmink, J. 32, 548, 554

von Glasersfeld, E. 623, 878
Vygotsky, L. 878

Wagner, S. 472
Wagner, V. 571, 575–6
Wainer, H. 278
Waits, B. K. 276, 303, 304, 312, 653
Walen, S. B. 842, 887–8
Walker, T. 402
Walkerdine, Valerie 51, 547, 554, 599, 735–6
Walsh, A. 654–5
Wang, H. C. 769
Wang, J. 166, 173–4
Warren, C. 422
Wassermann, S. 690, 708
Watanabe, T. 172, 181n
Waters, M. 187, 188
Watkins, D. A. 313
Watson, A. 698, 838, 849, 852, 854, 859, 869
Watson, D. M. 475
Watson, J. M. 404
Watson, L. 107
Watt, Sally 180
Watts, G. D. 675
Waywood, A. 832
Wearne, Diane 503–5, 800, 878
Webb, N. L. 45, 154, 650, 698, 703
Wedege, T. 7
  adult education 112–15, 117, 119
  cognitive conflict 553
  Denmark 108, 124
Weick, K. 656
Weiss, C. H. 476
Wenger, E. 117, 343n13, 416, 454, 676, 848,
    878, 898
Wenzelburger, E. 494
West, R. 363
Westbury, I. 37, 154, 158–9, 173
Weyer, J. 95
Wheatley, G. H. 277, 542
White, D. 662
White, M. 172
Whitehead, A. N. 796
Whitehead, J. 541
Whitfield, R. C. 729
Wiegel, Heide G. 639, 795–828
Wiggins, G. 692, 698
Wilensky, Uri 325, 328–9, 333, 342n4
Wiley, D. E. 155–6, 737, 769
Wiliam, Dylan
  assessment 513–15, 693, 698–9
  communication of research 513–15
  failure of research to impact
    practice 436–7, 471–90
  knowledge 845
  meta-analysis 626
  setting 26, 59–60

verification 505
Wilkin, M. 838
Williams, D. 616
Williams, H. 355
Williams, J. 554
Williams, M. D. 312
Williams, S. 650–1
Williams, S. R. 370, 842, 887–8
Willie, J. 273
Willis, Sue 48, 49
Wilmot, S. 381
Wilson, B. J. 39, 299–300, 304, 307, 311, 845
Wilson, K. 616
Wilson, M. R. 693, 704, 799, 806, 907
Wilson, P. 803
Wilson, S. M. 455–6, 462, 486, 509, 844
Wineberg, S. S. 509
Winicki-Landman, G. 902
Winslow, C. 380
Winters, L. 698
Wiseman, A. 106, 167–9
Wiske, M. S. 303, 307, 311
Witherell, C. 888
Witt, A. 366
Wittmann, E. C. 114–15, 610, 798, 810
Wolf, D. P. 698
Wolfe, R. G. 769
Wong, K. M. 279, 292–3
Wong, K. Y. 45, 58–9, 719
Wong, Ngai-Ying 41–2, 56, 234, 271–321
Wong, P. 312
Wood, D. 244
Wood, T. 506, 526, 537, 667, 679, 824, 847, 896
Woodhouse, G. 327

Woodrow, Derek 5, 9–30, 554
Woods, E. S. 402
Worcester, V. 655
Wu, C.-J. 739, 747, 749, 751, 753–4
Wu, D. 167
Wu, H. 305
Wu, Wen-Jin 275
Wu, Y.-Y. 751

Yackel, E. 358, 506, 661, 667, 679, 847
Yeidel, J. 382–3
Yelland, N. 328
Yerushalmy, M.
  software tools 333, 335, 653
  teacher problem-solving 904
  technology research 249–50, 268–9, 907
Yingkang, U. 653
Yoshida, M. 65
Young, M. D. 106, 110, 132, 580

Zack, V. 526, 626
Zaitun, T. 58–9
Zandieh, M. 365
Zandonadi, R. 123
Zangor, R. 359, 380
Zarinnia, E. A. 650–1, 697
Zaslavsky, Claudia 36, 47, 554
Zaslavsky, Orit 640, 869, 877–917
Zazkis, R. 376, 380
Zeichner, K. M. 500, 854
Zevenbergen, R. 7, 44, 119, 548, 554, 573
Zhang, D. 41–2, 56, 64, 292
Zhang, J. 275
Ziman, J. 479
Zimmer, J. M. 737
Zubrow, D. 691

Index of Subjects

a-didactical milieu   250, 255, 265–6
AAMT *see* Australian Association of
    Mathematics Teachers
abacus   306
ABE *see* Adult Basic Education
ability discrimination   26, 59–62
    see also streaming; tracking
Aborigines   204–5
absolutism   116, 736, 797, 802
abstract algebra   372, 375–7
abstract vector algebra   372
abstraction
    problem solving   86
    situated   341–2
ACACE *see* Advisory Council for Adult and
    Continuing Education
academic mathematicians   120–1
accountability
    internal   692
    league tables   460
    public spending   447, 462
    researchers   576
    standards movement   538
    teachers   437
achievement
    East Asia   216–17
    ethnicity   164
    gender differences   162–4
    IEA study   170–1
    international comparative research   144,
        150–1, 154, 158–9, 170–2, 175
    professional development link   678–9
    socio-economic status relationship   26–7,
        164, 476
    student solution strategies   710–12
    test design   694, 698
    see also attainment; performance
achievement-testing movement   690
act-utilitarianism   448–9
action
    APOS theory   355
    values influence   727–8
action research   572, 574, 576, 602–3, 813
    professional development   883–4
    research by teachers   525
    TACCOL project   420
    values   754
ACTIONAID   127–8
Activity Theory   118
Ad hoc Committee on Holistic Review of the
    Mathematics Curriculum (Hong
    Kong)   300–1
adaptive potential   6, 143, 145, 175, 179
adaptive practice   160–1
adaptive progressive sentiment   109
adaptive reasoning   664
Adult Basic Education (ABE)   120–4
adult education
    Latin America   220
    lifelong mathematics education   6, 103–42
        policy perspectives   106–11
        practice perspectives   122–31
        research perspectives   111–22
    numeracy   77
Adult Literacy and Lifeskills (ALL)   116
Adults Learning Mathematics
    (ALM)   111–12, 115
Advanced Certificate in Education   838
Advisory Council for Adult and Continuing
    Education (ACACE)   111
advocacy research   450–2, 457
AERA *see* American Educational Research
    Association
affective aspects of mathematics
    education   721, 731–2, 734, 738, 754
affective-cognitive dichotomy   723–8
Africa
    cultural values survey   721
    ethnomathematics   203–4
    inequalities   465
    research ethics   464–5
    socio-cultural needs   38
African American students   27, 173
African Mathematical Union   186, 206
Africanization   38, 548
age   108
aggregated data   155, 167
AI *see* artificial intelligence
AI-ED (Artificial Intelligence in
    Education)   254
AIDS model   95
algebra
    abstract   372, 375–7
    CBMS report   784
    Computer Algebra Systems   274–6, 306,
        380–1
    Australia   286–9
    de-emphasis of skill   307
    enactive representations   370
    as expressive tool   332, 336–9

France   305
handheld calculators   359, 361, 365, 379,
    386–7
integration   379
learning   369
linear algebra   371–5
meta-study on technology
    research   241–3, 244, 248, 264–5
constructivist teaching methodology   123
differential equations   365
graphing calculators   252–3, 261
ISETL program   357
linear   371–5
Mathematical Tasks Framework   886
microworlds   331
need to strengthen algebraic teaching   772
numeracy   77
representation   327
spreadsheets   306
symbolic computation   280
teacher education   795
technology research   238–9, 247, 252,
    260–2, 264–5, 268–9
United States   658, 660–1
vector   371–3, 375
algorithms
CBMS report   785
Computer Algebra Systems   242, 264
digital technology   327
numerology   96
alignment of curriculum   154–6, 158
ALL *see* Adult Literacy and Lifeskills
ALM *see* Adults Learning Mathematics
ambiguity   701–2
American Educational Research Association
    (AERA)   448, 451, 702
American Psychological Association
    (APA)   702
American Statistical Association   280
analytic rationality   436–7, 471, 473, 480–6
Annenberg/CPB   405
anonymity   448, 453–5, 464
'Ant-on-the-Wheel' investigation   815–24
ANTA *see* Australian National Training
    Authority
anti-racism   554
antiderivatives   366–7
anxiety
elementary teachers   808, 811, 843
students   34, 41, 123
APA *see* American Psychological Association
apartheid   453, 525, 550, 645, 839
APOS theory   244, 355, 368, 370, 375–6, 380
Appalachia Educational Laboratory   660
apprenticeship model   836, 847–8
appropriation, international comparative
    research   178, 180

Argentina
building workers   125–6, 128–9
collaborative research projects   222
UN classification   219
art   148
artefacts   83–4, 244, 341
artificial intelligence (AI)   254, 263
Artificial Intelligence in Education
    (AI-ED)   254
Asia
Colombo Plan   212
compulsory maths curriculum   41
elites   40–2
equity   40
imported curricula   206
international comparative research   155,
    158
manipulatives   737
pupils' attitudes   63–4
Second Asian Technology Conference in
    Mathematics   x
tracking   61
see also East Asia; South East Asia; tiger
    economies
Asia Pacific   186
Asian-American students   155, 173–4
assessment
adult numeracy practice   131
conservative influence   624
design   638, 689–716
development   630n2
formative   157, 485, 513–14, 698
power of   45–6
teacher education   412, 809–10
undergraduate mathematics   369, 384–5
see also examinations; international
    comparative studies; International
    Programme for Student Assessment;
    tests; Third International Mathematics
    and Science Study
assessment driven reforms   200
Assessment in Education (journal)   514
Assessment Performance Unit   594
Assessment Standards for School Mathematics
    (NCTM, 1995)   207
Association of Teachers of Mathematics
    (United Kingdom)   304
associationism   475, 600, 605
asymptotes   249, 268, 269
attained curriculum
curriculum documents   297
examination effect on   650
SIMS   198
TIMSS   154
attainment
East Asia   40–1

poverty relationship 25–8
see also achievement
attendance 15
attitudes 63, 720, 731, 750
  cultural conflicts 738
  East Asia 41
  internalization 724–5
  values relationship 723, 725–7, 729–30
  see also beliefs
Auckland, University of 126
Australia
  Aborigines 204–5
  adult numeracy teachers 121
  case study 208–14
  competency-based education 116, 119
  compulsory maths curriculum 41
  cultural pluralism 155
  cultural values survey 721
  ICME 192
  immigrant teachers 731, 739–40
  inequitable resource distribution 45
  international students 186, 209–12
  Learner's Perspective Study 166
  'Learning About Teaching' project 842
  LUDDITE study 404
  MERGA 524
  National Statement on Mathematics for Australian Schools 207, 285, 647
  non-English speaking students 155
  outcomes-based education 108, 209
  PISA results 153
  pupils' attitudes 63
  regulating entry into teaching profession 767, 774–6, 783
  social marketing 109
  student teachers 662
  technology 285–90, 299–300, 461, 653
  textbooks 738
  TIMSS reporting 146
  values 720–1, 738–9, 740–7, 754
  VAMP 739–47, 753, 757–8
Australian Association of Mathematics Teachers (AAMT) 82, 277, 299–300, 302
Australian Education Council 285, 647, 649
Australian National Training Authority (ANTA) 109
Australian Research Council 226n6, 620, 740
Austria
  PISA results 153
  power distance 722
authoritarianism 44, 49, 58–9, 313, 604
authorship, cultural 6, 79, 143, 145, 162, 165–6, 176–7
autonomy

collegiality 851–3
research ethics 450, 452, 465
student 424–5, 813
awareness 812–13
axiomatic objects 354

Bachelor of Education (BEd) degree 836–8
Back to Basics 215
BALID *see* British Association for Literacy in Development
Banana problem 709–10
Bangladesh, REFLECT programme 127
Basic Education Curriculum Material Development Centre (China) 292
Basic IT Competence (BIT) 312
basic skills 19, 20–3, 678
BEAR Assessment System 704
BEd (Bachelor of Education) degree 836–8
behaviorism 130, 600, 605, 609, 613
Belgium, PISA results 153
beliefs 720, 731, 750
  about teaching 410–13, 417
  assessment practices 158
  change 616–17, 639, 672–3, 677
  classroom practices 645–53
  communication of research 619
  cultural 179, 199, 738
  doubt 900
  identity development 755
  internalization 724–5
  national context 167
  resistance to change 616–17
  student teachers 662
  SummerMath programme 892
  teacher education 795, 799–802, 805, 812
  values relationship 723, 725–7, 728–30, 734
  see also attitudes
benchmarking
  Australia 209
  information technology 311
  international studies 199
  TIMSS 458–60
best practice 537–9
  East and South East Asia 218–19
  UK Best Practice scholarship 856
bias of international comparative studies 200
biographies 572
BIT *see* Basic IT Competence
Board of Studies (Victoria, Australia) 285, 290, 720
bookkeeping 93
bottom-up approaches 656–9, 678
Boxer 328–9, 331, 340, 463
boys
  abstracted techniques 53

association of mathematics with   36
community support against biases   66
international comparative studies   162–3
rationality   50–2
'brain drain'   15, 186
Brazil
    adult education   83, 118
    ethnomathematics   203, 568
    ghettoization   83
    income inequalities   219
    PISA   80
Brigham Young University   364
British Association for Literacy in
        Development (BALID)   128
British Columbia, University of   343n6
Brunei Darussalem
    authoritarianism   58
    values   719
building workers   125–6, 128–9
Burkina Faso, ICMI Solidarity
        Program   193

C&M project *see* Calculus and Mathematica
        project
C4L Reform Program   363
C View   398, 412
Cabri-Géomètre   275–6
    linear algebra   374
    technology research   251, 255, 265–7
    undergraduate mathematics   377
CAI *see* Computer Assisted Instruction
CAL *see* Computer Assisted Learning
calculational instruments   332, 336–9
Calculator Based Lab (CBL)   422
Calculator-Aware Number (CAN)
        project   654–5
calculators   161, 272, 276–7, 326, 461–2
    Australia   285–9, 299–300
    CAS   359, 361, 365, 379, 386–7
    China   292–3
    classroom practices   653–55
    Cockcroft Report   279
    graphing   276, 279, 286–9, 311, 386–7, 462
        'Ant-on-the-Wheel' investigation   820
        classroom practices   653
        data analysis   503
        integration   379
        limit concept   370
        teacher education   422
        technology research   252–3, 261, 336
    Hong Kong   276–7, 294
    Japan   295
    Kumon method/Singapore Math   652
    National Research Council
            recommendations   279
    Netherlands   291
    New Zealand   290

South Korea   295
Taiwan   293
teacher education   396, 422
technology research   240, 252–3, 255, 262
TI-89 calculator   359, 361, 370
TI-92 calculator   276, 280, 338, 370
TIMSS   474
United Kingdom   284, 654
United States   282–4
calculus
    'Calculus Reform'   278, 363, 384
    Colombia   223
    computer use   363–71, 386–7
    notation   327
    'procept' notion   248
    teacher education   795
Calculus and Mathematica (C&M)
        project   364
'Calculus Reform'   278, 363, 384
California Achievement Test (CAT)   696–7
California State Board of Education   282–4,
        301
Cambridge Institute of Education   594
Cameroon, ICMI Solidarity Program   193
CAN project *see* Calculator-Aware Number
        project
Canada
    cultural pluralism   155
    cultural values survey   721
    PISA results   153
    TIMSS reporting   146
Candle problem   706
Cape Town, University of   533–7, 540–1
capitalism   11–12, 23
    individualism   13
    inequalities   546
    neoliberalism   548
CARAPACE   264–5
Caribbean   89
Cartesian philosophy   796–7
CAS *see* Computer Algebra Systems
case studies
    case inquiry approach to teacher
            education   884–8
    Formal Adult Mathematics
            Education   125–7
    globalization/internationalization   208–23
        Australia   208–14
        Colombia   220–3
        East and South East Asia   214–19
        Latin America   219–20
    Informal Adult Mathematics
            Education   125–6, 128–9
    international research   167–9
    narratives   889
    Non-formal Adult Mathematics
            Education   125–8

professional development 669–70
research in conflict situations 558
rigor 504
teacher education 854–68
TIMSS 199
VIMT projects 750
see also narratives
CAT *see* California Achievement Test;
  Computerized Adaptive Testing
catalytic validity 575, 577
CBAM *see* Concerns Based Adoption Model
CBL *see Calculator Based Lab*
CBMS *see* College Board for the
  Mathematical Sciences
CBT *see* competency-based education and
  training
CCP *see* Connected Curriculum Project
CD-I discs 399
CD-ROMs 294, 399, 404, 406, 411, 422, 654
CEMI *see Collaboration for Enhancing
  Mathematics Instruction* project
Central Queensland University 383
centralization 208
CERME *see* European Society for Research
  in Mathematics Education
certification 775, 779–82, 787–91
CETP *see Philadelphia Collaborative for
  Excellence in Teaching Education
  Program*
CGI *see* Cognitively Guided Instruction
chalkboard use 313
change 606, 610–11, 628
  barriers to 596
  classroom practices 638, 643–87
  influences 612–17
  new habits 622
  professional development 640, 663–77
  resistance to 443, 616, 620–1, 656
  social 75–6, 85–6, 97
  system obstacles 624–5
  teacher 638, 643–87
  values 718, 730–1
  see also reforms
Chaos Theory 479, 534
Characteristic Pedagogical Flow
  (CPT) 168–9
CHC *see* Confucian Heritage Culture
child-centred education 475, 843
children's thinking 404–5, 413, 895
  see also student thinking
Chile, UN classification 219
China
  arguments with World Bank 197
  examination culture 42
  high attainment 41, 56–7, 64, 217
  international students 185–6

long-term orientation 722
PISA 80
technology impact on curriculum 292–3
textbooks 738
values 719
Chreods (journal) 187
CIAEM *see* Conferencia Interamericana de
  Educación Matemática
CIEAEM *see* Commission Internationale
  pour l'Etude et l'Amelioration de
  l'Enseignement des Mathematique
ciphering 711
citizenship
  mathematical literacy 6, 75, 76, 81, 85,
    89–90, 97
  numeracy 120
  Suzuki method of teaching 105
Clarion University of Pennsylvania 420
class *see* social class
classroom activity
  international comparative
    research 158–60
  public talk 165
  technology in teacher education 402–13
  see also lessons
classroom assessment 698–9, 712
Classroom Computing (journal) 401
classroom interaction
  conflict 551–3
  norms and routines 847
  reflection on teaching practice 848–9
  teacher education and technology 405–8,
    410, 413
classroom practice
  changes in 638, 643–87
  Cognitive Guided Instruction 892
  democratic 42–5
  international comparative research 159,
    161, 171–2, 180
Classroom with a View (C View) 398, 412
CLICK *see Computers and Learning in
  Classrooms: K-6*
co-learning 571, 576, 831, 882, 897–9
co-operation
  computers 363
  international research 435
  teacher values 742, 744, 746
  technology 379–80
  see also collaboration
Cockcroft Report (DES/WO, 1982) 76, 111,
  279, 599
codes of ethics 448
coflection 577, 580
cognition
  affective-cognitive dichotomy 723–8
  learning systems 595

situated   341–2
values   724, 726–7, 734
cognitive conflict   551–3, 674
cognitive dimension, technology
    research   242, 244–6, 249–51, 257, 263
Cognitively Guided Instruction (CGI)   485,
    648, 666, 811–12, 845, 891–2
cognitivist perspective   338, 342
collaboration
    action research   883–4
    case inquiry   885
    constructionism   328
    contrived collegiality   629
    global   7, 206–8
    internationalization   188, 195, 224
    narratives   890
    professional development programs   671
    research   145, 176, 180, 224–5
        action research   883–4
        Australia   213–14
        by teachers   532–3, 537–8, 540
        Colombia   221–2
        East and South East Asia   218–19
        researcher-participant   571
        researcher-practitioner   496
        teacher research   532–3, 537–8, 540
        web-based teacher resources   415–17
    see also co-operation
*Collaboration for Enhancing Mathematics
    Instruction* (CEMI) project   416, 420
collectivism   217, 722
collectivity   571–2, 575, 580
College Board for the Mathematical Sciences
    (CBMS)   768, 772–3, 783–6, 789
The College Mathematics Journal   275
collegiality
    autonomy   851–3
    contrived   629
    teacher research   532
Colombia
    case study   219–23
    conflict studies   556
    cultural values survey   721
    income inequalities   219
    UN classification   219
Colombo Plan   212
colonialism/colonization   186, 547–8, 582
    ethnomathematics   202, 204
    Latin America   221, 223
    South East Asia   214
COMET ('Cases of Mathematics Instruction
    to Enhance Teaching') project   885
Comité Interamericano de Educación
    Matemática   186
    see also Conferencia Interamericana de
        Educación Matemática

Commission Internationale pour l'Etude et
    l'Amelioration de l'Enseignement des
    Mathematique (CIEAEM)   ix, 33–5,
    191
Committee on Scientific Principles for
    Education Research   479
common sense   118–19, 132
communication
    Internet technologies   399–400, 413–18
    language styles   44
    of research   511–16, 618–19, 627–8
    teacher education   399–400, 413–18
    teacher values   746
communications software   396–7
communitarianism   449
communities of practice   416, 604, 878, 882,
    904
community
    individual dichotomy   614
    research   531
    support   66
    see also learning communities
community-based education
    lifelong education   110
    REFLECT programme   127–8
comparative international studies   6, 143–84,
    197–200, 436, 719
    less successful countries   850
    mathematical literacy   79
    research ethics   447, 458–61, 464
    technology   256
    see also International Programme for
        Student Assessment; Third
        International Mathematics and
        Science Study
competency assessment   704
competency-based education and training
    (CBT)   116, 118, 130
competition
    economic   133, 149
    global context   225
    international comparative research   149,
        153, 199
complementarity   558, 570
complexity
    dissemination of mathematics
        research   595, 600, 609
    environmental models   88–9
Complexity Theory   534
computational transposition   335, 338
Computer Algebra Systems (CAS)   274–6,
    306, 380–1
    Australia   286–9
    de-emphasis of skill   307
    enactive representations   370
    as expressive tool   332, 336–9

France 305
handheld calculators 359, 361, 365, 379, 386–7
integration 379
learning 369
linear algebra 371–5
meta-study on technology research 241–4, 248, 264–5
Computer Assisted Instruction (CAI) 255, 300, 326
see also Intelligent Computer Assisted Instruction System
Computer Assisted Learning (CAL) 273–5, 293–4, 300
computer conferencing 396–8, 400, 404, 414–16, 451
computer programming 326–31, 339–40
curriculum 280
ISETL 355–7, 363, 375–6
computer simulations 88–9
Computerized Adaptive Testing (CAT) 278
computers 272, 299, 311
algebra 260–2
Australia 285, 299–300
CARAPACE 264–5
changing role of teaching 307–8
China 292–3
classroom models 405–6
classroom practices 653
commercial interests 24
costs 423
France 290–1
generic organizers 267–8
Hong Kong 294
instrumental analysis 252
intelligent software tutors 254, 263–4, 278, 326
IT Competence 312
Japan 295
mediation 427
microworlds
characteristics 358–9
embodied objects 360–1
group theory 376
influence on curriculum 272–3, 299, 301
non-euclidean geometry 377–8
research projects 262–3, 267, 328–31, 339
teacher education 419
Netherlands 291
New Zealand 290
representation 327
South Korea 295
spatial visualization 302
Taiwan 293

teacher education 396, 400, 405–6, 419–22, 842
TIMSS 474–5
ubiquity of 324
undergraduate mathematics 351–94
abstract algebra 375–7
calculus 363–71, 386–7
changing curriculum 378–85
linear algebra 371–5
United States 282–4
viability 253
see also Computer Algebra Systems; information and communication technology; information technology; Internet; programming; software
Computers and Learning in Classrooms: K-6 (CLICK!) 422
Computers in the Primary Classroom resource kit 406
concept image 354
concepts of mathematics 353–62
process and objects 354–7
representations 357–62
Concepts in Secondary Mathematics and Science (CSMS) project 483
conceptual understanding 80, 369, 599, 664, 668, 773, 844–5
Concerns Based Adoption Model (CBAM) 674
condensed measures 90–3
conferences ix, x, 186, 194
East and South East Asia 216
increased number of 451
WCEFA 32
see also International Congress on Mathematics Education
Conferencia Interamericana de Educación Matemática (CIAEM) ix
see also Comité Interamericano de Educación Matemática
conferencing tools 396–8, 400, 404, 414–16, 451
confidence
newly qualified teachers 858
teacher values 744
see also self-esteem
confidentiality 448, 453–5
conflicts
cultural 551–3, 738
social/political 437–8, 545–91
Confucian Heritage Culture (CHC) 217, 313
Confucian influence 40–1, 56, 64, 217, 313, 722
conjecture 334–6, 352, 418, 784
Connected Curriculum Project (CCP) 383
connectionism 904

consent   450, 452, 465
conservatism   624
construction   251, 333–5, 340
   of meaning   82, 249–50
   teacher education   809
constructionism
   conflict   553
   programming research   328
   technology research   244
constructivism   19, 27, 201, 605, 609, 613
   adult mathematics education   117, 123
   beliefs   677
   collaborative groups   652
   conflict   553
   constructivist revolution   475–6
   descriptive nature of   623
   fallibilism   798
   learning   363, 600, 647–8, 672, 678
   the mind   796
   professional development   878
   radical   594–5, 601, 630
   reform-based approaches   824
   research   530
   social   553, 594–5, 599, 601
   SummerMath project   673, 892
   teacher education   411–12
   technology research   244, 246, 249–50, 257
Consultative Group on Early Childhood
      Care and Development   32
consumerism   189
contemporary liberal theory   449–50
content games   273
context   20–2, 157
   conflict relationship   552–3
   exclusion from mathematical
         problems   53–4
   global   185–229
   mathematical literacy   152
   professional development   670–1
contextualization   53, 250–1, 257, 578
continuing professional development
      (CPD)   384
Contour Analyser   332
contrived collegiality   629
conversation   534, 538, 540, 567
Corona Foundation   221
cost-effectiveness   617
Costa Rica, UN classification   219
costs, resource development   423–4
CPD *see* continuing professional
      development
CPT *see* Characteristic Pedagogical Flow
creativity   744–5
critical apprenticeship   848
critical hermeneutics   603, 614
critical mathematics education

mathematical literacy   85–6, 89–90, 97
   research in conflict situations   554, 568–9,
         579
critical pedagogy   85, 89
critical perspectives
   critical mathematical literacy   85–6, 97
   generalization   578
   power relations   576–7
   research in conflict situations   554, 568–9,
         572, 575–6, 579
   research discourses   603–4
critical theory   449–50, 569
cross-subject comparisons   509–10
Crowther Report (DES, 1959)   76
crucial descriptions   572, 576
CSMS *see* Concepts in Secondary
      Mathematics and Science project
Cuba   219
cultural authorship   6, 79, 143, 145, 162,
      165–6, 176–7
cultural capital   19, 25
   Bourdieu   12, 42, 49, 107
   social class   27
cultural difference   132
cultural diversity   68
   see also multiculturalism
cultural identity   68, 75, 82–4, 89
cultural imperialism   5, 156, 162, 180, 191–2
cultural myths   18–19
cultural psychology   179
cultural relativism   449
cultural reproduction   108
culture   3, 55–6, 63–5
   adaptive potential   175, 179
   case studies   199
   classroom practices   644, 679
   communication of research   619
   conflicts   551–3, 738
   cultural psychology perspective   179
   ethnomathematics   83–4, 201–5
   global curriculum   205–6
   globalization   189
   ICME conferences   195
   intellectual dominance   25
   internal variation   155
   international comparative research   6, 151,
         158, 171–2, 175, 200
   learning   108, 160
   mathematical literacy   6, 75–6, 81, 97
   professional development   638
   school   308–11
   societal values   163
   survey metrics   162
   values   721–3, 732, 735, 737–8
      changing classroom practices   645–53
      international comparative research   158,
            172, 175, 179

IT in mathematics curriculum 234
  societal 163
  see also socio-cultural issues
curriculum
  ability differentiation 61
  adult mathematics education 118–20,
    122–4, 132
  class divisions 47
  classroom practices 648–50
  cultural oppression 3
  cultural selection 43
  curricular alignment 154–6, 158
  development 607, 630n2
  globalization 188, 200, 205–8
  importation of Western curricula to
    developing countries 206, 215
  innovation 573
  international comparative research 144,
    148, 153–4, 155–9, 175, 200
  introduction of new 656–7
  linear algebra 374–5
  as obstacle to dissemination of
    research 624
  Portugal 657, 661
  pressures for change 610–11
  pseudo 20
  reforms 66–7, 218, 446
  repositioning 299–308
  SIMS 198
  social construction 110
  South Africa 549
  South East Asia 214–15, 218
  technology influence 234, 271–321
  traditional canonical 37–8
  undergraduate 378–85
  see also global curriculum
Curriculum Development Centre
  (Malaysia) 296
Curriculum Development Council (Hong
  Kong) 293–4, 298
Curriculum Development Institute (Hong
  Kong) 301
curriculum differentiation *see* tracking
*Curriculum and Evaluation Standards for
  School Mathematics* (NCTM, 1989)
  calculators 277
  changes in classroom practices 657, 670,
    679n1
  core knowledge base 39
  process-orientation 599
  technology 282
  US reforms 39, 207
Curriculum Planning and Development
  Division (Singapore) 295–6
Curriculum Reform Committee
  (Shanghai) 292, 293

Curriculum Reform Working Group
  (Macau) 294–5
cyber learning 278

Dakar Framework for Action 133
data
  aggregated 155, 167
  communication of research 511
  data-logging 286–9
  moving from particular to general 505–8
  records of practice 516
  rigor of analysis 502–5
data collection 90–1, 161, 566–7
  conflict studies 558
  Learner's Perspective Study 166–7
  research practices 500, 503–4, 511
  video studies 165
  VIMT projects 750–1
databases 284, 286–9, 336
  conflict 551–2
  MILE 412–13
  teacher case studies 531
  'Zentralblatt für Didaktik der
    Mathematik' 239, 551
Davidson series 273
de-professionalization 11, 207, 692
de-skilling 692
Deakin University 421
decentralization 208
decimals 803, 809, 866–7
decision-making
  gender differences 50
  moral 50
  values 727–30
decolonization 195–6, 582
decontextualization 22, 52–3, 82, 407, 734
deficit approach 849
definitions 902–4
democracy 57–8, 554–5
  ethical issues in research 447, 452–3, 457,
    463–4
  globalization 190
  individualism 12–13
  learning process 831
  as multileveled practice 47
  public debate 17
democratic classroom teaching 42–5
democratic participatory validity 455, 576
democratic progressive sentiment 108–9
democratization
  adult education 105
  developing countries 442
  Mathematics for All 62–3
  technology 463
Denmark
  conflict studies 556, 562
  labor market needs 108

PISA results   153
theoretical developments   124
deontological principles   448–9
Department for Education and Employment
    (DfEE)   626, 649, 655, 678
    adult numeracy teachers   121
    'Best Practice' scholarship   856
    cultural development   55–6
    information technology   284
    Moser Report   120
    setting   59
    skills   107, 119
Department of Education and Science (DES)
    adult education   76, 111, 119, 121
    Cockcroft Report   76, 111, 599
    information technology   284
    national curriculum   483
Department for Education and Skills
    (DfES)   649
DERIVE
    impact on curriculum   274, 276, 305
    incorporation into graphing
        calculators   463
    technology research   243, 258n4, 338
    undergraduate mathematics   369
DEs *see* differential equations
DES *see* Department of Education and
    Science
desktop publishing   286–9
DETEN *see* Digital European Teacher
    Education Network
developed countries
    achievement/GNP relationship   15–16
    economics discourse   11–12
    intellectual dominance   24–5
developing countries
    access to education   34
    'brain drain'   15, 186
    conflicts   545–6, 548–9, 573, 581
    cultural values survey   721
    culturally-orientated curricula   206
    economics discourse   11–12
    global collaboration   224–5
    ICME attendance   192, 195
    importation of Western
        research/curricula   206, 215, 582–3,
        606
    poverty   550–1
    qualified teachers   769–70
    REFLECT programme   127–8
    reform initiatives   441–2
    research   441–5, 447, 564
    resources   65, 68
    socio-cultural context   38
    textbooks   83–4
    TIMSS   458

'Western mathematics' influence   737–8
    see also Third World
development
    ethical issues in research   442, 447, 452,
        456, 461, 464
    research   605–12, 628
developmental research   625, 629
DfEE *see* Department for Education and
    Employment
DfES *see* Department for Education and
    Skills
DGS *see* dynamic geometry systems
dialogue   438, 570
    deliberative   577
    participatory validity   575–6
diaries   525–6
dictionaries   498
didactic model of assessment design   638–9,
    693, 698–9, 703, 712
didactical contract   506–8, 661, 847
didactical research   255–6, 268–9
didactics   601, 704
didaktikal tradition   851
difference, teaching for   132
differential equations (DEs)   360, 365–6
digital divide   302
Digital European Teacher Education
    Network (DETEN)   413
digital technology   323–39
dilemmas of teaching   408–10, 413
Discipline of Noticing   535
disciplined inquiry   492–4, 497, 499, 517–18
discrete mathematics   307
discrimination   48, 59–62
disequilibrium   672–4
dissemination of research
    obstacles to   593–634
    problems with   530–1
distance education   410, 418
diversity   68, 548, 580
doubt   899–902
dragging mode   334–5
drawing tools   251, 266–7, 334, 784
Duke University   363, 383
Dutch Ministry of Education, Culture and
    Science   291
dynamic geometry   275–6, 278, 284, 294, 822
    dynamic geometry systems   333–6, 340
    technology research   249, 251, 254–5,
        266–7, 463
dynamic geometry systems (DGS)   333–6,
    340

e-learning   413–14
E-Standards (NCTM)   415
EARCOME *see* East Asian Regional
    Conference on Mathematics Education

East Asia
  attainment 40–1
  case study 214–19
  opportunities for girls 52
  values 719
  see also Far East; South East Asia
East Asian Regional Conference on
  Mathematics Education
  (EARCOME) x, 216
Eastern Europe, achievement/GNP
  relationship 16
ECM *see* European Congress of Mathematics
ecological ethics 449–50
ecological perspectives 594–6, 600, 609
ecology of provision model 107–8
economic capital 27, 107
economic determinism 109
economic development 118, 201
  mathematics relationship 4–5
  qualifications in mathematics 769–70
  World Bank policies 196
economic imperative 12, 108–9
economic issues 4–5, 9–30
  Colombia 220
  competition 133, 149
  globalization 189–90, 447
  Latin America 219
  lifelong learning 109–11, 118–19
  mathematical literacy 646
  neoliberal economics 106, 109, 189, 548
  overseas students 210, 212
  reforms 617
  System for Integrated Environmental and
    Economic Accounting 92–3
  teacher education resources 424, 426
ecosystems 87
Edexcel Foundation 285
Education for All 104, 133
Education and Manpower Bureau (Hong
  Kong) 308–12
Educational Resource Information
  Center 646
Educational Studies in Mathematics
  (journal) 186–7, 553, 732
edutainment games 273
effectiveness of schools 19–20, 150
El Salvador, REFLECT programme 127
electronic communications 286–9
elementary education
  anxiety 808
  child-centred education 843
  IMPACT project 662
  Japanese curriculum 295
  Japanese teacher preparation 840–1
  lack of teacher
    knowledge/preparation 802–3, 809,
    811, 833

teacher qualification 770, 772–5, 778–9,
  782–3
  see also primary education
elites 15, 40–2
  economic imperative 12
  traditional canonical curriculum 37–8
elitism
  curriculum 43
  giftedness 42
  international comparative research 149
  league tables 14, 20
  national 17
embodied objects 354, 360–1
emotional intelligence 50
emotions 724, 731
employment *see* work
empowerment 603, 606, 613–15, 629
  adult education 118, 120
  international collaboration 225
  REFLECT programme 127–8
  teacher educators 638
Empresa Docente 221
enactivism 594, 599, 609, 613–14
  development 612
  enactive mathematics 360, 365, 370
  learning 600
  teacher research 534–6
encapsulation 355
energy issues 86–7
engineering 38–9, 90
England
  adult numeracy teachers 121
  basic skills 678
  curriculum research 565
  examinations 650
  Her Majesty's Inspectors 846
  international comparative research 173
  league tables 460
  learning of mathematics 813
  national curriculum 483, 649, 698
  National Numeracy Strategy 626, 649,
    656
  outcomes-based education 108
  prescriptive directives 679
  primary education 120, 624
  reforms 678
  SMILE project 621
  teacher boycott of national
    curriculum 698
  teacher preparation 835–8
  technology 461, 653
  TIMSS reporting 145
  see also Great Britain; United Kingdom
English Journal 531
enrolment
  Colombia 220

poorer countries   15
environmental issues
  globalization   189–90
  mathematical literacy   76, 86–9, 97
  System for Integrated Environmental and
      Economic Accounting   92–3
environmental mathematics   88
episteme   480–1, 486, 622
epistemology   341, 580
  epistemological dimension of technology
      research   243–9, 257
  epistemological values   735
  mathematics education   116–18
equality of educational opportunity   105
equations
  calculators   279
  differential   360, 365–6
equity   5, 36, 40, 654
  conflict   554
  exclusion   562
  international comparative research   144–5,
      154–5
  IOWME   193
  IT-disadvantage   302–3
  lifelong mathematics education   107–8
  REFLECT programme   127–8
  reforms   566
  research   495, 510
  standardized tests   698
  state role   190
  see also inequalities; social justice
Escuela Nueva project   221
essentialism
  gender   50
  knowledge   22
  numeracy ideal   21
  TIMSS   20
estimation   130–1
ethical issues
  ecological   449–50
  international collaboration   225
  relational ethics   449–50
  research   xiii, 436, 441–70
ethnic minorities
  achievement   476
  discrimination   48
  Mathematics for All   36
  United Kingdom   54–6
  see also marginalized groups; minority
      groups
ethnicity   54–7
  access to education   34
  aggregated data   155
  CIEAEM manifesto   35
  exclusion   547
  international survey research   162, 164

research   495
  see also race
ethnography   115, 278, 572
ethnomathematics   11–12, 20, 25, 299, 548,
    598
  common sense   118
  conflict   551–2, 554, 568
  critiques of   204, 206
  cultural practices   117
  Eurocentrism   38, 201–2, 205
  globalization   201–5
  mathematical knowledge   735–6
  mathematical literacy   75, 82–4, 97
  methodologies   118
  universal mathematics conflict   201–5
EU *see* European Union
Eurocentrism   3, 47
  ethnomathematics   38, 201–2, 205
  Manifesto   2000 for the Year of
      Mathematics   191–2
  research   582
Europe
  apprenticeship models   103
  compulsory maths curriculum   41
  teacher autonomy   851
  teacher education   526
European Congress of Mathematics
    (ECM)   ix
European Society for Research in
    Mathematics Education (CERME)   x
European Union (EU)
  international students   186
  internationalization   191
  lifelong learning   104
  T3 project   416–17
evaluation
  changes in classroom practices   678
  mathematical literacy   76–7, 89–90, 97–8
evaluative listening   534
Everybody Counts   279
everyday mathematics   105, 117–18, 598
evidence-based practice   539
examinations   471–2, 624, 650
  calculators   277, 292
  China   42, 217
  curriculum documents   297
  East Asia   41
  Japan   459, 650
  standardized   623
  undergraduate mathematics and
      technology   385
  see also assessment; tests
Excel   366, 817–18, 820
exclusion   48, 83, 85
  lifelong learning   106
  research in conflict situations   547, 549,
      562

exemplarity 572, 579
Exeter, University of 416
exploitation, international comparative
    research 178, 180
exploratory studies 629
expression 328–9
expressive software tools 325–8, 332–42

face-to-face learning 126–29
Fachseminar 836
fairness 154–5
fallibilism 19, 116, 797–8, 805, 825
FAME *see* Formal Adult Mathematics
    Education
family, learning trajectory concept 108
Far East
    technology impact on curriculum 234,
        279–80, 292–8
    see also East Asia; tiger economies
fast-track certification 787–8, 790–1
FDE *see* Further Diploma in Education
feedback
    internship scheme 858, 859, 861–2, 864,
        868
    research 484
    undergraduate mathematics 377, 379
femininity 722
feminism
    multiplicity of feminisms 189
    policy research 604
    power relations 576–7
    radical 118
    relational ethics 449
    research in conflict situations 573
file management 286–9
FIMS *see* First International Mathematics
    Study
Finland
    MILE project 412–13
    PISA results 153
First Class software 400
First International Mathematics Study
    (FIMS) 198
fiscal policies 27
Flag problem 693–7, 700, 702, 705
fluency 664
FME *see* Formal Mathematics Education
folk education 200
Folk Mathematics 118
For the Learning of Mathematics
    (journal) 186
Formal Adult Mathematics Education
    (FAME) 125–7
Formal Mathematics Education (FME) 106
formalism 639–40, 795, 797–8, 806–8, 826
    mathematical knowledge 736
    values 734

formative assessment 157, 485, 513–14, 698
forming research questions 499–502
Fourth World 549
fragmentation 189, 201
Framework for Action to Meet Basic
    Learning Needs 32
framing questions 499–502
France
    colonial education tradition in South East
        Asia 214–15
    Computer Algebra Systems 305
    cultural values survey 721
    international students 185–6
    learning of mathematics 813
    Ministry of Education 238
    national curriculum 279
    PISA results 153
    technology 240, 290–1, 653
    test scores 651
Freundenthal Institute 67, 413
Fundamental Theorem 365
funding xiii, 27–8
    Colombia 222
    international testing 147
    journals 582
    Latin America 220
    reforms 617
    research 476, 478–9, 532–3, 627
    school development 850
    Solidarity Program in Mathematics
        Education 193
    technology research 464
    universities 210–12
    values 736
Further Diploma in Education
    (FDE) 453–7
further education 121
FX2 calculator 359

game theory 94, 736
games 273
GATE(way) project *see Graphing, Algebra,
    Technology and Excellence* project
gay rights 189
gaze 204–5, 451, 581
GCSE Mathematics software 273
GDP *see* gross domestic product
gender
    access to education 34
    achievement 475–6
    advocacy research 451
    Asia 40
    CIEAEM manifesto 35
    community support 66
    conflict 552, 554
    exclusion 547, 562
    globalization 189

IEA study   171
inequalities   563
information technology   302
international comparative research   154–5,
    162–4
International Organization of Women and
    Mathematics Education   36, 193–4
learning trajectory concept   108
Mathematics for All   36
media creation of differences   17
power relations   43
rationality   49–52
research   495, 573
SMILE project   621
social deprivation   26
technology research   462
see also boys; femininity; girls; masculinity;
    women
general insights   505–8
generalizability   537, 574–5, 578–80, 618
generativity   572, 578–80
generic organizers   267–8, 358
genetic decomposition   355–6, 368, 370, 377
Geometer's Sketchpad software   275, 377, 418,
    422, 822, 908
Geometric Supposer software   653, 908
geometric vectors   371–2, 374
geometry   401, 784, 795
    adult education   123
    dialectic conceptualization   249–50
    dynamic   275–6, 278, 284, 294, 822
        dynamic geometry systems   333–6, 340
        technology research   249, 251, 254–5,
            266–7, 463
    microworlds   330
    professional development programs   667
    teacher education   823, 908–9
    technology research   249–51, 265–7
    undergraduate   377–8
Geometry Expert software   275
Geometry Inventor software   377
Georgia, University of   421
Germany
    achievement/GNP relationship   15–16
    classroom practices   652
    didaktical tradition   851
    Learner's Perspective Study   166
    Nazi ideology   550
    school development after TIMSS   850
    teacher preparation   835–6
    technology research   461
ghettoization   83
giftedness   34–5, 42, 66, 68
girls
    abstracted techniques   53
    community support against biases   66

exclusion   547
international comparative studies   162–3
Latin America   220
opportunities   36
rationality   50–2
see also women
Glenn Commission   651
Glenn Report   768–72, 786, 788–91
global context   185–229
global corporations   5, 9
global curriculum   144, 147, 178, 180, 205–8
global village   188, 566
globalization   xi, 6–7, 185, 187, 200–8, 224–5
    adoption of RDD model   606
    case studies   208–23
        Australia   208–14
        Colombia   220–3
        South East Asia   214–19
    conceptualization of term   187–91
    e-knowledge   24
    ethics in research   446–7
    from above   189, 208
    from below   189–90, 204, 208
    international comparative research   147–8
    lifelong mathematics education   106–7,
        111
    research in conflict situations   565–6, 582
    resources   11
    technology   308
    see also internationalization
GNP *see* gross national product
goals
    changing classroom practice   677–8
    cross-national variation   153, 171–2
    cultural authorship   176
    Education for All   104
    international comparative research   162,
        176
    learning outcomes   180
    national   199
    research   465
good practice   129–31
Graphic Calculus program   268, 365
graphical representation
    calculators   279
    differential equations   366
    expressive tools   333
    limit concept   370
    multimedia   399
graphical visualization   249, 267–9
graphics/graphing software   274, 284, 286–9,
    325, 336–7
Graphing, Algebra, Technology and Excellence
    [GATE(way)] project   419
graphing calculators   276, 279, 286–9, 311,
    386–7, 462

'Ant-on-the-Wheel' investigation   820
  classroom practices   653
  data analysis   503
  integration   379
  limit concept   370
  teacher education   422
  technology research   252–3, 261, 336
graphs
  as embodied objects   361
  Excel   817, 820
  preservice teacher problem-
    solving   815–20
  undergraduate calculus   366–7
grass roots ownership   656
Great Britain
  cultural values survey   721
  research   477
  see also England; Scotland; United
    Kingdom; Wales
Greece, uncertainty   722
gross domestic product (GDP)   93
gross national product (GNP)   15–16
grounded theory approach   504
group theory   376
groups
  learning   646
  teacher values   742
Guatemala
  collectivism   722
  income inequalities   219

habits   622
habitus   26–7
handheld technologies   333
Harvard Education Review (journal)   531
hegemony   540
Her Majesty's Inspectors (HMI)   846
hermeneutic listening   535
hermeneutics   601–3, 614
Hierarchical Linear Model analysis   161
high-tech industries   78
higher education
  Colombia   220–3
  Post Graduate Certificate of
    Education   836–9, 854–68
  teacher research   539
  World Bank policies   196–7
  see also tertiary education; universities
Hispanic students   27, 173
historical perspectives   796–9
History and Pedagogy of Mathematics
  (HPM)   ix
HMI *see* Her Majesty's Inspectors
Hogeschool of Drenthe   413
holistic spray   376
homework   170
homogenization   189, 203

Hong Kong
  achievement/GNP relationship   16
  colonial education tradition   214–15
  cultural values   172
  high attainment   16, 41, 64
  ICMI study   217
  justification and proof   156
  Learner's Perspective Study   166
  Personal Data Assistants   313
  reforms   678
  Second IEA Mathematics Study   500
  statistics   281
  technology impact on curriculum   276–7,
    293–4, 298, 300–1, 304, 308–12
  TIMSS reporting   146
Hong Kong Association for Mathematics
  Education   303
HPM *see* History and Pedagogy of
  Mathematics
human capital
  lifelong learning   108
  mathematical literacy   80–2
  policy emphasis   119
human rights   189–90
Hungary, gender differences   163

IALS *see* International Adult Literacy Survey
ICAI *see* Intelligent Computer Assisted
  Instruction System
ICC *see* item characteristic curve
Ice Cream problem   708–9
Iceland, PISA results   153
ICM *see* International Congress of
  Mathematicians
ICME *see* International Congress on
  Mathematics Education
ICMI *see* International Commission on
  Mathematical Instruction
ICT *see* information and communication
  technology
ICTM *see* International Commission on the
  Teaching of Mathematics
ICTMA *see* International Conference on the
  Teaching of Modelling and Applications
identity
  cultural   68, 75, 82–4, 89
  pedagogical   726, 733–4, 748–9, 755–7
  researcher   581
ideology   547, 550
  of certainty   13–14, 17
  definition   13
IEA *see* International Association for the
  Evaluation of Educational Achievement
IFAME *see* Informal Adult Mathematics
  Education
IFME *see* Informal Mathematics Education
IIT *see* Intermediate IT Competence

IJCAME *see* International Journal for
    Computer Algebra in Mathematics
    Education
ILF *see Inquiry Learning Forum*
Illinois, University of   364
illiteracy   33, 77
Illuminations   398, 415
imagery   866, 867
IMF *see* International Monetary Fund
immigrant teachers   725, 731, 738–40
IMPACT (Increasing the Mathematical
    Power of All Children and
    Teachers)   662–3
imperialism
    cultural   5, 156, 162, 180, 191–2
    economic   11
    intellectual   24
    research   582
implemented curriculum
    examination effect on   650
    SIMS   198
    teacher role   307
    TIMSS   154
    undergraduate mathematics and
        technology   379–84
implicit personal research   526
imposition   178, 180
improvement
    schools   538, 692
    technology research   242, 244
in-service teacher education
        programmes   640, 767, 811
    ethical issues   453–7
    Michigan Mathematics Inservice
        Project   893
    Problem-Solving Inservice
        programme   890
    professional development   877, 880, 882,
        885, 896–7, 901–2, 911
    research by teachers   525–7, 532, 539, 541
    teacher educators   896–7, 899
inclusiveness   108
incomes
    Latin America   219
    low-income jobs   107
incomparability   151
independent learning   123
India
    arguments with World Bank   197
    cultural values survey   721
    drain of expertise from   15
Indiana University   401, 415–16, 420
indigenous knowledge   83, 547, 582
indigenous land rights   189
individual differences   744–5
individual progressive sentiment   108

individualism   12–13, 600, 621, 722
Indonesia
    cultural values survey   721
    reforms   217–18
    US New Mathematics curriculum   214
    values   719, 721
inequalities
    access to education   31
    Africa   465
    blame shifting to individuals   18
    capitalism   11, 546, 548
    Colombia   220
    conflict situations   563, 575
    ethnicity   54
    ethnomathematics   568
    globalization   188–91, 447
    ignored by international comparative
        research   151
    information technology   302–3
    Latin America   219
    mathematical knowledge   83
    poverty   550–1
    power distance   722
    resource distribution   11, 45, 68, 107
    social reproduction   85
    socio-cultural approaches   554
    sources of   566
    South Africa   454, 457
    structural   570
    technological divide   461
    United States   173
    see also equity
Informal Adult Mathematics Education
    (IFAME)   125–6, 128–9
informal assessment   698
Informal Mathematics Education
    (IFME)   106
information and communication technology
    (ICT)   233–5
    adult education   123
    classroom practices   653–5
    influence on curriculum   234, 271–321
    multidimensional perspective   237–69
    teacher education   395–432
    technological divide   9, 11, 22–4
    technological revolution   474–5
    see also computers; Internet; software;
        technology
information technology (IT)
    Australia   285–90
    China   292–3
    Hong Kong   293–4
    influence on mathematics curriculum   234,
        271–321
    Macau   294–5
    Malaysia   296

mathematical literacy   78
   Singapore   295–6
   South Korea   295
   see also computers; Internet; software;
      technology
informational society   548
inner city school poverty   26
innovation   564–5, 618
   ICT   237, 242–3
   technology research   237, 256
inquiry groups   791
Inquiry Learning Forum (ILF)   400–1,
      415–16, 420
inquiry-based mathematics   441–5, 465
insider perspective   452, 456–7, 460
inspection
   Her Majesty's Inspectors   846
   UK Framework   515
Institute of Employment Studies, University
      of Sussex   477
Institute for Mathematics and Science
      Teaching, University of
      Stellenbosch   414
institutional approach to ICT   244–6, 252–3,
      258
institutional system of mathematics education
      (ISME)   556
instructionally embedded assessment   698
instrumental approach to ICT   244–5, 246,
      251–2, 256–8, 260
instrumental genesis   338–9, 342
instrumentation   257, 260, 301, 305, 339–40
integration
   technology   378–9, 386
      research   237–9, 243, 253, 258, 260
      teacher education   420–1
   theory and practice in teacher
      education   640, 829–75
   undergraduate calculus   365–8
   values education   754–5
integrity   756
Intelligent Computer Assisted Instruction
      System (ICAI)   278
intelligent software tutors   254, 263–4, 278,
      326
Intelligent Tutoring System (ITS)   278, 326
intended curriculum
   reforms   218
   SIMS   198
   technology impact on   278–9
   TIMSS   154
   undergraduate mathematics and
      technology   378–9
   values   737
intended values   740–8
Inter-American Committee on Mathematics
      Education   186

interactive chalkboard   273–4
interactive television   398
interiorization   354–5
Intermediate IT Competence (IIT)   312
internalization of values   723–24, 726, 730–1,
      734
International Adult Literacy Survey
      (IALS)   116
International Assessment of Educational
      Progress (IAEP)   163
International Association for the Evaluation
      of Educational Achievement (IEA)   79,
      169–71
   curriculum   278
   international comparative studies   154,
      198–9
   Second IEA Mathematics Study   500
International Commission on Mathematical
      Instruction (ICMI)   186, 191–5, 435,
      574
   Asian countries   64
   Australian educators   213
   collaboration   208
   Japan   216
   studies   x
   undergraduate teaching   121
International Commission for the Study and
      Improvement of Mathematics Teaching
      (CIEAEM)   ix, 33–5, 191
International Commission on the Teaching of
      Mathematics (ICTM)   435
international comparative studies   6, 143–84,
      197–200, 436, 719
   less successful countries   850
   mathematical literacy   79
   research ethics   447, 458–61, 464
   technology   256
   see also International Programme for
      Student Assessment; Third
      International Mathematics and
      Science Study
International Conference on the Teaching of
      Modelling and Applications
      (ICTMA)   ix, 37
International Congress of Mathematicians
      (ICM)   ix
International Congress on Mathematics
      Education (ICME)   ix, 3–4, 143, 186,
      205
   adult mathematics education   111, 115
   attendance   144, 147, 192
   Australian educators   213
   curricular tracks   39
   global inequalities   22–4
   internationalization   194–5
   Mathematics for All   33, 37

technology 463
TIMSS 10–11
Topic Study Group 216
vocational knowledge 21
International Group for the Psychology of
    Mathematics Education (PME) 186,
    193–4, 213, 495
conferences ix, x
ethical issues in research 452, 463
Mathematics Teacher Development
    Group 884
teacher research projects 525–6, 529, 533
International Journal for Computer Algebra
    in Mathematics Education
    (IJCAME) 242
International Mathematics Union 192
International Monetary Fund (IMF) 23
International Newsletter on Proof 187
International Organization of Women and
    Mathematics Education (IOWME) 36,
    193–4
international organizations 186, 191–7
International Programme for Student
    Assessment (PISA) 34, 151–3
classroom practice 646–7, 651–2
literacy 80–2, 115–16
media reporting 147
International Society for Technology in
    Education 312
international students 185–6, 188, 209–12,
    738
International Study of Achievement in
    Mathematics 436
International Study Group on
    Ethnomathematics (ISGEm) 203
International Study Group for the
    Relationship Between the History and
    Pedagogy of Mathematics 193
International Year of Mathematics 191–2,
    201
internationalization 6–7, 143–50, 185–7,
    224–5, 606
case studies 208–23
conceptualization of term 187–9
ICMI role 194–5
research in conflict situations 565–6
see also globalization
Internet
CAI 255
classroom practices 653
communication of research 512, 515
globalization 308
Hong Kong 294
impact on curriculum 272, 277–8
as new source of knowledge 463
on-line resources 282, 326

teacher education 396–401, 413–18
mobile teaching facilities 421–2
video streaming 406
United States 282–4
web-based teaching 382–3
see also web sites; World Wide Web
interns 855–68
interpretative research 258n5, 448–50, 529,
    574, 578
interpretive listening 535
intranets 294, 401, 421
intuition 437, 481, 483
intuitionism 797
IOWME *see* International Organization of
    Women and Mathematics Education
Iran, cultural values survey 721
Ireland, adult numeracy teachers 121
ISETL programming language 355–7, 363,
    375–6
ISGEm *see* International Study Group on
    Ethnomathematics
ISME *see* institutional system of mathematics
    education
Israel
achievement/GNP relationship 15–16
classroom practices 652
justification and proof 156
Learner's Perspective Study 166
technology 653
*Issues in Undergraduate Mathematics
    Preparation of School Teachers* 417
IT *see* information technology
Italy
technology 653
TIMSS reporting 146
item characteristic curve (ICC) 701
ITS *see* Intelligent Tutoring System

Japan
calculator use 161
chalkboard use 313
classroom practices 172, 647, 652–3
cultural scripts 168
cultural values survey 721–2
curriculum 158
examinations 459, 650
high attainment 40–1, 64, 651
ICME 192
ICMI 216
Kumon method 652
Learner's Perspective Study 166–7
learning goals 105
learning strategies 160
lesson study 527, 533, 652–3, 668, 775–6
masculinity 722
Open-Approach Method 67
PISA results 153, 651

professional development 675
recall emphasis 156
reforms 67, 218
regulating entry into teaching
    profession 767, 774–7, 783
SIMS 154
teacher preparation 639, 835, 839–41
teaching practices 771
technology impact on curriculum 234,
    295, 297
TIMSS results 147, 166, 652, 768, 846
Japan Society of Mathematical
    Education 295
*Journal for Research in Mathematics
    Education* 186, 732
journals x, 186–7, 451, 513, 567
    affective factors 732
    communication of research 619
    funding 582
    research ethics 455–6
    teacher research 531
    technology research 239, 242
    technology in teacher education 401
justice 450

Kantian approach 448–9
Kent-Medway-Oxfordshire Formative
    Assessment Project (KMOFAP) 485
Kenya, poor mathematics performance 145
'key incidents' 506
kinaesthetic devices 332–3
KMOFAP *see* Kent-Medway-Oxfordshire
    Formative Assessment Project
knowledge
    case inquiry 885
    CBMS report 784–5
    conceptual understanding 80, 369, 599,
        664, 668, 773, 844–5
    content 353
    contextualization of 250–51, 257
    creation 485
    cross-subject comparisons 509–10
    ecological perspectives 595–6
    educative 879, 880
    episteme 480–1, 486, 622
    ethnomathematics 735–6
    five types for teachers 810
    framing research questions 502
    inequalities 83
    logic 797
    mathematical 879–80
    Mathematical Knowledge for
        Teaching 868–9
    mathematical literacy 78
    mode of interaction 534
    pedagogical 879, 880
    pedagogical content knowledge

subject-matter knowledge 510
    teacher education 773, 784–5, 789, 844,
        866, 868
    values 749
    phronesis 480–1, 486, 622
    power-knowledge 546, 549
    preservice teachers 802–4
    professional development
        programs 666–8
    research practices 493–4, 496–7
    social construction of 201
    software tools 341
    tacit 538, 843
    teacher education 831, 833–4, 842–6, 866,
        868
    teacher-educators 869
    transfer 484
    transmission of 132
    verification 505
Korea
    examinations 650
    high attainment 41, 64, 651
    PISA results 153, 651
    problem-solving 156
    technology impact on curriculum 234,
        295
    TIMSS results 768
Korea Institute of Curriculum and
    Evaluation 295
Kumon method 652

labor force demands 4, 78, 108
    see also vocational education; work
LACSG *see* Linear Algebra Curriculum
    Study Group
Landless Peoples Movement (MST) 83,
    568–9
language
    CIEAEM 191
    class disadvantage 44–5
    communication of research 619
    economic 5, 9, 10, 17
    international comparative research 154–5
    mathematical 79
    programming languages 328–30, 355–7
    South African teacher education
        research 455–6
    values research 757–8
    writing skills 512–13
Language Arts (journal) 531
Laplace transforms 274
Latin America
    case study 219–20
    international students 186
Latvia
    achievement/GNP relationship 15–16
    PISA 80

leadership
  for change   658–9
  research   613
  support   660
league tables
  aggregated scores   157
  economics discourse   14–18, 20
  England   460
  TIMSS   458–9
learner-centred practice   441, 456
'learners of mathematics' concept   62–3
Learner's Perspective Study (LPS)   166–7,
    176
learning
  assessment   624
  basic learning needs   32–3
  beliefs   672
  calculators   277
  case inquiry   885
  classroom practices   406, 647–8
  Computer Algebra Systems   380–1
  concepts of mathematics   353
  Confucian influence   217
  constructivism   363, 600, 647–8, 672, 678
  culture specificity   159–60
  data analysis   503–4
  didactical contract   507
  disequilibrium   673–4
  e-learning   413–14
  enactive mathematics   360
  ethnomathematics   83
  IEA study   170
  Japan   105
  learning trajectory concept   107–8, 903
  microworlds   330–1
  mode of interaction   534
  models of learning situations   254
  opportunities for   170, 878–9
  outside-school   653–4
  practice   179–80
  professional development   665–7, 879–82,
      895, 899, 912
  reconceptualizing   341–2
  reform-orientated   878
  research   594, 599–600
  self-paced   130
  social practice theory   676
  'social turn'   495
  socio-cultural approaches   554
  software   325, 330–1, 339–40
  student teachers   831, 857–63, 868, 870
  systems   595
  teacher education   423–6
  teacher educators   897–8
  teacher/student similarity   813
  technology
    developments   234–5
    digital   326
    research   246, 248, 250, 252–3, 256
    software   325, 330–1, 339–40
    undergraduate mathematics   362–3, 387
  undergraduate calculus   366
  see also Computer Assisted Learning;
      lifelong learning
Learning About Teaching project   409–10,
    842
learning communities   415–18, 660
  networked   308
  software tools   341
learning society concept   104
learning trajectory concept   107–8, 903
*Learning the Unlikely at Distance Delivered as
    an Information Technology Enterprise*
    (LUDDITE)   404
Lebanon, conflict   550
lecturers   353, 381–4, 387, 420
lectures   381
legitimacy of research   436
lesson study   527, 533, 540, 652–3, 668–9,
    775–6
lessons
  Characteristic Pedagogical Flow   168–9
  cultural scripts   166, 168
  Japan   166–8
liberal theory   449–50
Liechtenstein, PISA results   153
life histories   572
lifelong learning   103–42
  professional   425
  teachers and technology   313
lifelong mathematics education   6, 46,
    103–42
  policy perspectives   106–11
  practice perspectives   122–31
  research perspectives   111–22
  vocational skills   21–2
limit concept   369–71
linear algebra   371–5
Linear Algebra Curriculum Study Group
    (LACSG)   374
listening   534–5
literacy
  adult   104, 116
  BALID   126
  Brazil   568
  critical mathematical   85–6, 97
  Latin America   220
  mathematical   5–6, 75–102, 646–7
    critical mathematical   85–6, 97
    international comparative
        research   152–3, 154
    PISA tasks   152

REFLECT programme 127–8
loans 196–7
local context 538, 644
local independence 700–1
local initiatives 613
location 204–5
logic 796–8
LOGO 325, 328, 330–1, 343n11
   epistemological shifts 463
   meta-analysis on technology research 251,
     263, 266–7
   turtle geometry 272
long-term orientation 722
longitudinal studies 404–5, 408, 500, 539
*Longitudinal Study of Children's Development
   of Mathematical Ideas about Justification
   and Proof* 405
Los Andes, University of 221
LPS *see* Learner's Perspective Study
LUDDITE *see* Learning the Unlikely at
   Distance Delivered as an Information
   Technology Enterprise

M²IP *see* Michigan Mathematics Inservice
   Project
Macau, technology impact on
   curriculum 294–5
Macdonaldization 25
macros 340, 343n10
Making Weighty Decisions 405–7, 420
Malawi, access to schooling 441–2
Malaysia
   authoritarianism 58
   colonial education tradition 214–15
   cultural values survey 721–2
   ethnic communities 56–7, 155, 164
   power distance 722
   reforms 217
   technology impact on curriculum 296,
     298
   values 719, 721–2, 739
managerialism 539, 613–14
Manifesto 2000 for the Year of
   Mathematics 191–2
Manor Project 666, 897
Maple software 363, 366, 368–9, 371–2, 374,
   381–3
marginalized groups 46–7, 548, 582
   adaptive progressive sentiment 109
   Mathematics for All 31, 49–62
   pathologized by research 560
   social reproduction 85
   see also ethnic minorities; minority groups
market principles 13, 23–4, 539
marketization of university research 213,
   224
Marxist perspectives 546, 603–4, 614

masculinity 722, 729
Masters in Education (Teaching) course,
   University of Cape Town 533–7, 540–1
Matematik faghoefte 12 647
Math Forum 398, 400, 415, 421
MATH (*Mathematics and Teaching through
   Hypermedia*) project 398, 407–8, 841–2
'math wars' 226n3, 282–3, 619, 768
Mathcad 383
mathemacy concept 569
Mathematica software 274, 364–6, 369, 371,
   375–6, 383
Mathematical Association of America 280
Mathematical Association (United
   Kingdom) 830, 870n6
Mathematical Knowledge for Teaching
   (MKT) 868–9
mathematical proficiency 79–80
Mathematical Sciences Education Board 77,
   825
Mathematical Tasks Framework 886
Mathematics for All 5, 31–73
   lifelong learning 105
   South Africa 645
Mathematics Case Methods Project 669
*Mathematics Classroom Situations
   Project* 669–70
Mathematics Education Research Group of
   Australasia (MERGA) 186, 524
Mathematics Education and Society (MES)
   conference ix, 194–5
mathematics learning centres 123
Mathematics Learning Study Committee 79,
   82
Mathematics Research Group (Taiwan) 293
Mathematics in School (journal) 401
Mathematics and Science Teaching
   Academies 790
The Mathematics Teacher (journal) 401
mathematics teacher-educator educators
   (MTEEs) 877, 880–2, 896–8, 912
mathematics teacher-educators
   (MTEs) 637–8, 849–50, 869–70
   educative power 879
   learning opportunities 879
   professional development 877, 880–2,
     896–902, 912
   research by teachers 526–7
   tasks 903–4, 908
   see also tutors
*Mathematics and Teaching through
   Hypermedia* (MATH) project 398,
   407–8, 841–2
mathematization 711–12
Mathsticks 331
Matlab 372, 374, 383

matrices, linear algebra   371–4
meaning
  construction of   82, 249–50
  internal mental operations   358
measurement   91, 693–6, 795
media   12, 623
  cultural myths   18–19
  language   17
  reporting of PISA results   147
  reporting of TIMSS results   145–6
Mediterranean Conference on Mathematics
    Education   x
Melbourne, University of   404, 422, 783
mental fitness   385
mental math   785
mentoring   830–1, 834–5
  collegiality   852–3
  England   837–8, 855–68
  internship case study   855–68
  Japan   841
  Mathematical Knowledge of
    Teaching   869
  professional development   898–9
  reflective practice   849–51
  selection of mentors   854
  South Africa   839
MERGA *see* Mathematics Education
    Research Group of Australasia
MES *see* Mathematics Education and Society
    conference
meta-studies
  dissemination of research   626
  technology and innovation research   233,
    237–69
metacognition   105, 109
methodology   444, 566–74
  adult mathematics education
    research   115–16
  Discipline of Noticing   535
  ethnomathematics   118
  international comparative research   161,
    179
  meta-studies   238–40
  paradigm wars   581
  quality of research   577–8, 580
  research practices   502–3
  TIMSS   459
  validity   575
  see also qualitative methods; quantitative
    methods
Mexico
  collaborative research projects   222
  UN classification   219
Michigan Mathematics Inservice Project
    (M²IP)   893
Microsoft   24

microworlds
  characteristics   358–9
  embodied objects   360–1
  group theory   376
  influence on curriculum   272–3, 299, 301
  non-euclidean geometry   377–8
  research projects   262–3, 267, 328–31, 339
  teacher education   419
middle-class students   44–5, 637
migrant students   738
MILE (Multimedia Interactive Learning
    Environment) project   398, 412–13,
    841–2
mind-body divide   534–5
Ministere de l'Education nationale, de la
    Recherche et de la Technologie   290–1
Ministry of Education, Culture and Science
    (Netherlands)   291
Ministry of Education (France)   238
Ministry of Education (Israel)   647
Ministry of Education (Japan)   839–40
Ministry of Education (New Zealand)   290
Ministry of Education (Portugal)   657
Ministry of Education (Republic of
    China)   293
Ministry of Education (Singapore)   295–6,
    719–20
Ministry of Education (South Africa)   645
Ministry of Education (Thailand)   719
Ministry of National Education
    (Taiwan)   293
minority groups
  classroom practices   645–6
  conflict   552
  restricted opportunities   34
  see also ethnic minorities; marginalized
    groups
mixed ability classes   59–60
MKT *see* Mathematical Knowledge for
    Teaching
Mobile Teaching Facilities (MTF)   421–2
model lessons   893–5
modelling
  computer   286–9
  environmental problems   86–9, 92–3
  parallel   329
models
  economic discourse   4
  numeracy   76
  Platonic   94–5
  surface-models   95–6
  tools and techniques   283
modern mathematics movement   473
Monash University   639, 717
moral philosophy   446
moral values   726

Morley's Theorem 377
Moser Report 120
Mozambique, colonialism impact 204
MST *see* Landless Peoples Movement
MTEEs *see* mathematics teacher-educator
    educators
MTEs *see* mathematics teacher-educators
MTF *see* Mobile Teaching Facilities
multiculturalism 3, 55, 654, 722
    cultural conflicts 738
    indigenous knowledge 83
    research in conflict situations 548, 554
    see also cultural diversity
multimedia 286–9, 294, 381
    teacher education 395–9, 402–3, 423–7
        children's thinking 404–5
        classroom interaction 405–8
        dilemmas of teaching 409–10
        MILE 398, 412–13, 841–2
        teachers' beliefs 411–12
    see also Internet; video
Multimedia Interactive Learning
    Environment (MILE) project 398,
    412–13, 841–2
multiple solution problems 693–6, 706–8
multiple-choice tests 459, 693, 696, 698–9
multiplicative structures 805, 810
myths 17–19

NACOME *see* National Advisory Committee
    on Mathematics Education
NAE *see* National Academy of Education
NAEP *see* National Assessment of
    Educational Progress
narratives 572, 604, 669, 888–91
    action research 884
    reflection 890–1, 912
    see also case studies
National Academy of Education (NAE) 496
National Advisory Committee on
    Mathematics Education
    (NACOME) 304
National Assessment of Educational Progress
    (NAEP) 164, 651
National Board of Employment, Education
    and Training (NBEET) 119
National Board for Professional Teaching
    Standards (NBPTS) 791
National Center for Educational Statistics
    (NCES) 177
National Center for Fair and Open
    Testing 698
National Commission on Mathematics and
    Science Teaching 651, 768
National Council for Accreditation of
    Teacher Education 312

National Council on Education and the
    Disciplines 77
National Council for Educational
    Technology 303, 312
National Council on Measurement in
    Education (NCME) 702
National Council of Teachers of Mathematics
    (NCTM)
    *Assessment Standards for School
        Mathematics* (1995) 207
    curricular changes 36, 649
    *Curriculum and Evaluation Standards for
        School Mathematics* (1989)
        calculators 277
        changes in classroom practices 657,
            670, 679n1
        core knowledge base 39
        process-orientation 599
        technology 282
        US reforms 39, 207
    E-Standards 415
    Illuminations 398, 415
    ISGEm affiliation 203
    Mathematics in Context 660
    *Principles and Standards for School
        Mathematics* (2000)
        constructivist learning theories 117, 647
        E-Standards 415
        equity principle 40
        influence on policy 772
        pedagogical content knowledge 785
        process-orientation 599, 799
        technology 282, 284
    *Professional Standards for Teaching
        Mathematics* (1991)
        action research 884
        changing classroom practices 657
        constructivist learning 117
        core knowledge base 39
        teacher education 407, 411
    reform-orientated education 882
    research 472
    skills for work 646
    teacher problem-solving 904
    technology 272, 282, 307, 906–7
    tests 705
    TIMSS 171
    training 119
national curriculum
    China 292
    diverse educational settings 565
    economic development 14
    research influence 483
    technology 292
    values 718–20
    Western systems 279

National Curriculum (United Kingdom) 14, 279, 483, 649, 866
  anti-multiculturalism 55
  criticisms of 206–7
  mathematics as empowering force 31–2
  teacher boycott 698
  technology 284
National Foundation for Educational Research (NFER) 61
National Numeracy Strategy (United Kingdom) 120, 626, 649, 656
National Office of Overseas Skills Recognition (NOOSR) 777
National Qualifications Framework (NQF), South Africa 838
National Research Council (NRC) 643, 652, 664–5, 667, 672
  adult education 119
  calculator use 279
  IT projects 277
  Mathematics Learning Study Committee 79, 82
  teacher education 786
  tests 691, 704
National Science Foundation (NSF) 86, 646, 662
National Statement on Mathematics for Australian Schools 207, 285, 647
National Taiwan Normal University 639, 717
national training targets 108
The National Writing Project Quarterly (journal) 531
nationhood 178
naturalism 574
Nazi ideology 550
NBEET *see* National Board of Employment, Education and Training
NBPTS *see* National Board for Professional Teaching Standards
NCES *see* National Center for Educational Statistics
NCME *see* National Council on Measurement in Education
NCTM *see* National Council of Teachers of Mathematics
neo-colonialism 224
neo-Deweyism 600
neoliberalism
  blame on individual 106–7
  economic determinism 109
  free market economics 189
  inequitable resource distribution 45, 548
  social construction of curriculum 110
Netherlands
  adult education 123
  MILE project 412–13, 841–2
  problem-solving 156
  Realistic Mathematics Education 67
  regulating entry into teaching profession 767, 777–9
  technology impact on curriculum 291
  technology research 461
networking technologies 326
New Math 11, 23, 37, 200, 473–4
  RDD model 605, 613
  resistance to change 656–7
  South East Asia 214–15
New South Wales, University of 210
New Zealand
  ethnomathematics 203
  PISA results 153
  prescriptive directives 679
  technology impact on curriculum 290
newly qualified teachers (NQTs) 857
NFAME *see* Non-formal Adult Mathematics Education
NFER *see* National Foundation for Educational Research
NFME *see* Non-formal Mathematics Education
Non-formal Adult Mathematics Education (NFAME) 125–8
Non-formal Mathematics Education (NFME) 106
non-governmental organizations 66
NOOSR *see* National Office of Overseas Skills Recognition
norms 836, 847–8
Norms and Standards for Educators (South Africa) 838
North America 203
Northumbria, University of 413
Norway, achievement/GNP relationship 15–16
notation 326–7, 330, 357
Nottingham, University of 300
novice researchers 492–4, 498–9, 502, 505–6, 516–18
NQF *see* National Qualifications Framework
NQTs *see* newly qualified teachers
NRC *see* National Research Council
NSF *see* National Science Foundation
number sense 77
numeracy 13, 75–7, 90
  adult 105, 127–8, 130–1
    assessment 123
    research 111, 113–14, 116, 119–20, 122
  constructivist approaches 117
  diverse forms of 79
  essentialism 21
  labor force demands 78

National Numeracy Strategy   120, 626,
  649, 656
  REFLECT programme   127–8, 130–1
  UK standards   654–5
numerology   96–7
Nuremberg Code   448

objectivism   85, 547, 732–3
objectivity   87, 97, 486, 567, 574
objects   354–7
  APOS theory   355–6
  grouping   906
  process-object approach   248, 250
obstacles to the dissemination of
  research   593–634
OECD *see* Organization for Economic
  Co-operation and Development
Office of Educational Research and
  Improvement (United States)   648
Open-Approach Method   67
opportunities
  learning trajectory concept   107–8
  to learn   170
  underrepresented groups   36–7
oppression   3, 450, 452, 456–7, 460
oral examination   215
Organization for Economic Co-operation and
  Development (OECD)
  curriculum   156
  innovative programs study   156, 175–7
  International Programme for Student
    Assessment   34, 151–3
    classroom practice   646–7, 651–2
    literacy   80–2, 115–16
    media reporting   147
  lifelong learning   46, 104
  mathematical literacy   80–2, 86, 90,
    115–16
  training   119
Organization for European Economic
  Co-operation   473
organizational approach   655–63
Oulu, University of   413
out-of-school mathematics   82, 97–8, 598
outcomes
  international comparative research   151
  learning   180
outcomes-based education   108, 118, 209
Overseas Development Aid   216
overseas students   185–6, 188, 209–12, 738
ownership
  of change   606
  grass roots   656
  research projects   455, 466, 613–14

Pacific region, compulsory maths
  curriculum   41
Pakistan

M.Ed programme   897–8
  short-term orientation   722
Palm Pilot   422–3
Panama, UN classification   219
paradigm wars   581
Paraguay, income inequalities   219
paramedics case study   437, 482–3
participation
  collaborative international comparative
    research   176–7
  lifelong mathematics education   107–8
  mandatory   662–3
  research   575–7
  teachers   656–8, 662–3
participatory validity   455, 576–7, 580
particulars   505–8
partnerships
  research   576
  university-school   854–68, 870
PCK *see* pedagogical content knowledge
PDAs *see* Personal Data Assistants
pedagogical content knowledge (PCK)
  subject-matter knowledge   510
  teacher education   773, 784–5, 789, 844,
    866, 868
  values   749
pedagogical identity   726, 733–4, 748–9,
    755–7
pedagogy
  adaptive potential   179
  adult mathematics education   122–4, 132
  Characteristic Pedagogical Flow   168–9
  conflict situations   570
  education separation   601
  international comparative research   200
  of investigation   844
  narratives   888–9
  of presentation   844
  representational   132
  research   594
  social class   52–4
  teacher education   427
'People's Mathematics'   550, 557
perceived objects   354
perception, dynamic geometry   249, 255, 266
perceptions
  interns   860–5
  mentors   861–4
performance
  international comparative research   150–1,
    158
  Kenya   145
  undergraduate calculus   364
  see also achievement
personal construct position   117
Personal Data Assistants (PDAs)   313, 326

personality 96
Peru, introduction of computers 23–4
PGCE (Post Graduate Certificate of
    Education) 836–9, 854–68
phenomenology 594
Phi Delta Kappan (journal) 177, 514
*Philadelphia Collaborative for Excellence in
    Teaching Education Program*
    (CETP) 402
Philippines
    colonial education tradition 214
    Learner's Perspective Study 166
    reforms 217–18
    textbooks 215
    values 719
philosophy 478, 481, 495–7, 796
Philosophy of Mathematics Education
    (journal) 187
phronesis 480–1, 486, 622
PISA *see* International Programme for
    Student Assessment
placement dilemma 834, 836, 854
Platonic models 94–5
Playgrounds 329, 340
pluralism 795, 798, 805–8, 812–13, 823–5
PME *see* International Group for the
    Psychology of Mathematics Education
policy xii, 3–7
    adult participation in tertiary
        education 121–2
    communication of research 515
    condensed measures 91
    cultural authorship 145
    developing countries 564
    development 630n2
    five levels of 597–8
    international comparative research 168,
        172–5, 199
    lifelong mathematics education 106–11
    policy-makers 625–6, 628
    political lobbying 619
    pressure groups 611
    regulation 627
    research influence 438, 476–7, 515, 565
    social 63
    United States 169
    World Bank influence 196
Political Dimensions of Mathematics
    Education conference 195
political issues 3–4, 467, 627
    assessment 713
    economic conditions 5, 9, 15
    international comparative research 172–4,
        200
    lobbying 619
    Mathematics for All 62–3

numerical arguments 93
political awareness 85–6
research in conflict situations 437–8,
    545–91
TIMSS reporting 10–11, 15, 145–7, 436,
    459–60
see also democracy; state
popular culture 17
population
    environmental problems 86–7
    models 95
portable devices 359
Portugal
    calculator use 161
    curriculum development 657, 661
    gender issues 52
positioned neutrality 11
positivism 575, 577–8
Post Graduate Certificate of Education
    (PGCE) 836–9, 854–68
post-Darwinism 600
postmodernism 157, 187, 449–50, 573
poststructuralism 604
poverty 5, 9, 20, 25–8, 550–1
    community support 66
    developing countries 34, 564
    environmental problems 89
    globalization 189–90
power
    educative 879, 899
    ethnomathematics 205
    international collaboration 225
    mathematical 879, 899
    pedagogical 879, 899
    relations 43, 446, 576–7
    research in conflict situations 546–7, 569,
        571–2
    technology 548–9
power distance 722
power-knowledge 546, 549
practical wisdom
    failure of research to impact practice 437,
        471, 473, 481–2, 484–5
    obstacles to dissemination of
        research 611–12, 622, 628
practice xiii–xiv, 636–917
    adaptive potential 174–5, 179
    adult mathematics education 122–31
    case studies 167
    Characteristic Pedagogical Flow 168–9
    crucial descriptions 572
    cultural authorship 176
    five levels of 597–8
    international assessment 157–8, 161,
        171–2
    learner-centred 441, 456

learning 179–80
records of 516–18
representing 515–16
research
failure to impact 436–7, 471–90, 496, 565
relationship with 114–15, 124, 608–10
research practices 437, 491–521
social 75, 81, 676–7, 878
teacher change 638, 643–87
teacher education 640, 829–75
theory relationship 124, 607–10, 829–75
see also best practice; classroom practice; communities of practice
practitioner research 529–30, 576
see also teachers, research by
pre-interpretative research 448–49
presentation
multimedia 381
pedagogy of 844
of research 514–15, 619
software 313
preservice teachers 639–40, 663, 801–5
'Ant-on-the-Wheel' investigation 815–24
implicit personal research 526
multimedia case studies 405–6
principles for teaching mathematics 806–13
problem-solving 814–15
regulating entry into profession 639, 767–93
video studies 402, 410, 412
see also student teachers; teacher education
pressure groups 611
primary education
cultural variation 166
lack of access to 33
Latin America 219–20
National Numeracy Strategy 120, 649
PCGE course 837
Singapore 296
teacher education 422
World Bank policies 196–7
see also elementary education
principals 660
Principles and Standards for School Mathematics (NCTM, 2000)
constructivist learning theories 117, 647
E-Standards 415
equity principle 40
influence on policy 772
pedagogical content knowledge 785
process-orientation 599, 799
technology 282, 284
privacy 450, 452–5, 465
private sector 769

The Private Universe Project in Mathematics 405
privatization 189
problem-solving
abstraction 86
'Ant-on-the-Wheel' investigation 815–24
calculators 277, 295
children's thinking 895
Cognitive Guided Instruction 891–2
cross-national variation 153, 156
dependent problems 708–10
Flag problem 693–7, 700, 702, 705
four stages of 814
geometry 377
intelligent software tutors 254
level of challenge 159
linear algebra 374–5
mathematical literacy 80–1
multiple solution problems 693–6, 706–8
narratives 890–1
Open-Approach Method 67
preservice teachers 814–24
research 352–3, 494
Singapore 720
software tools 325
strategies 710–12
teacher education tasks 904–6
technology assessment 385
technology impact on curriculum 301, 304
technology research 242, 254
undergraduate calculus 363–4, 366
Problem-Solving Inservice (PSI) programme 890
'problématiques' 240–6, 248–9, 252
'procept' notion 244, 248, 305, 354
process games 273
process-based teaching 799–800, 802, 806, 808–9, 812
see also reform-based teaching
process-content debate 304–5, 308
processes 354–7
APOS theory 355–6
process-object approach 248, 250
product-orientation 116, 613, 649
productive disposition 664
professional development 630n2, 640, 663–9, 877–917
changing nature of 882–96
continuing professional development 384
cultural variation 638
dynamics of 560
Glenn Report 770, 790–2
in-service programmes 454
interns 857
lecturers 384, 387

lesson study   527
lifelong process   612
mandatory participation   663
process and content   485–6
research   485
similarity to student learning   813
Solidarity Program in Mathematics
      Education   193
tasks   899–912
teacher research   526–7, 529, 531–2
teacher values   730, 753–7
technology   300, 313
    Internet resources   415–17
    research   235, 239, 252–3
    teacher education   399–401, 415–17,
        420–2
    tertiary staff   420–1
theory/practice integration   833, 870
see also teacher education
professional organizations   216
*Professional Standards for Teaching
    Mathematics* (NCTM, 1991)
action research   884
changing classroom practices   657
constructivist learning   117
core knowledge base   39
teacher education   407, 411
Professional Tutors (PTs)   856–9, 861–8
professionalism   xiii, 679, 835
autonomy   852
Japan   297, 840
technology impact on curriculum   308–13
professionalization   833, 835
proficiency   79–80, 150–1, 153
programming   326–31, 339–40
curriculum   280
ISETL   355–7, 363, 375–6
Project Calc   363
Project LINCS   667
proletarization   846
proof
axiomatic objects   354
dynamic geometry   335–6
studies   405
PSI see Problem-Solving Inservice
    programme
psychoanalytic perspectives   604
psychology   186, 194, 560
constructivism   475
cultural psychology perspective   179
mathematics relationship   558–9
research   435, 478, 494–5
see also International Group for the
    Psychology of Mathematics Education
The Psychology of Inservice Education of
    Mathematics Teachers working
    group   526

psychometrics
    test design   638, 689, 693, 699–705, 712
    TIMSS   458
PTs see Professional Tutors
public talk   165
puzzle-style software   326

QCA see Qualifications and Curriculum
    Authority
QTS see qualified teacher status
quadrilaterals   902–3
Qualifications and Curriculum Authority
    (QCA)   55–6, 284
qualified teacher status (QTS)   837, 849, 861
qualitative methods   574, 602, 603
    key incidents   506
    research ethics   447, 448, 464
    rigor of analysis   503, 504
    technology and innovation   240–6, 255
    TIMSS   198
quality
    reforms   566
    research   561, 574–80
quantitative methods   464, 478, 602–3
    limitations of   462
    rigor of analysis   503–4
    technology and innovation   240, 255
    TIMSS   449, 460
    traditional research   449
quantitative reasoning   77
QUASAR ('Quantitative Understanding:
    Amplifying Student Achievement and
    Reasoning') project   485, 670, 885
questions for research   499–502

R³M (Recognizing and Recording Reform in
    Mathematics Education Project)   659,
    661, 670
race
    advocacy research   451
    equity issues   40
    exclusion   562
    inequalities   563
    information technology   302
    power relations   43
    SMILE project   621
    social deprivation   26
    US achievement testing   173–4
    see also ethnicity
racial discrimination   66
    see also apartheid
racism   54, 132, 725
    see also apartheid
radical constructivism   594–5, 601, 630
radical feminism   118
rationalism   720, 732–3, 735, 796
rationality   87, 547
    analytic   436–7, 471, 473, 480–6

gender 49–52
technical 878
RDD (research-development-dissemination)
   model 605–7, 609, 612–13
reading 497–9
real life mathematics 79–81, 130–1
realism 20, 462–3, 530, 609
Realistic Mathematics Education (RME) 67
Recherche en Didactique des Mathématiques
   (journal) 187
recontextualization 500–1, 570, 579
records of practice 516–18
recruitment
   interviews 846
   United Kingdom 870n9
   US crisis in 785–91
REFLECT programme 125–8, 130
reflection 110, 805, 900
   case inquiry 885–6, 888, 912
   didactical 260
   internship scheme 859
   narrative 890–1, 912
   reflective practice 843–4, 846, 848–51, 879
   teacher-thinking seminar 895–6
reflexivity 450, 452, 577
reform movement (United States) 199
reform-based teaching
   professional development 878, 882, 898
   teacher education 799–801, 807–9,
     811–12, 824–5
   see also process-based teaching
reforms 446, 555, 564–6
   assessment driven 200
   critiques of 445
   developing countries 441–2
   Mathematics for All 66–7
   resistance to 443
   South East Asia 217–18
   undergraduate calculus 363–4, 384
   US teacher certification 789–90
   see also change
Regenerated Freirean Literacy Through
   Empowering Community Techniques
   (REFLECT) programme 125–8, 130
regional meetings 192–3, 203, 219
regulation of teacher training 767–93
relational ethics 449–50
relational understanding 720
relativism 449
representation 357–62
   differential equations 366
   dynamic geometry systems 333–4
   graphical
     calculators 279
     differential equations 366
     expressive tools 333

limit concept 370
   multimedia 399
international comparative research 155,
   177
linear algebra 371–2
mathematical knowledge 844–5
multiple 358–60, 364–5
syntonicity 332
of teaching 515–16
web-based teaching 383
representational pedagogy 132
representational versatility 359, 361
reproduction
   cultural 108
   power-knowledge 549
   social 57, 59, 85
research x–xi, xii–xiii, 435–634
   Australian universities 213–14
   by teachers 437, 523–44, 604
   collaboration 145, 176, 180, 224–5
     action research 883–4
     Australia 213–14
     by teachers 532–3, 537–8, 540
     Colombia 221–2
     East and South East Asia 218–19
   Colombia 221–2
   communication of 511–16, 618–19, 627–8
   Computer Algebra Systems 337–9
   cultural authorship 176–7
   cultural beliefs 179
   digital technologies 323–5, 339–42
   dissemination of 438, 530–1, 593–634
   East and South East Asia 218–19
   ethical issues 436, 441–70
   failure to impact practice 436–7, 471–90,
     496, 565
   lifelong mathematics education 111–22
   obstacles to dissemination 438, 593–634
   positioning of researcher 567, 571
   practice relationship 114–15, 124, 608–10
   research practices 437, 491–521
   similarities 201
   social/political conflicts 437–8, 545–91
   teacher education 401, 404–8, 420, 770–4
   technology 233–4, 237–69, 323–5, 339–42
   tools 511
   undergraduate mathematics 351–3, 384
   values 720–1, 731–5, 738–53, 757–8
   World Bank 196–7
   see also action research; case studies;
     international comparative studies;
     methodology
Research in Undergraduate Mathematics
   Education Community (RUMEC) 375
research-development-dissemination (RDD)
   model 605–7, 609, 612–13

researchers
  novice   492–4, 498–9, 502, 505–6, 516–18
  as obstacles to dissemination of
      research   618–19
resources
  access to   65
  home   170
  inequitable distribution of   11, 45, 68, 107
  international comparative research   155
  neo-colonialism   224
  poor countries   550–1
  research   626–7
  resource development   630n2
  South Africa   456–7
  technological   235
  technology in teacher education   397–8,
      401
    access to   421–2
    classroom interaction   407–8
    costs   423–4
    dilemmas in teaching   409–10
    MILE   412–13
    teachers' beliefs   411–12
    web-based   415–18, 423
  web-based   382–3, 415–18, 423
responsibility
  researcher   576–7, 613
  rigor   580
responsiveness
  researcher   576–7
  rigor   580
retention   170
Revised Secondary Education Program
    (World Bank)   215
Riemann integration   366–8
the right   12
rigor   502–5, 541, 574, 580
riots   548
risk society   106
RME *see* Realistic Mathematics Education
Roger Williams University   363
routines   836, 847–9
Royaumont Seminar   473
rule-expression   329
rule-utilitarianism   449
RUMEC *see* Research in Undergraduate
    Mathematics Education Community
Russian Federation
  international comparative research   173
  PISA   80
Rutgers University   405, 910

sabbatical programs   208
saber-tooth curriculum   314
salaries   32, 51
'scaffolding'   244

SCANS *see* The Secretary's Commission on
    Achieving Necessary Skills
schema   354, 386
  APOS theory   355–6
  values   728
school improvement   538, 692
School Science and Mathematics
    (journal)   401
School Survey movement   478
school-based experience   403
schools
  conflict studies   556, 559–62, 569
  culture   308–11
  effectiveness   19–20, 150
  IMPACT project   662
  improvement   538, 692
  low-performing   692
  as obstacles to dissemination of
      research   623–4
  partnership with universities   854–68, 870
  school development   850
science   14, 78
scientific calculators   276
  see also graphing calculators
Scotland, gender differences   163
SEACME *see* Southeast Asian Conferences in
    Mathematics Education
SEAMS *see* Southeast Asian Mathematical
    Society
Second Asian Technology Conference in
    Mathematics   x
Second International Mathematics Study
    (SIMS)
  aggregated data   155
  curricular alignment   154
  economic performance relationship   16
  investigation of curricula   198
  poverty   28
  United States   159, 173
second-hand values   729–30
secondary education
  attitude of teachers   811
  Japanese curriculum   295
  Japanese teacher preparation   840–1
  lack of teacher preparation   833
  Netherlands teacher preparation   778–9
  PCGE course   837
  preservice teachers' mathematics
      knowledge   803–4, 809–10
  Singapore   296
  teacher attitudes   843
  teacher education   422
  US teacher certification   780–2
Secondary Education Development Project
    (World Bank)   215
Secondary Mathematics Individualized
    Learning Experiment (SMILE)   621

The Secretary's Commission on Achieving
  Necessary Skills (SCANS)   119
SEEA *see* System for Integrated
  Environmental and Economic
  Accounting
segregation
  ability   59
  school mathematics role   49
  social class   54
selection
  curriculum   43
  social segregation   49
  of teachers   851, 853–4
self   749
self-actualization   105
self-esteem   743–4
self-paced learning   130
seminars   895–6
semiotic dimension, technology
  research   243–9
September 11th attacks   545–6
service mathematics   105
SES *see* socio-economic status
setting   59–62
Shell Centre for Mathematical
  Education   300
short-term orientation   722
SimCalc project   332–3
SIMMS IM ('Systemic Initiative for Montana
  Mathematics and Science Integrated
  Mathematics') project   887–8
SIMS *see* Second International Mathematics
  Study
Singapore
  authoritarianism   58
  classroom practices   652
  colonial education tradition   214–15
  cultural values survey   721–2
  ethnic groups   164
  high attainment   41, 64
  IT competence   312
  new curriculum   656
  streaming   59, 61
  technology   295–6, 298, 653
  textbooks   217, 738
  TIMSS results   146, 768, 772
  uncertainty   722
  values   719–22, 738
Singapore Curriculum Development
  Institute   273
'Singapore Math'   652
situated abstraction   341–2
situated cognition   118, 341–2
situational dimension, technology
  research   245–6, 253–5
situations, theory of   250, 257

size of studies   501
skills
  basic   19–23, 678
  Cognitive Guided Instruction   892
  de-emphasis of skill   277, 280, 303–4, 307
  informal education   129
  IT   78, 301, 312
  manual calculation   385
  mathematical literacy   78–9, 97
  REFLECT programmes   128
  research   508, 511–13
  vocational   20–2, 108
  World Education Forum goals   104
Slovenia, teacher professionalism   679
smart calculation   711
Smart Schools   296
smartboard technology   418
SMILE (Secondary Mathematics
  Individualized Learning
  Experiment)   621
Sneakers   398, 406
social capital   27, 107
social change   75–6, 85–6, 97
social class
  access to education   34
  advocacy research   451
  attainment relationship   26–7, 54
  CIEAEM manifesto   35
  community support   66
  conflict   550
  critical pedagogy   89
  decontextualized nature of mathematics
    education   53
  equity issues   40
  exclusion   547, 562
  globalization   189
  inequalities   563
  language use   44–5
  mathematics curriculum   47
  pedagogy   52–4
  power relations   43
  see also middle-class students; socio-
    economic status; working-class
    students
social construction   110, 201, 553
social constructivism   553, 594–5, 599, 601
social contract   91–2
social control   108, 446
social deprivation   26
social exclusion   48, 106, 562
social inclusion   133
social interactions   117, 553
social issues   118, 436, 467
  democratic social relations   58
  ICME   3–4
  language of mathematics   13

research in conflict situations   437–8,
    545–91
social policy   63
social role of mathematics education   47–9
see also socio-cultural issues
social justice   5, 475, 554, 566
    democratic progressive sentiment   108
    exclusion   562
    globalization   191
    Mathematics for All   34, 62
    radical feminism   118
    state role   190
    see also equity
social negotiation   849
social order   4, 53–4
social practice   75, 81, 676–7, 878
social relations   58
social reproduction   57, 59, 85
social sciences   451, 481
    critical perspectives   568
    paradigm wars   581
    research   448
social theory   528
social turn   495
socialization
    teachers   738, 836, 854
    young people   43
socio-cultural issues
    conflict   553–4
    developing countries   38
    epistemologies of education   117–18
    mathematical skills   79
    teacher education resources   396, 424, 426
    values   734–8
    see also culture
socio-economic status (SES)
    attainment relationship   26–7, 164, 476
    IEA study   170
    information technology   302
    NAEP data   164
    PISA   646
    see also social class
sociology   478, 495, 736
software   247–9, 255, 323
    appraisal   419
    'content-free'   301
    democratizing effects   463
    edutainment games   273
    expressive tools   325–8, 332–42
    geometry   251, 265–7, 275, 278, 377–8, 401
    graphics/graphing   274, 284, 286–9, 325,
        336–7
    intelligent tutors   254, 263–4, 278, 326
    interactive chalkboard   273–4
    learning   254, 325
    presentation   313

    puzzle-style   326
    representational perspective   326–8
    statistical thinking   280
    symbolic algebraic   269
    teacher education   396–7, 401
    see also Cabri-Géomètre; DERIVE;
        dynamic geometry; programming;
        spreadsheets
Solidarity Program in Mathematics
    Education   193, 208
Solution Sketcher   268
sorting tasks   906
South Africa
    apartheid   453, 525, 550, 645, 839
    conflict studies   556, 560–1
    curriculum reform   549
    development/democracy tension   447
    ethnic communities   155, 164
    Further Diploma in Education   453–7
    Learner's Perspective Study   166
    longitudinal studies   539
    on-line teacher education   414
    'People's Mathematics'   550, 557
    student teachers   500
    teacher preparation   835, 838–9
    teachers as researchers   525
    teaching materials   65
    TIMSS   458–9
    TIMSS-R   460–1
South Asia, Colombo Plan   212
South East Asia
    authoritarianism   58–9
    case study   214–19
    Colombo Plan   212
    values   719
    Western influence   737
    see also East Asia
South Korea *see* Korea
Southeast Asian Conferences in Mathematics
    Education (SEACME)   x, 62, 216
Southeast Asian Mathematical Society
    (SEAMS)   186, 214
Southern California, University of   788
Soviet Union, former
    controlled economy   190
    international students   186
Spain
    international students   186
    teacher professionalism   679
spatial games   274
specialized mathematics   105
spreadsheets   325, 336, 823
    teacher education   312, 401, 784
    technology impact on curriculum   284–9,
        291, 294, 301, 306
    vocational skills   21

stage-learning perspective 723
stakeholders 76, 149–50, 549
standardization 162, 207–8
standardized testing 638, 690–3, 704
   alternatives to 698–9
   beliefs 623
   objections to 697–8, 705
standards xiii
   China 217
   international comparative research 162
   multimedia teacher education 411–12
   National Board for Professional Teaching
      Standards 791
   standards movement 538
   see also Assessment Standards for School
      Mathematics; *Curriculum and*
      Evaluation Standards for School
      Mathematics; *Principles and Standards*
      for School Mathematics; *Professional*
      Standards for Teaching Mathematics
Standards for Educational and Psychological
   Testing (AERA/APA/NCME) 702
Stanford University 509
StarLogo 329, 340
state
   adaptive progressive sentiment 109
   blame shifting to individuals 18
   globalization 190
   statistics influence on 547
statistics 280–1
   condensed measures 90–3
   critical mathematical literacy 85, 97
   research skills 508
   state power 547
Statistics Canada 92
Stellenbosch, University of 414
stories *see* narratives
strategic competence 664
stratification 43, 52–3, 61
streaming 26, 53, 59–62
   see also tracking
street mathematics 105
student teachers
   Australia 774
   beliefs 662
   conflict study 557–8, 560
   identity development 756
   internship case study 855–68
   Japan 774–7
   Netherlands 777–9
   participation in research projects 525–6,
      541
   technology in teacher education 402–3,
      407–8, 421
      autonomy 424–5
      beliefs 411–12

dilemmas of teaching 409
   MILE 413
   web-based resources 417
   theory/practice integration 829–75
   United States 779–82
   see also preservice teachers; teacher
      education
student thinking 811–12, 891–2, 895, 900,
   909–12
   see also children's thinking
student-centred approaches 313, 402, 412,
   824–5, 891
students
   change 661–2
   international comparative research 160–1
   learning 665–7
   problem-solving tests 693–6, 706–12
   task-based interviews 895
   teacher-student interaction 890
Summer Institute Experiences 894
summer institutes 788, 791, 893–4
Summer Math program 658, 673–4, 889,
   892–3
support 66, 659–61
Supported Field Experiences 894
surface-models 95–6
survey studies 161–7, 573, 577
Sussex, University of 477
sustainable development 127–8
sustained conversations 538
Suzuki method 105
Sweden
   cultural values 172, 721–22
   femininity 722
   Learner's Perspective Study 166
   PISA results 153
   recall emphasis 156
   technology research 461
   vocational education 123
Switzerland
   cultural values survey 721
   PISA results 153
Sydney, University of 209
symbol sense 77
symbolic calculation 370
symbolic computation *see* Computer Algebra
   Systems
symbolic representation 77, 268–9, 330–1
symbolization 82, 357–8
symmetry
   group theory 376
   microworlds 262–3, 331
   quadrilaterals 903
syntax 356–7
syntonicity 332
System for Integrated Environmental and
   Economic Accounting (SEEA) 92–3

systemic change   659–60
systems theory   594

T3 project *see Telematics for Teacher
    Training* project
TACCOL *see Technology Advancing a
    Continuous Community of Learners*
tacit knowledge   538, 843
Taiwan
   achievement studies   651–2
   cultural values survey   721
   technology impact on curriculum   293
   values   719, 721, 739, 747–54
   VIMT projects   739, 747–53, 757–8
TAPPED IN   398, 415
target equity groups   107
targets for national training   108
tasks
   Mathematical Tasks Framework   886
   PISA   152
   professional development   899–912
Teach for America (TFA)   782, 787–8
teacher education   637–40, 795–828
   accountability   462
   adult mathematics education   114, 120–2
   Australia   774, 775–6
   crisis in   639
   impact on teaching   500
   Japan   774–7
   learning   599
   Netherlands   291, 777–9
   regulating entry into profession   767–93
   research ethics   453–7, 464
   teacher research projects   526–7
   technology   235, 260, 395–432, 813, 841–2
      classroom activity   402–13
      critical view   906–9
      impact on curriculum   291, 312
      Internet technologies   413–18
      preparation of teachers   418–23
   theory/practice integration   829–75
   United States   779–82
   University of Cape Town   533–7
   values   638–9
   see also in-service teacher education
      programmes; preservice teachers;
      professional development; student
      teachers
Teacher Training Agency (United
    Kingdom)   312
teacher-centred approaches   613
teacher-educator educators (MTEEs)   877,
    880–2, 896–8, 912
teacher-educators (MTEs)   637–8, 849–50,
    869–70
   educative power   879
   learning opportunities   879

professional development   877, 880–2,
    896–902, 912
research by teachers   526–7
tasks   903–4, 908
see also tutors
Teacher-Research (TR) movement   524, 528,
    538–9, 541
teachers
   assessment design   698–9
   assumptions on attainment   26, 44
   authority   57–9
   autonomy   208, 851–3
   beliefs   410–12
   blamed for failure   560
   boycott of national curriculum   698
   changing classroom practices   638, 643–87
   collaboration with researchers   438
   collegiate   811
   Colombia projects   221
   Computer Algebra Systems   338
   conceptions of mathematics   799–804
   conflict studies   556, 559–60, 562–3
   de-professionalization   11, 207, 692
   decision-making   729
   demoralization   207
   development   612
   didactical contract   506–7
   dilemmas of teaching   408–10
   dynamic geometry   336
   ethical issues in research   442, 444
   expansion of research   495
   failure of research to impact on
      practice   484–5
   Further Diploma in Education   453–7
   international comparative research   160,
      169, 172, 199
   knowledge transfer   484
   maintaining quality   476
   national context   167
   as obstacles to dissemination of
      research   620–4
   pedagogical identity   726, 733–4, 748–9,
      755–7
   policy/practice levels   597–8
   poor research communication   619
   professionalism   xiii, 679, 835
      autonomy   852
      Japan   297, 840
      technology impact on
         curriculum   308–13
   regulation of entry into profession   767–93
   research by   437, 523–44, 604
   resistance to change   616, 620–1
   scientific knowledge production   570
   selection   851, 853–4
   setted groups   60

shifting roles   307–8, 311
teacher privileging   384
teacher-student interaction   890
'teaching to the test'   650–1, 690–2
technology   235, 245, 247, 253, 257, 300, 313, 379–80
traditional assessment   46
US crisis in recruitment   785–91
values   717, 725, 728–30, 733–4, 739–57
VAMP   739–47
VIMT projects   739, 747–53
World Bank projects   215
see also lecturers; newly qualified teachers; preservice teachers; professional development; student teachers; teacher education
Teaching and Change (journal)   531
'teaching experiments'   564, 610
Teaching and Learning about Decimals   404
Teaching for Life Skills and Sustainable Development conference (UNESCO)   110
techne   480
technical rationality   878
technological divide   461
technology   xii, 13, 233–432
    classroom practices   653–5
    critical mathematics education   89–90
    digital   323–39
    environmental issues   87
    influence on mathematics curriculum   234–5, 271–321
    intellectual dominance   24–5
    mathematical literacy   78
    meta-study on technology research   233, 237–69
    as obstacle to dissemination of research   624
    research ethics   461–4
    as source of power   548–9
    teacher concerns   620
    teacher education   235, 260, 395–432, 813, 841–2
        classroom activity   402–13
        critical view   906–9
        impact on curriculum   291, 312
        Internet technologies   413–18
        preparation of teachers   418–23
    transfer   123
    undergraduate mathematics   234–5, 351–94
    see also Computer Algebra Systems; computers; information and communication technology; Internet; software
Technology Advancing a Continuous Community of Learners (TACCOL)   420

teleconferencing *see* computer conferencing
Telematics for Teacher Training (T3) project   398, 416–17
teleological principles   448–9
television   17, 398, 404
terrorism   545–6
tertiary education
    adult participation   121–2
    Colombia   220–1
    ICT impact   234–5
    research   625
    TACCOL project   420
    technology as teaching tool   351–94
    web-based teacher resources   417
    see also higher education; universities
tests   638, 644, 651–3
    adult numeracy practice   131
    assessment design   689–716
    content and format   650–1
    economic conditions   5, 9
    validity   458
    see also examinations; international comparative research; International Programme for Student Assessment; Third International Mathematics and Science Study
Texas Instrument   276
textbooks
    commercially produced   623
    cross-national variation   156
    developing countries   23, 83–4
    IEA study   170
    inappropriately sold to the Third World   23
    NCTM yearbook   272
    South East Asia   214–15
    values   735, 738, 758
    Western adoption of Eastern textbooks   217
TFA *see Teach for America*
Thailand
    achievement/GNP relationship   15–16
    reforms   217, 719
theory
    crucial descriptions   572
    definitions   831–2
    framing research questions   501–2
    integration with practice   829–75
    methodology   570
    practice relationship   124, 607–10, 829–75
    teacher education   640, 829–75
Third International Mathematics and Science Study (TIMSS)   34, 161, 174–5, 197–9, 679
    Attaining Excellence   159
    calculator use   474

CBMS report   773
computer use   474–5
critiques   14, 174, 458–9, 768
curricular alignment   154
curricular differentiation   155–6
curricular intentions   769
democratic classroom   43
East Asia   41
economic performance   14–18
equity issues   154–5
forming research questions   499–501
funding for school development   850
gender issues   40, 162–4
global politics   147–8
globalization   582
lesson study   527
mathematical literacy   78–9
politicized use of   10–11, 18–19, 145–7,
   177–8, 436
psychometric approach   703
pupils' attitudes   63
purposes of   169
quantitative methods   449, 460
research ethics   458–61, 464
school effectiveness   150
stakeholders   149
students   160
United States   146–7, 159, 177–8, 499,
   651, 768, 771–2
values   719, 722
video studies   165–6, 499–500, 648, 652,
   771, 845–6
see also TIMSS-R
Third World   3, 23–4
see also developing countries
TI-89 calculator   359, 361, 370
TI-92 calculator   276, 280, 338, 370
TICE   254
tiger economies   15
time factors   615–16, 628
   IEA study   170
   professional development   675–7
TIMSS-R
   East Asia   41
   girls' attainment   51
   South Africa   460–1
   US inequalities   173
'tinkering'   711–12
Tomorrow 1998   647
tools, software   325–6, 327–8, 332–42
Top Class software   400, 414
top-down approaches   656–7, 659, 678
TR *see* Teacher-Research movement
tracking   26, 59–62, 68
   see also streaming
traditional research   448–9

trainability   109
training
   adult education   119
   competency-based education and
      training   116, 118, 130
   mathematical skills for IT labor force   4
   research   516–17
   VET   119, 121–3
   World Bank projects   196, 215
   see also teacher education; vocational
      education
transactions   93
transformative practice   572
transparency
   research   572
   software tools   338, 339–40
trigonometry   268, 784, 816
Turtle Mirrors microworld   262–3, 331
TurtleMath   331
tutors
   adult education   120–1
   internship programme   854–9, 861–8
   see also intelligent software tutors

Uganda, REFLECT programme   127
UIT *see* Upper IT Competence
UN *see* United Nations
uncertainty   479, 722, 899–902
undergraduate mathematics   234–5, 351–94
Undervisningsministeriet   647, 657
UNDP *see* United Nations Development
   Program
UNESCO *see* United Nations Educational,
   Scientific and Cultural Organization
UNICEF *see* United Nations Children's
   Fund
unidimensionality   700
uniqueness of mathematics   593–4
United Kingdom
   achievement/GNP relationship   15–16
   calculator use   654–5
   Cockcroft Report   76, 111, 279
   colonial education tradition in South East
      Asia   214, 215
   conservative pedagogical agenda   464
   cultural contestation   65
   employers demand for numeracy   78
   ethnic minorities   54–6
   evidence-based practice   539
   Framework for the Inspection of
      Schools   515
   ICME   192
   inequitable resource distribution   45
   influence on Australia   208–9
   international comparisons   460
   international students   185–6
   IT competence   312

MILE project 413
National Curriculum 14, 279, 483, 649,
    866
  anti-multiculturalism 55
  criticisms of 206–7
  mathematics as empowering force 31–2
  teacher boycott 698
  technology 284
National Numeracy Strategy 120, 626,
    649, 656
PISA results 153
pupils' attitudes 63
puzzle-style software 326
reforms 200
resistance to change 616
the right 12
schools-university partnership 854–68
setting 59–61
smartboard technology 418
teacher education 829
teacher research grants 620
Teacher-Research movement 528
technology impact on curriculum 284–5,
    303
test validity 458
see also England; Great Britain; Scotland;
    Wales
United Nations (UN) 92, 186, 191
United Nations Children's Fund
    (UNICEF) 32
United Nations Development Program
    (UNDP) 32
United Nations Educational, Scientific and
    Cultural Organization (UNESCO)
  'brain drain' 186
  curriculum 41
  East and South East Asian
    conferences 216
  Escuela Nueva project 221
  ICME 192
  International Environmental Education
    Programme 86
  Latin America 219
  lifelong learning 103–4
  local history 196
  Mathematics Education and Society
    conference 194
  role 191, 195
  *Teaching for Life Skills and Sustainable
    Development* conference 110
  WCEFA 32–3
  World Education Forum 220
United States
  achievement studies 651–2
  achievement/GNP relationship 15–16
  adult education 123

algebra 658, 660–1
American Educational Research
    Association 448, 451, 702
bottom-up approaches 656
calculator use 161, 653
calculus 223
California Achievement Test 696–7
CBSM standards 783
classroom practices 647
colonial education tradition in South East
    Asia 214
compulsory maths curriculum 41
constructivism 117
cultural pluralism 155
cultural scripts 168
cultural values survey 721–2
curriculum 158–9, 279
disenfranchised communities 83
economic goals 11, 14
equity 40
ICME 192
IMPACT project 662
individualism 722
inequitable resource distribution 45
influence on Australia 208–9
international students 185–6
IT competence 312
IT development 277–8
Learner's Perspective Study 166
learning strategies 160
lesson study 527, 533
manipulatives 737
math wars 619
Mathematics Learning Study Committee
    report 82
National Assessment of Educational
    Progress 164, 651
National Center for Fair and Open
    Testing 698
NCTM Standards 207
New Math 656–7
policy debates 169
poor school funding 27–8
problem-based research 496
Project LINCS 667
pupils' attitudes 63
QUASAR project 885
recall emphasis 156
recruitment crisis 785–91
reforms 199–200, 218, 564
regulating entry into teaching
    profession 767, 779–83, 785–91
research 472, 479, 566
resistance to change 616
the right 12
school choice 658

School Survey movement   478
Science and Mathematics Education   157
SIMS   154–5, 159, 173
socio-economic status   26–7
standards movement   538
systemic change   659
teacher education   456, 767–9, 779–82, 785–91
Teacher-Research movement   528
teaching practices   771
technology   282–4, 461
tests   690, 692
TIMSS   146–7, 159, 177–8, 499, 651, 768, 771–2
top-down approaches   656
tracking   59, 61
vocational education   103
wealth   550
universal mathematics content   37–9
universal rules   481–2
universalism
    deontological research   449
    ethnomathematics conflict   201–2, 205–6
    research findings   565
    values   718
universalization
    curricular tracks   39
    globalization distinction   189, 203
    Mathematics for All   36, 38
universities
    academic mathematicians   121
    adult education   121–3, 126–7
    Colombia   221–2
    international students   186, 209–12
    mobile teaching facilities   421
    on-line teacher education   414
    partnership with schools   854–68, 870
    research   625
    sabbatical programs   208
    teacher education   774, 780, 782
    teacher preparation   835–7, 839–41
    teacher research   528, 532, 539–40
    technology as teaching tool   234–5, 351–94
    undergraduate mathematics   234–5, 351–94
    see also higher education; tertiary education
University of Auckland   126
University of British Columbia   343n6
University of Cape Town   533–7, 540–1
University of Central Queensland   383
University of Deakin   421
University of Exeter   416
University of Georgia   421
University of Illinois   364

University of Indiana   401, 415–16, 420
University of Los Andes   221
University of Melbourne   404, 422, 783
University of Monash   639, 717
University of New South Wales   210
University of Northumbria   413
University of Nottingham   300
University of Oulu   413
University of Rutgers   405, 910
University of Southern California   788
University of Stanford   509
University of Stellenbosch   414
University of Sussex   477
University of Sydney   209
University of Wisconsin-Madison   648, 780–3, 787
University of the Witwatersrand   453
Upper IT Competence (UIT)   312
Uruguay, UN classification   219
USA Goals   2000   11, 14
utilitarianism   22, 448–50, 737

validity   537, 574–8, 580
    data collection   567
    democratic participatory   455
    of tests   458
value-rationality   480, 486
values   xiii, 48, 56, 638–9, 717–65
    Asian   64
    classroom practices   645–53
    cross-cultural variation   721–2
    cultural   721–3, 732, 735, 737–8
        changing classroom practices   645–53
        international comparative research   158, 172, 175, 179
        IT in mathematics curriculum   234
        societal values   163
    decisions and action   727–31
    epistemological   735
    mathematical knowledge   98
    professional development   730, 753–7
    research   452–3, 720–1, 731–5, 738–53, 757–8
    social class   54
    societal   163, 735
    socio-cultural issues   734–8
    value indicators   722–5, 749
    VAMP   730, 739–47, 753, 757–8
    VIMT projects   739, 747–53, 757–8
    Western   547, 718, 732–3, 735
'Values and Mathematics Project' (VAMP)   730, 739–47, 753, 757–8
'Values in Mathematics Teaching' (VIMT) projects   739, 747–53, 757–8
VAMP *see* 'Values and Mathematics Project'
variable   330–1
vector algebra   371–3, 375

velocity 820–2
Venezuela, UN classification 219
verification 505
VET *see* Vocational Education and Training
video
  CGI program 666
  classroom practice 161, 171
  communication of research 512, 516
  Learner's Perspective Study 166–7
  MATH project 841–2
  MILE project 842
  records of practice 516–17
  reflection 886
  teacher education 396, 398–9, 402–3, 419
    children's thinking 404–5
    classroom interaction 406–7
    expert facilitation 425
    MILE 412–13
    teachers' beliefs 411–12
    teaching dilemmas 409–10
  teacher observation 644
  TIMSS studies 165–6, 499–500, 648, 652, 771, 845–6
  VAMP research 741
  VIMT projects 750–1
video-conferencing 400, 404, 416, 451
videodiscs 396, 399, 407, 410
Vietnam
  colonial education tradition 214–15
  engineering 38–9
  high attainment 41
VIMT *see* 'Values in Mathematics Teaching' projects
virtual classrooms 400, 405–6, 410, 414–15, 418
virtual communities 400, 401, 416
visualization
  CBMS report 784
  interactive 386
  microworlds 358
  spatial 302
  technology research 246–7, 250–1, 255, 257
    graphic representations 249, 267–9
    symbolic techniques 268–9
    undergraduate geometry 377
vocational education
  lifelong education 105
  skills 20–2, 108
  United States 103
  see also work
Vocational Education and Training (VET) 119, 121–3
voice
  ethnomathematics 204
  international collaboration 225

international comparative research 160–1, 176–7
research ethics 455

Wales
  curriculum research 565
  examinations 650
  national curriculum 483, 698
  see also Welsh Office
WCEFA *see* World Conference on Education for All
web sites
  teacher education 407, 417
  teacher research 541
web-based teaching 382–3
webbing 341
Welsh Office (WO) 76, 284, 483, 599
'Western mathematics'
  colonial legacy 547
  dominance of 205–6
  Eastern learning contrast 217
  ethnomathematics 83–4, 202–4
  influence on developing countries 737–8
  international comparative research 177
  technology influence on curriculum 280, 282–91, 297
  values 718, 732–3, 735
Whistle and Watch problem 707
whole-class approaches 130, 840, 866
Wisconsin-Madison, University of 648, 780–3, 787
Witwatersrand, University of the 453
WO *see* Welsh Office
women
  adult literacy 33, 104
  classroom practices 645–6
  exclusion 547
  globalization of concerns 189
  International Organization of Women and Mathematics Education 36, 193–4
  Latin America 220
  rationality 50–2
  see also femininity; gender; girls
word processors 275, 312
work
  building workers in Argentina 125–6, 128–9
  changing classroom practice 646
  Glenn Report 769
  key skills 21–2
  lifelong learning 109–10
  low-income jobs 107
  mathematical literacy 78, 82–3
  policy initiatives 118–19
  see also labor force demands; vocational education
Working Group for Action 463

working-class students
  alienation 53
  failure 465
  language use 44–5
  test validity 458
  tracking 26
World Bank 9–10, 186, 190–1, 195–7
  Colombia projects 220–1
  globalization 215
  SEEA 92
  WCEFA 32
World Conference on Education for All
  (WCEFA) 32–3
World Declaration on Education for
  All 32–3

World Education Forum 104, 220
World Federations of National Mathematics
  Competitions 193
World Wide Web (WWW)
  research 515
  teacher education 414
  technology influence on curriculum 278
  web-based teaching 382–3
  see also Internet
worthiness concept 723, 749, 757
writing 512–13
WWW *see* World Wide Web

Yokohama National University 776

'Zentralblatt für Didaktik der Mathematik'
  (ZDM MATHDI) database 239, 551

Kluwer International Handbooks of Education

Volume 1

International Handbook of Educational Leadership and Administration
Edited by Kenneth Leithwood, Judith Chapman, David Corson,
Philip Hallinger, and Ann Hart
ISBN 0-7923-3530-9

Volume 2

International Handbook of Science Education
Edited by Barry J. Fraser and Kenneth G. Tobin
ISBN 0-7923-3531-7

Volume 3

International Handbook of Teachers and Teaching
Edited by Bruce J. Biddle, Thomas L. Good, and Ivor L. Goodson
ISBN 0-7923-3532-5

Volume 4

International Handbook of Mathematics Education
Edited by Alan J. Bishop, Ken Clements, Christine Keitel, Jeremy Kilpatrick,
and Collette Laborde
ISBN 0-7923-3533-3

Volume 5

International Handbook of Educational Change
Edited by Andy Hargreaves, Ann Leiberman, Micheal Fullan,
and David Hopkins
ISBN 0-7923-3534-1

Volume 6

International Handbook of Lifelong Learning
Edited by David Aspin, Judith Chapman, Micheal Hatton,
and Yukiko Sawano
ISBN 0-7923-6815-0

Volume 7

International Handbook of Research in Medical Education
Edited by Geoff R. Norman, Cees P.M. van der Vleuten, and David I. Newble
ISBN 1-4020-0466-4

Volume 8

Second International Handbook of Educational Leadership and
Administration
Edited by Kenneth Leithwood and Philip Hallinger
ISBN 1-4020-0690-X

Volume 9

International Handbook of Educational Evaluation
Edited by Thomas Kellaghan and Daniel L. Stufflebeam
ISBN 1-4020-0849-X

Volume 10

Second International Handbook of Mathematics Education
Edited by Alan J. Bishop, M.A., (Ken) Clements, Christine Keitel,
Jeremy Kilpatrick, and Frederick K.S. Leung
ISBN 1-4020-1008-7